THE DONALD

HOW DID IT HAPPEN?

BLOOD, SWEAT, TEARS, & THE DONALD
How We Did It

Danforth Prince, President, Blood Moon Productions

This is a revised edition of a book which we hastily issued, with the (thwarted) expectation of elevated sales, eight years ago, just two "high stress, high-anxiety" months before Donald Trump won the Presidential election of November, 2016.

What could possibly have gone wrong? Moments before its anticipated release, perhaps with political motivations of its own, our then-distributor, the National Book Network, abruptly switched strategies and refused to sell it, throwing into last-minute chaos our carefully orchestrated hopes and dreams.

Hurriedly, we gathered our marbles and released it instead through alternative (but less extensive) distribution channels. Within a few months, its first edition garnered impressive reviews, a handful of prestigious literary awards, and cautious applause from both sides of the political divide.

Now, on the eve of Donald Trump's bid for a second Presidential term, we believe that some of the mysteries associated with SECOND TERM ("Comeback") DONALD lie in early clues he dropped, many of which we recorded in this book.

We present it to readers as a Rosetta Stone, an insight into VINTAGE TRUMP and THE WAY WE WERE at the time of its first introduction to the reading public, way back in 2016. This is a historic overview of THE DONALD and HOW HE DID IT, a horrified but compelling memoir for future generations.

God Bless Us All, and **God Bless America**. We salute, with reverence, the American concepts of Democracy, Free Speech, Prosperity, and Justice for All.

WHAT IS BLOOD MOON PRODUCTIONS?

"Blood Moon, in case you don't know, is a small publishing house on Staten Island that cranks out Hollywood gossip books, about two or three a year, usually of five-, six-, or 700-page length, chocked with stories and pictures about people who used to consume the imaginations of the American public, back when we actually had a public imagination. That is, when people were really interested in each other, rather than in Apple 'devices.' In other words, back when we had vices, not devices."

— The Huffington Post

THE DONALD
How Did It Happen?

Darwin Porter & Danforth Prince

THE DONALD
How Did It Happen?

Darwin Porter and Danforth Prince

Unless otherwise stated, all texts are copyright
© 2023 Blood Moon Productions, Ltd.
with all rights reserved.

www.BloodMoonProductions.com

ISBN 978-1-936003-90-7

Manufactured in the USA
Covers and Book Design by Danforth Prince

This book is distributed worldwide through
Ingram, Amazon.com, and internet vendors everywhere.

BLOOD MOON PRODUCTIONS

PROUDLY DEFINES THIS BOOK AS

VOLUME NINE

OF ITS
MAGNOLIA HOUSE
SERIES

CONTENTS

PROLOGUE   PAGE 1
    TRUMPOCALYPSE

CHAPTER ONE   PAGE 11
    THE DONALD AND THE PRINCESS (DIANA); THE MODEL (MELANIA) AND THE MOGUL; THE MINI-DONALD (BARRON); AT HOME WITH THE TRUMPS; LIKE-MINDED BILLIONAIRES (RUPERT MURDOCH AND THE DONALD); MARITAL WOES AND INFIDELITIES AMONG THE INSANELY WEALTHY; WAS MELANIA "TRUMPED" BY THE SHANGHAI LADY?

CHAPTER TWO   PAGE 25
    POLITICKING & POWER PLAYS: THIRTY YEARS OF SHIFTING ALLIANCES WITH DIVERGENT POLITICAL ALLIES; DONALD CONTEMPLATES WHITE HOUSE RUNS IN 2000, 2004, AND 2012. REFORM PARTY FRENEMIES & THE BIRTHER BLITZ; THE DONALD VS. WARREN BEATTY—WHICH WILL BECOME PRESIDENT? BUILDING MORE THAN SKYSCRAPERS: THE DONALD'S BUTLER CALLS FOR THE ASSASSINATINO OF BARACK OBAMA; THE DONALD'S HAIR: POOFERY AND PUFFERY; DONALD (EARLY AND LOUDLY) PLAYS THE TERROR CARD.

CHAPTER THREE   PAGE 39

A SALESMAN WITH THE MIDAS TOUCH (GOLDFINGER TRUMP); TRUMP UNIVERSITY AND THE (YOU'RE FIRED!) APPRENTICE; THE DONALD BECOMES THE PAGEANT WORLD'S MASTER OF THE UNIVERSE; FEUDS WITH ROSIE O'DONNELL, GRAYDON CARTER, AND BEAUTY QUEENS ALICIA MACHADO, TARA CONNER, AND MISS PENNSYLVANIA (SHEENA MONNIN); MISS WORLD (DISASTROUSLY) GOES TO NIGERIA; UNIVISION (DONALD AT WAR WITH LATINO AMERICAN TELEVISION).

THE SUMMER OF TRUMP

CHAPTER FOUR   PAGE 57

HOW A "SHOCK JOCK" TV ENTERTAINER ANNOUNCED THE DONALD'S RUN FOR PRESIDENT OF THE UNITED STATES; INSULTING MEXICANS, MUSLIMS, AND HIS GOP RIVALS; FORBES DISPUTES THE DONALD'S NET WORTH; THE DONALD AS "POSTER BOY" FOR THE JIHAD; LATINOS DENOUNCE TRUMP AS "THE AMERICAN HITLER." LOATHED BY THE ESTABLISHMENT AND HATED BY THE MEDIA, DONALD TAKES STANDS ON WHAT WILL "MAKE AMERICA GREAT AGAIN." THOSE PESKY REPUBLICAN PRIMARIES: WHEN THEY WERE OVER, AFTER EVISCERATING HIS ENEMIES, ONLY THE DONALD REMAINED.

THE AUTUMN OF TRUMP

CHAPTER FIVE   PAGE 85

INCREDULITY: (WHAT THE F#@%? THE DONALD FOR PRESIDENT?); INSULT BY INSULT, DONALD CLIMBS IN THE POLLS. "I FINANCE MY OWN CAMPAIGN, AND I'M TOO RICH TO BE BOUGHT LIKE HILLARY & JEB!" THE DONALD, THE KKK, BLACK LIVES MATTER, AND LATINO RAGE. DONALD AT WAR WITH THE GOP. HOW THE TERMINATOR (ARNOLD SCHWARZENEGGER) WAS ENROLLED AS THE REPLACEMENT HOST FOR CELEBRITY APPRENTICE; KANYE WEST (DISASTROUSLY) JOINS THE TRUMPETTES; STICK A FORK IN IT" ANTHONY WEINER AND THE SEXTING BROUHAHA; HOW TO WIN A TELEVISED DEBATE? LASH OUT AT THE MODERATORS.

THE WINTER OF TRUMP

CHAPTER SIX   PAGE 109

THE DONALD'S HOLY WAR (TRUMP VS. THE POPE); DONALD IS FORCED TO DEFEND THE SIZE OF HIS PENIS ("DO YOU KNOW WHAT THEY SAY ABOUT A MAN WITH SMALL HANDS?"); DONALD QUOTES FROM MUSSOLINI AND GETS THE SUPPORT OF THE KKK AND THE AMERICAN NAZI PARTY; THE GOP VS. THE TABLOIDS: PORN KINKS AND GAY PARTIES; REPUBLICAN VENOM, DISCORD, RAGE, & FRUSTRATION; "THE GRAND OLD PARTY IS DEAD"; DONALD'S ANTI-MUSLIM RANTS COST HIM MILLIONS; BURNING BUSHES: JEB! AND THE COLLAPSE OF A POLITICAL DYNASTY; BROMANCE: THE DONALD AND "THE SCOURGE OF RUSSIA"; LET ME ENTERTAIN YOU: THE TABLOIDS & DONALD'S DISH; SCHLONGED AGAIN: MONICA LEWINSKI AND BILL CLINTON; IVANKA'S SHOW-STOPPING CELEBRITY PREGNANCY.

CHAPTER SEVEN   PAGE 129

THE GOP: TRAPPED BETWEEN A BOMB AND A KAMIKAZE

"You can't make Chateaubriand out of cowpies, or chicken salad out of chicken shit." (Linda Stasi, in *The NY Daily News*)

"Trump Divides God's Voters" (Headline in a Des Moines, Iowa, Newspaper). PLAYGROUND BULLIES AT WAR—THE DON-

ALD VS. "PUSSY BOY TED CRUZ"; RADICAL EVANGELICAL JERRY FALWELL, JR., PRESIDENT OF LIBERTY UNIVERSITY, URGES STUDENTS TO "ARM THEMSELVES."

CHAPTER EIGHT PAGE 141

MAMA GRIZZLY (SARAH PALIN) ENDORSES TRUMP. CARTOONISTS MOCK THEM: "I'M WITH STUPID." POLITICAL ATHLETE CHRIS CHRISTIE ENDORSES TRUMP, EVISCERATES RUBIO; THREE-TIME NYC MAYOR, MICHAEL BLOOMBERG BECOMES A "VOICE OF REASON"; THE DONALD'S "PISSING MATCH' WITH MEGYN KELLY, A PREMIER NEWS ANCHOR AT FOX; TRUMP FANS HUSTLE VOTERS IN "THE CORNFIELD CRUCIBLE" BEFORE THE IOWA CAUCUS; BASHING FAGS: REPUBLICANS TARGET THEM, AGAIN, AS PUBLIC ENEMIES; REPUBLICAN JAWS OPEN WIDE TO DEVOUR "LITTLE MARCO" RUBIO.

CHAPTER NINE PAGE 155

ENROLLING JOHN WAYNE, FROM THE GRAVE, AS A TRUMPETTE; THE DONALD ACCUSES REPUBLICAN RIVALS OF COCAINE ABUSE; KID DONALD INSULTS THE POPE, AGAIN. DONALD DEMANDS TORTURE OF SUSPECTED "ENEMIES OF THE STATE"; DAWN OF THE BRAIN DEAD: "MINDLESS ZOMBIES" ELECT DONALD AS THEIR CANDIDATE IN THE NEW HAMPSHIRE PRIMARY; CAMELOT? DONALD AND MELANIA DISCUSS THE GLAM QUOTIENT OF THEIR PRESIDENCY; TED CRUZ AND THE PORN-INDUSTRY STAR OF *DEVIANT WHORES;* MOCKING "LOW ENERGY JEB!"; DONALD'S PUBLICITY MACHINE INSISTS THAT JEB! SHOULD HAVE BEEN IMPEACHED FOR THE WAR IN IRAQ; POLITICIZING SCOTUS: TRUMPETTES INSIST THAT SUPREME COURT JUSTICE ANTHONY SCALIA WAS MURDERED BY A HOOKER; THE "CRUZIFICTION" OF TED CRUZ; HOW THE DONALD INSULTED HIS WIFE; *MEIN KAMPF*: AFTER SOMEONE SENDS HIM A COPY, DONALD GETS AN ENDORSEMENT FROM THE KKK; TRUMP ENROLLS THE OWNERS OF *THE NATIONAL ENQUIRER TO TRASH HIS POLITICAL ENEMIES;* THE IRONIES OF FAME: DUBIOUS CELEBRITIES WEIGH IN WITH ENDORSEMENTS OF TRUMP.

2016: THE SPRING OF TRUMP

CHAPTER TEN PAGE 175

IN EUROPE, DONALD IS DENOUNCED AS "THE WORLD'S MOST DANGEROUS MAN—WORSE THAN DRACULA"; DEMOCRATIC STRATEGISTS DEBATE HOW THEY MIGHT CASTRATE A CANDIDATE "WHOSE COHONES ARE (ALLEGEDLY) MADE OF STEEL"; SUPER TUESDAY 2016: CARPETBAGGERS DONALD AND HILLARY SWEEP TO VICTORIES IN THE SOUTH (BLACKS FOR HER, WHITES FOR HIM); IT'S ALIVE! CONSERVATIVE REPUBLICANS REACT WITH HORROR TO THE FRANKENSTEIN THEY CREATED IN THEIR HATE LABS; NEW CHAPTERS IN THE SIZE WARS: DONALD CONTINUES TO DEFEND THE SIZE OF HIS PENIS AGAINST ASSAULTS FROM "LITTLE MARCO"; DONALD'S POLITICAL MASSACRE OF MITT (ROMNEY) AND THE SAD STORY OF BOWE BERGDAHL

CHAPTER ELEVEN PAGE 187

BRITISH PUNDITS INSIST THAT THE DONALD AS PRES WOULD LEAD TO MASSIVE GLOBAL DISASTERS; DONALD REBUTS GOP ATTEMPTS TO DESIGNATE ONE OF THEIR OWN AS A THIRD-PARTY INDEPENDENT, THREATENING VIOLENT PROTESTS IN CLEVELAND IF REPUBLICANS SABOTAGE HIS NOMINATION; SEXUAL POLITICS: CRUZ DENIES ANY ASSOCIATION WITH $1,000-A-NIGHT HOOKERS; SURVEYS REVEAL THAT MILLIONS OF AMERICANS—ESPECIALLY MEMBERS OF THE MILITARY—ADORE THE DONALD; PROTESTERS MOCK TRUMP WITH "MAKE AMERICA HATE AGAIN!"; DONALD CELEBRATES HIS LACK OF POLITICAL CORRECTNESS WITH "UNLEASH THE GENERALS ON ISIS"; MARCO RUBIO DROPS OUT OF THE PRESIDENTIAL RACE;

Compelling Sub-Plots from JOHN KASICK, JOE ARPAIO, and CAITLYN JENNER; PRE-PRESIDENTIAL PORN from MELANIA's Murky Past; a "Trade War Mini-Scandal" from IVANKA; The Embarrassing Rise of PAUL MANAFORT; FEMINISTS FLIP when The Donald calls for Punishments for Women Who Abort; FALLING ON HER SWORD: The Sad, Small Story of Bernie Sanders Vs. Debbie Wasserman Schultz

Chapter Twelve   PAGE 201

More Bellows, More Bluster, More Bigotry, More Buffoonery; Hothead Cruz Gets Denounced by the Speaker of the House as LUCIFER IN THE FLESH; The Donald Calls for a Cutoff of Millions of Dollars to MEXICO and calls for a Buildup of the U.S. Military on the Southern Border; After Riots in California, Radical Billionaire and Republican Mega-Donor CHARLES KOCH Denounces both Trump and Cruz and Threatens to Support Hillary; Trump Gets Creamed in Dairy Land Wisconsin; TANKING TED: CRUZ FLOPS in Donald's Home Town of NYC; SEGREGATED TOILETS FOR THE TRANSGENDERED Becomes a Republican Mega-Issue.

Chapter Thirteen   PAGE 211

"CROOKED HILLARY' Vs. "DANGEROUS DON" and the Pinocchio Factor; The Donald Becomes the Presumptive Republican Nominee; Hillary "Feels the Bern" from Sanders; BAY OF PIGS: Donald Accuses Ted Cruz's Father of Assassinating JFK; TED CRUZ and the Indiana Primary: The Battle of the Alamo; GHOSTS CAN'T DO IT, even with Bo Derek: The Donald's Stab as a Film Actor; The Donald's HATE SPEECHES lead to an increase in HATE CRIMES; Both the Mayor of London and the Former President of Mexico SNUB THE DONALD; THE DONALD endorses THE NRA; Introducing New Jersey's MISTER BIG: CHRIS CHRISTIE; CLIMATE CHANGE: Donald Enrages Greenpeace; More About MEGYN KELLY: Making Up is Hard to Do; Although Popularity Polls Rank Lice and Dumpster Fires Ahead of Both Candidates, REPUBLICANS COALESCE BEHIND THE DONALD.

Chapter Fourteen   PAGE 225

Donald Fires His Campaign Manager after Ivanka Tells Daddy "It's him (Corey Lewandowsky) or me!"; An Assassination Attempt on Donald is Blocked by Policemen; CRINGE-WORTHY COURT CASES AND MORE: Addressing Litigation against him, Donald Rages Against what he Defines as "a Biased (Mexican-American) Judge"; HILLARY MAKES HISTORY as the first Female Presidential Nominee; MASS SHOOTINGS in Orlando at a Gay Club ('But the Fag-Hater Was Gay!"); THE DONALD DOES DALLAS (and wears a big hat to prove it); JEFFERSON BEAUREGARD SESSIONS III: Stage One of Donald's Corruption of the Justice Department; YOU'RE HIRED! YOU'RE FIRED! and the rise of White Christian Religious Fanaticism; Trump's Enigmatically Veiled Son-in-Law: JARED KUSHNER: A Creature from the Twilight Zone; DONALD BUNGLES BREXIT; JAMES COMEY and his F.B.I. Screwup; IN PRAISE OF DESPOTS: The Donald Praises Saddam Hussein, Vladimir Putin, Mohammar Khadady, and Kim Jong Un; The Elite Gets Vocal: RUTH BADER GINSBURG vs. RUDY GIULIANI; GAY RIGHTS and THE RACE WARS: Donald Screws Them up, Bigtime; The Sad, Scary, and Unsettling Story of KATHY GRIFFIN AND THE SEVERED HEAD.

EPILOGUE AND THE PRELUDE TO CLEVELAND PAGE 245

THE DONALD CLAIMS THAT AS PRESIDENT, HE'LL URGE CONGRESS TO DECLARE WORLD WAR III; THE ODD COUPLE: DONALD DESIGNATES INDIANA HOMOPHOBE MIKE PENCE AS HIS RUNNING MATE; DAYS ONE, TWO, THREE, AND FOUR OF "THE GREATEST CIRCUS SINCE BARNUM & BAILEY"; LOCK HER UP! RANCOR AND HARD-EDGED RHETORIC AT THE REPUBLICAN CONVENTION; MELANIA, FIRST LADY IN WAITING, IS CHARGED WITH PLAGIARISM AFTER HER WARM-UP SPEECH. WHOSE INTELLECTUAL PROPERTY DID SHE STEAL? MICHELLE OBAMA'S!; BLATANT HOMOPHOBIA FROM ACROSS THE GOP; PRIME TIME BLAHS AT THE RNC. D-LIST SPEAKERS FROM SHOW BIZ'S DEAD ZONE BREATHLESSLY WITNESSING TO MILLIONS ABOUT DONALD. PRIME TIME STUMPERS AND TRUMPERS INCLUDE A CALVIN KLEIN UNDERWEAR MODEL AND A HAS-BEEN FROM *HAPPY DAYS;* BENGHAZI AGAIN, AND AGAIN, AND AGAIN, AND AGAIN, AND AGAIN; FROM THE PODIUM, A NEW CROP OF AMBITIOUS CONSERVATIVES SPIN FOR RECOGNITION. FROM THE CONVENTION DONALD'S CHILDREN EMERGE AS CELEBRITIES, WITH COMPARISONS TO THE KENNEDY CLAN OF THE 1960S; DADDY'S LITTLE GIRL, HIS #1 CHARACTER WITNESS IS IVANKA, BLONDE, COOL, AND CORRUPT

POST CONVENTION POSTSCRIPT: CHAOS, CONFUSION, TURMOIL, RAGE, & DESPAIR PAGE 274

POST ELECTION POSTSCRIPT: THE DIVIDED STATES OF AMERICA: PAGE 277

AUTHORS' BIOS PAGE 281

PREVIOUS WORKS BY DARWIN PORTER
PRODUCED IN COLLABORATION WITH BLOOD MOON

BIOGRAPHIES FROM BLOOD MOON'S MAGNOLIA HOUSE SERIES

Henry Fonda, He Did It His Way,
(Volume One —1905-1960—of a Two-Part Biography)

The Fondas, Henry, Jane, & Peter: TRIPLE EXPOSURE
(Volume Two—1962-1982—of a Two-Part Biography)

Lucille Ball & Desi Arnaz: They Weren't Lucy & Ricky Ricardo
(Volume One—1911-1960—of a Two-Part Biography)

The Sad & Tragic Ending of Lucille Ball
(Volume Two-1961-1989) of a Two-Part Biography

Marilyn: Don't Even Dream About Tomorrow (a 2021 revision of the best-selling
Marilyn at Rainbow's End: Sex, Lies, Murder, & the Great Cover-Up (2012)

The Seductive Sapphic Exploits of Mercedes de Acosta, Hollywood's Greatest Lover

Jacqueline Kennedy Onassis, Her Tumultuous Life & Her Love Affairs

Judy Garland & Liza Minnelli, Too Many Damn Rainbows

Historic Magnolia House: Celebrity & The Ironies of Fame

Glamour, Glitz, & Gossip at Historic Magnolia House

***

BIOGRAPHIES FROM BLOOD MOON
NOT ASSOCIATED WITH ITS MAGNOLIA HOUSE SERIES

Burt Reynolds, Put the Pedal to the Metal

Kirk Douglas, More Is Never Enough

Playboy's Hugh Hefner, Empire of Skin

Carrie Fisher & Debbie Reynolds,
Princess Leia & Unsinkable Tammy in Hell

Rock Hudson Erotic Fire

Lana Turner, Hearts & Diamonds Take All

Donald Trump, The Man Who Would Be King

James Dean, Tomorrow Never Comes

Bill and Hillary, So This Is That Thing Called Love

Peter O'Toole, Hellraiser, Sexual Outlaw, Irish Rebel

Love Triangle, Ronald Reagan, Jane Wyman, & Nancy Davis

Pink Triangle, The Feuds and Private Lives of Tennessee Williams, Gore Vidal, Truman Capote, and Famous Members of their Entourages.

Those Glamorous Gabors, Bombshells from Budapest

Inside Linda Lovelace's Deep Throat,
Degradation, Porno Chic, and the Rise of Feminism

Elizabeth Taylor, There is Nothing Like a Dame

J. Edgar Hoover and Clyde Tolson
Investigating the Sexual Secrets of America's Most Famous Men and Women

Frank Sinatra, The Boudoir Singer. All the Gossip Unfit to Print

The Kennedys, All the Gossip Unfit to Print

The Secret Life of Humphrey Bogart (2003), and
Humphrey Bogart, The Making of a Legend (2010)

Howard Hughes, Hell's Angel

Steve McQueen, King of Cool, Tales of a Lurid Life

Paul Newman, The Man Behind the Baby Blues

Merv Griffin, A Life in the Closet

Brando Unzipped

Katharine the Great, Hepburn, Secrets of a Lifetime Revealed

Jacko, His Rise and Fall, The Social and Sexual History of Michael Jackson

Damn You, Scarlett O'Hara,
The Private Lives of Vivien Leigh and Laurence Olivier

Film Criticism

Blood Moon's 2005 Guide to the Glitter Awards
Blood Moon's 2006 Guide to Film
Blood Moon's 2007 Guide to Film, and
50 Years of Queer Cinema, 500 of the Best GLBTQ Films Ever Made

Non-Fiction

Hollywood Babylon, It's Back! and *Hollywood Babylon Strikes Again!*

Novels

Blood Moon,
Hollywood's Silent Closet,
Rhinestone Country,
Razzle Dazzle
Midnight in Savannah

Other Publications by Darwin Porter Not Directly Associated with Blood Moon

Novels

The Delinquent Heart
The Taste of Steak Tartare
Butterflies in Heat
Marika (a roman à clef based on the life of Marlene Dietrich)
Venus (a roman à clef based on the life of Anaïs Nin)
Sister Rose

Travel Guides

Many Editions and Many Variations of The Frommer Guides, The American Express Guides, and/or TWA Guides, et alia to:

Andalusia, Andorra, Anguilla, Aruba, Atlanta, Austria, the Azores, The Bahamas, Barbados, the Bavarian Alps, Berlin, Bermuda, Bonaire and Curaçao, Boston, the British Virgin Islands, Budapest, Bulgaria, California, the Canary Islands, the Caribbean and its "Ports of Call," the Cayman Islands, Ceuta, the Channel Islands (UK), Charleston (SC), Corsica, Costa del Sol (Spain), Denmark, Dominica, the Dominican Republic, Edinburgh, England, Estonia, Europe, "Europe by Rail," the Faroe Islands, Finland, Florence, France, Frankfurt, the French Riviera, Geneva, Georgia (USA), Germany, Gibraltar, Glasgow, Granada (Spain), Great Britain, Greenland, Grenada (West Indies), Haiti, Hungary, Iceland, Ireland, Isle of Man, Italy, Jamaica, Key West & the Florida Keys, Las Vegas, Liechtenstein, Lisbon, London, Los Angeles, Madrid, Maine, Malta, Martinique & Guadeloupe, Massachusetts, Melilla, Morocco, Munich, New England, New Orleans, North Carolina, Norway, Paris, Poland, Portugal, Provence, Puerto Rico, Romania, Rome, Salzburg, San Diego, San Francisco, San Marino, Sardinia, Savannah, Scandinavia, Scotland, Seville, the Shetland Islands, Sicily, St. Martin & Sint Maarten, St. Vincent &

the Grenadines, South Carolina, Spain, St. Kitts & Nevis, Sweden, Switzerland, the Turks & Caicos, the U.S.A., the U.S. Virgin Islands, Venice, Vienna and the Danube, Wales, and Zurich.

BIOGRAPHIES

From Diaghilev to Balanchine, The Saga of Ballerina Tamara Geva

Greta Keller, Germany's Other Lili Marlene

Sophie Tucker, The Last of the Red Hot Mamas

Anne Bancroft, Where Have You Gone, Mrs. Robinson?
(co-authored with Stanley Mills Haggart)

Veronica Lake, The Peek-a-Boo Girl

Running Wild in Babylon, Confessions of a Hollywood Press Agent

HISTORIES

Thurlow Weed, Whig Kingpin

Chester A. Arthur, Gilded Age Coxcomb in the White House

Discover Old America, What's Left of It

THIS BOOK IS DEDICATED
TO THE UNSUNG HEROES OF THE AMERICAN CENTURY,

the unlucky, hardworking men and women, some of them pawns of fate, who collectively succeeded at making America great.

BIOGRAPHIES
FROM BLOOD MOON PRODUCTIONS

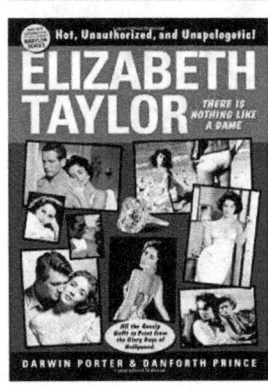

MORE BIOGRAPHIES FROM BLOOD MOON PRODUCTIONS

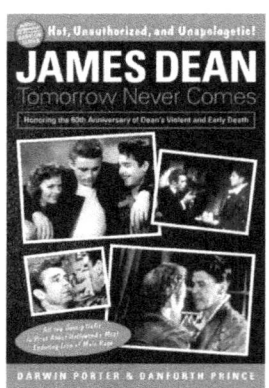

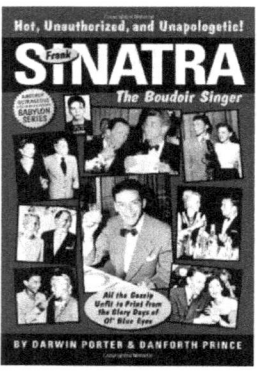

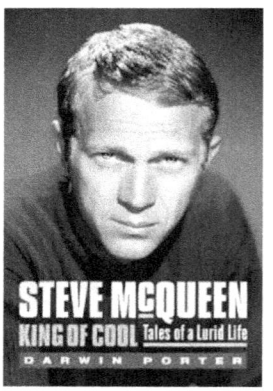

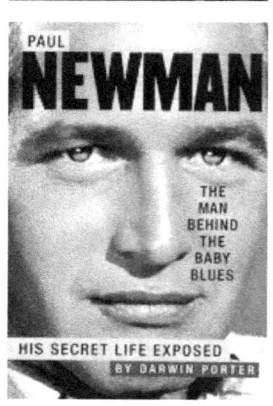

BOOK AWARD NEWS FROM BLOOD MOON PRODUCTIONS

ON FLAG DAY, 2023, IN HONOR OF A GREAT AMERICAN FAMILY AND A GREAT AMERICAN HOLIDAY, BLOOD MOON RELEASED **VOLUME TWO** OF ITS TWO-PART OVERVIEW OF THE FONDAS. ABOUT A MONTH LATER, AS A TWO-VOLUME SET, THEY DESIGNATED AS RUNNER-UP TO THE BEST BIORAPHY OF THE YEAR BY THE JUDGES AT THE SAN FRANCISCO BOOK FESTIVAL

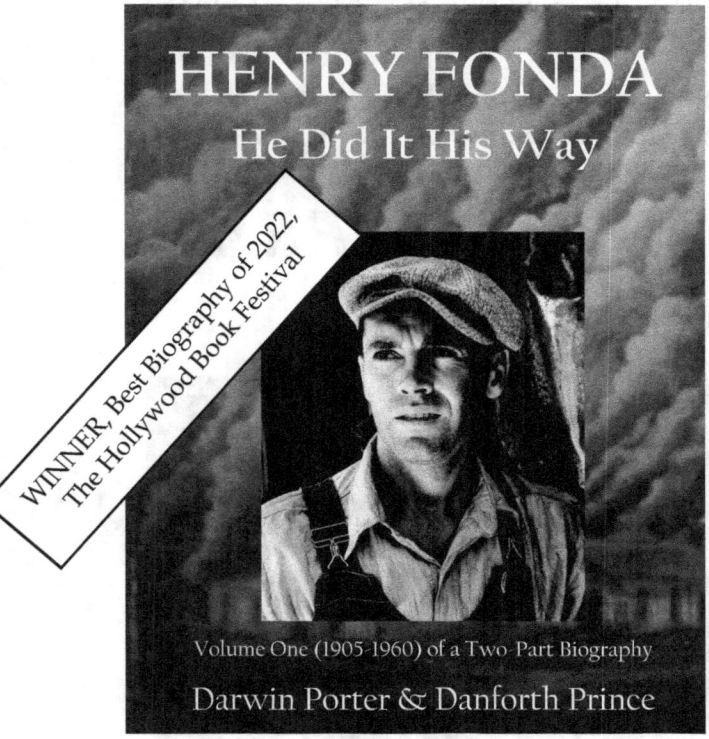

Throughout his forty-five year career, Henry Fonda—a stable, reassuring archetype of the American male—never gave a bad performance, immortalizing himself in such films as *Young Mr. Lincoln, The Grapes of Wrath,* and *Mister Roberts.* The torments of his introverted private life vied with his on-screen dilemmas.

Personal dramas included five wives (two of whom committed suicide) and involvements in many of the seminal events (including active service in the Navy during World War II) of the 20th Century. His affairs starred such mega-divas as Lucille Ball, Joan Crawford, and Bette Davis. With his second wife, Frances Seymour, he founded a Hollywood dynasty with movie star children, Jane and Peter.

The story of Henry and the legacy and children he spawned are now the subject of a two-volume set, the most detailed and insightful ever published

Volume One (1905-1960) covers Henry's origins in Depression-era Nebraska, his rise to fame, his complicated dynamics with other celebrities, and his middle-aged years navigating his passion for acting with the business realities of Hollywood.

Volume Two (1961-1982) turns kleig lights on three emotionally intertwined mega-celebrities, two of them Oscar winners: It's about Henry and his children: the eternal rebel, **Jane,** and his son, **Peter**, a preppy-looking thrill seeker indelibly linked to the "bad boy on a bike" narrative of the 60s. Unlike any other books published, these two volumes reflect the private agonies of a father, daughter, and son engulfed by the divisions of their respective generations and the ironies of the American Experience.

HENRY FONDA, HE DID IT HIS WAY; Volume One (1905-1960) of a Two-Part Biography, and
THE FONDAS: HENRY, JANE, & PETER, Volume Two (1961-1982 of a Two-Part Biography

Both are available now, everywhere, from internet booksellers worldwide

Hot, Show-Bizzy, Unauthorized, Unapologetic, and Newsworthy from Blood Moon Productions: **A NEW and EXPANDED EDITION of the SCANDALOUS ANTHOLOGY** that made us famous when its (smaller, thinner) predecessor first appeared in 2008. This Time, We're Calling It:

HOLLYWOOD BABYLON WITH DETOURS TO GOMORRAH

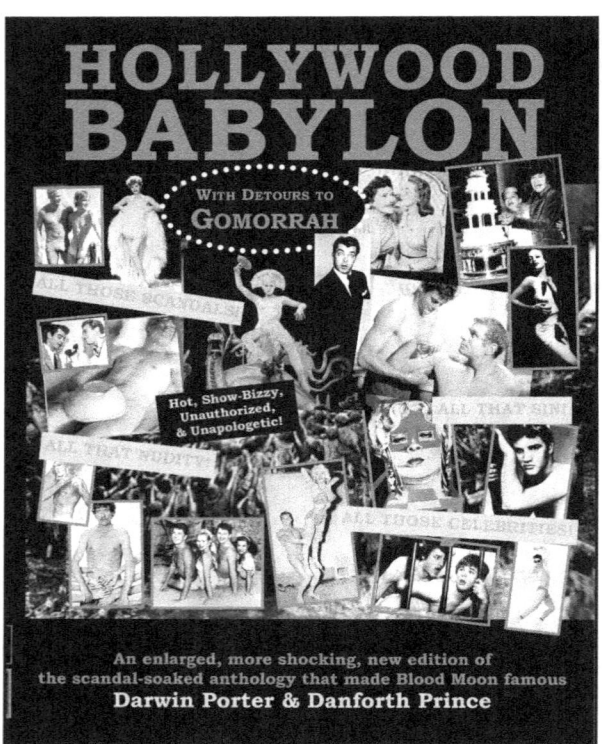

Dishing with abandon, the authors spare no one--especially not the dead. Marilyn Monroe had an affair with Ronald Reagan. Marilyn also had a tryst with Joan Crawford but refused to make it an ongoing affair. James Dean showed a disconcerting interest in a 12-year old boy in the early 1950s. Lucille Ball launched herself into show business as a hooker, and her husband Desi Arnaz had a fling with Cesar Romero. Cary Grant had an incestuous relationship with his stepson, Lance Reventlow. And this, by the way, is only the tip of the iceberg."

Rush & Molloy, *The NY Daily News*

HOLLYWOOD BABYLON:
MAKING AMERICA GREAT AGAIN
For Immediate Release, from Blood Moon Productions
Hollywood Babylon, with Detours to Gomorrah

In the tradition of GREAT AMERICAN GOSSIP, Blood Moon offers this COMPELLING ANTHOLOGY OF GOSSIP to anyone who ever had any nagging questions about show-biz indiscretion, mendacity, and excess.

WHAT IS IT? According to Blood Moon's President, Danforth Prince, "It's the best feature-length compendium of Hollywood gossip ever compiled, lavishly illustrated, and loaded with examples of the PR hurricanes generated by the false gods of fame, physical beauty, lust, greed, narcissism, and exhibitionism. This book might not be everybody's fantasy about what they really wanna crawl into bed with, but as a publishing phenomenon, it's the very best of its genre."

HOW HAS IT BEEN REVIEWED SINCE ITS FIRST EDITION?
ANSWER: With spectacular praise and enthusiasm from publications that include the NY DAILY NEWS, London's EXPRESS, a passel of entertainment-industry publications "Down Under," and show-biz blogsites around the world.

HOW BIG IS IT AND HOW MUCH DOES IT COST?
ANSWER: This anthology was conceived and designed as a softcover **COLLECTOR'S ITEM** for placement on COFFEE TABLES in living rooms that need a little nudge. It has a BIG footprint—something akin to an 8 1/2 x 11" news magazine—and the central image of its front cover is Fritz Lang's 1920s 'perhaps demented' image of THE WHORE OF BABYLON. Debauched and persuasive, she hovers over a passel of spectacularly famous, partially undressed celebrities culled from a century of show-biz mania. In this case, you can acquire her "favors" for $60.

Danforth Prince continued: "We're marketing this as the most lewdly sophisticated 'coffee table book' of the holiday season. It's a one-of-a-kind 'conversation stopper' or (depending on your point of view) 'conversation starter.' This is a 'hipster to hipster' gift you'd give to an embittered survivor who's already deeply familiar with the casting couch. It's the best accumulation of tabloid trauma ever published....a drunken sorority party's first prize; a 'I'm ready for another martini' cocktail *klatsch's* most embarassing panty raid."

"We've doubled its content from its previous edition," Prince continued, "by adding the 'concentrated cream' from rip-snorting OTHER biographies within Blood Moon's (very extensive) backlist. This anthology is what happens when Classic Hollywood gets down and low with the literary *avant-garde* of the Fabulous Fifties, the Free Love Sixties; the Sexy Seventies, and the big-haired teledrama-driven Eighties."

"WHO'S NEW? There's More about Ronald Reagan and Nancy than you might wanna know, and a cross-section of ONCE AGAIN IN THE NEWS stars you might, if not for this book, have forgotten."

IT'S BACK.! IT'S BABYLON! And it's available everywhere, now, through **Amazon.com, Barnes & Noble.com** and other online booksellers worldwide.

HOLLYWOOD BABYLON with DETOURS TO GOMORRAH
By Darwin Porter and Danforth Prince   www.BloodMoonProductions.com
488 pages, 8 1/2" x 11" softcover. ISBN 978-1-936003-88-4

A ONE-OF-A-KIND COLLECTOR'S ITEM AND COFFEE TABLE SHOWPIECE.
MSRP $60.

Challenging the Status Quo's Beliefs about Celebrity, The Ironies of Fame, Modern Politics, & Entertainment from Hollywood's Golden Age

TRUMPOCALYPSE

How a Loudmouthed, Pussy-Grabbing TV star, Casino Kingpin, and Real Estate Mogul won the Republican Nomination for President of the United States

The original 2016 edition of this book—which was "shakily and contentiously" published two months before Trump was elected President of the United States, won a trio of coveted and widely acknowledged First Prizes: They included BEST BIOGRAPHY OF THE YEAR Awards from the New York Book Festival, The California Book Festival, and the Florida Book Festival

MEDIA CULPA

In the immediate aftermath of Donald Trump's surprise upset in the November 8, 2016 presidential election, Fox and other members of the right-wing media crowed the news of his controversial victory. "The Donald" had triumphed in the Electoral College, even though Hillary Clinton had won the popular vote. Ever since, conservative pundits have attacked the "biased" liberal media for not seeing the oncoming *tsunami* (or *Trumpocalypse*).

The New York Times issued a statement: "After such an erratic and unpredictable election, there is the inevitable question:

Did Donald Trump's sheer unconventionality lead us and other news outlets to underestimate his support among American voters?"

Columnist Michael Goodwin claimed, "*The Times* decided that Trump's supporters were a rabble of racist rednecks and homophobes. It didn't have a clue about what was happening in the lives of the Americans who elected the new president."

Donald Trump occupies a unique place in the history of the Republic. In his bitter race for the White House, he aroused fierce passions and raging furies.

Trump is nothing if not a study in contradictions. He is also called "The King of Debt," owing, for example, millions of dollars to the Bank of China, even though he criticizes the United States for doing the same thing.

This is the first biography on the market to include many of the details of Trump's politically incorrect race for the Presidency, a campaign that shocked and sometimes horrified the world. Read what went on behind the scenes as he set out (in his words) "to kick ass"—mainly, Hillary Clinton's.

Lambasting the Pope, defending the size of his penis, castrating sixteen other GOP hopefuls, including a woman, he attracted millions of "Trumpkins." His throngs of outraged enemies denounced his followers as "mental midgets and xenophobic troglodytes."

Another outrageous title in Blood Moon's Babylon series, this is a world-class first, a post-recession overview of America during its 2016 election cycle, a portrait unlike anything ever published on Donald Trump and the climate in which he thrived.

***

From the moment in June of 2015, when "The Donald" descended that escalator at Trump Tower to denounce Mexicans as dangerous rapists, Darwin Porter and Danforth Prince at Blood Moon realized that he might not only have a chance at winning the presidential election, but probably would. Millions of Americans were ready for a change, almost any change, it seemed. The erratic venom of Trump had morphed him into the man of the hour.

Some journalists realized he was promoting a "whitelash," having focused on America's forgotten man who often couldn't support his family, some of whom lived in shabby, once-bustling factory towns where the jobs had gone with the summer wind. The unpaid bills were piling up, and the future looked bleak. Overall, there was an overwhelming nostalgia for a since-departed America—and Trump had tapped into it.

The puzzling riddle is how Trump, of all men, got millions of votes from some of the downtrodden. What an odd choice for them.

A man born into the lap of luxury knew nothing but the most lavish headquarters, the finest food, the most gorgeous of women, and a host of high-priced lawyers *(some of whom didn't get paid)* to keep him out of jail.

Prior to 2016, Porter and Prince had inhabited widely divergent regions of America, including sites on both seacoasts, the Rust Belt States, and a "residential immersion" into the small-town Deep South. At this point in The Donald's campaign, they sensed that a revolution of some sort was near at hand.

Naysayers (and some of their colleagues) in the publishing industry warned that they were wasting their time writing about the origins of the Trump dynasty and its unconventional campaign. They were warned, "After November 8, anything to do with Trump will be a dead duck as far as books are concerned. Whereas no one will want to read about Trump, sales of *exposés* about the new President (Hillary) will surge."

In spite of this reaction, they persisted and turned out their big, award-winning *The Man Who Would Be King,* a tabloid treatise on Trump's rise to power and how he slew his enemies one by one. Considered a "risky" publishing phenomenon at the time, it was the first book of its type on the market. It was released with fanfare and lots of self-doubt and controversy, just two months before the actual 2016 presidential election.

Despite impressive advance sales, in a last-minute reversal, Blood Moon's distributor, the National Book Network—based partly on the political preferences of its administration, and partly on fears of vengeful litigation from "The Donald" and his camp—severed its connection with the book and its premises.

That refusal by Blood Moon's then-distributor of the first edition *(which was nonetheless published a few months before the 2016 election but without access to any major distribution network)* put a massive dent in sales of that provocative and potentially blockbuster title. *(Editors Note: That quirky, then very radical book is still available through Amazon.com under its original title,* **Donald Trump, The Man Who Would Be King***; ISBN 978-1-936003-51-8.)*

Since then, the world has endured daily onslaughts of outrage from Donald Trump, amplified by Fox to the point of numbness. Donald-isms, while still horrifying and dangerous, have lost some of their shock value, and the world has grown more jaded and more *blasé*.

It is our hope, however, that this gently reconfigured new edition will replicate, almost as an educational tool, the dark, shady, and weirdly inexplicable context that got Trump elected in 2016.

This is an "only in America" tale about greed, envy, politics gone crazy, and an American populace terrified of an uncertain future and sinking deeper into a media-driven maze of distortions.

Here it is…fact-based and controversy-soaked, the story of how Donald Trump succeeded at seizing the most world's most powerful platform within the bizarre landscapes that fostered him. It's about **HOW IT HAPPENED**, presented with irony and (whenever possible) humor, from the writers and editors at Blood Moon Productions.

PROLOGUE
Was He America's Savior? Or The Anti-Christ?

A VIEW OF "VINTAGE DONALD" in 2016

In this revised configuration of Blood Moon's 2016 "The Donald" project, Darwin Porter and Danforth Prince present a revised and updated profile of "The Donald"—uncensored, unexpurgated, and sometimes embarrassingly intimate.

"Like Don Quixote, I've dreamed the Impossible Dream," proclaimed Donald Trump. "That involved marrying Princess Di after her 1996 divorce from that Charles guy. Alas, it was not meant to be. But, back to reality, I'm dreaming no more when I plan to become the next President of the United States."

This fast-moving *exposé* provides an unvarnished inside look at America's most famous oversized billionaire, empire builder, and *politico*. Trump is presented in all his glory (or vainglory) in a confusing medley of guises: corporate swashbuckler, modern day Midas, master wheeler-dealer, ubiquitous TV celebrity of cult status, Reagan-era Gilded Age mojo, guru for wannabe millionaires, master of *schmaltz*, choreographer of "The Deal," mogul Kahuna, a gossip columnist's steak dinner, the Barnum of hot press and self-promotion, global magnate, real estate tycoon, gambling casino kingpin, the previous landlord of such controversial tenants as Liberace and Michael Jackson, and finally, a Don Juan of the boudoir.

"To hell with political correctness. I call a rapist a rapist. What other politician has the *cojones* to tell the country the truth that Obama was born in Kenya, not Hawaii?"

Power and ambition are not Trump's only reasons for living. He also enjoys his favorite things—money ("piles of it"), women ("without them, there is nothing); Oreos, golf, juicy hamburgers, the James Bond movie *Goldfinger*, and bathroom toilets plated with gold.

In his quest for "the right woman," he has already bagged three beautiful wives—Ivana Zelníčková, Marla Maples, and Melania Knauss (aka Melania Knavs).. Along the way, he pursued European model Carla Bruni, who later married French president Nicholas Sarkozy. Reportedly, dozens of women "threw themselves at me," including movie star Kim Basinger and pop singer Madonna.

In 2015, during his first presidential campaign, another woman of a different stripe seemed poised to enter his life: Prior to his nomination, he asserted that "he might" enroll Oprah Winfrey as his vice-presidential running mate. "She's popular, brilliant…a wonderful woman. And she would take half the crucial African American vote away from Hillary, the most crooked Secretary of State in America's history. As President, I will see that she's locked up. At rally after rally, my fans screamed for her to be jailed."

Whether you loved him or hated him, Donald Trump—inspiration for legends and myths— fascinated millions of Americans. Mystery prevailed—even his enemies considered him "an enigma wrapped in a riddle." During one of his rare moments of introspection, he once famously said, "There is something crazy hot, a phenomenon out there about me, but I'm not sure I can define it. And I'm not sure I want to."

***

In September of 2016, right before the presidential election, Blood Moon released *Donald Trump, The Man Who Would be King.* With almost 800 pages, it was the biggest and most detailed book ever published on his life and dynastic origins. It traces his life from his trauma-inducing adolescence until his 2016 takeover of the U.S. government.

Prior to November of 2016, millions did not believe that he'd win, but he (thanks in part to the quirks of the Electoral College) proved them wrong.

Dozens of books since then have expounded on Trump's notorious first term as President. Despite the ferocious loyalty of his fans and members of his cult, he was widely excoriated in America and around the world, often with ridicule and mockery.

Our widely contested original book, *Donald Trump, the Man Who Would Be King*, also traced the swampy, Gold Rush origins in Alaska and the Klondike of the Trump Dynasty, the story of which should probably morph into interest to film producers.

Donald's grandfather, Frederick Trump, an entrepreneurial German immigrant from the Rhineland, joined the Gold Rush but not to hunt for gold. A restaurateur and "entertainment specialist," he arrived in the north with a reservoir of cash and a bevy of over-the-hill whores from Seattle, aiming their services at the miners who had poured into the Klondike, often with high libidos and inadequate provisions, from points East.

They also needed to be fed. Fulfilling that basic need, The Donald's grandfather (Friedrich, aka Frederick) ordered his staff to gather up the frozen carcasses of the overburdened mules and pack animals which had died *en route* to the gold mines. Steaks from their sometimes tainted corpses became one of Friedrich's profit-generating staples, served to newbie miners desperate for something to eat.

By the time Friedrich returned to the gentler climes of New York, he had accumulated $400,000, a fabulous fortune at the time.

From there, he briefly returned to Germany to marry a girl (Elizabeth Christ, aka "The Kallstadt Lily,") he had last seen when she was only five years old. (After having seduced many of the whores of the Klondike, he wanted a virgin for a bride.) She had grown up and blossomed. After persuading her to marry him, she returned to America with him and became The Donald's paternal grandmother.

They settled in Queens, a borough that had only recently been consolidated into New York City and raised a family. One of their children, Fred Trump, became the father of Donald. In time, Fred Trump—fueled by the boom in government-sponsored housing during and in the wake of the shortages of World War II— would evolve into one of the richest building contractors in the history of New York City.

Like his father, Friedrich, Fred too, went to Europe to find a bride. He settled on a bonnie lass from the remote islands of Northern Scotland, Mary McLeod.

He married her, and she bore him five children, the fourth of which evolved into the notorious future President. *[Some of his future enemies wished she had smothered the infant at birth.]*

Donald grew up wild, incorrigible, and rebellious, a "Baby Boomer Pit Bull." His father, Fred, feared (with good reason) that his son would evolve into a knife-wielding juvenile delinquent.

He shipped him off to a military school known for its rigorous discipline. There, the deeply controversial "problem child" excelled in athletics and became a "babe magnet," in part because of his good looks and perceived wealth. He also became known as a bully, terrorizing "the nerds."

In his early 20s, The Donald, now known as "The Cincinnati Kid," ordered tenants in a Trump-owned apartment complex in Ohio "to pay the rent or get kicked out." Rivalries, disputes over money, deals coming and going, and plenty of "wenching" occupied the young man's days.

Back in Manhattan one night at a singles bar, he spotted a Czech model and ski instructor, and was awed by her beauty. He moved in quickly, aggressively pursuing her until she agreed to become his wife. Ivana later became the hard-driving mother of his three children: Ivanka, Don Jr., and Eric.

With bluff, bluster, and the spread of deliberate falsehoods, Trump was on his way to creating a real estate empire. A peak victory involved the acquisition and reconfiguration of the Commodore Hotel in midtown Manhattan. With more acquisitions and some favorable tax breaks, he in time became known as a real estate tycoon, wheeling and dealing and up to his carefully maintained coif in lawsuits, scandals, and shady deals. Along the way, there was a "devil's pact" with the notoriously shady lawyer, Roy Cohn. *(Cohn had been an intimate of the "commie-baiting" Senator, Joseph McCarthy.)*

As a hotel owner with easy access to celebrities and their influence, Trump hosted and wheeled and dealed with Liberace, Michael Jackson and a slew of political kingmakers and sports stars.

Later, he became a "gambling czar" in the then-on-the-rise Atlantic City, famously tangling with TV host and casino owner Merv Griffin, and with the heir to the Hilton fortune.

Along the way he acquired the most fabled estate in Florida, Mar-a-Lago, at a fantastically low price. Back in New York, he acquired the Plaza Hotel and returned it to its days of glory.

But, with wide coverage from the tabloids, it soon became obvious that he had bitten off "more than he could chew," and faced bankruptcy. As "the master of the deal," he miraculously recovered, soon being hailed (accurately or not) as "The Wolf of Wall Street."

Dysfunctional and greedy, brash, self-centered, and brazen, Donald and Ivana lived a life that could be torn from the telecasts of *Dynasty*.

But the sun was setting on their marriage, and Donald's roving eye turned elsewhere.

A divorce followed, and Ivana walked off with a fortune, enough so that she could live in grand luxury, in homes and aboard yachts for the rest of her days. She could also employ as many "Italian stallions" as her heart desired.

Soon after that, a Southern beauty named Marla Maples entered Donald's life. In time, she would become his second wife, giving birth to his second daughter, Tiffany, who grew up to lead the life "of the one percent."

Marla, a shapely, beautiful, busty, and blonde Georgia peach from the "Tree of Life" was not First Lady material, at least not in the way defined by Eleanor Roosevelt.

During their brief marriage, Marla frequently repeated the same pivotal, four-word sentence: "Charge it to Donald."

In the meantime, Trump developed his own motto: "So many models, so little time."

His marriage to Marla eventually came to a crashing, widely publicized end.

***

The political saga that's explored in this book begins in 1998 as Donald shops around and eventually enters his third marriage—this time to the beautiful and exotic-looking Melania Krauss (aka Melania Knavs), a one-time model so stylish that it briefly appeared that she'd challenge the legacy of the very fashionable Jacqueline Kennedy.

Melania (some called her "the most visible trophy wife since Cleopatra brought Egypt into the orbit of ancient Rome") was at Donald's side as he descended that escalator to attack Mexicans and to announce his run for the presidency.

He then set out to "slay dragons" on the campaign trails, including Republican competitors Ted Cruz, Jeb Bush, and Marco Rubio.

Now, he faced his biggest challenge, the general election and Hillary Clinton, his Democratic opponent. In the words of one of his campaign workers, "On TV, The Donald cut that woman up into little pieces and fed her to the wolves."

Once ensconced within the Oval Office, he launched the most controversial and notorious presidency in the history of the Democracy. From Day One, he was mocked and caricatured, later making history by surviving two impeachment trials.

***

A Sweat-Soaked Search for the Holy Grail

WHAT THE DONALD SAID ABOUT HOW HE'D MAKE AMERICA GREAT AGAIN

"Install me as Prez even if it means tossing the Constitution aside."
—Donald Trump

"We'll Build a Wall and Mexico Will Pay for It."
—Donald Trump

"Why are we having all these people from shithead countries coming here?"
—Donald Trump

"To dream the impossible dream: Princess Di as my First Lady, Oprah Winfrey as my Veep."
—Donald Trump

"Shut your Pie Hole!"
—Donald Trump to Ted Cruz

"John McCain Was No War Hero—War Heroes Aren't Captured."
—Donald Trump

Crooked Hillary Should Be Jailed.
—Donald Trump

***

THE DONALD AS TABLOID FODDER

Never in the history of the presidency has any man been so ridiculed and satirized. Even before Trump became president, he made headlines across the United States, Mexico, Canada, and Europe. German newspapers mocked him, as did the French and Italian press.

During his term in office, the "Second Coming" headlines he generated were among the most mocking and provocative ever printed.

Bill Clinton's penis was the first such organ associated, in the news, with a U.S. president. But Trump topped him, his penis making headlines.

[Editor's Note: Neither President was as heavy-hung as Lyndon B. Johnson, who ordered his tailors to give him extra room in the crotch.]

HERE ARE SOME OF THE HEADLINES INSPIRED AND GENERATED BY DONALD TRUMP BEFORE, DURING, AND AFTER HIS PRESIDENCY

He's a porn queen humper

Trump's dick is deformed.

"Are you in yet?"

"American Prez is Craziest Man on Earth."
—London Tabloid

"He Needs to Shave His Balls—Hairy as a Neanderthal."
—Stormy Daniels

Trump claims All African Countries Are Poo-Poo Holes, and "All Haitians have AIDS"

Haitians tell Trump where to put it.

Trump is in Love: With a North Korean Despot

Trump's Family Company must pay $1.6 million to the Feds for Tax Fraud

"Shit for Brains" Trump spews vicious slur against immigrants.

Donald Trump's Trading Card Depicts Him as Superman—Big muscles, small basket.

Vengeful FBI Agents Trap Ex-President, Who May Go to Jail.

Epstein Madam Sells Out Trump.

Oh, Lardy—Trump Gains 60 pounds.

Explosive TV hearings Expose Betrayal, Lies, & Treachery.

Trump's insane Capitol Hill Coup.

Trump Entertains Nazi at Mar-a-Lago

After Years of Delay, Trump Is Deposed in Rape Accuser Suit. She wins.

Mike Pence signs a pact to Lie or Die for Caligula.

Trump Tries to Suppress Lesbian Nude Photos of his Wife.

Trump's Lawyer Roy Cohn Claims he Once Went Down on Trump.

Trump has Body of Seal—That's Why He's Afraid of Sharks

"Donald has Trouble Rising to the Occasion. He once raped me."
—Ivana Trump

"Stormy Daniels Screws Publicly and Trump Screws the Public."
—Columnist Linda Stasi

Clown runs for President

Hate for nonwhite immigrants—Love for Norway.

Trump Grabs Umbrella & Lets Barron and Melania Get Soaked.

Trump Denounced as Little Nero, Mad Caligula.

The Donald Likens Porn Queen as "Being Like My Daughter."

The Bastard King Turd

Mysogenistic, Homophobic, Racist, Vulgarian.

Trump's a Male Version of Medusa's Head.

Trump Issues Command at Mar-a-Lago: "No stinking Jews or Jungle Bunny Blacks."

Trump Would Invade Mexico.

Trump Would Launch an Atomic Bomb.

Trump Kicks Ted Cruz's Dingleberry-Studded Ass Out of New England.

Unhinged, Ranting, and Raving.

The Donald Would Deport All Muslims.

Donald Trump Would Bring Back Nazi Concentration Camps for illegal immigrants.

In private, Trump was Overheard Calling Hillary a Dyke.

Trump Tells a Lie Every Five Minutes.

Gun Nuts Back a Nut.

Trump Has a Ten-Inch Pinocchio Nose.

Popularity Polls Rank Lice and Forest Fires Ahead of Trump

Trump Will Nuke the U.S. Economy.

Trump is Charged with the Rape of a 13-Year-Old Girl.

Angry Caucasians Defend Trump as Last Stand of the White Man.

President Will Urge Congress to Declare World War III.

The Odd Couple—A homophobic, Bible-thumping Misogynist Is Trump's Choice for Veep.

GOP Switches Initials to BIFF (Bigots, Idiots, Fascists, and Fools)

Gays Should Be Stripped of All Rights Except Taxation.

Trump Becomes President—Let the Circus Begin.

Trump is to the Right of Attila the Hun.

Lucifer! He's Back!

Forecast for a Trump Reign—Confusion, Turmoil, Rage, and Despair

Trump Will Spend Eternity Rotting in Hell.

Trump Presidency will lead to Global Disaster.

Trump Turns America into a Banana Republic.

Trump Mocked Around the World.

Never Trump! He's a Miserable Son of a Bitch!

Trump Has Lizard Brain.

Trump Is a Modern Day Hitler.

Trump Is a Junkyard Dog with Rabies.

Trump Is a Pompous Asshole.

Trump is a Buffoon and a Phoney.

Potty Mouth Wants to Kick Disloyal Blacks off Football Field.

"Is Trump Worse than Dracula?" England Ponders

Trump Debates Hillary Like a Balls-Out Pissing Match.

Trump Has Tiny Cojones Made of Steel.

Trump Is the World's Most Dangerous Man.

Blacks for Hillary, Racist Whites for Trump

It's Alive! Republicans Back Modern-Day Frankenstein

Trump Defends the Size of His Penis from "Little Marco."

The Rise of Nastiness and Ignorance in the White House

The End of the GOP.

Dawn of the Brain Dead—Mindless Zombies Turn Out for Trump.

Dixie Ding-Dongs Back Trump.

KKK Endorses Trump.

The Donald Takes Viagra

(Trump is a) Fat Man Without a Plan.

Trump's Insane Capitol Hill Coup

The Donald: One Big Mac and Two Scoops of Chocolate Ice Cream Away from Keeling Over.

Trump Divides God's Voters.

From the Granite State to the Palmetto State, Donald Deflowers Pussy Boy Ted Cruz.

Trump: Elephant in the Room

Trump's a Big Pile of Blow

Trump Tells Jeb Bush to Shut Up

From the Grave, Trump is Endorsed by John Wayne

(Trump is a) Bloviating Billionaire & Idiot.

Send in the Dancing Bears

(Trump is a) Pathological Liar, Narcissist, & Serial Philanderer.

Trump's Butler Claims Obama Should be hanged for Treason.

Donald Reveals Secrets of His Orange Coif

He's a Mad Man, a Raving Lunatic, a Demented Fool, a Rotting Pile of Manure.

TRUMP IS IMPEACHED

TRUMP IMPEACHED AGAIN

TRUMP INDICTED

TRUMP INDICTED AGAIN

The Art of the Comeback: But is it Presidential?

In this 1997 book by Donald, he delivered this as one of his top ten comeback tips: **GET EVEN.**

"During the bad times, I learned who was loyal and who wasn't. I believe in an eye for an eye. A couple of people who betrayed me need my help now, and I'm screwing them against the wall! I am doing a number...and I'm having such fun."

Left photo: In 1984, an article in *Time* profiled **Donald**, including references to his cardplaying as a metaphor for his business-related (and perhaps political) games of chance: "At 6 ft. 2 in., real estate tycoon Donald J. (for John) Trump does not really oom colossus-high above the horizon of New York and New Jersey. He has created no great work of art or ideas, and even as a maker or possessor of money he does not rank among the top ten, or even 50."

"Yet at 42, he has seized a large fistful of that contemporary coin known as celebrity. There has been artfully hyped talk about his having political ambitions, worrying about nuclear proliferation, even someday running for President. No matter how farfetched that may be something about his combination of blue-eyed swagger and success has caught the public fancy and made him in many ways a symbol of an acquisitive and mercenary age."

Right photo: **Donald's Fall from Grace** after his botched election bid of 2020 was not the first time media outlets predicted his demise:

During his bid for the Presidency in 2016, the question was often asked, "How can a person who has filed for bankruptcy four times expect to be elected President of the United States? How is Donald Trump able to file for bankruptcy so many times?"

The answer is, "He didn't." Donald himself never filed for bankruptcy. His corporations, however, filed for Chapter 11 bankruptcy four times. All of these bankruptcies were connected to over-everaged casino and hotel properties in Atlantic City.

HOW WILL HISTORY JUDGE HIM?

Will Trump be interpreted as a George Washington, a Thomas Jefferson, Abraham Lincoln, or Franklin D. Roosevelt? Or will he go down as another Martin Van Buren, Franklin Pierce, James Buchanan, Warren G. Harding, Herbert Hoover, or Richard Nixon?   Until Trump, James Buchanan (1857-1861; *third photo from left*) was considered the worst President in U.S. History.

HOW DID HE DO IT? In this saga, we'll explore the historic, fast- unfolding tricks, traps, and trade-offs of the capture (some said "enslavement") of the American Presidency by The Donald, a president whose aftermath changed the world.

Chapter One

THE DONALD AND THE PRINCESS
Donald & Diana: The Fantasy Romance That Never Happened

MELANIA

How to Marry a "Bloviating Billionaire" and Emerge as a First Lady

Cinderella's Billionaire Baby: **BARRON TRUMP**
At the Age of Three, He Learns to Shout, "You're Fired!"

Long before he met her, Donald hoped to cash in on the publicity whirling around the royal heads of Princess Di and Charles.

When he was selling apartments at Trump Tower, Donald was allegedly the source of a rumor that Prince Charles and his Princess had purchased one of the high-end apartments, a 24-room, $5 million condo.

"They don't need bank financing," he told his associates.

In London, Buckingham Palace was asked to comment on the possible purchase, but they refused.

When cornered by reporters to confirm the rumor, Donald told them, "Only the best people in the world are buying my apartments. Charles and Princess Di are among the best people in the world. But that's all I'm saying for now."

Later, Donald would be introduced to Princess Di on at least five formal occasions in London, but it was his estranged wife, Ivana, who first got to shake her royal palm.

In July of 1990, Ivana boarded the Concorde and flew to London. Within the previous two months, she'd made three trips to Europe, treating it almost like flying from New York to Palm Beach. British tabloid readers were well aware of her marital woes with Donald.

She lodged with her friend, Eva O'Neill, on Eaton Square. Who was she?

Gossip columnist Nigel Dempster, writing for the *Daily Mail*, called her "a blonde woman of an uncertain age who lives in the right part of town but is not prominent in any way. Her friends have names like Von Panz and Hohenlohe."

Wearing Parisian haute couture and plumed hats, they were seen having tea at The Ritz, dinner at The Savoy, at the tennis matches at Wimbledon, and at the horse races at Ascot attended by the Queen.

At a fashionable luncheon attended by Diana, Ivana managed to pass, along with the other guests, in front of a formal receiving line to shake hands with the tastefully dressed and charming princess herself.

Di smiled demurely at the rather overdressed and overly made up wife of Donald Trump. When she passed on down the line, Diana was caught casting a disdainful look at Ivana.

By July 8, she was on her way back to New York to meet with attorneys to give depositions in her lawsuit against Donald, seeking half of his estate for all the work she'd done for his companies, both in Atlantic City and in Manhattan.

At a time when Diana's unhappy marriage to Charles was being widely reported, although she had not filed for divorce yet, Donald, along with millions of others, learned of her marital woes. It seemed that he wanted to be among the first in her lineup of new suitors.

He began to send her bouquets of flowers and love notes. It was reported that he sent her a rare piece of jewelry that had once belonged to Marie Antoinette, although that does not appear to be the case.

Besieged by his cascade of letters, flowers, and (unwanted) attention, Diana placed a call to her friend, Selina Scott, one of Britain's most recognized TV journalists. Scott had been a key player in a documentary about Donald for the BBC. It was so unflattering that he attacked her for years after its release. During her time in America, Scott had found that, "I was especially put off by Trump's behavior toward women."

A REAL ESTATE COUP THAT NEVER WAS The Prince and Princess of Wales, "in residence"—that is, if anyone believed Donald's hype during sales of condos in Trump Tower. Donald tried to convince buyers that Charles and Diana would be part-time residents.

In distinct contrast to how **Diana** snubbed Donald's (romantic) overtures, she related well to **Hillary**. Their 1997 meeting in the Map Room of the White House is depicted in this U.S. government photo.

"What should I do with all the flowers and solicitations?" Diana asked.

"My suggestion," Scott said, "is just bin the lot" [i.e., "toss them in the dustbin."]

Apparently, the Princess told Scott just how repulsive she found Donald to be, and that there would be no romance. Donald did not give up so easily.

He told his friends that the young Princes, William and Harry, "needed a strong macho image to be their father. I would take care of the boys while Charles was off pursuing the ugliest woman in Britain …what's her face?"

"And if Diana agreed to marry me, I would not insist on a prenup."

He had read that Diana once said, "When I was born, I was unwanted. When I married Charles, I was unwanted. When I joined the royal family, I was unwanted. I want to be wanted."

"When I heard that," Donald said, "I wrote her a very short note: 'I want you.'"

He became very miffed when Diana rejected his advances and turned to a different lover, Dodi Al Fayed.

In the late 1990s, shortly before Di's death, Alex Yemendijian, the CEO of MGM, reported that once in the Trump Tower, Donald was enraged that the Princess had been the focus of frontpage headlines and that he had been assigned "to the also-ran page three."

"Donald, surely you know that a pretty girl always wins out," the chairman said.

"This is crazy. It's not fair somehow. She's no longer in line for the throne, and is actually shacked up with this Arab. He's only an ugly Arab! Had she played her cards right, she could have had me! Women…I'll never understand them."

Weeks later, he said, "I don't think I'll ever get over the news." He was referring to August 31, 1997. "I couldn't believe she was gone. The news hit me like a shock wave."

He avidly followed world reaction in the wake of Diana's death, and was particularly interested in how Charles and the Queen were handling it. He immediately wrote sympathy notes to both William and Harry.

He learned that after hearing of Diana's car crash, the first person Charles called was not his mother, nor either of his sons, but his mistress, Camilla Parker-Bowles.

Around the same time, after her friends heard of Diana's death, some of them called Camilla to congratulate her. "My dear!" one of the ladies said. "You are going to wear the crown of the Queen of England!"

"It's ghastly," Donald told his friends, "how the royal family treated Diana. She should have been mine. I would have taken care of her. In fact, if she had married me, she'd still be alive and living in regal splendor on the top of Trump Tower."

Just eight weeks after Diana's violent death, Donald admitted on national TV that one of his biggest regrets was that he never got to date Diana. His interviewer, Stone Phillips, asked him, "Do you think she would have agreed to go out with you?"

"I think so," Donald said. "Yeah, I think she would. I would have had a shot. I don't recall ever being turned down by a woman."

Donald was very sympathetic to Mohamed Al Fayed, Dodi's father, who was chairman of Harrods in London. "Mohamed has gone through a rough time over the last several years. It was his son Dodi who was dating Princess Di. To many of us, it looked like they would be getting married at some point in the not too distant future, until their lives ended in that tragic car crash in Paris. Mohamed is an extremely loyal father who has fought so hard for his son and the memory of him. I wish people understood him better. He is truly a good man."

According to Selina Scott, **Donald** regarded the divorced **Princess Diana** as "the ultimate trophy wife. Of all the women in the world, she is the most desired and sought after now that Charles is out of the picture. **Donald and Diana**...I like the sound of that."

Selina Scott on the BBC describing her feud with Donald Trump. She was more impressed by his Scottish mother.

"What a couple Di and I would have made," he said. "Just imagine if I decided to run for President of the United States? With her charm and grace, she would have propelled me into the White House. There's no way we could lose."

"Di would be the greatest First Lady America has ever seen," he said. "Forget Jacqueline Kennedy and her so-called style. Di would have made Jackie look like a salesclerk in a department store."

"President Donald Trump and First Lady Diana Windsor Trump would have entered the history books, you know, along with such historical figures as Cleopatra and Marc Antony, Napoléon and Josephine, Franklin and Eleanor."

***

Since his romance with the Windsor lineage was not to be, Donald soon recovered from the shock of Di's death and turned elsewhere. "I was looking for love, and I soon found it."

When he set out on his search, he had two requirements: His new love had to be as lovely as Princess

Reportedly, **Donald** relished the marketing lure of **Princess Diana**. "She could make millions in endorsements," he claimed. "Also, I'd invite her to the inauguration of all my properties around the world. I think we could become the power couple of the 21st Century."

Di, or almost so, and she had to be regal enough to be a suitable First Lady if, in the future, he decided to (and was able to) move from the Trump Tower to 1600 Pennsylvania Avenue.

Fast forward from 1997 to 2004:

MELANIA'S BEAUTY:
Apprentice Contestants Invade Trump Tower. When They Meet Her, They're Awed

Once, on *The Apprentice*, Donald extended an invitation to the winning team to dine with him and his girlfriend, model Melania Knauss, at their lavish penthouse apartment atop Trump Tower. He called it "a filet mignon dinner at twilight."

Arriving promptly at 7PM, the contestants were awed by the beauty of their hostess and the stunning décor of Donald's private quarters, even though it has been parodied on *Saturday Night Live* as "having the same interior decorator as Saddam Hussein."

In the soft lighting, Melania appeared as an incandescent beauty, with lustrous skin a dusty bronze. Photographers spoke of her "aqua eyes" that sometimes appeared a bit squinchy but in person were much wider. When she entered a room, it was like Princess Diana herself had entered. Melania was lithe and limber, with the waist of a high-fashion model, moving her 5'11" frame across the lushly carpeted room like a model on a Versace runway.

Donald delayed his entrance for thirty minutes, but Melania shook each of the contestant's hands before showing them around. For the occasion, she wore a pink cap-sleeved Antonio Berardi sheath dress with matching Louboutin high heels.

The focal point of the penthouse, and its dramatic highlight, was a Hall of Mirrors, evocative of the one at the Palace of Versailles, through which Louis XV paraded with *la comtesse du Barry*. The wide-eyed contestants took in the white marble fountain and the hand-painted ceilings with fat cherubs.

Her voice was soft and seductive, and fluent in English, Slovenian, French, German, or Serbian.

After a tour of the gold leaf décor, Melania directed the contestants toward the panoramic view of the city and Central Park at night.

The butler arrived with champagne. One of the contestants held up her glass to praise Melania. "You're very lucky."

Raising her own glass, Melania shot back, "And he's not lucky?"

At this point attention focused on Donald, descending the stairs in a suit, red tie, and shoes far more expensive than the monthly wage of some of the contestants. He walked over to Melania, giving her a gentle kiss on her succulent lips. "Welcome to my humble abode," he told his guests. "The beef you're about to eat tonight is the most expensive cuts in the world."

The contestants, like any readers of the New York tabloids, knew a lot about Donald Trump and his two previous wives, Ivana and Marla. But who was this "trophy girlfriend" who was not some vapid model but an intelligent, sophisticated woman of immense charm? As one contestant said of the evening, "Melania is as regal a princess as Grace Kelly or Princess Di ever was."

At the time, little was known of her background, and most of the American public outside of New York had never heard of her.

THE MODEL AND THE MOGUL

Born on April 26, 1970, in the northern tier of what was then known as Yugoslavia, within a region now known as the independent nation of Slovenia, Melanjia Knavs would eventually change her name to the more Germanized Melania Knauss.

In Manhattan and in Palm Beach, although she would preside over two of the grandest residences in the U.S, she grew up modestly.

She lived in one of the anonymous concrete apartment complexes built during Josip Tito's socialist administration of what was then known as Yugoslavia. At the time, over-the-top capitalism, and full-blown Trumpism, did not exist for her.

She came of age in Slovenia's Sevnica district in the Lower Sava Valley. Her father, Viktor Knavs, owned a car dealership, and her mother, Amalija, was a seamstress who sometimes designed clothing. Melania also had an older sister, Ines.

Melania had brains as well as beauty, and she studied design and architecture

Ad slogan from the Slovenian Tourist Office. Locals define Melania as the greatest incentive to tourism her country has ever seen.

at the University of Ljubljana in Slovenia.

It seemed inevitable that she would attract the attention of a photographer. Now in his early 80s, he was Stane Jerko, who discovered her and asked her to pose for him. "She was striking even with baby-fat cheeks and a Madonna-style pony tail. It could be said that I discovered her. My pictures set her down the road to fame and fortune."

Jerko's pictures were seen by a talent scout for a modeling agency in Milan. Within months, Melania had launched her career as a mannequin, appearing on high-fashion runways not only in Milan but in Paris.

"It seemed that I came across a sleeping chrysalis that transformed herself into a glamourous butterfly," Jerko said.

She dreamed of coming to New York to advance her career, and migrated there in 1996. "I was no illegal immigrant that Donald would deport. I did it the long and hard way, but the legal way."

She was in America on a visa. When it was close to expiring, she returned to Europe but re-entered again. This went on until she became a permanent resident of the United States in 2001 and was granted a green card, becoming a full-fledged U.S. citizen in 2006.

"As a girl growing up in Slovenia, I was told that America was a place where dreams come true. But never in my pink-clouded fantasies did I think I would climb so far as to become a possible First Lady of my newly adopted country. I'm not there yet, of course, but one can dream. If I make it, I will use Nancy Reagan and Jacqueline Kennedy as my role models, although I will pioneer my own wardrobe."

Photographers in New York were immediately attracted to Melania's exotic beauty, and soon she was posing for Helmut Newton, Mario Testino, Patrick Demarchelier, Arthur Elgort, Ellen Von Unwerth, and Antoine Verglas.

She was the cover girl supreme, gracing the covers of such magazines as *Vogue, Harper's Bazaar, Style, Ocean Drive, Avenue, New York* magazine, *Self, Glamor*, and inevitably, *Vanity Fair.*

Her most revealing photo appeared in 2000 for the annual edition of *Sports Illustrated*'s swimwear edition in a bikini.

She was represented by several modeling agencies, including Donald Trump Model management, even though she had yet to meet the mogul.

She was also featured in a number of TV commercials, including one for Aflac, an insurance company that's associated with America's top duck icon. She would later co-host *The View* with Barbara Walters. "Behind all that beauty was one smart cookie," Walters said. "She is no mannequin, and has a passion for the arts, architecture, design, and fashion."

A person can thrive and grow in the cultural diversity of New York," Melania said. "It is, in fact, the cultural capital of the world."

One night during Fashion Week in 1998, Paolo Zampoli threw a chic party for the ID Modeling Agency. Separate and unconnected at the time, his guest list included the names of both Donald Trump and Melania Knauss.

Donald arrived with an "arm candy model," beautiful but vapid, and was soon surrounded by a bevy of beauties. He seemed disenchanted with his date for the evening. With his eagle eye for female pulchritude, he focused on this "stunning looker."

At the time, he had split from his second wife, Marla Maples, and was looking for another conquest.

When Donald's date went to the ladies' room, he turned to Zampoli: "That girl over there is incredible. I want you to introduce us." He was surprised to find that she had a link to his own modeling agency. Once introduced, he chatted briefly with her and asked for her phone number.

"Since he was with a date, I refused to give him my number," Melania said. "I won't give you my number, but you can give me yours," she told him. "I'll call you."

"Frankly, I wanted to see what kind of number he would give me," she said. "Perhaps it would ring through to a secretary or some aide. I was wrong. He gave me several private numbers, not only his private office number, but his penthouse number, even an unlisted number in Palm Beach."

In the spring of 2010, **Melania** posed for this sexy photograph for the cover of *Avenue* magazine, revealing an ample bosom and "Betty Grable" legs.

Obviously, at this point in her career, Melania never knew that in a few short years she would be considered a potential candidate for First Lady of the United States

Melania represents "photogenic razzmatazz," as one photographer phrased it, a glamourous figure well suited for the promotion of her beauty products.

Among her other achievements, she knew how to turn crushed fish eggs into an expensive beauty aide.

"I had this shoot in California when I phoned him," Melania said. "He was in New York. I was struck by his energy when we spoke. He has this amazing vitality."

Back in New York, on their first date, Donald picked her up in a black stretch limousine, and, along with Zampoli and the magician, David Copperfield, he instructed his driver to take them to the deluxe Cipriani Restaurant.

When she left the table to powder her nose, Zampoli told Donald, "When you get to know Melania, you will love her. It doesn't take long for people to fall in love with her, especially men, but she's very hard to get. She's not on the party circuit."

On the following night, he took her to dinner at Mooma, which in the late 1990s was the *ne plus ultra* of celebrity-studded hot spots. "It was a great place," she said. "It was a great date. A night to remember."

Within weeks, Donald and Melania became a power couple around Manhattan, and were seen at all the lavish galas and chic restaurants, including Le Cirque. He took her there only for dinner, because his previous wife, Ivana, often lunched there with her gossipy women friends.

Very quietly and discreetly, Melania moved into his lavish quarters at the Trump Tower, sharing all those rooms with her new boyfriend. In spite of the difference in their ages (he was born in 1946, she in 1970), they clicked as a couple.

Her life with limos, helicopters, deluxe restaurants, diamonds, penthouses, lavish estates, and a fabulous "to-die-for" wardrobe had begun.

It wasn't long before the tabloids started writing about "The Mogul and the Model." The *New York Daily News* reported that "Donald Trump's latest model friend has been selected to advertise BMW cars. Did she get the job through a powerful connection?"

The couple made an appearance at the gala honoring the restoration of the Grand Central Terminal.

To the delight of photographers, Donald and Melania dazzled when they came into the lavish Costume Ball at the Metropolitan Museum of Art, where much of *tout* New York feasted their eyes on her for the first time.

"Nobody seemed to take notice of me," Donald said. "All eyes were on Melania. Perhaps that was because I didn't wear a costume myself. Hey, wasn't that Anna Wintour approaching us?"

During her courtship with Donald, Melania could sometimes create a tabloid frenzy. Such was the case when she showed up, plunging *décolletage* and all, at the funeral of Fred Trump, who died in 1999 at age 93. The funeral was at the Marble Collegiate Church in Manhattan. In spite of all the distinguished guests from both the business and political worlds, the paparazzi focused on sexy Melania, although she faced criticism for dressing so provocatively at a funeral.

In Europe, Melania had frequented some of the most glamourous spots, including St. Tropez on the French Riviera, or a palace on Lake Como. But Donald claimed that she found Mar-a-Lago the most beautiful place on earth.

At the former estate of Marjorie Merriweather Post, Donald and Melania "moved through the rooms of the estate with her acting like a princess and him some turn-of-the 19th-century grandee," a reporter wrote. "They were warm and attentive, and she looked like she stepped off the cover of *Vogue*."

The relationship between Donald and Melania came to the attention of millions of Americans during a 1999 radio interview on *The Howard Stern Show*.

At one point, the shock jock asked Melania what she was wearing. "Not much!" she shot back. It was predictable that Stern would turn to the topic of sex. Donald admitted that he and Melania had watched the notorious sex tape of Paris Hilton. "I saw it in spite of the fact that I have known Paris

As this magazine cover demonstrates, **Donald** knew how to turn a hot fashion model into a symbol of domestic decorum.

In this article, **Melania** extolled his virtues as a husband and as a father, and then went on to say, "He would make one of America's greatest Presidents."

Since her involvement with Donald, **Melania** has become a legend in Slavic Europe, an adventurous personification of the postmodern American Dream.

Here, striding into a bold New World, she's depicted on the front cover of the Bulgarian edition of *Harper's Bazaar*.

since she was twelve years old, and I've been close friends of her family for years."

He told Stern that "Melania looks best—really hot—when she wears only a very small thong."

She confided, "We have sex at least once a day, maybe more. It's incredible sex. Donald is the greatest lover."

"Melania is great," Donald told Stern. "I've never heard her fart or make doodie." He also told Stern that he could trust her to take birth control every day. "She has great boobs, which is no trivia matter to me."

Stern wanted to know what Donald would do if she got into a horrible car accident, perhaps lost the use of an arm, or was disfigured in some way.

"How would the breasts look," Donald asked.

"The breasts would be okay," Stern answered.

"Then yeah, of course," Donald said. "Our relationship would continue if the breasts were okay."

A friend who did not want to be named claimed that "Melania is perfect for The Donald—as if a divine plastic surgeon had sculpted her out of his rib."

"I WASN'T NAKED. I WORE A DIAMOND CHOKER"

—*Donald's nude girlfriend, in reference to a photo-shoot aboard his private plane*

WHAT PEOPLE WERE SAYING ABOUT MELANIA:

"She ain't Bess Truman, and she ain't Mamie Eisenhower...But is she anything akin to Jackie Kennedy?

Ivana probably had a lot to say when *Bella* magazine, on its cover, defined Melania as "The First Lady of NYC."

Melania's sexy celebrity appeal received its greatest exposure through her appearance on the January 2000 cover of the British *GQ* magazine. The picture of her posing nude would later become a campaign issue in 2016, erupting into a bitter fight between Ted Cruz and Donald.

The photographer was Antoine Verglas. He had shot such models as Cindy Crawford and Claudia Schiffer. His assignment for *GQ* had been defined as a sexy photo essay about jet-setters, with a focus on "the sexiest model around," who was also the girlfriend of a mogul who traveled in his own private jet.

Wearing a sparkly diamond necklace—and "not a stitch of clothing"—Melania had never looked more seductive, with her icy, blue-green eyes, and her plump,

Sex at 30,000 Feet

GQ's Naked Supermodel Special

Widely berated, and with a lot of exposed flesh, this feature in GQ in 2000 was controversial even before Donald became a presidential candidate. Ted Cruz, in advance of the Utah primaries in March of 2016, aimed dire warnings at conservative Mormon voters, buying ads that screamed, **"Meet Melania Trump, your next First Lady."**

In response, Donald, through Twitter, released unflattering photos of Cruz's wife, Heidi, "looking like a gargoyle," according to a writer from *Maxim*.

His message to Cruz? "My wife is hotter than yours."

17

pouty lips, along with her shapely butt. However, she refused to pose for certain more revealing photos that Verglas wanted.

He was also a makeup artist and hair stylist, and he spent part of that day inside Donald's custom-built jet while it was stationary and sheltered within a hangar at New York's LaGuardia airport.

"It was for the cover of a men's magazine, so I was going for the sexy image," he said. "Melania is easy to shoot because her body, unlike so many models I've photographed before, has no flaws."

On that same day, he photographed her on a fur blanket handcuffed to a leather briefcase.

Another shot depicted her standing on the wing of the plane. Pointing a pistol, evoking a James Bond girl, she wore a red bra and thong, very dark sunglasses, knee-high leather boots.

The magazine's headline was "SEX AT 30,000 FEET. MELANIA KNAUSS EARNS HER AIR MILES."

That same year, Verglas also photographed Carla Bruni, who had previously dated Donald before marrying the French president Nicholas Sarkozy. "They both were gorgeous models, really gorgeous, with perfect figures," Verglas said. "But they were very different personalities. Before Donald, who was lusting for Princess Di at the time, Bruni had dated a lot of famous men like Mick Jagger and Eric Clapton. In contrast, Melania lived in a modest apartment and had no history of boyfriends—and that was most unusual for a model."

The ultimate vulgarian shock jock, **Howard Stern**, during a live interview with Donald, wanted to know, "What underwear are you wearing?"

Verglas later photographed Melania at Palm Beach. "The girl from Slovenia was now mistress of Mar-a-Lago! It was WOW! Like Cinderella!"

"Melania was America's Carla Bruni," said image consultant Christina Logothetis.

In the years to come, Melania would develop thousands of followers on Twitter, posting selfies of her beauty rituals, private jet rides, and her bikini-clad body. However, by July of 2015, as Donald was in the first days of his campaign, the window into her private life was shut down, the curtains drawn.

"LOVE IS BETTER THE THIRD TIME AROUND"

—*Donald Trump*

The relationship of Donald and Melania received a lot of publicity after the launch in 2006 of *The Apprentice* when he spoke of their long courtship. "We literally have never had an argument. Forget about the word 'fight.' We are very compatible. We get along."

After surviving painful and expensive divorces from his first two wives, Donald drifted for years before he contemplated marriage again. "I didn't want to get married until I was older and wiser," he said.

"Before I married Melania, it was a big decision for me. We had a comfort zone with each other. I believe strongly in the concept of 'the woman behind the man,' or vice versa. I was with Melania for five years of my life, during which I enjoyed great success. For example, *The Apprentice* became number one on TV, and my show got nominated for five Emmys. So if figured I'd better marry the woman who stood behind me (and in front of me) during this amazing and crazy period—and fast!"

In 2000, when Donald was contemplating a run for President of the United States on the Reform Ticket, a publicist came up with "a crazy idea" for a shot.

"I was out of my mind," Donald said, "but I agreed to it."

Provocatively draped in an American flag, and lounging across his desk, Melania was photographed gazing lovingly at her boyfriend.

When Donald saw the final print, "No way in hell!" he said. "The damn picture is over the top, even for me."

"I chose to be married because I didn't want to be single any longer," he said. "I have had a bad track record of being married, it is true, but I would rather live a married life than be single. That is because I have met the right

Here, as a fashion-savvy techie with a penchant for ambiguity, **Melania** clicked and distributed, via Twitter, a selfie showing her outfit of the day.

Distributed on May 29, 2015, it advised, with a lack of discretion the Secret Service later curtailed, "Bye. I'm off to my summer residence."

woman. I have learned something from my previous mistakes. I am determined to do much better in my eventual marriage to Melania."

He didn't need a special occasion, such as a wedding, to present jewelry to his girlfriend. He'd been known to pop into Asprey's flagship store, conveniently positioned within Trump Tower, to purchase a "trinket" for her.

"Asprey's has been around since the 18th Century, and its jewelry makes the most beautiful women even more beautiful," he said. "But if you're in the market for diamonds, go to Harry Winston or Graff. They sell the best diamonds in the world."

Weeks before his marriage, Melania was asked to sign a prenup agreement. He'd gone through that before with both Ivanka and Marla, and ultimately, neither of them had wanted to honor their original contract with him.

He told Melania, "I love you so much, and we're going to have the greatest marriage ever. It's going to be unbelievable. Listen, just in case it doesn't work out, sign on the dotted line."

In marked contrast to both Marla and Ivana, she willingly signed her name without any fuss. He later said "It was not the most romantic thing to do, but I really, really needed her to do that."

Melania's $200,000 wedding dress was designed by the controversial John Galliano of the House of Dior. An embroidered couture creation, it took 1,000 hours of hard labor to craft.

After many years of co-habitation, Donald Trump married Melania Knauss, his third wife. The date on the social calendar for many luminaries was January 22, 2005 in Palm Beach at the Episcopal Church of Bethesda-by-the-Sea.

Notables attending the wedding included Katie Couric, Matt Lauer, Rudy Giuliani, Heidi Klum, Star Jones, P. Diddy, Shaquille O'Neal, Barbara Walters, Conrad Black, Regis Philbin, Simon Cowell, Oprah Winfrey, and Kelly Ripa.

The veiled bride would appear as the focal point of a stunning cover of *Vogue*.

For her hair, Melania flew in a top stylist. Donald quipped, "I did my own hair...unfortunately for the world."

After the wedding, a lavish reception was staged at Mar-a-Lago. To entertain, Billy Joel serenaded the crowd with "Just the Way You Are," and supplied new lyrics about Donald to the tune of "The Lady Is a Tramp." The wedding cake was a fifty-pounder, a spectacular orange Grand Marnier chocolate truffle cake with a Grand Marnier butter-cream filling. It was covered with 3,000 dewy fresh red roses.

Tina Brown, the former editor of *Vanity Fair*, wrote in a column for *The New York Post*: "Bill and Hillary Clinton were there to do what they always like to do best for R&R: Raise money."

In 2015, early in his campaign for president, Donald was criticized for having invited the Clintons. "She had no choice but attend when I asked her to," he said. "After all, I had contributed generously to her foundation."

To explain what she was doing there, she said, "I happened to be in Florida and I thought it would be fun to go to his wedding because it was certain to be entertaining."

Brad Johns, a celebrity colorist who added "caramel highlights" to Melania's hair, said, "She's incapable of being mean. She's not gossipy at all, not bitchy and just really nice, though I know that's not exciting to hear."

Tina Brown wrote of Melania: "Underneath all the fabulousness and gloss, Melania Knauss's staying power in Donald's life is based on a shrewd understanding of her quasi-commercial role. One feels she will not make Ivana's mistake of competing with the Trump brand. But she also knows, as second wife Marla Maples did not, the difference between being mere arm candy and high-definition product enhancement. As one of her friends puts it, 'For Melania, it's never ask what Donald can do for you, it's ask what you can do for The Donald.'"

And the magazine covers just kept coming, and coming, and coming... prompting voters to ask, "Will the Secret Service allow photo-ops of **Melania** at the White House? And if they do, what will she wear?"

As the campaign blustered on, a relentlessly fashionable **Melania**, like Liza Doolittle in *My Fair Lady*, was coached —diction, grammar, what not to say—during situations she was likely to face.

THE MINI-DONALD
Barron Trump, the 21st Century's Little Lord Fauntleroy

"Those jerks running against my dad are creeps—Cruz is a liar and Hillary is a crook."
—Barron Trump

When the cover of *Vogue*, featuring Donald's beautiful bride #3, was released, viewers had trouble recognizing (or even seeing) **Melania** through the faux-virginal *froufrou*, the frills, the lettering of the cover design, the accessories, and the *whoopla*.

In the aftermath of the Trump-Knauss wedding, his enemies released this photograph of **Donald at his wedding with Melania.** A friendly and charming **Bill and Hillary Clinton** were sandwiched between them.

Widely distributed by both campaigns, it emerged as controversial and, for Donald, embarrassing. Its implications and bragging rights, and (perhaps false) professions of respect and friendship would become a furiously contested campaign issue.

Hillary later said, "I thought attending the wedding would be fun—and it was!"

Responding to his critics, Donald said, "I am a businessman. It was important to me to be friendly with people in both political camps."

Before giving birth to her first child, Melania posed again for *Vogue*. She was seven months pregnant, but wore a golden bikini.

In March of 2006, she gave birth to a son. Donald suggested the aristocratic first name of "Barron," with Melania supplying the middle name of William.

In the beginning, Barron occupied a crib in his parents' room.

"Donald did not change the diapers," his mother said. "He did not view that as a proper role of a man, and I agree."

As he grew older, Barron was given practically a floor to himself on top of the Trump Tower, decorating it according to his wishes. He liked pictures of helicopters and airplanes on his walls.

In a corner of one room was placed a miniature red Mercedes-Benz with "BARRON" on the license plate. "That's a preview of the gift from my father when I get my driving license," said the six-year-old.

Unlike many rich kids, Barron wasn't reared by nannies, Melania preferring a much more hands-on approach. In an interview with *People* magazine in October of 2015, she said, "Donald and I don't like a lot of help raising our boy. We keep it down to a minimum. If you have too much help, you don't get to know your kid."

She claimed that when Donald was off on the campaign trail, she devoted nearly all of her time to Barron. "He is the light of my life. He's also an athlete, liking tennis and baseball. As he grew older, Donald took him with him to the golf course. But we don't have time for that anymore."

The longtime Trump butler, Anthony Senecal, claims, "Young Barron is more like his father than any of his other offspring. He learned to speak at an early age and issued orders when he was three years old to the staff."

Senecal told *Inside Edition* that, "I was serving the tot breakfast. He was sitting in his high chair. He looked at me and ordered, 'Tony! Sit down! We need to talk.'"

According to Melania, "Donald and Barron have a mutual admiration society. Before the campaign, Barron traveled often with us to Mar-a-Lago. Many people think he will grow up to fulfill Donald's shoes. I already call him 'Mini-Donald.'"

He likes suits and ties when he goes out, just like Donald. Of course, we always have to order an array of new suits because he's a growing boy. He is meticulous about his dress."

As Barron entered the pre-teen stage, he became enamored of his mother's skin care products. Every night he generously dips into containers of her caviar skin cream (priced at $150 an ounce). He likes to have baths in her apartment spa, generously pouring perfume from some of the world's most expensive bottles into the bath water.

He is fluent in English and Slovenian, and he also speaks adequate French.

Melania, on *The View*, told Joy Behar: "He's very mature, and he bosses everybody around. He fires housekeepers who anger him. Sometimes, he hires them back…sometimes. They have to learn who's boss. He's just adorable."

People magazine published a feature on Barron, calling him the "Billion Dollar Baby. He has his mom's eyes, his dad's lips, his own floor in Trump Tower, and doting parents. Welcome to the world of Barron William Trump."

***

In 2015, at the beginning of the Republican presidential race, Melania Trump was kept in the background. The other leading candidates quickly established their marriage credentials, Senator Rand Paul of Kentucky citing his 25-year marriage to his wife, Kelly; Senator Ted Cruz of Texas referring to his longtime Heidi, a former employee of Goldman Sachs (he left that out). Next, Senator Marco Rubio of Florida claimed that he'd been married for seventeen years. Then, both Ben Carson and Carly Fiorina made pointed references to their long-term spouses. In contrast, one billionaire candidate said nothing of his wife. "I am Donald Trump, and I wrote *The Art of the Deal*."

For a while, Donald configured his 33-year-old daughter, Ivanka, as an "unofficial campaign spouse." She made compelling speeches on behalf of her father, and did much to soften his image, as did Melania when she became more involved in the campaign during the months ahead.

Melania kept a low profile, although she was seen at certain events. As autumn came, she had a red or pink overcoat often draped over her shoulders.

During the early years of her dating Donald, she usually wore gowns that displayed an ample bosom. But since she was campaigning as the wife of a Republican candidate, she began to wear clothing that discreetly concealed her upper torso.

"No matter what she wears, she looks glamourous," said image consultant Christina Logothetis.

***

When Donald decided to run for President, he met with Melania and Barron for a family conference. "He talked it over with us, and Barron gave his own opinion," she said.

The boy said that Donald "will make the greatest president ever…and I know he'll win. My dad is not a loser like those jerks I see on TV. Ted Cruz looks like he could play a movie monster."

Reportedly, Barron becomes furious when he hears pundits attack his father on TV. He's also had some arguments at school when his fellow classmates mock Donald. "They probably picked up that crap from their moronic parents. My father is the greatest man in America."

In 2015, when Donald announced for the presidency, Melania

Two views of "The Mini-Donald," **Barron Trump,** whose future appears fascinating.

"People had better treat my dad fairly—or else they'll have me to deal with."

said, "I encouraged him because I know what he will do and what he can do for America. He loves its people and wants to help them."

The New York Times asked Melania what kind of First Lady she'd be. "I'd be like Betty Ford and Jackie Kennedy, and support my husband."

If Melania becomes First Lady, she would be the second First Lady born outside the United States. Louisa, the wife of the 6th U.S. president *[John Quincy Adams (1825-1829)]*, was born in England.

"I give Donald my opinions," Melania said. "Sometimes he takes them in. Sometimes he does not. Do I agree with him all the time? No!"

Like Donald, Melania can also be critical of the press, although she expresses her resentment more discreetly. "Reporters talk to people who do not even know me, and then publish their opinions, which often are not true. These people have their fifteen minutes of fame talking about me. They most often distort the facts. Make up stuff really. The press can be very unfair to both Donald and me."

"Donald is not always politically correct, but he tells the truth," Melania claimed. "He is handling everything very well. Everything is not roses and flowers and perfect. He wants America to be great again, and he can make it so. He's a great leader and an amazing negotiator."

An interior view of **the White House**. After Trump Tower, would its decor be a letdown for the Trumps? Could Melania and/or Ivanka fix it?

Before Donald ran for President, Melania had posed for a series of very sexy photographs of herself, a kind of public flirtation unknown within the histories of any other potential First Lady. As one of Donald's campaign workers said, "You won't see that ugly witch, Heidi Cruz, posting photographs of herself, and certainly not that ugly, aging hippie, Bernie's wife, Jane, showing off all her blubber. And if Hillary ever posed for a magazine centerfold, the publisher would have to make it a three-page spread to take in her elephantine butt."

One reporter who checked out Melania's Twitter images claimed, "There is a touch of Kanye *[West]* and Kim *[Kardashian]* to her luxury-streaked romance with The Donald."

Even though she is in her forties, Melania is sometimes asked, "Will you have more children?"

"I don't like to say 'never,' but my life is very busy. We are happy and my hands are full with my two boys—my Big Boy and my Little Boy."

As for her stepchildren, she said, "They are adults. I don't see myself as their stepmother. I am their friend. I am there when they need me. Of course, most of my life revolves around Donald and my remarkable son, Barron. The boy is the center of my life. I taught him to speak Slovenian, and quite a bit of French. Donald remains a monoglot."

Like Ivana, Melania also showed that she could be a business woman on her own. She nets at least one million dollars a year hawking her beauty products or her jewelry collection, "Melania Timepieces and Jewelry."

At its launch in February, 2010, her jewelry sold out in 45 minutes. Donald was the first customer. For the most part, her jewelry consists of cheaper versions of expensive gems from her private collection.

"I like to help women to spend not a lot of money—to feel powerful, elegant, glamourous, to feel good about themselves," she said.

When the distribution outlet charged with her "Melania Caviar Complexe C6" did not, in her view, adequately promote her new skin care product made with caviar, she sued them for $50 million for damages.

In an interview with *Parenting* magazine, Melania said, "It's a lot of responsibility for a woman to be married to a man like my husband. I need to be quick, smart, and intelligent."

"I think the mistake some women make is when they try to change the man they love after they marry him. You cannot change a person."

Were truer words ever said?

RUPERT MURDOCH & DONALD TRUMP
LIKE-MINDED BILLIONAIRES
Marital Woes and Infidelities Among the Insanely Wealthy

The Nude Slovenian Model & "The Lady from Shanghai" in their Respective Roles as Trophy Wives

Mr. and Mrs. Rupert Murdoch, the press baron and his "China Doll," Wendi Deng, before their estrangement.

Born in Australia in 1931, Rupert Murdoch, who owns both 21st Century Fox and the News Corporation, was destined to meet Donald Trump at some point. With a net worth of more than $5 billion, he is richer than Donald, owning some 800 companies in more thatn 50 countries.

As the owner since 1976 of the tabloid, the *New York Post*, Murdoch brought his right-wing politics to Manhattan, introducing British-style tabloid screaming headlines and lots of scandal. His chief rival was the *New York Daily News*.

Later in the 2016 presidential race, the *News* would become the chief media attacker of Donald, aften portraying him as a clown. Murdoch guided the *Post* into right-wing journalism, concentrating on celebrities. Donald became a regular feature as the tabloid revealed his triumphs in business and tales of his marriage to Ivana.

The left wing often attacked the *Post*. Osborn Elliott, dean of the Columbia School of Journalism, called it "a force for evil."

Donald and Murdoch had something in common: Both of them eventually married their "trophy girlfriends," the often scantily clad Slovenia-born beauty, Melania Knauss, for Donald, and Wendi Deng of China for aging Murdoch.

When introduced, Wendi seemed to find Melania charming…and vice versa.

By 1999 the cover story of *Punch*, the satirical London-based magazine, revealed the romance to the world under the headline "MURDOCH'S MISTRESS, THE SECRET LIFE OF THE WOMAN WHO SNARED THE BIG ONE." The story by Steve Vines claimed, "The Viagra-chomping Rupert Murdoch has been dating a Cantonese cutie."

A colleague said, "The boss may be old enough to qualify for a bus pass, but they giggle like lovestruck teenagers."

One of the wealthiest men in the world, the owner of newspapers around the globe, Murdoch met Wendi Deng in China. In her high boots and faux fur, she was called one of the "Shanghai Girls." This burgeoning subset of upwardly mobile young Chinese women were labeled that in the 2010 book, *Shanghai Girls*, by Nina Hanbury-Tenison. It seemed that the goal of these beautiful young women was to succeed at all costs—and that part of the definition of "success" involved marrying a multi-millionaire businessman like Donald Trump or Murdoch.

Re: **Wendi Deng Murdoch**'s "endorsement" of Melania: Was a recommendation from a trophy hunter as notorious as the "Shanghai Girl" Wendi Deng an asset or a curse?

"Wendi got Murdoch, the ultimate, a billionaire with a private jet," said one of her envious former girlfriends. "Oh, what a gold digger. Great success story."

The couple married in a spectacular wedding in 1999. He had divorced his second wife just seventeen days before. At the time, he was 68, Wendi 30. Together they would have two daughters.

The Murdochs moved in the same circles as Donald and Melania.

Wendi told the press how much she admired Melania. "She's wonderfully supportive of Donald and a lovely person."

As it turned out, Wendi wasn't that loyal to Murdoch, at least not when handsome Tony Blair, former Prime Minister of Britain, was introduced to her.

It wasn't long before she fell for the "sexually insatiable" Blair. Even his own wife, Cherie, reported that "sex five times a night…even more," was not unusual for her husband. "He's always *up* for it."

Wendi apparently agreed. A passionate note surfaced amid the flotsam of a shipwrecked marriage to Murdoch when he divorced her in 2013. She wrote: "Oh, shit, oh shit. Whatever why I'm so missing Tony. Because he is so so charming, and his clothes are so good. He has such good body and has really really good legs. Butt… and what else and what else and what else?"

In her note, she didn't describe that 'what else," but it was obvious to readers what she was referring to.

In 2012, Murdoch endorsed Mitt Romney, hoping he "could save us from socialism."

At first, Donald wanted Murdoch's endorsement. But in October of 2015, the media czar stirred up a controversy after he tweeted, "Ben and Candy Carson terrific. What about a real black President who can properly address the racial divide and much else?"

After that, he tweeted his apologies. "No offense meant. Personally, I find both Obama and Carson charming."

In January of 2016, with Wendi gone from his life, Murdoch announced his engagemenbt to former model Jerry Hall (ex-lover of Mick Jagger). He was just a week short before his 85th birthday, and she was still looking good at 59.

Donald reportedly said, "Rupert is an inspiration for all of us older guys. Will Melania still love me when I'm eighty-five? By then, they'll have something better on the market than Viagra."

WAS MELANIA "TRUMPED" BY THE SHANGHAI LADY?

During his 2016 race for the presidency, Donald was frequently cited in the newspapers for his "bromance" with Vladimir Putin. But his friend, Wendi Deng Murdoch, did him one better. According to rumors, she actually sleeps with the Russian dictator, who has dreams of restoring the former Soviet Empire. She had seen many pictures of the ruler shirtless, so, as Melania reportedly said, "Wendi saw at least half of what she was getting."

What does a 40-year-old woman do when her aging husband divorces her?

Wendi seemed to like seducing powerful men. Rumors circulated that she spent some nights with Eric Schmidt, CEO of Alphabet (the multinational conglomerate created in 2015 as the parent company of Google) at the Beverly Hills Hotel.

Where to go after that? A world leader, like Blair, a media mogul like Murdoch, and even a king of technology like Schmidt were a hard act to follow.

Tony Blair, the former prime minister of Britain. Privately, he was known as "the lover who couldn't get enough."

But Wendi, Dahling..Is It True that Love, or at Least Lightning, with a Mogul Can Strike FOUR SEPARATE TIMES?

For Wendi, it did. A recent romance with Vladimir Putin was detailed by, among others, *US magazine, Vanity Fair, the Daily Mail,* and *The Mirror*. Putin is freshly single, following a 2014 divorce from his wife of 30 years.

The size of his fortune, like so much about the strange dictator, is perhaps known only to himself. He cites his salary at $100,000 a year. A former fund manager in Russia, however, estimated his net worth at $200 billion. That would make Donald, his partner in bromance, only a poor acquaintance.

Putin is believed to be the richest person on earth, owning a vast network of assets in and (secretly) outside of Russia, nearly 60 airplanes, 700 automobiles (most of them custom made), and countless villas, palaces, and manor houses. Okay, so he's a former KGB spy accused of heinous crimes and unrelenting torture of his victims.

Perhaps one day, Putin and Wendi will be photographed riding together as the sun sets in the West, territory that the dictator…perhaps…would one day want to rule, or so it is said.

Autocratic, egomaniacal, deadly, and primed for a bromance with the future U.S. President: **Vladimir Putin** (aka"Vlad the Terrible") strips for his subjugated brethren.

" I would be willing to bet I would have a great relationship with Putin. It's about leadership. "

Donald Trump,
interview on Fox News

Chapter Two

POLITICKING & POWER PLAYS:
THIRTY YEARS OF SHIFTING ALLIANCES
*Donald, from Divergent Political Allegiances,
Contemplates White House Runs
in 2000, 2004, and 2012*

THE REFORM PARTY &
THE BIRTHER MOVEMENT
*Warren Beatty ("the Sexiest Man Alive") vs. "the Skyscraper King of Manhattan"
Which of Them Will Become President?*

BUILDING MORE THAN SKYSCRAPERS
*"Donald Trump Is the Apotheosis of Our Gilded Age"
On Facebook, Donald's Longtime Butler Calls for Obama to Be Killed*

"The Moral Lepers of the Reform Party insist I give up my live-in mistress if I want to be President."
—Donald Trump

Donald Trump once allowed his long-term butler, Anthony Senecal, to talk to the press. A colorful character, he wore horn-rimmed glasses and had a walrus mustache. According to Senecal, "At Mar-a-Lago, Donald is the king. When he first thought of running for President, I had the bugler play 'Hail to the Chief' when he stepped out of his limousine. If his cap is white, the boss is in a good mood. If it's red, it's best to stay away."

Senecal revealed that Donald was obsessively worried about Islamic terrorist attacks on America. He recalled the days when Ivana was there. "She liked to swim naked in the pool. But she was horrified that any member of the staff would see her nude. She demanded that all the staff go in hiding when she stripped down for a swim."

He also said that when Donald showed visitors around Mar-a-Lago, he sometimes stretched the truth a bit. "Mr. Trump claimed that the décor in the children's suite was actually painted by a young Walt Disney. Well, we don't know for a fact that he didn't."

Senecal also said that Marjorie Merriweather Post had a well-stocked library. But when the Trumps moved in, the library didn't get much use. "Mr. Trump installed a bar instead and had a large portrait of himself painted in his tennis whites. The portrait, lit at night, dominates the room. The staff calls Mr. Trump 'The King.'"

The butler confirmed what was already known, that Donald is more a "meat-and-potatoes kind of guy than a caviar-and-truffles dandy."

Then he added a tantalizing culinary tidbit: "He likes his steaks so well done that they're like rocks on his plate."

Senecal also revealed that he wanted to retire but "Mr. Trump insisted that I stay on at Mar-a-Lago, perhaps as its historian, if nothing else."

"THIS PRICK (OBAMA) NEEDS TO BE HUNG FOR TREASON!"
Or So Says Donald's Butler

Donald with his opinionated butler, **Anthony Senecal.** He obviously believed in speaking his mind, calling Hillary "the lying bitch of Benghazi" and Obama "the Asshole of Allah."

In mid-May of 2016, Donald's faithful butler, Anthony Senecal, at the age of 84, became the target of a national scandal after his rantings on *Facebook* were revealed to the world. He was denounced in blaring headlines as a "KILL BAM HATE NUT."

In a series of unhinged and racist online posts, he urged that President Obama "should be taken out by our military" or else "hung for treason." He also denounced Obama as "a pus head."

Then he praised his boss: "Now comes Donald J. Trump to put an end to corruption in government. The so-called elite, who are nothing but dog turds on your front lawn, are shaking in their boots because there is a new sheriff coming to town. I can't believe that a common murderer is even allowed to run ("Killery Hillary") or a commie like Bernie. Come on, America. put your big boy pants on—GET YOURS ASSES OUT AND VOTE!!!"

One of his posts read: "It is time for the SECOND AMERICAN REVOLUTION!!! The only way we will change this crooked government is to douche it!!! This might be the time with this Kenyan fraud in power!!! With the last breath I draw, I will help rid this America of the scum infested in its government--if this means dragging that ball-less dickhead from the White Mosque and hanging his scrawny ass from the portico--count me in!!!"

Another post followed. "If Obama gets hung, then "Sasquatch" (Michelle) does, too. Amen. Two of the most DISGUSTING individuals on the face of God's Green Earth!!! Puke!!!"

He also referred to the former Secretary of State as "the Lying Bitch of Benghazi!" He suggested "she should be in prison right now awaiting the gallows."

Under a photo of Obama, Senecal wrote: "IF ALLAH HAS AN ASSHOLE, IT WOULD LOOK LIKE THIS!!!"

He followed that with another post: "Obama is an unfeeling sack of camel feces. I don't believe he's an American citizen. I think he's a fraudulent piece of crap that was brought in by the Democrats."

"Once the President leaves office, only a FEW Negroes and Josh Earnest will even remember him."

He also had scorn for former Speaker John Boehner and Senate Majority Leader Mitch McConnell. "Both are FUCKING CROOKS and should be run out of D.C. on a rail and covered in hot tar."

Donald: "Had I wanted it, I could have become Vice President in 1988, but I preferred to conquer other worlds—more real estate...and **Reality TV** lay in my future."

1987: DONALD'S FIRST CAMPAIGN SPEECH
"The World Is Laughing at Us"

The date was October 22, 1987, when Donald Trump, future presidential nominee of the Republican Party, made his first political speech.

As twilight fell over southern New Hampshire, his shiny black French-made helicopter landed on a grassy airfield.

He emerged from the craft, a 41-year-old mogul wearing his classic scarlet tie and a well-tailored navy blue suit. He got into a waiting stretch limousine for the seven-mile ride up U.S. 1 to Portsmouth.

There, just before entering a restaurant named Yoken's, where political cronies in Portsmouth had gathered for years, he waved at the crowd, members of which brandished "TRUMP IN '88" signs.

Mike Dunbar, a woodworker (specializing in the crafting of Windsor chairs), novelist, and local Republican party activist, was on hand to greet him. Previously, he had written to Trump, urging him to take on George H.W. Bush and Mike Dukakis in the 1988 presidential election.

At the podium, Donald addressed the crowd and launched into a speech in which he claimed that the United States was on a disaster course. "Other countries such as Japan, Iran, and Saudi Arabia are kicking us around. They're laughing at us. It makes me sick." Unless trade and other policies changed, he predicted a catastrophe for America.

By 2016, this point of view had catapaulted him into a position as the Republican Party's frontrunner.

Dunbar had hoped that the restaurant would be the venue for Donald's announcement that he was seeking the presidency, but that was not to be. Loudly, the crowd expressed their disappointment when he told them that he would not be a candidate during the Presidential Race of 1988.

With adaptations, the speech that Donald delivered that day would be repeated again and again, especially during Barack Obama's occupancy of the White House. But when he first declared that America was being shoved around by other governments, Ronald Reagan was President.

Later, some staid New Englanders told reporters that they found the New York real estate mogul "brash and egotistical."

Before he headed back in his limo, he told a disappointed Dunbar that he didn't think he could "put up with all the false smiles and red tape that a presidential candidate would have to face."

That relatively unknown speech in New Hampshire in 1987 represented a milestone in Donald's long-running attack on "gridlock and incompetence in government," in which he blamed both the Republicans and the Democrats.

***

Seven months later, in April of 1988, Donald appeared on *The Oprah Winfrey Show*, complaining about America being "a debtor nation."

Oprah asked him if he planned to run for President that year. "Probably not," he told the audience. "But I do get tired of seeing the country ripped off. Right now I don't have the inclination to seek political office."

He later told reporters that if he ever did run for President, Oprah would be the ideal running mate as his Veep. "She's popular, she's brilliant, and she's a wonderful woman."

For years to come, despite a statement to *The New York Times* ["I believe if I did run, I'd win"], he would repeatedly deny that he was a presidential candidate.

Dunbar had been among the first to plant a presidential seed in Donald's brain, and he later admitted that. "It was that speech that got the whole thing started," he said.

At the time, Donald was a registered Democrat.

[Dunbar later wrote at least eight romantic/sci-fi/adventure books as part of the "Castleton Series." Aimed at "teenagers, young adults, and the young at heart," they're united with a common theme— "Time travel messes with your mind and your heart." Within some of them, a character

---

The Granite State in the Late 1980s, Site of The Donald's Official POLITICAL DEBUT

Trump holds a press conference following his speech at a Rotary Club luncheon in Portsmouth, New Hampshire, on October 22, 1987.

A local Republican Party activist, woodworker **Mike Dunbar** listens at left, as **Donald** states, "I will not be your candidate in the 1988 race."

In his 2007 book, *Think Big*, Donald wrote about how sweet getting revenge is. His advice: "When somebody screws you, screw them back in spades. When someone attacks you publicly, always strike back. If you want to stop a bully, hit them right between the eyes. Go for the jugular so that people watching will not want to mess with you."

named Jack Lincoln is portrayed as the manager of The Sirens, a fast-rising teen band. As part of the story line, after money started rolling in, Lincoln cheats The Sirens out of royalties that belong to them.

The author admitted that his Jack Lincoln was a "Trump-like figure, bigger than life, one who moves like a bulldozer, and one who has an office that's an entire floor of a Manhattan skyscraper."]

In 2016, when a reporter asked Dunbar if he'd vote for Donald for President, he answered, "The last two—even the last three—Presidents have been so horrible that Donald can't be any worse."

A REALITY CHECK FROM BUSH COUNTRY
(AKA: HOT NEWS)
Did "Daddy Bush" Consider The Donald as His Vice-Presidential Running Mate in 1988?

In November of 2015, Donald Trump revealed that way back in 1987, George H.W. Bush ("Daddy Bush") had seriously considered nominating him as his vice presidential running mate, a decision that would have spotlighted him in 1988 at the Republican Convention in New Orleans.

Donald said that Lee Atwater, the former chairman of the Republican National Committee—and the notorious, widely loathed, master of dirty political tricks—contacted him, asking him if he would allow himself to be vetted as a potential vice presidential candidate.

"Lee told me that he thought I would be a great vice president," Donald claimed.

Atwater also held out the possibility that after Bush served eight years, it would be a natural progression that he would pass the Oval Office for another eight years to Donald. "You'd be President in 1996, and you'd do such a fabulous job you'd be a shoo-in to get re-elected in 2000. That means you'd be America's first President in the 21st Century."

"At the time I was approached, I was in the midst of building my real estate empire, and wasn't raring to devote my life entirely to politics," Donald said. "He was very frank with me, telling me, I'd be a great running mate for George."

"You should go for it, you really should," Atwater said. "I want to talk it over with George, but I'll think he'll go for it big time. George can be a bit dull, and I think you'd provide the high energy needed—call it a big shot of baby-making testosterone."

Donald was disappointed when Bush named a relatively unknown Danforth Quayle as his vice presidential pick. Many insiders told Donald that Quayle was a political lightweight. "He's rather good-looking, but tepid," Atwater said. "He's lily

According to author John Meacham, when queried, about Trump having been considered as a Veep running mate to **Daddy Bush,** the ex-President flatly refuted Donald's claim that he'd ever been considered.

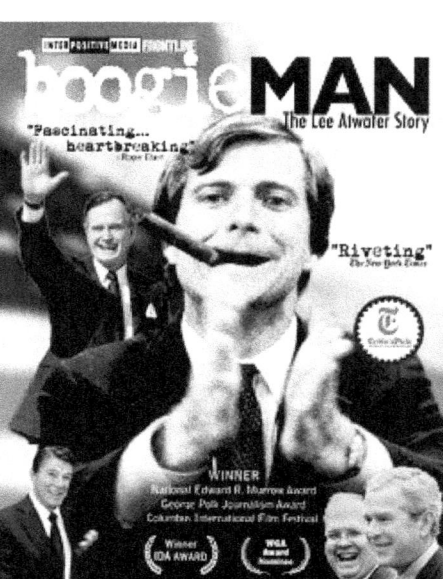

Lee Atwater, the dirty trickster of the far right: "I'll meet all my enemies when we arrive at the Gates of Hell," he once said, strictly off the record.

George H.W. Bush looks skeptical as his vice presidential running mate, **Danforth Quayle,** delivers one dumb remark after another. Lee Atwater added his private assessment: "As Greta Garbo said of her co-star (Robert Taylor) in *Camille*, Quayle is so pretty but so dumb."

white, very conservative, a homophobe, Blacks won't go for him. Neither will the Jews."

Atwater had told his associates, "Quayle's wife Marilyn is the ball-clanker of the family."

Years later, Donald allegedly told his associates, "I'll never know why Bush picked this guy. He can't even spell potato. A little black kid spelled it correctly, and Quayle told him to add an extra 'e.'"

Atwater died in 1991 at the age of forty from a brain tumor when he was at the height of his political power.

Donald's claim that he had almost become the Republican's candidate for Vice President at the 1988 Republican Convention was later treated skeptically by Jon Meacham, a Pulitzer Prize winner who was allowed unlimited access to George H.W. Bush. In 2015, he published *Destiny and Power*, a book whose revelations shocked many conservatives. He even provided a critique of George W. Bush's two terms as President—including many of his father's "harsh words for Dubya." ["Dubya," according to the UrbanDictionary.com, is a slang term for the most inept President the United States has ever had, i.e., George W. Bush, George H.W. Bush's son.]

As laid out in Meacham's biography, Daddy Bush also fired missiles at Dick Cheney, his son's Vice President, and at Secretary of Defense Donald Rumsfeld.

Meacham maintained that he asked the senior Bush if he had considered running in 1988 with Donald Trump as his vice president.

"What a strange and unbelievable idea," Bush shot back.

***

[Donald's opinion of the Bush vs. the Clinton Dynasty hasn't always been consistent. In one of his books, *Thinking Big* (2007), Donald weighed in with a description of his preference for Bill Clinton over his opponent, Daddy Bush.

"A friend of mine from Arkansas, Bill Clinton, ran and won against the first President Bush. Bill has the ability to think big. His wife, Hillary, is a fantastic person, who also has the ability to think big. That's why Bill Clinton won the election and sent Bush back to Texas. When others were unwilling to tread against Bush's huge poll numbers, Bill had no fear. Bill Clinton is a great guy with courage."

Donald's opinion, of course, would be considerably altered during his 2015-2016 run for president.]

DONALD'S HAIR:
THE NATIONWIDE RUMPUS

Time *Reveals the Secrets of His Orange Coif*

"Today, no one seems to care if you're a good person. People only care if you're good looking and rich."

—Dr. Rosalyn Weinman

Donald in his youth was considered a handsome man. He was not only good looking, but very rich and with enormous style and panache—a "babe magnet" as some of his admirers described him.

Although in the eyes of many, his allure continued, with the onset of middle age, he struggled to keep his weight under control. He also, as documented by television cameras around the world, made extraordinary efforts to camouflage a tendency for a condition that's widespread within the general population, male middle age baldness.

His enemies zeroed in on his sensitivity on the subject: "The worst thing a man can do is let himself grow bald," he told Mark Grossinger Estess, one of this casino executives who would die in a helicopter crash.

Donald's coiffure had come under scrutiny and was often talked about—or mocked—on TV. The most notorious assault came from Rosie O'Donnell [*more about that later*].

Donald told *Playboy* in 2004 that he styles his own hair and lets only one person trim it—"My girlfriend, Melania."

For a time, many viewers thought Amy Lasch, veteran of a thirty-year career as a hair stylist for the TV and film industry, was responsible to some de-

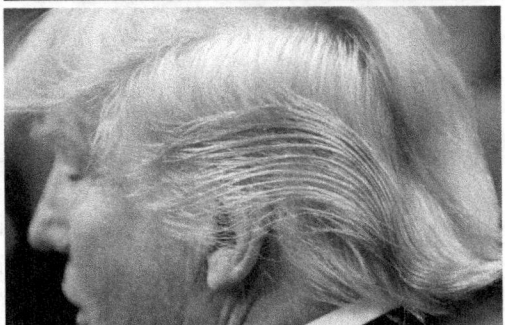

Upper photo: **Donald** with **Farouk Shami**, developer of his favorite hair products. Did the presidential candidate really hate Muslims?

Donald's controversial, even infamous, coiffure, not only inspired satire, but also a cottage industry of orange-colored Donald Trump "fright wigs."

gree for Donald's coiffure. (She worked on the set of *The Apprentice* during its first two seasons.) But she later revealed, "Donald wouldn't let me near his controversial mane."

It seemed that everybody had an opinion about Donald's hair, and windblown photos of his "bad hair days" appeared everywhere. Louis Licari, who colored Ivana's hair for some twenty years, claimed, "I think it's all his hair—but through transplants. I saw him several times in the office of Dr. Norman Orentreich *[a NYC dermatologist known as "the father of hair transplants]* in the early 1980s.

Even the editors at *Time* magazine, who don't usually muck about with such nonsense, made it a point to publicize the secret of Donald's controversial coif. Within its pages, perhaps in an attempt to help other men afflicted with hair loss, "Losi," a well-known men's stylist, described how the look could be replicated:

> "1. Blow dry the hair forward. Don't confuse this with a classic side-part comb over."
> "2. Fold and blow the hair back and to the side. That would be in the manner of cartoon character Wilma Flintstone or the TV talk show host, Conan O'Brien."
> "3. Sweep and blow the remaining hair on both sides. This maneuver anchors the edifice."
> "4. Apply ozone-depleting amounts of hairspray. Voila! Boardroom fabulous!"

Once, during a televised interview on a golf course with a newscaster on Britain's *Channel 4*, **Donald** was asked about his hair. Removing his trademark cap, he revealed this not-unattractive "natural look" with the comment, "It might not be pretty, but it's mine."

Men with previous "bad hair" moments everywhere applauded his grace.

The man behind Donald's hair spray, Farouk Shami, claimed, "I like the cut, not the color." The hair guru once sent Donald a box of medium-blonde hair coloring, but Donald nonetheless stuck to orange.

"To get that soft-swerve, he uses an aerosol hair spray," Shami said. "I know environmentalists want to eradicate hair spray!"

At a rally in South Carolina in 2015, Donald said, "They say hair spray is going to affect the ozone. They want me to use a pump spray. But that comes out in big blobs. I want my own hair spray."

He wouldn't name the brand, but it's been said that one of his preferences is Farouk Systems CHI Helmet Head, a humidity-resistant and fast-drying spray.

During the weeks before Halloween of 2015, novelty stores did a rocketing business hawking orange-colored Donald Trump wigs.

BULWORTH AND THE REFORMERS
Warren Beatty's Satirical Overview of Presidential Politics

"Everybody Should Fuck Everybody Until Everyone Is All the Same Color."
—**Warren Beatty as Senator Bulworth**

Many pundits compared Donald's flirtation with the presidency to the 1998 movie *Bulworth,* an American political comedy co-written, co-produced, and directed by Warren Beatty, who was also its star. Ironically, Beatty considered declaring a run for the White House in 2000, at the same time Donald was contemplating entering the race.

The madcap film follows the title character, California Senator Jay Billington Bulworth (Beatty), as he runs for re-election while trying to avoid a hired assassin.

His frank but offensive remarks make him an instant media darling and propel him forward in the polls. Along the way, he becomes romantically involved with a young black activist named Nina (Halle Berry).

There are many parallels between the film and the narratives of Donald's campaign. But Bulworth radically departs from the trajectory pursued by Donald when the Senator urges that "everybody should fuck everybody until everyone is all the same color."

At the end, Bulworth is assassinated by an agent of insurance company lobbyists, terrified by the senator's recent push for single-payer health care.

In an "only in America" chain of events that raised eyebrows within the Washington beltway, Hollywood star **Warren Beatty** gave consideration to a White House run in 1999. The previous year, he'd released a controversial political satire, *Bulworth*. The outspoken senator in that film was later compared to Donald.

Above is an ad for that provocative movie.

Despite many differences, in hindsight, some aspects of Bulworth seem like an early preview of Donald's campaign for the presidency. The hero (or protagonist) of the film, along with his wife and children, have expressed their deep-seated fears that he might be assassinated. Consequently, both Beatty (as a film character) and Donald Trump are flanked by security guards.

But whereas Senator Bulworth did everything he could to deliberately lose the race by being offensive and wildly inconsistent, the real life Donald found that being offensive only made his poll numbers rise, as did Bulworth's in the film.

Donald proclaimed, "I am the winner, not a loser like the rest of the jerks running against me—Lyin' Ted Cruz, who opposes me, along with Little Marco (Rubio) and Low-Energy Jeb (Bush)."

For the first presidential election of the 21st Century, **Warren Beatty** considered a run for the White House.

One of his biographers called him, "The sexiest man alive." But could the actor have turned his sex appeal and *charisma* into a successful presidential bid?

"I know a Hollywood actor who became President," Beatty said.

As a Hollywood actor with a passionate interest in politics, Beatty had made a cinematic impact on progressive politics through his films Reds (1981) and Bulworth. He also campaigned for two liberals, Bobby Kennedy and George McGovern. Rare for an A-list actor, the Hollywood films he made portrayed socialism in a positive light long before Bernie Sanders arrived on the scene.

On August 12, 1999, *The New York Times* ran a story headlined: "BEATTY REPORTEDLY FLIRTING WITH WHITE HOUSE RACE."

As stated by Beatty: "I have some very strong feelings, the most important of which at the time is campaign finance reform because its tentacles reach into every other issue. I fear we're getting closer to a plutocracy than we want to, and I believe that deep down the people want to do something about that."

John Bredin, talk show host, educator, and writer, said, "Though Beatty never ran for President himself, he flirted with the idea, and the closest he ever came was in 2000 when he was urged on by Arianna Huffington. I believe he could have won easily—as a charismatic, intelligent, left-wing Hollywood antidote to Reaganism—in the 1980s, 90s, and beyond."

Beatty met with members of the Reform Party to talk about his being their candidate.

[The Reform Party of the United States of America (RPUSA), generally known as the Reform Party USA or the Reform Party, was founded in 1995 by Ross Perot as a viable alternative for independent voters disillusioned with the traditional division of the U.S. Government into the traditional two-party system. In 1992, Perot had famously and feistily run as an independent against (the Republican) George H.W. Bush and (the Democrat) Bill Clinton.

Citing corruption, ineptitude, and waste as incentives for sweeping changes to a government mired in bureaucratic stalemates, the party was most famously associated with Perot himself, the ultra-conservative Pat Buchanan, consumer advocate Ralph Nader, the former professional wrestler, Jesse ("The Body") Ventura, and—if his stories aren't exaggerated—Donald Trump.]

Beatty confessed that he didn't see himself as the best candidate. "There certainly should be someone better. That's not to say that I don't have strong feelings on a lot of things that aren't being spoken."

Biographer Ellis Amburn, author of *Warren Beatty, The Sexiest Man Alive*, wrote:

> *"Beatty didn't have the time, energy, will, or desire to go directly to the public and ask them to finance his campaign. It was sad, because his platform would have been good for the nation, espousing campaign finance reform, Medicare for everyone, increasing teachers' salaries, and rebuilding the educational infrastructure, and end, through world trade sanctions, environmental abuse and cruel labor practices."*

In September 1999, perhaps terminally discouraged with the political process, Beatty announced that it was "extremely unlikely" that he would run. Several months later, he said, 'I'm not running now.'"

EARLY AND LOUDLY, DONALD PLAYS THE TERROR CARD

"A Terrorist With a Bomb in a Suitcase Could Turn Manhattan into Hiroshima."
—**Donald Trump in his first campaign book**

As he was contemplating his 2000 race for the White House, Donald decided to release another book, *The America We Deserve*. It was to be his "first campaign book" (with many more to follow). To help him write it, he hired author Dave Shiflett, a veteran writer who had previously penned articles for both the *National Review* and *The Wall Street Journal*.

In this book, Donald took lethal aim at many of his rivals from across the political spectrum. He claimed that Pat Buchanan "has totally lost it," and that Al Gore "is an able, underrated man who seems confused."

In terms of its role as a political tract that laid out the scope, scale, and ambitions of a newcomer to a political and electoral setting, some readers compared it to *Mein Kampf*.

In it, he came down hard on America's enemies abroad, especially China, North Korea, and Cuba, and he was "tougher than tough" on crime. The book revealed, as described by reviewer Ron Hogan, a "straight-shooting personality and policy-wonk data points."

Donald praised the "diversity of American culture," denounced the murder of Matthew Shepard, a young gay man in Wyoming, criticized the harassment of Jews and all other hate crimes.

Shiflett later claimed that the platforms Donald espoused in 2015, as opposed to his platforms of 2000, sounded "more like those of a political shock jock than a statesman." But even before the 9/11 attack on the World Trade Center, Donald had expressed fear that "a terrorist with a suitcase bomb could turn Manhattan into Hiroshima II."

In reference to his collaboration with Donald in 2015, Shiflett told *The Wall Street Journal*, "We made a pretty good team. He needed words. I needed money. I have long considered the resulting book my first published work of fiction."

Shiflett likened his 2000 presidential aspiration to a "rich guy out on a lark, bombastic enough to make headlines, not history. It was a short-lived dance through the spotlight—and plenty of fun."

Historians are still debating the effect that a rich Texan, **Ross Perot,** had on the 1992 race for the White House.

At the time, a sitting President, George H.W. Bush, was up against a relatively unknown Democratic governor from Arkansas with a "woman problem."

The question is still being debated: Did Perot's entry cost Bush his re-election?

***

The political bug continued to bite deep into Donald's skin. What was a mere flirtation in 1988 had become something of an obsession by 1999, eleven years later.

He told a reporter, "If I decide to run for President, the beauty of it is that I'm very rich."

He commissioned an exploratory committee to determine his chances for victory if he ran as a possible Reform Party candidate in November of 2000 against the Democratic nominee (Vice President Al Gore), or against the Republican nominee (George W. Bush, the governor of Texas).

When the results of the polling came in, Donald was bitterly disappointed to learn that if he participated, he would receive only seven percent of the vote.

***

Despite the miserable prognosis for his chance at election, Donald appointed Roger Jason Stone Jr. to form a sort of "Trump for President in 2000" Committee.

Stone, a political consultant, lobbyist, and strategist, was noted for his far-reaching use of "destructive opposition research." In other words, he dug up dirt "on the enemy."

The Daily Beast described him as a "self-admitted hit man for the GOP," and *The New York Times* more kindly referred to him as "a renowned infighter and a seasoned practitioner of hard-edged politics."

With Donald, Stone shared his battle plan to advance a candidate: "Attack! Attack! Attack! Never defend! Admit nothing! Counterattack!"

On October 24, 1999, at the urging of Stone,

Posters and magazine articles, including rundowns in a 2004 edition of *Esquire* depicted above, addressed Donald's previous but not-so-serious attempts to run for the White House. In 2000, he would have run not as a Republican or Democrat, but on the Reform Party ticket.

In contrast, a **"Trump for President"** movement in 2012, in which he would have opposed Obama, was never really launched.

Donald made a TV appearance on *Meet the Press* to announce that he would officially resign from the Republican Party and join the Reform Party. "The Republicans," he charged, "have become too crazy right!"

He was asked if his previous life as a womanizer might harm his chances of becoming President. "I would not run if I believed there was anything in my past that would be an impediment to my winning the race for the White House."

Donald entered the race, giving interviews that outlined his platform. On social issues, he was progressive, supporting gays in the military. "They would not disturb me. After all, I live in Manhattan."

For the Reform Party nomination, he faced opposition from Pat Buchanan, who also wanted to run as their candidate. Buchanan had left the Republican Party in October of 1999, denouncing it as "The Beltway Party."

Donald was supplied with a detailed background, some of it explosive, on Buchanan and his career. A paleoconservative *[extreme conservative]* political commentator, author, and broadcaster, he had been Director of Communications at the White House under Ronald Reagan. He had also been a senior advisor to Presidents Richard Nixon and Gerald Ford, and was one of the original hosts on CNN's *Crossfire*. He had sought the Republican nomination for President in both 1992 and 1996, and had, each time, lost badly.

In addition to Donald, John Hagelin, a physicist from Iowa whose platform was based on Transcendental Meditation, was also running.

For Donald, Buchanan was just too controversial. "He's to the right of Hitler!" Donald charged. "I guess he's an anti-Semite. He doesn't like the blacks, and he doesn't like the gays."

Buchanan was labeled a "Holocaust Denier." He once wrote that it was impossible for 850,000 Jews to have been killed by diesel exhaust fed into the gas chamber at Treblinka. "It was not a death camp, but a transit camp used as a pass-through point for prisoners," he wrote.

[In truth, some 900,000 Jews were slaughtered at Treblinka.]

The Anti-Defamation League denounced Buchanan as "an unrepentant bigot who repeatedly demonized Jews and minorities and openly affiliates with white supremacists."

"I can't support such a man," Donald claimed. Consequently, he pushed ahead with his own pursuit of the nomination, running on a platform of fair trade, elimination of the national debt, and universal health care.

His political positions were outlined in *The America We Deserve*, a book released in January of 2000. Dick Morris, former advisor to Bill Clinton, claimed that Donald was only running for President because of the publicity it generated which "might boost his book sales."

Hatchetman **Roger Stone** *(above)* was the attack dog of the far right. He described his political "standard operating procedure" as "Attack, attack, attack, never defend," and "Admit nothing, deny everything, and launch a counterattack."

If **Pat Buchanan** — a cultural warrior of the far right—had been nominated as a presidential candidate in 1992, he would have been one of the most controversial men ever to seek that office.

Homosexuals were often his main target, although he was no champion of civil rights for other minorities either.

Even before **Donald** officially announced he was a candidate for the presidency in June of 2015, he appeared on Fox, hosted by anchorwoman Megyn Kelly, with whom he would later enter into a well-publicized feud. He was blunt: "This country is a hell-hole!"

MEDIA FRENEMIES & REFORM PARTY ENEMIES
Donald Becomes Politically Notorious

"He's a fraud...the greatest con artist."
—NYC Mayor Ed Koch

As his opinions became more widely publicized, and as his visibility increased, critics lined up to attack Donald. One of them was the outspoken Mayor of New York City, Ed Koch, who called him "a fraud and the greatest con artist when it comes to trumpeting his own name. My gut tells me he knows nothing about policy."

Controversies continued on the Latino front: Donald appeared in Miami and spoke before the Cuban American National Foundation. He denounced Fidel Castro and favored the continuing U.S. embargo against Cuba. He was met with VIVA DONALD TRUMP! signs.

"I have two words for Castro," he told the assembled Cubans. "*Adios, amigo!* Fidel is a killer and should be treated as such."

After he returned from Miami, Donald met with Reform Party leaders who objected to his living openly with his mistress, Melania Knauss. He promised "to remedy the situation."

He was said to have temporarily separated from her, so he would not be charged in the upcoming campaign with having a live-in mistress. "Melania will be missed," he said. But on the day of his withdrawal from the Reform Party, he asked for her to move back into Trump Tower.

That was not the only trouble facing him.

All hell broke loose in the Reform Party when John Hagelin supporters claimed that the party's open primary, which favored Buchanan by a wide margin, was "tainted."

That led to the party holding dual conventions simultaneously in separate areas of California's Long Beach Convention Center. One gathering nominated Buchanan while the other backed Hagelin, with each camp claiming to be the legitimate Reform Party.

Because of all this infighting, Donald planned to withdraw from the party, and Ventura also said he was going to bow out.

Donald gave his reasons to the press. "The Reform Party now includes a Klansman, Mr. David Duke, a neo-Nazi and former leader of the KKK, and Mr. Buchanan, as well as a communist, Miss Fulani."

He was referring to Lenora Fulani, a psychologist and political activist, who became the first woman and the first African American to achieve ballot access in all fifty states. She received more votes in a U.S. general election than any other woman in American history, and ran on a platform of racial equality, gay rights, and political reform.

Jesse Ventura may have ended his future in politics when he told *Playboy*, "Organized religion is a sham and a crutch."

When Donald heard that, he said, "There goes the evangelical vote."

Donald officially ended his 2000 campaign and his association with the Reform Party on February 14, 2000 during an appearance with Matt Lauer on the *Today* show. During that interview, he claimed that the Reform Party was "a total mess on the verge of self-destructing."

He did hold out, however, the possibility that he might seek the presidency again in 2004.

The Chairman of the Reform Party, Pat Choate, vigorously disputed Donald's claim. "Trump campaigned for the presidency only to smear Pat Buchanan. Trump will be unwelcome to seek our party's nomination in 2004. Actually, I think his campaign was nothing but a Republican dirty trick orchestrated by Roger Stone."

Donald said that "running for President was enormous fun, but doesn't compare with completing one of the great skyscrapers of Manhattan."

***

As a politician contemplating a presidential race, Donald had begun to pick up enemies who opposed him. One of the most vocal was the 85th Governor of Connecticut (1991-1995), Lowell P. Weicker, Jr. He had sought the Republican nomination for President in 1980, but had lost to Ronald Reagan.

Weicker and Donald had conflicted in 1993 when the real estate mogul wanted to expand his gambling empire to Bridgeport. Weicker had vigorously opposed that, telling Donald that he had already entered into a compact with the Mashantucket Pequot Tribal Nation to build the Foxwoods Resort Casino.

Donald challenged the tribal recognition process, claiming, "They don't look like Indians to me."

During a TV interview, Weicker denounced Donald as a "dirtbag and a bigot."

Lenora Fulani richly deserved her footnote in American history.

In 1988, this African American psychotherapist and political activist ran on the ballots in all fifty states, receiving more votes than any other woman ever had, years before Hillary.

As Donald moved deeper into expanding his gambling interests and his role in politics, he made a strong enemy of long-time Republican **Lowell P. Weicker Jr.,** who served during his long career as a U.S. Senator, a U.S. Representative, and as the former governor of Connecticut.

"He favored the redskins over me," Donald protested, in reference to Weicker's objections to the establishment of a Trump-controlled casino in Weicker's state.

Years later, in a review of his years of public service, Weicker evaluated Trump as "a dirtbag," "a con artist," and "a racist."

Donald reciprocated by calling him "a fat slob who couldn't even get elected dog-catcher."

[In 2015, when Donald announced his bid for the presidency, Weicker, then in his mid-80s, had nothing but disdain for Donald. "I think the man is a total con artist. Maybe it's a reflection of the Republican Party more than Donald Trump if it allows any nut case like Trump to make it as if he were a valid presidential candidate. The party has drifted. The man's a disgrace. But the Republican Party is a disgrace. If I were a Democrat, I'd hope for nothing more than Trump to become the candidate. Do I want an American President to identify with prejudice toward different minority groups? I certainly don't."

J.R. Romano, head of the Connecticut GOP, said, "Weicker is still clueless. Donald Trump has tapped into the angst and anger that many Americans feel toward politicians like Weicker."]

Jesse ("The Body") Ventura was a pro wrestler who somehow managed to capture the imagination of the voters of Minnesota, who elected him governor of their great state.

Donald reportedly told his aides, "**David Letterman** should be more careful when he suggests that I'm a racist. That could get him into deep shit."

***

By 2004, Donald once again considered challenging George W. Bush for the presidency but ultimately decided not to. He'd been critical of Bush's handling of the Iraq War. For a while, his friend Jesse Ventura, considered running in his place and asked Donald for his support, but the Minnesota governor decided that he, too, would bow out once again.

Donald spoke out on certain issues, suggesting that vaccination might cause autism, and he also criticized advocates of global warming, deriding the claim it was a phenomenon catalyzed by the actions of humans.

In 2009, Donald changed his voter registration from Democrat to Republican, and once again, he considered a 2012 run for the White House, taking on Barack Obama, whom he claimed was one of America's worst presidents. He sharply criticized the President's trade policies, and questioned his citizenship and the authenticity of his birth certificate.

He also questioned whether Obama's grades (and by implication, his intelligence level) had been good enough to warrant entry into Harvard Law School.

Some critics suggested that Donald was toying with the idea of launching a presidential run as a means of gaining free media publicity for *The Apprentice*.

It came as a surprise even to him that a *Wall Street Journal/NBC* poll released in March of 2011 found Donald leading among other contenders for the GOP nod.

A *Newsweek* poll showed him one point ahead of Mitt Romney (too close to call) and just a few points behind President Obama himself.

Executives at NBC gave him a deadline for deciding if he were going to sign a new contract for his hit show, *The Apprentice*. The question was this: Should he run for President and subject himself to a bruising race, or "go for the gold?"

He made a decision: He notified NBC executives that he would sign on for another season of *The Apprentice*. Consequently, on May 16, 2011, in reference to the upcoming 2012 elections, Donald announced, "I will not seek the nomination."

At the time, Public Policy Polling described his race for the White House as "one of the quickest rises and falls in the history of presidential politics."

Even though he donated money for the campaign of Mitt Romney, Donald later mocked him. "He's a small business guy who walked away from some big money from a company he didn't create."

When Romney didn't beat Obama, he denounced the Mormon as "a god damn loser. I backed a loser, and I don't like losers."

***

As each month went by, Donald became embroiled with one media personality after another, usually in response to mocking attacks they'd made on him.

Bill Maher, the very liberal TV talk show host and comedian, offered to donate $5 million to Donald's favorite charity if "he could produce a birth certificate that showed he was not fathered by an orangutan."

Donald then had his lawyers send Maher a copy of his birth certificate with a demand that he receive a $5 million cashier's check. When Maher refused, Donald threatened legal action.

The case never made it to court, like so many other legal suits that Donald used to threaten various pundits and media figures.

The wildly popular liberal talk show host and atheist, **Bill Maher,** in a $5 million dollar bet with The Donald.

Maher wanted Donald to prove that his father was not an orangutan.

In another television interview, Donald said, "I would love to be a well-educated black because they have an actual advantage."

Later, David Letterman, the TV talk show host, attacked Donald during an on-air appearance of "Dr. Phil."

"It's all fun, it's all a circus, it's all a rodeo, until it starts to smack of racism," Letterman said. "And then it's no longer fun."

A talk show host himself, Phil McGraw, known as "Dr. Phil," considered Donald a friend. "I don't think Donald is a racist," he said. "Perhaps a bit rash at times. I don't think he always thinks everything through. I think sometimes he's a little from the hip. I don't think he has a racist bone in his body."

Donald watched the program that night. He fired off a response to Letterman: "I was disappointed to hear the statements you made about me last night on your show that I was a racist. In actuality, nothing could be further from the truth, and there is nobody who is less of a racist than Donald Trump."

Then-President **Barack Obama**, in April of 2011, at the podium for the White House correspondents' dinner, skewered Donald Trump on the eve of the long-plotted death of **Osama bin Laden.**

Four years later, in 2015, at an equivalent forum, Obama repeated his scathing attacks on Donald: "I know he's taken some flack lately. But no one is prouder to put this birth certificate issue to rest than Donald, and that's because he can get back to the issues that matter, like, did we fake the moon landing? What really happened in Roswell? And where are Biggie and Tupac?"

On April 30, 2011, at the annual White House Correspondents Association dinner, both Seth Meyers (a key player and later, host of *Saturday Night Live*) and President Obama ridiculed Donald as he sat grim-faced in the audience. Meyers mocked Donald for claiming, "I have a great relationship with the blacks."

Meyers said he didn't question Donald's statement—"that is unless the blacks are white people."

Meyers didn't let up. "Donald Trump has been saying he would run for President as a Republican, which is surprising because I thought he would be running as a joke."

Obama then rose to the podium. "All kidding aside, we all know about Donald Trump's credentials and breadth of experience. For example—no, seriously, just recently, in an episode of *Celebrity Apprentice*—at the steak house, the men's cooking team did not impress the judges from Omaha Steaks: And there was a lot of blame to go around. But you, Mr. Trump, recognized that the real problem was a lack of leadership. And so, ultimately, you didn't blame Lil' Jon or Meatloaf. You fired Gary Busey. And these are the kind of decisions that would keep me up at night. Well handled, sir. Well handled."

While Obama made these mocking comments, U.S. Navy SEALS were flying in helicopters into Pakistan with the intention of killing Osama bin Laden as a payback for 9/11.

Columnist Maureen Dowd remained a continuing critic of Donald, calling him "The Apotheosis of our Gilded Age, where money, celebrity, polling, and crass behavior in politics and the TV show, *Who Wants to Be a Millionaire*, dominate the culture."

THE BIRTHER BLITZ
Donald Launches New Battles in His War Against Obama

(Did you know that the term "Birther-ism" originated in Hillary's camp?)

Contrary to popular belief, theories about a conspiracy surrounding Obama's birth did not originate with Donald.

During the closing weeks of the Democratic Party's presidential nomination process of 2008, when Hillary Clinton was competing with Barack Obama for the party's nomination, her supporters, in an attempt to revive her then-faltering campaign, sent anonymous e-mails that questioned the legitimacy of Obama's U.S. citizenship and his birth certificate.

Vermont Senator **Bernie Sanders,** seen here challenging Hillary for the Democratic nomination, was known as "the Giveaway Candidate," promising free college tuition and everything else.

Economists added up the cost, finding his proposals would levy $15.3 trillion in new taxes, plus another $2 trillion for his health plan. They also claimed that his plans would "slow GDP growth by 9.5%."

One e-mail from Hillary's camp claimed, "Barack Obama's mother was living in Kenya with his African father late in her pregnancy. She was not allowed to travel by plane then, so Obama was born in Kenya and later flown to Hawaii."

Politico investigated the charge that the birther issue originated from within the Hillary campaign, and not (at least originally) from Donald's.

"In fact, the claim was first advanced by Hillary supporters as her nomination hopes faded in 2008," *Politico* revealed. "So was the suspicion that Obama was a secret Muslim."

In February of 2008, *The Guardian* reported that a Clinton staffer had been forced to resign after forwarding an e-mail that suggested that Obama was a Muslim. "There is no moral high ground for the Clinton team here; there is only hypocrisy."

Ironically, eight years later, during a February 2016 CNN Democratic Town Hall broadcast from Columbia, South Carolina, Vermont Senator Bernie Sanders referenced the birther movement. Even though it had originated with the Democrats, Sanders charged that, "There is racism inherent in the Republican base. Nobody asked for my birth certificate. Maybe it's the color of my skin."

In February of 2011, Donald spoke at the right-wing Conservative Political Action Conference (CPAC). At that point, he'd become a convert to the Birther movement. "Our current President came out of nowhere. Came out of nowhere! In fact, I'll go a step further. The people that went to school with him never saw him. They don't know who he is. Crazy!"

Right to left: **Barack Obama**, born in 1961, and **Maya Soetoro**, born 1970, with their mother **Ann Dunham** and grandfather **Stanley Dunham** in Hawaii in the early 1970s.

Obama's mother was born in Wichita, Kansas. She was of predominantly English ancestry with a very American pedigree: Wild Bill Hickok was her sixth cousin, five times removed.

Although Donald was a Johnny-come-lately to the Birther rumor, he quickly became its most famous advocate.

Later, on Bill O'Reilly's nighttime TV program, the most-watched news show on television, Donald launched what became known as "the Birther Blitz."

He said that he used to believe that Obama was born in Hawaii, "but I have come to have my doubts, since I've seen evidence to the contrary."

Although a right-wing commentator, O'Reilly could also be a tough questioner, and he challenged Donald's claim.

In response, Donald continued: "Now he may have a birth certificate, but there is something on it he doesn't want us to see—maybe religion, maybe it says he's a Muslim. I don't know."

O'Reilly concluded the interview with, "I don't think you believe your charge."

During the weeks that followed, Donald appeared on a number of shows questioning the circumstances of Obama's birth and consequently, his legitimacy as the U.S. President. He even claimed that he had sent a team of investigators to Honolulu to get to the truth of the matter.

The implications of Donald's words were serious, indeed: If it were revealed that Obama had been born in Kenya, it would have invalided his election as a U.S. President. *[Only a native son (or daughter), according to U.S. law, is allowed to serve as the nation's President.]*

Under more intense questioning, Donald, on another TV show, claimed that Obama's grandmother, who spoke only Swahili, was present at his birth in Kenya: "We have her on tape."

However, it turned out that the tape was a phone interview with Sarah Obama, the President's stepmother. In an interview with Ron McRae, a police officer who became a bishop for the Anabaptist Churches worldwide, Sarah told him that she was present at the birth of Barack Obama and that the birth took place in Kenya.

Later, on *The View*, Donald said, "I want Obama to show his birth certificate. There is something on that birth certificate that he doesn't like."

That comment led to Whoopi Goldberg defining that remark as, "The biggest pile of dog mess I've heard in ages."

When Donald took up the Birther issue and promoted it, he was accused of racism by both *CBS News* and *The New Yorker*.

Rumors can have a devastating effect. Early in 2011, a poll showed that half of all Republicans surveyed by Public Policy Polling believed that the President had, indeed, been born in Africa.

One particularly vicious cartoon widely available across the Internet depicted the Obama family as chimps living in trees. "Now you know why no birth certificate," the caption read.

On April 25, 2011, Donald called for Obama to end the Birther issue by releasing the long form of his birth certificate.

Melania Trump weighed in, too. "It would be very easy if President Obama would just show us the documents. It is not only Donald who wants to see them. It's the American people who want to know the truth."

In a formal move by the White House, Obama released the long form, showing that he was born in Hawaii's Kapiolani Hospital.

Donald, however, did not seem satisfied. "I hope it checks out for his sake. We have to see, is it real? It could be a fake, you know. I am really honored and I am really proud that I was able to get him to do something nobody else could."

On October 24, 2012, Donald offered to donate $5 million to the charity of Obama's choice in return for the publication of his college and passport applications. Obama did not respond to the offer.

During September of 2015, on the campaign trail for the 2016 elections, Donald flew once again to New Hampshire. During a question-and-answer period, an irate New Englander said, "We have a problem in this country. It's called Muslims. We know our current President is one. You know, he's not even an American. Birth certificate, man! We have training camps growing where they want to kill us. That's my question: When can we get rid of them?"

Donald replied, "We're looking at a lot of different things. And you know that a lot of people are saying that bad things are happening out there. We're going to be looking at that and at plenty of other things."

"He dodged the bullet on that question," one reporter claimed.

When pressed on the Muslim question, a Donald spokesman said, "Christians need to fear in this country. Their religious liberty is at stake."

Unless some document surfaces somewhere, it now appears beyond a reasonable doubt that the President's father was born in Kenya, his mother in Kansas, and Obama himself saw the light of day in Hawaii.

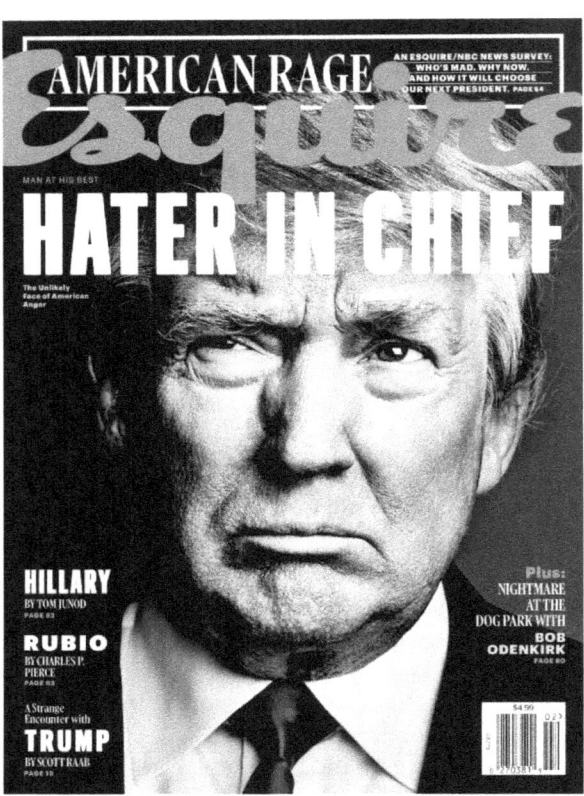

Il Duce: Donald's detractors began comparing his arrogance to that of Mussolini.

Chapter Three

GOLDFINGER TRUMP
A SALESMAN WITH THE MIDAS TOUCH
Living Large & Living Loud

TRUMP UNIVERSITY

"Professor Trump," the Big Hair on Campus, Promises that for $35,000, Any Member of the "Great Unwashed" Can Become a Millionaire

THE APPRENTICE
"You're Fired!"

DONALD AS THE PAGEANT WORLD'S "MASTER OF THE UNIVERSE"

*The Beauty Industry's Triple Crown:
Miss USA! Miss Universe! Transgenders Can Compete!*

In and Out of Court, Donald Feuds with Pageant Winners & "That Fat Pig," Rosie O'Donnell

In 2004, as one of his worst business decisions, Donald Trump, with two of his associates (Jonathan Spitalny and Michael Sexton), launched Trump University.

At fees ranging from $1,500 to $35,000, it offered courses "taught by experts" in real estate, asset management, and wealth creation. Most of all, it promised courses in entrepreneurship itself "taught by the greatest entrepreneur on earth, who makes more in a day than most people earn in a lifetime."

Promoting Donald as "a professor" was a bit of a stretch. Although prospective students expected to be taught by the master himself, their courses would be delivered via web-based, long distance seminars. Lessons were neither conducted nor taught by "The Donald."

The Trump University website had promised, "In a highly competitive world, the one sure way of being successful is to know everything you can about what you do. And of course, you will have the opportunity to learn directly from Donald J. Trump himself."

For many men and women, dreaming of getting rich, the prospect of learning from "the sorcerer" who spearheaded *The Apprentice* was a formidable enticement.

From the beginning, *exposé* editors at TheSmokingGun.com were skeptical—with good reason. The staff noted that Donald had graduated from the Wharton School of Finance. "Perhaps he can lecture on the importance of having a rich father. Or maybe he can offer a somber Founders' Day reflection on how he actually managed to lose money operating a casino?"

If it's one thing that Donald knew how to do, it involved generating free publicity. He boasted that, "Trump University is going to be very big in investment banking and education."

He was heralded in promotional material as a financial swashbuckler, "The Errol Flynn of real estate," or at least a Douglas Fairbanks Sr.

Trump University (aka Trump Wealth Institute and later Trump Entrepreneur Initiative LLC) was not an accredited university or college, and conferred no college degree.

Those who paid the fees were offered access not directly to Trump, but to Trump U's website, where articles, lectures, and videos about salesmanship were made available. Within some of its videos, they also got some gossip from The Donald himself.

In one sequence, he delivered his thoughts on the pop singer Britney Spears: "She has seen better days. She performed five years ago at the Trump Taj Mahal in Atlantic city, and was great. But today, everything seems to be slipping away from her. Britney, don't let that happen. Keep your shaved head on straight!"

Students also received a primer, a book called *Trump 101*, that featured his picture on the cover. Since he wasn't around to pose for selfies, students had to settle for having their pictures snapped as they stood beside a life-sized, free-standing cutout of the master.

They heard rags-to-riches stories, one instructor claiming that as a young man, he slept on the subways in Manhattan before becoming a real estate mogul.

Trump U coasted under the radar for a few years, but by 2010, a growing coven of dissenters had emerged. The offices of Attorney Generals in six states were bombarded with complaints from former students, and the *New York Daily News* published some of them.

The most serious charges involved allegations that students had been urged "to max out their credit cards to pay for extra courses and seminars." It had also been suggested that graduates of the university would be introduced to powerful tycoons who had made "a killing in real estate."

That never happened.

The most serious challenge to Trump U came in 2013 when Eric Schneiderman, Attorney General for the State of New York, launched an investigation that led to him suing both Donald and Trump U for $40 million on grounds that students had been defrauded. Immediately, Donald dropped the name "university" from his school, renaming it Trump Entrepreneur Initiative. The state required accreditation for any institution calling itself a uni-

Donald made a powerful enemy over the issue of Trump University. New York Attorney General **Eric Schneiderman** filed a $40 million lawsuit against him, claiming that students had been defrauded.

Donald fired back, calling the AG "a political hack" and even tying Obama into a so-called conspiracy to bring down lawsuits on him.

versity.

As was his custom, Donald went on the offensive, charging that no college or university, even Harvard and Yale, ever received complete approval from their students. He told the *New York Daily News* that "ninety-eight percent of Trump U's students praised the courses. Lots of pupils left their seminars with us and became very successful in making big deals with little money."

Vanity Fair ran an article about Trump U by William D. Cohan, headlining Donald as the BIG HAIR ON CAMPUS. The magazine's editor, Graydon Carter, labeled Donald "a short-fingered vulgarian."

He shot back, "Carter is a sleazebag and highly overrated."

Of all the politicians he'd tangled with (up to that date), Eric Schneiderman became Donald's worst enemy, charging him with operating an enterprise "that is nothing short of an out-and-out fraud."

In his suit, during August of 2003, the Attorney General claimed that between 2003 and 2011, Donald and Trump U intentionally misled more than 5,000 students nationwide, including 600 in New York State alone. He charged that Donald made $5 million for his contribution to the "university," a profit that he had promised to donate to charities.

Graydon Carter, editor of *Vanity Fair*, exposed Donald and Trump University in an article in his prestigious magazine. Donald was ridiculed as the "Big Hair on Campus."

Donald denounced Carter as a "sleazebag."

Later, in response, Donald revealed that legal fees had eaten up all the profits, and that there was nothing left to contribute.

Before the New York press, Schneiderman claimed, "Mr. Trump used his celebrity status and personally appeared in commercials making false promises to convince people to spend tens of thousands of dollars they couldn't afford for lessons they never got."

Appearing on the right-wing TV show, *Fox & Friends,* Donald shot back attacking Schneiderman's character and calling him "…a political hack. The lawsuit was cooked up immediately after he visited Barack Obama at the White House. The two met on Thursday, and he filed the lawsuit on a Saturday. It was a helluva coincidence. Obama wants to get back at me over the Birther issue. I'd had a lot of litigation. I have never heard of a lawsuit being filed on a Saturday."

The response from the AG was immediate. "President Obama and I had more important things to discuss than my busting this penny-ante fraud of Trump University. Donald Trump seems to be the kind of person who goes to the Super Bowl and thinks the people in the huddle are talking about him."

"The Attorney General is a disgusting human being," Donald responded, "a sleazebag and a crook, who is driving business out of New York. He once came to me begging for a campaign contribution, and now he's trying to screw me."

The AG defended himself, as the battle between adversaries was waged in the tabloids. "The fact that Donald Trump has a larger megaphone than most fraudsters is what gets all the attention here. It is true that he did not support me in the primary of 2010, but once I won, he gave me one contribution—and that was it."

Schneiderman attempted to "out-blitz the Blitzer." He wrote an Op-Ed piece for the *New York Daily News,* and appeared on TV talk shows. "Trump's outlandish accusations are not surprising for a showman who has built a career around bluster and hype. But I am not in the entertainment business: I am in the justice business. Instead of going to court, he chose to try the case in the press."

Later, both in and out of court, the AG aired his accusations, asserting that the so-called free seminars "were the first step in a bait-and-switch to induce prospective students to enroll in increasingly expensive seminars starting with the three-day $15,000 fee that led to advanced seminars—the Gold Elite Program—costing $35,000."

Jackie Loughery, Miss USA 1952.

Modesty in bathing suits was the custom back in the year that Dwight Eisenhower was elected President.

Jackie Loughery became the first Miss New York USA and the winner of the first Miss USA beauty pageant.

Among her husbands were the popular singer Guy Mitchell and the famous TV actor Jack Webb.

"Schneiderman, for tarring me as a fraud, will pay politically for his accusations against me," Donald threatened. "My legal response will blow Schneiderman out of the war."

On the campaign trail in 2016, "Little Marco Rubio and Lyin' Lion's Head Cruz" (Donald's appellations) repeatedly brought up charges against Trump U and its pending litigation.

"I could have settled for peanuts," Donald said, "but if you give in too easily, then skunks start emerging from the underground to file more lawsuits against you. My lawyers are going to fight this thing, and we will win."

"BLONDE BEAUTIES
—That's What I Like"

—Donald Trump

It was a lovefest when the popular gossip columnist, **Cindy Adams**, met Donald Trump, courtesy of his lawyer, Roy Cohn. They formed a beneficial relationship, and he often gave her insider tips to run in her column.

Ivana meanwhile had won the backing of Cindy's rival columnist, Liz Smith.

In *The Art of the Comeback*, Donald wrote that Cindy Adams, columnist for the *New York Post*, "knew way back when that I loved beauty. Loved blondes and loved the Miss Universe Pageant."

[That was before he bought a trio of Beauty Pageants.]

At a party, his attorney, Roy Cohn, introduced Donald to Cindy Adams, claiming, "This guy will own New York one day."

She replied, "Oh yeah, pass me the gravy."

She later said, "Who knew he'd own the world some day? His dinner partner that night was a drop-dead gorgeous blonde, with a neckline so low she probably still has bronchitis. And brainy? Couldn't spell CIA. He and I kept talking across Blondie's puffy chest. We laughed all night. Loved one another instantly."

From 1996 to 2015, Donald owned, at least partially, three beauty pageants, of which Miss Universe was the most celebrated. The trio of pageants fell under the baton of the Miss Universe Organization.

The origin of Miss Universe went back to 1926 when it was called the International Pageant of Pulchritude. It flourished for nine years until the Great Depression and war clouds over Europe brought it to a (temporary) halt in 1935.

Revived in 1952, it was sponsored by Pacific Mills, the California-based clothing manufacturer.

Its chief rivals were Miss World and Miss Earth. Miss Universe drew beauty queens from 190 countries worldwide, and the pageant was seen every year by half a billion TV watchers.

Deep into his ownership of the pageant, Donald claimed that it was worth $40 to $50 million. "I plan to make Miss Universe the world's most dominant beauty show. As far as I'm concerned, Miss America is as dead as the Model T."

"The backers of Miss America don't know what they're doing. It's all fucked up. They're beset with problems. They have this talent contest. Who cares? Beauty pageants aren't about talent. No contestant is a budding Judy Garland. The viewers don't give a shit if a girl can play the piano or the violin. They want to see what she looks like in a bathing suit."

The second pageant he acquired, Miss USA, formed in 1952, is an annual competition that determines America's entrant in the Miss Universe contest. The pageant originated when Yolande Betbeze, winner that year of the Miss America contest, refused to pose for publicity pictures in a bathing suit.

The first Miss USA was Jackie Loughery, who had been Miss New York before any links had been forged between the pageant and the TV networks.

The pageant aired from 1963 to 2002 on CBS. In 2002, Donald brokered a deal with NBC for broadcasting rights to the show, ceding half ownership of the annual event to the network.

Famous hosts of Miss USA had previously included John Charles Daly, Bob Barker, John Forsythe, and Dick Clark.

Since its inception, eight Miss USA titleholders have gone on to wear the Miss Universe crown.

When Donald owned the pageants, he gave the winners the use of a deluxe apartment within Trump Place in Manhattan.

Miss Teen USA, formed in 1983 and open to girls ages 14 to 19, was broadcast on NBC until 2007. Since then, the competition has been held at the Atlantis Paradise Island Resort, across from Nassau in The Bahamas.

In a remarkable concession to LGBT rights, Donald showed a noteworthy liberal streak when he allowed transgendered women to compete—if they'd previously won their national pageant—in his beauty pageants. This policy was markedly more liberal than that of the Republican legislators of North Carolina and Mississippi, who, in 2016 passed laws that insisted that a transgendered person must use whichever bathroom corresponded to the gender listed on his or her birth certificate.

Since his acquisition of the pageants, Donald has become involved in some widely publicized feuds, even lawsuits, with his beauty queens, some of which are described in the pages that follow:

ALICIA MACHADO: MISS UNIVERSE 1996
"She's an Eating Machine" Donald Charges

"God, what problems I had with this woman," Donald said, referring to Alicia Machado. As Miss Venezuela, she won the 1996 Miss Universe competition, becoming the fourth Miss Venezuela to hold that title. Her reign began at around the same time that Donald took over the pageant.

"First, she wins," he said. "Second, she gains fifty pounds. Third, I urge the committee to fire her. Fourth, I go to the gym with her in a show of support. Then she trashed me in *The Washington Post* after I stood by her the entire time. What's wrong with this picture? Anyway, the best part was the knowledge that next year, she would no longer be Miss Universe."

When Donald publicly defined her as "an eating machine," it be-

OTHER THAN HIS WELL-PUBLICIZED PLEDGE TO BUILD A WALL, WHAT'S ANOTHER REASON HISPANICS DON'T LIKE DONALD TRUMP?

It involved his long-standing feud with **Alicia Machado**, Miss Venezuela, an icon of the Latino world, depicted in all her glory in the three photos above.

came a tabloid scandal. More scandal was on the way. In February of 2006, she posed nude for the Mexican edition of *Playboy*, thus becoming the only Miss Universe to pose as a centerfold for any franchise of that magazine.

In 2005, she became engaged to baseball's Bobby Abreu. Then, during their engagement, she appeared on *La Granja*, a Spanish-language reality show, where she was filmed having sex with another character on the show. Shortly after that video surfaced, Abreu abruptly ended their engagement.

TARA CONNER
Should Donald Have Dethroned Miss USA 2006?
(Or Should He Have Given Her Another Chance?)

The belle of Kentucky, Tara Conner, won three beauty contests in her home state before winning the Miss USA crown in 2006.

After her coronation, reports surfaced that she'd been drinking in a setting where she was underaged at the time. Even worse, the tabloids reported that she'd been using heroin, cocaine, and crystal meth.

Some of the pageant's officials wanted to take her crown, but after she agreed to enter a drug rehabilitation program, Donald stood by her.

On *The Oprah Winfrey Show*, Donald said he wanted to give Tara a second chance for personal reasons. "My brother, Fred Trump, died of alcoholism. I believe in second chances."

Tara admitted that she had turned to drugs when she was only fourteen in the wake of her parents' separation and the death of her beloved grandfather.

Donald had moved her into an apartment at Trump Place, along with that year's title holders from the *Miss Universe* and *Miss Teen USA* pageants. Tara was alleged, as reported in an *exposé* in the *New York Daily News*, to have invited—in defiance of pageant rules—young men into her quarters. One of her defenders (unnamed in the tabloid) claimed, "Tara is just a small town girl who went wild in New York. She just couldn't handle herself. She was sneaking those nightclub guys in and out of her apartment."

Donald's defense of Tara, and his indulgence in allowing her a second chance, ballooned into one of his most notorious celebrity feuds.

Tara Conner, according to the New York tabloids, had gotten into trouble with drugs and alcohol. As owner of the *Miss USA* contest, Donald wanted to give her a "second chance."

This led to Rosie O'Donnell mocking his self-imposed status as "a moral authority." Her ridicule led to one of his most famous feuds.

ROSIE O'DONNELL

DONALD: "She's a Degenerate, Ugly, Third-Rate Fatass."
ROSIE: "He's a Gelatinous, Goopy Garden Slug with a Jell-O Orange Comb-Over."

Before her feud with Donald, Rosie O'Donnell knew him well enough for him to invite her to his wedding (to Marla Maples) reception at Mar-a-Lago in Palm Beach.

But after watching him on television granting Tara Conner a second chance, she became furious and attacked him the next day on *The View* when Barbara Walters, its host, was on vacation.

Before millions of TV viewers, Rosie mockingly said, "Donald Trump a moral authority?" Then she tossed her hair to one side to mock his orange coif.

Two views of **Rosie O'Donnell.** On the *right*, she's parodying Donald for his sanctimonious judgments—"As if he's a role model!"

"Left his first wife. Had an affair. Left the second wife. Had an affair. But now he's the moral compass for 20-year-olds in America? Donald, sit and spin, my friend."

She also called him "a snakeoil salesman."

Donald fired back at Rosie in the media, calling her "a slob and a fat pig. I plan to sue her. I look forward to taking lots of money from fat little Rosie."

In an interview with the *New York Daily News*, he told a reporter, "When I saw that tape of *The View*, I said, 'you'd better watch out, Rosie, or I'll send one of my friends over to take your girlfriend.' I imagine it would be pretty easy to take her away, considering how ugly fat Rosie looks."

[*The TV star was one of a handful of openly lesbian celebrities at the time, living with her partner, Kelli, in a household with four children.*]

Donald continued to hit back, claiming that "Rosie was really interested in having some sort of romance with Miss USA herself, Tara Conner." He also claimed that his friend, Barbara Walters, "can't stand Rosie. Fat Rosie hurts the program that Barbara created. I'm worth billions of dollars, and I have to listen to this fatass slob!"

[*Since Rosie joined* The View, *its TV audience rose some thirteen percent. On her web site, Rosie claimed, "The emperor has no clothes. The comb-over has gone ballistic."*

Gallup took a poll, finding that most of the viewers sided with Donald.]

In her 2007 memoir, *Celebrity Detox*, Rosie wrote:

> "Donald groaned in a strange way, almost salivating over his attack on me. Totally creepy. He was sadistic in a deeply disturbing way. It was like seeing a specimen squirming in a slide in a high school science class. Poke here and it lashes its tail. Add salt to the brine and it shrivels up."

> "Donald also reminded me of a lot of garden slugs we used to get on our front steps after rains—gelatinous, goopy slugs, some five inches long, sleek and wet, leaving sticky trails in their wake."

Madonna, as she's interviewed by Meredith Viera on the *Today* show, defending Rosie against Donald.

Reporters later suggested that the real reason Madonna dropped by the show was to drum up support for her new film, the animated feature, *Arthur and the Invisibles*, which had received horrendous reviews.

Even Madonna got in on the act. The pop singer had been a friend of Rosie's since they had starred together in *A League of Their Own* (1992).

Appearing on NBC's *Today Show* for an interview by Meredith Viera, Madonna said she'd heard of the Donald/Rosie feud while vacationing "in the middle of the Indian Ocean."

According to Madonna, she had e-mailed Rosie: "I wanted to hear it from the horse's mouth. Rosie is a stand-up comic, and they're known for talking about provocative things in their monologues. I feel that if every stand-up comic was penalized for saying politically incorrect things, they'd all be hung in the public square."

In her memoir, Rosie wrote that Donald "was not a human being, but a wind-up toy with Tourette's, a man who had allowed himself to get pulled so deeply into capitalism that he had turned his entire being into a product with a price tag on it; he was gift wrapped and stuffed with Styrofoam."

On TV, Donald revealed that he had spoken to Barbara Walters herself, while she was on vacation. He quoted her as saying, "I am no fan of Rosie's." The talk show host had also warned him, "You should never get in the mud with pigs."

Rosie later wrote, "Trump outed Barbara, dragging this septuagenarian into the fray. He wounded two women, and for what? The worst part of it was that I knew, from the get-go, twisted that he was, I knew in my heart that Barbara had said those things. In one way or another, she had betrayed me. I was Trumped."

CARRIE PREJEAN
Same-Sex Marriage & The Culture Wars

Semi-Nude Photos & Miss California 2009

Few beauty contestants have ever been as controversial as Carrie Prejean, recipient of the double-barreled honor of having been crowned Miss California in 2009 and the first runner-up in the Miss USA pageant that same year.

The blonde-haired, green-eyed beauty was reared in an evangelical Christian household in Vista, California. A year after her birth in 1987, her parents separated.

Her opinions about homosexuals were formed when she was growing up during the long divorce proceedings of her parents, who allegedly made homosexual allegations against each other. She heard such false statements as "all men who have mustaches are gay."

As Prejean matured, her modeling career skyrocketed, leading up to her winning the Miss California competition.

She then went on to enter the Miss USA contest, competing with exceptionally beautiful women. The contest was going fine until, in front of millions of TV viewers, the controversial Perez Hilton, who is gay and was one of the judges, asked her to share her views on whether same-sex marriage should be legalized nationwide.

Prejean responded, "In my family, I believe that marriage should be between a man and a woman. No offense to anybody out there. But that's how I was raised."

Before that utterance, which was broadcast across the country, a beauty pageant title holder had almost never become embroiled in the fight over homosexuality.

Hilton, who was known for posting hot gossip across the internet, added a video blog to his website, disparaging her and calling her "a dumb bitch."

"She gave an awful, awful answer," he wrote. He also told ABC News that her Miss California crown "should be taken away because of her homophobia."

She later responded, "I was being dared—in front of the entire world—to give a candid answer to a serious question. I knew if I told the truth, I would lose all that I was competing for: the crown, the luxury apartment in New York, the large salary—everything that went with the Miss USA title. I also knew, or suspected, that I was the front-runner, and if I gave the politically correct answer, I could be Miss USA."

Donald defended her response, saying, "It wasn't a bad answer. She simply stated her belief. The question was a bit unlucky, and no matter which way she answered, she was going to get killed."

Even the liberal *New York Times* weighed in, stating that her belief was representative of mainstream public opinion on the issue. "While a majority of Americans believe that

Carrie Prejean later claimed that she lost the *Miss USA* crown in 2009 for expressing her "heartfelt opinion against same-sex marriage."

Whether that was true or not, she angered millions of viewers, but also won millions of followers from the homophobic far right.

Of course, there was a book deal...of course.

gay couples should be able to enter into unions with some of the legal protection of marriage, only a minority believe that gays and lesbians should be permitted to 'marry' per se."

[Of course, that opinion would soon evolve in favor of same-sex marriages.]

Prejean's opposition to same-sex marriage endeared her to the right-wing National Organization for Marriage, which used footage of her answer for a TV ad that warned that "same-sex activists want to silence the opposition."

More trouble was on the way. Pageant organizers investigated reports that Prejean had violated the terms of her contract by not disclosing that she had posed for semi-nude photographs. When confronted, Prejean claimed, "It was legitimate modeling."

Donald more or less agreed with her. "We are in the 21st Century. We have determined the pictures are fine. In some cases, the photos are lovely."

Prejean continued to speak out, doubling down on an incendiary position that she might have been wise to have softened. She went on to assert a statement that many liberals denounced: "Marriage is good. There is something special about unions of husband and wife. Unless we bring men and women together, children will not have mothers and fathers."

[Thus from the mouths of babes emerges "wisdom."]

The tabloids immediately erupted with rumors that Prejean was dating the Olympic champion swimmer, Michael Phelps. He denied it, claiming "I'm not dating anybody. I'm single. My private life stays private."

When quizzed, although Prejean ducked the issue, her grandmother, Jeanette Coppolla, asserted, "Carrie and Michael go on dates—baseball games, dinners. When he's in town, he always calls her and they go out."

Phelps was also asked for an opinion about the same-sex marriage issue. On a morning TV talk show, he said, "I'm not saying I support her. I'm not saying I don't support her."

More trouble was on the way. On June 10, 2009, Donald terminated Prejean's contract, claiming that she had continued to violate its terms.

Prejean fought back, claiming that the producers of the Miss California pageant wanted her to pose nude for *Playboy*. Executives responded that they had merely passed the magazine's offer on to her, as they did all the other offers coming her way.

In August, she sued Miss California USA, charging that she had been both slandered and libeled and was made to suffer religious discrimination. She also alleged that there had been a release of her private medical records.

Pageant officials countersued, seeking profits from a book she'd written in violation of her contract. It was entitled *Still Standing: The Untold Story of My Fight Against Gossip, Hate, and Political Attacks*. The pageant also sought a repayment of $5,200 lent to her for breast implants.

By November, a settlement was reached, the terms of which were not revealed. CNN later reported that the settlement was prompted by the alleged discovery of a "sex tape" involving Prejean.

The most eligible bachelor of that moment, **Michael Phelps**, did not want to get involved in the same-sex marriage controversy.

Nor did he want to admit or deny that he was dating Carrie Prejean.

SHEENA MONNIN
MISS PENNSYLVANIA 2012??
A Judge Orders a Miss USA Contestant to Pay Donald $5 Million for Denouncing His Pageant as "Rigged"

A brunette beauty, Sheena Monnin, seemingly made a career out of winning beauty pageants. Her titles, among many others, included Miss Florida USA (2006), Miss Texas USA (2009), and Miss Pennsylvania USA (2012). She was also, amid huge controversy, a (losing) contestant in the *Miss USA Pageant* in 2012.

Sheena Monnin...lawsuits, accusations that the contest was rigged, denunciations. "I'm taking a stand against that bully, Mr. Trump."

She later became the founder and CEO of Custom Life Design, an employee assessment and training company. A psychologist, she is also the author of a self-help book, *Hands on the Wheel: Getting Control of Your Life*.

On the night Monnin lost the Miss USA contest, she posted on Facebook the accusation that the pageant was "fraudulent, lacking in morals, inconsistent, and in many ways trashy." She also accused pageant organizers of working from a script in which the final sixteen contestants and the top five finalists were all pre-determined.

Donald called her a "beautiful young woman who had sour grapes because she was not among the final contestants."

In protest, she relinquished her titles of Miss Pennsylvania "rather than compromise my values. I feel the world has a right to know the truth about the pageant. I'm standing up against this bully, Donald Trump."

He sued her for $5 million, charging defamation. Because she failed to show up in court on the day of her hearing (based on what was later defined as faulty legal advice from her lawyer) a default judgment was rendered against her for that amount.

"We applaud the judge's very articulate thirty-page decision," said Michael Cohen, Donald's attorney. "We will pursue our rights available to Mr. Trump."

Later, Monnin—after months of inconvenience, expense, and despair—sued her attorney and was able to recover expenses and also resolve the lawsuit.

BIKINIS, BOSOMS, & HIGH HEELS: MISS WORLD GOES TO NIGERIA
(With Death Threats, Decapitations, Mob Violence, & Religious Fanaticism)

In 2002, Donald had set his sights on acquiring the Miss World pageant, which he viewed as the major competition to his Miss Universe Pageant. It was owned by Julia Morley, a Londoner and the widow of Eric Morley, who had organized it in 1951 and controlled it until his death in 2000.

As reported in *Vanity Fair*, Donald's intention was to wrest control of the Miss World Pageant from her at a bargain price.

"Every time I try to put my head up there in the United States, Trump used to try to blow it off," Morley alleged. "He actually took legal action against me for having a Miss World USA contest."

When Judy Bachrach of *Vanity Fair* contacted Donald for his response, he neither admitted nor denied the charge. "He fairly crowed about the hopes of acquiring the Miss World competition," Bachrach wrote.

"Yeah, I'd buy it for almost nothing," he said. "If I did, I would make it better—or maybe I'd shut it down."

He was informed that Morley was trying to make the swimsuits of the contestants more modest.

He chuckled at that: "When I bought Miss Universe, the bathing suits got smaller and the heels got higher—and the ratings skyrocketed."

Weeks later, Donald avidly followed the gory details of the Miss World pageant. It was staged that year in Nigeria, a nation with a large Muslim population, during the holy month of Ramadan.

It was a disaster—a cultural clash of epic (and for the contestants, terrifying) proportions. Some ninety scantily clad beauty queens from around the world were flown to Nigeria's capital of Abuja.

The November pageant with so much naked flesh on display set off a series of bloody riots that led to 250 people dead and thousands injured. Machetes were used to chop off heads; mosques were burned to the ground, and bystanders were "necklaced" with burning tires. Hundreds of protesters attacked others.

"Down with beauty!" was the rallying cry of the day. "Miss World is an abomination! *Allahu Akbar!*"

A Nigerian woman journalist, age 21, who had written about the pageant, had to flee for her life. The young contestants also fled Nigeria. On the way to the airport, their buses passed charred bodies and burning cars. Muslim fundamentalists had been outraged at the provocation of the pageant.

Back in London, headlines screamed SCRAP MISS WORLD.

Morley defended her decision. "To tell the truth, before I left, I thought Sharia was a girl's name. I did! I swear to you. I was totally ignorant. I got into big shit trouble because I hardly realized what I was letting myself in for."

Julia Morley, depicted above at one of her contests in 2001, operated the *Miss World Pageant*, but in the mistake of her life brought all that exposed flesh and all those "western decadent" photo-ops to a Muslim nation, Nigeria, during Ramadan.

THE RESULT?: Mob riots, beheadings, and multiple deaths by "necklaces" crafted from burning tires.

Harrassed and terrified, the scantily clad contestants fled from Nigeria and from *Miss World*, grateful to escape with their lives.

In New York, Donald was no longer interested in acquiring the Miss World pageant. "I was shocked at Morley's decision to fly the girls into Nigeria. The pageant has been so tarnished by the stupidity of going to Nigeria. I wouldn't consider a purchase now. Not unless the price was ridiculously low. You can't go to Nigeria! Everybody knows that!"

UNIVISION
Donald at War with Latino American Television

When Donald made remarks against Mexicans that his partner, **Univision**, considered racist, the Spanish language TV network withdrew their ties to him, which led to lawsuits. But the network had long had trouble for broadcasting anti-gay slurs and shows that treated women like disposable objects.

The scene above depicts finals for "**Miss Mundial Brasil 2014**" on the entertainment talk show El Gordo y la Flaca. The show—entitled "Eight Reasons to Fire up the Jacuzzi"— invited guests to take a dip in an on-set hot tub.

In September of 2015, in a decision based on Donald's comments in June about illegal immigration, both NBC and Univision, the Spanish language TV network, dropped the *Miss USA* pageant and backed off from their business relationships with Donald.

As part of their settlement, he bought out NBC's fifty percent ownership of the pageant, thereby emerging as its sole owner.

Three days later, he sold the company to WME (William Morris Endeavor), a talent agency founded in Beverly Hills in 2009, and its satellite, IMG, which WME had acquired for $2.4 billion in 2013. Trump then filed a $500 million lawsuit against Univision, alleging defamation and breach of contract.

In February of 2016, he and Univision reached a settlement, the terms of which were not made public. Also in 2016, in the void created by the departures of NBC and Univision, Fox signed on to broadcast the *Miss USA* pageant.

Donald told a reporter, "I've exited the beauty contest business. I've got the most beautiful woman in the world waiting for me every night atop Trump Tower."

THE APPRENTICE:
HOW TO BE A WINNER
(aka How Not to Get Fired)

It was a hot day on Venice Beach, south of Los Angeles, as a young man, transplanted to the West Coast from London, hawked T-shirts hoping to eke out a living. One of them was emblazoned with the large message FUCK ME NOW! In his chocolate brown felt Akubra, the young man, known as Mark Burnett, evoked Indiana Jones.

This son of Archie and Jean Burnett, both of them factory workers at Ford Motors, he had enlisted in the British Army at the age of seventeen, advancing into a Section Commander in the Parachute Regiment. He had seen action during Britain's short war with Argentina over the Falklands.

In 1982, he'd emigrated to the United States, where, for a while, he worked as a live-in nanny, looking after two boys for $250 a week. Wanting a bigger slice of "the American pie," he had saved his money and was able to purchase *Eco-Challenge*, a TV show devoted to competitions. This was the doorway to his career as a TV producer, which, in time, would bring him untold millions.

One of Mark Burnett's greatest successes, pre-Donald, was **The Bible**, a ten-hour *History Channel* series seen by millions of viewers.

He continued to work his way up the ladder, and by the summer of 2000, he was producing the hit TV reality show, *Survivor*. By 2009, it had been designated as the Number One reality series of all time.

Burnett's single greatest success was *The Bible*, a ten-hour History Channel series based upon Biblical stories. It was seen by 100 million viewers, becoming in 2013 the top mini-series ever.

[The Bible was developed and produced after Burnett met Donald Trump.]

One day, when Burnett was hawking those $18 T-shirts on Venice Beach, a friend handed him a book called *The Art of the Deal* by Donald Trump, an author he'd never heard of. However, by the following morning, he said., "I have become a Donald Trump fan."

A week later, he called Donald in New York, and the mogul, familiar with Burnett's name because of *Survivor*, took the call. Burnett immediately made his sales pitch, claiming that he wanted to produce another reality show to be entitled *The Apprentice*. "I see you as the star of the series, a kind of businessman's *Survivor*."

"Donald was all ears," Burnett said. "A lot of big CEOs shun publicity. Not Donald. It was obvious to me that he loved the limelight. That was just the kind of celebrity host I needed."

A meeting was set up at Trump Tower. In terms of millions of dollars, this might rank up there with Stanley meeting Livingstone in darkest Africa. "Within fifteen minutes of talking to Donald, I knew he was THE MAN. He could make fast decisions, and quick ones at that. He didn't waste time. He gets right to the point. He's a creation of instinct, and his instinct is invariably right. Most of all, he's a natural born showman."

"I wanted this charismatic businessman for my partner," Burnett said. "Ronald Reagan might have been called 'The Great Communicator,' but I found that Donald was even more skilled than the former President. Unless it's inherited wealth, no billionaire is a damn wallflower. It takes intelligence and aggression to get where Donald is."

After reading a synopsis, Donald agreed with Burnett that the New York business world "is a jungle filled with wild flesh eaters."

"There are more snakes here and more things that can kill you than any other jungle in the world. Even Tarzan would get snake bite walking the canyons of Wall Street. A wannabe may be a genius but lack the killer instinct to survive in the dog-eat-dog business world. The city can eat some of these kids alive."

When their meeting ended, Donald and Burnett shook hands. "It's going to be a big hit," Donald said. "I have this gut instinct. Let's go for it."

Before Burnett had walked through his door, Donald had turned down at least seven TV producers who wanted him to go before the cameras with a reality show.

"They wanted to follow me around with cameras, watching me make deals, brush my teeth, and, most certainly, comb my hair. None of this appealed to me. I don't do business that way. Who do they think I am? Anna Nicole Smith?"

A secret deal was worked out between Burnett and NBC. Donald would host the first season, a sixteen-episode series. If *The Apprentice* were moderately successful, with the intention of boosting ratings, they would, for the second season, hire a big CEO name like Microsoft's Bill Gates, or perhaps Virgin Atlantic's Richard Branson to take over for him.

After the first casting call went out, an estimated 215,000 contestants applied from twenty of America's biggest cities. The show was billed as "The Ultimate Job Interview."

After signing the contract, Donald said, "I was a real schmuck to believe what Mark told me, that the TV show would take up only three hours of my time each week. It ended up taking some thirty hours, but I didn't mind."

He admitted that as the series was launched, he became somewhat of a babe magnet. "All the women on the show flirted with me—consciously or unconsciously. That's to be expected. A sexual dynamic is always present between people, unless you're asexual."

The Apprentice was first telecast on January 8, 2004, and the ratings "went through the ceiling" in Donald's words. An average of some twenty million viewers—he claimed twenty-five million—tuned in. Eventually, it outdistanced the enormously popular CBS hit, *CSI*, which aired during the same time slot.

The first season's finale, which aired on April 15, 2004, was a blockbuster, helping the series emerge as the most highly rated on any network for viewers aged 18 to 49.

According to Donald, "I appeal to millions out there who have dreams of caviar and wishes for the bubbly instead of water."

The degree to which it became a hit came as a surprise. It was one of the highest-rated entertainment shows of the 2003-4 season. Donald was

The fine print on this cover of industry magazine *Ad Week* described **Mark Burnett** (*depicted above*) as " the man behind *Survivor, Shark Tank,* and *A.D. Now.*"

Burnett was also the genius who pitched the idea of hosting a TV show called *The Apprentice* to Donald Trump.

on a roll. The telecast of his Miss Universe Pageant (2004), broadcast from Ecuador, drew an audience of ten and a half million viewers.

Not only that, his 2003 book, *How to Get Rich*, hit *The New York Times'* best-seller list. He subtitled it, "Big deals from the star of *The Apprentice*."

The so-called "smoochathon" of TV, Robin Leach, who pioneered *Lifestyles of the Rich & Famous*, said, "Donald made rich people not ashamed to be rich and brash. He is the American Dream."

As a billionaire and "household name," he didn't want to stray too far from Trump Tower. "Let the fuckers come to me," he said.

For access to "the boardroom" where many of the scenes were filmed, he had only to take an elevator to one of the building's lower floors for shooting to begin.

In another area within Trump Tower, a studio for filming commercials was installed. Every day, right from his desk, he broadcast to 400 radio stations for the Clear Channel Communications Group.

He was a star and an entertainer, although for a time, he didn't want to play up his status as a TV reality show star, fearing it might turn off some investors who might have preferred a more staid and conservative business mogul with less of a "show-biz" style.

With all of his new-found fame, he was soon inundated with deals calling for him to endorse products at very lucrative terms. *Fortune,* in its April 26, 2004 edition, extolled his status as a TV celebrity. "He's never been hotter," the magazine proclaimed. "Just ask him!"

A month earlier, *Newsweek* had featured him on its cover.

In the 21st Century, a Gallup Poll found that ninety-eight percent of all Americans knew the name of Donald Trump, even some children twelve and below.

After the success of *The Apprentice*, the rap artist and hip-hop star, Jay-Z, boasted, "I am the ghetto's answer to Donald Trump!"

Thousands of business requests flooded into Donald's office. "People all over the world were requesting a job in Mr. Trump's organization," said his chief aide and "gatekeeper," Norma Foerderer.

During these tsunamis of publicity, he claimed, "I'm selling apartments like crazy. And I'm still the biggest real estate developer in New York. I've even been asked to be the grand marshal marching in the annual Israeli parade down Fifth Avenue."

He also like to brag about the success of his books, beginning with *The Art of the Deal*, first published in 1987. "My books sell like hotcakes. I get a great kick at looking at my name on top of all the bestseller lists and telling everybody to go fuck themselves."

He was even picking up endorsements from seasoned politicians who thought that he should run for President of the United States. "Henry Kissinger urged me to do the run, and he told me he suspected I would win. A lot of other big politicos thought the same—I won't name them. I listened to them, but right now, I love what I'm doing. I don't want to give up my day job."

Eliot Spitzer, the New York Attorney General, said, "Donald has transformed himself, and his name is one of the most identifiable brands in the world. He's not Coca-Cola, but he knows how to capture the imagination of the public. When people see his name, they associate it with good quality and a certain degree of flamboyance. He's part showman."

"If Bill Gates is the quintessential innovator, then Donald is the quintessential deal maker, and part of *The Art of the Deal* is marketing, a certain flamboyance, and tons of self-promotion," Spitzer said. "No one in America knows how to promote himself more than Donald."

"I'm not a celebrity," Donald proclaimed. "I'm a super-celebrity. I showed that money isn't everything. It doesn't guarantee happiness. In real life, money isolates you from other people."

At the conclusion of any year's series, the one person who remained unfired and still standing among the sixteen other wannabes would emerge as the

Robin Leach made a career on TV of invading the lifestyles of the rich and famous.

His astonishment at "The Donald" is reflected in his open mouth gaping.

Eliot Spitzer was the former Attorney General and later Governor of New York State before he was disgraced for pursuing—and paying off—prostitutes.

Even he was impressed with the marketing power of the Donald Trump name.

50

supreme victor and become an apprentice to Donald at the salary of $250,000 a year. He or she would be assigned with managing a project for the Trump Organization, perhaps (but not necessarily) one associated with real estate.

During the run of the show, Donald featured all three of the children he'd fathered with Ivana: Ivanka, Don Jr., and Eric. Melania Trump was also a regular on the show, hawking her fashion and cosmetic products. Ivanka's fashion products were also featured.

Jeff Zucker, president of NBC Universal Television Group, had liked Burnett's proposal. "Donald is a tireless promoter, especially of himself, and Mark—based on the success of *Survivor*—was the ideal producer."

Zucker immediately saw the allure of the "Trump *zeitgeist*. He's the quintessential made-in-America story: He's been up. He's been down. He's been back up again. After all, he wrote *The Art of the Comeback*."

Of course, there were those behind the scenes, who objected to the show, citing the fact that "Donald is fodder for the gossip columns, especially tabloid scandal. That might diminish how seriously he would be taken as a business executive."

Zucker disagreed. "He combines gossip, a razor-sharp business brain, and a social presence that could be intimidating on camera. No social figure in New York can top him."

Incredibly, many at NBC initially interpreted Donald as a has-been, belonging to the previous century and "all that debacle with his Atlantic City casinos."

Appearing on *The Larry King Show*, on February 27, 2004, in reference to *The Apprentice*, Donald said, "We have a really good system, where I go into the board room and rattle like a lunatic to these kids, and I leave and go off and build my buildings. And then it gets good ratings, and they pay me. Can you believe this?"

He received enormous praise from people in the industry. Producer Harvey Weinstein called from the West Coast, telling him, "You're the number one star in Hollywood."

Donald's youthful dream of being a mover-and-shaker in the entertainment industry had come true. "In the history of TV, nothing like this has ever happened," crowed Donald. "You know you're a star when Melania and I walk down the street. Taxi drivers slow down and shout at me, 'Trump! You're fired!'"

From Bayonne, New Jersey, to Santa Monica, California, eager contestants arrived to be on his show. Some of them were "token" African Americans and Asians. One black woman, Omarosa Manigault Stallworth, stood out. She was said to air her claws and bring up the charge of racism. Donald himself admitted, "The audiences soon found out she was the Wicked Witch."

One ominously terrifying contestant, when he was fired, gave Trump that same look that Tony Perkins in *Psycho* gave Janet Leigh in the shower before he slashed her nude body. Sometimes, a candidate would beg, "Mr. Trump, please don't fire me...pretty please!"

Fired during the fourth episode of the first season, Jennifer Crisafulli appeared on the *Today* show. "What you don't see is there are little ittybitty bullets that come flying, invisible bullets, out of Trump's fingers into your chest, and you're like *pu-pu-pu-pu-pu*. Oh, it was awful, just awful. I got canned in front of forty million people, maybe more. I was devastated."

The 32-year-old bodacious brunette from one of Manhattan's top real estate brokerages had made a slur against "old fat Jewish ladies." That had sealed her fate. After being so politically incorrect, she was shown to the door.

***

"Most people think I'm a fucking flamethrower," Donald said. "Historically, I've had people who stay with me for a long time. There is one exception. If I find an employee stealing from me, I fire them with dragon fire, an act they'll remember the rest of their thieving lives."

After seeing his father perform, Don Jr. told his Dad, "You missed your calling. You should have been an actor."

Donald was no stranger to TV. He had made appearances as a caricature of himself on TV and in films which included

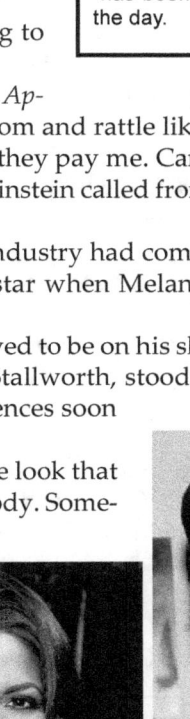

Jeff Zucker, president of NBC, formed a triumvirate with Donald and Mark Burnett to launch *The Apprentice*. He felt that Donald's flamboyance would be ideal in making the reality show a hit on TV.

There were many naysayers at NBC, many of whom viewed Donald as a "has been," but Zucker's wisdom won the day.

Omarosa Stallworth was a contestant on the first season of *The Apprentice* and later returned for its sequel, *Celebrity Apprentice*.

TV Guide listed her as one of the "60 Nastiest Villains of All Time."

On *The Apprentice*, contestant **Jeniffer Crisafulli** got the boot because of an indiscreet remark she made.

In trying to explain why her team "failed" at their task of opening a restaurant, she said, "It was because of those two old fat Jewish ladies...the pinnacle of the New York jaded old bags."

The next words she heard were, "You're fired!"

Home Alone 2, Lost in New York; The Nanny; The Fresh Prince of Bel-Air; and *Wall Street: Money Never Sleeps.* He also appeared in a cameo in an episode of the TV series, *Sex and the City*. A member of the Screen Actors Guild, based on previous earnings and dues paid during the course of his membership, he receives an annual pension of some $110,000 a year.

For the most part, his appearances got rave reviews. Steve Wynn compared his deadpan delivery to the master of deadpan delivery, Jack Benny himself.

Robert Wright, president of NBC, praised Donald's acting ability: "Marilyn Monroe might have required 58 takes to utter three words. But Donald Trump is known as 'one take.' He's better at getting it right the first time than any other actor or performer I've ever met."

Donald also won praise for his on-camera presence from a Hollywood bigwig, Alex Yemenidjian, CEO of MGM. "He has a narcissistic self-confidence that is truly amazing. There's never been a scene-stealer like him since W.C. Fields. He has the strong presence of any of the superstars of Hollywood's Golden Age. I could just hear him as Rhett Butler telling Scarlett, 'Frankly, my dear, I don't give a damn.'"

COMPETITION AMONG THE ÜBER-RICH?

Bill Gates: "Compared to Donald, I'm the modest type."

The co-founder of Microsoft, Bill Gates, defined by many experts as the wealthiest person in the world, said, "Unlike the rest of us, Jack Welch and myself, maybe Warren Buffett, we are not braggarts, touting our success. Donald goes against the grain. He flaunts his achievements without shame, certainly without modesty."

"There can be no doubt, present Donald with a microphone or a camera, and he performs," said Regis Philbin, his friend. "He has the look, the reputation, and a ton of charisma."

Russell Simmons, the hip-hop mogul, said, "Donald is a real life Richie Rich. He shares his toys with you. A lot of rich white guys tell you to go to hell as they munch their creamy cakes. They're fucking cake-aholics. That's not Donald. He not only enjoys his toys, he plays with his toys. He is the official bling-bling white guy."

In his book *TrumpNation*, Timothy L. O'Brien wrote:

"The Apprentice *showcased Donald Trump's one-of-a-kind, carnivalesque traits: The* High Plains Drifter *glower, the eyebrows that wandered around his forehead like fuzzy Slinkies, the bicycle helmet hairdo, the toughest-guy-in-the-bar swagger, the Day-Glo silk ties, and above all his unfailing on-spot assessments of contestants' strengths and weaknesses—and an unflinching willingness to say exactly what every viewer was already thinking about the ambitious, conniving, befuddled, and aspiring apprentices. Donald, as ringmaster and court jester, was channeling America.*"

In trying to explain the success of the show, Burnett said, "People always stop to watch a train wreck. People like rubbernecking on the freeway. On *The Apprentice,* they watched the train wreck in living color."

Jeff Zucker at NBC claimed, "*The Apprentice* is really about making it big in the Big Apple with the Big Guy."

In case anybody didn't already know it, Donald claimed, "In the history of the business world, all the Wall Street Greats, not a single man has ever risen to be the Number One star on television."

For his first season on *The Apprentice,* he was paid $700,000—that's about $50,000 per episode. When the show became a big success, he was paid $3 million per episode, making him one of the highest-paid personalities in the history of the medium. During the summer of 2015, right after he announced his run for the presidency, a press release stated that NBC/Universal had shelled out some $215 million for his fourteen seasons as host of the show. That earned him a star on the Hollywood Walk of Fame.

In spite of the praise for Donald's performance, he came in for his share of criticisms, notably from Jeffrey Sonnenfeld, an associate dean at the Yale School of Management. He called *The Apprentice* a "vulgar show, peddling deception, trickery, and sex. The lesson is that leadership selection is developed in a process similar to musical chairs at a Hooter's Restaurant."

Donald responded to the attack. "That guy claims there's too much sex, that it doesn't exist in the business world. What a laugh! Believe you me, it exists and bigtime. I know from personal experience."

Actually, Donald had to lecture some of his female contestants for "making their hawking look too much like hooking." He told them not to rely too much on mini-skirts and plunging *décolletage.*

In one episode, when male and female contestants were sent out on Wall Street to sell lemonade at a stand as part of their "assignments," the women offered kisses or gave out their phone number to male clients. Donald warned the women that "sex for sale" was more appropriate for a Hollywood casting couch than a Wall Street boardroom.

Penn Jillette, the magician, TV host, and author, attacked the contest as "venal people clawing at stupid, soulless stuff in front of the modern day Scrooge McDuck in order to stay famous. Trump just does what he wants, which is mostly pontificating to people who are sucking up to him."

***

During the second season of The Apprentice, one reporter was invited to fly to Palm Beach with Donald where he learned some personal data about him: His two favorite movies were Orson Welles' Citizen Kane and Gone With the Wind; he liked to devour a package of Oreos while he was watching movies; and his favorite movie star was Clint Eastwood.

"All those Sergio Leone westerns…" Donald said. "Nobody was cooler. He's a Republican, you know."

Donald and Burnett packed each episode with product placements, hawking various Trump enterprises along with Crest toothpaste or Pepsi-Cola. In the first three years of the show's run, this dynamic duo shared $100 million for product placement, the fees averaging some $1.5 million per episode. During the run of the series, Donald raked in an estimated $500 million in entertainment-related income, cashing in on books, speeches, beauty pageants, all of it based around The Apprentice.

Forbes magazine jokingly suggested: "Imagine President Donald J. Trump giving his inaugural address on a chilly afternoon in early 2017. Between grand pronouncements, he sips an Aquafina bottle sitting on his lecture—and gets a seven-figure check for his trouble."

DONALD'S FAVORITE MOVIES: In Gone With the Wind, he could identify with the swashbuckling Rhett Butler as played by **Clark Gable** holding Scarlett O'Hara (**Vivien Leigh**) in his powerful arms.

In Citizen Kane, he identified with the **Orson Welles** character, based on the real life William Randolph Hearst, the press baron.

The success of The Apprentice, where he portrayed "the titan tycoon of the business world" caused him embarrassment.

Although a business genius on TV, in his personal life, he was going through his worst financial crisis, declaring bankruptcy for his Atlantic City casinos.

Many associates, even his own sister, Maryanne Trump Barry, warned about the danger of overexposure. "There is such a thing as the public tiring of a media star," she said to him. "Where Donald Trump is concerned, I wonder if there is such a thing as over-exposure."

In response, Donald answered. "The more famous I get, the more offers pour in."

On August 12, 2004, he starred in a TV ad for a toy company, Hasbro, which had created Trump…the Game in which players made Trump-like deals, perhaps earning a million (play-money) dollars in the (fictional) aftermath. He later claimed that the Manufacturers Hanover Bank, which owned Hasbro, had paid him $5 million for his appearance and endorsement.

As a public speaker, Donald was in great demand for appearances at lecture halls as far away as Australia. He was getting $350,000 per speech, the highest speaker's fee in America, far more than Hillary Clinton got. One day, he was offered a deal to present three separate speeches, the first at 10AM and the third and final one scheduled for sometime in the late evening. "Had I accepted, I could have made $850,000 in just one day."

When he hosted Saturday Night Live, he told the audience, "Television is just a hobby for me. I'm primarily occupied with my real estate holdings; my best-selling books, and making love to women who have won prizes for their beauty—but not anymore, because I have a girlfriend."

He was referring to Melania Knauss.

On October 15, 2004, Donald made a difficult decision: He would appear at the New York Hilton for a Friars Club roast. He knew it could be brutal, even though the "roasters," for the most part, were his friends.

The zingers delivered that night were devastating. One of the best of them came from Jeff Zucker at NBC. He told the audience that he was unable to attend Donald's wedding, "but I'll catch the next one."

In another swipe, Zucker declared, "Donald has his dating down pat. There's the picking of the ring, the meeting of the parents, the meeting of the grandparents, and then the realization that he went to school with the grandparents."

At the end, struggling to conceal his annoyance, Donald urged the audience, "Go home, go to work, and watch your language."

The New York Times called it "A slash-and-burn salute from a bunch of foul-mouthed comedians lobbing off-color remarks about Trump's career, his looks, his spouse or spouses, his sexual prowess, and even—God forbid—his hair.'"

CELEBRITY APPRENTICE
A Forum Where Nearly Forgotten "Has-Beens" Could Resuscitate Some Public Recognition

After six seasons, a format for a spinoff series was introduced, *The Celebrity Apprentice,* a variation of *The Apprentice* series. Like its precursor, the show's opening theme song was "For the Love of Money" by the O'Jays.

Whereas the original version had focused on unknown wannabes striving against each other, this variation on the original theme focused on apprentices culled from among famous, or moderately famous, celebrities who would compete against other celebrities. Frankly, many of these celebrities were has-beens who still had some degree of name recognition. All of them competed to win money for the charitable organizations of their choice.

Celebrity contestants derived from the worlds of sports (Dennis Rodman, for example), or music, radio, reality TV, and dozens of other professions.

British tabloid editor and later talk show host Piers Morgan was once declared the winner for a season. The late Joan Rivers triumphed in the 2009 season. Season three was won by musician Bret Michaels.

MARTHA STEWART

Donald at War with the Doyenne of Domesticity
"Martha Stewart should Stick to Baking Her Cakes"
—Donald Trump

Martha Stewart was better at baking cakes than she was in hosting her version of *Celebrity Apprentice*, at least according to The Donald. Her show soon faded from the air.

There was yet another spin-off from the original theme. In 2005: *The Apprentice: Martha Stewart,* featuring the lifestyle mogul, was launched. It only survived for a single season.

Stewart had excelled in publishing, broadcasting, merchandising, and electronic commerce, and had written numerous best-selling books (one of the most successful of which had been entitled *Martha).* She had also published and been the creative force behind a magazine called *Martha Stewart Living*, and hosted a TV show, *Martha Stewart Living* (1993-2005).

In March of 2004, based on charges related to the ImClone insider trading affair, she was found guilty of felony charges of conspiracy, obstruction of Justice, and making false statements to Federal investigators. In July of 2004, she was sentenced to serve a five-month term in a Federal correctional facility and a two-year period of supervised release, five months of which were electronically monitored.

After her (hugely embarrassing) stint in prison, she made a comeback in 2005, and launched *Martha,* a TV show that ran from 2005 to 2012.

Both Donald's *The Apprentice* and its short-lived spinoff, *Martha Stewart Apprentice,* were produced by Mark Burnett. From the beginning, her ratings were poor.

Lloyd Allen, her biographer *(Being Martha),* wrote: "On *The Apprentice,* Martha showed the side of her that is a kinder, gentler boss. The contestants ate off beautiful Martha Stewart plates and slept on Martha Stewart sheets from Kmart."

On the air, whenever she had to fire one of her contestants, in contrast to the "show-no-mercy" tradition of Donald, she let the poor soul down nicely, saying "You just don't fit in."

Originally, or so it was rumored, the executives thought Stewart could be so successful that she might replace Donald altogether. "Millions would watch if Martha came on his show and shouted at him, 'You're fired!'" said the executive.

When Donald heard that rumor, he exploded in anger. "Having Stewart on a spin-off has been a mistake for everybody," he charged. "She's hurting my own ratings. What moron thought she'd be so successful that she could replace me on a hit TV show?"

She shot back, "Donald's criticism of me is mean-spirited and reckless."

When he heard that, he fired back: "Your performance was terrible, boring."

Appearances can be deceiving. **Donald** and **Martha** were not friends—more like jealous rivals.

Ostensibly based on its poor ratings Martha's spin-off series was not renewed for a second season.

When she failed, Donald had only kind remarks to make. But before it was over, however, she and Donald tangled. Then she accused him of not wanting her to have a successful series. "You wanted it jinxed," she charged. He denied that.

"YOU'RE FIRED !"
—NBC to Donald about the renewal of his contract for another season of The Apprentice, based partly on his divisive image, and partly on legalities associated with his upcoming bid for the presidency

Donald, who had not fully defined himself as a politician way back in 2004, fully supported President George W. Bush for re-election that year.

[Twelve busy years later, in May of 2016, neither Baby Bush nor Daddy Bush would return the favor, announcing they were not going to endorse Donald as the Republican Party's nominee. Both of them harbored ill will toward Donald for continuously trashing their brother and son, "low energy" Jeb Bush, during the Republican Primaries.]

Donald, however, remained friendly with 2004's Democratic nominee, John Kerry.

According to Donald, "He (Kerry) praised my negotiating skills and even suggested that when he was elected President, he might appoint me to be his Middle East envoy."

Kerry allegedly told him, "You'd be the best person to settle the Arab-Israeli conflict."

Donald boasted, "It would take me just two weeks to reach an agreement between these two bitter rivals."

When Donald learned that NBC had hired **Arnold Schwarzenegger** to replace him as host of *The Apprentice*, he reportedly said, "The Terminator will probably end up terminating my hit TV series."

***

Early in 2015, NBC was prepared to proceed with a renewal of *The Apprentice* for its 15th season. But Donald—perhaps tired of the series after such a long involvement—was not ready to sign on. Privately, he was discussing with friends and associates a possible run for the presidency.

Actually, his past and present roles might have, to an increasing degree, been in conflict. When Donald raised the issue about President Obama's birthplace, suggesting that he might have been born in Kenya, some pundits publicly called for NBC to fire him from *The Apprentice*. Liberal political commentator Lawrence O'Donnell led the attack, as did former congressman Anthony Weiner.

Media experts speculated about the extent to which Donald's controversial political statements had contributed to the decline in ratings for *The Apprentice*. It was also noted that after the debut of his campaign for the presidency, many other Trump-associated businesses had a fall-off in sales.

By the end of June, 2015, NBC was deluged with negative reactions to Donald's campaign speech—infamously known as the "Mexican Rapist Proclamation."

In a statement, and in reaction, NBC said, "Due to the recent derogatory statement by Donald Trump regarding immigrants, NBC/Universal is ending its business relationship with him."

There was another problem that made it impossible for Donald to return to his job as the series' host: After he announced his bid for the presidency, he was subject to a Federally mandated policy requiring that TV stations give equal time to every candidate involved in the same electoral campaign.

In September of 2015, NBC announced that the faded actor, the former Mr. Muscleman and Mr. Universe, and the former governor of California, Arnold Schwarzenegger, would become the host of *The Apprentice* for the 2016-2017 season.

As *Forbes* magazine later wrote, "Should Trump tire of politics, he can take comfort in the fact there's always a place in the entertainment business for washed-up elected officials, as evidenced by his replacement on *The Apprentice*, Governor Arnold Schwarzenegger himself."

MSNBC's implacable anti-Donald fixture: **Lawrence O'Donnell.**

 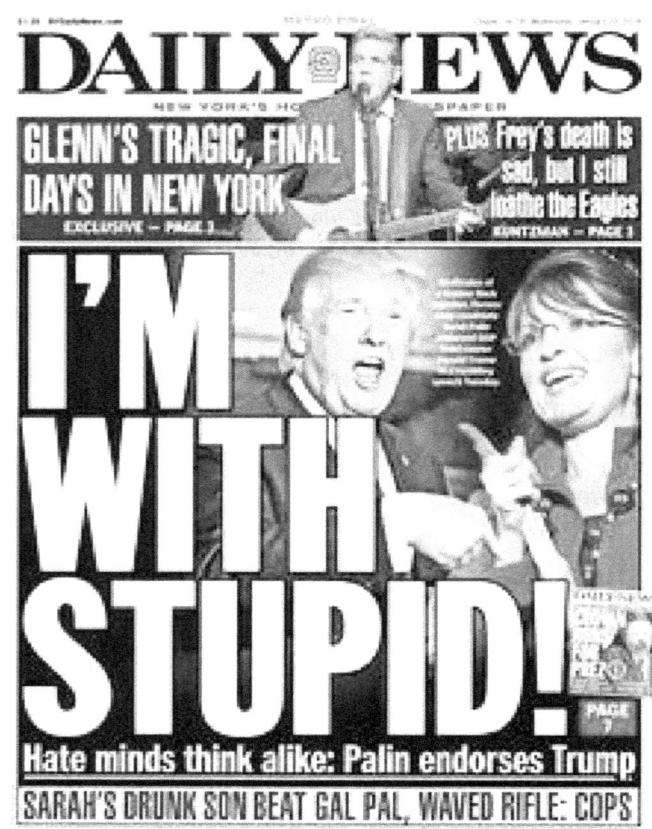

Early retrospectives on the Trump campaign, as published by **Mad magazine** and the **New York Daily News** featured insights from "What, Me Worry?" Alfred E. Neuman and **Sarah** ("*la Stupida*") **Palin.**

PART TWO
THE SUMMER OF TRUMP

DONALD ANNOUNCES HIS PRESIDENTIAL CANDIDACY

IN THE BEGINNING

With Melania,
Donald descended an escalator and moved toward
a podium, some microphones, cameras, and news reporters.

CHAPTER FOUR

A shady Real Estate Mogul & "Shock Jock" TV Entertainer

ANNOUNCES HIS RUN FOR PRESIDENT OF THE UNITED STATES

MEXICANS
"They're Bringing Drugs. They're Bringing Crime. They're Rapists!"

MUSLIMS
Donald Pledges to Bar Them from Entry into America

INSULTING HIS GOP RIVALS
"They're Losers! And They're Pathetic. Especially Low-Energy Jeb Bush."

Although Bloggers and Pundits Predict His Downfall, Donald Emerges "With More Lives Than Rasputin"

In 2014, supporters of Donald Trump had approached him in his office at Trump Tower and invited him to run for governor of New York. After politely thanking them, he said, "I have much bigger political plans than that. Stay tuned!"

As his political advisor, Roger Stone said, "Donald wanted to climb a higher mountain. How many great hotels, great buildings, great golf courses, can you build?"

On June 16, 2015, the height of the mountain he wanted to climb was made evident to the world. Hundreds of supporters gathered in the atrium of Trump Tower listening to the sounds of Neil Young's "Rockin' the Free World."

Down the escalator descended Donald Trump, preceded by his wife, Melania, in a couture dress. As a former model, she posed as stiff and photogenic as a mannequin.

During a forty-minute speech, Donald made history, as he announced that he was running as a candidate for President of the United States on the Republican ticket, an alliance from which he had bolted so many times before. His goal, he stated, was to "make America great again."

Donald Trump singled out Japan, China, and Mexico for taking advantage of the United States. "When do we beat Mexico to the border?" he asked. "They're laughing at us, at our stupidity."

"And now they're beating us economically. They are not our friends, believe me. And they're killing us economically."

Then he delivered an anti-immigration speech heard around the world.

"America has become a dumping ground for everybody else's problems," he charged. Then he paused a moment to listen to the applause.

"When Mexico sends you its people, these aren't the best and the finest. They're sending people who have a lot of problems, and they're bringing those problems to us. They're bringing drugs. They're bringing crime They're rapists. And some, I assume, are good people."

"It's coming from more than Mexico. It's coming probably from the Middle East. But we don't know. Because we have no protection, and we have no competence, we don't know what's happening. And it's got to stop and it's got to stop fast. As President of the United States, I will build a great wall on our southern border. And I will have Mexico pay for that wall."

As he moved through his stunning diatribe, he pronounced the American dream dead. He attacked President Obama as incompetent, and criticized American trade deals, lambasting Obamacare and the dour U.S. economy. He promised, "I will be the greatest jobs President God ever created. Our country needs a truly great leader, and we need a truly great leader *now*. We need a leader who wrote *The Art of the Deal*."

As for his opponents also seeking the GOP nod, he denounced them as "sweating dogs. How are they going to defeat ISIS? I don't think it's going to happen."

His well-groomed family, each member looking like a model transplanted from the pages of *Vogue* or *GQ*, came under the immediate scrutiny of television cameras. Collectively, they generated a portrait of the American Dream come true: A family who had everything, even good looks (not an ugly one among them). His entourage was the best dressed, the best fed, and the best educated, living a lavish lifestyle. Donald could be safe in the knowledge that his children and their children's children would be provided for during decades to come.

When his speech was over, the sound of the Neil Young song once again blared through the atrium, and Donald and Melania disappeared into their Versailles-like apartments "on top of the world," at the summit of Trump Tower.

"The Man Who Would Be King" had officially entered the presidential race.

Although his cheering squad applauded wildly, the worldwide reaction was mostly negative. His anti-immigration rhetoric seemed to appeal to the dark side of millions of Americans.

His hometown paper, the *New York Daily News*, ran a shocking frontpage Photoshopped picture of Donald with a red nose and lips under the "Second Coming" headline: CLOWN

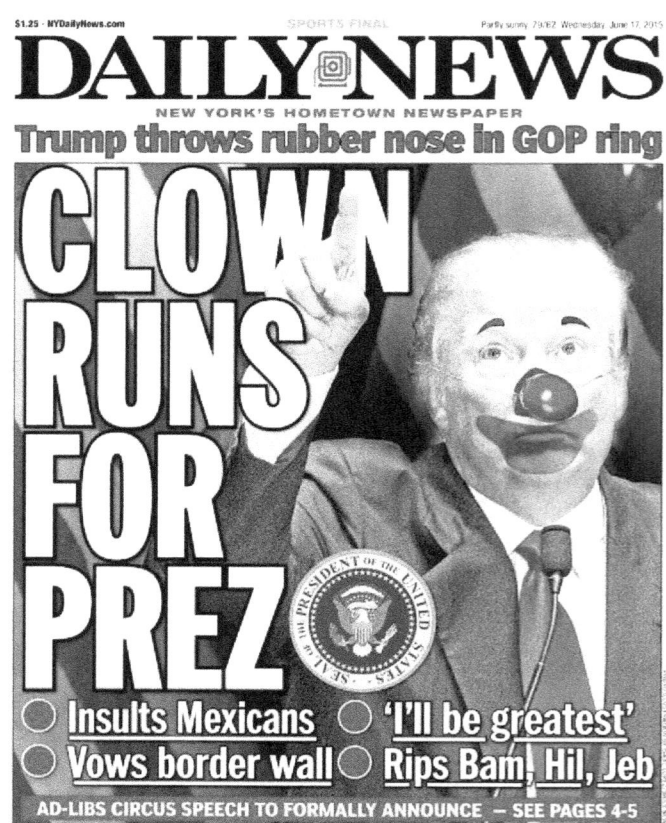

RUNS FOR PREZ.

Of course, he would become fodder for late night comedians on television.

Donald had tangled with David Letterman before, but the once popular TV talk show host emerged from retirement to present his "Top Ten List of Interesting Facts About Donald Trump." The one that met with the most derisive laughter was the charge that "during sex, Donald calls out his own name."

What came to be known as "The Summer of Trump" descended on America…and ultimately, the world.

***

Immediately, the question arose: Was Donald J. Trump really a Republican? Politically, he'd been called "a nativist," a "populist," a "protectionist," an "America Firster," and an "autocrat." Most voters viewed him as a moderate Republican, although some extreme right-wingers denounced him as "just another Hillary Clinton."

[For the record, Donald had been a Democrat until 1987, switching to the Republican Party from 1987 to 1999, when he was a backer (1999-2001) of the Reform Party. From 2001 to 2009, he came back into the Democratic fold, switching his allegiance to the Republicans again from 2009 to 2011. He registered as an independent from 2011 to 2012, before returning to the GOP in 2012, when he endorsed ("to my ever-lasting regret") Mitt Romney for President.]

During the opening days of that long, hot summer, Donald would launch his campaign, and then proceed to break just about every time-tested political strategy in the rule book. Defying political logic, he went on to dominate both TV news and political gossip in America. His style of campaigning was eventually accepted as "the new normal."

"I plan to be me," he proclaimed.

And so he was. The Republican field was forced to adjust to this new lightning rod, who began to attract supporters who had never voted before.

Whereas some candidates recognized his political allure and tried to channel their own "inner Trump," others chose to remain uncommitted, "laying low," in the futile hope that "The Donald would just disappear," drowning in his own outrageous rhetoric.

But, as history would show, thanks to some degree to his bigger-than-life personality, he would make all the flowers in the garden wilt except one, and that was Donald himself.

In many ways, even from the beginning, he had already outdistanced his competitors. He didn't need to spend millions on political advertising to make himself known. He was already known. As the summer progressed, cable TV news, with its 24-hour coverage, was dominated by his every utterance, no matter how off-the-wall his political proclamations became. Political junkies fell asleep with the television on, awakening hours later as it continued to blast out facts, opinions, and argumentative punditry about Donald.

As a result of the controversies he raised, some of his business contacts withdrew from him. Four TV networks, including NBC's *The Apprentice*, and even Macy's, which carried his clothing line, canceled the marketing partnerships they'd established with enterprises he controlled based on remarks he'd made about Mexicans.

In addition to NBC/Universal, Televisa, Ora TV, and Univision cut ties with Donald. Mexico's largest TV network, Televisa, said that Donald's remarks offended the entire Mexican population. Ora, owned by Carlos Slim, the world's second-richest man, defined Donald's comments as "racist."

"What we've been doing from day one is building something that's much bigger and broader than most people thought and understood," said Corey Lewandowski, Donald's campaign manager.

"Donald likes making history. He likes his name up in lights. And he's having fun," said political advisor Roger Stone.

During his campaign, Donald made frequent references to his ability to self-finance it, citing his "bank full of money. I can't be bought." As events unfolded, he ultimately spent much less on political ads than his competitors (Marco Rubio, Jeb Bush, and Ted Cruz), whose paid ads frequently blanketed the airwaves. In contrast, Donald was the beneficiary of huge blocks of free media coverage, something that TV networks generated in massive amounts in the form of talk shows, interviews, and (supposedly unbiased) news coverage.

Journalists have always found it hard to resist broadcasting details about the wealth (or lack thereof) of a candidate seeking the highest office in the land. Donald claimed he was worth $10 billion, but in September, *Forbes*, the arbiter of American wealth, defined his worth at $4.5 billion.

"I'm worth much more than that," Donald protested.

During his critique of *Fortune's* conclusion, Donald insisted that his 'brand" (that is, the ability of his name to increase the value of entities it promoted) was worth $3 billion alone. And as the value of his endorsements have shown, there is, indeed, promotional value—lots of it—associated with his name.

[When Donald's father died in 1999, his estate was valued at $200 million, of which Donald got $40 million.

"Doubting the Donald" Trump: What he's really worth. Is it really $10 billion?

Forbes estimated that Donald in 1988 was worth $20 million. The Associated Press claimed that by using an S&P calculator, if Donald had invested that money in an index fund [a conservative, not-particularly flashy mutual fund with a portfolio whose components reflect the makeup of a market index, such as the Standard & Poor's 500 Index], he would be worth $13 billion today "and could have just sat back and watched the dividends flow in."]

***

From the sales site of the **Donald Trump** *"(Don't let him up and into your ass")* **butt plug.**

On the campaign trail, polling results revealed that Donald's supporters praised him for "telling it like it is," and they relished his disdain for political correctness. Although frequently defined as a "bully," and denounced as "divisive and "unserious," and despite his inclusion within the much-mocked one percent of rich Americans, he maintained a massive appeal among working class voters. As such, he continued his high-profile attacks on the press, on other politicians (especially Hillary Clinton and President Obama), and also on GOP rivals who challenged him for the nomination. Every morning, he shot off rapid volleys of Twitter comments, lashing out at the critics who had attacked him as recently as the night before.

As a means of pandering to Jewish voters, Donald let it be widely understood that he had Jewish grandchildren, and a Jewish daughter. Ivanka had converted to Judaism before her marriage to Jared Kushner. "I am very honored by that. It wasn't in the plan, but I am very glad that it happened."

[In January of 2013, Donald emerged as a popular figure in Israel, and he owns land there, the Elite Tower Isle, a building site in Ramat Gan, Israel, in which various skyscrapers—including, if and when it's finished, what's conceived as the tallest building in Israel. During the 2013 Israeli elections, he endorsed Benjamin Netanyahu as Prime Minister. Later, however, Netanyahu objected to Donald's proposal to ban Muslims from traveling to the United States.

In March of 2016, when Donald addressed the American Israel Public Affairs Committee—a group that self-identifies as "America's pro-Israel lobby," he received wild applause for denouncing President Obama's lack of support for Israel.]

Those surges of popularity were soon replaced with expressions of mockery and rage. By July, novelty merchants were busy hawking Donald merchandise, regardless of how vulgar, insulting, or obscene.

The most controversial novelty was a butt plug (a rectal dildo) with a cartoon version of Donald's image implanted into it in low relief. Derived from a prototype developed on a 3D printer, it replicated Donald's trademark orange hair, whipped up into a comb-over, and the look of defiance he displayed whenever he came under fire from a rival candidate. It was the creation of Fernando Sosa, a 32-year-old Florida artist, who told the press, "I like the mental picture of Donald going into people's asses."

Although the model portraying Donald eventually emerged as a bestseller, Sosa didn't spare any of Donald's rivals. He also distributed a line of sex toys and dildos that unattractively depicted cartoon images of Ted Cruz, Marco Rubio, and Rand Paul.

In a post-purchase evaluation of the products, a consumer said, "The Jeb Bush butt plug was designed to give you the least thrill of all. As for the Cruz butt plug, a user had to ask, "Are you in yet, Ted?"'

In New York, a street artist named "Hanksy" went even further, depicting Donald in a mural he painted on a wall in Manhattan's Lower East side as a "pile of poop crowned with lemon yellow hair and circled by flies. I started with the fact that Trump kinda rhymes with dump, so I decided to paint him like a giant pile of shit," the artist tweeted.

The bald eagle is an opportunistic carnivore with the capacity to consume a great variety of prey, especially fish. It is both the national bird and the national animal of the United States, and appears on its seal.

It was removed from the U.S. government's list of endangered species in 1995 and transferred to their list of threatened species. As a rule, the bald eagle is a poor choice for up close and person displays, prone to becoming highly stressed, frightened, and unpredictable.

Horrified that his image would be depicted on a butt plug, Donald wanted to be photographed "looking presidential" for the upcoming cover of *Time*. The photographer assigned to him for that project was Martin Schoeller, who claimed that Donald "was very difficult to photograph. If you asked him to look up a little bit, he says no or he just doesn't do it. He literally has one angle. If I ask him to smile, he puts on a big grin and then goes back to his Zoolander 'blue steel' look."

For one of Schoeller's portraits, Donald agreed to pose with a 27-year-old American bald eagle, named "Uncle Sam." The bird had been transported from Texas to the Trump Tower, even though Donald was hesitant about too close a proximity to a ferociously carnivorous wild bird which can't be trained.

Hit by a car in 1994, Uncle Sam had been evaluated, because of his injuries, as "non-releasable into the wild." One of the most widely photographed bald eagles in history, he had appeared in movies, TV shows, and commercials, and had been seen by millions.

He posed with Donald and did not attack him, and the subsequent double portrait was incorporated into *Time* magazine's front cover. "Donald is an icon, and Uncle Sam the bald eagle is an icon, so it was a big success," said Jonathon Wood, the bird's owner, a falconer and wildlife rehabilitator.

***

In his pursuit of the presidency, Donald not only had to look presidential, but he had to pursue the evangelical vote. At the time, it was being "courted" by Ted Cruz, who more and more was sounding like a messenger sent directly to Earth from God.

Until he ran for President, attracting evangelicals, Donald was not known for expressing his points of view about religion. During an April 2011 interview with broadcasters from the right-wing religion-oriented *700 Club*, he claimed he was a Presbyterian and "have had a good relationship with the church over the years. I think religion is a wonderful thing."

During that interview, he said that he attended Marble Collegiate Church in Manhattan, where he'd married Ivana in 1971. The church later said he was not an active member.

He admitted, "I have not asked God to forgive me of my sins. I think if I do something wrong, I just try and make it right. I don't bring God into the picture."

He went on to assert that "The Bible is my favorite book. Nothing beats the Bible!" He refused, however, to designate his favorite Bible verse—"I don't like giving that out to people that I hardly know."

He said his second favorite book was *The Art of the Deal*.

"EVERY VAGINA IS A POTENTIAL LAND MINE."
—*Donald to "Shock Jock" Howard Stern*

During the summer of 2015, an anti-Trump movement coalesced and become more vocal. Activists hunted through old television archives for previous interviews he'd delivered in front of cameras. They found that some the most embarrassing of the tapes had been videotaped during Donald's appearances on *The Howard Stern Show* way back in 2004.

On air, he had revealed to Stern that he "felt lucky not to have picked up an STD *[Sexually Transmitted Disease]*. Having sex in the 1980s was dangerous and scary like Vietnam. It was my personal Vietnam. I felt like a great and very brave soldier."

During the same interview, he also admitted that at the age of 22, he had avoided the military draft "because of bone spurs in both of my heels."

Stern chimed in, "A lot of guys who went to Vietnam came out unscathed. And a lot of guys who've gone through the 1980s having sex with different women came out with AIDS and all kinds of things."

Donald also admitted on air that he had arranged for many of his potential sexual partners to get screened for STDs with his own personal doctor.

"Was that a difficult thing to ask a potential partner?" Stern asked.

"The whole romantic process is terrible," Donald replied, "because you meet somebody, and you start getting with that person, and

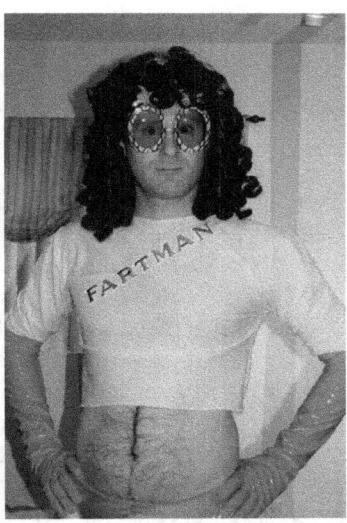

Donald's political enemies dug into TV archives to replay his provocative and vulgar comments made on *The Howard Stern Show*.

During his interview with Donald, Howard seemed to goad him on, even getting the future presidential candidate to talk about the toilet habits of both Ivana and Melania, his first and third wives.

Donald's scat talk fitted in well with the mode of the Stern show, which often featured Joe Tyler Gold (right photo above) as "**Fartman,**" a fictional superhero who attacks evil using his super-powered flatulence, which allows him to fly through the air.

Fartman even reached the screen in director Tammy Caplan's *Fartman: Caught in a Tight Ass*, which starred Fartman and introduced the evil villain, Tight Ass, who had the ability to squeeze weapons from his ass.

Donald seemed to glide smoothly into this scat world spearheaded by Howard Stern,, although confessing, on the air, "I'm not into anal."

you're really going at it and you say, 'excuse me, we have to stop now.' The 80s are not like… you know, the 70s, which was the best time for sex."

In one bizarre segment with Stern, broadcast widely over the airwaves, Donald discussed the toilet habits of both Ivana and Melania, wives #1 and (eventually) #3. He claimed that Ivana's bowel movements were a "little more normal than Melania's. Melania never poops, not that I know about. She's such an elegant and dainty lady."

He also admitted to what he liked sexually: "I'm not into anal."

After the show and in private, both Stern and Donald agreed on one concept: "Every vagina is a potential land mind. There is real danger there."

[Sam Clovis, a 25-year Air Force veteran, said, "I was offended by a man who sought and gained four student deferments to avoid the draft and who has never served this nation a day—not a day—in any fashion or way."

Ironically, after denouncing Donald in several e-mails, Clovis went to work for his campaign in Iowa after Rick Perry suspended his pursuit for the presidency.]

DEFIANT DONALD AS POSTER BOY
For Jihadist Recruitment Videos

During 2015's "SUMMER OF TRUMP," in one of his most shocking proposals, Donald called for the exclusion of Muslims attempting to enter the United States "until we can figure out what the hell is going on."

Republican leaders, including Senate Majority Leader Mitch McConnell and Republican House Speaker Paul Ryan, strenuously voiced their objections.

Denunciations also poured in from foreign leaders, including Canadian Prime Minister Justin Trudeau, British Prime Minister David Cameron, and French Prime Minister Manuel Valls.

Reince Priebus, the Chairman of the Republican Party, also protested. GOP leaders argued that banning Muslims violated the party's conservative values and was in violation of both the First Amendment and America's immigrant heritage.

Then *The Washington Post* reported that Donald had been featured as an enemy of Islam in a new Jihadist recruitment video. Even the U.S. Pentagon issued a statement: "Anything that bolsters' ISIL's narrative and puts the United States against the Muslim faith is certainly not only contrary to our values, but contrary to our national security."

On Fox News, Donald claimed that France and Belgium have been blighted by the failure of Muslims in these countries to integrate. "Living in Brussels is like living in a hellhole because of the dire failure in Muslim assimilation."

Growing ever more provocative, Donald made a public statement in which he advocated police surveillance of mosques in the U.S. "as possible terrorist cells." He cited U.S. General John J. Pershing who, during the Moro Rebellion, allegedly shot Muslim terrorists with bullets that had been dipped in pig's blood as a deterrent to other radicals. *[Most historians cite the pig's blood story as an urban legend.]*

World leaders, at news of Trump's ascendency in the American polls, were horrified.

David Cameron (upper photo) in front of #10 Downing Street; **Manuel Valls** *(center)*; whom the French press had defined as "an adroit leftist;" and movie-star-fabulous **Justin Trudeau** of Canada each loudly denounced Donald's racist views.

As would be expected, The Council on American-Islamic Relations denounced Donald and his remarks.

[The Moro Rebellion was an armed conflict between indigenous Muslim groups in the southern Philippines (the Moros) and the U.S. military between 1899 and 1913. A bloody incident within a context of four centuries of conflict between the ethnic Muslims and whomever happened to be in control of the Philippines at the time, the Moro Rebellion was not directly associated with other elements of the Spanish-American War of 1898.]

Hillary issued a response. "Donald Trump not denouncing false statements about POTUS (President of the United States) and hateful rhetoric about Muslims is disturbing—and just plain wrong. Cut it out!"

LATINOS DENOUNCE TRUMP
"He's the American Hitler"

In August, Donald shocked a good deal of the world with a claim that as President, he would forcibly deport more than 11 million illegal immigrants from the U.S. Then he forged forward in his promise to erect a wall along the U.S.-Mexico border, continuing to insist that he'd devise a way to make Mexico pay for it.

Although each of these positions met with ferocious opposition, they added to his legion of hard-core supporters.

Former Mexican President Vicente Fox, in February of 2016, said, "I'm not going to pay for that fucking wall." Felipe Calderón, another former President of Mexico, said, "We are not going to pay a single cent for such a stupid wall—and it's going to be completely useless if built, which I doubt."

Yet throughout the course of that summer, Donald continued to hit hard on the issue of U.S. border security. At his first town hall campaign rally in Derry, New Hampshire, he said, "On Day One of my presidency, illegal immigrants are getting out and getting out fast."

He also announced that he opposed birthright citizenship, attacking "anchor babies like Ted Cruz, who was born in Alberta, Canada. Anchor babies should not be protected by the 14th Amendment of the U.S. Constitution. All illegal immigrants should be deported but some—the non-criminal element—might be allowed to return if they went through proper channels. But that's not going to happen under my presidency until the border is strengthened."

Figures in the Latino community responded in fury, including singer Ricky Martin, who authored a scathing article condemning Donald and urging Latinos to unite against him. In spite of all these objections and outrage, Donald continued to maintain that he "will win the Latino vote."

Anti-Latino attitudes in the U.S. didn't originate with fans of Donald Trump.

This cartoon by Clifford Berryman first appeared in 1916, and advocated a more aggressive imperialism on the part of Uncle Sam in "disciplining" the rebellious guerillas of Pancho Vila.

Despite the outrage, throughout the course of July, Donald continued to reinforce his claim that Mexican immigrants are responsible for a large number of rapes in the U.S. "There is a mind-boggling link between rape and illegal immigration," he said. "Latino immigrants are more likely to perpetrate rape than the wider population." He cited an article that had appeared in *Fusion* magazine, a Paleolibertarian monthly with links to conservative newscaster Glenn Beck. *[In 2012, it changed its title to TheBlaze.]*

It claimed that "Eighty percent of women crossing the Mexican border are raped along the way, often by criminal gangs, traffickers, and corrupt officials."

[There is no centrally recorded government statistics on the ethnicity of convicted rapists in America.]

Hoping to clarify the issue, *The Washington Post* spearheaded an investigation about crime rates among immigrants, later admitting that the present data is incomplete. However, during the course of their investigation, a tantalizing fact emerged: "Crime rates increase as generations of immigrants assimilate into America. Second generation immigrants, who are born in the U.S. (and thereby become citizens), with at least one foreign-born parent, are more likely to commit crimes than first-generation immigrants." It was also pointed out that first-generation immigrants tend to stay out of trouble, hoping to avoid deportation.

At an August 26 news conference in Dubuque, Iowa, tension between Donald and Jorge Ramos boiled over. *[At the time, Ramos was the main news anchor for the Spanish-language media group, Univision, whom Donald was suing at the time because of its refusal to broadcast his Miss Universe pageant. Ramos, whose programs were aimed at Latinos and their role as a critical voting block in U.S. elections, has been called "The Walter Cronkite of Latino America."]*

Without being formally "recognized," from the podium *[i.e., "granted permission to speak"]*, Ramos began a long, rambling question-cum-political-statement. Refusing to respond, the candidate signaled to his security guards to remove the TV journalist

Employed as a news anchor for Univision, Mexico-born **Jorge Ramos** is the most powerful newscaster for Latinos. He voiced opposition to Donald's anti-Mexican rants.

But he learned at a rally that disobeying protocols would get him ejected from the sea of Donald's faithful supporters.

from the audience.

"Don't touch me!" Ramos shouted at the guards marching him out of the room. He was eventually allowed to return and his questions and comments were addressed.

Donald's action was condemned by the National Association of Hispanic Journalists.

He may have been responding to Ramos's earlier declaration, in which he had defined Donald as "the loud voice of intolerance, hatred, and division in the United States."

By August, more and more Latinos attacked Donald, none more vocally than Ricardo Sánchez. Known as "El Mandril" *[a name that translates as "a spindle or an axle used to secure or support material being machined or milled"]* on his Spanish-language radio show in Los Angeles, he labeled Donald as "El hombre del peluquin" *[the man with the toupée]*. Other more vocal Latinos compared him to Hitler.

Sánchez claimed that if Donald became President, "It would be like giving a loaded gun to a monkey. But a gun that fires automatic bullets."

During discussions of his anti-immigration stance, Donald cited "Operation Wetback," a program sponsored by President Dwight D. Eisenhower in the 1950s which rounded up and deported illegal aliens. He referenced an article in *The Christian Science Monitor*:

> *"Fifty-three years ago, when newly elected Dwight Eisenhower moved into the White House, America's southern frontier was as porous as a spaghetti sieve. As many as three million illegal immigrants had walked or waded northward over a period of several years for jobs in California, Arizona, Texas, and points beyond. President Eisenhower cut off this illegal traffic. He did it quickly and decisively with only 1,075 U.S. Border Patrol agents—less than one-tenth of today's force."*

The New York Times launched an attack on Donald's immigration stand. "Because the plan is so naked—in its scapegoating of immigrants, its barely subtextual racism, its immense cruelty in seeking to reduce millions of people to poverty and hopelessness—it gives his opponents the chance for a very clear moral decision. They can stand up for better values, and against the collective punishment of millions of innocent Americans-in-waiting."

In late summer, CNN took a poll of Republicans, finding that 44% of them believed that Donald was the best candidate to handle the immigration issued. No other candidate in the poll even came close.

***

As early as August, Donald launched an attack on Hillary, thinking she would beat Vermont Senator Bernie Sanders in the Democratic presidential primary.

On August 28, he accused her of spilling classified government secrets during her tenure as Secretary of State. To a crowd on August 28 in Massachusetts, he claimed she had misused her private e-mail server and demonstrated a flagrant lack of security standards.

He also attacked her top aide, Huma Abedine. "She, too, is getting classified secrets, and she's married to Anthony Weiner, who's a perv and a sleazebag."

[As a congressman in 2011, Weiner had been caught up in an online sexting scandal. He sent out pictures of himself in tight-fitting, virtually see-through underwear.]

From the campaign trail, Hillary shot back, claiming "The party of Lincoln has become the party of Trump."

She denied that any classified government secrets were on her server. "Material may have been classified later, but it wasn't when I received it in 2009 and 2010," she claimed.

LOATHED BY THE ESTABLISHMENT & HATED BY THE MEDIA,
Donald Takes Stands on Issues He Claims
"WILL MAKE AMERICA GREAT AGAIN"

Even fellow Republicans made it a point, early and loudly, to denounce Donald and his presidential aspirations.

Top to bottom, **Paul** *("I can't hear you")* **Ryan; Mitch** *("the man you'd least want to have a beer with")* **McConnell;** and **Reince** *(the oft-horrified chairman of the GOP)* **Priebus**.

As he outlined his views, Donald often found himself opposed to the Republican Party establishment. He was a strong supporter of Social Security, and he called himself a "free trader," though claiming that trade must be reasonably fair. "Right now our political leaders are wimps, allowing other nations like Japan and China to take unfair advantage."

His tax plan called for reducing corporate tax rates to 15%, concurrent with the elimination of various loopholes and deductions. He did not believe the minimum wage should be raised, claiming that it would hurt "the economic competitiveness of the United States."

A CNN poll revealed that Donald was the choice of 45 percent of Republicans who believed he was best able to handle the economy. Jeb Bush, his closest competitor, got only eight percent. Donald also won 32 percent of a CNN poll as the best candidate to handle ISIS, which was double the percentage attributed to Jeb.

The latter came about after Donald had warned that, "We're in danger of the sort of terrorist attacks that will make the bombing of the World Trade Center look like kids playing with firecrackers."

In marked and acrimonious contrast to Hillary and Bernie Sanders, Donald took the opposite point of view on global warming. "This very expensive global warning bullshit has got to stop. Our planet is freezing, record low temps, and our GW scientists are stuck in ice."

He came down hard on China, laying out a series of plans to help make up for the towering trade deficit it faced with that country every year.

Declaring China a currency manipulator, he advocated bringing it to the bargaining table. He also stated his goal of reclaiming millions of American jobs and reviving manufacturing by putting an end to "China's illegal export subsidies and lax labor standards." He called for a lowering of the corporate tax rate as incentives to keep American jobs and companies at home.

On health care, he announced his opposition to Obamacare, preferring a free market plan and competition to lower costs. He had stated support for a single-payer system in the past.

He also came out for a strong support of "our veterans who are horribly mistreated," advocating an overhaul of the Veterans Health Administration. He supported satellite clinics for veterans within hospitals in remote rural areas. On education, he advocated support for school choice and local control of primary and secondary schools. He attacked Common Core *[a legally sanctioned educational initiative that defines and standardizes what students in the U.S. should know in mathematics and English language arts at the end of each grade between kindergarten and a senior year in high school]* as "a disaster that must be ended."

To pander to right-wing members of the party, he stated that he supported traditional marriage between a man and a woman, but he didn't really want to make this an issue like Ted Cruz did. Gay activists labeled the Texas senator as "a homophobe like hate-spewing Mike Huckabee."

The June, 2015 Obergefell v. Hodges ruling at the Supreme Court legalized same-sex marriage nationwide. Donald said, "I would have preferred states, you know, making the decision, and I let that be known. But the judges made the decision. So, at a certain point, you have to be realistic about it."

On another social issue, Donald described himself as pro-life, claiming he would ban late-term abortions except in cases of incest, rape, or health of the mother. In previous years, he had defended a woman's right to choose.

He supported the 2nd amendment, and was opposed to gun control in general. He admitted that he has a "New York concealed carry permit for a weapon." He also supported fixing the Federal background check system so that criminal and mental health records are entered into a law enforcement database.

On another front, although he opposed legalizing recreational marijuana, he supported medical marijuana, while being in favor of states' rights on drug-related issues.

Many pundits on the right denounced Donald for "being a traitor to his class"—in other words, they vilified him as a member of the monied elite appealing to blue collar workers, many of whom were without a job. References and comparisons were made between Donald and Franklin D. Roosevelt, another rich, well-connected member of the New York power elite.

Ross Douthat, writing for *The New York Times*, said, "So far, Trump is running against the Republican establishment in a more profound way than the Tea Party, challenging not just deviations from official conservative principle, but the entire post-Reagan matrix. He can wax right wing on immigration on one moment and promise to tax hedge fund managers the next. He can sound like Pat Buchanan on trade and Bernie Sanders on health care."

MELANIA?
A Foreign-Born, Bikini-Clad Fashionista With Oodles of Sex Appeal and Ample Cleavage

In August, newspapers for the first time began to "discover" Melania

Trump, Donald's Slovenia-born third wife, a former model. Pictures of her from her modeling days were published and widely distributed. Most of them showed her tremendous cleavage and bikinis made of so little fabric they barely covered her vital zone. Some of the more provocative ones had been snapped as late as 2011 at Mar-a-Lago, the luxurious Palm Beach estate she shared with Donald.

"She'll make a great First Lady," Donald said triumphantly. "She's got a great heart."

She has a lot of other assets he discreetly opted not to mention.

Nicole Lyn Pesce, writing in the *New York Daily News*, said, "The stunning 45-year-old ex-model looks more suited to *Women's Wear Daily* than the White House, with her figure-hugging designer dresses, mini-dresses, and sky-high stilletos."

Celebrity stylist Philip Bloch, said, "She would be the most stylish First Lady we've ever had, beyond a shadow of doubt—beyond Jackie Kennedy, beyond Michelle Obama."

Melania shares Nancy Reagan's taste for *haute couture*, appearing often in perhaps a slinky gold Alexander McQueen gown or draping herself in a Valentino. She does not shy away from being sexy.

If Donald were elected, it would mark the first time an American President came to power after two divorces. Ronald Reagan had had only one divorce (from movie star Jane Wyman) when he was elected president.

A recent gun show in Houston, Texas, displaying weapons for sale.

Among the nations of the world, the United States is often cited as an "armed camp," and the National Rifle Association is accused of controlling the Republican-dominated Senate and House.

OPPONENTS DONALD DEFINED AS LOSERS
They Were Anti-Gay, Anti-Abortion, Anti-Black, Anti-Muslim, and Anti-Immigrant, but They're Fervently

PRO-GUN

During 2016s race for the White House, some seventeen major candidates, including Donald Trump, announced they would seek the nomination of the Republican Party.

Noting the crew of dark-suited men and the lone female standing on the stage, one reporter, John Winslow, called the race "a hysterically underwhelming contest of bumblers, second-raters, extremists and religious loonies. You could work your way to the top by not looking obviously demented at first blush to the national media—that is, if you did not use former candidate Michelle Bachmann as your role model."

"Perhaps I'm wrong," Winslow continued, "but Donald Trump showed that having opponents who look demented might advance you in the polls. He surfaced to the top because so many of his challengers held views that put them to the far right of Josef Goebbels, a coven that would make Hannibal Lecter, the serial flesh eater in *The Silence of the Lambs*, look like a Presbyterian deacon."

"All that was missing from this posturing was an open raincoat showing a raging boner," Winslow claimed.

2015, The Summer of Trump: Dirty Linen on Parade

CANDIDATES FOR THE REPUBLICAN NOMINATION FOR PRESIDENT OF THE UNITED STATES

THE LOSERS

*First There Were Seventeen
And Then There Were Three,
And Then There Were Two,
And Then, Only The Donald Remained.*

Like characters in an Agatha Christie mystery, what began as an overcrowded, seething-with-ambition cast of seventeen eccentric Republicans degenerated throughout 2015s "Summer of Trump" into a brawl that had all parties denouncing one another by autumn.

Although each of the candidates for the Republican Party's nomination brought carloads of ironies and dramas to the summer calendar, we've opted to present a brief thumbnail description of each of them, with apologies for too brief an overview of political careers that, in at least 50% of the candidates, were, indeed, historically brief.

Here, below, therefore are thumbnail portraits of competitors that Donald managed to trivialize into historical footnotes of political careers that might have been but never were.

"Jeb Bush is an embarrassment to himself and his family."
—Donald Trump

John Ellis Bush (born February 11, 1953) entered the world in Midland, Texas, where his future sister-in-law, Laura Bush would run through a stop sign at an intersection and kill the high school athlete, Michael Douglas, when she was still a teenager.

Jeb was the second son of former President George H.W. Bush and former First Lady Barbara Bush. He had wanted to run for President earlier, but his older brother, George W. Bush, beat him to it, winning the office after a stint as governor of Texas.

"I had two sons who made it as governor," Barbara said. "Jeb in Florida and George W. in Texas." Privately, she told friends, "Jeb is the smart one."

A graduate of Phillips Academy in Andover, Massachusetts, Jeb later attended the University of Texas, earning a degree in Latin American affairs while becoming fluent in Spanish.

In 1980, he moved to Florida to pursue a career in real estate development. Six years later, he became Florida's Secretary of Commerce until 1988, when he joined his father's successful campaign for the presidency.

In an attempt to escape from "the curse" of his brother's name and legacy, **Jeb** ordered his campaign to print posters that avoided any mention of "Bush" and read only JEB!.

Donald said, "When Jeb speaks, the audience falls into a deep coma."

In 1994, Jeb made his first run for office, seeking the governorship of Florida, and losing it to incumbent Lawton Chiles. He ran again in 1998 and won, becoming the 43rd governor of the state from January 5, 1999 to January 5, 2007.

As governor, he was viewed as a moderate, at least by Republican standards. That meant he opposed same-sex marriage and abortion, except in the event of rape, incest, or the mother's health. He questioned the arguments for climate change, but then suggested that global warming might be real. He felt that immigrants should have a path to legal status.

Donald tweeted that "Jeb Bush has to like illegal aliens because his wife, Columbia, is Mexican born."

Jeb campaigned for President, beginning on June 15, 2015, and was viewed as an early frontrunner. To escape the "curse" of the Bush name, he authorized posters to read "JEB," omitting "Bush" as a means, it was surmised, to minimize an association to the family's (controversial) political past.

From the beginning, he tangled with Donald, attacking his plan to erect a wall along the Mexican border. "It won't work. Part of the border is rugged terrain. What we need is more law enforcement from the Border Patrol. Trump's plan is impossible and would cost hundreds of billions of dollars."

"Low-energy Bush is a weak candidate," Donald charged. "He's a total disaster as a campaigner. He's gone nasty with lies about me. By far, this sad sack has zero chance of winning…a weak candidate."

Ben Carson:
Although He Attacks His Mother With a Hammer and Stabs a Friend, He Becomes a Neurosurgeon and Candidate for the Republican Nomination

Benjamin Solomon Carson, Sr. (born September 18, 1951) came from parents with families growing up in rural Georgia. Sonya was thirteen years old when she married Ben's father, Robert, a minister, who was 28. She later discovered that her husband had another family, for which he abandoned her when Ben was eight years old. His mother, a domestic, had to work two or three jobs at a time to support Ben and his brother, Curtis.

Ben Carson, the soft-spoken African American neurosurgeon who aspired to be President, admitted to a violent past, compared Obamacare to slavery, and attacked gays as pedophiles.

In a memoir, *Gifted Hands*, Carson related that in his youth he had a violent temper and once tried to hit his mother over the head with a hammer because of a dispute over clothing. He also claimed that in the ninth grade, he got into an argument with a friend and attempted to stab him, but the knife thrust was blocked by his intended victim's belt buckle.

Although as a boy, he survived on food stamps, he managed to educate himself, graduating from Yale University in 1973, where he majored in psychology, later receiving his M.D. from the University of Michigan Medical School in 1977. By 1984, he had been appointed the Director of Pediatric Neurosurgery at Johns Hopkins Hospital in Baltimore. His most publicized achievement involved the surgical separation of conjoined twins. Another of his achievements focused on the development of a drastic surgical procedure known as a hemispherectomy, in which part or all of one hemisphere of the brain is removed as a means of controlling severe pediatric epilepsy.

His medical achievements led to his 2008 winning of a Presidential Medal of Freedom Award.

He won the heart of conservatives for his widely publicized speech at the 2013 National Prayer Breakfast, during which he criticized President Obama.

He made some of the most controversial statements of any candidate running for the Republican nomination, after announcing that he was seeking the presidency on May 4, 2015. He compared homosexual relationships to pedophilia and bestiality, and he claimed that modern day America is like Nazi Germany. One of his most controversial statements compared Obamacare to slavery.

Donald's campaign managers heard those comments and concluded that, "This Carson wacko will be easy to dissect. Just turn his surgical knife over to us."

Carson claimed, "I have a surgical personality, which means I look very, very carefully before I leap, and I measure the temperature of the water before I put my foot in."

Chris Christie:
Did "Bridgegate" and "Exteme Obesity" Disqualify His Run for the Presidency?

Christopher James Christie (born September 6, 1962), nicknamed "Chris," is the 55th Governor of New Jersey, even though it is a "blue" (i.e., predominantly Democratic) state and he is an ardent Republican.

Born in Newark, he's the son of Sondra, a telephone receptionist, and Wilbur, a certified public accountant. His mother is of Sicilian ancestry, his father of Irish, Scottish, and German descent.

He graduated from the University of Delaware with a Bachelor of Arts in political science in 1984, wining his law

Pilloried by dozens of cartoonists, both for his obesity and for his alleged pettiness as exemplified by the Bridgegate scandal, New Jersey Governor **Chris Christie** morphed from Trump's competitor to his attack dog, with mixed results from his increasingly fed-up electorate.

This cover illustration from *The New Yorker* shows a fat child playing in, and disrupting, the traffic across the George Washington Bridge.

degree in 1987 at Seton Hall University School of Law.

George W. Bush appointed him U.S. attorney for New Jersey, a post he held from 2002 to 2008.

In 2009, he filed to run for governor of his state, and, after a tough campaign, defeated Democrat Jon Corzine by winning 49% of the vote.

On many issues, he adopted stances that were more moderate than those of most other right-wing politicos from his party. As would be expected, he opposed abortion, but was soft on immigration. "It is not a crime, but a civil wrong," he said.

He also opposed same-sex marriages, but favored the protection offered by same-sex civil unions. "I believe that homosexuality is innate. If someone is born that way, it's very difficult to say that it's a sin to be gay."

In 2011, there was much speculation that he should seek the presidency of the United States. But he finally decided not to, claiming, "Now is not my time. New Jersey, whether you like it or not, you're stuck with me." He did, however, deliver the keynote address at the Republican National Convention in August of 2012.

When Hurricane Sandy devastated parts of New Jersey later that year, he praised President Obama's aid in Federal disaster relief and hugged him when he flew in to a stricken New Jersey. That act of support subjected Christie to a severe backlash from more right-wing members of his party.

In 2013, Christie ran for re-election as governor and won. That same year, he was also elected Chairman of the Republican Governors Association, succeeding Bobby Jindal of Louisiana.

In September of 2013, Christie became involved in a scandal called "Bridgegate." From September 9-13 of that year, two of three strategic and high-volume traffic lanes in Fort Lee were (needlessly and, it was suspected, vengefully) closed. They provided access to New York City via the George Washington Bridge, one of the most heavily traveled routes in the United States.

A massive morning rush hour resulted, and there was outrage in New Jersey, with calls for an investigation of what was believed to have been a deliberate sabotage of Fort Lee's ability to cope with its commuter infrastructure.

It was reported that the lane had been closed by Christie's aides in retaliation against the Democratic Mayor of Fort Lee, Mark Sokolich, for not having supported Christie in his run for a second term. Christie denied all knowledge of the events leading up to the closing of the traffic arteries, but several of his appointees and aides resigned in the aftermath.

Christie formally entered the U.S. presidential race on June 30, 2015.

Based on his potential status as a presidential candidate, the weight and health of the governor became an issue. The columnist Eugene Robinson applied the term "extremely obese" to him, citing medical guidelines of the National Institutes of Health. Christie claimed that in spite of his weight, he was relatively healthy. It was revealed that during February of 2013, that he had undergone "lap-band" *[laparoscopic adjustable gastric band]* stomach surgery, a radical procedure intended to slow the consumption of food.

The Obesity Society, a nonprofit scientific group, issued a statement. "To suggest that Governor Christie's body weight discounts and discredits his ability to be an effective political candidate is inappropriate, unjust, and ong."

Ted Cruz:
"I'm Not the Kind of Guy You'd Want to Have a Beer With"

Two Cubans ran for President in 2015-2016, including one that Donald called "the Anchor Baby born in Alberta" in 1970. He was Rafael Edward Cruz, nicknamed "Ted." A graduate of Princeton University, fellow classmates remembered him as "creepy." Other words used to describe him were "arrogant," "abrasive," "intense," "strident," and a "crank."

He admitted, "If you want someone to grab a beer with, I may not be that guy."

After graduating from Harvard Law School, Cruz, in time, became an advisor to George W. Bush (no great recommendation.).

From 2004 to 2009, he became the first Hispanic and the longest serving Solicitor General in Texas's history. In 2012, he ran for the Senate seat vacated by fellow Republican Kay Bailey Hutchison, and won, becoming the first Hispanic American to serve as a U.S. senator representing Texas. His Senate win was called a "true grassroots victory against very long odds."

Much to his later embarrassment during his campaigns in the Northeast, he was caught on tape saying, "When we used to see a New Yorker in Texas, we'd say, 'Get a noose!'"

A stunning moment that reinforced Cruz's notoriety came in October 2013, when he staged a government shutdown. To make it happen, he delivered a 21-hour fili-

The "Wacko Bird and Anchor Baby," as Donald called him, Texas Senator **Ted Cruz** is the most hated senator.

He wanted to head the U.S. government, but had only succeeded in shutting it down in an attempt to prevent Obama from providing health care for the poor.

bustering speech in the Senate, with the stated intention of delaying a key vote associated with approval of the federal budget. He orchestrated that (widely denounced) filibuster with the intention of defunding President Obama's Affordable Care Act.

As his months in office went by, he increased the venom of his accusations against President Obama, claiming he was "openly desirous to destroy the Constitution and this Republic." In effect, he was accusing the President of high treason. He followed that with a claim that the 2015 nuclear deal with Iran would define the Obama administration as "the world's leading financier of radical Islamic terrorism."

As a freshman Senator, Cruz also attacked fellow Republicans, calling them a "surrender caucus to Obama. They're squishes on gun control."

John McCain called Cruz a "wacko bird," and Lindsey Graham said, "If you killed Cruz on the floor of the Senate, and the trial was in the Senate, nobody would convict you."

In a heated speech in July 2015, Cruz accused Senate Republican leader Mitch McConnell of telling "a flat out lie" over his intention to reauthorize the Export-Import Bank.

Cruz began campaigning for the presidency as early as March of 2015.

Carly Fiorina: Could a CEO Who Laid Off Thousands, Botched a Merger, & Departed with a $21 Million "Golden Parachute" Ever Become President?

On *Twitter.com@alecmadrigal*, the "twenty-something" captain of a men's JV varsity basketball team said, "**Carly Fiorina** looks like Voldemort with a nose."

During her widely denounced tenure as a corporate CEO, Fiorina told more employees "YOU'RE FIRED!" than Donald.

Cara Carleton Fiorina (*née Sneed*), nicknamed "Carly," was born on September 6, 1954 in Austin, Texas. She attended three different universities, including Stanford and the Massachusetts Institute of Technology, before climbing to the top of the corporate ladder.

She became known primarily for her controversial tenure as CEO of Hewlett-Packard (HP) from 1999 to 2005. She was the first woman to lead a *Fortune* magazine Top-20 company In 2002, she supervised the largest technology sector merger in history, with HP acquiring rival personal computer manufacturer, Compaq, thereby creating, through that merger, the world's largest seller of personal computers. In the aftermath, she was bitterly resented for laying off 30,000 U.S. employees.

By February of 2005, after HP lost half of its value, she was forced to resign. For her failure as a CEO, she was awarded a $21 million bonus, called "a golden parachute." Pundit David Corn called Fiorina "a real American success story—for a corporate Republican."

In *Mother Jones*, Corn wrote: "Her sole claim to president-ish experience is her tenure at HP, and that stint was marked by layoffs, outsourcing, conflict, and controversy—so much so that several prominent HP colleagues recoil at the idea of Fiorina managing any enterprise again, let alone the Executive Branch. She developed a reputation of a manager who knocked heads together—and who chopped them off."

After her ouster, stock prices rose seven percent as Wall Street shouted "hooray."

In 2008, she flirted with politics, becoming an advisor to Republican Senator John McCain during his futile quest for the presidency. However, two years later, she won the GOP nomination for a U.S. Senate seat from California, but lost the general election to the popular incumbent, Democrat Barbara Boxer.

In May of 2015, Fiorina announced her race for the White House on *Good Morning America*. During its broadcast, she claimed, "I'll be the best person for the job because I understand how the economy really works. I'm best equipped to destroy Hillary Clinton, since pundits can't claim a gender bias."

During the coming months, many of her extreme right-wing positions were widely denounced, and her corporate record as CEO of HP was lambasted.

She entered the presidential race at a time when the other candidates, mostly Donald Trump, were demanding that manufacturing jobs to be returned to America.

But Fiorina stood as "the poster girl" for an industry campaign aimed at blocking any legislation that would restrict a company's ability to can U.S. employees and hire foreign laborers instead. She argued that an adoption of any Donald Trump's policies about returning jobs to mainstream Americans would seriously imperil the American economy.

"There is no job that is America's god-given right anymore," she announced at a press conference in Washington. "We have to compete for jobs."

That remark led to a massive outcry against her, her critics denouncing her as a "spokesperson for corporate insensitivity."

When Donald heard her remarks, he said. "Let's replay that video clip of Ugly Carly in the Rust Belt. Run her up the flagpole and no one will salute her."

Jim Gilmore:
A Virtual Unknown Marked by 45 Minutes of Fame.

James Stuart Gilmore III (born October 6, 1949), nicknamed "Jim," was the 68th Governor of Virginia from 1998 to 2002. He once served in the U.S. Army as a counter-intelligence agent.

For one year, beginning in January, 2001, he was chairman of the Republican National Committee, promoting the Republican Party's usual stands against abortion. He made the claim, "I represent the Republican wing of the Republican Party."

He entered the 2008 presidential race when it was dominated by John McCain, running against Barack Obama after Hillary lost the Democratic nomination. But on July 14, 2007, Gilmore bowed out claiming it was too difficult to raise campaign funds.

Eight years later, during the 2016 presidential race, Gilmore announced himself as a candidate on a platform to preserve the 2nd Amendment *[the right to bear arms]*. In an anti-immigrant stance, he called for greater border surveillance. He was also opposed to Obamacare, but urged a restoration of the American economy.

He struggled but gained no traction. Inevitably, he suspended his campaign on February 12, 2016. Poll after poll indicated that he had garnered virtually zero support. Mostly, he'd been met with the question: "Who is Jim Gilmore?"

The Washington Post wrote: "Like a well-oiled light switch, 'Gilmentum' silently flicked off."

Gilmore appeared at the second debate at the kiddie's table. His 45 minutes of fame came when thousands of Americans googled to find out who he was. His poll numbers later were so low that he did not qualify for inclusion in the second debate.

It seemed that no one, according to polls, wanted the relatively obscure **Jim Gilmore**, the former Governor of Virginia, to be President.

Some commentators wondered why he bothered to enter the race.

Lindsey Graham: The Outspoken, Self-Contradictory, and—at the beginning, at least—Relatively Moderate Republican Senator from South Carolina

When one of the most controversial senators of all time, the segregationist, Strom Thurmond, retired, Lindsey Olin Graham (born July 9, 1955) ran for his seat and won. It was in 2003. He has held the seat since then.

A reporter for *The Atlantic* described him like this: "Graham is small, wiry, and energetic, with bulging eyes in a round, ruddy face topped with bristly, spit-combed hair. His bared-teeth grin and frenetic manner might give him the effect of a high-spirited French bulldog."

He was born to parents, Millie and Florence James, who ran "The Sanitary Café," an all-inclusive rendezvous that incorporated a restaurant with a bar, pool hall, and liquor store. He received his Juris Doctorate from the University of South Carolina School of Law in 1981. From 1982 to 1988, he served in the U.S. Air Force and was a lawyer before getting elected to the U.S. House of Representatives, serving South Carolina for four terms (1995 to 2003) always with 60% of the vote.

During his second term in Congress, he was more sensible than his fellow Republicans. He was the only member of the GOP on the House Judiciary Committee who voted against the impeachment of Bill Clinton, asking his colleagues, "Is this Watergate or Peyton Place?"

Conservative blogs and right-wing radio talk show hosts nicknamed him "Flimsy Lindsey" or "Grahamesty."

He never married and has no children, as far as it is known, which had led to some gossipy speculation in "family values" South Carolina.

As a senator, he managed to remain more reasonable and cooperative than many of his colleagues, often working in a bipartisan fashion with Democrats on such issues as global warming and immigration reform. He's a strong believer in national defense, advocating that the U.S. take a greater leadership role.

On May 18, 2015, he announced his run for President.

Donald denounced him as "all talk—no action. He's a nasty, dumb mouthpiece."

In retaliation, Graham called Donald "a jackass."

Senator Lindsey Graham of South Carolina was the only bachelor in the presidential race. (Rumors were rampant.)

In the early days, he attacked Trump as unfit to be president, but later, during the Trump presidency, he became—in the world of one commentator, "Trump's major rimmer."

Mike Huckabee:
Bible Thumping on the Road to Political Oblivion

Michael Dale Huckabee (born August 24, 1955) is nicknamed "Mike," although his critics call him "Hickabee."

He was born in Hope, Arkansas, in the town where Bill Clinton (whom he despised) grew up. He made much of his working class upbringing when he ran for political office, citing his father (Dorsey) as a fireman and mechanic, and his mother (Mae) as a clerk at a gas company.

He read the news and weather on Christian Radio when he was only fourteen years old. He attended schools steeped in Southern Baptist Theology and became an ordained minister, his whole life shaped by "moral absolutes."

He decided to go into politics in 1992, running for lieutenant governor of Arkansas, but lost to incumbent Democrat Dale Bumpers. That was the year that Clinton was elected President. When Clinton resigned as Governor of Arkansas before heading to D.C. as the nation's newly elected president, his lieutenant governor, Jim Guy Tucker, became governor.

In the vacuum created by Tucker's promotion, Huckabee then won the race for Lieutenant Governor of Arkansas, serving in that office from 1993 to 1996. He became the second Republican since Reconstruction to be Lieutenant Governor of that state.

In 1994, Huckabee was re-elected to a full term as lieutenant governor of Arkansas. When incumbent governor Tucker resigned in the wake of fraud and conspiracy convictions, Huckabee automatically became governor in 1996. In 1998, he was elected to a full four-year term and in 2002, was re-elected to a second four-year term.

He ruled the state with a ferociously far right agenda, supporting Intelligent Design and opposing Darwin's theory of Evolution as part of the public school curriculum. He wanted to increase defense spending and urged immigration reform. Of course, he opposed abortion, same-sex marriages, and even civil unions. He outlawed gay marriage in Arkansas and opposed gay adoptions, becoming despised by millions in the LGBT community.

He ran for President of the United States in the 2008 election. On August 11, 2007, backed by evangelicals, he came in second in a Straw Poll in Iowa. Although for a time, he surged forward, winning victories in Alabama, Arkansas, Georgia, and Tennessee, he finally withdrew from the race for the Republican nomination after John McCain forged ahead to win it instead. For a brief moment, Huckabee was seriously considered as McCain's Veep, until that slot was grabbed by Sarah Palin.

In spite of national poll numbers in his favor, Huckabee announced that he would not be a candidate in the 2012 race. "All the factors say go, but my heart says no."

After four years of reflection, or perhaps boredom, the presidential bug bit him again in time for the 2016 elections. As a candidate, he maintained that he had the political backing of God himself. As regards fundraising, he urged his supporters "to give something in the name of your children and grandchildren."

He was bitterly opposed to abortion, calling for the reversal of *Roe vs. Wade*, and he vigorously continued his attacks on same-sex marriage and Obamacare.

In one of his most notorious maneuvers, earning even more outrage from the LGBT community, he made a well-publicized visit to Kentucky to lend his support to a bigoted redneck

Mike Huckabee wrote an autobiography (see above) that proved "what an Arkansas redneck hick he really is," in the words of one reviewer.

In the Republican field, he was the most ardent attacker of same-sex marriage. For a time, he scored big with the most rabid of Bible thumpers.

Hate and intolerance can be taught at a young age, as evidenced by these horrid signs. Obviously, this boy reflected the hostile environment in which he was reared. As a respected Episcopal priest, the Reverend Victoria Duncan, noted in New York City, "God had nothing to do with the bigotry this poster boy was promoting."

A mug shot of the notorious and grim-faced **Kim Davis**, a scary fanatic and county clerk from Kentucky.

She defied the rulings of the Supreme Court and refused to issue marriage licenses to same-sex couples.

"It violates my conscience," she claimed, "and it's against the teachings of the Bible."

county clerk, Kim, who claimed that—based on the teachings of God, and in brazen defiance of Federal law—she could never issue marriage licenses to same-sex couples.

Huckabee was joined in his support of Davis by what some members of the press had labeled as "the other religious nuts." They included Ted Cruz, Rand Paul, and Bobby Jindal.

On September 8, 2015, the day Davis was released from jail, Huckabee was on hand to support a crowd of homophobes, many of them waving Confederate flags. Ted Cruz had made it a point to be there, too, but Huckabee's "goons" pushed him aside so that their man would could stand alone alongside the dour and unattractive Davis, who wore no makeup and whose hair was long and untamed. Davis' husband, looking like a hayseed, also appeared on the platform with her, wearing bib overalls and a straw hat.

Huckabee called Davis "a victim of judicial tyranny."

The next day, a poll of Americans revealed that 65% wanted her to resign for not following the law.

As a role model, Davis herself was seriously flawed. During the course of her life, she had received four marriage licenses during her four marriages to three different men. After a dubious life, she claimed she experienced a religious awakening in 2011.

Her uncompromising right wing stance caused her to be ridiculed across the nation, including a parody on *Saturday Night Live*. She was easy to caricature. Actress Jennifer Lawrence claimed, "She makes me embarrassed to be from Kentucky."

Huckabee was attacked in the press for his endorsement of Davis. One writer claimed that "He seems to think Jesus is coming back to blow up the planet." Another said, "This hayseed from Arkansas thinks Democrats are controlled by a Satanic demon called Jezebel."

"Huckabee is bound to get all the votes of those crazy ass pastors," wrote another journalist. "His campaign theme song is 'Give Me That Ol' Time Religion.'"

But all the "crazy assed votes" in Red-state America weren't enough to propel Huckabee forward this time around. He suspended his campaign on February 1, 2016, throwing his support behind frontrunner Donald J. Trump.

Bobby Jindal: How an Indian-American "Anchor Baby" Steered Louisiana Politics "To the Right of Rush Limbaugh"

Piyush Jindal (born June 10, 1971), nicknamed "Bobby," was a former U.S. Congressman and the 55th governor of Louisiana from 2008 to 2016. As governor, he became the first Indian American ever elected to high office in the United States, and he was re-elected in a landslide in 2011, though despised by thousands upon thousands of voters.

His parents, who were from the Punjab region of India, came to the United States shortly before the birth of their child as a means of ensuring their son's citizenship, a situation that forever after marked him in some conservative circles as "an Anchor Baby."

His views against same-sex marriage and abortion were formed when he became a faithful Roman Catholic, later writing about his "spiritual journey."

In March of 2001, George W. Bush made him Assistant Secretary of Health and Human Services for Planning and Evaluation, but he later resigned to return to his native state to run for governor. He lost, but in time won a seat in the U.S. House of Representatives (2005-2008), becoming the second Indian American ever elected to Congress. In office, he warned of the growth of Medicaid.

Returning to Louisiana once again, he entered the contest for governor, winning the 2008 race. He was re-elected. Nearing the end of his second term, he witnessed a sharp decrease in his popularity, facing a budget deficit and painful cuts in public expenditure.

Throughout his tenure as governor, he always had an eye toward changing his address to 1600 Pennsylvania Avenue. As early as 2008, the attack dog of right-wing radio, Rush Limbaugh, cited

Sycophantic **Bobby Jindal,** governor of Louisiana and lackluster 2016 candidate for President of the United States, poses with his mentor, George W. Bush in 2008. They try to look like they know what they are doing.

"Dubya" was disgraced for his inept handling of Hurricane Katrina that devastated New Orleans in 2005.

him as a possible Veep running mate for John McCain.

On June 24, 2015, Jindal announced that he was a candidate for the Republican nomination for President in the 2016 election. *Time* magazine, in an article entitled "Let's Get the Party Started," claimed that his ethnic background would bring diversity to the GOP.

At that point, however, polls showed that he couldn't even carry the vote in Louisiana. On a national level, he gained no traction at all. On March 3, 2016, he withdrew from the race, announcing that he'd vote for Donald Trump.

The only sane adult in the GOP circus. **John Kasich,** Ohio's finest.

Donald called him "a dummy."

John Kasich:
"The Prince of Light & Hope" Is Hailed as the Only Sane Candidate in the GOP Primary

The current governor of Ohio, John Richard Kasich (born May 13, 1952), was descended from parents with a mixed Czech and Croatian background.

He was actually born in Pennsylvania in McKees Rocks, an industrial town near Pittsburgh. He later moved to Ohio, where he attended Ohio State University. While enrolled there, he wrote a letter to President Richard Nixon about his concerns for the nation, and, to his surprise, was granted a 20-minute interview. He later said, "He did it for Elvis, so why not me?"

In 1978, he ran a strong campaign for an Ohio Senate seat, and he became the youngest person ever elected to the Ohio Senate, launching a four-year term. He stunned voters by refusing himself a pay raise.

With a Ringo Starr coiffure, he ran for the U.S. House of Representatives and won, serving there from 1983 to 2001. His tenure included eighteen years on the House Armed Services Committee and six years as chair of the House Budget Committee, where he was a key figure in the passage of both welfare reform and the Balanced Budget Act of 1997. The following year, he voted to impeach Bill Clinton, based on the many charges brought against him.

He was married to Mary Lee Griffith from 1975 to 1980, when he divorced her. He knew that if he ever ran for President, he would not be the first divorced man to compete for that office. Ronald Reagan had divorced movie star Jane Wyman before marrying MGM starlet Nancy Davis.

As early as 2003, Kasich formed an exploratory committee to run for President, but when fund raising turned pale, he dropped out. For a while, he hosted a news show on the Fox Network.

In 2009, he ran for governor of Ohio, defeating incumbent Ted Strickland in a close contest. He was viewed as a successful governor, and he won re-election in 2004 with Tea Party support. However, he lost much of that backing when he favored expansion of Medicaid.

In April of 2015, he decided to run for President again, announcing his "New Day in America" campaign. On the campaign trail, he projected himself as "The Prince of Light & Hope." As governor, he was viewed as rather abrasive, but running for President, he evoked a gentler, kinder side. "I won't be an attack dog like Donald Trump," he promised.

However, Donald fired back anyway, claiming that "Kasich is one of the worst presidential candidates in history. He's a dummy falling in Obama's trap for Obamacare."

The New York Times endorsed Kasich's candidacy in January of 2016, attacking Donald and Ted Cruz. "Though a distant underdog, Kasich, a long shot contender, is running unapologetically as a candidate with experience even as others run as outsiders."

Reporter Alan James felt that "John Kasich is the only one of the sixteen candidates seeking the GOP nomination who is not insane. Nor is he a Bible Thumper. Perhaps I should say fifteen candidates, since I don't know how religious Donald Trump is. I got the impression that he likes to spend Sunday morning in bed with some knockout beauty, even his stunning wife."

George Pataki: Donald Claims
He Couldn't Get Elected Dog-Catcher

George Elmer Pataki (born June 24, 1945) was an attorney who became the 53rd governor of New York (1995-2006). In 1994, he ran against three-times-incumbent, Mario Cuomo, defeating him in the "Republican

George Pataki's presidential campaign--it seems long ago and far away--with memorabilia destined as tomorrow's quaint collectibles on e-bay.

Revolution." Pataki was one of only three Republican governors elected since 1923 to serve three consecutive terms. The other two included Thomas Dewey and Nelson Rockefeller.

Pataki had ancestors who came from the old Austro-Hungarian Empire, arriving in the United States to work in a hat factory or to become a mailman and a volunteer fire chief. Born a Roman Catholic, young Pataki grew up to attend Yale University, later earning his law degree from Columbia.

In July of 2000, Pataki's name surfaced near the top of the possible Veep candidates that George W. Bush was considering as running mates. Pataki lost to Dick Cheney, the former Secretary of Defense.

During the next presidential cycle (2004), Pataki was instrumental in bringing the Republican National Convention to Madison Square Garden in Manhattan, which had been viewed as hostile terrain, since the Democrats were to carry 78 percent of the vote that year. Pataki's most famous quote was, "This fall, we're going to win one for the Gipper. But our opponents, they're going to lose one with the Flipper," a snide reference to John Kerry.

President George W. Bush appointed Pataki as a U.S. delegate to the 2007 United Nations Assembly. In 2010, he rejected an offer to run for the U.S. Senate, setting his eye on a presidential bid in 2012 instead.

He later bowed out of the race during the 2012 cycle, but although he re-entered it in 2016, he didn't seem to take his race too seriously, missing filing deadlines in Alabama, Arkansas, Florida, Idaho, Ohio, Oklahoma, Texas, Utah, and Virginia. Ultimately, he failed to gain traction, generating national poll numbers that hovered at around one percent.

As 2015 was coming to an end, he realized how hopeless his Don Quixote quest for the presidency was and bowed out, endorsing Florida Senator Marco Rubio.

Donald Trump held Pataki's campaign in contempt, claiming he couldn't get elected dog-catcher. "He was a terrible governor of New York…one of the worst."

Rand Paul

"Donald Trump is an Orange-Faced Windbag."
—**Rand Paul**

"Rand Paul Reminds Me of a Spoiled Brat Without a Properly Functioning Brain."
—**Donald Trump**

Randal Howard Paul (born January 7, 1963), nicknamed "Rand," is a Republican Senator from Kentucky, the son of former presidential candidate Ron Paul. Both father and son are skeptical of big government, advocating Libertarian ideas as channeled through the ultra-conservative Tea Party.

Of the candidates, Paul believes the GOP needs a bigger tent and that they should repair their hostile relationship with Black America. That would include reforms within the criminal justice system.

As such, both Paul and his father picked up thousands of students who supported them, at least until Bernie Sanders took many of them away.

Rand Paul claimed that the GOP had to reach out "to the young, to Hispanics, and to blacks."

The senior Paul had had a compromised relationship with neo-Confederates.

Before becoming a politician, Rand Paul was graduated from the Duke University School of Medicine, and began a private practice of ophthalmology.

In 2010, he entered politics and ran for the U.S. Senate, labeling himself a conservative and a supporter of the Tea Party movement, advocating a balanced budget, term limits, and privacy reform. He stands against gun control.

In other positions, he predictably claimed, "I am 100% Pro-life. He also stated that "same-sex marriage offends me, but I would not support a Federal ban." In spite of his anti-gay stance, he contradicted himself by claiming, "The government should stay out of your private life."

Appearing on *The Nightly Show* with Larry Wilmore, Paul denounced Donald Trump as "an orange-faced windbag. A delusional narcissist. Have you ever had a speck of dirt fly into your eye? It's annoying, irritating, and might even make you cry. If the dirt doesn't go away, it will keep you scratching your cornea until eventually it blinds you with its filth. A speck of dirt is way more qualified to be President than Trump."

He also likened Donald to Josef Goebbels, the shrill-voiced Nazi propaganda minister. "I'm not sure I would say Trump is Hitler—Goebbels, maybe."

He later compared Donald to Gollum from *The Lord of the Rings*, referring to the deranged, embittered cave dweller who was abnormally obsessed with a magical golden ring.

Paul's remarks infuriated Donald, who claimed, "Rand Paul is a lowly candidate who's made a fool of himself. Why is he allowed to take advantage of the people of Kentucky?

Rand Paul: a fiercely independent political iconoclast who hated "The Donald" and all of his "outrageous platforms."

He's truly weird. Reminds me of a spoiled brat without a properly functioning brain."

Rick Perry: From Joke Candidate to Donald Trump's First Martyr

James Richard Perry (born March 4, 1950), nicknamed "Rick," was the 47th Governor of Texas, in office from 2000 to 2015. First elected Lieutenant Governor in 1998, he assumed the governorship when George W. Bush resigned to become President of the United States.

Perry was described as a "tall, perma-tanned Bible-thumping Texan, with the physique of a retired underwear model."

Rolling Stone wrote, "The description of Perry's early political career sounded like the first chapters of true-crime books about serial killers, where nobody notices anything special about the protagonist until the bodies start piling up."

Perry had spent several years denying he had presidential ambitions, even claiming that he would not serve as John McCain's Veep in 2008. "I have the best job in the world—and that's Governor of Texas."

In 2012, he entered the race for President, although early on, he was viewed as "the joke candidate" and considered "not all that bright."

Rick Perry, the Texas governor with good looks, the body "of a retired underwear model," and a reputation for ultra- conservative politics that made him a demon to most of the feminists of his home state.

He had a history of spectacularly corrupt old-boy favoritism that made him a frequent target of the liberal media.

Perry is depicted here in a detail from his oh-so-patriotic official portrait.

Writing about the GOP primaries, Rolling Stone defined the candidates as "a cast of hopefuls who are historically underwhelming, a contest of bumblers, second-raters, extremists, and religious loonies."

At first, Perry seemed to count on his "eelish good looks" and countrified manner to outshine another 2012 frontrunner, Mitt Romney, a Mormon whom Perry fully expected would turn off Southern Baptists and other evangelicals.

During the launch of his 2012 campaign, Perry denounced Social Security as "an illegal Ponzi scheme" and promised that, as President, he would repeal the Federal income tax.

Early polling positioned Perry as a frontrunner, garnering 29% of the vote, with Romney a distant second at 18%.

Perry turned out to be a lousy debater, telling millions of TV viewers that, when he was President, he would eliminate three government agencies. On the air, under pressure, he named two but couldn't remember the third.
[It was the Department of Energy.]

More trouble arose along the campaign trail as embarrassments from his past surfaced. It turned out, and was widely publicized, that his family had once leased and occupied a hunting camp in Texas called "Niggerhead."

He also ran an anti-gay campaign. "There's something wrong in this country when gays can serve openly in the military but our kids can't openly celebrate Christmas or pray in school."

Despite his poor *[some said "catastrophic"]* campaign, Time magazine wrote that "Everything is aligned for Rick Perry to be the Republican nominee for President in 2016."

***

True to that prediction, he officially launched his race for the White House on June 4, 2015 in Addison, Texas, to the sound of the Colt Ford song, "Answer to No One."

Only a year before, Perry had been indicted by the Travis County Grand Jury, charged with abuse of office for threatening to veto $7.5 million in funding for the Public Integrity Unit, an Statewide agency charged with prosecuting Corruption in Texas Politics. But by February of 2016, he was cleared of all charges.

In a field heavily laden with candidates, Perry gained no traction, and was an early casualty, withdrawing from the race on September 11, 2015. He was the first in an overcrowded field to drop out, after poor polling deriving from his first debate.

He left his campaign in dire financial straits, having spent nearly four times more money than he raised.

He later endorsed a fellow Texan, "Anchor Baby" Senator Ted Cruz. When Cruz dropped out on May 5, 2016, Perry endorsed Donald for the presidency, having previously denounced "the cancer of Trump-ism, a toxic mix of demagoguery and nonsense."

Previously, Donald had said, "As Governor of Texas, Rick Perry did a horrible job of securing the border. He should be ashamed of himself. He also should be forced to take an IQ test."

Marco Rubio

"A Lightweight like Little Marco Rubio will never make America great again."
—Donald Trump

A Cuban-American, Marco Rubio (born May 28, 1971), an attorney, is the junior U.S. Senator from Florida. His parents grew up in Cuba, but immigrated to the United States in 1956, prior to the rise of Fidel Castro in January of 1959. Neither of his parents was a U.S. citizen at the time of Rubio's birth, leading to some charges that, like fellow Cuban, Ted Cruz, "Little Marco" is also an Anchor Baby."

His later statement that his parents were forced to leave Cuba in 1959, after Castro seized power, was a lie.

After graduating from the University of Miami Law School, Rubio was later elected to the Florida House of Representatives, where, according to NBC News, "He aggressively tried to push Florida to the political right." He became Speaker of the Florida House of Representatives at the age of 34, becoming the first Cuban American to ever hold that post.

During his tenure as Speaker, Rubio shared a house in Tallahassee with David Rivera, another representative. After several missed mortgage payments, the bank foreclosed.

In Tallahassee, Rubio became a *protégé* of then-governor Jeb Bush. In 2009, he ran for the U.S. Senate seat from Florida, clashing with Charlie Crist, who had been the incumbent governor of Florida. Since they had opposed many of Crist's policies as governor, the Tea Party endorsed Rubio

Rubio was a critic of Crist's strategy to fight climate change, although many experts predicted that Miami Beach will be under water one day because of rising tides.

Dream on, Marco...The Florida senator with the big ears promised to restore "the American Dream to the Middle Class," but his race for the White House turned into a nightmare, largely because of Donald's barrage of insults and widely publicized denunciations.

Attacking him as "the Absentee Senator," and a "political lightweight," Donald carried Rubio's home state in the Republican primaries.

Despite Rubio's having stated that he would not run for office again, in the summer of 2016, after his failure to win the Republican party's presidential nomination, he announced that he would run again in a bid for his former Senate seat.

On November 2, 2010, during Florida's general midterm election, Rubio was elected Senator with 49% of the vote, in marked contrast to Crist's 30%.

Although he'd just arrived in Washington, a Senatorial newcomer, there was speculation that he might be a potential Republican candidate for the 2012 presidential election. Despite the hype, Rubio opted not to run during that election cycle.

But on April 13, 2015, he officially threw his hat into the ring, becoming a candidate for President in the GOP primaries. That would eventually bring him into conflict with Donald Trump. Rubio's campaign was based on his promise to restore "The American Dream" for the middle class. As justification for his passion, he cited his own background as the son of a working immigrant family living from paycheck to paycheck.

At first, Donald and Rubio refrained from criticizing each other, at least until Donald began to interpret him as a serious candidate. Then, one reporter noted, "They launched World War III."

Donald denounced Rubio as "Dishonest…He's scamming Florida. He treats America ICE *[Immigration and Customs Enforcement]* officers like absolute trash in order to pass Obama's amnesty to criminal aliens guilty of sex offenses. He is the puppet of the special interest Koch brothers."

He also cited Rubio's poor attendance record in the U.S. Senate, asserting that during one year alone, he had missed 35% of the Senate votes because he was out of town.

Rick Santorum:
"I Compare Homosexuality to Bestiality"

Rick Santorum, "family man."

"How?" his legions of haters asked, "did this fanatical, pro-life, anti-gay, semi-permanent fixture at the 'Kiddies' Table' manage to remain in the presidential race as long as he did?"

If any other candidate had taken a turn as sharp to the right as Rick Santorum, he would surely have run off the road. Richard John Santorum (born May 10, 1958), nicknamed "Rick," represented Pennsylvania in the U.S. Senate from 1995-2007. During his tenure there, in his capacity as "Conference Chairman," he was the Senate's third-ranking Republican.

Self-identifying as a devout Roman Catholic, he became a leading social conservative vehemently opposing same-sex marriage and even artificial birth control. He was also the author of the Santorum Amendment, promoting the teaching of Intelligent Design in schools.

On the foreign front, he favored the War on Terror and declared that weapons of mass destruction had been found in Iraq. He defended the harsh treatment of prisoners in Guantánamo Bay and favored waterboarding during his assault on "Islamic fascism."

On the home front, he lashed out at "radical feminism," comparing pro-choice Americans to Nazis.

He became the major "family values" advocate within the Senate, endorsing only monogamous, heterosexual relationships and traditional (male-female) marriages. He opposed both same-sex marriages and civil unions, too. "I favor laws against polygamy, sodomy, and other actions antithetical to a healthy, stable, traditional family. I compare homosexuality to bestiality."

[In 2015, he signed an online pledge vowing not to respect any law from the U.S. Supreme Court that endorsed same-sex marriage, claiming that such unions were against a "natural created order."]

He went on to describe contraception "as a license to do things in a sexual realm that is counter to how things are supposed to be." He also promised, if elected President, he would get rid of porn, which he claimed "causes brain damage."

Finally, on November 7, 2006, the voters of the very sane state of Pennsylvania wised up about the right wing firecracker, voting him out of office. He lost by more than 700,000 votes to the very sane and rational Bob Casey, Jr.

In 2012, Santorum decided to seek the presidency. He won the Iowa caucuses, getting only 34 more votes than Mitt Romney. He seemed on a roll, winning in eleven state primaries and garnering four million votes, more than any candidate except Romney. But he finally had to concede the race to his rival, whom he endorsed at the Republican National Convention.

In 2015, he decided to run for President once again. But this time he didn't generate any enthusiasm and was assigned to "the kiddies' table" in early debates.

He campaigned as a "culture warrior," and as a "true Christian conservative." Critics accused him of wanting to abolish the tenants of the U.S. Constitution in favor of a "Christian theocracy."

Santorum likened Obamacare to apartheid in South Africa in a Nelson Mandela tribute speech.

One of Donald's campaign workers said, "I've heard of extreme views, and there is Rick Santorum. Up to now, I thought Obama was the worst President in U.S. history. But that's because we won't survive a Santorum presidency. I'm sure he would bring back the Spanish Inquisition."

Santorum ended his campaign on February 3, 2016, endorsing Senator Marco Rubio, although he couldn't really give any good reason for doing so.

Scott Walker: He Survived a Recall from Voters in His Home State, but Not the GOP Rat Race for the White House

"Scott Walker is not presidential material…He's a not a very smart puppet."
—Donald Trump

The 45th Governor of Wisconsin, Scott Walker (born November 2, 1967) received national attention in 2012 when he survived a recall election. Democrats wanted to kick him out of the governor's mansion when he introduced a budget plan that limited collective bargaining among state workers and public employers. The centerpiece of rage and controversy, he became the first American governor ever to survive a recall effort.

Another controversial move was in 2011, when he defunded Planned Parenthood from Wisconsin's State budget. Two years later, he signed a bill that required women seeking an abortion to undergo an Ultrasound so doctors could show the patient the image of her fetus, presumably to shame them into canceling their abortions.

In addition to fighting the unions of Wisconsin, Walker signed a "no-climate tax," opposing any legislation that would raise taxes to combat climate change.

He did not rule out sending U.S. troops to Syria to oppose ISIS, and he said that, if elected President, he would send arms to Ukraine to fight Russia.

He also opposed the U.S.'s growing ties to Cuba, and claimed that he would rescind any prior deal brokered with Iran. He also declined to answer a question about whether he thought Obama was a true Christian.

Scott Walker during the heady moments of victory in the immediate aftermath of his 2010 victory in the Wisconsin Republican primary.

After a disturbing tenure as a lightning rod for the ultra-conservative Tea Party right, his appeal died fast.

Walker had not been born in Wisconsin, but in Colorado Springs. He had been reared, however, in both Iowa and Wisconsin before attending Marquette University. He did not graduate, but left school to accept a full-time job with the Red Cross.

He followed that by winning an election to the Wisconsin State Assembly in 1992, a venue where multiple future protests would be lodged against him. Later, he was elected county executive in Milwaukee County, and followed that in minor posts until he decided to seek the governorship in 2006. He didn't make it in 2006.

He tried again in 2010, this time defeating Democrat Tom Barrett.

In late January of 2015, he set up an organization called "Our American Revival," which, in essence, was his first shot at running for President. "Within a month, he'd quickly vaulted into the top tier of likely candidates for the Republican presidential race," or so said *The New York Times*. On July 13, he officially declared himself a candidate for the Republican nomination.

In June, he emerged as a comfortable frontrunner in a *Des Moines Register* poll placing him at 17%, but by the end of August, he'd fallen to 7%. He seemed to wilt during debates, overshadowed by Donald's larger-than-life stage presence. A national survey from Monmouth University that August (2015) had Walker dropping to 3%, in contrast to his 10% in June.

For weeks, despite focused attention from the media, Walker "seemed to walk all over the map, trying to articulate his positions on immigration and other issues, but it was obvious that he was not connecting with the voter," one reporter wrote. "On immigration, he seemed to take three different positions over the period of a month."

Facing declining support, Walker proposed an even more controversial stand than Donald. He suggested that America's northern border with Canada should have a wall built, "stretching from sea to sea." It would be similar to the one Donald was proposing for Mexico.

"It is a legitimate issue for us to look at," Walker said. "Secure the border, enforce the laws. No amnesty," he proclaimed.

His proposal was met with ridicule and scorn. The 5,525-mile-long U.S.-Canadian border is the longest undefended international border in the world, but only a small percentage of illegal immigrant come across it.

Walker and his campaign began a meltdown, plagued with the perception that he would not become a viable candidate, nationally. His campaign funds dried up.

On September 12, 2015, he suspended his campaign, asking other candidates to do the same, so that the GOP could rally around what he defined as the "conservative alternative" to Donald Trump: Ted Cruz. On March 29, 2016, he endorsed Cruz, a senator whose views were even miles to the right of Walker's own ultra-conservative positions.

For doing that, Donald lashed into him, calling him "a puppet, not presidential material. As Governor of Wisconsin, he ran up a massive deficit. He made of mess of jobs, delivering a bad forecast, a mess really. He's not very smart, a dumb fundraiser who hit me very hard—not smart at all."

"I OUTDID ALL THOSE LOSERS"
Donald Trump in Reference to His Performance at His First GOP Debate

The first live broadcast of a Republican National Debate was on August 6, 2015 at the Quicken Loans Arena in Cleveland, the same city in which the Republican Nominating Convention would convene in July of 2016

Broadcast on Fox News Channel, it was watched by 24 million viewers, making it the most-watched event in the history of cable TV.

Because there were so many candidates in an overcrowded race, Fox aired two separate debates.

Candidates at the bottom of the polls were assigned what was derisively called "the kiddies' table." Appearing at 5PM, the low-ranked candidates included Rick Perry, Bobby Jindal, Rick Santorum, Lindsey Graham, Carly Fiorina, George Pataki, and Jim Gilmore, in a debate moderated by Bill Hemmer and Martha McCallum.

The main debate, scheduled for the prime-time TV hour of 9PM, included Donald Trump (prominently positioned as

The lineup for the contenders from the "adults table" at **the first Republican debate** in Cleveland, August, 2015. It was compared in the press to an "apocalyptic sect of loopy Christian fundamentalists evoking a frat-house dong-measure contest."

the lineup's centerpiece), and his chief rivals, Ted Cruz, Scott Walker, Jeb Bush, Ben Carson, Marco Rubio, Mike Huckabee, Chris Christie, Rand Paul, and John Kasich. The Moderators included Bret Baier, Megyn Kelly, and Chris Wallace.

Even though he was leading in the polls, many of Donald's Republican enemies demanded that he should not be included in the debate, since he was not viewed "as a serious contender."

In an unrelated grievance, Santorum, Graham, and Fiorina complained to Fox based on their banishment "to the boondocks," The trio claimed that their assignment to a second rank position would make them less competitive in the upcoming primaries and caucuses. Fox turned a deaf ear.

A review of the debaters at the kiddies' table noted that Fiorina "was swimming in bright pink in a sea of dark-suited men." Her strong performance catapulted her into the national spotlight, bouncing her up in the polls. Based partly on that, she maintained, "I deserve a prime position on stage with the big boys."

After the early debate that evening, Jindal also got some scant praise, but, for the most part, Pataki, Graham, Gilmore, Perry, and Santorum were punched by critics. The lower tier debate was the first and only one for Perry. His post-debate poll numbers were so dismal that he didn't qualify for inclusion in any future debates. Reacting to that, he decided "to throw in the towel," as he phrased it.

Before going on, Donald had been skeptical, saying, "I'm not a debater, and I don't know how well I will perform. I question the value of debates. Politicians are always debating with little in the way of results."

At the debate, Donald was the chief attraction, being granted the most "voice time" time at 10 minutes, 32 seconds. Jeb Bush trailed at 8:10 minutes. Rand Paul got the least time, at 5 minutes.

Press reaction to the candidates' individual performances was divided. For the most part, Donald was criticized for being "rude and erratic."

In vivid contrast, "his supporters mopped it up," said Ohio voter Greg Benson. "The others were like a Bloody Mary without the vodka."

In post-debate analysis, the press tended to praise Jeb's tolerance, while attacking Donald's harsh rhetoric that called for the deportation of millions. At the debate, Jeb had described immigration as "an act of love," a statement that Donald later mocked.

Megyn Kelly: The moderator who became almost as famous as the characters in the news cycle she was covering.

Was the blood coming from her eyes—or from somewhere else? Donald raised that point after her intense probing of him.

Notoriously competitive (and some say "mutually vindictive,") the two big tabloids of New York City differed in bloodthirsty ways about virtually everything associated with Donald Trump.

When a Trump fan, a top editor endorsed by Rupert Murdoch at the New York Post retired, the Daily News exposed and celebrated his departure.

Donald also clashed with moderators Kelly and Wallace on the issue of sexism and illegal immigration.

Kelly launched into Donald like a tigress smelling fresh kill. She listed shocking derogatory remarks she said the GOP hopeful had made about women, describing them as "fat pigs, dogs, slobs, and disgusting animals."

He reserved his defense for later, trying to escape from her trap, although admitting to a feud he'd previously maintained with Rosie O'Donnell, after she'd attacked him in front of millions of talk-show viewers.

But later, with Don Lemon on CNN, in reference to Megyn Kelly, he said, "There was blood coming out of her eyes, blood coming out of her whatever."

[In a subsequent interview, he backed down, claiming he'd meant blood coming from her nose when he said, "wherever." But audiences knew he was suggesting that she was menstruating.]

He later attacked her as "being highly overrated, so average in so many ways. Crazy, sick, not worth watching, always complaining about me, yet she devotes entire shows to me. Get a life, Megyn! Without me, your ratings would tank. I refuse to call her a bimbo, since that would not be politically correct."

After the debate, polls showed Donald outperforming his rivals. "I was winning at every stage of the debate," he claimed. "*Drudge* put me at the top, and so did *Time* magazine."

In spite of the controversy, many polls showed that Donald was appealing to thousands upon thousands of voters who had never cast a ballot before.

When Kelly appeared in an interview with Charlie Rose that October, she stated her case, claiming that she had not wanted "any sort of war with Trump. He was obviously upset. That's fine: He's running for President. It's not a fun business. There's gonna be ups and downs, and I know he considered that a down. So we just wanted to forge forward and try to put it behind us, not pour any more fuel on that fire."

She defined the feud she and Fox News had had with Donald as "bizarre. I became the story. You know, you never want to be the story when you are a news person."

She told ABC's George Stephanopoulos, "You want to be covering the story so it was like an Alice-through-the-looking-glass experience."

Fox released a statement of its own. "Donald Trump's vitriolic attacks against Megyn Kelly and his extreme, sick obsession with her is beneath the dignity of a presidential candidate who wants to occupy the highest office in the land."

One reporter wrote: "More and more, Trump is sounding like an eight-year-old confused by his feelings for his third-grade teacher and lashing out."

At CNN, Anderson Cooper claimed, "The Kelly-Trump feud fuels the narrative that Trump is a misogynist and too thin-skinned to be President."

Kayleigh McEnany, the conservative columnist, said, "It plays well with the Republican base any time you attack the media."

Kelly claimed that broadcasting news "is a fickle business. Everything is rolling along fine and then you accidentally call Mike Huckabee 'Fuckabee'—and you're gone."

She was asked what her dream interviews would be, responding, "I'd love to interview Putin, Assad, Bill Clinton, Melania Trump, and most definitely Hillary Clinton…and also the Pope."

To Hell with Political Correctness! Donald Trump Is THE MAN WHO WOULD BE KING

Trumpus Rex

Throughout the "Summer of Trump," Donald received both praise and brickbats. Conservative columnist Ted Wrobleski lauded him, while others used such expressions as "a blowhard," "a TV huckster," a "buffoon," and "a soulless one-percenter."

"He may not be the best person for the job, but Donald Trump has saved us from the play-it-safe, poll-driven, stage-managed, social-media-drenched tedium that passes for presidential politics," Wrobleski wrote. "We can be thankful for that. The political ruling elite can't stand it. American culture and politics are all about money and celebrity—and Donald Trump's got both."

Talking on Sirius Radio, Chris Spatola, a former U.S. Army captain, attacked Donald. "He is reality TV in an age in which sound bites and sensationalism proliferate. He reflects the public's anger about politics. He appeals to those who feel left behind economically, culturally, and politically. He is not rooted in dogmatic ideology. No one knows what he really believes on policy."

"He plays to a part of the Republican Party that traffics in prejudice and feat. A part that believes immigrants are rapists and drug-dealing criminals, and that homosexuals are corrupting the 'sanctity of marriage'…and yada, yada, yada," Spatola charged.

Finally, he concluded, "Trump is not going to win the Republican nomination."

The Doomsday threat for candidate Donald was also echoed by Chris Cillizza in *The Washington Post*. "The question is what exactly does Trump's popularity (gulp) mean? There is no way he'll get nominated."

The normally savvy Bill Kristol, editor of *The Weekly Standard*, said, "Trump is a mere showman who will not last through the debates. He'll drop out along the way."

Senator Rand Paul, who at first viewed himself as the frontrunner, claimed, "There is no way voters in this country will nominate Trump. He's on every channel, all the time, and people have gone gaga. But it won't last. Trust me."

Donald's attacks in the media swelled into an avalanche. James Fallows, a correspondent for *The Atlantic*, wrote: "He is a novelty, a candidate akin to Herman Cain or Michele Bachmann. He has no experience in appointed or elected office, or in the military. His derisive remarks about Mexicans would not bear scrutiny."

In spite of all these dire predictions, Donald continued to dominate the polls as summer moved toward its inevitable end. On the *National Interest* website appeared this comment:

"Donald Trump is egotistical, vain, bombastic, often mean-spirited. He revels in his financial superiority, which he conflates with human goodness. When he contorts his mouth into a kind of tube as he talks, you brace yourself for something outrageous. His likability quotient, at least in terms of public persona, is down somewhere in the single digits and yet, he has just taken hold of the American political system by the neck and doesn't seem inclined to let go anytime soon."

In late August, Sarah Palin became one of Donald's early supporters, bringing him onto her right-wing TV talk show. "You're bringing back the Silent Majority," she told him. "I need you to set the record straight because I think we're not getting the truth from the White House. The idiots in the press are misrepresenting your positions."

At the end of the interview, she told Trump, "You're a terrific person. Before going off the air, she praised Curt Schilling *[The American major league baseball pitcher, a former video game developer, and right-wing political blogger]* "for comparing Muslims to Nazis."

The political heat wave generated by Donald continued through the dog days of August. Polls showed him beating Carson, Cruz, and Rubio, his chief rivals. He also picked up more support, even from former presidential candidate Pat Buchanan. Buchanan expressed praise for Donald, even though Donald had once compared Buchanan to Hitler.

Donald continued to convert thousands upon thousands of voters to his cause, perhaps based on his rather abrasive approach to politics, a style that was likened to "shooting from the hip—and to hell with political correctness."

He feared no competition from such candidates as Paul, Perry, and Graham. "They spent all summer at the bottom of the polls. I predict all these bottom feeders are losers."

The losers shot back: Paul mocked Donald's credentials as a true conservative; Graham threatened to "beat his brains out"; and Perry compared his politics to a fatal disease. In the polls, Paul came in at 6%, Perry at 1%, and Graham at 0%.

Jeb Bush lost more ground than he'd gained, despite an outlay of millions from his fat campaign war chest. Many pundits had considered Jeb a shoo-in, but as the summer ended, his polls had dropped to 6%. Jeb attacked Donald, calling him "a germaphobe trying to insult his way into the presidency."

Hoping to appeal to Hispanics, the bilingual Jeb often spoke Spanish at campaign rallies.

Donald attacked him for this, claiming, "He should really be speaking English in the United States."

Jeb appeared on ABC News, saying that, "Immigration and multi-lingualism that comes with it contributes to the vitality of America."

"Jeb tries to look cool, but can't make it," Donald said. "He's even dropped those glasses in favor of contact lenses to make him look more masculine. He's spending a fortune in campaign funds to defeat me. But he's a weak, desperate candidate."

As the Trump summer sun continued to blaze, Ben Carson forged ahead in the polls, as did Carly Fiorina.

Carson, Fiorina, and Donald were each "outsider candidates," and the public responded to that, viewing Establishment politicians with disdain. Donald attacked Bush, Cruz, and Rubio as career politicians.

At 18%, Carson rose to second place. Donald attacked Carson as "incapable of understanding foreign policy and illegal immigration. He has never created a job in his life"

He accused Fiorina "of running a dead campaign. If you listen to her for more than ten minutes, you develop a massive headache. She has zero chance." He also attacked her record as CEO at Hewlett-Packard: "She got fired for doing a terrible job!"

During the first months of the campaign, Donald and Cruz were accused of having a "bromance," based on not having mutually attacked each other. In the coming months, however, that would downgrade into "a wild dog fight."

When Cruz was interviewed by right-wing radio talk show host, Hugh Hewitt, the Texas senator said, "I think people are ticked off at Washington, and they want someone who will stand up to the corrupt power elite, someone who will take them on and tell the truth. I think that's why Donald has attracted the early support he has."

In roughly similar phraseologies, Donald, on CNN's *State of the Union* said, "There's a movement going on that's more than me. People are tired of these incompetent politicians in Washington. For that reason, I'm not surprised they're turning to me."

To the shock of many within the Republican Party, Donald went on to attack John McCain, the Arizona Senator who had run for President in 2008. "He was not a war hero," Donald charged. "The war heroes were soldiers who weren't captured. Not only that, he let the public down and didn't defeat Obama in 2008. He's made us pay an awful price for putting that guy in office."

As the first autumn winds blew down from the north, and the dog days of August cooled into early autumn, September unfolded with another big debate.

A pundit, Jimmy Connors, wrote: "For now, we may just have to sit back and marvel as the 'Summer of Trump' comes to an end. We must recognize that it's the real thing…and spectacular. All the naysayers were wrong. Donald Trump, or so it seems, has more lives than Rasputin."

Grigori Rasputin (1872-1916) was the demonically terrifying Russian mystic, priest and confessor to the Empress Alexandra at the Romanov court of Czar Nicholas II. By 1914, he had become an influential and divisive factor in Russian politics.

He proved hard to kill, but was done in by a group of Russian noblemen.

PART THREE

THE AUTUMN OF TRUMP

INCREDULITY VS. CREDIBILITY

("What the F#@%? Donald Trump?? For President???)

"Donald Trump is here for the duration—and gaining strength and traction by the hour."
—Reporter Paul Solotaroff

CHAPTER FIVE

INSULT BY INSULT
Donald Climbs in the Polls

Although Naysayers Insist, "There's No Way He Can Ever Win"
DONALD KNOCKS OFF HIS REPUBLICAN RIVALS

POLARIZATION AND PROTESTS
Attacks on The Donald Intensify

"I FINANCE MY OWN CAMPAIGN
And I'm Too Rich to be Bought Like Hillary & Jeb"

BLACK LIVES MATTER
AT PRO-DONALD RALLIES, PROTESTERS DRESS UP LIKE THE KKK

By the beginning of September, 2015, many journalists had reconsidered their initial rejection of Donald as a candidate for the White House. Reports cautiously surfaced that "the billionaire frontrunner's demise may be premature." In begrudging admiration, one headline read "THE SUMMER OF TRUMP MAY NOT BE OVER."

One thing, at least, was certain: Donald, his comments, and his points of view made for very interesting reading. His entry into the presidential race had sparked a series of blood feuds, pitting the GOP establishment against dozens of diehard conservative grassroots movements. As one reporter evaluated the antagonists: "The (Republican) party's nativist constituency is pitted against its globalist elites."

As Donald rose in the polling, it was speculated that he would never be awarded with the actual nomination, but that he might play a kingmaker at a brokered convention. Again and again, it was cited that Herman Cain, Rick Perry, and Michele Bachmann had each been short-term frontrunners in 2012, only to crash, burn, and then fall down from out of the sky.

Nate Cohn in The New York Times wrote: "Trump's surge in the polls has followed the classic pattern of a media-driven surge. Now it will most likely follow the classic pattern of a party-backed decline."

On one point, nearly every reporter and TV pundit agreed: Already, although the political season had just started, it had been one of the most unpredictable on record. Donald continued to dominate hour-to-hour media coverage and remained at the top of GOP polls.

"He has seen 'dragon Scott Walker' turn out to be a mere harmless lizard," wrote a reporter in Wisconsin.

Donald needed evangelical support and, with that in mind, tried to show off his theological depths: "When I go to church, and I drink a little wine—the only wine I drink since I shun alcohol—and I eat a little cracker, I guess that's a form of forgiveness."

"Not since Billy Graham," mocked one reporter in response, "have we seen such an uplifting display of Christian sentiment."

***

Through it all, Donald remained witty, provocative, outrageous, and always telegenic, despite makeup that somehow managed to resonate as orange-toned, except for white highlights around his eyes.

Much of the media continued to treat and interpret his candidacy as a TV reality show.

He glossed over his business failures and highlighted his successes. Even so, David Segal in The Washington Post wrote: "The people who know the least about business admire him the most, and those who know the most about business admire him the least."

Reporter Paul Solotaroff wrote: "Since Trump announced his candidacy, he has been mocked and reviled, worshipped and courted, and, till very lately, dismissed as a fever dream of the torch-and-pitchfork segment of the Republican Party. His negatives, however, have been through the roof."

"Even so, he stays on message: 'I am strong. Politicians are weak.'"

"If you're waiting for Trump to blow himself up in a Hindenburg of gaffes or hate speech, you're in for a long, cold fall and winter," said Solotaroff. "Donald Trump is here for the duration—and gaining strength and traction by the hour."

Donald told the world, "I'm tired of the party hacks—the Jeb Bushes, Scott Walkers, and Karl Roves. The people look at these jokers and say, 'This one's owned by David Koch, that

An anti-Trump rally near San Francisco turned into a STOP HATE gathering. A sea of protesters accused Donald of using racism to seize power in America.

Signs also protested his anti-immigration stance and his call for American Muslims to wear special IDs, evoking the Yellow Star that Jews were forced to wear in Nazi Germany.

one's owned by Sheldon Adelson, and so on. As for me, I'm owned by the people, and I'm going to do right by them."

John McCain, whom Donald had called "not a war hero," spoke up against him during the closing days of August. "Trump has fired up the crazies. It's very hurtful to our party."

The Arizona Senator (the one who had disastrously selected Sarah Palin as his candidate for Veep during his own bid for the presidency in 2008) appeared worried that he might lose his own re-election.

In retaliation, Donald shot back: "McCain is all talk, no action. He spends too much time on television and not enough time doing his job."

On September 11, 2015, a poll revealed that Donald continued to appeal to the most extreme members of the GOP—"Those whose views are way out in right field," Sixty-one percent of those polled believed that President Obama was not born in Hawaii. These same voters also felt that Obama was "lying about his religion and was a secret Muslim."

They supported changing the 14th Amendment, which guarantees citizenship to all U.S.-born children, regardless of their parents' immigration status, the so-called "Anchor Babies."

"My Rival Candidates Are Wacko Birds"

—Donald Trump

At mass rallies, Donald jangled the nerves of many in the GOP establishment, who had for years run on the promise of cutting taxes. In contrast, he said he might raise taxes in certain areas, especially on corporations which "do not act in the best interests of America."

He also threatened to impose tariffs on American companies that transferred their factories to other countries to take advantage of "slave labor."

Republicans shot back, claiming that Donald's policies were "anti-growth and would drive the American economy into the ground with huge drops in the G.D.P." Many predicted massive job losses.

In retaliation, he denounced hedge fund managers, defining them as "paper pushers who tend to get lucky on the road to riches."

He also jumped into the health insurance controversy, suggesting that to lower health care costs, insurers should be allowed to sell their policies across state lines. "My plan would eliminate a lot of red tape and lower administrative costs, which would lead to price reductions for the consumer."

His style was loud, pushy, and bombastic, a delivery that seemed to go over with voters. But, almost unnoticed, at first, the soft-spoken Ben Carson was slipping upward in the polls, coasting on his reputation as a Bible-loving Christian with a low-key personality. Polls had him in second place, some having him tied neck-and-neck with Donald.

The two men had completely different styles, with Donald being mad as hell, combative, and unfiltered, and Carson almost professorial.

Carson's campaign advisors told him to backpedal from his highly provocative anti-homosexual views. One observer noted that he went through the summer of 2015 in the shadow of the Trump supernova, and therefore never really came under scrutiny for his many dubious and off-the-wall observations and statements.

Carson advocated a repeal of Obamacare and the imposition of an annual flat tax that could be filed in fifteen minutes. He denounced global warming theories as "irrelevant." He also said that Planned Parenthood opened most clinics in black neighborhoods to control that population.

For most of these statements The Washington Post assigned Carson "four Pinocchios," a graphic illustration that implied a low quotient of truthfulness and/or accuracy.

He appealed to the same "hungry-for-change" conservatives that Donald did, but he packaged his message alongside an inspirational life story, aggressively resisting most of Donald's street-fighting tactics.

"He's not going to be a screamer or a bomb-thrower," said Carson's campaign manager, Barry Bennett. "He's in it for the good of the country. Carson by far is the more likable guy."

The unflinching stream of media attacks on Donald continued as columnist Bill Hammond claimed he "was morphing from a sideshow to a virus of the body politic—exposing and exploiting weakness in its immune response to claptrap hucksterism, especially on the Republican side."

Doug Muzzio, a political scientist at Baruch College, claimed, "What Trump says bypasses the cerebral cortex and goes right from the base of his spinal column out of his mouth."

There were reports that Donald's attacks on Mexicans were whipping up hate crimes. After a pair of thugs in Boston beat up a Mexican immigrant, they told police after they were caught, "Trump was right. All these illegals need to be deported."

There was growing concern that if Donald failed in his race to win the Republican nomination, he might establish a splinter party, rejecting the GOP altogether and running as a third party candidate like Ross Perot did in 1992.

Based partly on that possibility, and in light of Donald's notorious unpredictability, the RNC demanded that each of its candidates sign a statement vowing not to run as a third party choice. Reince Priebus, the RNC's chairman, promised to personally negotiate with Donald to get him to sign.

On September 3, Donald signed the pledge. "I see no circumstances in which I would tear up that pledge, although it is not legally binding."

In exchange for signing the pledge, Donald claimed he got nothing from the RNC. A reporter said he "sounded like Marlon Brando at the beginning of The Godfather." In a show of one-upmanship, Donald demanded that Priebus fly into New York to meet him at Trump Tower.

One of the first major protests outside Trump Tower was launched on September 3, after he'd signed the pledge to support whatever candidate the GOP ultimately endorsed.

Angered by his comments about immigration, protesters waved signs denouncing Donald as a racist. Many of them wore white hoods and KKK robes. A security guard at the tower was caught on video punching a protester in the face after he ripped up an anti-Trump sign. The guard later claimed, "I was jumped from behind."

It would be the first of many protests to come during the months ahead.

Through it all, Donald's best-funded rival, Jeb Bush, consistently failed to connect with millions of voters. Although he kept snipping at Donald's heels, he remained largely ineffective in bringing him down. Columnist Paul Krugman wrote: "[Jeb] Bush may pose as a reasonable, thoughtful type—credulous reporters even describe him as a policy wonk—but his actual economic platform, which relies on the magic of tax cuts to deliver a doubling of America's economic rate, is pure

Even the ultra-conservative **National Review** ridiculed Donald's quest to change his address from Trump Tower to 1600 Pennsylvania Avenue.

supply-side voodoo."

Although she'd been relegated to the outer fringes of the campaign, Sarah Palin continued to insert herself. During the first week of September, she claimed she'd serve as Energy Secretary in a Trump administration, but followed that pronouncement with the immediate vow to shut down the agency altogether. "I think states should have more control over their lands. Energy is my baby when I was governor of Alaska. I was known for my 'Drill, baby, drill!'"

Donald came under attack from rival candidate Carly Fiorina, who faulted him for not understanding the difference between Hamas and Hezbollah. She cited an interview Donald had delivered to radio host Hugh Hewitt, in which he had confused the Quds Force, a special Iranian military unit, with the Kurds.

Later, he accused Hewitt of asking him "gotcha questions," and denounced him as a "third-rate radio announcer."

As his campaign moved forward, Republicans were growing concerned that his inflammatory language would damage their party. There was a real fear that the aggressive tone of his rhetoric would turn off voters, especially Hispanics and African Americans, both of whom, polls showed, viewed him unfavorably at the rate of 80%.

"If we're going to be a majority party in the 21st Century, we're going to have to be a multi-racial, multi-ethnic, and an inclusive party," intoned (Republican) Representative Tom Cole of Oklahoma.

Donald also alienated many in the Black Lives Matter movement, based partly on his calls for law and order, as he defended the police and cited incidences of crime, raising anxiety and prejudice among white voters. He promised he would rid heavily black Ferguson, Missouri, of "gangs and tough dudes. The same goes for Chicago and Baltimore."

He delivered a speech in Nashville, in which he claimed that 99.9% of the police were good. "That first night in Baltimore, officials allowed that city to be destroyed by the blacks. They set back the city 35 years because the police were not allowed to protect people."

Echoing the same sentiment, Ted Cruz expressed a different slant on the assault on cops, blaming Obama for any attacks on the men in blue. Scott Walker also criticized the Black Lives Matter movement, calling for a change in tone "from chants and rallies that fixate on racial division."

With his hawk eye, Donald kept close watch on his competition. Subsequently, he was delighted that Carson, a surgeon and so-called scientist, did not believe in evolution.

Donald heard that Jeb was wounded that Donald found him boring, and promised "to unleash my American animal spirits at the next debate."

"As for Rubio, the high point of his summer was when he hit a kid in the head with a football," Donald told an aide. "As for Christie, he's got the Bridgegate thing, and now he's exposed for taking free plane rides to football games. Cruz seems to be joining himself to me at the hip so no one will look too closely at his wacko bird proposals."

Again and again, many of Donald's detractors stated that they didn't think he'd go over with evangelicals. Carson said, "My faith is a very big part of who I am. I doubt if that is true of Mr. Trump. I don't get that impression from him."

Although for the most part, Donald seemed to defend Planned Parenthood, his did not endorse its platform on abortions. "I would look at the legal aspects of it," he told CNN. His position was in marked contrast to candidates like Cruz, who was willing to escalate another government shutdown as the vehicle that would enable him to strip the organization of its $500 million in Federal funds, none of which went to pay for abortions.

Even Donald's attendance at Marble Collegiate Church in Manhattan came under fire. "That's where this married man met his next mistress, Marla Maples," one anti-Trump campaigner charged.

"Nothing beats the Bible," Donald said. "Not even The Art of the Deal."

David Brody, chief political correspondent for the Christian Broadcasting Network, tried to explain Donald's appeal to evangelicals. "We're sick and tired of being used as political pawns in the Republican leadership's Game of Thrones. Along comes Trump, who, for better or worse, is coming across as honest and truth-telling. And evangelicals are loving every moment of it."

When Donald heard that Fiorina, based on her surging polls, would move up from the "kiddies' table" to a prime time position among the main candidates during the upcoming debate, he backed down on his charge about how ugly she was. "I was talking about her persona, not her looks," he said, by way of explanation during his appearance on Fox & Friends on September 10. "The fact is, I probably did say something about Carly in a jocular manner."

[What he said was, "Look at that face. Would anyone vote for that? Can you imagine that, the face of our next President? I mean, she's a woman, and I'm not supposed to say bad things, but, really, folks. Come on. Are we serious?"

Fiorina had responded, "I'm getting under his skin a little because I am climbing in the polls."]

In spite of the attacks, a CNN poll in September showed Donald's support at 32%, an eight-point gain since August.

Hillary Clinton, perhaps as a preview of how she'd be handling unchivalrous comments from Donald, weighed in on the Trump/Fiorina controversy. At a rally in Washington, D.C., she said, "He seems to delight in insulting women every chance he gets. I must say, if he emerges, I would love to debate him."

To divert attention away from his remarks about women, Donald brought up the subject of foreign affairs: "The Ukraine crisis is rooted in the weakness of President Obama. Vladimir Putin felt free to invade the Crimea because he lacks respect for the President. Obama is not strong."

On September 12, Donald received news that the Texas governor, Rick Perry, had withdrawn from the presidential race. Headlines blared: "TRUMP CLAIMS HIS FIRST VICTIM AS PERRY EXITS." Texas' longest-serving governor had ended his second run with a whimper. [His first race was in 2012. In July, Perry had declared war on his billionaire rival, accusing him of "being a cancer on conservatism who will destroy the Republican Party if unleashed." In the first weeks of the campaign, the governor had been a leading voice in the anti-Trump movement.]

When Donald heard the news, he was in Iowa. "Mr. Perry, he's gone. He was very nasty to me. Good riddance!"

Cruz, a fellow Texan, declined to address what Perry's departure meant for the race.

"We have a tremendous field of candidates," Perry said before he left. "Probably the greatest group of men and women. I step aside knowing our party is in good hands, as long as we listen to the grassroots, listen to the cause of conservatism."

Before making his final curtain call, Perry issued one final warning to the GOP, claiming it was experiencing its most serious identity crisis in a generation. He reminded voters that Donald had supported abortion rights, given campaign money to Hillary, and "said good things about Obamacare."

As he bowed out, Perry made a parting shot at Donald on the radio: "Demeaning people of Hispanic heritage is not just ignorant, it betrays the example of Christ."

Donald appeared on The Tonight Show simultaneous with its host, Jimmy Fallon. Together, before a conventional sit-down interview, they jointly performed a skit during which Fallon pretended to be Donald's image in the mirror, mimicking his movements, clothing, and hair, responding with approval, at Donald's reflection, to everything he said. As part of his performance (and in the spirit of the late-night venue), Donald, as a good sport, was game for the sendup and used the late-night appearance and interview to promote his image and his brand.

Later, with Fallon, Donald talked about his aversion to apologizing. "I fully think apologizing is a great thing, but you have to be wrong. I will absolutely apologize if I'm ever wrong."

One of his greatest selling points was that, "I'm too rich to be bought, to be, like Hillary Clinton, the toady of the monied interests. In politics, if a man gives, he gets. As a businessman, I gave to many candidates. When they called, I gave, and you know what? When I needed something from them two years later, I phoned them. They were there for me. That's how the system works in this country."

DONALD AT WAR WITH THE GOP
LATINO RAGE

Just before the second Republican debate [conducted September 16, 2015, at the Reagan Presidential Library in Simi Valley, California, as moderated by CNN's Jake Tapper, Hugh Hewitt, and Dana Bash], Donald stepped up his campaign. "Our leaders are babies who are so stupid they stand by helplessly as we become a third world country."

Cruz was also gloomy, citing the "tyranny and lawlessness of jailing a county clerk in Kentucky who refuses to issue a same-sex marriage license." He also condemned Obama for making a pact with Iran. "Americans will die."

These dire doomsday theories seemed to fit in with the grim mood of the country. Polls showed that two-thirds of Americans believed their country was adrift. Pollsters found some of the reasons for the gloom: Slow economic growth, dysfunction in Washington, threats from abroad.

"Conservatives today are more mean-spirited, angry, not optimistic, and much more viscerally divisive," said Matthew Dowd, former top strategist for George W. Bush.

The former President, who, in disgrace, was sitting out the race and in a position where everyone was weighing whether his endorsement would be a help or a hindrance. He was quoted as having said, "Nobody ever bought a product that made them feel worse."

Hours before the debate, the Club for Growth, a deep-pocketed conservative coven of right-wingers, announced the launch of a major ad campaign to take down Donald. The group warned conservatives, "He's really just playing us for chumps. It's astonishing that he's running as a Republican."

On Twitter, Donald shot back, calling the group "little respected," and claiming that as recently as a few months before, its leaders had solicited a $4 million contribution from him. "They are spending lobbying and special interest money."

On September 13, 2015, in anticipation of the feverishly anticipated Iowa caucus, scheduled for February 1, 2016, Donald flew in the Trump jet into Iowa, where he was greeted like a rock star. His arrival was strategically timed to coincide with the most frenetic and most emotionally charged football game in the state, the Cy-Hawk game.

[If you don't follow college sports, the Cy-Hawk game was between perennial rivals the Cyclones from Iowa State University (which is located in Ames) and the Hawkeyes from the University of Iowa (which is in Iowa City).]

As a local reporter claimed, "The star-struck crowd greeted him like a stadium rocker during a sprawling tailgate party before kickoff."

Encircled by his security guards, Donald heard one young man call out, "Donald, you rock!"

The candidate jokingly responded, "Did he take me for Mick Jagger? I don't have that kid's wrinkles."

Not all Iowans were so friendly. One activist compared him "to the bad boy you date over the summer before returning to college."

Noting Donald's rise in the polls, and reflecting a pessimistic evaluation for the wannabe Bush Dynasty, Republican fundraiser John Jordan said, "A lot of Jeb donors wish they had their money back."

In visible contrast to his swell of support in Iowa, Donald's visit included an occasional protester. One of them carried a sign, "MR. HATE, LEAVE MY STATE."

Scott Walker, who had once led in the polls, made a brief appearance in Iowa too, even though he'd promised that if elected, he would "wreak havoc" in Washington." During his time there, he took a swipe at Donald, warning, "It takes more than just talk. It takes action. Action speaks louder than words."

When Iowans told Donald that Carson was moving up in the polls, he took a swipe at him. "I don't think Ben, like Jeb Bush, has the energy to make America great again. Ben is a nice man, but when you're negotiating with China, or Japan, they're going to come against you in waves. They think we're all a bunch of jerks, because our leaders are so stupid, and so incompetent, so inept. We need people that are really smart, that have tremendous deal-making skills, and that have great, great energy, unlike Jeb and Ben."

Many Latino pundits viewed Donald's surge in popularity as perhaps a blessing in disguise, claiming that his anti-Latino rhetoric would propel Latinos into an accelerated involvement in activism and voter registration drives. "We must defend ourselves at the ballot box," said Ben Monterroso, Executive Director of the Familiar Vota Education Fund. "We've got to convince Latinos that not participating in civic life has its consequences. In 2016, it showed that nearly 27 million Latinos would be eligible to vote. Mexicans were shown to have been the least likely to naturalize, even though eligible to become U.S. citizens."

Ernest Londoño, an editorialist who has blogged for both The New York Times and The Washington Post, said that what Trump was really saying was "Make America White Again."

Cristóbal Alex, President of the Latino Victory Project, said, "When you're attacked, belittled, characterized as being unworthy and subhuman, it has an effect of unifying and leading the collective action. It has folks like Ricky Martin and Gloria Estefan angry. Our job is to take that anger and turn it into action at the voting booth."

Vanna Slaughter, the head of the Dallas chapter of Catholic Charities, said, "Donald Trump can disappear tomorrow, but the damage is done."

On September 13, Donald responded to Hillary's claim that she'd like to debate him. "She's not a natural. I'm not sure she's even going to make it to the starting gate. She'd be easy to beat. So much baggage. When she talks, it's like reading a script written by a pollster."

Comedian Larry Wilmore claimed, "Hillary is getting Obama-ed by an old white guy."

"Sometimes, Hillary acts insulted that she even has to run at all against that communist, Bernie Sanders," Donald was said to have told his aides. "I think she wants a coronation."

Right before the second GOP debate (September 16, 2015), it was revealed that if "Donald doesn't succeed in making America Great Again, he could launch a Trump for Governor of New York campaign in 2018. Then, a spokesperson for realtors in New York chimed in. "Donald has been informed of our plans. Maybe Trump wouldn't be happy living in Albany, but we think he's smitten at being a politician. A governor is not like being POTUS, but at least it would be the Empire State."

Rudy Giuliani, when informed of the real estate mogul's plan, suggested an alternative post. "I think Trump should run for mayor of New York, because a mayor has to be wild and crazy. Ed Koch was. So was I. To be President, you have to be a little bit circumspect."

The Trump campaign did not immediately respond to these suggestions and recommendations.

AS DONALD PLOTS TO TERMINATE HIS RIVALS,
"The Terminator" Is Designated as the "Replacement Host" of
Celebrity Apprentice

Before this debate, NBC announced that it had signed Arnold Schwarzenegger to take over Donald's hosting role beginning with the upcoming new season (2016-2017) of The Celebrity Apprentice. The bodybuilder and movie action hero, of course, had served (2003-2011) as the Republican governor of California.

The 68-year-old former citizen of Austria said, "I'm thrilled to bring my experience to the boardroom to continue to raise millions for charity."

Ostensibly for legal reasons associated with the need to give equal air time to all candidates of a political race, the network had canned Donald's edition of the popular TV series when he entered the presidential race.

The campaign's second Republican debate, scheduled for September 16, 2015 at the Ronald Reagan Presidential Library in Simi Valley, California, was broadcast through a collaboration of CNN with Salem Radio.

Carly Fiorina was moved up to prime time from her previous status at the Kiddies' Table during the first debate in Cleveland. Moderators were Jake Tapper, Hugh Hewitt, and Dana Bash. This prime-time debate drew 23 million viewers, a million less than had tuned into the first debate on August 6th in Cleveland.

[By now, the phrase "The Kiddies' Table" had emerged as an acceptable term in the 2016 election cycle. It had entered the lexicon to describe the first cluster of participants within a doubleheader debate.

It was established as a way to choreograph the large number of participants into a limited time slot. In a two-hour span, each member of the collective horde would barely have enough time to introduce himself or herself.

As a solution to that dilemma, it was decided to divide the participants, based on their ranking in the polls, segregated into an early debate for candidates performing badly in the polls. That "Kiddies' Table" debate would be three or four hours before the main event, populated with contenders scoring high in the polls, would be scheduled for prime time, usually at either 8PM or 9PM.

No one had agreed on nomenclature for the first debate in Cleveland, but by the second debate, more and more people were calling it "The Kids' Table" or "The Kiddies' Table." The implication of that term was that these losing candidates had "not yet grown up" enough to be included among the adults debating in primetime.

Polling almost at the bottom of the polls, Lindsey Graham, the feisty Senator from South Carolina, said, "Well, when I'm in the first debate, which is the happy hour debate, at five o'clock, start drinking. By nine o'clock, Donald may make sense to you if you drink enough."]

During the early-hour debate at the Kiddies' Table in Simi Valley, Bobby Jindal said, "Trump is not a liberal. He's not a Democrat. He's not a Republican. He's not an Independent. He believes in Donald Trump."

At the time of the debate, a package of Oreos had been one of Donald's favorite snacks, but he claimed, "I'm weaning myself from them now that their parent company, Nabisco, is moving some of its operations from Chicago to Mexico." He then offered his reporters Tic Tacs, saying "They are made in America."

At the (second) debate, Donald uttered the baseless conspiracy theory that childhood immunization can cause autism. However, he did say he favored vaccines, with the stipulation that their applications be extended over longer periods.

Some aspects of the poster on the left, advertising Donald's *Celebrity Apprentice*, evokes a protest at one of his political rallies. Even the headline at the top ("All in for an all-out brawl.") seems to demonstrate the media value of discord, something Donald's enemies were quick to point out in association with his campaign.

On the right, **Arnold Schwarzenegger** is announced as the new host of Celebrity Apprentice. Ironically, as an Austrian immigrant, he had amply demonstrated how far a "New American" could advance. Elected governor of California, and sporting an accent he was never able to lose, he had generated millions and managed the seventh largest economy in the world.

The next day, Alison Singer, president of the Manhattan-based Autism Science Foundation, fired back, claiming, "What he said last night puts children at risk. Trump was reckless in airing this debunked theory in front of millions. We need to put this issue at rest."

Correspondent James Warren wrote: "Donald Trump was a snide, petty, and trashed human being piñata. A sophomoric entertainer. His so-far-winning air of unbridled candor seemed more like peevish arrogance. The prize fight morphed into a rhetorical Ringling Bros. circus."

In post-debate analysis, Marco Rubio was viewed as a strong candidate, and both his and Fiorina's poll numbers increased. Frontrunners like Donald, Jeb Bush, and John Kasich came in for heavy fire, and Rand Paul continued his downward fall.

One journalist described Donald as "Just another face on the crowded stage."

Columnist **Linda Stasi:** A pretty face and, when it came to Donald, an acid tongue and a point of view that was ready to rumble.

His weak command of several key issues was exposed. Bruce Haynes, President of Purple Strategies [a PR and communications firm headquartered in Virginia whose name reflects its bipartisan blend of strategies from both the "blue" (Democratic) and "red" (Republican) camps], said, "Trump didn't meet the moment. Call it the disappearance of Donald Trump."

Hungry for blood and eager to climb over Donald's wounded body, his Republican opponents attacked him head-on. Fiorina shot back at him for calling her ugly. "Women all over the country heard very clearly what Mr. Trump said," she intoned in a voice loaded with disapproval.

Her words were rewarded with wild applause.

Columnist Linda Stasi wrote: "The debate was sort of like watching a ship of fools slowly sink under the weight of so many whoppers that Burger King should sue for copyright infringement. Hell, these clowns even lied about Hillary's lies, which are so great they can stand on their own."

Carly Fiorina lied about the Planned Parenthood abortion video as part of an emotional anti-abortion appeal later denounced both for its insincerity and lack of accuracy.

The candidate falsely claimed, "Watch a fully formed fetus on the table, its heart beating, its legs kicking, while someone says we have to keep it alive to harvest its brain."

As Stasi phrased it, "I defy her to watch it herself, since the video doesn't exist. Oops."

***

In the wake of the debate, although Ben Carson continued to gain support, a poll of Republicans found that 39% still thought that Donald had the best chance of winning the presidency.

He continued to maintain that he was prepared to spend more than $100 million of his own money in the race to the White House. "I will spend $1 billion if need be. Actually, it's not been necessary to spend a lot of money because of the free media coverage I get."

At a post-debate rally in New Hampshire, a Trump supporter addressed the candidate on stage. "We have a problem in this country. It's called Muslims. You know our current President is one. You know he's not even an American."

Donald chuckled. "We need this question."

The unidentified questioner in a Trump shirt continued. "We have training camps growing where they want to kill us. When can we get rid of them?"

Donald responded with a sense of ominous portent, like a thundercloud looming overhead. "We're going to be looking into a lot of different things. We are going to be looking at that and plenty of other things."

Attacks from Hillary and the White House followed in the aftermath of Donald's Muslim response. Hillary said that she was appalled: "He should start behaving like a President and repudiate the level of hatefulness in such a questioner."

The White House fired back, too, its Press Secretary (Josh Earnest) asking, "Is anybody really surprised that this happened at a Donald Trump rally?"

THE WHITE MAN'S LAST STAND
Donald Responds to Cries from an Anguished, Receding America

Many William Buckley-type conservatives were to an increasing degree lamenting the drift of the GOP during the previous decades. One New York voter, David Carnivale, said: "The hatred the Republicans show toward the Mexicans, blacks, gays, and foreigners has become indistinguishable from the positions of the Ku Klux Klan. Republicans adding science, education, the environment, women, liberals, Muslims, all minorities in general, the poor, the sick, and those in need of welfare to the list of despicable things make the more focused hatred of the KKK seems nearly quaint in their narrow specificity."

Hillary seemed to be on the same page as this voter, charging that Donald was, "Lighting the fires of paranoia and prejudice. When you light those lights, you'd better recognize that they can get out of control. He should start dampening them down and putting them out."

Also at the same time, Ben Carson weighed in, outraging millions, when he said, "I would not advocate that we put a Muslim in charge of this nation."

He also told NBC's Chuck Todd, "I do not believe Islam is consistent with the Constitution."

On September 22, angered by Club for Growth's ads, Donald threatened to sue the political action committee. He attorneys sent them a cease-and-desist letter, accusing them of defamation and libel. Alan Garten, Donald's lawyer, said: "The ads of the pitiful little group were replete with outright lies, false, defamatory and destructive statements, and downright fabrications."

That announcement brought tabloid headlines—POOR LITTLE DONALD WILTS UNDER BLITZ. Pundits claimed, "He can dish it out, but he sure can't take it."

On September, Donald announced that he would not be appearing on any more Fox News Channel programs because the network had not been fair to him. He attacked Megyn Kelly but also news host Bill O'Reilly. He challenged O'Reilly "to have, for a change, guests on his show who were not Trump haters."

Thousands gathered along Fifth Avenue to see the motorcade of Pope Francis arriving in Manhattan.

Donald arrived at Trump Tower, where a large midtown crowd caught sight of him entering the skyscraper. The mostly Hispanic crowd angrily shouted, "Feo! FEO!" [In Spanish, that word translates as "ugly."]

From a second floor balcony of Trump Tower, above the Gucci store, Donald had a panoramic viewing platform from which he watched Pope Francis' motorcade proceed down Fifth Avenue.

In Washington, before a joint session of Congress, the Pope's message was markedly different from Donald's. He said, "Millions of people came to this land to pursue their dreams. We are not afraid of foreigners, because most of us were once foreigners."

Around the time of the Pope's visit, Donald aimed his fire power on "Low Energy Jeb." He was informed that his rival candidate had the backing of a Super PAC which was shelling out $37 million to finance a raft of anti-Trump ads on TV that was scheduled to continue, unrelentingly, until February. "Ads alone can't save a hopelessly drowning candidate," was Donald's response.

Throughout most of August and September, Donald had attacked Bush. But with the advance of autumn, he began to view Marco Rubio as an enemy. In a speech before the Family Research Council Values Voter Summit, he said, "You have this clown, Marco Rubio," That pronouncement was met with boos. Donald looked shocked. His subsequent words were softer: "Rubio is really weak on immigration."

Rubio shot back the next day. "Mr. Trump has had a tough week. Carly Fiorina really embarrassed him." Then he continued his attack, suggesting that Donald would not be capable of being commander-in-chief.

On the defensive, Donald accused Rubio of running up personal credit card debt. "He's got no money! Zero!" He also declared that he had a superior head of hair and attacked Rubio for "sweating too much."

In his speech the following day, a reporter approached Donald about Rubio, asking if Donald viewed him as a threat.

"I think he's a baby," Donald answered.

Author James B. Stewart wrote: "One thing is undeniable. Trump is a master of self-promotion, unrivaled even by the likes of the Kardashians. Whatever the outcome of the current presidential campaign, it has made him as famous, as instantly recognizable, and as talked about as anyone in America. Trump figured out early on that fortune follows fame, which is all but undistinguishable from notoriety."

Seth Grossman, a filmmaker and reality TV producer, said, "I've been working in reality TV for ten years, and I can tell you that Mr. Trump is exactly what we look for in our casting process. He's uncomplicated and authentic. You can understand his entire personality from a 15-second sound bite."

"His buildings are big and bold, shouting TRUMP in all caps. The Donald has absolute confidence even in his most wrong-headed opinions, and doubles down on every mistake, comfortable in the assurance that his wealth provides evidence for his intelligence. He doesn't need to be good in his job—if he fails, he creates chaos, and chaos makes good TV."

At Trump Tower on September 29, Donald laid out his plan for revamping the tax code by reducing taxes across the board on both individuals and corporations while eliminating certain deductions. The tax cuts would include not only the middle class, but billionaires like Warren Buffet, worth $62 billion, and Bill Gates, worth even more at $76 billion.

Denounced by hundreds of critics, the tax proposal, as predictable, won the praise of Grover Norquist, the anti-tax activist. "It's pro-growth, it's pro-fairness."

Most economists predicted that Donald's tax plan, if activated, would add trillions of dollars to the national deficit during its first decade.

"ADIOS, AMERICA—

A Reactionary Land of the Sour Tongue, the Frozen Heart"

Ann Coulter is the Darling of the Far Right, and a frequent guest on the O'Reilly Factor on Fox.

Her latest book was the controversial anti-immigration rant, *Adios, America*. She was also an early supporter of Donald. One reviewer said, "Ann and Donald have something in common—both of them would like to kick ass across the Mexican border."

Abraham Lincoln, a Republican, said, "America is the last best hope on earth." But as September rolled into October, Donald and the controversial extreme right-wing author, Ann Coulter, envisioned a different America altogether.

Coulter's latest book had been Adios, America. In it, she described "the philosophy of the receding roar, the mourning for an America that once was and is now being destroyed by foreign people and ideals."

Donald was hearing this anguished cry across the land. As one columnist described it, "There is now a reactionary attitude toward life. This is an attitude that sours the tongue, offends the eye, and freezes the heart."

WEIRD ENTERTAINMENT NEWS:
KANYE WEST BACKS DONALD IN 2016
THEN DESCRIBES HIS VISION ABOUT BECOMING *POTUS* HIMSELF IN 2020

At the MTV Video Music Awards at the end of August, Kanye West [the African-American hip hop recording artist, songwriter, record producer, and fashion designer, who famously married an icon of the social-media industrial complex, Kim Kardashian, in 2014] announced his candidacy for President in 2020. He delivered this surprise as he accepted the Video Vanguard Award.

He facetiously claimed that after his election, by presidential decree, all future music-industry prizes would have to be cleared through him, with at least half of the prizes going to Beyoncé.

Eugene Craig, chairman of the Young Minority Republican Fund, said, "I don't think there's a better way to reach out to minority voters than to bring Kanye into the fold."

Then there was press speculation about possible cabinet posts, Kanye suggesting that after his occupany of the Oval Office, he would "sex it up," appointing his wife, Kim Kardashian, as Energy Secretary. Perhaps Rihanna as Secretary of State and Taylor Swift as Secretary of the Treasury.

"Pot would become legal and mandatory at all White House dinners," Kayne said.

Donald responded to this with, "Even Kanye West loves Trump. He goes around saying, 'Trump is my all-time hero.' He says it to everybody."

One TV pundit mocked the endorsement. "With Kanye's blessing, Trump is almost moving into the White House."

Donald continued to pick up support from unlikely quarters, even from Quarterback Tom Brady. Although it was not an actual endorsement, Brady called him, "A good friend who has done amazing things. He obviously appeals to a lot of people, and he's a hell of a lot of fun to play golf with."

Brady had met him in 2002, when he was a judge at one of Trump's beauty pageants.

It might be a bit of a stretch, but Richard Nixon was cited as the source of an endorsement of Donald delivered way back in 1987, after his wife, Pat, had praised him to her husband after seeing him on an episode of the Phil Donahue Show.

"As you know, Pat is an expert on politics," Nixon later told Donald. "She predicts that whenever you decide to run for office, you will be a winner. Pat was impressed at how you talked about how you could fix

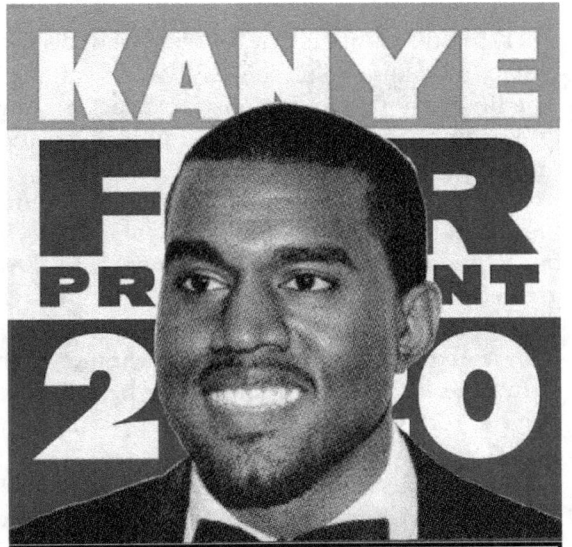

A 2016 supporter of Donald Trump for President, the hip hop mogul, **Kanye West**, was the first to anounce his run for the presidency in 2020.

"America needs another African American President—This time a real African American!"

America."

ANTHONY WEINER
& THE SEXTING BROUHAHA
Donald Attacks Him as a "Perv Sleazebag"

Although Hillary and Donald had once been acquaintances on speaking terms, she joined the fray during the autumn of 2015 and attacked him. "His campaign is all about who he's against, whether it's immigrants, women broadcasters, or aides of other candidates. He is the candidate of—you know—being against. He's great at innuendo and conspiracy theories and really defaming people. That's not what I want to do in my campaign."

To answer her charges, Donald decided to fight back by humiliating Huma Abedin, Hillary's top aide. She was married to Anthony Weiner, a former New York congressman forced to resign because of having been caught in a sexting [text messaging with sexually explicit attachments] scandal. Donald renewed his attack on Weiner, calling him "the perv sleazebag. And his wife is the chief advisor to Hillary. Is that who we want advising her as President?"

Donald continued: "Abedin was a major security risk, and may have shared classified government secrets with Weiner, who might have included them in his sexting to bimbos he has the hots for."

Donald had heard Hillary admit she made a mistake for channeling her e-mail through a private server when she was Secretary of State. "But I plan to keep after her on her fuck-up," he told aides. "My prediction is, she'll end up not at 1600 Pennsylvania Avenue, but in the darkest jail cell."

The Disastrous Cinematic Premiere of Anthony Weiner
"I'M CARLOS DANGER"

Donald's campaign aides seemingly decided that a way to "get to Hillary's vulnerable underbelly" was to attack Weiner and, indirectly, Abedin. He hoped to demonstrate a lack of judgment on Hillary's part by keeping Abedin as her chief aide, even though her husband was mired in scandal.

His attack was made easier when a feature film Weiner, was previewed at the Sundance Film Festival in Park City, Utah, and then sent out to general distribution to theaters across America. The movie was greeted with tidal waves of derisive laughter, which must have brought joy to Donald's heart.

He actually made a cameo appearance in the movie. As part of its its footage, he provides a comment when Weiner dared to run for Mayor of New York City: "We don't want perverts running our city," Donald says. "No perverts!"

The movie focused on the doomed 2013 New York mayoral run. He'd sent revealing cellphone photos of his privates to young women, using the nom de plume (or nom de porn) of "Carlos Danger."

Almost unbelievably, Weiner, after his resignation, was caught in another sexual scandal, also by sending explicit sexual material via a cellphone. This second scandal could not have come at a worse time for him.

Whereas the first scandal had been dubbed in the tabloid press as

Donald attacked former congressman **Anthony Weiner** and his wife, **Huma Abedin**, who was one of Hillary's closest political advisors.

In a scandal identified forever after as "Weinergate," the congressman was forced out of office when it was revealed that he sent sexually explicit photos of himself to young women. In some, his erect penis was partially concealed by boxer briefs. He'd married Huma in July of 2010 in a ceremony officiated by Bill Clinton.

WEINERGATE, the second sexting scandal—dubbed SEVEN INCHES—broke during his attempt to return to politics by announcing his candidacy for Mayor of New York City.

The news of the second scandal broke in July of 2013 and concerned three young women. Weiner admitted sexting the women. Consequently, he had to confront a call from the editorial board of The New York Times, among others, to bow out of the mayoral race, but he refused. He remained in the race until the very end, taking fifth place in the Democratic primary, attracting only 4.9% of the vote.

Donald beefed up his attack on Weiner, emphasizing Hillary's association with him.

Weiner asserted that he will not go to see the film. ("After all, I know the ending.")

He accused its filmmakers, Josh Kriegman (Weiner's former chief of staff) and Elyse Steinberg, of exploiting the fact that his wife, Huma Abedin, 39, is one of Hillary's closest aides. One segment in the film depicts Hillary's campaign workers urging Huma to split from her "deviant husband."

One headline read: "WEINER SHOWS HIS JUNK IN HIS SKIVVIES."

Columnist Andrew Peyser wrote, "He got a sleazy thrill sexting pictures of his engorged manhood to random babes."

During the peak of the controversies that raged, in a dig at Bill Clinton, Weiner said: "I didn't rape anyone, didn't sexually assault anyone, and didn't commit adultery."

Ironically, Weiner's comment about the rape charges that had been brought against Bill Clinton during his presidency provided an excuse for Donald to bring them up again during the presidential campaign.

The news of the Wiener film's upcoming release sparked numerous articles in newspapers across the country. Both "Hillary and Huma," based on unfounded but lurid accusations and insinuations, have faced endless rumors about their own "special friendship."

Donald was made aware of these accusations, and had even read tabloid headlines accusing Hillary of having engaged in lesbian affairs. But, as he told his aides, "We'd better hold off on that for the moment."

Both women have been hailed (even celebrated) for standing by their men. And in Hillary's case, she's been accused of working to destroy her husband's attackers, while simultaneously championing women's rights.

In the sexting scandal, newspapers had a field day drawing parallels between Anthony's penis and its nickname, "Weiner."

After resigning from Congress and a "dignified" delay, **Weiner** entered the 2013 mayoral race in New York City.

Amazingly, seemingly undeterred by the previous brouhaha, he once again transmitted over the internet more sexually explicit pictures of himself for—as it happened—most of the world to see. Obviously, he lost his bid to become the mayor of New York City.

The right-wing New York Post, dredging up the scandal yet again in anticipation of the 2016 race, summed it up: "Hill & Bill, Huma & Carlos—are two political couples mired in sex, lies, and enabling. Not what any presidential campaign wants displayed on the big screen."

Perhaps in response to the unrelenting attacks, Hillary was overheard telling her staffers: "Contrary to popular belief by Trump, I am not the Bride of Frankenstein. Nor do I make lampshades out of human skin. I just want to be a Baby Boomer grandmother lifting Americans out of their current malaise."

In its review of Weiner, film critic Stephen Holden, in The New York Times, wrote: "This cringe-inducing portrait of an arrogant politician's self-immolation, like John Edwards, Bill Clinton, and Eliot Spitzer, shows that even at the risk of career suicide, the penis will not be denied."

OCTOBER, 2015

"In Politics, It's All About Kicking Ass to Win."
—Donald Trump

Donald had driven much of the national news cycle every day during the previous four months with his disruptive presidential campaign.

At Trump Tower, he had time only for crisis-level business emergencies. He told his aides, "That's merely a brush fire. Let Ivanka put it out."

When informed that 60 Minutes wanted to interview him, he said, "Tell those guys to get in line. Everybody in the whole fucking world wants to talk to me."

By early October, the Rasmussen Report revealed that 58% of Republicans believed that Donald would be their presidential nominee for 2016.

Reporters branched out to determine Donald's unique support among voters. Many of them answered his rallying cry "as a yearning for a great leader to restore a lost swagger."

In the words of reporter Mark Leibovich, "The voters wanted a return to a less complex, less politically correct, and more secure nation. Trump's war on political correctness is especially pleasing to many of the white voters of the GOP, who feel usurped by newcomers and silenced by progressive gains that women, Hispanics, and gays have enjoyed."

In a 70-minute speech in Dallas, Donald ridiculed John Kerry for breaking his leg in a bicycle accident during nuclear negotiations with Iran. "So weak, so pathetic. The people from Iran are saying, 'What a schmuck.'"

"Even if I lose, and I won't, but if I did, I'll go back to being Donald Trump, only bigger. I've had more than my 15 minutes of fame," he said.

Occasionally, he mentioned a former Democratic president. "Jimmy Carter used to get off Air Force One carrying his luggage. I don't want a President who is gonna come off carrying a large bag of underwear. We want someone who is going to go out and kick ass and win."

It wasn't just Democrats that Donald ridiculed. He also attacked figures from the Republican Establishment, calling Karl Rove "a totally incompetent jerk."

When it came to criticizing front runner Hillary, he had a lot of help.

A copy of Edward Klein's explosive new tell-all arrived at Donald's office. It is not clear if he read it or even riffled through it, but he was told about it.

The book was Unlikeable—The Problem With Hillary. Klein claimed that during her tenure as Secretary of State, she became unhinged and exhibited violent psychotic behavior. He wrote of her confrontations with Obama, during which she accused him of feeding stories about her Email server to the media.

At one point, Klein quoted her as yelling at the Commander-in-Chief, "Call off your fucking dogs."

In another episode, he wrote that Bill Clinton accused his wife of looking old, telling her "to get a face-lift."

Donald also kept a keen eye trained on Vice President Joe Biden, suspecting that he might enter the race competing with Hillary for the Democratic nod. "What's that goof ball saying now?" he asked his aides.

There was long-standing speculation that **Joe Biden,** Vice President of the United States, would toss his hat into the presidential ring, challenging Hillary for the Democratic nomination.

Many of Donald's aides feared that the popular Biden might be more serious challenger than Hillary. "We've got a lot of shit to throw at her," said one aide. "Less so at Joe."

From the sidelines, Biden made an occasional headline, as there was increased speculation that he might enter the race for the Democratic nomination. He was the first to endorse same-sex marriage, long before Obama and Hillary.

Biden was the keynote speaker on October 4 at the Human Rights Campaign's annual star-studded dinner. He claimed, "There are homophobes still left. Most of them are running for President."

He also threw his support behind allowing transgender people to serve openly in the U.S. military. "All Americans are qualified to serve. Transgender rights are the civil rights of our time."

Biden also said that "Gays and lesbians shouldn't fear those shrill voices trying to undo same-sex marriage and other advances, because Americans have moved so far beyond them and their appeals to prejudice and fear."

Donald was an early riser, and every day, his aides prepared an early-morning dispatch of press comments about himself, both favorable and unfavorable. Sometimes, the negative comments would cause him to explode with fury.

Columnist Nicholas Kristof wrote about the frontrunners in the GOP, many of whom, it seemed, didn't have even the most basic qualifications. "If I wanted a circus ringmaster, I'd hire Trump. If I wanted advice on brain surgery, I'd turn to Carson. Fiorina would make an articulate television pundit. But for President?"

Pundits continued to write columns or analyze the political situation on TV shows, vigorously stating: "Trump as President of the United States? No Way! It's not going to happen! A slow fade leading to a weak finish in Iowa is possible," wrote Jonathan Bernstein for Bloomberg View. "Trump is not going to be the GOP nominee, or even come close."

On October 14, Donald claimed that he needed Secret Service protection, because of the many large crowds he was drawing as frontrunner. He cited presidential hopeful Barack Obama receiving protection during May of 2007, about a year and a half

Throughout the 2015-2016 presidential race, **Frank Bruni**, columnist for *The New York Times*, wrote some of their most perceptive articles about Donald's race for the White House and the dilemma he posed for the GOP.

He described Donald's campaign as "a carnival."

before the November 2008 election that propelled him into office. "Because I'm a Republican, they don't give a shit," Donald said.

Columnist Frank Bruni summed it up: "The slow torture of the Republican primary knows no limit. First, Donald Trump turns it into a carnival, then Ben Carson comes along with his insanity about the Holocaust and guns. Between them, they own nearly 50% of the Republican vote, according to the most recent national surveys."

Donald wasn't the only Republican attacking Republicans. The Texas Senator, Ted Cruz, was becoming a threat. Donald read with glee when George W. Bush told the press, "I just don't like that guy Cruz. He's cynically opportunistic and self-serving."

Cruz had worked as a policy advisor to George W. in his race for the White House in 2000.

Almost daily, Donald uttered something that morphed into a headline. Told that Ben Carson was now leading in the polls in Iowa, Donald said, "Too much Monsanto in the corn creates issues in the brain."

He continued his attacks on Muslims, claiming he was "absolutely certain that he'd close certain mosques—centers of terrorism—and revoke passports from U.S. citizens in our fight against the Islamic state. If a man goes out and fights for ISIS, he can't come back here."

La divinissima—grand chic of the old-time feminists, **Gloria Steinem**. The slogan on her T-shirt widely publicized her stand on abortion.

She found Donald a horror. On a scale of one to ten, she had rated him less than a one, especially if he lost all his money.

He also claimed that if he'd been President, he could have prevented 9/11. "I am extremely, extremely tough on illegal immigration. I'm extremely tough on illegals coming into this country," he said on Fox News.

He told a biographer, "For the most part, you can't respect people, because most people aren't worthy of respect. People are really vicious, and no place are they more vicious than in their relationships with the opposite sex."

Donald aroused fury among the Muslims, but leading feminists also attacked him, including Gloria Steinem, who had been defending women's rights for half a century. The 81-yesr-old author said she was still baffled about Trump saying that model Heidi Klum was "no longer a 10."

"Why did nobody bother to say Trump hasn't ever been a one, much less a ten? If he lost his wallet, how many women would be interested? I just don't understand why what he dishes out isn't equalized and coming back at him."

The bombastic billionaire was said to have become even more bombastic when the latest poll showed that Carson had overtaken him in the race, garnering a 26% approval rating, in contrast to his 22%. This was the first time in more than three months that the real estate mogul had not led in a national poll, a New York Times/CBS News survey revealed.

He was skeptical of the polls, suggesting that Carson—"a lot of contradictions"—will face greater scrutiny from the press. "One thing I know about a frontrunner is that he gets analyzed 15 different ways from China. A lot of things about Carson will come out!"

He also questioned Carson's Seventh-Day Adventist faith.

At the Third Debate, GOP Candidates
LASH OUT AT THE MODERATORS
Donald Wins an Endorsement from a Non-Mexican Rapist

The third Republican debate was held on October 28, 2015, at the University of Colorado at Boulder. CNBC moderators included Carl Quinatanilla, Becky Quick, and John Harwood, each destined to endure "a night of hell" before millions of viewers.

The debate was supposed to have focused on the economy, but it quickly disintegrated into a generalized attack on the media, especially as it applied to their propensity for formulating "gotcha" (entrapment) questions.

The two frontrunners, Donald and Carson, each threatened to withdraw if the debate were not trimmed to two hours instead of three. Their wish was granted, even though the shortened venue virtually guaranteed that not every participant would be able to express him or herself within the moments allocated.

The number of participants at "The Kiddies' Table" had by now been reduced to four "losers" (Donald's words). Rick Santorum hopelessly continued his pursuit of the presidency, as did Bobby Jindal, Lindsey Graham, and George Pataki.

The main debate began at 6PM MDT (Mountain Daylight Time, aka 8PM on the East Coast), and soon, the candidates, while relatively restrained with one another, became involved in a slugfest with the moderators, calling them biased.

"The questions from the so-called moderators were designed to garner ratings rather than a substantive discussion of the issues," Donald said. "The questions revealed just why most Americans don't trust the media."

Ted Cruz entered the fray, claiming, "A debate should not be a cage match."

Donald also charged that "The Democratic candidates and their moderators get a love fest, while the attack dogs are unleashed on us."

During the commentary that followed the debate, most television pundits defined Ted Cruz, Marco Rubio, and Chris Christie as the winners, primarily because of their take-no-prisoners attack on the moderators. Donald and Ben Carson had no memorable moments, but squeaked to the finish line, unlike Jeb Bush and John Kasich, who delivered lackluster performances.

Cameron Joseph of the Washington Bureau of the New York Daily News wrote: "Rubio shined, Kasich punched, Trump squirmed, and Jeb Bush fizzled. Republican candidates spent more time beating up the media than they did targeting each other."

When attacked, which was often, Donald counterpunched, but failed to refute a single charge.

Shortly after the debate, Donald stood next to a microphone facing the press. Alongside him was Mike Tyson, whom Donald had promoted so heavily years before during the boxer's glory days in Atlantic City. The disgraced ex-boxer, who had since then been imprisoned for rape, heartily endorsed Donald's presidency.

As one reporter wrote, "Trump attacks Mexican rapists but accepts the endorsement of an American rapist."

CAMPAIGN FEUDS FROM MARRIAGES PAST
Ivana Says That Melania, as First Lady, Would Be HORRID

In early November, Donald released one of his seemingly endless books, this one called Crippled America: How to Make It Great Again. Basically, it was a self-promotional claim that only he could make America great again, and only if he were elected President. Seventeen pages were devoted to "About the Author," listing his properties—and aircraft—and detailing the buildings either developed or licensed in his name. The book opened in seventh place on Amazon's best-seller list.

November also opened with Ivana, "the would-have-been First Lady," trashing Melania, Donald's third wife. Despite Ivana's attack on the woman who had supplanted her, Ivana was supportive of Donald's seeking the presidency. "The problem is," Ivana wrote, "what is he going to do with that third wife of his? She can't talk, she can't give a speech, she doesn't go to events, she doesn't seem to want to get involved."

As for Donald, Ivana claimed, "He was always meant to be a politician."

"Donald's dalliances with Marla Maples while married to me may have derailed his political ambitions for a couple of decades," Ivana said. "At that time, America came to hate him because of how badly he treated me."

NOVEMBER, 2015

"Some mosques are terrorists' cells."
—Donald Trump

Potential First Ladies aside, Donald moved into November forging forward with some of his most controversial positons. "I will certainly implement a database to track Muslims in this country," he proclaimed. "There should be a lot of systems beyond databases." That comment came in the wake of an earlier suggestion that, as President, he might have to close down certain mosques used for terrorist cells.

Asked how his database would differ from how Nazis tracked Jews and forced them to wear the Yellow Star, Donald said, "You tell me."

In the wake of enormous backlash, he tweeted, "I didn't suggest a database—a reporter did. Nonetheless, we must defeat Islamic terrorism—words Obama can't

WOMAN ESCORTED OUT OF TRUMP RALLY

Across the country and across the world, Muslims turned out at protest rallies with slogans, signs, and rants against Donald's threat to bar them from the United States.

In the photo above, **Rose Hamid**, standing in silent protest wearing a logo that announced "Salam, I come in Peace" was evicted from a Trump rally in Rock Hill, South Carolina.

even utter—and have surveillance, including a watchlist, to protect America."

His position drew fire from his rivals, with Hillary calling it "shocking rhetoric," and Jeb Bush attacking Donald "for manipulating people's angst and their fears."

Carson, however, seemed to lend his support to Donald's position. "If there's a rabid dog running around in your neighborhood, you're probably not going to assume something good about that dog. It doesn't mean you hate all dogs, but you're putting your intellect into motion."

To the same degree he attacked Muslims, Donald defended veterans. On November 1, headlines read: "TRUMP WOULD AX BIGS AND REDO FED AGENCY"

[The headline, of course, referred to the U.S. Veterans Affairs Department, the "bigs" being the officers who ran it.]

In a speech in front of the warship Wisconsin in Norfolk, Virginia, he outlined his plan to reform the U.S. Veterans Affairs Department. As part of his proposal, he would create a more streamline agency and allow veterans to opt for a private health care provider. "They have earned the freedom to choose."

He revealed no plan, however, about how his new programs would be financed.

As Donald Calls Jeb! "Forrest Gump" and Denounces Dr. Carson's Theories as "Bullshit"
OBAMA MOCKS THE GOP CANDIDATES

On November 3, 2015, at a Democratic fundraiser, Obama poked fun at the other GOP candidates, claiming that they can't handle the tough questions. "Every one of them says I am weak, and that Putin is kicking sand in my face. But then the Republicans' frontrunner claims he can straighten Putin out. But then it turns out these wannabe Presidents can't handle a bunch of CNBC moderators."

"If a candidate can't handle those guys, I don't think the Chinese and the Russians are going to be too worried about any of them," Obama said.

At around the time Obama was mocking GOP candidates, so was Donald. Early on the morning of November 4, he unleashed a slew of nasty images targeting Jeb Bush. He compared the former Governor of Florida to a Nazi, mocking his ties to Mexico, and claiming he was intellectually disabled. "ADIOS JEB, AKA JOSE!"

The tweet contained a collage of derogatory pictures, one of them showing Jeb next to a swastika, another depicting him as Forrest Gump. A third jeering cartoon had Jeb in a Mariachi costume and sombrero, standing in a desert studded with cacti.

The following day, Donald released his first batch of ads on radio, mostly a rant against immigrants and the articulation of a "pro-veteran hawkish platform."

"Obama is a total disaster," a voiceover proclaimed. "Donald promises to repeal Obamacare and replace it with something better."

Then, Donald himself chimed in with: "I'll take care of

Left photo: **Jeb Bush** and his overused, never-very-effective campaign logo.

Right photo: **Tom Hanks** playing the title role (a slow-witted but kind and well-intentioned child of god), in *Forrest Gump* (1994).

veterans and make our military so strong that nobody will mess with us. I'll secure our borders, and yes, we'll have that wall."

Based to some degree on the distribution of ads like that, the Department of Homeland Security announced that both Ben Carson and Donald would soon have Secret Service protection. Both candidates had requested such security a month earlier.

Some of Donald's aides felt that they didn't need to go after Carson since he seemed to be self-destructing with his every utterance.

"WHAT THE TUT?" a headline had screamed when, for seemingly no reason at all, Carson claimed that the Biblical character of Joseph built the pyramids of Egypt to store grain and not as monuments for the burial of the Pharoahs. He made this silly pronouncement, which didn't contain a "grain" of truth, at Andrews University, the flagship educational institution of the Seventh-day Adventist Church, in southwestern Michigan.

Donald denounced Carson's "idiotic theory as strange."

In the same speech, Carson called for transgendered people to have their own bathrooms. "It's not fair for them to make everybody else feel uncomfortable. It's one of the things I don't particularly like about the LGBT community."

Carson's latest prattles included affirmations that the Jews could have prevented the Holocaust if they had been armed, and that men entered prison straight and came out gay.

By the first week of November, Carson's lies on the campaign began to catch up with him. He had previously asserted that he had been granted a prestigious scholarship to West Point, although later, when confronted with facts to the contrary, he backed off from that boast. In the wake of these and a number of other embarrassments, Carson lost his lead in Iowa, receiving 23% of the vote, in contrast to Donald's accumulation of 25%.

The West Point claim had earned Carson the headline: "HE'S FULL OF BULL."

Other stories soon appeared, some of them debunking Carson's rejection of the theory of evolution. Carson, despite his training as a surgeon and scientist, had asserted, "It's a bunch of fairytales encouraged by Satan."

Some columnists concluded, "Carson is about the craziest person ever to seek the presidency."

He continued to get blasted in the media. On November 8, exposé articles appeared questioning statements he had made in his autobiography, Gifted Hands. In it, he had claimed that he protected white students in his high school the day after Martin Luther King's assassination in 1968. Detroit was riddled with race riots. One of them ravaged the city's Southwestern High School, whose enrollment of blacks exceeded that of whites.

His account was widely discredited by witnesses on the scene at the time.

To defend himself, as it applied to the media's perceived obsession with negative slants on politicians and celebrities, Carson said, "There's got to be a scandal. There's got to be some nurse a candidate had an affair with—there's got to be something. They have gotten desperate. Next week, it will be my kindergarten teacher who claims to the press that I peed in my pants. It's ridiculous!"

On November 8, Donald was thrust into the orbit of millions of Americans when he hosted Saturday Night Live. Before his appearance, some 200 protesters rallied to denounce his appearance on SNL, defining him as "a racist piece of shit." The demonstrators massed outside Rockefeller Center in Manhattan, where the broadcast had been scheduled. Protesters included Mexicans whose signs displayed the words, "I AM NOT A RAPIST!"

One of the late-night skits presented on SNL depicted Donald in the Oval Office in 2018, after having defeated ISIS, after having persuaded Mexico to pay for the wall, and after having made Putin cry.

A moment that drew laughs and applause occurred when the show's co-anchor Michale Che, who is black, said "Whenever rich old white guys start bringing up the good old days, my Negro senses start tingling."

Despite its flashes of humor, most reviewers panned the broadcast as "boring."

In the wake of the SNL satire, James Parker, a contributing editor for The Atlantic, advocated a new journalistic standard wherein Donald's hair would be defined as off-limits, unsuitable for future satires.

"By all means, lampoon or deconstruct Trump's opinions, which I don't believe are really opinions at all, but random clots and thrombi of rhetorical ectoplasm gathered from the ether with high-end paranormal pooper-scoopers. Yes, make hay with inconsistencies, stick your satirical probes in the hinds of his fascinating and possibly apocalyptic personality. But leave his hair alone."

"His hair is in the strictest sense powerless. It's doing its best—as hair, as a hairstyle. It lies there and tries and makes no replay. It's quite a nice color. I once described (in print) an actor in a Harry Potter movie as 'sturgeon-lipped.' Why did I do that? Seeking the cheap high of invective, nothing more. Lay off that stuff, is my advice. Going for the hair may not bother him (who knows?) but it's not good for you—or your satire."

Donald was aboard his private plane when it flew into Iowa in mid-November. The rise of Carson in the polls had baffled him. During a 95-minute appearance on an Iowa stage, he used terms like "pathological" to describe his opponent. He mocked Carson's account wherein he tried to stab a friend only to have his large belt buckle deflect the blade.

Donald stepped from the podium to perform the most unpresidential "show and tell." Thrusting his arm as if stabbing and pulling on his own belt, he asked. "Anyone have a knife you want to try on me?"

The buckle wouldn't have stayed in place!" he said. "Give me a break!" he cautioned the voters of Iowa. "Don't be fools. Don't vote for this irrational man!"

As Donald continued to campaign in anticipation of the Iowa caucus, there were stories about recent developments linked to a former frontrunner for the GOP presidential nomination in 2012. News about Congresswoman Michele Bachmann had popped up during her November, 2015 tour of Israel. The former Republican presidential candidate had asserted her desire to convert as many Jews as possible to Christianity. Her tour of Israel had been organized by the Family Research Council, which she said was in preparation for the Second Coming of Christ. In a (horrified) response, Rabbi Avi Shafran, a spokesperson for Agudath Israel of America, told The Jerusalem Post, "Ms. Bachmann's mission should be a reminder of the importance of Jewish education, since the surest defense against missionizing is authentic Jewish knowledge."

THE FOURTH DEBATE
"Ignorance and Arrogance"

Staged in Milwaukee, Wisconsin, on November 10, 2015, the fourth debate was a joint production of the Fox Business Network and The Wall Street Journal, and as such was aired with the stated intention of focusing on business policies and the economy. The moderators included Gerard Baker, Neil Cavuto, and Maria Bartiromo.

Removed from the debate, based on their low showings in the polls, were Christie and Huckabee. The main lineup featured Donald, positioned front and center in the lineup of the prime-time participants, flanked by Carson, Rubio, Cruz, Jeb Bush, Fiorina, Kasich, and Rand Paul.

At the Kiddies' Table, Bobby Jindal appeared for the final time, just before he ended his run for the White House based on his abysmal showing in the polls.

For the most part, the fourth debate was generally rather staid, and didn't seem to generate many firecrackers. Mostly, the candidate argued with each other over jobs and spending. Many reporters evaluated it afterward as a "snoozefest."

Donald returned to his familiar anti-immigrant stance, praising a Federal court for ruling earlier in the week for the blockage of several of President Obama's executive orders on immigration. He tangled with Kasich over the issue. "I've built a company worth billions of dollars—I don't have to hear from this man," Donald said, casting a bitter look at the Governor of Ohio.

Of the many Republican candidates campaigning in Iowa in anticipation of the much-watched Iowa caucus (scheduled for February 1, 2016), Donald was the only one who kept referring to Vladimir Putin.

"If Putin wants to go and knock the hell out of ISIS, I'm all for it, 100 percent, and I can't understand how anybody would be against it."

Jeb Bush and Donald tangled onstage over foreign policy. There was little love or charity evident between the two candidates. Jeb called Donald's world view "that of a child playing a board game. Monopoly is not how the world works."

In a post-debate evaluation, Bush was described as "still inarticulate" by columnist Charles Krauthammer.

"I suppose Cruz and Rubio did well, which I guess they did if you like illogical economic programs and totally terrifying views on foreign affairs," wrote columnist Gail Collins.

Under the headline "TRUMP MAY TAKE GOP DOWN WITH HIM," Dick Polman of the Cagle Syndicate wrote, "If success is measured in ignorance and arrogance, then the winner of the Republican fourth debate was Donald Trump. I can't tell the difference between his real-life schtick and his Saturday Night Live act."

Reporter Maggie Haberman summed up Donald's dilemma in Iowa: "Mr. Trump's seemingly steady flow of support in those polls could begin to give way, especially as more Republicans turn to more sober-minded candidates with military and national security experience following the terrorist attacks in Paris."

Dave Carney, a Republican political strategist who ran Rick Perry's failed presidential race in 2012, said, "Trump is walking a tightrope. He loves the applause of the crowd 100 stories down. But when you start to make fun of being Born Again and Redemption and Christian faith in our party, you can talk yourself right off the tightrope."

"Trump's attacks on Carson could be the hole in the dike," said Ed Rollins, a veteran GOP consultant.

"Pray for Donald," Carson said in the wake of Donald's denunciation of him based on his many untruths that had been baldly exposed in the press. At one point, Donald had called him pathological and even compared him to a child molester.

"Give me a break," Donald said. "How stupid are the people of Iowa to fall for Carson's crap?"

Donald's voice offered no comfort to the unemployed or to those who were at the lower end of the wage scale, some of

---

Donald received a report that **Michele Bachmann**, the former (notorious and ill-informed) congresswoman from Minnesota, was in Israel, urgently warning its people, much to the consternation of local rabbis, about the imminent second coming of Jesus Christ.

In 2013, Bachmann was under investigation by the House Ethics Committee, the Federal Election Commission, the Iowa Senate Ethics Committee, the Urbandale Police Department and the Federal Bureau of Investigation because of alleged campaign finance violations in her 2012 campaign for President.

them holding down two jobs as a means of supporting their families. "I hate to say it, but we have to leave the minimum wage the way it is," Donald said on the campaign trail. "People have to go out, they have to work really hard and to get into that upper stratosphere."

Columnist Albor Ruiz wrote: "Say what you will about Trump, you have to admire this guy's gall. For a filthy rich guy, born with a proverbial silver spoon in his mouth, poor people are so because they do not work hard enough—and not because despite being overworked, they are paid hunger wages by greedy bosses like him."

Donald might have faced an uphill battle in Iowa, but in New Hampshire, he was clearly the favorite, beating out "JEB!" and "Little Marco Rubio," each of whom were stuck in the mud of single-digit approval ratings. The conclusion of the pundits was this: A New England state that's usually a force for moderation wasn't following that script this time around in going all out for "The Donald."

Whether he used them or not, Donald was supplied almost daily with controversial material and issues he could use against his rivals if he chose to do so. At a point in the campaign where Iowa polls indicated almost equivalent approval ratings between himself and Cruz, he was supplied with information about the background of Rafael Cruz, Ted's father.

In the 1950s, Rafael was said to have been a Cuban revolutionary and a devoted supporter of Fidel Castro. When he opted to emigrate to the United States, although the U.S. government granted him political asylum, he chose instead to move to Alberta, where he became a citizen of Canada. Consequently, the Texan senator (Ted Cruz) was born in Alberta, a fact that later provided ample fodder for Donald's allegations that Cruz, if nominated, would be legally ineligible for election to the nation's highest office.

Donald claims that his chief rival, **Ted Cruz**, was an "Anchor Baby" born in Alberta, Canada, and therefore not eligible to run for President of the United States.

He also learned that in the 1950s, Rafael Cruz, Ted's father, had been a Cuban revolutionary who supported the communist overthrow of the Cuban government by Fidel Castro.

Trump's Murky Misuse of
BOGUS CRIME STATISTICS

On November 22, Donald tweeted a rant called "USA Crime Statistics—2015."

A photo depicted a dark-skinned man with a bandanna and a mask holding a gun. The abbreviated and loosely defined "statistics" supplied alongside the illustration listed, with very few modifiers, and with no statistical breakdown, the percentages of "Blacks Killed by Whites" (2%); and "Whites Killed by Blacks," (81%). The figures it cited derived, the tweet claimed, from the "Crime Statistics Bureau—San Francisco," an entity that didn't exist.

His tweet was expedited just a day after he'd been jeered by a protester wearing a Black Lives Matter shirt. The man was kicked out of a Donald rally in Birmingham, Alabama. In a video, several pro-Trumpers were seen tackling the man, one white man punched him, and a woman kicked him while he was on the ground, CNN reported. From the podium, Donald demanded, "Get him the hell out of here!"

Forced to leave, the protester left, shouting FUCK DONALD TRUMP! No arrests were made.

After his tweet, the press revealed that almost all of the murders happen within a race, the Department of Justice claimed that 84% of white murder victims are actually killed by white perpetrators.

Columnist Shaun King, an African American, wrote: "America has grown to love Donald Trump, not in spite of what we saw as unelectable gaffes, but because of them. Whether we like it or not, the horrific white supremacy of Trump is a reflection of a very real portion of America. Worse than David Duke, he is the most racist, offensive, presidential candidate in modern American history…and he's in the lead."

In the wake of the November, 2015, ISIS terrorist attacks in Paris, in which 130 people were killed, the approval ratings of Donald in national polls increased. Even so, still plagued with the perceived lack of support and cooperation from the "Establishment GOP," he refused to rule out an independent run for the White House in 2016.

On ABC's This Week, he was asked what he'd do if GOP opponents "try to take you out."

"I will see what happens," Donald said. "I have to be treated fairly. If

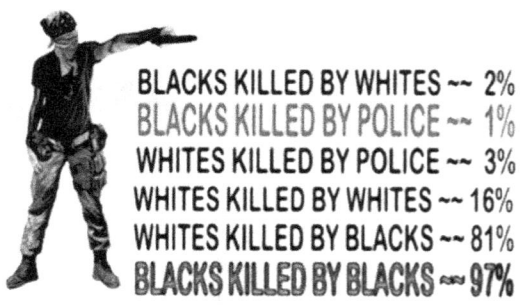

Some of Donald's tweets—including this ambiguous and confusing attachment demonstrating dubious statistics about perpetrators and their race—were loudly denounced by sociologists as dangerous, divisive, and misleading.

I'm treated fairly, I'm fine."

He pledged that he would be "the toughest of the candidates" running for President.

***

Reporters assigned to Donald quickly noted that he often relied on generalities to dodge hard questions about policy. He had an avoidance of specifics, often sidestepping delivery of direct answers in a generalized refusal to be pinned down.

Rich Lowry of The National Review, noted, "Trump has an amazing ability to backtrack without incurring any political harm from doing so. His supporters don't seem to care very much about consistency from one interview or statement to the next, as long as he's projecting strength."

Virtually every campaign speech delivered by Donald contained anti-Muslim rhetoric.

One of the low moments for Donald's campaign came in late November when he claimed that thousands of New Jersey Muslims had been televised dancing at the news of the September 11 attacks on the World Trade Center.

When he was challenged to prove that assertion, he said he watched it on television, and he cited a story by reporter Serge Kovaleski in The Washington Post.

One of the most controversial moments in Donald's campaign came when he mocked the disabilities of reporter **Serge Kovaleski** of the Washington Post.

Kovaleski suffers from a disabling malfunction of his limbs. From a televised podium at one of his rallies, **Donald** delivered a cruel and mocking parody of the man's disability.

Kovaleski suffers from a disabling malfunction of the limbs called arthrogryposis [a congenital defect of the limbs characterized by severe contractures of multiple joints.]

Kovaleski later came forward to tell the press that the reports of Muslims dancing in the streets after 9/11 were never verified.

[In fairness to Donald, such news was indeed broadcast on television on September 11, and millions of New Yorkers heard it. However, much misinformation was broadcast amid the horrified confusion and consternation of that fateful day.]

When Donald, at a South Carolina rally, heard that Kovaleski was backing down on what he had presented as news within his earlier story, Donald ridiculed him cruelly. "You have to see this poor guy," Donald said, as he flailed his arms around in spastic gestures, mocking Kovaleski's disabilities. It was caught on video, fomenting outrage and denunciations.

He later defended himself. "I would never mock a person who has a disability. I have long donated money to groups supporting people with disabilities. Nobody gives more money to Americans with disabilities than I do. I don't mock people who have problems, believe me."

Appearing with Chuck Todd on NBC, the broadcaster challenged him on the "Dancing Muslims" assertion. Donald stuck by his charge, insisting that he saw this "dance of death" on television.

Near the end of November, Donald became alarmed when polls showed Ted Cruz doubling his support in Iowa, bypassing Carson and nearing Donald's own lead. Cruz stood at 23%, Donald at 25%, newspapers revealed. Carson had surged ahead, but a series of negative stories associated with claims about his past had harmed him with evangelicals.

Voters cited America's foreign policy and the rise of terrorists as the issues that made them favor Cruz. Donald was cited as the candidate best able to deal with economic issues. Carson clearly won out among evangelicals, based partly on his anti-abortion and anti-gay rhetoric.

Before Cruz and Donald launched World War III during the coming year, he praised the rebellious senator from Texas. "He's backed everything I've said. Ted's agreeing with me 100%."

Reporter Cameron Joseph wrote: "Selecting Cruz as his Veep would give Trump someone on the ticket with government experience—even if the highlight of his work history was shutting down that government. The pick of Cruz might shield him—a tiny bit—from charges of racism against Hispanics, as Cruz is half-Cuban."

As for Marco Rubio, in contrast to Donald, who was 69, the junior senator from Florida accented his youth. "If I am your nominee, we will be the party of the future." Whenever he could, he seemed to disparage the grandmotherly Hillary and the grandfatherly Donald as relics of a bygone age. History and voting patterns have shown, however, that GOP primary voters tend to value experience above youth.

Many reporters such as Matt Flegenheimer noted that foul-mouthed terms and language never heard in equivalent settings before were cropping into the campaign, "shit" being a favorite of Donald's in particular.

"The reasons for saltiness seemed varied—a play for machismo, perhaps, particularly as national security becomes a chief focus, or a signal of vitality, rawness, a willingness to break through the din of the overstuffed field of competitors."

As was noted, candidates hoping to outcurse Donald were outmatched. He often called things "political bullshit," and was fond of the expression, "You bet your ass."

He warned his enemies on Twitter, "Treat us fairly or otherwise, I'll tweet the fucking daylights outta ya."

In defense of his penchant for cursing, Donald cited Joe Biden, whose sometimes equivalent epithets were famously called into use during his description and defense of Obama's then newly inaugurated health care law as "a big fucking deal."

This photo seemed harmless at first, as candidates **Donald Trump** and **Hillary Clinton** came together on stage. Bullets and flames soaked in "industrial scale hatred" were about to begin.

Never in the history of American politics has any woman been so attacked and reviled. Even the "Bitch of Buchenwald," who made lampshades from Jewish skin, got a better press than the former Secretary of State. Across the nation, Trump-pumped crowds roared, "Lock her up."

Trump mocked and attacked her handling of government documents, claiming that as president, he would be a diligent custodian of the secrets of the U.S. government. Should his devoted fans have believed that?"

PART FOUR
THE WINTER OF TRUMP

THE POPE VS. THE BILLIONAIRE
Pope Francis and Donald Launch a "Holy War of Words"

"DO YOU KNOW WHAT THEY SAY ABOUT A MAN WITH SMALL HANDS?"

Rubio Asks a Crowd of Mocking Voters.
Donald Is Forced to Defend the Size of His Penis

DONALD QUOTES FROM MUSSOLINI
And Gets Offered the Support of the KKK & the American Nazi Party

The GOP vs. THE TABLOIDS
The National Enquirer Assaults Republican Candidates With an Exposé of Porn Links, Gay Parties, & a Police Record of an Arrest in Miami's "Hustler Park."

CHAPTER SIX

VENOM AND DISCORD
"Trumpkins are Mental Midgets and Xenophobic Troglodytes."

"HILLARY GOT SCHLONGED
by Obama"

—Donald Trump

REPUBLICAN RAGE & FRUSTRATION
Donald's Rivals, & Their "Long, Bootless Slogs through Alligator-Infested Swamps"

December of 2015 began with what appeared to be a clever political move: Donald Trump would meet with about a hundred black ministers and, after some spirited conversations, would perhaps emerge with their endorsement of his candidacy.

Donald himself had called for such a meeting, hoping that the endorsement of so many black ministers would help dispel charges that he was a bigot.

But despite his intentions, the meeting, as it had been planned, never really materialized. Perhaps bowing to pressure from the Black Lives Matter movement and to other activists, there was much backtracking among the ministers, many of whom refused to appear with him at Trump Tower in Manhattan.

Only a few ministers showed up, and of those who did attend, some seemed out of place. Brebon Hall, a preacher from Toledo, Ohio, told the press, "It appears as if Trump is a possible racist based upon some of the things he's said about black America."

After the "scaled-down" confab, Donald, as was his custom, put a good spin on it, claiming, "There was great love in the room. They liked me, and I liked them."

The discussion had centered on unemployment in the black community, police shootings, and deficiencies in urban education.

Many pastors claimed that although they'd been invited, they'd refused to attend. Corletta J. Vaughn, Senior Pastor at the Holy Spirit Cathedral of Faith in Detroit, said "My constituency would murder me if I showed up."

The meeting, even in its scaled-down format, drew fiery denunciations from many African-Americans. The Rev. Jamal Bryant, pastor of the Empowerment Temple Church in Baltimore, called the ministers who went to Trump Tower, "Prostitutes seeking their 15 minutes of fame. My objection to Trump is that he is flagrantly against humanity."

For having said that, The Rev. Darell Scott, who had helped organized the event, sharply rebuked Bryant. "For respectable preachers to be called 'prostitutes on a pole' is very insulting, demeaning, and misogynistic to say the least. If Trump called black preachers 'prostitutes on a pole,' the entire nation would be in an uproar."

Donald did get another endorsement from the Rev. James David Manning, known as "the Harlem Hate Pastor." He had compared President Obama to Hitler and had accused both George H.W. Bush and George W. Bush of each having had sex with some one hundred men.

There was a sign outside his Atlah Worldwide Church on Lenox Avenue in Harlem that proclaimed: "Obama has released the homo demons on the black man. Look out black woman! A white homo may take your man!"

Manning claimed that "Donald Trump will help black people escape the abyss created by Bill Clinton *and* Martin Luther King, Jr."

By Christmas of 2015, Donald Trump had invaded virtually every aspect of popular culture. Feature writers at Halloween had managed to associate Pumpkins with Trumpkins in the popular imagination to the point where consumers began to confuse the terms.

In the upper photo, a charity "pumpkin carve" in Pennsylvania made special note of the award-winning "Donald Trumpkin."

In the lower photo, artist Jeanette Paras of Dublin, Ohio, locally famous for "pumpkinizing" celebrities and political figures every year since 1988, displayed this image on Facebook ("Paras Pumpkins") as part of her annual "unveiling" of her newest celebrity pumpkin on her front porch.

Never one to avoid a controversy, the Rev. Al Sharpton said, "I wonder why black religious leaders would seek to bask in the glow of a billionaire while offending their congregants and offending their cloth? I don't know how you preach Jesus, a refugee himself, on Sunday, and then deal with a refugee-basher on Monday."

Donald dismissed Sharpton's rebuke. "Deep down inside, Al likes me a lot. That I can tell you. He's just doing his thing like he always does."

***

Millions of voters-at-large "detested" Ted Cruz, yet by the first of December, approval ratings were moving upward. Donald appraised Cruz's rise with skepticism, noting that whereas Cruz was strong with evangelicals and those defining themselves as "very conservative," among moderate or liberal Republicans *[is there such a thing?]* he drew a low 6%.

As polls showed, the very far right candidates could do well in Iowa because nearly half of the GOP electorate self-defined as "very conservative," standing firmly against abortion and same-sex marriage, among other issues.

During the weeks ahead, Cruz would spew a cobra-like venom against Donald. But in December, he seemed to align himself with Donald, perhaps hoping to expand his appeal to voters other than those from the extreme right wing—many of whom had been labeled as "fanatic" in the liberal press.

Columnist Frank Bruni wrote a diatribe entitled ANYONE BUT CRUZ.

"Cruz is the antithesis of a team player. His thirst for the spotlight in unquenchable. His arrogance is unalloyed. He actually takes pride in being abrasive. His roommate at Princeton said, 'I would rather pick someone from the phone book to be President rather than Ted Cruz.' He never backs down. It's the fruit of a combative style and consuming solipsism that would make him an insufferable, unendurable, President. And if there's any sense left in the election, and mercy in the world, it will undo him soon enough."

The much-photographed, shame-inducing sign in front of the hatemongering **Harlem congregation of Atlah.**

This World Missionary Church is the platform from which the Rev. Manning calls for the death of homosexuals by stoning. He refers to himself as "the sodomite slayer." From the pulpit he rants against Obama, whom he calls Hitler, claiming that he is going "to use gay people to destroy the black community."

He also calls for Harlem to become a "homo-free zone," and maintains that both of the Presidents Bush engaged in anal sex with hundreds of men.

BUT AT LEAST HE LIKED DONALD:

Born in North Carolina, where he later picked cotton and pulled tobacco, the Rev. **James David Manning,** as a young man, burgled some 100 houses and was imprisoned for 3 1/2 years. While in prison, he became his version of a Christian and grew into the most controversial African American minister in the United States.

He reserves his harshest criticism for Ben Carson, whom he calls "a pathetic nigga" and a "demon," and defining Carson's supporters as "closeted sodomites, lesbos, and buttlickers."

He also asserts that Obama and Vladimir Putin will soon be outed as "fags," and that Starbucks puts semen in its coffees. He has also referenced Marco Rubio, Ted Cruz, and George W. Bush as "sodomites and homos."

BUT HE SUPPORTED DONALD TRUMP

***

The final month of 2015 had hardly begun when headlines exposed the dilemma of the Establishment: "Fellow Republicans want Trump pushed out, as long as someone else does the pushing," wrote one journalist. "The fear was that if Donald were the standard bearer, he would imperil the political careers of other "downticket" Republicans.

The end of the year poll conducted by *ABC News/The Washington Post* revealed that Donald's unfavorable rating derived from 65% of women and 74% of nonwhite voters.

"Trump would be a disaster," said Senator Lindsey Graham of South Carolina, who wanted the GOP presidential nomination for himself. "If you're a xenophobic, race-baiting, religious bigot, you're going to have a hard time being President, and you're going to do irreparable damage to the party."

Many in the GOP seemed equally horrified that if not Donald, then Ted Cruz would be an even less desirable standard-bearer.

Donald was growing less fearful of Ben Carson in the wake of the carnage inflicted by terrorists on innocent people in Paris. Tied with Donald in November, polls in December showed the mild-mannered, soft-spoken Carson slipping as terror reshaped the race.

A new national poll from Quinnipiac University revealed that the neurosurgeon had slipped seven points. Republican strategist Ron Bonjena said, "Carson is failing the commander-in-chief test that Republican primary voters require, especially around national security."

Carson made a highly visible, much-reported gaffe when he claimed that China was engaged in a military incursion in Syria when he meant Russia. He also called Syrian refugees "rabid dogs."

MANY JEWISH VOTERS DISMISS DONALD
As a "Meshuggina Goy"

Both Carson and Donald hoped to rally Jewish voters to their respective causes. *[There are some Jews, believe it or not, who are not Democrats.]* As such, both candidates appeared at a rally of wealthy, influential Jewish Republicans.

Carson, with dismal results, misspoke several times during his speech. He mispronounced Hamas, pronouncing it like "hummus," which, of course, is a food product made with garbanzos. His attempt at a joke about Jews and money was greeted with boos.

The major insight he proffered involved telling his hip Jewish audience that, "The Middle East is complicated." He expressed that with ominous portent, as it had been a revelation, sharing it with a group whose members were far better informed about the Middle East than he was.

Carson revealed that he had just returned from Israel where "I feared I might be shot."

"That went over like a coven of Tennessee evangelical snake-handlers shouting the glory of Jesus Christ at a convention of rabbis," said Bernard Goldstein from Dallas.

Donald fared better than Carson, but then almost any candidate could have done better. However, Donald was jeered when he refused to answer a question about whether Jerusalem should be split into two.

Like Carson, he seemed to associate Jews with money, bringing up the link three times. "Stupidly, you want to give me money," he said. "But Trump doesn't want your money."

As one of the donors in the audience later said, "That remark went over like a Jew drinking a pint of pig's blood."

During his speech, Donald promised to fly to Israel for a meeting with Prime Minister Benjamin Netanyahu, but the highly publicized trip was canceled. It was speculated that Donald's mere presence with the prime minister at holy sites could have caused domestic turmoil. "Bibi," as he is called, presides over a country that is one-fifth Muslim.

Donald told the press that he would schedule a visit with Netanyahu after he became President.

A New York stockbroker later told the press, "Jackie Mason, Trump isn't. *Oy gevalt!* 'Billary' Clinton he isn't either. What he is, however, is a *ganze macher (larger-than-life schemer/arranger who can make things happen).* He's dismissed by the *chochem (clever people or wise guys)* as a *meschuggina goy (mad, crazy, or insane non-Jew)."*

Benjamin Netanyahu after a "working dinner" with **Hillary Clinton** in 2009.

Netanyahu seemed to shy away from an endorsement for Donald, who avidly sought the support of Jewish voters, frequently asserting that his daughter, Ivanka, had converted to the Jewish faith.

Since "Bibi" presides over a country whose population is 20% Muslim, he did not extend a welcome for Donald, as a presidential hopeful in the heat of a contested campaign, to visit Israel.

"THE WORST PRESIDENTIAL RACE
In the History of the Republic"

Since the early 1970s, the Iowa caucuses have been the first major electoral event of the nominating process for President of the United States. As such, they're frantically pursued by candidates because of the massive media attention they generate during U.S. presidential election years.

In 2016, they were scheduled for February 1, and as their preludes began to heat up, candidates, including Donald, turned to the relatively cheap medium of radio to get their messages across.

Consequently, hour after hour, motorists driving along highways were pummeled with appeals. Whereas some chatter dismissed Marco Rubio as "no more than a pretty face," other broadcasts droned on, calling Cruz "the worst kind of politician."

Since the media seemed intent on giving him hour after hour of free exposure, Donald didn't purchase any TV ads. But he did buy radio ads.

On December 2, as more and more voters began to interpret Donald as a possible strong military leader, he revealed that he "sometimes felt bad for not having served in the military. *[He had used four college deferments to avoid being shipped off to Vietnam. His final rejection was based on bone spurs in his foot.]*

Many former military men criticized him, including retired Marine Lt. Col. Orson Swindle. "I just find Trump to be a huckster, and he's very good at it. Such comments he's made are distasteful to veterans." *[Swindle had been shot down during a jet fighter mission in 1966 in Vietnam and had spent six years as a prisoner of war.]* "Trump took the easy way out," he said.

With support for Donald mounting, in spite of critics, columnist David Brooks weighed in. "Trump is what GOP voters want at the moment. He reflects their disgust with the political Establishment. He gives them the pleasurable sensation that somebody can come to Washington, kick some tail, and shake things up." He suggested that when voters face the final decision about who to put in charge with having their finger on the nuclear trigger, it would not be Donald.

"In contrast to Carson, Trump, even when he misspeaks, voters see him as someone who projects strength and confidence," said Ford O'Connell, a GOP strategist who was on John McCain's campaign team in 2008.

Whereas only 5% of GOP voters in Iowa thought Carson would be best at handling terrorists, an impressive 30% thought Donald was the man for the job.

Columnist Mike Lupica called the 2016 presidential race "the worst in this country's history."

America's most famous—some say, notorious—African American pastor, **Al Sharpton**, inserted himself into the presidential race.

"Black celebrities and luminaries live in a world that is much more engaging to Trump, and parallel to his world, than those of us that have been in politics and civil rights on the ground for a long as Trump has been out there."

"He has little understanding of the lives of the vast majority of African Americans. It's not like there's a Trump building in Harlem."

"Donald Trump is the angry face of it all, able to out-talk everybody on radio and television, and out-tweet them, and shock the world with his theories about Muslims. But Trump isn't alone. He's just the one with the biggest bullhorn, able to out-shout even the bullhorn media."

Hip-hop impresario Russell Simmons, who has been a pal of Donald's for more than three decades, told him, "It's time to find a new rap. You seem to be like a one-man wrecking ball willing to destroy our nation's foundation of freedom. Stop the bullshit! Stop fueling fires of hate."

On December 9, President Obama appeared to use the 150th anniversary of the constitutional amendment abolishing slavery to challenge the incendiary rhetoric of Donald. At a ceremony at The Capitol, he rebuked Donald for saying that as President, he would bar Muslims from entering the United States. "Our freedom is bound up with the freedom of others," he said, "regardless of what they look like, or where they come from, or what their last name is, or what faith they practice."

Even the best-selling author of the Harry Potter series, J.K. Rowling, voiced her view, comparing Donald to her evil and scheming (fictional) villain, Voldemort.

During an interview with Barbara Walters, Donald denied he was a bigot. "Probably the least of anybody you've ever met. I just have common sense."

After White House spokesman Josh Earnest denounced Donald "as a carnival barker." even David Cameron, the prime minister of the U.K. weighed in, calling Donald's remarks "divisive, unhelpful, and quite simply wrong."

Establishment Republicans were among his loudest critics: House Speaker Paul Ryan (R-WI) told the press, "This is not conservatism."

Columnist Linda Stasi wrote that "Donald is a bald-faced liar—even if he's not bald-headed. What he is and what Trump has always been is the greatest showman since Michael Jackson. If The Donald really believed the disgusting, incendiary, and nut-job things he said about Muslims, Mexicans, and everyone who isn't him, he would have stayed in Palm Beach with all those other white, WASPy types!"

Yet in spite of the outrage he'd generated, Donald's "shoot-from-the-hip" style of proclamations only seemed to enhance his poll numbers.

As a potential warning (some said "threat") to such GOP critics as Rand Paul and others, Donald tweeted: "A new poll indicated that 68% of my supporters would vote for me if I departed from the GOP and ran as an independent."

Reporter Patrick Helay wrote: "While many candidates appeal to the passion and patriotism of their crowds, Trump appears unrivaled in his ability to forge bonds with a sizable segment of Americans based on anxieties about a changing nation, economic insecurities, ferocious enemies, and emboldened minorities (like the first black President, whose heritage and intelligence he has all but encouraged supporters to malign)."

At times, Donald seemed to threaten his antagonists, vowing to attack his political opponents "ten times harder than they criticize me." He even evoked the horrors of Hiroshima, when he said, "We'll bomb hell out of our enemies."

Many pundits claimed that in using fiery language to win favor from frightened Americans, Donald was following in the tradition of Barry Goldwater, George Wallace, Joseph McCarthy, Huey Long, and Pat Buchanan.

Jennifer Mercieca, a political expert at Texas A&M, said, "Trump's entire campaign is run like a demagogue's, a language of division, his cult of personality, his manner of categorizing and maligning people with a broad brush."

It was noted that Donald seemed to believe in what Vince Lombardi once said: "Winning is not everything. It is the only thing."

THE GOP'S RHETORIC GETS HOTTER
"Homicidal Maniacs Are Trying to Kill Us!"

Two massacres, one in France, another in California, strongly affected the style of Donald's race for the White House. Each became a controversial topic in his continuing anti-Muslim rants.

On November 13, a series of coordinated terrorist attacks occurred in Paris and

Darth Vader from Hollywood's *Star Wars* trilogy incited frustration and terror as the most destructive force in the Universe.

Because of his destructive after-effects of (among others) the government shutdowns he engineered, Cruz's enemies made frequent comparisons.

Ted Cruz's electoral campaign was said to have generated more weird commercial products than any other candidate.

Among them was this poster, as crafted by the conservative artist Sabo, on sale for $50 through Cruz's websites, likening him to a "blacklisted and loving it" tough guy who'd wreak havoc in Iran.

its northern suburb, Saint-Denis, in which 130 innocent people were slaughtered, 89 at the Bataclan Theater. Another 368 people were injured. Three suicide bombers struck targets in Paris' Saint-Denis, followed by suicide bombing and mass shootings at cafés, restaurants, and a music venue. ISIL and the Islamic State of Iraq claimed responsibility.

On December 2, fourteen people were slaughtered and 22 seriously injured in a terrorist attack (a mass shooting and an attempted bombing) on the Inland Regional Center in San Bernardino, California. Within a rented banquet hall, the assassins, Syed Rizwan Farook and Tashfeen Malik, a married couple, carried out the barbaric act. They fled in a rented SUV but, four hours later, police pursued their vehicle and killed them in a shootout.

The FBI revealed that the perpetrators were "homegrown violent extremists" inspired by foreign terrorist groups and trained through lessons on the Internet. The murderous duet had stockpiled weapons, ammunition, and bomb-making equipment within their home.

In the wake of the shootings, Obama urged Americans to avoid a war on Muslims. "ISIL does not speak for Islam. They are thugs and killers, part of a cult of death."

When Donald heard those words, he tweeted, "Is that all there is? We need a new President—and FAST!"

In the wake of the massacre of Americans by Islamic terrorists in San Bernardino, GOP candidates ranted and raved. Some, including Ted Cruz, blamed Obama "for failing to protect lives."

He also warned of the "gathering storm of homicidal maniacs who want to kill us."

Donald was the least hysterical among the field of GOP hopefuls, calling for a "moment of silence for the victims."

In the aftermath of J.K. Rowling's designation of her fictional character of **Voldemort** (portrayed above in one of the Harry Potter movies by Ralph Fiennes) as "**worse than Donald,**" the internet witnessed a sudden burst of Voldemort images sporting orange wigs, mocking Donald.

When the GOP battleground relocated to New Hampshire, he became harsher in his rhetoric, blaming Obama's failure to stop "radical Islamic terrorism." He warned voters that "something really dangerous is going on with Muslims in mosques. There is also something going on between Muslims and the President we don't know about."

Although accused of being inconsistent in his positions, he remained steadfast in talking about "you" and "we," while attacking the "dangerous them."

On December 7, in the wake of the husband-and-wife attack in California, Donald delivered his strongest counterattack yet.

In a widely publicized speech, he endorsed a platform calling for "a total and complete shutdown of Muslims entering the United States," not just immigrants and tourists, but even Muslims who are U.S. citizens, but who travel abroad.

At a rally in Mount Pleasant, South Carolina, he cited the danger posed by Muslims, and said they wanted to be governed by *sharia* law.

Donald's call for an anti-Muslim ban was not universally condemned. Many talk radio hosts defended his position. "Anyone who thinks Trump's comments will hurt him doesn't know the temperature of the American people," said radio host Laura Ingraham.

In the wake of wide-

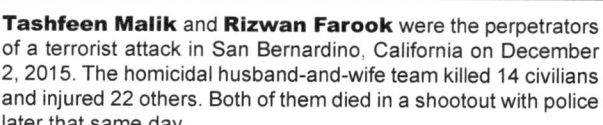

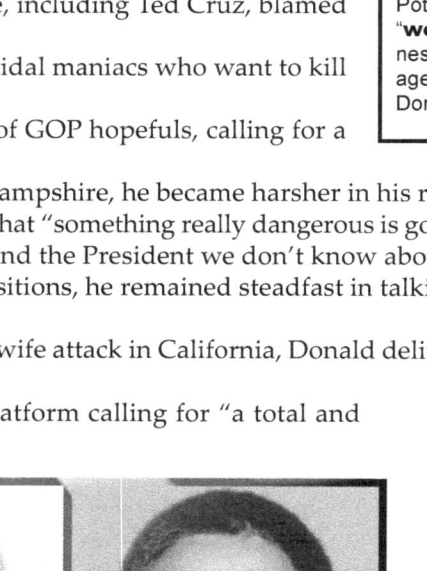

Tashfeen Malik and **Rizwan Farook** were the perpetrators of a terrorist attack in San Bernardino, California on December 2, 2015. The homicidal husband-and-wife team killed 14 civilians and injured 22 others. Both of them died in a shootout with police later that same day.

The FBI concluded that they were "homegrown violent extremists inspired by foreign terrorist orgaizations." Their enormous stockpile of weapons led investigators to conclude that they intended to inflict further terror attacks as part of their "Hate America" campaign.

Shortly before his death in June of 2016 at the age of 74, **Muhammed Ali** came out swinging one final time.

"I am a Muslim and there is nothing Islamic about killing innocent people in Paris and San Bernardino or anywhere else in the world. True Muslims know that the ruthless violence of so-called Islamic jihadists goes against the very tenets of our religion."

spread criticism, Donald weakened his stand. "If a person is a Muslim, goes overseas, and comes back, they can come back," he said. "They're a citizen. That's different."

Many newspaper editorials condemned Donald's stance against Muslims. As the *New York Daily News* phrased it, "a creature of ego, overweening ambition, barstool intellect, and vision that extends further than the mirror, Trump, the inquisitor, made a lie of American exceptionalism. Never could he take the oath of office to preserve, protect, and defend the Constitution without committing perjury."

Donald's attacks on Muslims had catalyzed the special outrage during the second week of December, with some headlines greeting him with: *HATE YA BACK, DON. GOP HAS TO SHUN HIM OR SUFFER. HIS BIG LIE HAS SINISTER NAZI ECHO.*

A response came fast from Nihad Awad, the executive director of the Council on American-Islamic relations. "Trump sounds more like the leader of a lynch mob than a great nation like ours."

In spite of his anti-Muslim attacks, or perhaps because of them, mid-December polls put Donald in a strong lead ahead of his rival GOP candidates. Those voters who had cited security as their top reason for voting seemed overwhelmingly to approve of Donald.

However, the situation in Iowa was different. For the first time, the firebrand Texas senator, Ted Cruz, became the frontrunner, registering a 24% approval rating to Donald's 19%. As recently as October, Ben Carson had led the pack at 32%.

Even the tabloids suddenly became models of righteous good citizenry.

Here, one of the biggest tabloids in Donald's home town denounced his implicit potentiality as an autocrat.

PAYING THE PRICE
Donald's Anti-Muslim Rants Cost Him Millions in Middle Eastern Deals

Donald's call to bar Muslims from entering the country threatened to diminish his brand's golden appeal in the Middle East, including in such countries as Dubai. The Dubai-based Landmark Group, responded to his threatened bar by removing all Trump-derived products from the shelves of its Lifestyle retail stores.

Before his denunciations, the name Trump was synonymous with American luxury and bigtime success. In the Middle East, his name had been applied to golf courses, residences, home accessories, and, in Turkey, some major hotels.

At the Trump Towers in Istanbul, a complex that housed both upmarket stores and luxurious condos, resident Melek Toprak said, "I feel ashamed to live in a building associated with such a vile name."

The business world estimated that Donald's incendiary remarks had cost him millions of dollars, if not tens of millions, in lost licensing and other deals.

But he said he was unbowed, that he had many friends in the Middle East, and that they had told him he had addressed a difficult problem that other world leaders had studiously avoided.

Business leaders were quick to point out that Donald had worked with Muslim investors in the Middle East for years. A $325 million investment in 1995 from a Saudi prince had helped him refinance ownership of the Plaza Hotel in Manhattan. And in Dubai, Donald already had a fully operational golf course and another under development.

Ironically, his Muslim partner in the United Arab Emirates was Hussain Sajwani. Together, they were building a massive luxury complex seven times bigger than the Pentagon.

New billionaire **Hussain Sajwani** has transformed the skyline of Dubai with luxury apartments, deploying extreme marketing strategies. He is now called "The Donald of Dubai."

In one of his most lavish gated communities, he made a golf course bearing the Trump name as its centerpiece. "We made a deal with the Trump Organization," Sajwani said. "They know how to run golf courses. We stay away from politics."

But Donald's comments about Muslims had a ripple effect. Damac Properties, owned by Sajwani, removed the Trump name from a stone wall in front and also replaced images of Donald and his daughter, Ivanka, from a billboard nearby.

Their images were replaced with an enormous photo of Marlon Brando as Vito Corleone in *The Godfather*.

NEO-NAZIS AND HATE GROUPS
Feel Emboldened by Donald

As another result of Donald's anti-Muslim tirade, he breathed new life and new energy into the KKK and the American Nazis. Many white supremacy covens suddenly felt emboldened and even legitimatized.

In an article in *Politico,* Don Black, founder of *Stormfront,* a white supremacist group, spoke out: "Demoralization has been the biggest enemy, and Trump is changing all that. He's certainly creating a movement that will continue independently of him even if he does fold at some point."

George Lincoln Rockwell (1918-1967) was the godfather of the American Nazi Party, and his beliefs and writings have continued to be influential among white nationalists and neo-Nazis in the 21st Century.

On August 25, 1967, Rockwell was assassinated in Virginia by a member of his own group. He threatened that if he came to power in the United States, he would execute at least ninety percent of all Jews.

To counter the Black Panthers rallying cry of "Black Power," he started calling for "White Power," which later became the name of the party's newspaper and the title of a book he wrote.

Donald had also suggested that Black Lives Matter activists "deserved to be roughed up" for disrupting free speech rallies.

In August, he received the endorsement of David Duke, the former imperial wizard of the KKK. "How come it's against American values to want to preserve the heritage of this country?" Duke asked. "I'm for Donald Trump."

HAIL DONALD TRUMP—the ULTIMATE SAVIOR, was positioned as one of the headlines in the neo-Nazi website, *The Daily Stormer.*

The Southern Poverty Law Center's Intelligent Project said that Donald's words had contributed to a resurgence of the "main-streaming of hate."

DONALD AS A GUERRILLA FIGHTER
Popping In and Out at Rallies Along the Campaign Trail
Attacking "Lyin' Ted," "Little Marco," & "Crooked Hillary,"

"I'll be the most high-energy guy ever to occupy the Oval Office."
—Donald Trump

As 2015 entered its final weeks, Donald's method of campaigning was different from that of any of his GOP rivals. He was light on travel and heavy on media time. At least once a day he was interviewed on camera or over the phone for a "call-in chat," often provocative.

What do **Donald Trump** and **David Duke** have in common? Both are interpreted as heroes by American Nazis.

When he did leave his home base in New York, he flew on a private jet, touching down in such places as New Hampshire, Florida, and South Carolina, among other stops. He'd appeared at pro-Trump rallies, greeting hundreds of supporters, mired only by protesters, some of them violent.

Characterizing his travels as "pop in, pop out," he managed to keep his national lead in the polls, although Cruz and even Marco Rubio "seemed to be breathing down my neck with their bad breath," he told aides.

His wife, Melania, admitted, "Donald is a homebody who prefers to sleep in his own bed."

At a rally in Orlando, Florida, he said, "I came in, I spoke for twenty minutes, and then I got the hell out."

Two primary battles that especially concerned him included New Hampshire—"a more advanced electorate"—than in "evangelical Iowa." In contrast to his lackluster performance in Iowa, the New Jersey governor, Chris Christie, was surging ahead in New Hampshire, and "Little Marco Rubio" and "carpet bomber," Ted Cruz, were showing strong wins there, too.

What if this slogan is true, that **the Republican Party** died because of a changing demographic and intolerance (or stupidity, or self-interest and/or greed) on the part of its ruling elite?

In Iowa, Donald looked upon Rubio with great skepticism as he "became another Bible thumper," appealing to the evangelicals. "Not many evangelicals come out of Cuba," he said, seemingly disbelieving Rubio's "Ol'-time" religious credentials. To Donald, they evoked a cynical ploy to attract right-wing voters.

He read a confidential report about Rubio's much-vaunted religious background. Born a Roman Catholic, he converted to Mormonism, like Mitt Romney, before returning to the Catholic fold. At present, he seemed to be attending both a Southern Baptist Church and a Catholic one.

To appeal to the evangelicals, Donald threw his support behind those who felt same-sex marriages were being forced upon them, in spite of their religious objections. Or, as John Kasich jokingly said, "These people think they might have to serve a gay person a cupcake."

Both Donald and Rubio were supplied with polls that showed that 70% of white evangelical Protestants opposed same-sex marriages, whereas only 39% of the general voting public opposed such unions.

In the middle of his campaign in Iowa, Rubio encountered unwelcome headlines: KISS OF DEATH: BILLIONAIRE WHO FUNDED SAME-SEX MARRIAGE ENDORSES RUBIO.

The reference was to financier Paul Singer, a high-profile contributor to efforts to legalize same-sex marriage. For reasons known only to himself, he was a strong supporter of Rubio.

Perhaps to counter the negative publicity, Rubio hired Eric Teetsel, an anti-gay conservative activist, to join his campaign. TV ads appeared in Iowa attacking Rubio. "Can anyone think of anything Marco Rubio has ever done in the few times he's shown up on the Senate floor—anything at all except amnesty. He looks good on TV—and that's about it."

For a change of pace, for a while, at least, Donald stopped attacking his GOP rivals and aimed heavy ammunition at Hillary instead. He outrageously accused her of being responsible for the Syrian refugee crisis. "And she calls me dangerous."

Not letting up on her, on December 11, at Manhattan's Plaza Hotel, which he had once owned, he addressed the annual luncheon of the Pennsylvania Commonwealth. It was here that he adopted a new nickname for his major Democratic rival, calling

Nikki Haley began her tenure as Republican governor of South Carolina in 2011, the first woman to serve in that capacity in that red state.

In 2016, she endorsed Marco Rubio for President, angering Trump supporters. In the call for attendance to an upcoming Republican debate, depicted above, a heavily muscled superman (with Donald's head superimposed onto its torso) is seen overpowering Haley after she denounced him.

her "Crooked Hillary," a moniker he'd maintain in the public conscience throughout the remainder of his campaign.

Inside the hotel, a small group of protesters interrupted his speech and had to be escorted out. One woman who refused to budge was thrown to the floor. Outside, Marnie Halasa, dressed in a red, white, and blue uniform, carried a sign that read— "Trump Makes America Hate Again."

Within two days after his appearance at the Plaza, Donald loaded his verbal arsenals and went after Ted Cruz. In the latest national poll, Donald still commanded a lead at 27% but Cruz was moving up at 22%, a 12-point gain since October. Carson seemed to have lost his footing and fallen from his mountain peak.

"BRUISE CRUZ" screamed a headline as Donald went after the Texas senator, calling him "a maniac. Look how he's dealt with the Senate. I don't think he's qualified to be President. You can't walk into the Senate screaming and calling people liars and not be able to cajole and get along with people." He delivered that attack on *Fox News* to Chris Wallace.

At every event, Donald was met with protesters, and often there was violence. At a rally in Las Vegas, a black protester, pastor Ender Austin, interrupted Donald's speech. Police grabbed Austin, who sat defiantly on the floor, almost defying security to drag him out of the building.

One Trump supporter shouted, "*Set the motherfucker on fire!*" Another screamed "*Shoot him!*" Yet another yelled out, "*Kick his ass!*" One Trump supporter was caught on camera barking the Nazi salute, "*Sieg heil!*"

The GOP Establishment was building its own wall against Trump, but many celebrities he'd known stepped forward to either endorse him or to speak kindly of him.

Quarterback Tom Brady didn't exactly endorse Donald, but had kind words for him and called him a good friend.

For that, Brady was denounced, the *New York Daily News* splashing out in "Second Coming Headlines" that "BRADY HAS NO BALLS!"

Donald had come to Brady's defense during the "Deflategate Scandal," in which the football player was linked to charges involved letting some of the air out of footballs used in high-stakes games.

Amara Grautski, a reporter, wrote: "Patriots' quarterback Tom Brady went from deflated balls to no balls. The four-time Super Bowl champ turned big-time chump when he fumbled a perfect opportunity to condemn his good friend, Donald Trump, for his dangerous demagoguery and racist rhetoric."

As Donald came to be perceived more and more as a serious candidate, investigative reporters delved into his past, and revelations appeared.

Reporter Isabel Vincent came up with an *exposé* about Donald and his charities. She discovered that the last check Donald had written for his foundation had been way back in 2008 for the amount of $35,000.

"He hasn't coughed up a dime for his charitable foundation in six years, but has used the donations of others to give to the private school attended by his son, Barron. The Donald J. Trump Foundation doled out half a million dollars in 2014, $50,000 of which went to the Columbia Grammar and Preparatory School at which Barron was a student.

More and more was being learned about Donald's personal life and even his eating habits. He constantly battled a weight gain, since his preferred foods were steaks, hamburgers, pastas, and French fries. This unhealthy diet seemed to have little effect on his health. "I am fortunate to have been blessed with great genes— both from my parents who led long and very productive lives. If elected President, I would be the healthiest holder of that office in the history of America."

To back up his claim, his doctor, Harold Bornstein, a specialist in internal medicine and gastroenterology, claimed that his patient's health was "astonishingly excellent. Only positive results from many tests such as for high blood pressure," the doctor maintained. "He's lost fifteen pounds. His physical strength and stamina are extraordinary."

An active player in Republican politics and a Marco Rubio supporter, **Paul Singer** is an American hedge fund manager, activist investor, and philanthropist, and a financial supporter of LGBTQ rights.

Since his son came out as gay in 1998, he has sought to persuade other Republicans to support gay marriage. "The fact that gay couples want to marry is a kind of a lovely thing and a cool thing and a wonderful thing."

It's estimated that Singer has donated $10 million to gay rights.

Tom Brady, a football quarterback for the New England Patriots, took a beating in the press for his having touted his friendship with Donald Trump. Brady is considered among the greatest quarterbacks of all time.

The football player and Donald have played several rounds of golf together, and Donald stood by Brady when he was alleged to have played a role in the "Deflategate" scandals. Charges were filed that there was evidence of "football tampering" by letting some of the air out of the balls used in the game.

BURNING BUSHES
THE COLLAPSE OF A DYNASTY

"You're not going to insult your way into the presidency!"
—Jeb Bush, shouting to Donald onstage

The fifth GOP debate was held on December 15, 2015 at the Venetian Resort in Las Vegas. This was the second debate to air on CNN, with Wolf Blitzer being the chief moderator along with Dana Bash and Hugh Hewitt.

The debate was split into primetime and pre-primetime, with the Kiddies' Table occupied in their hopeless quest by Mike Huckabee, Rick Santorum, Lindsey Graham, and George Pataki. For Pataki and Graham, it would be their last hurrah, as each would suspend their respective campaigns before the end of the month.

Eighteen million people watched as Donald, Cruz, Rubio, Carson, Bush, Fiorina, Paul, Christie, and Kasich squared off. The audible coughing heard from onstage during the debate came from the only medical doctor among their ranks (Ben Carson), who had suffered from a lingering infection for the previous few weeks. At the debate, he seemed to be "sharing his cough" with the candidates close to him.

Donald and Rubio became prime targets during the debate, which focused on toughness, with immigrants and foreign intervention showing glaring divisions among the candidates.

From the beginning, one of the top contenders, Cruz, went aggressively after Rubio, questioning his conservative credentials and his judgment on national security and immigration. The Texas senator accused Rubio of lining up with liberals in favoring amnesty for immigrants.

Bush tore into Donald for his anti-Muslim rants, hoping to move his lackluster campaign forward in spite of, or because of, his famous name. Yet despite strenuous efforts and mountains of cash, he seemed to be failing to connect with the voters.

"Donald, you are not going to be able to insult your way into the presidency," Bush said. "That's not going to happen. Leadership is not about attacking people and disparaging them."

"With Jeb's attitude, we will never be great again," Donald said. "That I can tell you."

His remarks were greeted with loud boos.

Cruz claimed that his position on immigration, and that of Rubio's, was "like suggesting the fireman and the arsonist have the same record because they were both at the scene of the fire."

Donald, as anticipated, came in for his share of brickbats, and Rand Paul compared him to "totalitarian governments" because he supported monitoring the Internet for suspicious activity. Bush entered with his own bricks tossed at Donald, saying, "Trump is not a serious candidate, but merely great at one-liners."

"He's a chaos candidate," Bush said, "and would be a chaos President."

THE GOP'S FINEST, LIVE FROM LAS VEGAS!

Donald decimated all of them.

Columnist Frank Bruni described "the sparring and preening, the puffed chests and sound bites over nuanced policies and earnest reflection. Cruz was the defining figure, his certainty verging on cockiness, his ambitions transparent, his attempts to tap into some warmth a mesmerizing exercise in futility."

Regardless of what was happening on the campaign trail, radio's bombastic **Rush Limbaugh** could always be counted on to weigh in with an opinion. Although he rarely had a kind word for Donald, his pronouncements could sting his rivals too.

Limbaugh entered the anti-immigration fight by claiming, "Rubio was part of the 'Gang of Eight' trying to secure amnesty and wishes now that he hadn't done that."

"Jeb doesn't believe I'm unhinged," Donald shot back. "He said that very simply because he has failed in this campaign. It's been a total disaster. Nobody cares."

In the lower tier of candidates, Huckabee and Santorum, among others, valiantly chased after an elusive dream. Desperate to attract attention, Santorum said, "We have entered World War III. We have a leader who refuses to identify it and be truthful to the American people," a libelous reference, of course, to Obama.

Huckabee seemed to agree. "We have an enemy out to kill us, and we have a government we don't trust any more." The former New York Governor, Pataki, called Donald "the know-nothing candidate of the 21st Century."

Lindsey got in his licks, claiming that Donald's stand on the Muslims "has made us less safe." Asked if he would support him if he were the nominee, he said, "Like Bob Dole, I may sleep late that day" [i.e., the day he'd have to cast a vote].

In some corners, the most hated man in America, and the bane of many local police departments, **Wayne LaPierre,** CEO of the NRA.

With more bluster than details, each of the upper-tier candidates, including Carly Fiorina, tried but failed to convince voters that they would "make us safe." But as the evening ground on, it degenerated into tedious, even puerile, bickering.

Reporters ridiculed Cruz for equating Obamacare to "Nazi appeasement." As one reporter wrote, "There are those who say Cruz is smart. But how dumb can you get, comparing Nazis killing millions of people to Obama trying to give everyone some form of health insurance to save their lives? Smart? Sounds like an idiot to me."

Columnist Linda Stasi wrote: "Donald is bombastic and boorish, but Cruz? Now you're talking a bully without respect for the very government he claims to love for all his slimy, sweet words. His spoiled brat screaming and stomping his feet helped shut down the government which cost the U.S. economy $23 billion."

Although Jeb (and most of his Republican candidates) extolled the direct links between gun ownership and their lobbyists definition of freedom, many thousands of voters heartily, even passionately, disagreed.

A New York Republican, Peter King, referred to Cruz and his Tea Party as "government terrorists."

With devastating accuracy, Stasi attacked and ridiculed Cruz's Senate filibuster, wherein, for hour after hour, as a means of blocking a timely Senate approval of the budget, he had droned on, overnight about "'Green Eggs and Ham;' delivered a Darth Vader impression; and spoke of 'The Little Engine that Could' and other nonsense."

Many persons in the media attacked the candidates' weak stands on gun control. In 2000, Donald had favored a ban on assault weapons. But in 2015, he pledged to veto gun controls. In reference to recent schoolyard shootings, he said, "You're going to have these things happen, and it's a horrible thing to behold."

Jeb Bush, a so-called "moderate," addressed the National Rifle Association and declared, "The sound of our guns is the sound of freedom."

In the wake of the debate, the newspaper offices were flooded with letters to the editor, some quite articulate, as in the case of John Amato of New York City: "The debate was full of sneers, weird looks, anger, teeth-grinding, and verbal explosions. It looks like who is left standing next November will win. It's kind of like a 'third world' country during a *coup d'état*."

One of Ted Cruz's memoirs came up for scrutiny at the time. Published in 2015, it was entitled *A Time for Truth*. As many reviewers pointed out, "Truth had nothing to do with it."

An excerpt from it was shown to Donald, in which he learned that Cruz had described himself as "a geeky kid." In his self-appraisal, Cruz had claimed that he changed his name to Rafael Edward Cruz [*nicknamed Ted*] when he was a teenager.

At school, his classmates had ridiculed him when he was first known as "Rafaelito" and as "Felito."

"The problem with that name was that it seemed to rhyme with every major corn chip on the market," Cruz wrote. "Fritos, Cheetos, Doritos, and Tostitos."

For two years, Rafael, his born again Christian father, refused to call him Ted, viewing the Anglicization of his name as a rejection of both him and his heritage.

When the final verdict on the Las Vegas debate came in, it was generally assumed that Donald had established his alpha dog dominance over the other candidates in the overcrowded field. It was noted that many of the weaker candidates were afraid to take him on because he was known for his venomous pushbacks.

Bush's assault against Donald was seen "as a long, bootless slog through the alligator-infested swamps associated with virtually everything about Donald and his candidacy."

One caller, speaking on a talk-show radio program in Las Vegas, called Cruz "Donald's pussy," suggesting he was afraid to really take him on. That, of course, would change during the weeks ahead.

Up until then in the campaign, Cruz showed, or at least pretended, respect for Donald, probably with hopes that he might avoid as many direct confrontations until much later in the campaign.

All of that was about to change.

The more viable Cruz appeared, as reflected by increasingly favorable polls, the stronger became the attacks on his character (or lack thereof).

Reporter Jennifer Steinhauer wrote, "It is the hate that dare not speak its name. Since his arrival in 2013, Ted Cruz has managed to alienate, exasperate, and generally agitate the plurality of his 99 colleagues in the Senate. He stands out for this widely held reputation for putting Ted first."

After the debate, Rubio struggled in third or fourth place, coming under fire for having made a big bet on immigration overhaul. He now seemed to try to back away from it. But Cruz wouldn't let him.

The "bromance" between **Vladimir Putin** and **Donald Trump** reached the tongue-kissing stage in a now notorious mural that was spread to millions through social media. Evaluated as a political masterpiece, it brought world-wide attention to a barbecue restaurant in Vilnius, Lithuania, on the NATO border with Russia.

Locals have been using the mural as a backdrop for romantic kissing photos of their own.

***

Newspapers continued to play up the **"BROMANCE OF DONALD AND VLAD."**

According to Donald, as expressed on MSNBC's *Morning Joe,* "Putin is at least a leader, unlike what we have in this country. "

Larry McShane, a reporter, wrote: "The two men—despite matching egos—remain an unlikely mutual admiration society. Trump all sculpted hair, tailored suits, and golf clubs; Putin all toned pecs, shirtless photo ops, and hunting rifles."

CARPET BOMBINGS VS. MAGIC CARPETS
Just Imagine If Aladdin Had Had a Nuclear Weapon!

How did **Aladdin** become an issue in the 2016 race for the White House?

Aladdin, of course, is the hero of a Middle Eastern folk tale that appeared in *The Book of One Thousand and One Nights.* He was "revived" in 1992 as part of a Disney animated film. In the yarn, Aladdin becomes rich and powerful with the aid of "the Genie of the Lamp," and goes on to marry the Sultan's daughter.

In a survey, nearly half of Donald's supporters favored the U.S. bombing of Agrabah, Aladdin's home town, not realizing it was fictional.

Some polls seemed deliberately to mock Donald's supporters, including one conducted by Public Policy Polling. When presented with whether they'd be in favor of bombing the city of Agrabah *["the (fictional) city of mystery and enchantment," aka, the home of Aladdin and his true love, Jasmine, "Princess of Agrabah," as depicted in Disney's animated film,* Aladdin *(1992)]*, results indicated that 41% of people self-identifying as Trump supporters claimed they were in favor of bombing it.

[According to Justin Mayhew, a communications specialist for PPP, the polling group that conducted the survey, "We made the question intentionally vague. We wanted to see how far this would go."]

In the aftermath of the survey's (horrifying) implications, headlines shouted "WATCH YOUR ASS, ALADDIN!"

Only 13% of Trump supporters opposed the bombing. Among Democrats, 19% favored the bombing.

At around the same time, Katrina Pierson, a spokeswoman for Donald, appeared on Fox's *The O'Reilly Factor*, and seemed to encourage the use not only the bombing of some (vaguely defined) point in the Middle East, but a full-out nuclear strike. "What good does it do to have a good nuclear triad if you're afraid to use it?"

LET ME ENTERTAIN YOU
"I Watched Every Episode of The Apprentice. *That Trump is One Hell of an Entertainer"*
—A Trump Fan at a Rally

Hoping to revive his campaign, Bush arrived in New Hampshire, where he didn't seem too articulate, or at least very artful. "I've got to get this off my chest. Donald Trump is a jerk!"

A Granite State poll conducted near the time of his arrival put Donald in first place at 26% of the vote to Jeb Bush's 10%.

Despite that success, the Trump camp felt that its ground plan wasn't working as well as they wished. Demographics revealed that his supporters were younger and without a college degree.

A disturbing element was cited in as a result of the polling. Although hordes of people were turning out at Donald's rallies, the survey showed that many of them had never voted before—and it was not certain if they would in 2016.

Another factor emerged as expressed by rally attendee Phil Beaton: "I'm not political, and I don't plan to vote. I came to be entertained. I watched every episode of *The Apprentice*. That Trump is one hell of an entertainer."

A retired Jersey City police captain, Peter Gallagher, on December 21, entered the fray over whether Muslims did hail and celebrate 9/11. He told the press that Muslims in New Jersey had celebrated 9/11 on rooftops and in street parties until they were dispersed by "disgusted cops," thereby backing up and corroborating Donald's much-disputed comments.

"Some men were dancing, some held kids on their shoulders. The women were shouting in Arabic in the high-pitched wail of Arabic fashion."

Other witnesses also came forth to back up Donald's previous claims, including yet another police officer, who claimed that he witnessed "a jubilant Arab celebration" on John F. Kennedy Boulevard. That was near the Masjid Al-Salam Mosque, where the 'blind sheikh," Omar Abdel-Rahman, screeched his sermons of hate before the 1993 bomb attack on the World Trade Center.

During his fielding of the rage generated by his widely refuted charges associated with Muslims who celebrated 9/11, Donald, campaigning in Michigan, stumbled into yet another controversy, based entirely on comments he (unchivalrously) delivered in front of thousands of his supporters.

At a rally, he commented on Hillary's battle against Obama for the Democratic nomination during the 2008 race.

Evaluating the outcome of that competition, Trump told his audience, "She got *schlonged*." Of course, as every New Yorker knows, *schlong* is a (Yiddish) word for penis.

Someone at the rally who was unfamiliar with the word asked a supporter what it meant. "It means Hillary got fucked by Obama," the Trump supporter in a red cap bluntly extrapolated.

Abdel-Rahman is currently serving a life sentence at the Butner Medical Center which is part of the Butner Federal Correctional Institution in Butner, North Carolina. Formerly a resident of New York City, Abdel-Rahman and nine others figured into a prosecution derived from investigations of the World Trade Center bombing of 1993.

Abdel-Rahman was accused of being the leader of Al-Gama'a al-Islamiyya (also known as "The Islamic Group"), a militant Islamist movement in Egypt that is considered a terrorist organization by the U.S. and Egyptian governments. He, with his alleged cohorts, were convicted of seditions conspiracy, which requires only that a crime be planned, not that it necessarily be attempted.

TRUMP SUPPORTERS
Perceived as "Peasants in Revolt"

In spite of their differences, Hillary and Donald, according to a Gallup Poll, each ended up among the most admired men and women in the world. Obama and Hillary tipped their respective lists, but Donald came in second, tying with Pope Francis.

Donald and Hillary certainly didn't admire each other. Their holiday spirit didn't last long. The Christmas season's last broadcast of "Jingle Bells" was played as Donald went on the attack, citing Bill Clinton "as a notorious philanderer. He's fair game in this campaign. Bill was a liability that Hillary suffered during her 2008 campaign against Obama, and this time around, it will be no different."

More and more talking heads on TV were claiming that without the support of African American voters, Donald could never win the presidency. A poll conducted by Quinnipiac University revealed that 88% of black America viewed Donald unfavorably.

The Rev. Jesse Jackson claimed that Donald's speeches on the campaign trail were "devastating, painful, and hurtful." The pastor was asked if he felt that Donald was a racist. "I don't use that kind of language."

Donald and Jackson had known each other for some three decades, and he had given Jackson free office space in one of his building in the Wall Street district.

During the course of his business career, Donald had known many African American celebrities, such as boxer Mike Tyson and his wife, Robin Givens, as well as the king of pop, Michael Jackson. Don King, Tyson's former promoter, said, "Donald's my man. That's who he is. As for those outlandish remarks, that's Donald. This is not a presidential endorsement. It is a humanistic endorsement."

For the most part, Obama stayed out of the campaign, but right before Christmas, he blasted Donald for exploiting the fears of the working class man—"Joe Sixpack"—claiming that much of the contempt he faced was for being the first black commander-in-chief.

The President also asserted his belief that the relentless charges about being born in Kenya, and that he was therefore not an American, or the lie that he was not a Christian, were all tied in with the fact that he was the first black President.

***

With his wife Melania, and his son, Barron, Donald flew to Mar-a-Lago in Palm Beach for the Christmas holidays. For one day, he quit tweeting attacks on his enemies.

But on the night before Christmas, 2015. Hillary and Donald weren't singing Christmas Carols, but exchanging barbs instead. She claimed that Donald had "a penchant for sexism," and would not be the best candidate to advance women's rights.

Blasting back, he accused her of "playing the woman card." On Twitter, he wrote, "Be careful, Hillary, as you play the war-on-woman-being-degraded card. When you complain about a penchant for sexism, who are you referring to? I have great respect for women."

Without saying so, he was actually threatening to introduce her husband's 1990s reputation—"his abuse of women"—into the 2016 race,

"The Mini-Donald," as Melania called him, appeared at Christmas in a matching blue suit and tie, as he made the rounds of the various tables at Mar-a-Lago. "A future President in the making," said one of the guests. Another guest at a nearby table called Barron "the best dressed nine-year-old in America."

After dinner, when Barron retired for the night, Donald and Melania went to a midnight service at the Episcopal Church of Bethesda-by-the Sea, where they had been married in 2005.

"Hillary has some nerve to talk about a war on women and other bigotry toward women when she has a serious problem with her husband," Katrina Pierson, a Trump spokesperson said on CNN. "I can think of quite a few women who have been bullied by Hillary in an attempt to hide her husband's misogynistic sexist secrets."

She was getting stabbed on all sides, both by Donald's forces and by her aging rival, Senator Bernie Sanders of Vermont. On CBS's *Face the Nation*, he revealed that he might also be Donald's worst enemy, as he planned to win over much of his constituency in his support of a $15-an-hour wage, the creation of new jobs, and his making college tuition free.

At year's end, economists began to analyze not only Sanders' giveaways, but also those among the GOP frontrunners. Shockingly, it was determined that the Trump plan would increase the U.S. deficit by $12 trillion over ten years.

His chief rival, Cruz, had a plan that called for a flat tax rate and the elimination of all payroll taxes used to fund Social Security and Medicare. Most economists denounced this plan as "irresponsible fantasy."

Back on the campaign trail, Cruz proved himself to be the major "culture warrior" of the GOP, unless one counted the losing evangelical, Mike Huckabee. The Texas senator continued with his anti-gay chant, insisting that as President, he would be under no obligation to accept the Supreme Court's decision on same-sex marriage.

***

Despite her pregnancy, Ivanka had been on the campaign trail advocating for her father. Right after Christmas, she posed for a picture of herself as a pregnant mother.

A business woman, Ivanka was set to give birth to her third child.

She leveraged the occasion into a vehicle for the promotion of "Daddy Don," claiming that he was one of the campaign's greatest advocates for women. "He 100% believes in quality of gender."

The 34-year-old daughter was asked about political ambitions of her own. "At this point, I would never contemplate it, but that doesn't mean when I'm fifty, I might have a change of heart."

***

Many members of the Republican Establishment, including both John McCain and Mitt Romney—each a failed presidential candidate in his own right—continued to express their total contempt for Donald and his campaign. Yet despite ferocious opposition from the Old Guard, poll after poll continued to document his amazing depth and breadth of his support.

His attackers trivialized his supporters as "Trumpkins." In the words of journalist Michael Walsh, they were "mental midgets and xenophobic troglodytes who've crawled out from their survivalist caves to destroy the Beltway Establishment."

A headline read THE PEASANTS ARE REVOLTING, as national polls put Donald at 40% in the GOP race, with Cruz trailing at 8%.

Rick Wilson, writing in *The Daily Beast,* said that Trump supporters "put the entire conservative movement at risk of being hijacked and destroyed by a bloviating billionaire with poor impulse control and a profoundly superficial understanding of the world."

One conservative writer concluded, "The Trumpkins are sick of winning and having nothing to show for it, and their vengeance will be terrible."

Spy magazine dubbed Donald "the short-fingered vulgarian—neither a real Republican nor a real conservative."

Donald's hometown newspaper, the *New York Daily News,* awarded him its annual "New York Knucklehead of the Year Award for his superstorm of stupidity." The paper stated that the award was "to identify people who make asses of themselves with acts of vanity, ambition, and plain stupidity at levels far beyond those of mere morons."

Donald was determined not to let the year end without dredging up discord associated with the embarrassments of "Bubba" Clinton, appearing on the *Today Show* to bring up the old charges of his infidelities that marred his presidency in the 1990s.

"There was certainly a lot of abuse of women," Donald charged. "You look at whether it's Monica Lewinsky or Paula Jones or many of them, and that certainly will be fair game, certainly if they play the woman card with respect to me."

"I like the fact that Bill Clinton is out campaigning for his wife. He failed badly in 2008, really badly. He did a poor job of campaigning, if you wanna know the truth."

When Bill Clinton as president was mired in scandal in 1998, Donald appeared on CNN. He told the audience, "Bill is probably got the toughest skin I've ever seen. I think he's a teriffic guy."

After the Clintons left the White house, Donald pitched the idea to them of settling into one of his gilded properties in Manhattan. But instead, they moved to Westchester County, into a verdant suburb north of the city.

Donald even praised Bill's golfing abilities (or lack thereof). The former President is only a so-so golfer known for taking mulligans.

He also claimed that Hillary "would be the worst president ever."

However, back in 2008, Donald had said, "I know Hillary, and I think she'd make a great President or Vice President."

On December 29, GOP presidential candidates temporarily slowed their attacks on Donald, firing instead upon Marco Rubio. Recent polls had indicated that he was running in second place to Donald.

Governor Chris Christie slammed Rubio for repeatedly not showing up for

GETTING SMEARED

(OR WAS IT SCHLONGED?) BY DONALD

Here we go again. Donald Trump, as part of a smear campaign, decided to revive the most notorious sex scandal of **Bill Clinton**'s presidency.

Monica Lewinsky and Bill were all smiles when this photograph on the White House grounds was taken, but soon they would not have anything to smile about.

A French newspaper (in English translation) wrote: "Only in America can the act of fellatio at the U.S. presidential palace lead to the impeachment of a sitting president. In Paris, we are far more sophisticated about such matters."

In lashing out at Hillary, some of the points Donald made about the sexual embarassments of the Clintons were true.

Blood Moon's award-winning biography **Bill & Hillary, So This Is That Thing Called Love** lays out—in a style equivalent to this overview of Donald Trump—most of the embarrassments, scandals, compromises, and pain associated with the Clintons.

work. Ads attacked Rubio for attending big fund raisers and missing key Senate hearings that had been scheduled after terrorist attacks in Paris and San Bernardino. One ad claimed, "Over the last three years, Rubio has missed important national security hearings and missed more total votes than any other senator."

The year of 2015 might be labeled "The Year of the Polls." When Civis Analytics, a Democratic data firm, released the results of its latest survey, it indicated that Donald was strongest in the South, in Appalachia, and in the industrial North. He showed his greatest strength among Republicans who are less affluent, less educated, and less likely to turn out to vote. Donald was particularly upset over that latter revelation. His most ardent fans were new Republicans, some of whom were nonetheless registered as Democrats.

His most loyal state was West Virginia, followed by New York. He fared well in Florida, in spite of the fact that two of that state's sons, Rubio and Jeb Bush, were also in the race.

His strength faded as the survey moved west, with an especially low approval rating in staunchly Republican Utah.

As 2015 ended, columnist Timothy Egan summed up the GOP state of affairs. "The Republican Party is now home to millions of people who would throw out the Constitution, welcome a police state against Latinos and Muslims, and enforce the religious test for entry into a country built by people fleeing religious persecution. This stuff polls well in the party, even if the Bill of Rights does not."

Famously pregnant, and, as breathlessly headlined by *Town and Country*, "in charge of a growing American Dynasty," the cover girl was once again **Ivanka**, by now an overexposed regular with some mileage under her belt.

In the throes of a show-stopping *haute mode* pregnancy, the press headlined her situation as **"Trump and Bump."**

Mitt Romney, the GOP nominee for President in 2012: "I will not endorse Donald Trump."

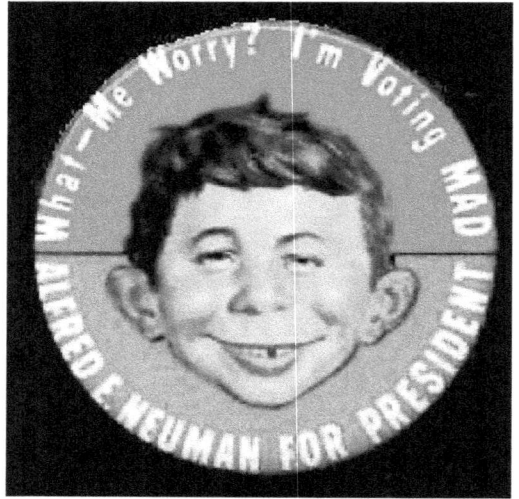

John McCain, the GOP nominee for President in 2008: "I will not endorse Donald Trump."

CHAPTER SEVEN

BOILING WITH HATRED
CAMPAIGN VITRIOL

ENRAGED, MUTUALLY ANTAGONISTIC CANDIDATES
UPGRADE THEIR ARSENALS AND INTENSIFY THEIR VENOM

TRAPPED BETWEEN A BOMB AND A KAMIKAZE
THE GOP IS HORRIFIED

"You can't make Châteaubriand out of cowpies, or chicken salad out of chicken shit."
—**Linda Stasi,** columnist for the *NY Daily News* in reference to **Ted Cruz**

Donald Trump opened January of 2016, the year of the presidential election, attacking President Obama for taking time out from his duties to attend a special screening of *Star Wars: Episode VII – The Force Awakens* (2015).

Seizing the opportunity as a sound bite, Donald accused him of prioritizing *Star Wars* over the War on Terror. The attack came in an ad posted on Instagram. "He prefers to watch the latest installment of the storied sci-fi franchise instead of using the force to fight ISIS," Donald charged. "We are in a serious war."

The ad ended with a film clip wherein the President ends a press conference with the words, "OK, everybody, I gotta get to *Star Wars.*"

The Trump video left out a major point: Obama was going to a special event for Gold Star families, those who had lost loved ones in the Iraq War. At his press conference, the President had tackled the subject of terrorist threats, global climate change, and Guantánamo Bay.

Donald revealed that he planned to spend $2 million of his own money over the upcoming months on ads in early primary or caucus states such as Iowa, New Hampshire, and South Carolina. He was still leading in the national polls, although evangelicals were converging around Ted Cruz, who had spent a lot of time campaigning in Iowa in anticipation of feverishly anticipated February 1 caucus.

Dr. Ben Carson, who had once been a frontrunner in Iowa, began 2016 with deep rifts in his campaign staff, as evidenced by the resignation of its manager, Barry Bennett. Carson's spokesman, Doug Watts, also resigned after multiple fumblings by Carson, many of them exposing his *naïveté* in foreign affairs. Despite strenuous efforts to stop it, Carson's campaign continued its downward spiral.

As America moved into 2016, arch conservatives, such as columnist Peggy Noonan, was asking, "Will Donald Trump unite or divide the GOP? We could see a great party split. The question is whether his race will play out over the next few cycles, or turn abrupt and fiery. Some in Washington speak giddily of the prospect, wondering aloud if the new party's logo will be a lion or a gazelle."

Other columnists, such as Ross Douthat, weighed in on the strange turn the GOP had taken. He admitted, "I underestimated Donald Trump. I sold him wildly short, and his entire campaign to date has proven it. Trump has had a very easy time turning his celebrity fan base into a meaningful constituency."

Douthat also wrote, "I'm not completely humbled. Indeed, I'm still proud enough to continue predicting, in defiance of national polling, that there's still no way that Trump will actually be the 2016 Republican nominee. Trust me: I'm a pundit."

Top photo: **Detail from an anti-Rubio poster** distributed widely during the caucases.

Lower photo: Donald Trump attached this illustration directly to his Twitter feed with this (devastating) message:

"Little Marco Rubio, the lightweight no show Senator from Florida is just another Washington politician."

Donald's major competition was also being examined, and not faring well, either. According to odds makers and prediction markets, Marco Rubio, the "absentee" senator from Florida, was a probable nominee, even though he was still a distant third behind Donald and Cruz in the polls.

As columnist Frank Bruni noted: "For those who could not stomach either Cruz or Donald as the nominee, Rubio was the flawed, rickety lifeboat they clung to, the amulet they clutched. Trump is too perverse, Cruz too cruel."

Unattractive episodes from Rubio's past emerged. During his tenure as majority whip in the Florida House of Representatives, he used Statehouse stationery to write a letter of support for the issuance of a real estate license for his sister's husband, who had served twelve years in a Federal prison for distributing $15 million worth of cocaine.

Rubio was often called "The Republican Obama," owing to his youth (age 44) and his elevation to a presidential contender while still a first-term senator.

But one GOP strategist called him "the Republican Bill Clinton, a Slick Willie who straddles ideological divides carrying the Tea Party banner while still cozy with Wall Street donors."

Journalist Eleanor Clift claimed, "He is triangulating," a Clintonian verb used to describe Rubio's evolving position on the issues. He was often denounced as "fuzzy."

Donald continued his assault on his GOP rivals, but saved much of his fire to burn Hillary. He made outrageous accusations against her, suggesting she caused tremendous deaths in the Middle East and that she was the chief architect of the migration of millions of refugees from Syria. He blamed her for voting for the war against Iraq and for the U.S. intervention in Libya that resulted in the killing of Moammar Khadafy in 2011, followed by a civil war. He further blamed her for the deaths of four American citizens at the U.S. consulate in Benghazi.

"The entire world has been upset by her wrong judgments," Donald charged. "She did a terrible job as Secretary of State."

At a rally in Mississippi, he accused both Hillary and Obama of being the "twin founders of ISIS." He claimed that their "reckless decisions" inspired the birth and survival of the terror group, which burns men in cages and beheads others. He called for Hillary to end up "behind bars for her misuse of her private email system. She should be in jail for what she did. What she did with those emails is a disgrace."

His New Year's celebration was brief, and by January 3, he was admitting to the press that, "I feel guilty. My campaign for the White House has cost me so little. I was going to have to spend some $35 to $40 million by now. But I have spent almost nothing. That's why I feel guilty." He made these remarks on CBS's *Face the Nation*.

He claimed that thousands of supporters were attracted to him because he was self-funded and wasn't a "bought candidate like Jeb Bush or Marco Rubio." He survived on endless appearances on TV and call-ins on talk radio shows, and—lest we forget—his provocative tweets. [*Melania confessed around this time that she wished "he wouldn't tweet so much."*]

As he moved deeper into his campaign, comparisons were inevitable with the communist witch hunter, Senator Joseph McCarthy, who, in the early 1950s, had terrified (and sometimes ruined) liberals and leftists.

Columnist Richard Cohen said, "Trump is not quite ready yet to fill McCarthy's boots. He has the late senator's gift for exaggeration and self-worship, and he needs the spotlight the way a vampire needs blood. We've been down this road before. But this time, instead of a demagogue on his knees like McCarthy shooting craps ('Come on babies, Papa needs a new pair of shoes!'), we've got one who owned the gaming tables in Atlantic City."

A poll released January 6 was deeply disturbing to leaders of the Republican Party. In essence, voters said, "It's Donald Trump—or nobody."

In the latest NBC/Survey Monkey Poll, he grabbed 35% of the voters, with Ted Cruz trailing at 18%. Most of Donald's supporters said they'd vote for him because they saw him as a strong leader. The majority of voters claimed that if Donald failed to get nominated, they would sit out the presidential election in November.

Despite Donald's sizable lead, he turned on Cruz, his closest rival. "The fact he was born in Alberta, Canada, is a big problem. He was, in fact, an Anchor Baby."

Donald had once demanded a forensic audit of Obama's birth certificate. Now he predicted an equivalent problem for Cruz. "The GOP may be tied up in court for two years if Cruz wins, because he was born to an American mother and a Cuban father in Canada. I would not call that a 'natural born' U.S. citizen."

Every day from his campaign trail, Donald promised to "Make America Great again." In defiance, outside his rallies, protesters sometimes carried signs—"AMERICA WAS NEVER GREAT!"

Many older voters recalled a time half a century ago when non-Hispanic whites made up more than 83 percent of the population. By 2016, that figure had fallen to only 62% of the demographic. It was predicted that Hispanics might be in the majority in 20 or 30 years, far outnumbering African Americans. The ongoing shift in voting power deeply alarmed many of Donald's most ardent supporters.

Columnist Eduard Porter wrote: "The reaction of whites who are struggling economically raises the specter of an outright political war along racial and ethnic lines over the distribution of resources and opportunities."

"Racial animosity in the U.S. makes redistribution to the poor, who are disproportionately black, unappealing to many voters," wrote economist Alberto Alesina.

The eminent sociologist, William Julius Wilson, said, "White taxpayers have opposed welfare because they see themselves as being forced, through taxes, to pay for stuff for blacks that many of them could not afford for their own families,"

In-depth surveys showed that Donald appealed to this white voter, who feared he or she would soon be disenfranchised by the rising tide of minorities.

Throughout most of his campaign, Donald had avoided an outlay of cash for expensive ads, having concluded that the daily 24-hour news cycle, as broadcast on cable TV, usually spotlighted him as the lead-off news event.

His monopoly of the nation's daily news cycle was defined as a "chokehold" by some pundits.

But in the first week of January, he launched his first-ever TV ad campaign, an anti-immigration video that, before 2PM on the day of its release, made him an international laughing stock.

On TV, swarms of desperate refugees were depicted running (presumably) toward the U.S. border, as a voice intoned,

The ferociously anti-communist Republican Senator from Wisconsin, **Joseph McCarthy** *(left)* with attorney **Roy Cohn** during Senate hearings.

In the 1950s, the gay attorney was "the brain" behind McCarthy. He later became Donald Trump's "take-no-prisoners" lawyer.

Collusion, collaboration, and betrayals from the then-president of the Screen Actors Guild, **Ronald Reagan**.

"Donald will stop illegal immigration by building a wall on our southern border that Mexico will pay for."

It was later revealed that the immigrants depicted in the video were not racing from within Mexico toward the U.S. border. The refugees depicted were Moroccans attempting to flee from their native land into Mellila.

[Mellila, along with nearby Ceuta, are autonomous Spanish ports, much-disputed remnants from Spain's imperial age, on the Mediterranean coast of Morocco.]

"I'M NO DUMBO."
—Melania Trump

The increased visibility (and perhaps the increasing defensiveness) of **Melania** made its way into increased media exposure.

"Growing up as a little girl in Slovenia, never in my wildest dreams did I ever think I might be a candidate for First Lady of America."

At a chic party in Miami's Design District, Ivana, the "dumped" first wife of Donald, continued her rather catty attack on Melania, suggesting she might be too ill-informed, too shy and retiring, to make a suitable First Lady. However, she totally endorsed Donald's candidacy.

She didn't say so, but the inference was that he'd need a First Lady like herself, with an energy and capability equivalent to how she'd supervised the restoration of the Plaza Hotel in Manhattan and a major Trump casino hotel in Atlantic City, to help him run the country.

These remarks seemed to push Melania out of the shadows and into the light. At the beginning of the campaign, she'd chosen to remain within Trump Tower with her beloved son, Barron, as Donald flew in and out of Manhattan. She told the press that when they were separated, she spoke to him at least five times a day.

She told a reporter for *Harper's Bazaar* that, "I have chosen not to go political in public. That's my husband's job. They say I'm shy. I'm not shy."

"I also am not behind in the issues," she said, "as some of my critics have suggested. Behind closed doors, I am very political. Between me and my husband, I know everything that is going on. I follow politics from A to Z."

"I have my own mind, my own opinions," she maintained. "I am my own person. I think my husband likes me for that."

Her increased visibility on the campaign scene earned her big headlines, including one in *The New York Post*. TRUMP'S WIFE SPEAKS OUT: "I'M NO DUMBO!"

MEANWHILE, IN THE U.K...
"If Britain Bans Donald, Would He, as President, Carpet Bomb London?"

Throughout the campaign, and during the spring months to come, Donald generated headlines virtually every day. Some of them were unexpected, as when the House of Commons in London debated whether he should be banned from the British Isles. Members of Parliament were responding to a petition that had circulated and had garnered some 580,000 signatures, calling for a blockage of his presence from the U.K., based on his call to ban Muslims from entering the United States.

"If Trump came to visit our country, he'd unite all of us against him," said the British Prime Minister, David Cameron, who had previously expressed his widely distributed distaste for the GOP frontrunner.

In reference to Donald, among the bizarre letters the PM received was one from a British survivor of World War II: "Are you considering breaking off diplomatic relations with the United States if voters put Mr. Trump in the White House? Please remember that the Yanks helped us in World War II...and be kind, won't you?"

Donald answered his detractors in England, those who had objected to his suggestion that America seal its borders as a response to the global threat of terrorism.

Whereas Donald will be indelibly associated with NYC and its idiosyncracies, across the pond in London, **Boris Johnson**—in terms of braggadoccio and media swagger—was a more-than-adequate counterpart.

Donald-isms that made him unpopular in the U.K., some of them uttered as early as 2012, included: "Wind farms are a disaster for Scotland like **Pan Am 103,** an abomination, only sustained with government subsidy."

Boris' coif was sometimes compared to Donald's.

George Osborne, Chancellor of the Exchequer, denounced Donald's "hate speech" but rejected the call to bar him from entering the U.K., asserting that his "nonsense" views must be defeated through debate rather than banning him. "Bloody hell! He might be the next President of the United States."

Many Londoners were angered when Donald told *MSNBC* that "Parts of London are so radicalized that the police are afraid for their lives." Boris Johnson *[London's Mayor from 2008-2016]* dismissed that assertion "for being simply ridiculous. The only reason I wouldn't go to some parts of New York is the real risk of meeting Donald Trump."

In the House of Commons, lawmakers attacked Donald as "a demagogue," "an idiot," and "a joke."

Jack Dromey, a Member of Parliament, said, "It would be dangerous and deeply divisive" to let Trump fly into London."

It was even suggested that he might fear for his life if he wandered into Birmingham, based on that city's large Muslim population.

"Donald Trump is free to be a fool, but he's not free to be a dangerous fool in Britain," said Tulip Siddiq, another member of Parliament who labeled Donald's words as "poisonous. They are not comical."

Not every lawmaker agreed, some of them pointing out that barring Donald might make him a martyr. Time and time again, lawmakers kept pointing out that the United States was Britain's major ally and barring a U.S. President from its borders was "unthinkable."

One member of Parliament asked, "What if the Queen invited The Donald for tea at Buckingham Palace?"

"His mother, a fine woman, was born in Scotland," another member pointed out. "British blood flows through his veins."

The Trump Organization eventually issued a statement: "We will pull back from plans to invest about $1.03 billion, or £700 million, in Scotland if the government votes to bar Mr. Trump from entering Britain. Barring Mr. Trump will alienate millions of Americans who wholeheartedly support him."

Mark Hughes of Edinburgh said, "Trump threatening to pull millions out of Scotland and abandon his planned golf course near Aberdeen, I say good riddance. We're just fine without whatever vulgar monstrosity his money would build."

Jeanetta Baratta tweeted, "Go then, pull out: No one wants you in Scotland anyway."

One of Donald's most ardent supporters, Glenn Forrest, of Chicago tweeted: "When he's elected President, Mr. Trump would be justified to carpet bomb London to bring back memories of the Blitz."

Many American columnists, such as Ted Wrobleski, chided the Brits for their anti-Trump rants. "BUTT OUT ON TRUMP!" headlined one of his columns. "Let Americans deal with the stuff on our side of the pond. After all, we won the Revolutionary War. It's not your country anymore. On migrants, Trump's position was better safe than sorry. What if they banned him if he were the U.S. head of state? What are we to do? Break off all diplomatic relations with us? Close the embassies? Drive us back into the arms of the French?"

Eventually, despite the fiery British rhetoric, both in and out of Parliament, the House of Commons, as it turned out, discreetly opted not to hold a vote about barring, or not barring, Donald from the U.K.

DONALD PREFERS A POTTY MOUTH TO A SILVER SPOON

"This Is a Campaign Worse Than Voters Have Ever Seen"

With alarming frequency, polls revealed just how polarized America had become, and as he continued his campaign, it seemed that Donald was making it even worse. For the first time in history, polls demonstrated that both of the frontrunners, both Donald and Hillary, were unpopular by record-breaking margins. "We're given a choice," said Brett Halper. "We'll have to vote for Hillary or Donald and decide which one we hate the least."

As he neared the end of his administration, Obama, as evaluated in the words of writer Ed Criscoll, had presided over "the hateful eight years." As America's first black President, he had been the single most polarizing President in American history.

However, many savvy politicians said Obama would soon lose that label, transferring it onto his successor after the November 2016 elections. "Take your choice: it's either Donald or Hillary. Talk about polarizing," wrote one GOP activist.

Pollsters found the public "ready to lay down their switchblades and switch to howitzers," in the words of one reporter. Donald's latest disapproval rating had him at 57% opposed, with Hillary a close rival.

Donald's other rival, Ted Cruz, "did not come across as a day at the beach," in the

The Immigration Wars: HATING RUBIO and (ANCHOR) BABIES

Some Donald supporters said, "DON'T LOOK NOW, BUT IT ISN't JUST TED CRUZ WITH THE ELIGIBILITY PROBLEM."

This illustration appeared on the conservative website patriotretort.com with the caption BABY MARCO: "EL CUBANO."

words of *MSNBC*'s Chris Matthews.

Columnist Kyle Smith wrote: "Cruz is worse than a used-car salesman. He's more like a used car salesman's lawyer. GOP candidates are chasing the most extreme, stubborn, and confrontational members of their party. It'll be a campaign season nastier than anything you've ever seen. There won't even be a pretense of playing to our better instincts. Forget hope and change. It's time for nope and rage."

Most of Hillary's supporters seemed unmoved by Donald's onslaught. "Same old, same old," said Ann Poe, a Democratic City Councilwoman in Cedar Rapids, Iowa.

David Brock, founder of the pro-Clinton Super PAC, *Correct the Record*, said, "These are desperate moves by Trump to appeal to the right wing. He's throwing red meat at his conservative base."

Donald was not satisfied in going after just Hillary. Once Bill Clinton hit the campaign trail, he attacked the former President "as an abuser of women."

Hillary shot back at Donald. During one of her interviews on CBS's *Face the Nation*, she said, "Talk about my husband's infidelity is a dead end, a blind alley for Trump."

In an appearance in Cedar Rapids, Bill Clinton didn't snap at the bait tossed by Donald. Instead, he brushed aside issues associated with his former dealings with women. "I'm in this campaign only to help Hillary, not to answer Trump's ridiculous charges. I have no response. He says a lot of silly things."

When not either joining in the assault on Hillary, or firing shots at Donald, the other frontrunners went after each other. Jockeying for position from way behind, Chris Christie told Laura Ingraham, the right-wing radio talk show host, that "Hillary Clinton would pat Rubio on the head and then cut his heart out if they squared off in a general election. That guy's been spoon fed every victory he's ever had."

Competing for the evangelical vote, Rubio and Cruz each began a tirade about which of them was the most religious. Cruz presented himself as a man so devout that he seemed to wake up to the sound of "Onward Christian Soldiers" with trumpets blaring. "Put on the full armor of God," he exhorted his campaign volunteers.

Later that day, he told a rally in Iowa, "Any President who doesn't begin every day on his knees isn't fit to be commander-in-chief."

He was speaking at a convention of Faith & Freedom, screeching about "religious liberty." Translated, that meant the freedom to refuse gay people's access to same-sex weddings.

As one LGBT activist said, "In other words, these people wanted their freedom while denying it to millions of others. What bullshit!"

Back on the east coast, *The New York Daily News* took a dim view of both Trump and Cruz. One of its blaring front page headlines read "DROP DEAD, TED." Inside, another headline proclaimed "WHAT AN ASS HE IS."

In one of its editorials, it claimed, "Cruz and Trump are sorry specimens. Neither is blessed with the character of a New Yorker."

The paper concluded that, "Trump is one white guy even Al Sharpton can't bamboozle or threaten with a racial demonstration—the kind that can end with Sharpton getting a nice fat seat on whatever board he's threatening with racism at the moment."

On January 13, Cruz's finances were exposed by *The New York Times*, the paper claiming that the candidate solicited and received a loan of more than $1 million from Goldman Sachs and Citizen's Bank. *[His wife, Heidi, worked for Goldman Sachs.]*

According to the paper, whereas he had spent the money to finance his 2012 Senate race in Texas, he had failed to disclose the loan on his campaign finance report.

Ted and Heidi had decided at the time to liquidate their entire net worth to finance their campaigns. A spokesperson for Cruz claimed, "The failure to report the loan was inadvertent."

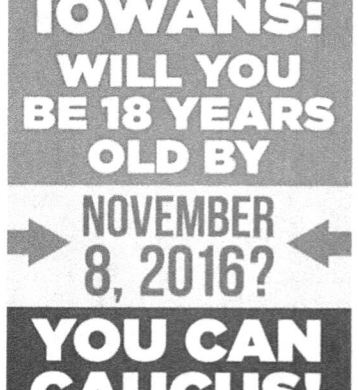

Pundits from all sides of the political spectrum denounce **the Iowa Caucus** as irritating, misleading, and undefinitive.

But as a PR tool and bellwether for heartland America's political groundswells, each of the 2016 candidates threw themselves into it with something approaching passion.

Early in January, Donald daringly decided to invade Burlington, Vermont, staging a bigtime rally in the hometown of Bernie Sanders, who had once been its controversial "commie mayor." For fans or detractors hoping to get into the rally, security was told to "eliminate the riff-raff" and invite only Donald's faithful. "I'm planning to take care of my people—not the morons voting for Bernie or the undecided," Donald said.

Hiss rally in Burlington unfolded within the Flynn Center for the Performing Arts, attracting a heady mix of supporters, protesters, and the merely curious. His speech was interrupted by protesters who had lied about their loyalties to security guards at the entrance.

"Confiscate their coats," Donald urged from the platform. "Turn those loose outside where it's ten degrees below zero."

After they were removed, he told the faithful. "Oh, I would like to run against Bernie. A dream come true."

When Sanders heard that, the socialist said, "And I would love, love, love to run against Trump."

As the campaign moved forward, Donald became increasingly known for his tweets, which at times became notorious. He even tweeted that he would "kick the ass of drug lord El Chapo."

Surprisingly, from somewhere deep within Mexico, El Chapo tweeted back. "Keep fucking around, and I'll make you eat those god damn words, you fucking whitey."

In January, the drug lord was captured at his hideaway in Mexico.

The "oily" Ted Cruz, as some members of the press had dubbed him, also tweeted anti-Trump messages. "Can that kind of slime *[a reference to Donald]* even be showered off with a firehouse?" he asked.

On January 10, Donald appeared on *MSNBC's Meet the Press,* hosted by Chuck Todd. He was told that once again he had been compared to Kim Kardashian or else to circus king P. T. Barnum. By this point in his campaign, the association of Donald with that entertainer and impresario had become widespread. The *National Review* had called Donald "the P.T. Barnum of American politics," and in a roughly equivalent phraseology, *Salon.com* had deemed him "the Second Coming of P.T. Barnum."

Donald opted for and seemed to cheerfully endorse the Barnum comparison. "We need a little bit of Barnum," he said, "because we have to build up the image of this country. We have to be a cheerleader for America. Obama is not. He's the great divider."

As tension increased, more and more Old Guard Republicans like John Cain expressed fears that a lasting split along class divisions might erupt because of provocations from mavericks like Donald and Cruz. "I haven't seen this large a division in my career," said McCain. "Ronald Reagan and Gerald Ford were tense in 1976, but not like this."

In 2016, in response to Donald's negative comments about Mexicans, "**El Chapo**" ("Shorty," *aka* **Joaquín Archivaldo Guzmán Loera**), depicted here after an arrest in 1993, sent a threat to "whitey Trump."

Identified by U.S. officials as Public Enemy no. 1, he was, at various periods of his saga, the most powerful drug trafficker in the world, a billionaire kingpin responsible for the transport of some 500 tons of cocaine into the United States.

Political strategists within the GOP claimed it might be hard to suppress the passions of an angry, hard-core, anti-immigrant base in the future. It appeared that the nativists weren't going away early; if anything, they appeared to be becoming more feverish.

Columnist Frank Bruni wrote: "If you're not with them, you're a loser (Trump's words) or godless (Cruz's words). The duo markets name-calling as truth-telling, pettiness as boldness, vanity as conviction. And their tandem success suggests a dynamic peculiar to the 2016 election. A special rule prevails: Obnoxiousness is the new charisma."

David Von Drehle in *Time* magazine wrote, "The GOP has awakened to find itself in bed between a bombshell and a kamikaze."

Many analysts concluded that Independents—and not traditionally defined Republicans or Democrats, who seemed to be running neck and neck—would decide the outcome of the general election in November, and that Independents appeared to be far from sold on the GOP frontrunners, Cruz or Donald.

In the 2012 election, 41% of all voters had self-defined as moderate, with 29% weighing in as conservatives.

In contrast, polls also showed that Donald's unfavorable ratings were higher than those of any candidate in the GOP field.

Ted Cruz didn't fare much better. According to Dean Stroker, a Hillary campaign aide, in reference to Cruz, "'That wacko bird,' *[a label coined by John McCain]*, seemed to have stuck to his *[i.e., Cruz's]* slimy feathers like tar."

CHARLESTON
THE DARKEST OF THE GOP DEBATES

RESEMBLING A CARTOON SIDESHOW, IT FEATURES A TEXAS IDEOLOGUE WITH A PROFESSIONAL HATRED FOR NEW YORKERS AND AN AGENDA TO THE RIGHT OF ATTILA THE HUN

PLAYGROUND BULLIES AT WAR
When Donald Defines Cruz as a "Canadian Anchor Baby," Cruz Rips Donald's "New York Values"

"WE DON'T WANT YOU!"
Horrified Canadians Lash Out at Bible-Thumping Cruz

The sixth GOP debate was held on January 14, 2016 in North Charleston, South Carolina, by the Fox Business Network at that town's Coliseum. Moderators included Neil Cavuto and Maria Bartiromo. In the prime time debate, Donald occupied center stage, adjacent to such other "mainliners" as Ted Cruz and Marco Rubio.

The 5PM "Kiddie Table debate" had featured Mike Huckabee, Rick Santorum, and Carly Fiorina. Rand Paul had been invited, but he had bowed out, resenting his demotion from prime time "to the losers' debate." In spite of, and in defiance of, his low poll numbers, he insisted he was a first tier candidate running a first tier campaign.

Voters did not agree. One voter in South Carolina said, "I sort of like Donald's hair, but I find Rand Paul's hair a big turn-off for me."

Other polling of South Carolina voters showed that many opinions were based on very personal reactions. "I was for Ted Cruz," said a garage mechanic from Charleston, "because I think he believes in Jesus. Then I saw that wife of his, this Heidi thing, on TV. I found her disgusting. If there's one thing I hate, it's a god damn Texas broad."

The rising heat of the debate was fueled by acidic exchanges between Cruz and Donald, as they engaged in bitter rivalry, their former "bromance" long buried with the ashes of yesterday. Donald questioned the Texas senator's eligibility to run for President, calling him an Anchor Baby born in Alberta, Canada, to a Cuban father from Castro's communist island of Cuba.

"You might drag the party into a legal fight with Democrats since you were born outside the United States," Donald said. "That's the question mark over your head. The Constitution calls for a natural-born citizen. Alberta is not part of the United States. Neither is Kenya for that matter."

Cruz, who had frequently touted his credentials as a constitutional lawyer, angrily shot back. "I'm not taking legal advice from Donald Trump. I recognize that Donald is dismayed that his poll numbers are falling in Iowa."

Cruz then assailed Donald for having so-called "New York Values," reminding his audience in contemptuous tones that "not many conservatives come out of Manhattan. I think most people know exactly what New York values are. Everyone understands that the values in New York City are socially liberal."

In Donald's best moment throughout the debates, he eloquently defended New Yorkers. "When the World Trade Center came down, I saw something that no place on earth could have handled more beautifully, more humanely. That was a very insulting statement Cruz made."

That debate was one of the darkest of the campaign. Each of the candidates depicted America suffering through a great malaise, declining economically and militarily, its once lofty position as leader of the Free World fading.

Rubio tried to slip an occasional comment into a debate otherwise virtually monopolized by Donald and Cruz. "I hate to interrupt this episode on *Court TV*," the Florida senator said to laughter and applause. But when he eventually got to speak, Rubio offered little that was new, for the most part referencing canned, overused, overexposed comments from the campaign trail.

Several candidates attacked Donald's endorsement of a 45% tariff on all goods entering the U.S. from China. He denied having ever made that comment.

"During the mutual hatred that by now was obvious between Donald and Jeb, Hillary was mentioned too. Jeb! charged that if she were elected, she would spend the first 100 days of her office going back and forth between the White House and the courthouse, facing charges about her improper use of e-mails.

Rubio joined in the assault, claiming, "Hillary would be a disaster as President. She is not qualified to be the commander-in-chief. Someone who cannot handle intelligence information cannot be in charge. Nor can someone who lies to the families of those victims in Benghazi."

After the debate, which was widely watched in Cruz's native-born Canada, most Canadians were horrified by Donald's suggestion that Cruz should return north to run for Prime Minister.

Canadian newspapers were inundated with letters to the editor. Everad Soares wrote: "Please, Americans, do us a favor and keep him. We're enjoying watching your soap opera—what a script!"

"We don't want this jerk who has already rejected his Canadian citizenship," claimed Michael Reece. "Get lost and stay lost, Cruz!"

"The last thing Canada needs is another politician who sounds like he's on crack," claimed blogger John Ignatowicz.

Nothing generated more anti-Cruz hostility than his attack on "New York Values."

Columnist Mike Lupica wrote, "Cruz really must think he can get the nomination of his party by simply working the slower-thinking precincts, sharing a world view that could fit inside a shot glass."

Lupica ended his tirade by claiming, "It is the other party who has a donkey as its mascot. But Cruz is the one who is a jackass."

By the thousands, New Yorkers fired back at Cruz. Even Hillary said, "Just this one time, I applaud Donald Trump for defending New York. New Yorkers value hard work, diversity, tolerance, resilience, and building better lives for their families."

New York's Mayor, Bill de Blasio said, "On behalf of all New Yorkers, I'm disgusted at the insult that Ted Cruz threw at this city and its people."

"What are New York values?" tweeted Scott Wooledge of Manhattan. "We dominate the world of finance, medicine, science, fashion, art, music, theater, publishing, media, and hospitality."

New York State's Governor, Mario Cuomo, said, "If the jerk has any class at all, and I suspect he doesn't, Cruz should apologize to the people of New York."

Even the conservative *Wall Street Journal* weighed in on Cruz's assault on New York, "The problem with the Princetonian's anti-New York riff is that it echoes Sarah Palin's 2008 disdain for the part of the country that she said wasn't the real America. Cruz is playing the same kind of polarizing politics to win over conservatives in Iowa, by showing contempt for half the country. This is not the way to build a conservative majority."

In an analysis of the debate, columnist Gerald F. Seib wrote: "After months of dancing around each other in crystallizing anti-establishment anger, the two (Trump and Cruz) now know they are fishing from the same pond with less than three weeks to go before voting in Iowa begins."

Cruz emerged as a slashing, skilled debater, even if he wandered down some dark backwoods road in the rotting sagebrush wastelands of Texas. For most of his career in the Senate, he had been dismissed as a "cartoon sideshow—an ostrich boot-wearing ideologue."

Reporter Michael Barbaro wrote: "Cruz just didn't dominate much of the debate, he slashed, he mocked, he charmed, and he outmaneuvered everybody else on stage, but none as devastatingly and as thoroughly as this campaign's most commanding performer, Donald J. Trump."

At the time of the debate, news broke that Donald had picked up the dubious backing of White Nationalist Groups, including the Ku Klux Klan. Members were leading the "Bias Bandwagon," agreeing with Donald's proposed crackdown on illegal immigration—"those Mexicans coming here to rape our women and take our jobs."

These "Second Coming" tabloid frontpages made **Ted Cruz** as welcome in New York as the Second Coming of the Bubonic Plague.

Voters in Iowa were bombarded by robo-calls. Many of them encouraged voters to turn out for Donald, "The Great White Hope to Save America."

Jared Taylor, founder of *American Renaissance*, a webzine sometimes described as a white supremist publication, said, "We need smart, well-educated white people who will assimilate to our culture. Vote Trump! We don't need Muslims in this country!"

Donald also picked up support from other white supremacist groups for having tweeted inaccurate crime statistics used by various KKK sympathizers. He suggested that Black Lives Matter activists deserved to be "roughed up." He was also receiving signs of support from virtually every Islamaphobe in America.

GOP candidates, especially Donald and Cruz, shifted to the right as it applied to their point of view about climate change, as the campaign trail became studded with rocks. In 2008, Rubio had backed a cap-and-trade program to combat climate change, but in a ploy to win the right wing, he shifted to the side of those who denied climate change, opposing remedies like cap-and-trade. "It will hurt the U.S. economy," he maintained.

Ironically, Republicans had once championed market-based systems to control pollution as a way to avoid more direct regulations.

But now, as part of a concentrated effort to thwart their (black) President and his Democratic supporters, the GOP took the night train out in another direction, questioning scientists, and perhaps the scientific process itself, in an attempt to win votes among the ill-informed.

As the days of January moved forward, Donald appeared to be losing in Iowa, yet nationwide, he was still the favorite among the Republican electorate. He actually went up in polls in December and January, as Cruz voters seemed to be leveling off.

"I smell blood on the battlefield," Donald told his aides. "Tainted Cruz blood."

As Trump's insults and rhetoric got hotter, so did the **implicit threats of violence** from gun advocates and/or members of the Tea Party.

"Brashness Becomes Boorishness, Peacockery Becomes Peevishness"

In Sioux Center, Iowa, just before the all-important Iowa caucus in early February, Donald delivered one of his most controversial statements: "I could stand in the middle of Fifth Avenue and shoot somebody, and I wouldn't lose my loyal voters."

[Surprisingly, that remark was uttered at—of all places—Dordt College, a private, Christian, liberal arts college that's closely affiliated with the Christian Reformed Church in North America.]

He used the speechifying venue there to bash radio talk show host Glenn Beck for having appeared at GOP rallies hyping the dubious candidacy of his rival, Ted Cruz. "Beck is a loser and sad sack," Donald proclaimed.

Many pundits had been recently evaluating the Republican campaign as if it had evolved into a contest exclusively dominated by Cruz and Donald. Charles Krauthammer, who appeared frequently on TV talk shows, wrote: "The 2016 race had turned into an epicontest between the ethno-nationalist populism of Donald Trump and traditional conservatism, though in two varieties; the scorched-earth fundamentalist version of Ted Cruz, and a reformist version of Marco Rubio—and articulated most fully by non-candidate Rand Paul and a cluster of productive thinkers and wonks dubbed 'reform-icons.'"

As the Republicans of Iowa were still trying to make up their minds about which candidate to endorse, columnist Michael Walsh summed up the race as a "cage match" between Donald and Cruz. "Brashness becomes boorishness," he wrote of Donald. "Peacockery becomes peevishness, and ostentation becomes obnoxiousness. A decisive loss for Trump in Iowa might mean a reversal of fortune to rival that of Oedipus. But betting that Trump will implode on his own accord has been a fool's game since he announced in June of 2015."

Walsh also wrote that, "The prickly charm of Cruz lacks Obama's easy charm, and as the 'first half-Cuban President,' that just doesn't have the same ring to it that the first black President has. Further, he lacks Marco Rubio's boyish earnestness, and the kind of urban *machismo* exemplified by Chris Christie. That doesn't fit the Harvard debater. Cruz is going to have to keep the knives out until he's the last man standing. There is no other way for him."

Tea Party rally in Hartford, Connecticut, in 2009. The movement's nascent roots went viral, just in time to feed the fires of Donald's rhetoric.

Columnists across the country kept writing about the GOP's Holy War, especially those aspects launched and perpetrated by Cruz and Rubio. At one rally, an evangelical conference, Cruz paraded onto the stage after a right-wing preacher, a real nutbag, talked about the death penalty, "according to the Bible," for gay people.

The Texas senator came out and pointedly did not renounce the horrendous "Biblical mandate." His strategy for changing his address to 1600 Pennsylvania Avenue hinged on evangelical support. He seemed shocked that the thrice-married Donald was capturing a lot of his voters.

On the campaign trail, Cruz hit harder against abortion and same-sex mar-

Trump fans called the act of affixing **this bumper sticker** to the backside of their cars an act of honest polical activism.

Opponents defined it as another incentive for road rage.

riage. Many observers claimed that his so-called political rants were nothing more than "hell's fire sermons," with constant invocations of God or Jesus Christ, with whom Cruz seemed in constant Facebook contact.

Jeb Bush even questioned Donald's professed faith. Rubio referenced "Judeo-Christian values," so frequently that many voters began to wonder if he knew that there was, within the constitution, a separation of church and state.

"If Rubi gets elected," wrote one reporter, "Muslims and Asians will have reason to fear for their future in Born Again America."

Hustling to South Carolina on his private jet, Donald addressed a Tea Party rally at Myrtle Beach.

From the podium, he lit into Cruz with rattlesnake venom. "Nobody likes Ted Cruz. Nobody in Washington likes him. He didn't report his bank loans from Goldman Sachs, and he's got bank loans from Citibank—and then he acts like Robin Hood. His wife worked for Goldman Sachs, which helped fund his Senate race. He's beholden to rich campaign donors…*Nasty Ted!* Nobody likes him anywhere once they get to know him. He's a hypocrite."

Donald's opinion of the nastiness of Cruz was echoed by many, some of them attacking him with better skills than Donald had.

One of the best of the New York columnists, Linda Stasi, wrote: "Ted Cruz is as disingenuous as he is despicable. You can't make Châteaubriand out of cowpies, any more than you can make chicken salad out of chicken shit. So from New York to Texas Ted: Screw you and the horse you rode in on. *Yeehaw!*"

Reaction against **Ted Cruz** from across the internet was swift. This went out to thousands of Twitter accounts from Cruz opponents across the political spectrum.

Some of them included the twittered message "**Cruz for PM** (Prime Minister)."

***

Donald continued to label Cruz as an "Anchor Baby," citing his birth in Alberta.

Retaliating, Cruz referred to his American "roots," asserting, "As an expert on the Constitution, I say there is no issue at all about my right to seek the Presidency."

Actually, he was misleading his followers. Other scholars of Constitutional law claimed that the definition of "natural born" had, in its 230-year history, never been fully resolved by the Supreme Court.

Although he'd been born in Calgary, Cruz claimed U.S. citizenship through his mother. He had moved to Houston when he was four, and "didn't realize" (his words) that he was still a Canadian citizen until the *Dallas Morning News* pointed it out to him in 2013. Subsequent to that, he renounced his Canadian citizenship in 2014.

The Constitution (and Cruz knew it) states that "No person except a natural born citizen of the United States shall be eligible to the office of President." The interpretation hinged on the phrase "natural born." [*In a twist on an example that Cruz's fellow Republicans had been chanting in reference to Obama for years, Cruz's opponents were saying: "If Cruz's mother had given birth to him in Kenya, or in Canada, would he therefore be a "natural born" U.S. citizen?*]

On the campaign trail, Cruz continued to hammer Donald relentlessly, accusing him of "being nothing but a deal-maker who will capitulate to the Washington Establishment."

The 1996 Republican presidential nominee, Bob Dole, had never liked Cruz. He told reporters, "The GOP would suffer cataclysmic and wholesale losses if Cruz were the Republican nominee. Trump would fare better."

Dole, a former senator from Kansas, also questioned Cruz's allegiance to the Republican Party. "I wouldn't call him a conservative. Extremist is the word. Trump probably could work with Congress because he's a kind of dealmaker. Cruz has falsely convinced Iowa voters he's a kind of mainstream conservative."

Dole's favorite candidate had been Jeb Bush, but even he had to admit, "Jeb has trouble gaining traction."

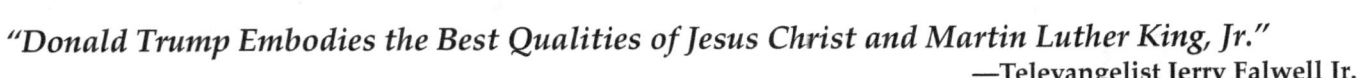

"Donald Trump Embodies the Best Qualities of Jesus Christ and Martin Luther King, Jr."
—Televangelist Jerry Falwell Jr.

At around the same time, even Donald became a "Bible Thumper," as demonstrated at his rally at Liberty University, a prominent evangelical Christian institution in Lynchburg, South Carolina.

He had pledged to defend Christians "under siege," citing a reference from "Two Corinthians 3:17." [*That phraseology raised eyebrows among the many Bible students in attendance, who knew that the book he was citing was almost universally referred to as "Second Corinthians."*]

Jerry Falwell Jr., [*son of Jerry Falwell (1933-2007), the ultra-conservative founder of Liberty University, a megachurch in Lynchburg, Virginia (The Thomas Road Baptist Church) and the political activist organization "Moral Majority"*] compared Donald favorably to both Jesus Christ and the Rev. Martin Luther King Jr.

The pastor also said that, "Donald is a wonderful father and a man who I believe can lead our country to greatness again."

However, other evangelists, including those ardently supporting Cruz, feared, "Donald is like a wolf in sheep's clothing, invading the flock."

As January deepened, polls showed Donald still out in front, often winning over more and more evangelicals who might have otherwise supported Cruz. The Texas Senator, in the words of one reporter, was practically conducting "holy-roller revivals."

Jerry Falwell Jr., President of Liberty University, gave what history will record as the single most over-effusive, over-the-top introduction of Donald Trump in the history of academia.

A *New York Times/CBS* poll had Donald, a Presbyterian, dominating the field with 42% of the evangelical vote.

A retired police officer from Oklahoma City claimed, "Trump is the only one who can pull America back from the abyss."

Along the way, Donald picked up a number of controversial endorsements, not just from the KKK. He won praise from America's most controversial sheriff, the immigrant-hating Joe Arpaio of Maricopa County in Arizona.

He also won praise from sources that included ultra-conservative author Ann Coulter; boxing champion Mike Tyson; Minnesota governor and previous pro wrestler Jesse Ventura; actors Stephen Baldwin and Gary Busey; wrestler/stuntman Hulk Hogan; and basketball star and "bad boy" personality Dennis Rodman when he wasn't extolling the virtues of North Korea's crazy dictator.

Another Trump endorsement came from gun advocate and rock guitarist Ted Nugent, who, on the warpath against Obama, referred to the President's supporters as "Pimps, whores, and welfare brats, soulless supporters electing a President to destroy America."

Then, a dubious "for Donald" endorsement came in from the New York-hating, has-been pitcher, John Rocker. In 1999, he had said, "The biggest thing I don't like about New York are the foreigners. How the hell did they get into this country?"

"You can walk the entire block of Times Square and not hear anybody speaking English. Donald Trump is my guy."

"Imagine having to take the subway to the ballpark," Rocker said: "It's like you're riding through Beirut. You sit next to a kid with purple hair on one side. On the other, some queer has AIDS. They get off and new passengers come on. The seat is taken by a dude who just got out of jail for the fourth time. On your right is a 20-year-old welfare mom with four kids—fathers unknown. It's depressing."

Editorial writers across the country continued with barrages, the *National Review* writing: "Donald Trump is a menace to American conservatism who would take the works of generations and trample it underfoot on behalf of populism as heedless and cruel as 'The Donald' himself."

Others disagreed, including John Feehery, a Capitol Hill lobbyist. "Trump won't do long-lasting damage to the GOP coalition. Cruz will."

Back in Donald's hometown of New York, the *Daily News* continued to mock Donald with its tabloid covers depicting him as a clown. The paper lamented the fact that Donald was still running strong and then editorialized, "The latest polls are a horrifying Rorschach test of the mentality of the GOP base. If only forced medication were available on a mass scale."

Although subjected to mounting criticism from around the world, Donald continued to win new voters every day. "I'm running my campaign from the heart—and the brain," he told the press.

However, Peter Wehner, a former White House adviser to the Bushes, said, "Trump's style degrades people and public discourse. His keen sense to go for the jugular and play to the Kardashian culture is effective, but dangerous for failing to offer a positive vision for the country."

"A lot of times I sound negative, but I'm really positive," Donald maintained. "Make America Great Again is a very positive campaign. I'm either going to get this campaign right, or else I'm not going to do it at all."

CHAPTER EIGHT

MAMA GRIZZLY ENDORSES DONALD
Sarah Palin Emerges from Her Troglodyte Cave

"BIRD BRAINS FLOCK TOGETHER"
Media reaction to Palin's endorsement of Donald Trump

PALIN BLAMES OBAMA
After Her Violent Son Is Arrested for Abuse of His "Gal Pal"

CHRISTIE, "LOOKING LIKE A HOSTAGE," ENDORSES TRUMP, THEN EVISCERATES RUBIO

Early in 2016, Sarah Palin, "the rogue Vice Presidential candidate" who helped John McCain lose his Republican bid for the presidency in 2008, emerged from the snow drifts of Alaska (from whose vantage point she could see Russia) to endorse Donald Trump. In Ames, Iowa, on January 19, she threw her Tea Party credentials behind him.

From a podium at Iowa State University, the wilting Venus's flytrap, by now beloved only by the Republican Party's most extreme right-wing fanatics, pumped up an audience with, "Are you ready to vote for the leader to make America great again? Are you ready to stump for Trump? I'm here to support the next President of the United States."

Then, repeating her faded, much-discredited signature phrase, she said, "He's been going rogue left and right!"

Columnist Gail Collins noted the half-smile on Donald's face as he stood uncomfortably next to her onstage, hearing her sing his praise as she warbled off-key and off-message.

According to Collins, it was "hard to tell if it were a half smile of self-satisfaction or the look of someone trapped at a dinner party next to a stranger who's describing how she met President William Henry Harrison in a past life."

Previously, Palin had thrown her endorsement to Ted Cruz during his run for the Senate of Texas. As payback for having switched allegiance, Cruz supporters later stigmatized Palin as a "deserter" and a "Trump turncoat."

Donald used his pulpit at the Iowa rally to denounce Cruz as "worse that Hillary Clinton. He didn't disclose his bank loans from Goldman Sachs," he continued, "because that greedy Wall Street firm owns him."

Palin's contract as an analyst with Fox News had ended (and pointedly not been renewed) in 2015, and since then, she had maintained a relatively low profile.

Cynics claimed that she had opted to endorse Donald as part of a cynical ploy to propel herself back into the media spotlight during the 2016 presidential race. Some pundits went on to speculate that she was seeking a cabinet position, or perhaps—although this was far-fetched— a nomination as his vice-presidential running mate.

Negative reactions to Palin's association with, and endorsement of, Donald were loud and immediate. One headline blared "A TRUMP/PALIN TICKET?—WHAT IS AMERICA COMING TO?" Columnist James Hyland wrote: "It's hardly surprising that a nattering nabob of narcissism like 'The Donald' would easily win the endorsement of another self-infatuated public celebrity—that nattering nemesis of the caribou, Sarah Palin. Perhaps she's gunning for the job of energy secretary in a Trump administration."

Most *politicos* pondered if Palin's backing would make a dent in the Trump campaign. "Palin's brand among evangelicals is as gold as the bathroom faucets at Trump Tower," boasted Ralph Reed, chairman of the ultra-conservative extreme right-wing Faith and Freedom Coalition, a group he defined as "a bridge between the Tea Party movement and evangelical voters."

Palin's endorsement of Donald could not have come at a worse time for the failed Veep candidate, who had been derisively nicknamed "John McCain's idiot Alaskan squaw" during the 2008 race for the White House.

Palin's eldest son, Track, an Iraq war veteran, was arrested by the police at Wasilla, Alaska, at the Palin family home. He was jailed overnight following an alleged attack on Jordan Loewe, 26, a woman whom news-

Sarah Palin *en famille* in 2008, photo courtesy the Alaska governor's office. Palin family photo shows then-Alaska Governor **Sarah Palin** (*center*) surrounded by her tribe. From *left to right*, back row: son **Track** and husband **Todd**; second row: daughter **Willow**, **Governor Sarah Palin,** daughter **Bristol**; at front, daughter **Piper.**

Columnist Gail Collins claimed, "Republicans are currently okay with blaming the President for anything, even sunspots. But some of them may have found Sarah Palin's latest charge a little creepy."

Palin blamed Obama for her son's death threats and reported assault upon his girlfriend.

papers labeled as his "gal pal."

The battered young woman charged that Track had punched her in the head and kicked her before grabbing a rifle and holding the barrel "just a few inches from my face."

Reportedly, he had yelled at her, "Do you think I am a pussy? Do you think I won't kill you?"

The following day at another Trump rally in Tulsa, Oklahoma, Palin said, "I guess I have to address the elephant in the room," referring to her son's arrest, details of which had been splashed all over newspapers and featured on cable news.

She began by attacking Obama, asserting that he "wore political correctness like a suicide vest. He's the weak-kneed capitulator-in-chief. He causes us to bend over and say thank you to our enemies."

Commentators suggested that she was hinting that the United States "was getting rectally fucked by its enemies."

"With Donald Trump as President," she shouted, "there will be no more pussy-footin' around! Our troops deserve the best!"

Reporters noted that perhaps for the first time in American political history, three figures prominently associated with the political news cycle—Donald (in New Hampshire), Track (in Alaska), and Sarah (in Tulsa)—had each, within a short span of time, invoked use of the word "pussy" as an insult and putdown.

At the Tulsa rally, Palin claimed that the domestic violence incident associated with her son was the result of post-traumatic stress based on his previous tour of military duty in the Middle East. "My son was changed by the horrible experience he endured while serving his country. Track, like the sons of so many other mothers, came back a different person, a bit hardened. He and his fellow soldiers and airmen, and every other member of the military, came back wondering if their country appreciated the sacrifices they'd made for our freedom."

"Everything stops at the top, and Obama is the commander-in-chief. Look at how bad he runs the Veterans Administration. Just hear Donald talk about how awful our vets are treated. My son is a victim of Obamacare, or the lack of care. His weak veterans' policy is the reason Track got off-track."

ENTER MICHAEL BLOOMBERG

*Richer than Donald, Could this Republican "Gazillionaire"
And Three-Term Mayor of New York City
Banish Donald to His Lair in the Trump Tower?*

Michael Bloomberg: Well-informed, well-connected, sometimes visionary, and sane.

In January, word leaked that Michael Bloomberg, the three times Republican Mayor of New York City, was contemplating a run for the White House. The stony-faced, self-made "gazillionaire" had been one of the most liberal high-profile Republicans of his era. As mayor, he had championed same-sex marriage and was pro-abortion.

Described as "rich as a double chocolate fudge cake," he had a lot more money than Donald and could finance his own campaign. It was speculated in some quarters that the White House could be within the reach of this "short, Jewish, divorced billionaire."

Early in the race, he had hired a team to formulate plans for his potential run as an independent in the already overcrowded presidential race. Some of his aides, speaking off the record, said, "Mike didn't think Donald Trump or Bernie Sanders would make a good President—perhaps each of them would be a disaster."

In years past, Bloomberg had also contemplated a run, but rejected the idea, saying, "I can't win."

On January 24, Donald uttered a completely insincere statement. "I would welcome the entrance of Michael into the race. We've been friends over the years. I don't know if we are friends anymore. If he runs, I think I would do well against him."

But behind the scenes, he feared a run from Bloomberg, predicting it would siphon off much needed votes.

When Bloomberg's wealth was reported at $37 billion, Donald scoffed at that entry as it appeared in *Forbes* magazine, evaluating the former mayor's media tech company as "very fragile."

"His is a technology company, which in a short time could be easily replaced. I think real estate is a far more secure bet."

Bloomberg set a March deadline for an announcement of whether he'd become a can-

To Donald Trump: "Keep your money. We won't be used as a political pawn."

Depicted above: **US soldiers** on a successful rescue mission near Baghdad in 2003.

didate. For a potential candidate, March was the final date access that could be granted to the ballots in all fifty states.

His backers studied previous third-party runs. It was rumored that the former mayor would have been willing to spend $1 billion of his own fortune to finance his presidential campaign.

Bloomberg, aged 73, was four years older than Donald, and he said that he had no personal *animus* against him. He did express his fear that Donald might have a "devastating lasting hold on the GOP field."

An aide said that Bloomberg strongly disagreed with Donald's political positions, especially his stance on immigration.

Bloomberg feared that Hillary's personal scandals, including the notorious private e-mails she sent during her tenure as Secretary of State, might seriously harm her candidacy.

The founder of the financial news and information provider, Bloomberg, LP, had been a political novice when he launched an unlikely bid for mayor in 2001. A longtime Democrat, he became a Republican as a vehicle for entering the race, although he later listed himself as Independent.

Jonathan Lemire, writing for the Associated Press, said, "Bloomberg oversaw a gilded age in the nation's largest city, as Manhattan shed its gritty image to become a sparkling star of film and television. Record numbers of tourists arrived, as did young professionals seeking their future. But critics noted the growing gap between rich and poor."

Bloomberg also became the nation's most vocal proponent of gun control, and used his vast fortune to bankroll candidates who clashed with the National Rifle Association.

"Liberals found fault with his cozy ties to Wall Street," Lemire wrote, "and also his unquestioned support for the New York Police Department, which drove down crime during his tenure, but engaged in tactics that a Federal judge later ruled discriminated against minorities."

MEGYN KELLY

DONALD ENGAGES IN WHAT THE PRESS CALLS "A PISSING MATCH" WITH A PREMIER NEWS ANCHOR AT FOX

The seventh debate had been scheduled for January 28 in Des Moines, Iowa. Donald had announced that he would not appear. "Let's just see how much money Fox is going to lose in advertising revenue with me not showing up," he told reporters.

He said that "Roger Ailes and Fox News think they can toy with me, but I don't play games."

"I don't like being used by this lightweight," Donald said of Kelly. "She's trying to use attacks on me to win ratings. I have zero respect for her as a reporter. She is totally biased against me."

Ted Cruz mocked Donald's refusal to join his opponents in the latest GOP debate. "He's such a fragile soul," Cruz said in his most sarcastic voice. "You know if Kelly

DONALD TRUMP SAYS HE WILL NOT PARTICIPATE IN REPUBLICAN DEBATE

QUESTION:

"DURING A TELEVISED PRESIDENTIAL DEBATE, IF A CANDIDATE IS EMBARRASSED BY THE DIRECTION AND TONE OF A REPORTER'S QUESTIONS, WHAT SHOULD HE (OR SHE) DO?"

TRUMPISH ANSWER:

DESTROY HER

To her horror, then-hotshot Fox anchor **Megyn Kelly**—because of the thorny and piercing questions she aimed at Trump during one of his televised debates, "became the news" rather than an objective observer in the process of reporting it.

Their feud raged on both sides of the media for weeks, until they (unconvincingly) made up and (unconvincingly) embraced after a stormy meeting—later (unconvincingly) described by Kelly in TV interviews with CNN and other (not Fox) outlets—in Trump Tower.

Ironically, despite Kelly's loud and frequent statements of loyalty to her mentor at Fox, chairman Roger Ailes, she later sued him (and won) for sexual harassment. Her "disloyalty" was later interpreted as a "cringeworthy' advance insight into the chronically murky self-interest and flamboyant mismanagements prevailing within Fox throughout the course of their coverage of Donald Trump before and during his presidency.

Some newshounds interpreted how Ailes and the Fox administration played this as the beginning of the end of Megyn Kelly's career as a newscaster.

asks him mean questions, his orange hair might stand on end."

Three miles away, Donald presented his "dual screen" rally at a packed auditorium at Drake University, claiming that his one-man show was staged to raise much-needed money for veterans.

"We have to stick up for ourselves as a people, and we have to stick up for our country when we're being mistreated," he said.

Right before he appeared, word had leaked that he might be in the GOP debate after all. It was broadcast, but unconfirmed, that Fox News had apologized to him for Kelly's "excessive questioning." That apparently turned out not to be true.

Donald discounted the rumor, saying, "Once this ball started rolling, we can't stop it." He claimed that his rally had already solicited $5 million in contributions to veterans' charities, and he was definitely going through with his competing event.

"I plan to out-Fox Megyn," he said. "I will not call her a bimbo, since that is not politically correct. However, I can safely say she's a bad reporter."

Before going onstage at the rival rally, many of the candidates mocked Donald's boycott. The mean-spirited Cruz, "the man everybody loves to hate," referred to him as "Ducking Donald," and called for a "*mano-a-mano*" contest with Donald.

When he heard about that, Donald responded, "Can we stage such a debate in Canada?" Of course, he was drawing attention to the senator's birthplace in Alberta.

In a review of Donald's one-man act, columnist Michael Barbaro wrote: "Trump put on a show all right—and it was entirely about him: His hurt, his feelings, his vanity, and his revenge."

Looking sheepish, Rick Santorum showed up at Donald's event, although he refused to be photographed in front of a TRUMP FOR PRESIDENT sign. He said, "I'm supporting another candidate."

Mike Huckabee also showed up at Donald's rally, and this "guns, grits, and gravy" losing candidate had kind words for Trump, suggesting a possible future endorsement.

In references to Donald's rally, many veterans claimed they would not accept any of his charity. Paul Rieckhoff, founder of the Iraq and Afghanistan Veterans Association, told the press, "If offered, we will decline donations from Trump's event in Des Moines. We need strong policies from candidates. We will not be used for his political stunts."

***

At 8PM on January 28, the seventh GOP debate opened in Des Moines, minus Donald. Sponsored by Fox News Channel, it was moderated by Bret Baier, Chris Wallace, and the controversial Megyn Kelly. Fox had refused Donald's request to have her removed.

The 5PM debate at the "Kiddies' Table" was significant in that it marked the final appearances of losing candidates who included Carly Fiorina, Jim Gilmore, Mike Huckabee, Rand Paul, and Rick Santorum. In February, all of these candidates, whom Donald always referred to as "the losers," would suspend their presidential bids. When Donald learned about this, he said, "They didn't have a chance. I ripped them to shreds."

The debate opened with Kelly "addressing the elephant in the room"—that is, the absence of the leading candidate.

In a burlesque, the Texas senator said, "I'll stand in for Donald." He then pretended to be him, saying: "Ted Cruz is a maniac, and everybody on this stage is stupid, fat, and ugly. Ben Carson, you're a terrible surgeon."

Then, slipping back into his own character, he said. "Now that we've gotten Donald Trump out of the way…"

The audience roared with laughter.

Cruz and his arch rival on stage, Marco Rubio, filled the void left by Donald, clashing over immigration and other issues. Trying to get a word in, Rand Paul of Kentucky questioned Cruz's authenticity, claiming he had "a shifting sands stance on immigration and amnesty."

Although Cruz was condescending to Rubio, he avoided any reference to the nickname ("Little Marco") Donald had assigned to him.

"I like Marco," Cruz said, barely concealing his hostility.

An Iowa reporter would later write: "At

The state has long suffered from jokes decrying it as the corniest state in the union. It's quiet around here UNTIL the every-four-year hysteria of **THE CAUCUS**.

Despite the warnings of front-page pundits like this headline writer from **Donald's "Home Town Newspaper,"** Trump as a presidential candidate, miraculously survived outrages, derisions and predictions that "he'll never be elected."

His vow, according to insiders within his campaign?

To wreak vengeance and slow, excruciating torment on each of his critics and opponents, one by one.

least Cruz didn't say that both of them were Cuban refugees trying to take over the control of the U.S. government, as if we didn't have enough native homegrown boys who could do the job better."

When an opportunity arose, the other candidates on the stage tried to work in a word or two. But Jeb Bush, Carson, John Kasich, and Rand Paul delivered lackluster remarks, and failed to win any traction with the already biased audience, many of them Donald's supporters.

During his time in the spotlight, Christie directed most of his fire at Hillary, claiming, "She'll never get within ten miles of the White House. Do you want a white Obama in the Oval Office?"

Both Cruz and Rubio appeared as "holier-than-thou" preacher-politicians. In a last-ditch appeal to evangelicals, Rubio claimed that if he were elected, his faith would play a great role in his administration, assuring his audiences, "Jesus Christ came down to earth to die for your sins."

"The Florida senator said those words as if the all-Christian audience had never heard that theory before," said a TV newscaster in Des Moines. "What does he take us for? A pack of heathens? Perhaps he's stayed out in the Florida sunshine too long."

The candidates weren't the only ones attacked. Kelly came in for her fair share of criticism. One sarcastic late night radio caller labeled her "a true bimbo!"

Another unidentified caller on radio said, "What on God's earth convinced these pathetic jackals on stage tonight that either of them could be President of the United States? I hope Donald Trump, when he becomes President, deports Rubio back to Castro's little Commie island of Cuba, and sends Ted Cruz back to Alberta where he'll probably freeze his balls off—that is, if he has any. As for Jeb Bush, he reminds me of my third-grade English teacher. ISIS would laugh at him before they caged him, doused him with gasoline, and lit a match. As for the others, ISIS, when it invades Washington, would probably toss them off some very high rooftop. That fat boy, Christie, would probably splatter into a million pieces of blubber."

Another call-in to the station asked, "Where is Donald Trump now that we need him"? Instead of Donald making us great again, we were treated to a third-rate vaudeville show at the last GOP debate."

"TRUMP DIVIDES GOD'S VOTERS"
—*Headline in a Des Moines Newspaper*

In the wake of the debate, editorial writers and reporters went into high gear dissecting what had taken place.

Under a banner headline, "TRUMP DIVIDES GOD'S VOTERS," a reporter wrote, "Evangelicals still wield power, but both their unity and influence have faded by 2016. Once, the faithful voted overwhelmingly for Michele Bachmann, Mike Huckabee, and Rick Santorum. But no more. This coven of homophobes and anti-abortion avocates have lost their allure."

Author Sarah Posner said: "Many evangelicals are abandoning Cruz and Rubio to support Trump, who is unabashedly ignorant of biblical imperatives that form the foundation of evangelical culture. Polls show Trump attracting a quarter to a third of white evangelical support."

Columnist Steve Hewitt wrote: "Trump doesn't really seem to give a damn about religious issues. As for the fight over providing insurance coverage for contraception, Trump would probably say 'Get a fucking condom, god damn it! There are enough starving kids in the world already.'"

In-depth polling discovered that the far-right wing of the Republican Party was not appealing to the millions of more moderate or independent Americans. That discontent was expressed by Walter Bennett of Shenandoah, Pennsylvania.

"Domestically, all the Republican debaters wanted to repeal the Affordable Care Act, casting millions back to uninsured status, and slash domestic spending, creating an ever wider gap among the haves, have-at-least-a-little, and having nothing at all. Most Americans will be in the latter two categories."

"The GOP rivals want to set fire to the social compact of this nation at home while marauding in search of conflicts to exacerbate wars abroad," Bennett said. "Oh, and Rand Paul wants to declare every fetus a citizen. By his very absence, Donald Trump proved that without him, the choice is 'none of the above.'"

***

Around the nation and abroad, everybody seemed to have formed an opinion about The Donald, including both his former wife, Ivana, and a Holocaust survivor in Amsterdam.

In honor of Holocaust Memorial Day, Auschwitz survivor Eva Schloss, the stepsister of Nazi victim Anne Frank, told the press, "Donald Trump is acting like another Hitler. If he becomes President of the United States, it will be a complete disaster. Like Hitler, he would incite racism, maybe not against the Jews but against Muslims and Mexicans."

At a chic party in Palm Beach, First Wife Ivana was taking credit for Donald's run for the White House, claiming that it was she who had first suggested that he enter politics.

Married to Donald from 1977 to 1992, she seemed to have regretted that she had lost her chance to become First Lady.

A so-called friend, who did not want her name used, said, "I think Ivana was asked to stop attacking Melania—perhaps by Donald himself, but she has continued to dish her. She can really pile it on about what a terrible choice Melania would be as First Lady. Real pissy stuff. She endorses Donald but not Melania."

Several of Ivana's friends thought that with her business background and proven track record of "getting things done," she would have been a far better choice as First Lady.

One of her critics disagreed: "As First Lady, Ivana would be a loose cannon."

As Trump's fame and venom increased, so did the notoriety of his past and present wives. From *left to right*, above, is **First** (1977-1990) **Wife Ivana Zelníčková**: "I'd have made a better First Lady than Melania"); a cover girl photo of **Second** (1993-1999) **Wife Marla Maples;** and the official White House photo of **"the winner"** in the glam and perhaps notoriety division, **Melania Knavs** (married 2005).

One thing was certain: All three of them, contrary to public statements they made, hated each other.

FEBRUARY, 2016
From the Granite State to the Palmetto State, Donald Deflowers
"Pussy Boy Cruz"

"I haven't left my house in days. The best election commentary I've heard so far. I watch the news channels incessantly. All the news stories are about the election. All the commercials are for Viagra and Cialis. Election…erection…election…erection…Either way, we're getting fucked."

—*Bette Midler*

***

Donald Trump began the month of February by presenting his favorite tabloid, *The National Enquirer,* with a ten-point plan to fix America.

"We're being laughed at by the rest of the world," he claimed. *"I'm running for President because I see no one else capable of doing the job! "When I was growing up, I saw the respect that other countries had for us—but not anymore. When Ronald Reagan was President, we were respected. But today it's much different. People in this country feel we are the whipping post for other countries."*

In a nutshell, he promised to:

1. *Protect the U.S. from ISIS and radical Islamic terrorism.*
2. *Find the next General Douglas MacArthur.*
3. *Reopen the debate about Obamacare and replace it with something that benefits everybody.*
4. *Create jobs.*
5. *Rebuild the country's infrastructure.*
6. *Save Medicaid, Medicare, and Social Security.*
7. *Renegotiate foreign trade deals.*
8. *End Obama's executive actions on immigration.*
9. *End border crossings from Mexico, and*
10. *Build a "great, great wall" along the U.S.'s southern border.*

In its same issue, the *Enquirer* revealed that "hefty Hillary" had gained more than thirty pounds and had started to waddle. "She has been gorging on all manner of fatty, high-calorie foods," claimed the article. "Soon, she will have to be rolled down the campaign trail."

The magazine went on to claim that in addition to gorging on pizza, hot dogs, tacos, and Dairy Queen ice cream, she "continues to hit the bottle with reckless abandon after a long day."

The *Enquirer* also ran a tabloid headline about a possible blip in Rubio's sexual background. The writer suggested that the Florida senator had a "zipper problem," and predicted some "shady lady" might surface to ruin his run for the presidency. It was alleged that when Rubio was Speaker of Florida's House of Representatives in Tallahassee, he paid this mystery lady's expenses, charging them to his American Express card.

When contacted, the woman told the *Enquirer,* "The allegations that I had an inappropriate relationship of any kind with Marco Rubio are absolutely false. Expenses were incurred when I worked for the GOP House campaigns in 2007."

***

Celebrities from movie stars to leading feminists backed certain candidates. Deserting Hillary, Susan Sarandon threw her support to Bernie Sanders.

Meanwhile, Gloria Steinem pronounced Donald a "total fraud." She told *Women's Health* magazine, "He was, as they say, born on third base, but thinks he hit a home run. His father was a very successful developer, and nothing makes money as successfully as already having it. The buildings outside of New York that bear his name, he didn't build. He is not competent in understanding social issues."

Steinem, as expected, came out for Hillary, claiming "She represents the interest of women very well, very fiercely, and very devotedly."

CORNSTALKERS IN "A CORNFIELD CRUCIBLE"
Hustling Voters in the Hawkeye State Before the Iowa Caucuses

Late in January, newspapers photoshopped Donald, Rubio, and Cruz, along with Hillary and Sanders as "cornstalkers" hustling the voters of Iowa. At the time, candidates were blitzing the Hawkeye State before its caucus on February 1.

To demonstrate how religiously observant he was, Donald attended a nondenominational church (the First Christian Orchard Campus in Council Bluffs) with his wife Melania. As part of a minor gaffe, during a ceremony where communion wafers were passed among the congregants on a silver tray, Melania correctly took a communion wafer from the silver plate when it was passed. But in what some observers described as a "cringeworthy moment," Donald mistook the communion plate for the collection plate. Digging some money from his pocket, he tried to put in an offering, something which *The Daily Mail* reported he later laughed off to members of his staff.

Polls showed that in the Iowa Caucus, Cruz would be his chief rival. Reacting to these polls, Donald attacked him as a "total liar" on ABC's *This Week.*

At a Cruz rally, someone rose from the audience shouting, "Ted Cruz looks so weird!"

To that, Cruz shot back, "Is that Donald Trump out there?"

Right before the caucus, a former Iowa staffer for the Trump campaign filed a sexual discrimination lawsuit. She alleged that during her stint with the Trump campaign, she was paid less than the male staffers, and she also had to endure crass comments from Donald about her looks.

In her complaint to the Civil Rights Commission, Elizabeth Mae Davidson, 26, said that when Donald met her and a female volunteer, he said, "You guys could do a lot of damage."

Davidson was fired on January 14. She stated that the alleged discrimination caused her to suffer "lost wages, mental anguish, and damage to my career."

During an interview with *Bloomberg Politics,* Donald denied her accusation, defining her as "a disgruntled employee who wanted to come back to the campaign, but she didn't do a good job."

Hours before the Iowa caucus, the candidates were still slinging mud and trying to outmuscle each other. Races on both the Democratic and the GOP sides seemed too unpredictable to call. Bradley Todd, a veteran GOP strategist, said, "Betting on the caucuses would be like divining chicken bones."

Before the voting began, Iowa reporters ran articles headlined CAN CRUZ TRUMP TRUMP? and WILL RUBIO SNEAK BY BOTH?

The night before the caucus, whereas bombastic Trump had the lead at 30%, with Cruz trailing at 24%. Rubio racked up only 15%.

Reporter Alan Rappeport wrote: "Candidates have munched on pork chops in the heat of summer and hunted game in the dead of winter. Spouses and children have been dispatched as surrogates across the plains of Iowa."

In the final hours, candidates were leaving nothing to chance, furiously crisscrossing the state and making direct appeals to voters.

Iowa was hardly a microcosm of America, since it is mostly rural, overwhelmingly white, and very evangelical.

It seemed that the battle in Iowa had evolved into a two-way race between Cruz and Donald. At best, Rubio could only hope for a third place finish in Iowa, and Jeb Bush and Chris Christie had more or less moved on, focusing on the next battleground, New Hampshire.

No one worked harder for votes than Cruz, who visited all 99 of the state's counties, sounding like a hell-raising preacher on the stump. At one point at a town hall meeting, he asked the audience to get down on its knees and pray that the Supreme Court would not recognize same-sex marriage. Fortunately for the GLBT community, God opted not to grant his prayer.

The New York Times labeled Iowa "THE CORNFIELD CRUCIBLE" in one of its headlines.

On the campaign trail in Iowa, Donald notoriously suggested that the primary voters of that state were "stupid," and to prove his case, evangelical voters turned out in droves to give Senator Cruz an unexpected victory. If anyone read the results of previous contests, this surge of support for this extreme right-wing candidate should have come as no surprise. After all, these were the same evangelicals who had awarded victories to both Rick Santorum and Michele Bachmann.

Humbled by his defeat in the cornfields of Iowa *[which many sociologists have concluded do not represent the voting preferences of large swaths of the rest of the U.S.]*, Donald made it clear that he did not like to lose.

Despite the limited conclusions the Iowa caucus provides, many reporters, failing to take into account that the fanatical religious right does not represent the scope of the United States at large, claimed that the Cruz victory brought into question the depth of support for Donald's unconventional candidacy.

In Iowa, Cruz won 28% of the vote, with Donald getting 24%. Rubio was breathing down Donald's neck, winning 23%. Ben Carson, who had once been a frontrunner, suffered the biggest setback, receiving only 9% of the vote.

In defeat, Donald demonstrated his gracious side, claiming he was deeply honored by the support he received. In a salute to Iowa, he said, "I think I might come here and buy a farm—I love it."

That's what he said: What he must have thought was, "Get me the hell out of this cornfield. I want to go back to Fifth Avenue."

During his acceptance speech, Cruz sounded like an old-time Elmer Gantry. "Let me first of all say, to God be the glory."

Reacting to its shameless pandering, some of Cruz's enemies asserted that that remark "libeled God's good judgment."

In a dig at Donald, Cruz said, "No one personality can right the wrongs done by Washington."

Meanwhile, Rubio, boasting about his strong third place showing there, said, "The people of this great state have sent a very clear message—after seven years of Barack Obama, we are not waiting any longer to win our country back."

Polls showed that evangelicals made up 62% of Iowa's electorate.

Right before voters turned out, a rumor spread that Carson had quit the race for the Republican nomination, and that he was flying back to his home in Florida.

The most embarrassing (and most widely publicized) defeat was suffered by Jeb Bush, who despite vast expenditures and a lot of on-site campaigning, had garnered only 3% of the vote—a humbling rejection, perhaps of the Bush dynasty itself.

Columnist John Podhoretz wrote: "The voters of Iowa did not fall for Trump's vainglorius and solipsistic blather about making America great again. In fact, 75% of the voters rejected his nonsense, not wanting to place their party in the hands of an insult comedian character assassin."

In 2008, the Protestant pastor, Mike Huckabee, had been declared as the winner in that (long-ago) Iowa caucus. But voters had, since then, grown disenchanted with him. He won a meager 1.8% of the vote and subsequently suspended his disastrous campaign.

As for the Democrats, in their own neck-and-neck contest, the Vermont senator, Bernie Sanders, rode a wave of support from young and first-time Iowa caucus-goers. Hillary Clinton, however, by the narrowest of margins (mostly winning voters aged 45 and older), carried the state. Even though her margin of victory had been narrow, she was at least able to avoid the embarrassing rejection she'd suffered in 2008, when she had lost to both Barack Obama and to the soon-to-be-disgraced John Edwards who had come in second.

The third contender among the Democrats was Martin O'Malley, perhaps the finest—and most sane—of all the candidates. But Iowa voters rejected him, granting him only one-half of one percent of the vote. Consequently, his campaign leaked news that he would drop out of the "rat race" even before all the votes had been tallied.

The morning after the caucus, headlines blared that Donald had been "CRUZIFIED," but he showed no letting up, no change in his tactics, as he, along with Hillary,

Martin O'Malley, running for President on the Democratic ticket, might have scored victories in a different time and place. In a field of extreme views or candidates who carried "too much baggage," he was a fine and decent man.

Confronted with the Black Lives Matter movement, he dared say, "All lives matter," and was booed off the stage.

rushed onward to the next battleground, New Hampshire, a state markedly less conservative than Iowa.

In New Hampshire, Donald expected to win big. In contrast, Hillary—based on that state's close links to Bernie's home state of Vermont—anticipated losing.

During the Iowa campaign, many of the GOP candidates had made many false statements. Donald nailed Cruz on several of his off-key messages, calling him a "liar." Perhaps the biggest lie of all was spread by Sarah Palin, who accused the Republican Congress of giving Obama "a blank check."

In point of fact, GOP members of Congress had opposed virtually everything the President had proposed.

Before leaving Iowa, perhaps never to return, Donald privately was heard chiding primary voters for picking candidates who had not won the nomination in sixteen years. "They pick losers. That's why they went for Lyin' Ted."

"PUBLICITY IS THE DONALD'S COCAINE
and Right Now, in New Hampshire, He Has the Biggest Pile of Blow in His Life"

—Fortune Magazine

The very imposing and formidably ferocioous **Chris Christie** never became either the fervent friend or the fervent foe of Donald Trump in 2016. Will he more clearly define his intentions in 2024? Enquiring minds, especially ones with a "soft spot" for New Jersey, find him fascinating.

SCOTT BROWN

During the first week of February, Donald's battleground moved to New Hampshire, where his rivals felt energized after his defeat in the Iowa cornfields.

Jeb Bush, as he continued his spectacular descent, attacked Donald as "a man of deep insecurity and weakness."

Former New Hampshire governor, John Sununu, branded Donald "a loser because of his string of business failures, especially in Atlantic City."

Chris Christie sarcastically called him, "Donald the Magnificent."

Bleary-eyed and "dog tired," Rubio flew into Manchester and encountered an "army" of campaign volunteers willing to stump for him, many asserting that he was the best-equipped candidate to unite the splintered Republican party.

Soon after his arrival in Milford, New Hampshire, Donald won the "male beauty vote," as one female reporter noted. Scott P. Brown, former nude model and ex-Senator from Massachusetts, endorsed him. In 2012, as incumbent Senator, he had lost his bid for re-election to his first full term to Elizabeth Warren. *[After that defeat, he moved to New Hampshire where, two years later, as an obvious transplant, he ran unsuccessfully for the New Hampshire Senate, eventually losing to Democrat Jeanne Shaheen.]*

"Donald Trump is the one person who has the independence and can be the change agent to get Washington working again," Brown claimed.

In Windham, New Hampshire, Cruz said, "Six weeks ago, Trump was saying every day that I was his friend, that he loved me. That I was terrific, and that I was nice. And now I'm an Anchor Baby from Canada."

Those words, although intended as a put-down, would be the last kind remark Cruz would make about Donald in the

In attacking Donald, **Elizabeth Warren**, the outspoken senator from Massachusetts, and the bitter rival of Scott Brown, delivered the sharpest attacks on Donald, even more cutting than Hillary's.

In retaliation, mocking her claim to have Cherokee blood, Donald labeled her "goofy-looking," and "Pocahontas."

Former Massachusetts Senator, **Scott Brown,** threw his "weight" behind Donald Trump.

The former nude model, on this resumé, gave vital statistics, but left out his penis size, which became a topic of debate during the GOP race.

His resumé did reveal that he had "excellent hands" and that he wore a size ten shoe, if that provides any clue.

coming weeks. "The Texas rattler was released spewing his venom," said one of Donald's aides.

In the wake of his terrible defeat in Iowa, Ben Carson shot back, accusing Cruz's campaign of spreading false rumors about him, claiming without any formal authority that he was quitting his campaign. The neurosurgeon denounced the rumors spread by Cruz aides as "lies and dirty tricks."

Minutes before voting had begun, Rep. Steve King, Cruz's campaign co-chair, tweeted, "Carson looks like he is out. Iowans need to know that before they vote. Most of his supporters will switch to Cruz, I hope."

E-mails from Cruz's campaign urged precinct captains to be aware that Carson had withdrawn from the race. "Spread the word," they urged Republican voters.

In a look back at Iowa, Donald blamed his loss on his boycott of the most recent debate. Nonetheless, he insisted that he'd have done the same thing over again, since he had raised a reported $6 million for veterans that night.

Once again, Donald warned potential supporters of Cruz, "If you guys get the nomination, the Democrats are gonna sue the ass off this Canadian Anchor Baby."

Under the headline "POLLSTERS—YOU'RE ALL FIRED," it was revealed that thirteen polls in Iowa had pre-determined the winner as Donald days before voting began.

In New Hampshire, Rubio even thanked Jesus for the Second Amendment [*i.e., the right of the people to bear arms*]. In response, a pundit said, "After all, Jesus loved nothing more than a good, American-made assault weapon to kill people in greater numbers."

Another columnist noted, "Pretty boy Rubio thanked 'My Lord and Savior Jesus Christ.' He ignored all the Jewish, Hindu, and Muslim voters, to name just a few. Oh, screw 'em if they won't come to Jesus."

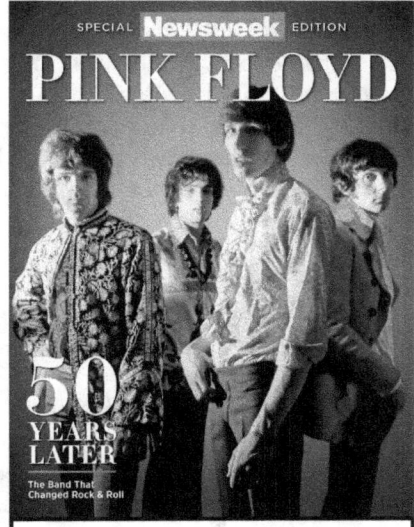

Although Cruz had emerged as the victor in Iowa, he came under devastating attack from many newspapers. The *New York Daily News* wrote, "On issue after issue—guns, taxes, gay rights, foreign policy—Cruz offers himself as an uncompromising zealot. The architect of one government shutdown desperately wants another. In his long, rambling victory speech, he saluted the 'heroes who rushed into burning buildings in the wake of 9/11.' Those are the same heroes Cruz turned his back to by refusing to support the bill offering health care and financial assistance to responders who served on the smoldering pile after 9/11."

In New Hampshire, failing candidate John Kasich, the governor of Ohio, came up with a vote-winning idea. He promised that, if elected President, he would reunite the iconic rock band, Pink Floyd, for a musical concert.

"I'll get the group at least to play a couple of songs," he vowed. "Since we have so many troubles in America about finances, I'll ask the band to start with a little song they created called 'Money.'"

"Ohio" **John Kasich**, ethical and relentlessly hard-working, canvassed every county in Iowa prior to the caucus, and always reflected his basic sanity in a field of sometimes bizarre eccentrics.

Admittedly, his idea—if he became president, as expressed on a TV interview—to bring back **Pink Floyd** was sort of eccentric.

Under a provocative headline "HERE'S NOBEL PEACE OF CRAP," a News Wire Services story broke the revelation that Donald had been nominated for a Nobel Peace Prize, thereby elevating him into a position alongside Pope Francis and Nadia Murad.

[Nadia Murad was a 21-year-old Yazidid tribeswoman who escaped from ISIS terrorists and brought the story of her plight as a sex slave ("ISIS forced us to pray—then raped us") to the attention of the international community, the United Nations, and, through broadcasts in Egypt, to the Muslim world.]

Nobel Watcher Kristian Berg Harpviken said that Donald's nomination letter cited "his vigorous peace through strength ideology, used as a threat weapon of deterrence against radical Islam, ISIS, nuclear Iran, and Communist China."

Ever the Voice of Enlightenment, Cruz mocked Donald claiming that "if he became President, he would throw a fit and nuke Denmark."

In a moment of restraint, Donald said, "I'm trying to be a little bit more understated and statesmanlike. Some people like that."

But within moments, Donald found his inner Machiavelli and accused Cruz of stealing the Iowa caucus. He demanded a "do-over."

Many of his fans believe that **the Nobel Peace Prize**, whose Medal is depicted above, should be awarded to Donald Trump.

In the words of one of his sponsors, "They gave it to Barack Obama in 2009, and Donald deserves it more than he ever did."

"Lyin' Ted Cruz didn't win Iowa, he illegally stole it," Donald charged. "That's why all of the polls went so wrong and why he got more votes than anticipated." Then he lashed into the Cruz campaign for fomenting what Trump and Carson supporters described as a choreographed conspiracy to mislead voters. It involved the dissemination of a false rumor that Carson had dropped out of the race. "Based on the fraud Cruz committed, a new election should take place and the present results nullified. And this liar calls himself a Christian!"

***

To the LGBTQ community, at least those who bothered to find out who this man was, **Tony Perkins**, president of the co-called Family Research Council, is the most hated man in America.

He's hysterical on the subject of same-sex marriage, defining such unions as a symbol for the collapse of Western civilization.

With schoolyard insults and a chest-thumping *machismo*, Donald trudged through the snows of New Hampshire. It was a radically different political terrain from that of Iowa. As regards the hot-button issue of abortion and birth control, polls showed many Republican women there supported a woman's right to choose.

Some 35% of male voters were for Donald, but only a quarter of the women planned to vote for him.

Clara Frechette, a tax analyst, said, "I don't think Trump really cares about women's issues, and their being equal to men. As for Cruz, he'd be looking at the Bible and quoting it, 'The man should be the head of the household and the women should do what the men say.'"

Cruz continued with his anti-gay hysterics, calling into the radio show of Tony Perkins. *[For reasons known only within the darkest recesses of his soul, Perkins is the most vehement opponent of gay rights in America.]*

During that call-in, Cruz lamented, "Our heart weeps for the damage to the traditional marriage that has been done." Quoting Biblical scripture, he addressed an audience of homophobes, exhorting them, "To be as wise as serpents and as gentle as doves."

Yet when Cruz, with his hand out for money, visited the Manhattan office of a supporter of same-sex marriage, he cooled his rhetoric. He told the billionaire mega-donor, Paul Singer, "If New York politicians want to legalize it, that is their business."

That wasn't enough to convince Singer, who later endorsed Rubio, even though he, too, opposed same-sex marriage.

When the Supreme Court, by one vote, legalized same-sex marriage, Cruz told a conservative rally that the decision "was one of the greatest threats to our democracy we have seen in modern times."

"And people call Cruz educated," said Ernest Bellows, a Trump supporter. "Cruz sounds just like any other redneck rodeo cowboy. Time his horse tossed him onto the dusty ground."

Sensing Rubio as one of this major rivals, Governor Christie attacked him. "Let's get the boy out of the bubble. His appearances are scripted. One New Hampshire reporter compared Rubio to a computer algorithm designed to cover talking points.

"Rubio is not really progressive," said reporter Julie Fleming. "He's so far right of Ted Cruz, if such a thing is possible, only he conceals it. He's anti-choice even for victims of rape and incest. He's against Obamacare. He was part of the infamous 'Gang of Eight,' pushing for immigration reform. Now he *hates* amnesty. His ads in Iowa were about the 'free gift of salvation' offered by Christ. Perhaps if he fails as a politician, he could become a fire and brimstone preacher. He plays both sides, a Baptist one week, a Catholic the next."

Both Cruz and Rubio were attacked by a fellow *latino*, Jorge Ramos, the Univision anchor, who said, editorially, to an audience that included thousands of *latinos*, in reference to these *(latino)* candidates' anti-immigration stances, "There is no greater disloyalty than the children of immigrants forgetting their own roots. That is a betrayal."

On February 4, it was announced that Megyn Kelly, Donald's nemesis, who had, to wide acclaim, emphasized Donald's designation of women as "fat pigs, dogs, slobs, and disgusting animals," had won a victory. It was reported that Harper-Collins had offered her $10 million for a memoir.

Reaction from the public was generally unfavorable, one TV viewer claiming, "Kelly will never contribute anything of value to society—just a dressed-up doll sucking up the money."

[Kelly anchors the Fox News Channel program, The Kelly File. *Her show is the no. 2 rated cable news program.]*

"Low Energy Jeb" continued to hustle for votes in New Hampshire. He hoped to win supporters who wanted to censor some of the things coming out of "the bloviating billionaire's potty mouth."

"Enough with the cursing," said Bush at a campaign rally. "I'm tired of the profanity, tired of the vulgarity. There are kids listening to him, for crying out loud."

"Bush was responding to Donald's dropping 'shit bombs' along the campaign trail and crowing that he'll "kick ISIS' ass," wrote one reporter.

Meanwhile, Donald eased up on his war on Megyn Kelly, claiming that he would appear at the next Fox debate, scheduled for March 3 in Detroit.

On February 5, Bush unveiled his "secret weapon," calling for the assistance of his formidable mom. Consequently, a frail Barbara Bush showed up in New Hampshire, looking every bit –and more– her ninety years on this earth.

She retained a bit of her famous spark, tearing into Donald in a TV interview. Like her son, she attacked Donald's foul language. "I don't know how women can vote for someone who said what he said about Megyn Kelly. It's terrible. Money doesn't buy everything. It's incomprehensible to me why people are voting for this man."

Appearing on *This Morning*, she said, "I don't advise Jeb, but if I did, I would say, 'Why don't you interrupt like the other people in the debates?'"

Two years before, Barbara had candidly admitted that America "had had enough Bushes." But she came around. Or did she? Perhaps she spoke the truth originally. Voters in New Hampshire and Iowa seemed to agree.

Detail from the official White House portrait of stern, no-nonsense former First Lady, **Barbara Bush**, *grande dame* of the Republicans.

She hated Donald Trump for, among other reasons, his attacks on Jeb!.

Barbara was also opposed to Hillary. She received a copy of the latest Edward Klein book, *The Problem with Hillary*. In it, an alleged quote was attributed to Bill Clinton. Reading it, the quote must have warmed the cockles of Barbara's tired heart.

"Trump is a generational challenge," Bill said, "and a challenge for the Hispanic vote. We've got to destroy him before he gets off the ground."

"Maybe the Clintons will do Trump in and allow Jeb to move up," Barbara told one of her son's campaign workers.

But as Marco Rubio surged in the polls, Barbara watched with dismay, noting that Rubio had once been a *protégé* of her son. "Jeb did so much for him."

She was surprised at the young women who flocked to Rubio's rallies, although their numbers didn't surpass the number that Bernie Sanders attracted.

JAWS OPEN WIDE IN NEW HAMPSHIRE
Otherwise Known as "the Shark," Chris Christie Begins
DEVOURING "LITTLE MARCO"
As Donald Tells Jeb! To Shut Up

The eighth GOP debate was held at Goffstown, New Hampshire, on February 6, and this time, Donald showed up to star in the middle of the stage at the event organized by *ABC News* and the *Independent Journal Review*. The debate at St. Anselm's College Institute of Politics was the first not to feature a "Kiddie Table." (The losers had dropped out.) The moderators were relatively unknown: Josh McElveen, Mary Katherine Ham, David Muir, and Martha Raddatz.

The debate opened with mishaps. Kasich's introduction was inadvertently skipped, and Carson missed his cue.

To winnow down the field and perhaps to score a lethal blow at Rubio, Chris Christie led

Many young women, flocking to a **Marco Rubio** rally, seemed more interested in his "male beauty" than they were in his campaign.

A female Rubio aide said, "When Marco speaks, young women swoon, old women faint, and toilets flush themselves."

Barbara Bush told a Jeb supporter, "Here's one old woman who won't faint. And I'll flush my own toilet, thank you!"

an all-out assault as only a native of New Jersey can do. He hammered Rubio as "callow, ambitious, and lacking in accomplishment."

It was the fiercest attack the Florida senator had ever suffered, and he seemed to wither in the spotlight. He gave his best "deer-in-the-headlights" look, and seemed rattled. He pushed back with scripted lines, but failed utterly under Christie's prosecutorial glare.

As if Christie needed any help (he didn't), both Bush and Donald sliced Rubio into ribbons, but they were weak compared to Christie's personal derision. "He cut into Rubio with a beheading machete," observed a New Hampshire reporter.

Rubio at one point became so flustered he repeated the exact sound bite four times, thereby confirming Christie's point.

"There he goes," Christie said. "The memorized 25-second speech."

He attacked Rubio for taking credit for policies "although he skipped out on the vote. That's not leadership! That's truancy! You do nothing but utter your rehearsed sound bites. How many times in one night all you can say over and over again is that Obama is leading the nation to disaster?"

Columnist Frank Bruni wrote: "Christie's last-gasp strategy was to turn Rubio into a limp, soggy, chew toy, and the New Jersey governor was all jaws."

Despite Christie's strong and very macho performance, it would ultimately be his curtain call. The New Jersey governor suspended his campaign four days later after finishing sixth in the New Hampshire primary.

Donald attacked Jeb Bush: "He wants to be a tough guy, but it doesn't work very well." Bush tried to interrupt him, but Donald told him. "QUIET!" The audience booed Donald, but he claimed they were just Bush donors and special interest lobbyists.

No review of Donald's performance in the New Hampshire debate was as devastating as that of columnist John Podhoretz. "He was awful, so horrible, so disgusting in the debate—his lies, his distortions, his deceits, and his libels thicker and fouler than they've yet been. The man some Republicans want for their President is a disgusting jerk they somehow believe will have their backs when the only backs he'll ever have is his own."

"IMPOSSIBLE TO HEAR TRUMP OVER CHRISTIE'S EYES"

After New Jersey governor, **Chris Christie**, dropped out of the race, he threw his considerable weight behind Donald Trump's.

On CNN, as Donald delivered his standard anti-immigrant, anti-foreign trade speech, a gloomy Christie looked on as if in a trance.

Rumors spread that he was too unpopular to get re-elected as governor of New Jersey, so his hope for a political future hinged on Donald naming him as his Veep or at least appointing him Attorney General.

Before politics took its toll, there was a time when bearded **Chris Christie** looked relaxed, relatively thin, and not like a shark.

Here, he is, younger and perhaps happier, long before his entanglements in Bridgegate and his entry into the orbit of Donald Trump.

The acid tongue of columnist **John Podhoretz** turned on Donald with lacerating venom, defining him as "a disgusting jerk, a comedian character assassin, and a mouthpiece of vainglorious and solipsistic blather."

This artwork—ambiguously marketed as "**political comedy**,"—has appeared in homes, offices, and "mancaves" where few outsiders might have expected it.

As for its laugh quotient, foes of Trump never really found it funny. What one wit said *"He never came close to looking that good in real life,"* is probably its single biggest takeaway.

During the 2016 campaign, Marco Rubio ridiculed Trump's small hands. Perhaps in reaction, in this cartoon from the 2020s, his hands were morphed into paws that evoke Dracula.

Chapter Nine

John Wayne, at home on the range

Here's **HEE HAW!** configured as the self-proclaimed spiritual heir and presidential choice of MAGA's favorite ultra-conservative dead cowboy.

John Wayne's effigy, available for sale as a Christmas ornament.

ENROLLING JOHN WAYNE, FROM THE GRAVE
How a Dead, Slow-Drawling Movie Icon Endorsed The Donald

"BERNIE'S LOVE CHILD"
Is Exposed and Publicized in the Tabloids

One of their Former Aides Accuses Jeb! and Dubya of
"IMPORTING AND USING COCAINE"

DONALD INSULTS THE POPE

By February, the lives of all the candidates—as exposed by some of that month's editions of *The National Enquirer*, had heated up to the point where even the snows of New Hampshire seemed on the verge of melting.

One of the stories that widely circulated involved a Donald endorsement supposedly derived from the film star and icon of the far right, actor John Wayne (1907-1979), a tough-as-nails Republican diehard, who, along with his faded career, had retired to "Boot Hill" thirty-seven years before.

Aissa Wayne, the actor's daughter, a California attorney speaking at the John Wayne Museum near her father's birthplace in Winterset, Iowa, had said, "America needs help. We need a strong leader. We need someone like Mr. Trump with leadership qualities, someone with courage, someone who is strong like John Wayne."

Aissa told Donald, "My father would be very proud of you right now."

Donald once met Wayne, and was impressed. At the museum, posed in front of a fake desert background, a horse saddle, and a gun-toting effigy of the actor, he claimed, "He represented real strength—an inner strength you don't see very often. That's why his endorsement means so much to me."

The *National Enquirer* also revealed that one of the White House wannabees, Vermont Senator Bernie Sanders, was alleged to have fathered "a love child."

On his website, the socialist presidential hopeful had revealed that he had four children and seven grandchildren.

Actually, three of his kids are stepchildren born to his wife, Jane, from her previous marriage. Sanders was said never to have wed the mother of his only biological child, a 46-year-old son named Levi.

The senator, according to the tabloid report, was reported to have fallen in love with Levi's mother, Susan Campbell, during the sexual revolution of the 1960s. Reporter Sharon Churcher wrote: "Levi sometimes went hungry and lived in the dark in a rental apartment where the electricity was frequently turned off. Bernie wouldn't pay the bills."

In the same issue, in an "equal opportunity" exposé of the Bushes, the legendary CIA drug smuggler and pilot, Barry Seal, revealed that he had "orchestrated an elaborate sting at the Miami-Opa Locka Executive Airport in which the DEA got a videotape of Jeb and his brother, George W., bringing a kilo of cocaine into Florida for resale."

This exposé came from Roger Stone's book, *Jeb! And the Bush Crime Family*.

In it, Stone alleged that Jeb snorted coke the night his father, George H.W. Bush, was elected President in 1988.

It also made the claim that Jeb, during his tenure as governor of Florida, had snorted cocaine because he found the slow pace of Tallahassee "so boring."

The book was co-authored by Saint John Hunt, son of the notorious Watergate figure, E. Howard Hunt. Jeb was criticized for his war on drugs, the book labeling him a hypocrite "since he was a heavy drug user himself."

The John Wayne Birthplace and Museum in Somerset, Iowa mixed patriotism with Hollywood myths and politics, Donald style. According to its director, "This is a hard place to miss."

DONALD DEMANDS TORTURE
of Terrorists Using Methods "Worse Than Waterboarding."

GAWKER'S COMPILATION OF DEROGATORY NAMES FOR DONALD

To live up to his John Wayne toughness, Donald, on February 7, doubled down on his call for harsh interrogation techniques of suspected terrorists. "I want to go a lot further than waterboarding."

"In the Middle East, you have people chopping off other people's heads. This hasn't happened since medieval times. There's never been anything like this." Donald was speaking on NBC's *Meet the Press*.

"Believe me, going beyond waterboarding in terms of getting information would really work. Enhanced torture wouldn't bother me a bit. Look, when terrorists fly planes into the World Trade Center and kill thousands of people, you can't handle psychos like that with kid gloves made of unborn lamb."

On the eve of the New Hampshire primary, Donald called Cruz a "pussy," based on his objections to tough stances on waterboarding "or something even more horrendous."

It all started when a woman in the audience rose up at one of Donald's rallies. She was the first to accuse Cruz of being "a pussy" for opposing waterboarding.

"She just said a terrible thing," Donald told his audience. "OK, you're not allowed to say it—and I never expect to hear that from you again. She said, 'Ted's a pussy!'"

Trump's "Ted Cruz is a pussy" comments helped catalyze TV funny guy **Jon Stewart** to showcase his own promotion of the newest Donald Trump lawn ornament, one of his own design, as part of a relentless late-night anti-Trump ridicule campaign.

As Trump's campaign continued to churn out raw material for late-night comedy commentary, Stewart said, "I want to thank Donald Trump for making my last six weeks my best six weeks."

Hoping to ambush Bush "coming around the pass," Donald also fired at him, too. "Jeb is just desperate, even though he called on his mammy to bail him out in New Hampshire. He's a mama's boy. This sad person had gone absolutely crazy. The guy's a nervous wreck. He's having some kind of breakdown."

When Jeb heard that, he told the press, "Donald Trump is not just a loser. He's a liar and a whiner."

Indeed, the real estate mogul called Cruz a pussy, a name never before uttered with such abandon in association with a presidential campaign, but in context, it was only one of an armada of names his opponents had associated with The Donald.

In an attempt to document some of them, *The Gawker*, a web and blog site focusing on political and entertainment industry gossip, rounded up an array of names that Donald had been called by his enemies. They included, in no particular order: **"Off-Brand Dr. Seuss villain," "Fan-mail order meat salesman," "Delusional cheese creature," "Orange-tufted sentient troll doll," "Flopped-over traffic cone," "Cheeto-dusted bloviator," "Hot pork balloon,"** and **"Brightly burning trash fire."**

And, as Donald faced New Hampshire voters in that state's upcoming primary, he was assigned yet another new name: **"Fossilized meatball."**

DAWN OF THE BRAIN DEAD
"Mindless Zombies Turn Out in Droves to Make Donald the New Hampshire Winner"

No tabloid in America was harsher than Donald's hometown newspaper, the *New York Daily News*, which featured his February 9 win in the New Hampshire primary. He was depicted on the cover in clown makeup with vastly overpainted scarlet lips.

A second headline read: "CLOWN COMES BACK TO LIFE IN N.H."

Under his Photoshopped caricature was this caption: "Like a Chucky doll, this monster just won't go away. Donald Trump won the first-in-the-nation New Hampshire GOP primary handily—and scarily."

[Iowa had been a caucus, not a primary.]

More than three out of ten Granite State GOP voters had flocked to the polls to give Donald a spectacular win, with 34% of the vote. Ted Cruz came in with 12%. And in a surprise move, it turned out that John Kasich, the Ohio governor, won second place with 16% of the vote.

At his victory rally, Donald announced, "We're going to beat China,

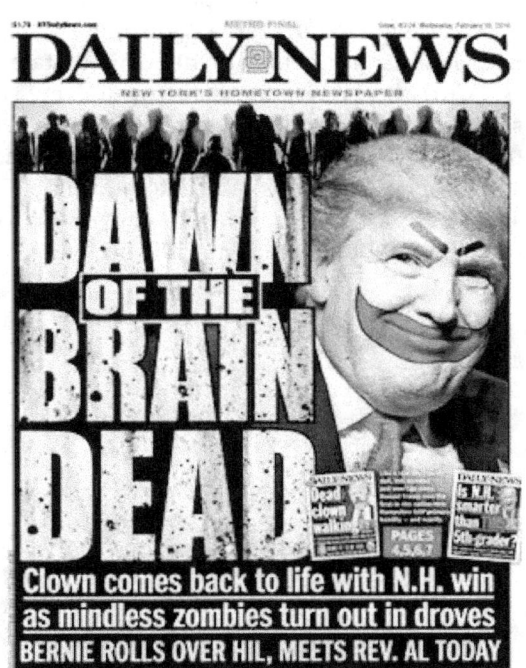

DO ZOMBIES SUPPORT DONALD?

The New York Daily News compared Donald's supporters in New Hampshire to "mindless zombies."

The *upper photo* shows a gone-viral photo still from the 2004 horror-comedy *Shaun of the Dead*. Currently, zombie culture and its spinoffs is a market estimated to bring more than $5 billion to the U.S. economy every year, according to *24/7 Wall St*, a financial analyst agency.

Pop authority Steven "The Zombie" Uden, one of the participants in World Zombie Day, said, "**Everyone can be a Zombie**. We have no prejudice, we are unselected. Zombies, differently from vampires, do not have a beauty pattern. You can be tall, small, thin, or fat—that does not matter for zombies."

Japan, Mexico. We're going to beat all those countries. The world is going to respect us again, believe me."

In fourth place, Jeb Bush polled only 11%. Donald at this point seemed to crush his rivals as badly as he had promised to eradicate ISIS.

The most embarrassing loss was suffered by Rubio, probably based on his utter failure during the New Hampshire debate. He received only 1% of the vote.

On the Democratic front, Bernie Sanders scorched Hillary in the New Hampshire Democratic primary. He won 69% of the vote, compared to her paltry 39%.

Polls showed that an astonishing two-thirds of New Hampshire voters agreed with Donald's proposal to temporarily bar Muslims from entering the United States.

Christie had hoped for a surge in New Hampshire, but like Rubio, he was greatly disappointed. He finished in a distant sixth place. He had little money left in his campaign purse, and a slim chance of being eligible for the next GOP debate. He told his few supporters that he was returning to New Jersey "to take a deep breath."

Despite strenuous efforts to humiliate Donald with a crushing debate, the opposite happened. "I left all of them in a snow bank," he proclaimed. "Now, it's on to South Carolina and another sweeping victory."

The GOP was left to muddle on with Cruz and a severely weakened Rubio, Kasich, and Jeb!

CAMELOT?

In a 21st Century Replay of Jack & Jackie, Donald and Melania Discuss the Glam Quotient of Their Presidency

After a thundering victory in New Hampshire, Donald returned briefly to his estate, Mar-a-Lago, in Palm Beach.

There, he discussed re-defining it as a "Winter White House," with his *fashionista* wife and former model, the Slovenia-born Melania.

"It'll be like the Kennedy compound in Palm Beach, only far greater in size, elegance, and culture," Donald predicted. "Of course, I'll have to retrofit the 90-year-old estate to accommodate Secret Service agents. I'll pay off the expenses myself, saving the taxpayers money."

It was surmised that the commissioning of Donald's very large portrait hanging in the building's main hall had, in some way, been clairvoyant of his upcoming presidency. In it, he was depicted in a white tennis sweater with a full head of hair like JFK. It was described as "very Kennedyesque, oh so WASPY, and so young." The staff already referred to it as "Mr. Trump's presidential portrait."

In the meantime, Melania was reported to be rehearsing her role as the future First Lady, and said to be consulting "image coaches" about how to act, speak, and behave.

"She's modeling herself as Jackie Kennedy," an insider told the press. "She's been trying out hair extensions similar to those worn in the early 1960s by Jackie."

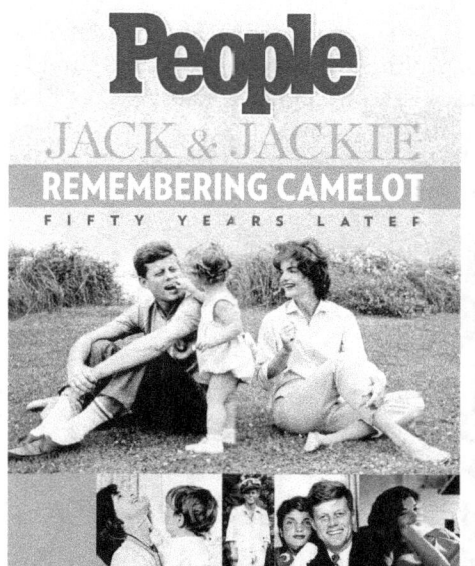

DON'T LET IT BE FORGOT

From reports, Donald and Melania want to bring "**Camelot**" back into the White House, but if they try, they'll face some stiff competition from previous residents.

"Camelot" is often used as a reference to the presidency of John F. Kennedy. The Lerner and Loewe Broadway musical was in vogue following JFK's assassination in 1963, and his widow Jackie quoted its lines in a history-making interview with the press:

"Don't let it be forgot, that once there was a spot, for one brief shining moment, that was known as Camelot," adding that "there will be great Presidents again, but there'll never be another Camelot again… It will never be that way again."

On stage on Broadway, in the musical version of the legend that inspired Jackie's quote, **Richard Burton** *(left figure in right-hand photo, above),* starred as the tragic King Arthur, with gay actor **Roddy McDowall** playing a treacherous courtier.

TED CRUZ AND THE PORN-INDUSTRY STAR OF
DEVIANT WHORES

"Lyin' Ted" Mistakenly Casts "A Woman With a Past" Into One of his Political Ads.

Soft porn queen **Amy Lindsay,** pictured in the revealing photo above, was selected by the Ted Cruz campaign as the star of a TV ad aimed at "Onward Conservative Christian Soldiers."

In February, a skin-flick babe, a former actress in the soft-core porn industry, starred in a political ad for holier-than-thou Ted Cruz, the (ostensibly) God-fearing candidate of the Republican Right.

A thirty-second TV and internet ad, entitled *Conservatives Anonymous,* had featured the body beautiful Amy Lindsay. Before her "Cruz gig," she had starred in such soft-corn porn films as *Deviant Whores; Carnal Wishes;* and *Timegate: Tales of The Saddle Tramps.*

[Other, more mainstream gigs had included an appearance in Star Trek: Voyager *and a secondary role in the 1996 film adaptation of Henry James'* The Portrait of a Lady, *starring*

Nicole Kidman.]

When Cruz was told of this, he ordered his staff to halt distribution of the ad immediately. It had featured actors cast as a group of dismayed, ex-Marco Rubio supporters gathered together in a group therapy session. Lindsay told *Buzzfeed* that she had not yet made up her mind about how to vote: Donald or Cruz?

She claimed that she had not duped the Cruz campaign, saying she thought they were aware of her previous porn work. She thought the Texas senator wanted to get rid of his "stuffy image."

"I didn't think they wanted some old white Christian bigot, but a cool, open-minded woman like me."

DONALD SHOOTS SOME VIAGRA

Into Low Energy Jeb! and Publicly Asserts that Dubya Should Have Been Impeached for the Iraq War

George W. Bush was not on stage at the next Republican debate staged on February 13, 2016 at Greenville, South Carolina. But he emerged as the hot topic at the debate, nonetheless.

Organized by *CBS News*, it was moderated by John Dickerson in Greenville's Peace Center for the Performing Arts starting at 9PM and lasting for 90 minutes. This would mark the ninth and final debate appearance of Jeb Bush, who suspended his hideously expensive and ill-fated quest to follow his brother and father into the White House.

During the debate, the name of the 43rd President of the United States was invoked multiple times, with varying degrees of reverence and/or scorn, as the tensions erupted between Jeb and Donald, the debate's chief combatants.

Provocatively, Dickerson asked Donald if he stood by his previous position that "Dubya" [*George W. Bush, son of George H.W. Bush*] should have been impeached for leading the country into the Iraq War.

"Obviously, the war in Iraq was a big fat mistake," Donald said. "We spent $2 trillion, thousands of lives. Iran is taking over Iraq with the second largest oil reserve in the world. George Bush made a mistake. We can make mistakes, but that one was a beauty. We should have never been in Iraq."

"You can do whatever you want, call it whatever you want," Donald continued in his assault on the former President. "I want to tell you, they lied. They said there were weapons of mass destruction. There were none, and they knew there were none."

Jeb sprang to the defense of his (disgraced) older brother.

"Here's the deal. I'm sick and tired of Barack Obama blaming my brother for all of the problems he's had. And frankly, I could care less about the insults that Donald Trump gives to me. But I am sick and tired of him going after my family. My dad is the greatest man alive, in my mind. And while Trump was building a reality TV show, my brother was building a security apparatus to keep us safe. And I'm proud of what he did."

"The World Trade Center came down during your brother's reign, remember that?" Donald interjected.

His remark, though completely accurate, was met with loud boos from the right-wing audience, which was overwhelmingly packed with diehard Bush dynasty fans and (according to Donald) their paid lobbyists.

"My mom is the strongest woman I know," Jeb continued.

"So she should be running," Donald tartly responded.

In spite of Dubya being one of America's worst Presidents, he was

Donald's attacks on **"Low Energy Jeb"** was reflected in political ads. Upper photo is from an ad from the Trump campaign suggesting that Jeb's speeches could put a potential voter to sleep.

Viagra was recommended as a means of correcting Jeb's "E.D."—in this case, "Electoral Dysfunction."

After the unexpected death of **Anthony Scalia**, the ultra-conservative Supreme Court justice, conspiracy theories abounded. They inluded commentary from across the political spectrum, including headlines from the right-wing Breitbart (*upper photo*) reacting to a lurid headline (*lower photo*) in the *National Enquirer*.

On the campaign trail, Donald fanned the flames, spreading his suspicion that Scalia may have been murdered by a lethal injection into his butt from a hooker.

absurdly defended by other Republican candidates. Rubio chimed in with, "I thank God, all the time, that it was George W. Bush in the White House on 9/11 and not Al Gore."

At that, Ohio Governor John Kasich interjected "This is just crazy. This is just nuts. Jeez, oh man."

The Bush family was still popular in South Carolina, a state that has a high concentration of veterans, at least those not killed in Iraq. The crowd loudly booed Donald any time he denigrated Dubya, but applauded any candidate who defended him. The vitriol seemed to take Donald by surprise as he had never been so pummeled at a debate before this.

As expected, the debate centered at times on the recently deceased, notoriously conservative Supreme Court Justice Antonin Scalia, as a battle raged over his successor. Beloved by arch-conservatives, he opposed abortion, gun control, and same-sex marriage.

As for gay rights, he had charged that "homosexual activists are trying to eliminate the moral opprobrium that has traditionally been attached to this perversion."

That claim, and countless other prejudicial utterances, earned him the loathing of millions of Americans. On the other hand, millions on the far right praised his three decades on the Supreme Court as the "voice of conservative Renaissance."

As was noted, Justice Clarence Thomas followed Scalia's every pronouncement "like an Uncle Tom heeding his master."

Donald criticized Chief Justice John Roberts, a usually conservative Dubya appointee who had been vilified for his role in two recent decisions whose outcome had upheld Obama's Affordable Care Act.

Onstage, Donald contemptuously said to Jeb, "Your brother wanted Roberts on the Court. He twice approved Obamacare. Good going, man!"

Donald then continued his assault on Dubya, claiming that he should have been impeached for his role in inaugurating America's involvement in the War in Iraq.

During the debate, Donald did not ignore his most serious rival, Ted Cruz. In fact, Donald lost his cool when Cruz charged that if Donald were President, he'd nominate a liberal to fill Scalia's seat. He also told the audience that Donald had once endorsed abortion.

"You are the single biggest liar," Donald shot back. "This guy will say anything. Nasty guy. Now I know why he doesn't' have a single endorsement in the Senate."

Donald repeated his charge that Cruz had undermined Ben Carson's race in Iowa.

"I will say it is fairly remarkable to see Donald defending Ben after he called him pathological and compared him to a child molester."

Even Dickerson, the debate's moderator, seemed to turn on Donald, asking him why he used language that many voters found offensive.

"On occasion, in order to sort of highlight something, I'll use a profanity," Donald said.

Ted's wife, Heidi Cruz, of course, was not on stage for the debate. However, on the radio in South Carolina, she made a claim that would even cause the right-wing evangelist, Pat Robertson, to blush: "Ted is running to show us the face of God that we serve. The God of Christianity is the God of freedom, of individual liberty, of choice and of consequence."

Earlier, Ted's father Rafael, had claimed, "It is the Holy Ghost who has called on my son to run for President."

Before the debate, Bible-thumping Ted himself said, "We can win if we awaken and energize the body of Christ."

So far, there is no evidence that either God or Jesus ever endorsed Ted's candidacy—far from it.

"TED CRUZ

Is mentally unstable & the biggest liar I've ever come across"
—*Donald Trump*

"DONALD TRUMP

is a creature from the fever swamps of the far left."
—*Ted Cruz*

The war between Donald and the Bush dynasty did not end on the evening of the South Carolina debate. "If Dubya had gone to the beach during his presidency, we would have been better off," Donald said.

After heavy losses in Iowa and New Hampshire, losing candidate Jeb had summoned the Bush family to his political deathbed in South Carolina. Dubya arrived with his wife Laura, the former First Lady. Prior to the debate in upstate Greenville, Laura showed up in Charleston to inform a rally about what a fine and decent man Jeb was.

Addressing that same rally, her husband, the former President, told the crowd, "There seems to be a lot of name-calling going on. But my father told me that labels were for soup cans. My brother Jeb has a deep and genuine faith that reveals itself through good works, not loud words."

To retaliate, Donald at a news conference, mocked Dubya's widely ridiculed "Mission Accomplished" appearance aboard the *U.S.S. Abraham Lincoln* in May of 2003. "The country was not safe during this jerk's presidency," Donald charged.

"The worst attack on this country came during 9/11."

A former President was not the only one butting into the South Carolina primary. A sitting President, Barack Obama, also mocked Donald. "Being President is a serious job. It's not hosting a talk show or a reality TV show. An inexperienced man like Donald Trump is unworthy of handling nuclear codes.'

In California, Obama said, "I continue to believe in the American people, and I think they will not elect Donald Trump President."

Donald dismissed Obama's attack, accusing him of doing "a lousy job. He has set us back so far. You look at our budgets, at our spending. We can't beat ISIS. Obamacare is terrible. Our borders are like Swiss cheese."

Obama is lucky I didn't run the last time when Mitt Romney ran—or else Obama would have been a one-term President."

Desperate for a win in South Carolina, the Christian Warrior, Ted Cruz, continued his Holy War against Donald, attacking him for claiming that George W. should have been impeached, and referring to Donald as "a creature from the fever swamps of the far left."

He made the unproven charge that Donald, if elected President, would replace Scalia with a choice "that would be indistinguishable from those of Hillary Clinton and Bernie Sanders."

Despite his self-avowed status as defender of the Constitution, he decided that, as a Senator, he would not fulfill his constitutional duty.

"I will block anyone—I mean, anyone—Obama names to the Supreme Court. Let me repeat: Any nominee Obama might name."

In one of his biggest attacks on Cruz to date, Donald charged, "He's a mentally unstable individual and the biggest liar I've ever come across. It's hard to believe that a Christian could be so dishonest and tell that many lies."

On February 15, Donald stunned an audience of supporters, saying that he might have to renege on his pledge not to run as an independent, and denouncing the GOP élite for not playing fair with him.

Early on the morning of February 17, Donald woke up to shocking news. The latest polls by *NBC* and *The Wall Street Journal* revealed that Cruz was polling ahead of him at a rate of 28% to 25%.

Christian warriors and Trump haters, **Heidi and Ted Cruz** appear at a rally in Houston.

Alleged to be intelligent, Cruz continued to make one dumb remark after another. "If Trump becomes President, the Second Amendment will be written out of the Constitution."

The Texas senator had endorsed ads revealing remarks that Donald had made during his so-called liberal past. One ad depicted Donald endorsing abortion. To answer that charge, Donald reconfirmed and reinforced his credentials as an anti-abortion candidate.

His attorneys sent Cruz a "cease-and-desist" letter, warning him to stop airing those ads.

At a CNN-sponsored town hall rally, Cruz told Anderson Cooper, "I laughed at his threat. I have practiced law for twenty years, and his letter was one of the most ridiculous and frivolous I've ever received."

The tension between the two rivals increased, markedly, during the weeks ahead.

Both Marco Rubio and Jeb Bush tried to gain traction in their obsession with toppling the frontrunners. Rubio hauled out Nikki R. Haley, the Indian-American governor of South Carolina and a rising star in the GOP. Before the cameras, she endorsed the Cuban-American, emphasizing their respective immigrant backgrounds. Haley herself was the daughter of Sikh immigrants from India.

It was also noted that both of them shared youth as a trait in common. "We are the future of the GOP," Haley declared. "Rubio is the best chance for Republicans in November."

Jeb! was not to be outgunned. Currently in sixth place in pollings, he posed with a gun bearing his name on it, plus the short caption, "AMERICA." His sudden macho posturing and swagger "triggered" a fusillade of mockery. On Twitter, a random outsider chided him with "Suicide is never the answer, Jeb!"

He was also criticized in countless tweets for not having engaged the safety device on the FNX-25 pistol, something that was obvious to gun aficionados from the photo. The pistol had been a gift from a gun maker, FN Manufacturing, in Columbia, SC.

Outside scrutiny heated up, too. Reporters such as Joe Nocera explored Donald's business background, concluding, "Trump made real estate blunders that turned billions in potential profits into mere millions. His foray into Atlantic City brought him close to personal bankruptcy. He claims about owning a sprawling business empire, but what he actually runs these days is a licensing company that slaps the Trump name on everything from buildings to steaks to an education company that's being sued for 'persistent fraud, illegal and deceptive conduct.' My conclusion—and I say this as a grizzled veteran of business journalism—is that Trump's business acumen (not to mention his net worth) has been widely overstated, by Trump himself. His core business skill is self-promotion."

A poll of potential Trump supporters in South Carolina revealed to Donald the political priorities of his supporters.

At least 70% believed that the Confederate flag should fly over the South Carolina State Capitol; 38% wished that the South had won the tCivil War, and a stunning 80% supported his ban on Muslims. At least 31% thought that homosexuality should be outlawed, and another 56% wanted the practice of Islam made illegal in the United States.

Donald avoided a direct answer when confronted with the astonishing and bigoted results of those pollings.

"All I can say is that my supporters are strong believers in what they believe. Good Christians, each and every one. Evangelicals love me!"

"KID DONALD" VS. THE POWER OF THE PAPACY
Pope Francis Suggests Wall Builders Are Anti-Christ

By mid-February, a "Holy War" of sorts was waged between Pope Francis, during a visit to Mexico, and Donald Trump on the campaign trail.

Time magazine claimed that the war that erupted "could not involve more polar opposites. Trump's name is synonymous with billions of dollars. Francis chose to be named after the patron saint of the poor, Francis of Assisi."

Both men, who tied for second place in a poll of "the world's most admired men," have an uncanny knack for getting their different messages across.

Near the end of his historic tour of Mexico, Pope Francis arrived in Ciudad Juárez, a city that's a hellhole of drug violence, poverty, and crime. He visited a prison filled mostly with criminals imprisoned on drug-related offenses, often murder, and later prayed at the border between Mexico and the United States. He lamented and prayed for the migrant dead, and condemned the "grave injustices" inflicted upon those who were forced by poverty and violence to cross illegally into America's great Southwest.

Il Papa waited to make his incendiary remarks when he was on the papal plane *en route* back to Rome and the Vatican. "A person who thinks only about building walls, wherever they may be, and not building bridges, is not Christian."

The Pope was responding to a direct question from a reporter. He'd been asked about Donald's claim that, as President, he would build a very high border wall.

"This is not in the gospel," the Pope said.

Within the hour, Donald had been alerted to the Pope's point of view. In the broadest sense, Francis' statement could implicate the religious tenets of such Republican candidates as Ted Cruz, who is evangelical, and it might have had implications for Jeb Bush, a Catholic, and Rubio, a sometimes Catholic, and even for John Kasich, who was reared as a Catholic and once considered becoming a priest before he entered politics.

But it was Donald, as was his custom, who fired back. Almost no major political candidate in the history of the Republic had ever directly confronted a sitting Pope before. "I think it is disgraceful for a religious leader to question a person's faith," he charged. "I am proud to be a Presbyterian. I am not a Catholic, but a Presbyterian. As President, I will not allow Christianity to be consistently attacked and weakened."

When reporters contacted Cruz, he stayed out of the confrontation, unwilling to get dragged into it. "I'm not going to come between Donald and the Pope," he said.

Privately, he told an aide, "Let those two duke it out."

Donald's rebuttal of the Pope's statement was conveyed to Francis, who by then was safely within the walls of the Vatican. Diplomatically, he responded that he wanted to give

Smiles and brilliant PR prevailed from the Obama camp during most of the Pope's visit, as shown by this assemblage on the balcony of the White House. In this official White House photo, Michelle, Francis, and Barack wave to their adoring fans.

(P.S. The Pope has a long tradition of waving from balconies.)

Donald the benefit of the doubt because he had not heard about his border plans independently.

Donald, however, didn't let up. He called the Pope "a pawn and an instrument of the Mexican government. I don't think the Pope understands the problems we have with our border. I don't think he understands the danger of an open border with Mexico. He has been fed only Mexico's propaganda."

Then one of Donald's senior advisers, Dan Scavino, claimed, "The pontiff's words were startling, considering the Vatican is 100% surrounded by massive walls."

When informed of Donald's latest shot at him, Francis said, "Aristotle defined a human person as '*animal politicus.*' So at least I am a human person."

Donald wasn't letting up in the Holy War. "If and when the Vatican is attacked by ISIS, which as everyone knows is ISIS's ultimate trophy, I can promise you that the Pope would have only wished and prayed that Donald Trump would have been President because this would not have happened. My opponents are using the Pope as a pawn for their policies. They should be ashamed of themselves for doing so, when so many lives are involved and when illegal immigration is so rampant."

In his final statement, *Il Papa* tried to elevate the conversation. He urged the faithful to see migrants as brothers and sisters. At no point did he recommend that Catholics should withdraw their support from Donald. "Let us together ask our God for the gift of conversion, the gift of tears. Let us ask him to give us open hearts. Not more death. No more exploitation. There is still time to change. There is still a way out and a chance, time to implore the mercy of God."

"I don't like fighting with the Pope," Donald said. "He's got a lot of personality...very different. But that wall around the Vatican is very, very big."

Pundits compared and contrasted the two world famous leaders, concluding that whereas Donald lived in a gilded marble palace in New York, the Pope lived in a gilded marble palace in the Vatican.

Reporter Carl Campanile wrote: "Trump makes shocking statements in the most bombastic way possible, and *Il Papa* makes shocking statements in the meekest way possible."

In the wake of the conflict between The Donald and *Il Papa*, the most recent poll showed that 78% of possible Republican voters favored a wall between the U.S. and Mexico.

Reporter Patrick Helay wrote: "Politicians rarely rebuke the Vatican so forcefully for fear of alienating Catholic voters. Trump's attack on Pope Francis reflected a political calculation that criticizing the Pope would not hurt him with conservatives. Some Southern evangelicals take a dim view of the Catholic church."

A Vatican spokesman, the Rev. Frederico Lombardi, denied that the Pope was trying to tell Catholics how to vote. "It was not a slap at the GOP presidential candidate. The Pope's opposition to the border wall is his general view, which is very consistent with his courageously following the indications of the Gospel offering welcome and solidarity."

Perhaps as a last word, Donald said, "If I ever meet the Pope, perhaps as President of the United States, I will enlighten him about our side."

Columnist Ross Douthat provided the most satirical overview of the "Clash of the Populists," referring to "The Donald" vs. Pope Francis.

Douthat wrote: "*The Book of Daniel* predicted it. *The Book of Revelation* confirmed it. The Necronomicon [*the fictional textbook of magic appearing in the horror stories of H.P. Lovecraft*] spelled it out in language too terrible for human ears to hear. And if you read Trump's *The Art of the Deal* backward in the original Sanskrit, you'll find it foretold there as well: Before the Seventh Seal is opened, before Famine and Pestilence are loosed, the Man in White must do battle with the combed-over Titan, amid the ravening shrieks of Twitter and beneath the unblinking eyes of Cable News."

Douthat also noted that the two men often shared a certain rhetoric. Whereas Donald preferred phrases like "low energy," "liar," and "loser;" *Il Papa* preferred "Pharisee or self-absorbed Promethean neo-Pelagian, though he might also use "whiner" or "sourpuss."

In the meantime, gossip columns were filled with endorsements and rebuttals from various celebrities, many of whom weighed in on one side or another. Joe Pantoliano [*the actor who interpreted the character named "Joey Pants" in* The Sopranos] joined in the attack on Donald, claiming "I'm with Pope Francis 100%. Trump promotes bigotry, exclusivism, racism. He's like Raid. You spray it in the corners, and all the cockroaches come out."

"Y'ALL CRAZY!"
Journalists Assert: "Dixie Ding-Dongs Go for Trump as Jeb! Quits"

On February 21, the *New York Daily News* conveyed the results of the South Carolina primary to its readers. Reporter Denis Slattery was blunt: "The piggish voters of South Carolina gobbled up the slop that Donald Trump served, handing the bloodthirsty billionaire his second straight Republican presidential primary."

Throughout the course of the race in the Palmetto State, Donald had tangled with Pope Francis over the border wall; called Ted Cruz a "maniac" and a "liar," and promoted a story about his support of a U.S. general shooting renegade Muslims with bullets dipped in pigs' blood.

At a rally of his supporters, Donald delivered his victory speech. "It's rough running for President. It's mean, it's nasty, it's vicious…and it's beautiful."

With most of the precincts reporting, Donald had made off with 33% of the vote, with most of the evangelicals going for him—and not for Ted Cruz or Rubio, each of whom came in with about 22% of the vote.

An emotional Jeb Bush, on the verge of tears, came in at fourth place. Soon after, he announced that he was dropping out of the race.

"Poor little mama's boy," Donald said mockingly, referring to the aging Barbara Bush showing up in South Carolina to urge voters to support the losing campaign of her second son.

The former First Lady and Jeb's older brother, "Dubya," had hoped to play on their lingering popularity in South Carolina.

The elusive Melania, Donald's wife, made a rare appearance, telling the crowd of beer drinkers (from plastic cups) that, "My husband Donald will make the best President ever." It can be assumed that her knowledge of previous American presidents was limited.

Donald's triumph in South Carolina was on the dawn of the "Ides of March." In just nine days, the nominating race would be fought in a dozen states stretching from Massachusetts to Texas.

Privately, the Trump campaign had more or less written off Texas, fearing it would go to that state's Senator, Cruz. However, Donald had hoped for a sweep through most of the other contests.

Newspapers continued to attack him as fact checkers reported that his campaign speeches "departed from the truth" at the rate of 77%. Just 6% of his statements were judged to be "true or mostly true."

Economists attacked his threat to impose a 45% tariff on goods from China, predicting that such a hostile act "would punish the world with a devastating trade war."

Even though Donald, still on shaky ground, was far from assured of the GOP nomination, he was eagerly devouring news from the Democratic battleground. Sanders was mounting a robust challenge to Hillary, attracting young voters by "offering them a lot of free stuff such as college tuition."

Donald followed the returns from Nevada, noting that Hillary had "Berned the Bern" in that state's caucuses. She had swept to victory over the "grumpy old man" (as his enemies called Sanders), garnering massive political support from workers in the Las Vegas casino hotels. Her fans and allies, often in reactions against Donald's candidacy, included blackjack dealers, pit bosses, cooks, room maids, janitors, and others who catered to the high rollers who flocked to this gambling mecca in the West. In the aftermath, among the Democrats, Hillary won 52% of the vote, with Sanders drawing less than 47%.

With the South Carolina results in, both Cruz and Rubio realized that each of them had to knock out the other before taking Donald on. An embittered Cruz did not take defeat lightly, labeling Rubio a "Donald Trump with a smile. Rubio and Trump are both liars, although Rubio lies with a smile."

On the campaign trail in South Carolina, Rubio sounded like a deranged Pat Roberson, running a "holier-than-Thou" campaign in his attempt to woo evangelicals from both Cruz and Donald. Rubio constantly repeated invocations of God and attacked the Supreme Court for legalizing same-sex marriage.

Since all three frontrunners were shouting about their commitment to religion, pollsters set out to determine why voters preferred one "priestly candidate" over the other.

A resident of Columbia, Betsy Bullis, said, "I voted for Rubio because we both love HBO's *Ballers,* and Rubio, like myself, thinks Batman could win a war against Spiderman. He told his supporters that."

Jack Daven, of Greenville, said he had been a Cruz supporter but that at the last minute had switched his vote to Rubio. "When Ted Cruz at this rally broke into this silly song, telling us how he serenaded his wife, Heidi, while courting her, it made my rebel blood squirm. He also said he wakes up scared every day and prays to God for mercy. I didn't want a little coward like that in the White House."

Theresa Kostrzewa, a former fundraiser for Jeb Bush, predicted that his backers would now throw their support behind Rubio. "I've talked to voters who want fresh blood. South Carolina is like the parting of the Red Sea. Republicans, this is your sign from God."

So far, the backers of Rubio and Cruz had spent a staggering $220 million for attack ads during their campaigns, with pitiful results. Bush had spent the most money, to no avail.

One of his wealthy Florida backers, who did not want to be named, said, "I put a ton of money on his ass, and he let us down. I think the 'Bush Dynasty' had ended not with a blast, but with a whimper. Good riddance, I say."

Katie Packer, a GOP strategist, said, "Our hope is that the field will winnow and conservatives will coalesce behind one candidate who is a real conservative."

Columnist Paul Krugman wondered why the GOP establishment viewed Rubio as a moderate and a sensible candidate. "Not long ago, someone holding his policy views would be considered a fringe crank. His statements on foreign policy are terrifying, as is his evident willingness to make a bonfire of civil liberties. His tax cuts would be almost twice those of George W. Bush. That means that millionaires like Mitt Romney would pay precisely zero in Federal taxes. It's not a fight between a crazy guy (Donald) and someone reasonable (Rubio). It's idiosyncratic, self-invented crankery vs. Establishment-approved crankery—and it's not at all clear which is worse."

February was moving toward an inglorious end on the campaign trail as one event after another provided fodder for the tabloids and cable TV news.

In a surprise move, Cruz fired his top adviser, Rick Tyler. Tyler had been asked to resign after a video was released with a false quote by Rubio, who was depicted as saying, "The Bible doesn't have all the answers."

The Cruz campaign had also spread the (patently false) rumor during a key voting moment that Ben Carson was dropping out of the race in Iowa. A Photoshopped, cobbled-together photograph of Obama with Rubio, shaking hands, was distributed suggesting that the Florida senator should drop out of the race for actually having shaken the hand of the President of the United States.

Donald also came in for his share of issues associated with dirty tricks and doctored videos. Cruz campaign aides arranged for audio clips from Donald's speeches to be inserted into visual scenes from the hit TV series, *Game of Thrones.* Donald talks about torturing people with the blunt brutality of a medieval king.

He was portrayed as a member of Night's Watch, a fraternal order whose members had been assigned to deflect any assault on a massive wall under siege by a "race of outsiders."

In this sword-and-sorcery fantasy epic, Donald is portrayed as saying, "Our enemies laugh at us. They protest our waterboarding, but they chop off heads…We need to build a wall and build it quickly."

Whereas attacks on Donald continued, Cruz and Rubio received a barrage of charges thrown at them, too. Columnist Frank Bruni claimed, "Ted Cruz makes angelic claims that are diabolically hypocritical. The Texas senator is some piece of double-talking, disingenuous work. His dirty tricks do stand out in the context of his flamboyant claims of rectitude and righteousness. He directs you to his halo as he surreptitiously grabs a pitchfork."

"The Bible talks about if someone treats you unkindly, repay them with kindness," Cruz told a rally in South Carolina.

In the Senate, Cruz had likened GOP senators who claimed it was logistically impossible to defund Obamacare to "Nazi appeasers."

Quote after quote attributed to Cruz depicted him as a bit unhinged, as in 2012 in a presidential debate when he claimed, "Mitt Romney actually French kissed Obama."

Throughout the campaign, Cruz continued to rant about same-sex marriage, calling it "the greatest scourge of our time." He seemed to view such unions as catalysts for the doom of civilization.

Even though he had by now already trounced both of his Cuban American competitors (Cruz and Rubio), Donald continued his attacks. He'd already accused Cruz of being a Canadian anchor baby. Now, he questioned Rubio's credentials to run for President, sowing seeds of doubt about his place of birth. "Ted Cruz and Marco Rubio are ineligible to run for President, Donald tweeted. "Cruz was born in Canada. I don't know where Rubio was born."

An unnamed aide to Donald made an outrageous charge. "I heard it on good authority in Miami that Rubio was born in Havana, and may have been the bastard son of Castro."

Donald chimed in: "I was told that Rubio's parents were not U.S. citizens when he was born. They were citizens of Castro's communist island of Cuba."

The latest poll showed Donald leading in ten of the next fourteen states to vote in the GOP primaries or caucuses. He was leading in Nevada, Alabama, Georgia, Alaska, Massachusetts, Tennessee, Virginia, Oklahoma, Minnesota, and Louisiana. As expected, Cruz was ahead in Texas, and Donald also trailed him in Arkansas, Colorado, and Kentucky.

In New York, Donald's fellow New Yorkers had a keen eye focused on the GOP race. In Albany, Governor Mario Cuomo signaled that he was ready to run for President if a Democrat failed to win in November. A source said, "Mario is seeing the light of a rapid leftward turn of the grass roots. His entire future rests on the defeat of a flawed Hillary and "the Abominable Snowman of Vermont" (i.e., Sanders).

In New York, Donald's fellow billionaire, Mike Bloomberg, was disheartened at a recent poll that revealed that his fellow New Yorkers weren't ready to vote for him for President, although they had already elected him mayor three times.

Nearly 60% of the voters claimed they preferred other candidates.

Another former New York Mayor, Rudy Giuliani, once a presidential candidate himself, revealed that he was an adviser to Trump's campaign. "People like that Donald tells it like it is. I like that he is eschewing political correctness."

Super Tuesday loomed for Donald. He told his aides, "After that, we could almost have the nomination locked up."

***

One by one, the once-leading candidates for the GOP presidential race began to fade from the radar screen. Perhaps in an attempt to regain more exposure, Ben Carson, who had distinguished himself as a neurosurgeon, continued to stir up controversy with his bizarre opinions.

Donald reacted with amusement when he heard Carson's views on President Obama. Carson claimed America's first black President didn't understand African Americans "because he was raised white." He was, of course, referring to the commander-in-chief's white mother.

"He grew up in white America," Carson said. "That doesn't mean there is anything wrong with that. It's just that when a claim is made that he represents the black experience, it is not true."

Carson's rebuke of Obama brought the strongest satirical attack of the neurosurgeon from Linda Stasi, who continued to swing the sharpest ax among columnists.

"Ben Carson needs to drop out of the race—the human race—and return to Mars, or whatever planet he came from. You don't have to be a brain surgeon to know that the guy is one step away from a tinfoil hat."

It was with trepidation that many GOP leaders, such as Senate majority leader Mitch O'Connell, watched as the candidates, mainly Donald, headed west to Nevada to compete in the races leading up to Super Tuesday.

Republican leaders faced a dilemma, privately proclaiming "anyone but Trump."

However, the party's second frontrunner, Ted Cruz, seemed to be loathed even more by party leaders, and hardly emerged as the proper candidate for voters to rally around.

Rubio was a possibility, although it was feared that he was too far to the right to attract moderate Republicans, Independents, or "Reagan Democrats."

In Nevada, where Donald owned a hotel, he was widely viewed as the favorite.

The caucus in Nevada, on February 23, turned out to be a voting disaster. Its procedures and its integrity were widely denounced on radio, TV, and in print. Voter fraud was alleged, along with insufficient ballots and general pandemonium at the precincts. Some fights broke out between Donald's supporters and those promoting the candidacy of Cruz. There were also allegations that many of Donald's supporters had cast ballots multiple times. Some Trump supporters showed up at the voting precincts wearing KKK robes.

As the results poured in, Donald, receiving the lion's share of the vote in Trump-friendly Las Vegas, became a new "American Idol," winning 33% of the vote, taking another giant step toward becoming the Republican nominee.

Rubio trailed at 24%, with "God's anointed," Cruz, getting only 21%.

In the wake of his provocative comments, Carson got 6.6% of the vote, with John Kasich, viewed as the most sensible of the candidates, receiving a meager 3.8%. The so-called "voice of reason" emanating from the Ohio governor had not seemed to resonate.

At a "watch party" at the Treasure Island Hotel in Las Vegas, Donald received thundering applause. There were screams of joy and delight. "Thank you, Nevada," he said. "We will make America safe and great again."

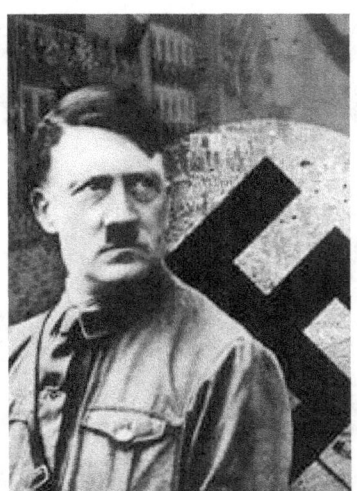

After years of suppression, **Adolf Hitler**'s *Mein Kampf* was republished in Munich in 2016 and became a bestseller.

A copy of the Führer's manifesto was rushed to Donald.

ADOLF HITLER'S *MEIN KAMPF*
After Someone Sends Him a Copy,
Donald Gets an Endorsement from the KKK

A scholarly edition of Adolf Hitler's infamous autobiography, *Mein Kampf*, first published in 1925 and filled with the Nazi dictator's anti-Semitic and genocidal rants, was outlawed in Germany for many years after World War II. It was republished in Munich in 2016 and became a bestseller.

One neo-Nazi in Munich sent Donald a copy of the *Führer's* manifesto, with a note: "Read it! There are lessons to be learned. Don't go after the Muslims. Go after the Jews! The *Führer* got it right."

Around that time, Hitler had re-entered the news cycle when his recently uncovered medical records were revealed. It had long been known that one of his testicles had never descended, but recently, he'd been exposed for having a "teeny tiny Wiener."

"Poor Eva," wrote a journalist in Stuttgart, referring to Eva Braun, Hitler's longtime mistress, who actually had wanted to go to Hollywood to become "another Lana Turner."

On February 24, Donald received an endorsement from a coven of admirers, who might also have supported Hitler had they lived in Germany in 1933. David Duke, the former Grand Wizard of the KKK, and once a presidential candidate himself, announced his support of Donald.

"Not voting for Trump would be a treason to your heritage,"

Throughout the campaign, Donald was frequently compared to **Adolf Hitler** (*left*).

From the campaign trail, he also quoted from **Mussolini** (*right*). "A good quote is a good quote, even if Mussolini said it," Donald insisted.

Duke claimed over the radio, addressing his followers. Duke implored them to volunteer to rustle up some votes for the New York billionaire.

"Voting for him is a strategic action. I hope he does everything we hope he will do." Duke urged KKK members to "Get off your duff. Get off your rear end that's getting fatter and fatter for many of you every day on your chairs. Among other Trump volunteers, you're going to meet the same kind of mindset you have."

Many politicians and civic groups called upon Donald to disavow the KKK's controversial endorsement. "I disapprove," he said at the time, and then changed the subject.

Duke had come out for Donald before, especially when he promised that a wall would be built during his administration to keep out Mexican rapists, and had called for a ban on Muslims entering the United States.

"I praise the fact that Trump has come out on the immigration issue," the former "Wizard" said. "I'm beginning to get the idea that he is a good salesman."

DENOUNCING DONALD
Cruz and Rubio Attack Donald at the Houston Debate As "An Empty Suit Without a Plan" and "a Bloviating Billionaire"

The tenth GOP debate, in Houston, had been heralded as a "do-or-die" for the remaining candidates in the race. At this point, whereas Cruz and Rubio remained as Donald's only serious competitors, Kasich and Carson would be onstage as well.

The debate was conducted on the evening of February 25 on Cruz's home turf in Texas, broadcast by CNN from the University of Houston. It had been scheduled just five days before Super Tuesday (March 1, 2016), a day when either primaries or caucuses would be held in fourteen states.

It was to have been sponsored by *NBC News*, but the RNC chairman, Reince Priebus, had previously denounced the network for having "bad faith" during the October 28, 2015 debate in Boulder, Colorado. That debate had drawn "dragon fire" from Donald, who didn't like the tough, often embarrassing, questions the moderators asked.

During the debate in the Lone Star State, all five remaining candidates—Donald, Cruz, Rubio, Carson, and Kasich—were invited for their input. This would represent the tenth and final debate for Carson, who skipped the following (March 3) debate in Detroit, and then dropped out of the race the following day.

As in a Hollywood rendition of a boxing match, perhaps one starring Sylvester Stallone, Rubio came out swinging, giving his most aggressive performance after his embarrassingly robotic debate in New Hampshire. He lit into Donald with a verbal assault weapon, ridiculing his health care proposal, immigration deportation plan, and even deriding him for inheriting millions from his father, Fred. The billionaire was depicted as a blowhard—"an empty suit without a plan."

"You're the only person on this stage who's ever been fined for illegally hiring people to work on your building projects," Rubio said.

"No! No! No!" Donald shouted back, "I'm the only one on this stage who's hired people. You haven't hired anybody."

"Donald hired workers from Poland and had to pay a $1 million fine for doing so," Rubio claimed."

He wouldn't let up on Donald, as he attacked his business acumen. "If you built that wall between the United States and Mexico, like you constructed Trump Tower, you'd be using illegal immigrants. If you hadn't inherited $200 million, you'd be selling watches on the streets of Manhattan."

When he finished his blitz against Donald, Cruz entered the fray to deliver some "sucker punches."

"When I was fighting against amnesty, where was Donald? He was firing Dennis Rodman on *Celebrity Apprentice*." Cruz uttered that charge with a smug mockery as Donald glared at him.

Both Cruz and Rubio bitterly attacked Donald for an impending lawsuit in which former students of Trump University were charging fraud and demanding refunds of their tuition.

Never at a loss for words, Donald called Rubio "a choke artist" and denounced Cruz as a "liar. Ted Cruz lacks the ability to get along with anybody." Then he turned to his Texas challenger. "You should be ashamed of yourself."

Inevitably, the subject of Hillary came up, with Cruz reminding Donald that polls showed that she could beat him in the November election.

"Hell, she would really kill you," Donald countered.

The debate degenerated into indecipherable shouting and name-calling.

Showing the ravages of their respective ages, Barbara Bush sat in the auditorium with her husband, former U.S. President, George H.W. Bush.

Despite the exit from the race of their son, Jeb, they were on hand to watch what Barbara later described as "a horror show." Their faces reflected their disillusion not only with the candidates, but perhaps with the state of the Republican race as well.

The weatherbeaten pair, survivors of many a political brawl, had never participated in something like this. There was a bitterness reflected in their faces as they looked on in disgust, still licking the wounds of the GOP's repudiation of their son, Jeb, during his spectacularly expensive and ill-fated quest for the presidency.

The next day, television's talking heads and many editorial writers awarded the debate to Rubio, claiming that he had stung Donald with his quick jabs and sharp denunciations. Rubio appeared to have benefitted from debate training, perhaps with coaches. Conveying a kind of desperation, he was sweating profusely as his chance of becoming America's first Cuban-American President faded.

Reporters described him as "newly pugnacious," as he tore into Donald, even attacking him for outsourcing the manufacture of his clothing line, including those "tasteless ties," to China.

When Donald protested, Rubio outshouted him. "Make them in America!"

Rubio may have won the debate, but many editorial writers agreed: "The Florida senator did not look or sound very presidential."

"NO MORE TIME FOR CLOWNS
& Dancing Bears"

—*Ted Cruz, After the Tenth Republican Debate*

In an almost desperate last-ditch effort to defeat Donald in the Super Tuesday GOP primaries, Cruz and Rubio stepped up their fire power. Campaigning hard in Texas, where polls had him in the lead, Cruz drew upon the massacre at the Alamo in 1836. "America is besieged," he claimed. Some Texas reporters claimed, "If Cruz loses Texas, he's a dead coyote on the trail"

Appealing to evangelicals, he claimed, "Texans will not give up their freedom quietly." He never spelled out exactly what freedom Texans had lost during the Obama years. "The time for the clowns and dancing bears has passed," he said, in an insulting reference to Donald.

Rubio also didn't let up, calling Donald a "con artist." He mocked his misspelled words in his endless tweets and even claimed he got "so flustered by my attacks during our last debate that he wet his pants."

"Donald Trump is Mr. Meltdown and can't spell. He writes 'chicker' instead of choker, and 'honer' instead of honor. A third grader could have done better."

Donald fired back: "Lightweight choker Marco Rubio looks like a little boy on stage—not presidential material."

Cruz also sent out tweets, one of them cringe-inducing: "Trump called me a soft, weak little baby. Hope he doesn't eat me."

One columnist responded to that: "I can only hope he does."

The homophobic Cruz didn't seem to realize that "eat me" in gay parlance referred to a blow-job.

The anti-Trump forces were marching as to war, with the Cross of Jesus going on before. Sometimes, however, Rubio quit claiming he was the candidate of Christ and reverted to character assassination.

At a rally in Kennesaw, Georgia, Rubio mocked Donald's appearance. "He likes to sue people. He should sue whoever did that orange face of his. It's the worst spray tan in America."

Donald responded with: "Little Marco applies makeup with a trowel before a debate."

Rubio might have found his voice, but Donald never lost his own. "Little Marco has a fresh mouth, and he's a very nasty guy. I see him starting to sweat. Thank God he has really large ears, the biggest ears I've ever seen, since they protect him from the profusion of sweat running down."

"Unlike Little Marco and Lying Ted Cruz, I won in Nevada with the young, I won with the old. I won with the highly educated. I won with the poorly educated. I love the poorly educated."

No one had ever accused Donald of being a Christian soldier, a Bible thumper like his chief rivals, Cruz and Rubio. Those two Cuban attack dogs had entered the race, hoping to divide the evangelical vote between them. It was estimated that 72% of the GOP electorate in the primaries consisted of "Born Again

Realizing that they were each losing their race for the nomination, both Ted Cruz and Marco Rubio reverted to cruel mockery of Donald in their campaign speeches.

At one point, Cruz compared Donald's rally speeches to the kind of entertainment you'd expect from "circus clowns and dancing bears."

evangelical Christians." However, Rubio and Cruz were surprised to see Donald appealing to evangelicals, even in Texas.

Writing for *Bloomberg View*, Francis Wilkinson said, "Unfortunately for those two senators, many conservative evangelicals have concluded that they don't need a candidate who shares their values. They can tolerate, even embrace, a candidate who is profane, greedy, vain, shifty, and thrice married with a loud history of sexual conquest."

He suggested that evangelicals were "nostalgia voters, eager to return to an idealized, socially conservative, and white-dominated past."

In-depth surveys of Tea Party diehards, most often evangelicals, discovered that they had strong, hardcore beliefs. They seemed convinced that Obama was not an American citizen, having been born, they claimed, in Kenya.

They were also convinced that he supported Islamic terrorists and was not a Christian, "but a Muslim tyrant, with a goal to turn the United States into a godless communist nation."

As one of Trump's most ardent supporters in Dallas told a pollster: "Trump will put the white man on top again, like he used to be, like it was before all the niggers, queers, Jews, Islamic terrorists, Hillary lesbians, and Mexican rapists steal our country forever."

The swiftness of the cultural change disturbed many evangelicals, who longed for a return to a perhaps illusionary golden yesteryear. "We now have gays in the military," said one evangelical from Fort Worth. "In the good old days, like in the Eisenhower era, faggots could not serve in the military. Homosexuality should be made illegal like it was back then. These guys should be put in prison along with the nigger murderers and Mexican drug dealers. Now there is talk of even letting transgendered people, whoever the fuck they are, serve in the military. Faggots have never served in the military and shouldn't now. Trump will see to that."

[In point of fact, thousands upon thousands of gay men and women fought and died during World War II, many of them heroically.]

As Rubio continued with his assault that Donald "had urinated in his trousers," Donald mocked Rubio's excessively parched throat. At one rally, he brandished a plastic water bottle, mocking "Senator Choke." Once, Rubio was caught on camera reaching desperately for a bottle of water, which he proceeded to noisily gulp down as millions laughed at him on TV.

Waving a water bottle at a Texas rally, Donald poured half of its contents onto the floor before ostentatiously gulping from it in a mocking imitation of Rubio. "That night, he looked like he had survived five days in the Sahara without benefit of a single drop," Donald said.

Cruz also claimed, "*ABC, CNN,* and multiple news reports have cited Trump's dealings with S&A Construction, which was owned by 'Fat Tony' Salerno, who is a mobster, who is in jail."

Appearing on *Meet the Press,* Cruz brought up Donald's alleged ties to the Mafia. "The reason he won't release his income tax forms is that it would reveal his link to organized crime," Cruz charged.

Just when American voters thought the GOP primary cat-and-dog fight could sink no lower, Rubio became the "bottom-feeder." Even the Queen of England reportedly asked, "Just what is happening to the United States?"

On February 28 at a rally at Roanoke College in Virginia, and on a Christian Sunday, no less, a smirky Rubio told the crowd, "Donald's hands are the size of someone who is 5 foot 2. And you know what they say about a man who has small hands."

Then he paused, as the crowd mockingly laughed. As if to protect himself, he added, "That is, you can't trust 'em."

He knew exactly why the crowd was laughing. "Small hands, small dick," was the reference, according to the (tired, old, and frequently disproved) urban myth.

Donald did not immediately defend the size of his penis. That would come later.

***

To recover from the onslaught of attacks from his two bitter rivals, Rubio and Cruz, Donald won the endorsement of a former rival on February 26. The governor of New Jersey, Chris Christie, endorsed him as the best GOP candidate to beat Hillary in November.

At a campaign stop in Fort Worth, Texas, Christie, who had already dropped out of the race, claimed, "There is no one better prepared to provide America with the strong leadership it needs than Donald Trump."

Donald gushed over the endorsement, and there was speculation that

"Small hands, small dick," or so goes the disproven American myth.

At a contentious debate, **Donald** held up his hands to show the world, "They're not that small." He also told voters that "I'm more than adequate down there, too."

Rubio of the big ears also revealed his hands, showing that they were larger than Donald's, thereby suggesting that he was better hung.

Actually, women who have gone to bed with either man confided that both candidates are "far larger than average," without providing exact measurements.

the losing candidate, Christie, wanted Donald to name him as his vice-presidential running mate.

Only a year before, Christie had told Fox News anchorwoman Greta Van Susteren that, "I don't think Donald is suited to be President of the United States."

Many greeted the endorsement with ridicule. On Twitter, David Kochel cracked, "New lessons, kids. Sometimes the best option for the fat kid is to hand over his lunch money to the schoolyard bully!"

On the campaign trail, Christie vowed, "We're gonna kick Obama's ass out of the White House. We're going to show up at 1600 Pennsylvania Avenue with an eviction notice."

Back in his native New Jersey, a local *politico* tweeted, "The bright lights are going out for our disgraced governor. He's got troubles at home. But right now, he's become the opening act for the star of the show…Donald Trump."

One newspaper headline read: "I HATED DONALD TRUMP. NOW I LOVE HIM"—CHRISTIE.

In the wake of his weak showing at the debate in Houston, Donald, in the words of one reporter, "fought back like a wildcat."

Columnist Rick Lowry wrote: "Now Trump has a prominent wingman who shares his taste for no-holds-barred political combat."

The acerbic columnist, Linda Stasi, couldn't resist jumping into the fray. She noted that Donald had been called a "carnival barker/jackass/a cancer/loser/narcissist egomaniac/pants wetter/bully."

But Christie, "traveling a bridge too far," had forgiven Donald all his failings and was now his chief surrogate.

"Peter only denied Jesus three times, and he went down in history as one of the world's biggest hypocrites," Stasi said.

Facing Super Tuesday, Donald continued to reveal just how thin-skinned he was. On February 26, he claimed that he would reverse the First Amendment when he became President. In a threat to the news media, he said, "We're gonna open up those libel laws, folks, and we're gonna sue you like you've never been sued before."

That his patience was wearing thin was obvious.

[*Around the same time, Donald's adversary, Bill Clinton, also had his nerves tested in South Carolina by a heckler, a retired marine sergeant in Bluffton. "We had four lives in Benghazi that were killed," the man said. "And your wife tried to cover it up."*

The crowd booed the heckler, and the former President of the United States said: "Shut up and listen to my answer."

Donald couldn't have done it better.]

In Washington, Hillary told the press, "It's been surprising to me to see somebody who was affable and was good company, and had a reputation of being kind and bigger than life, really traffic in a lot of prejudice and paranoia like Donald Trump. He doesn't fit into what I thought I knew about him."

News reached Donald on February 27 that Hillary had demolished her rival, Bernie Sanders, in the South Carolina primary, thereby reinforcing her frontrunner status as the Democratic nominee. An overwhelming turnout of African American voters propelled her to victory, as she defeated the aging Vermont senator by 47 points.

Meanwhile, Karl Rove went on the offensive. During the administration of George W. Bush, he had been called "Baby Bush's brain." The President in power at the time had a name for him: "Turd Blossom," inspired by a wildflower that thrived in decaying cowpiles in the grasslands of Texas.

At a luncheon of Republican governors gathering in Washington on February 19, Rove told his fellow right wingers that nominating Donald would be catastrophic for the GOP. "It's not too late to stop this onslaught," Rove predicted. Last-ditch efforts to block Donald's inexorable advance were energetically debated.

Perhaps in desperation, many members of the Republican Establishment seemed to think that "Little Marco" might be their man, although during the previous few months, millions of dollars had been spent on ads touting his glory. As one donor said, "We ran the flag up the pole and found few voters ready to salute it."

The baby-faced 44-year-old was told by the power brokers to continue "with his slash-and-burn night of the long knives, cutting into Donald with his recently sharpened vitriol." As the Old Guard of the GOP fumed and fussed over the emergence of Donald, he and Rubio continued in their sarcasm.

"If elected President, Donald would be flying 'Hair Force One,'" Rubio said, mockingly.

"Little Marco is too dim to have attended my Ivy League *Alma Mater*," Donald charged.

Rubio shot back, "Donald brings to mind the lunatic North Korean dictator with nuclear ambitions."

Satire ruled the day, none better than that of Frank Bruni who, in *The New York Times*, came out with a gender-bending appraisal:

"Imagine for a moment the presidential candidacy of a rich, brash, real estate magnate and reality TV star named 'Donna Trump.' Quizzically coifed and stubbornly sun-kissed, she's on her third marriage. There's clear evidence that infidelity factored into the demise of her first. One of her children was conceived out of wedlock."

"Her sexual appetites had been prodigious, at least according to her frequent chants and claims and vulgar cants. She has a tendency to talk about men as sirloins and rump roasts of disparate succulence. She denigrates those who displease her on cosmetic grounds. So-and-so used to be a 9, but, with that male-pattern baldness and desperate comb-over, is down to a 6. So-and-so thinks he's covering up that fat around the waist with baggy suits, but we know better."

Bruni went on to predict that "Donna Trump" would not have a chance in the race for the White House.

Donald had hoped that he could move on with a quick disavowal of his KKK support, but at the very last day of February, it returned to haunt him when he appeared on CNN's *State of the Union.* The subject of David Duke was brought up again.

"I don't know anything about David Duke," Donald said on camera, even though millions watching him knew that he did. "I don't know anything about white supremacists."

For that, he was severely attacked from many quarters for not having denounced Duke and the KKK. Cruz immediately tweeted, "You're better than this, Donald. We should all agree that racism is wrong, the KKK is abhorrent."

Then, one of New York's (Republican) Congressmen, Peter King, weighed in, telling Jake Rapper on CNN, "Donald says he doesn't know who David Duke is or what the white supremacist group stands for. If his statements are true, it means Trump is genuinely dumb. If he is lying, that is shameful. In any case, he should not be running to lead the United States."

Of course, the Rev. Al Sharpton had to weigh in too. "How can Trump not know who David Duke is if he is saying to people he has enough knowledge to run the Free World?"

Reporter Adam Edelman pointed out, "Trump's dumb act was particularly odd because the real estate mogul had once condemned Duke. In 2000, he said he would not run for President on the Reform Ticket because the party included Duke as a member."

To make matters worse, Donald tweeted a quote from Benito Mussolini. The Italian fascist had once said, "It is better to live one day as a lion than 100 years as a sheep."

Asked to defend having been inspired by a fascist, Donald responded, "It's a very good quote. It's a very interesting quote. I know who said it, but what difference does it make whether it's Mussolini or someone else?"

TV host Chuck Todd asked him if he wanted to be associated with a fascist.

Donald demurred. "No, I want to be associated with interesting quotes."

***

Donald's detractors weren't confined just to the United States. He was attacked around the world. Reporter Dan Bilefsky wrote, "Trump has been depicted as a snarling demagogue in France, equated with Donald Duck in Spain, and described as worse than Lord Voldemort in Britain. With his series of election wins, the reaction has become one of befuddlement, outrage, and panic, along with admiration in some unlikely quarters."

El Pais, one of the most influential newspapers of Spain, even published an imagined quote from the grave of Philip I, Spain's ascetic, empire-building 16th-century king. *El Pais'* editors wrote that if Philip had been alive, he'd have suggested that Donald should define himself as the agent who'd bring back the Inquisition.

In Germany, the front cover of *Der Spiegel* depicted Donald with the American flag behind him engulfed in flames. Its headline blared: "MADNESS: AMERICA'S AGITATOR."

Support for Donald came from surprising quarters, including from *Mlada fronma Dnes,* the leading newspaper of the Czech Republic. It seemed that Donald had evolved into a sort of folk hero among the disillusioned populace of Eastern and Central Europe. Many citizens equated Donald's rise to that of Ronald Reagan.

Fans were drawn to his showmanship and swagger. "To many Czechs, Trump signifies American values like show business and working hard to achieve success," wrote editor Jaroslav Plesi.

Donald also enjoyed massive popularity among the Russians, who wrote of his "budding 'bromance'" with Putin. The Russians took delight in Donald's lack of political correctness, as when he referred to the "protruding nipples" of the gay former Congressman, Barney Frank.

The newspapers consistently quoted the new legend that Putin and Donald were part of a mutual admiration society.

TRASHING DONALD'S COMPETITORS
What They're Hiding: The Enquirer Reveals All

On the last day of February, 2016, *The National Enquirer* released an exposé that shocked millions of Americans.

The headlines read: "WHAT THEY'RE HIDING!"

The tabloid ran pictures of Marco Rubio, Hillary Clinton, Donald Trump, Bernie Sanders, and a gloomy-looking Ted Cruz, followed by subheads blaring, "Gay Sex Arrest," "Rape Cover-up," "Child Sex Scandal," and "Suicide Shocker."

The paper did not identify which of those headlines belonged to which candidate—and with the intention of avoiding libel, we don't want to either. To play it safe, it was suggested that we replicate the words as they appeared.

Inside, a photo was published that was alleged to be of Rubio "wallowing in bubbles at a guys' foam party in Miami" when he was a young man. Yet another photo purported to be his image at a dance bar "in the swing with other topless men."

Reporter Sharon Churcher wrote that Rubio was hiding a "secret gay past."

Political blogger Wayne Madsen claimed, "People in the gay community have told me it was well known that Rubio frequented gay nightclubs and attended almost exclusively gay events."

The Enquirer also revealed (allegedly) official records that Rubio had been arrested, along with two other men, at 9:37PM on May 23, 1990, in Miami's crime-plagued Alice C. Wainright Park.

A homeowners' association newsletter stated that the park was "a haven for gang warfare, gunfire, prostitution (gay and straight), drug dealing, and muggings.

Police major Delrish Moss said, "It was very dark and had lots of trees. People went there to smoke illegal substances, have sex, and drink."

Charges made against the men were later dismissed. The Enquirer quoted Rubio aide Todd Harris, who claimed that the young men were merely caught drinking beer after hours.

The tabloid also headlined a story with "SUICIDAL WIFE DRIVEN CRAZY BY HIS RUTHLESS AMBITION!" It was an *exposé* of Cruz and his wife, Heidi. The two had met while working on George W. Bush's presidential campaign in 2000.

On August 22, 2005, in Austin, policemen discovered Heidi sitting "with her head in her hands" on the grass near an expressway. An officer later alleged that "she had walked away from her home after having two sips of a margarita an hour before dinner." He also said she was in danger, as she was sitting in despair only ten feet from the rushing traffic."

Cruz's campaign admitted that his wife "experienced a brief bout of depression."

Bernie Sanders came in for his share of scandal. The paper had already reported that he was alleged to have fathered a love child during the hippie era.

Now, the tabloid claimed that he had written smutty essays when he had a stint as a freelance journalist in the 1970s. He wrote of a man who goes home and masturbates to fantasies about being with a woman on her knees, a woman tied up, and a woman abused.

One woman, as described in one of Sanders' essays, was said to have fantasized "about being raped by three men simultaneously." He also wrote an article advocating that six-month old babies should be allowed to romp naked on the beach so "they can see each other's sexual organs—and maybe even touch them."

According to the article, Sanders also confessed to a fascination with stories about sexual assaults on kids. He was said to have written, "Do you know why porn magazines sell so well if they run such articles as 'Girl Raped by 15 Men?'"

As Congressman from Vermont, in 2003, Sanders opposed measures that cracked down on pedophiles who traveled overseas to such countries as Thailand to prey on kids. He also voted against outlawing some Internet child porn.

The allegations in that edition of the Enquirer against Bill and Hillary had been (frequently) aired before—that her "horndog husband" engaged in a series of affairs not only with Monica Lewinsky, but was accused of molesting Kathleen Willey, a volunteer at the White House, and of an actual rape of Juanita Broaddrick when he was governor of Arkansas. Hillary was accused of turning a blind eye to her husband's indiscretions, even though an advocate of women's rights.

Cruz had accused The Enquirer of being kind to Donald, and indeed, his biggest "scandal," as reported by that edition of that publication, was a glowing endorsement from has-been singer Pat Boone, who said, "Donald would make a great President. He would tell it like it is."

Our Media Age:
CELEBRITIES & CELEBRITY-DRIVEN POLITICS
*TV Icons, Dubious, Ill Qualified, or Indifferent,
Weigh in with Endorsements*

The tabloid also reported that other entertainers, including Wayne Newton and Gary Busey, had endorsed Donald. Other celebrities supporting various candidates were revealed to include Jennifer Lopez and Michael Douglas, each of whom supported Hillary. ("I think it's time for a woman," Lopez said.

Bernie Sanders won endorsements from Danny DeVito and Will Ferrell; and his fellow Canadian, Justin Beiber, endorsed Cruz.

Marco Rubio picked up the support of actor Orson Bean and Olympic hero Kurt Angle.

Ben Carson drew support from Mickey Rourke and Kelsey Grammer, with NBA Hall of Famer Charles Barkley wanting another Bush (Jeb!) in the White House.

In a TV ad, Cruz picked up a controversial endorsement from the so-called "redneck of all rednecks," Phil Robertson, a reality TV clown, star of *Duck Dynasty*. He endorsed Cruz at a rally in South Carolina.

At one point, Robertson had been temporarily suspended from his A&E TV show after making homophobic comments. He said, "I just can't understand why they prefer a hole to a pussy."

In a blatant attempt to win the support of the most "redneck of redneck voters," **Ted Cruz** "The Commander" *(right)* donned a hunter's "black face" camouflage for a duck hunt with the controversial **Phil Robertson**, a reality TV star, a noted homophobe, and a personality that his detractors perceived as gauche, menacing, unlikable, utterly without humor, and to some, terrifying.

Cruz believed he'd earn the votes of Duck Dynasty fans as a camera recorded his plot to penetrate and kill, with shotgun pellets, some harmless duck, which had—until this ad was shot— been flying freely through the air.

At the end of this gruesome and utterly distasteful ad (entitled "Cruz Commander,") voters were urged to "**JOIN THE FIGHT TODAY!**"

PART FIVE

2016: THE SPRING OF TRUMP

"NEVER TRUMP"
Republicans Rage & Scream
About Their Party's Presumptive Nominee

TRUMP REVEALS
How He'd Get Mexico To Pay for the Wall

DONALD SWEEPS TO VICTORY
IN THE NORTHEAST

DONALD TRUMP
Is a "Pathological Liar, Narcissist, & Serial Philanderer"
—Failing GOP candidate Ted Cruz

Chapter Ten

EUROPE PONDERS THE QUESTION "IS TRUMP WORSE THAN DRACULA?"
Journalists Wonder If America Is On the Road to Fascism

"THIS DEBATE MARKS THE DEMISE OF THE DIGNITY OF THE AMERICAN POLITICAL PROCESS"
—*The New York Daily News*, in reference to the March 3, 2016, Republican Debate in Detroit

DEMOCRATIC STRATEGISTS DEBATE HOW THEY CAN CASTRATE A CANDIDATE "WHOSE COJONES ARE MADE OF STEEL"

"The Hot, Hot, GOP Race Has Devolved Into a Huge, Balls-Out, Pissing Match"

March came in with a blast, as Mexico unveiled its strategy to counter slurs from Donald Trump. All of this followed in the wake of the billionaire's plan for a massive wall to divide the two nations. Both Marco Rubio and Ted Cruz had also proposed building a wall along America's southern border.

Mexico was greatly offended to have endured its immigrating nationals designated as "drug runners and rapists," and it was horrified by Donald's call for a mass deportation of eleven million undocumented immigrants.

In Mexico City, Francisco Guzman, the chief of staff to President Enrique Peña Nieto, said it was time "to push back." He announced a major public relations campaign to highlight the rewards of U.S./Mexican relations, both to the U.S. economy and its people.

Until March, the Mexican government had avoided any direct confrontations with Donald, although some of its diplomats had labeled his projected policies "ignorant and racist." But now, Vicente Fox and Felipe Calderon each denounced Donald, comparing him to Hitler.

Guzman said, "With our top trading partner (the United States), we need more bridges and fewer walls. America is the destination for about 80% of our exports. We also share many cultural and family links. I want the man or woman who becomes President in November to view Mexico not as a threat but as an opportunity."

Donald's harsh language against Latinos, especially Mexicans, was leading to a massive incentives for Latino immigrants to become naturalized U.S. citizens so—in the event he received the GOP nomination, they'd be able to vote against Donald in the November election.

Overall, according to Federal figures, applications for naturalization jumped 14% beginning in January. Nearly nine million legal residents had been able to naturalize, which would, it was surmised, contribute to an increasingly significant voting block if the subjects continued the process of becoming citizens. The majority of Latinos in the U.S. are Democrats. Naturalization drives were particularly effective in Colorado, Florida, and Nevada, states likely to be fiercely contested in November.

IN EUROPE, DONALD IS DENOUNCED
As "The World's Most Dangerous Man"

Mexico was not alone in sounding alarms against Donald. Headlines on the Continent blared—UNITED STATES EMBRACES LATTER-DAY MUSSOLINI.

In Rome, readers were warned, "Donald Trump could become Silvio Berlusconi with nukes," a reference to that country's disgraced ultra-conservative prime minister.

In Europe, Donald was labeled as "the anti-Obama, the loud mouth that spews hatred." The influential German news magazine, Der Spiegel, wrote that Donald was "the most dangerous man alive," before waxing nostalgic for George W. Bush. "Faced with the choice of Trump, we could suddenly discover a soft spot for Dracula," wrote one columnist.

From London, David Cameron attacked Donald, claiming that he "fuels hatred." In contrast, the French rightist and ultra-nationalist, Jean-Marie Le Pen, sang his praises.

Nearly all newspapers noted that Fascism had flourished on European soil during the mid-20th Century. "Could it possibly be coming to America in the 21st Century?" asked one Italian journalist.

Although at first, Donald had been dismissed as part of America's "lunatic fringe," by March, Donald was being taken seriously by Democratic campaign strategists.

Matthew Dowd, chief strategist for George W. Bush, said, in reference to her vulnerability, "Hillary has built a large tanker ship, and she's about to confront Somali pirates."

She launched her campaign on the high ground, saying, "Instead of building walls, we need to be tearing down barriers. Trump's rants do not represent American values. Racism, sexism, bigotry, discrimination, inequality are not American values."

She faced a problem with white men who were marching under Donald's banner by the millions.

David Pfouffe, architect of Obama's 2008 campaign and its calls for hope and change, said, "Today, it's more like hate and castrate."

Before the end of the month, Democratic strategists had concluded that despite intense opposition, Donald was now a formidable candidate. As his power grew, so did his opponents: As one Hillary campaign aide pondered, "What blade can we use to castrate him? His cojones seemed made of steel."

YANKEE CARPETBAGGERS (Donald & Hillary) SWEEP TO VICTORIES IN THE SOUTH
Blacks for Her, Whites for Him

At long last, Super Tuesday, March 1, dawned.

[Super Tuesday refers to one or more Tuesdays early in the presidential primaries when the greatest number of U.S. states hold caucuses or primary elections. Because greater numbers of delegates to the presidential nominating conventions can be won on one of these election days than on any other single day of the primary calendar, they are fraught with competitive emotion and intensely scrutinized by pundits.]

Donald, according to polls, showed a 33-point lead over his nearest rivals, Cruz and Rubio.

Some 49% of Republican voters in the CNN/ORC poll gave him a giant lead, with Rubio trailing at 16%, and Cruz a tardy 15%. Cruz, however, appeared set to "steal" Texas with its whopping 155 delegates. The only poll that put Rubio ahead was Minnesota at 23% of the vote. But that was a statistical three-way since Cruz got 21%, Donald 18%.

On the Democratic side, Hillary appeared in a strong position to topple Bernie Sanders, having drawn hordes of African Americans to the polls. Like Rubio, Sanders was "banking on Minnesota."

Super Tuesday produced a massive turnout for both Hillary and Donald. His victories swept across the South and New England, although Cruz carried his home state of Texas. Donald scored big in Alabama, Georgia, Tennessee, and Massachusetts, with narrow victories in Arkansas, Vermont, and Virginia. He showed he had broad appeal, even in the Evangelical Deep South and the more moderate, secular Massachusetts.

At his Mar-a-Lago estate in Palm Beach, he proclaimed, without justification, "I am a unifier. Once I knock down my rivals, I am going to go after one person: Hillary Clinton."

His strongest support came from low-income white voters, especially men and those without college degrees.

Whereas Cruz boasted of victories, not only in Texas but in Oklahoma, Rubio suffered grievous setbacks. As predicted, Rubio limped along, scoring only in Minnesota, which is not known for deciding presidential elections.

On his home turf in Miami, the greatly weakened candidate urged voters "not to give in to the fear and anger, by listening to sham artists and con artists who try to take advantage of your suffering."

In Palm Beach, Donald trivialized that advice by tweeting, "The Little Absentee Senator has spoken."

Hillary proved that she could pull together widely diverse voters, scoring wins over Bernie Sanders in both Texas and Virginia, and showing very strong support across the Southern states. She overpowered Sanders in predominantly black and Hispanic districts of the country. She also swept Massachusetts.

In Miami, she shouted to a rally, "America never stopped being great." She won sizable victories in Arkansas, where she was once First Lady, as well as in Alabama, Georgia, and Tennessee. Sanders carried his home state of Vermont.

Hispanics helped Hillary carry Texas with 66% of the vote, as opposed to Sanders getting 33%. However, Sanders swept to victory in neighboring Oklahoma, with 53% of the vote as opposed to her 42%. Sanders also beat her in Colorado, with 58% of the vote to her 41%. As anticipated he carried Minnesota with 60% to her 40%.

Cruz won Alaska, but no one seemed to notice except Sarah Palin, its former governor. She would later desert Cruz and back Donald in the presidential race.

Charles Krauthammer reacted with: "Cruz didn't have the great night he needed to put away Rubio and to emerge as Trump's only remaining challenger."

Donald's win embittered the GOP's Old Guard, even to the point that many of them vowed to quit the party and vote for Hillary. "I signed up for the party of Lincoln, not the KKK," said Ben Sasse, Republican Senator of Nebraska.

Donald's strong showing in the South was summed up by one voter, Mark Harris, 48, of Canton, Georgia. "He's not afraid to get in the trenches and fight for you. He's going to be a bully, and he's going to tell them what he thinks, and he's going to push to get it done. He don't care who he makes mad in the process."

At Mar-a-Lago, in reference to Rubio's attempts at humor, Donald said, "Little Marco decided to become Don Rickles, but Rickles has a lot more talent."

Stunned by Trump's strong approval ratings, many Americans threatened to move to Canada or elsewhere if the bombastic billionaire were elected President.

Al Sharpton said, "I'm planning on leaving if Trump becomes President…but only because he'd probably have me deported anyhow."

Samuel L. Jackson, the Washington, D.C.-born actor, said, "If that motherfucker becomes President, I'll move my black ass to South Africa."

Columnist Leonard Greene summed it up: "Donald Trump is to racism what Chris Rock is to a monologue on Oscar night. And Chris Rock killed it. Trump is to bigotry what Stephen Curry is to a jump shot, what Adele is to a song, what guns are to the NRA."

Entertainment News:
HOW, ON FILM, DONALD CONTRACTED AIDS

Writer-producer-star Sacha Baron Cohen opened The Brothers Grimsby in the United States, although its distributor, Sony Pictures, limited the marketing of this satiric comedy. As a plot device within its script, Donald gets AIDS in one gasp-inducing scene.

The world premiere for this film was in London, where that macabre scene was met with loud cheering from the audience. Elsewhere in Europe, at the end of that scene, there were standing ovations.

In Hollywood, Sony had protested the scene to Cohen, and wanted it removed, but he refused. Studio executives were nervous about angering the vengeful and litigious Donald.

Ryan Grim, writing for *The Huffington Post,* said, "Trump, with his perfectly balanced combination of bluster, hypocrisy, and ignorance, is almost a lampoon version of the 'ugly American,' the loud, brash, U.S. tourist whom much of the world loves to hate."

Frankenstein. IT'S ALIVE! Harry Reid, the Democratic Senator from Nevada, said, "Donald Trump is appealing to some of the darkest forces in America. It's time for Republicans to stop the **Frankenstein** they created in their hate lab."

Sacha Baron Cohen continued with his satiric range of movies with the release of his latest, The Brothers Grimsby. Appearing in a black thong, he announced his character in the movie as a "brand new tool."

But what brought audiences to their feet cheering was when the character playing Donald Trump contracted AIDS.

IT'S ALIVE!!
Conservative Republicans React with Horror
to the Frankenstein They Created in their Hate Labs

Anti-Trump Republicans spent much of March figuring out ways to deny him the nomination, fearing he might taint the public image of their party for decades to come. They began to spend millions of dollars on attack ads in Florida, which they hoped would propel Florida's native son, Rubio, into the lead.

In reference to the ads, Hope Hicks, spokeswoman for Donald, said, "This is yet another desperate attempt by the out-of-touch Establishment élites and dark money people, who control the weak politicians, to maintain control of our broken and corrupt system."

Jeff Berkowitz, a former RNC official, said, "The best case scenario for the NEVER TRUMP backers is to throw the convention into disarray, either by ensuring that Trump does not reach the eight-state threshold so the rules have to be changed, or by changing the rules even if he does."

"In failing to confront the most divisive forces of the [tea party] movement, Speaker Paul Ryan may have set the party up for its current crisis," wrote reporter Jenifer Steinhauer

Donald said, "Paul Ryan, I don't know him, but I'm sure I'm going to get along great with him. And if I don't, he's going to have to pay a big price."

Ryan faced a dilemma: Whereas he wanted to remain true to the values he had spent his career promoting, he confronted a Republican frontrunner who repudiated them.

A small but influential group of Republicans met together, emerging from their huddle to suggest that a third-party option might spare voters "the odious choice of Hillary or The Donald."

"I would sooner vote for Josef Stalin than I would vote for Trump," said Max Boot, a foreign policy advisor to Rubio.

Columnist Mark Cunningham claimed that the Republican Party had invited "a hostile takeover by The Donald. Ever since the Reagan years, the GOP regulars have been aiming for the Gipper's 'second coming' merely by imposing ever-stricter ideological tests. Today, the main alternatives to Trump are Ted Cruz and Marco Rubio—each a specialist in pushing one or another set of right-wing buttons."

"Cruz's best moment," Cunningham claimed, "came when he talked about trying to get his sister out of that crack house—everything else is a rehearsal performance."

Emerging from the lunar dust of his failed 2012 presidential bid, Mitt Romney made headlines again in March. He led the charge of the Old Guard in attacking Donald, whom he seemed to despise, even though Donald had supported and contributed money to his dismal campaign.

Romney claimed that a Donald nomination would "imperil the GOP. He's a fraud and a phoney who would drive the country to the point of collapse. He's playing American voters for suckers. He has neither the temperament nor the judgment to be President."

One reporter, after hearing this, whispered sarcastically to a colleague, "Mitt should tell us what he really thinks."

Donald counterattacked, deriding Romney as a "failed candidate, a choke artist, and a loser for his defeat by Obama."

Then, Senator John McCain of Arizona, another failed presidential hopeful, also denounced Donald. He called him "ignorant of foreign policy who has made dangerous utterances on national security."

These warring factions, as noted by columnists, were forcing the GOP to the point of rupture. In Salt Lake City, stronghold of his fellow Mormons, Romney continued his assault, claiming that Donald "embodied a brand of anger that has led other nations to the abyss."

Romney also blasted Donald for his "affairs and for lacing his speech with vulgarities. "Dishonesty is Trump's hallmark. He commits offenses—the bullying, the greed, the showing-off, the misogyny, the absurd third-grade theatrics."

In a New York Times editorial entitled, "The GOP's Monster in the Mirror," appeared this indictment:

"It is an excellent thing that Republican leaders have noticed the problem they've fostered, now embodied in the Trump candidacy. But until they see the need to alter the views and policies they have promoted over the years, removing Trump will not end the party's crisis."

NEW CHAPTERS IN THE SIZE WARS
(AMERICA'S FASCINATION WITH SEX)
"PRICKLY" DONALD CONTINUES TO DEFEND THE SIZE OF HIS PENIS AGAINST ASSAULTS FROM "LITTLE MARCO"

On March 3, the eleventh GOP debate took place at the Fox Theater in the center of economically depressed Detroit. It was the third debate hosted by Fox News, with anchors Bret Baier, Chris Wallace, and the controversial Megyn Kelly, who had previously been denounced by Donald.

When the conservative news anchor arrived in the auditorium, a Trump supporter yelled at her, "Brought any Kotex, Megyn?" Of course that was a reference to Donald having suggested that she had been menstruating at the last debate.

This reunion of Kelly with Donald was the first since their televised feud six months before.

Body language expert Susan Constantine, said, "The body language of both Trump and Kelly was clearly adversarial. The language was loud and clear: Those two can't stand each other."

The Detroit debate was a prelude to the upcoming primaries in Maine, Kansas, Kentucky, Louisiana, Michigan, Mississippi, Idaho, and Hawaii.

Rubio and Cruz, Donald's leading competitors, were in a fight for their political lives. Behind the scenes, Rubio had

A national landmark, the 1928 **Fox Theater** in downtown Detroit was selected as the venue for the eleventh Republican debate.

The anchor and namesake of a neighborhood nicknamed "Foxtown," the movie palace is the largest surviving of the great cinema showcases of the 1920s. Long before Donald mounted the stage here, the theater hosted Elvis Presley and Frank Sinatra.

announced to his aides, "Tonight the gloves come off. It's going to be a bare-knuckled prize fight."

The following morning, the New York Post carried the tabloid headline—"PRICKLY DON RIPS BELOW THE BELT—SIZE MATTERS."

During the debate, Donald mounted a defense of his lower anatomy to score points against Rubio.

"I called Rubio a lightweight," Donald said. "I would like to take that back. He's really not much of a lightweight. And he referred to my hands. If they are small, something else must be small. I guarantee you, there is no problem there."

That line drew the most boisterous laughter of the evening.

Then Cruz rebuked both Rubio and Donald for bringing up such a subject. "I don't think the people of America are interested in a bunch of bickering school children."

Turning to Rubio, Donald called him, "Little Marco."

The Florida senator shot back in mocking tones, "Big Donald."

A reporter later wrote, "Donald defended the size of his male member before ten to twenty million of his fellow Americans. For the real truth, we need to interview perhaps 24 of his former bathing beauty contestants, get their estimated measurements before arriving at a general consensus. For example, if one beauty says 10 inches, another claims 6, we'll average that out to a studly 8 inches."

An editorial in the New York Daily News said, "Mark the time at approximately 9:06PM on March 3, 2016, when the dignity of the American political process expired. Trump's insinuation in a presidential debate that he is well-endowed genitally unpardonably demeaned the office he seeks and the nation he hopes to lead."

[After the debate in Detroit, since the size of Donald's penis had become the topic of a national debate, some researchers weighed in with their comments.

Although to some it reeked of "junk science," a study in 2011 by the Asian Journal of Andrology claimed that men with shorter index fingers than ring fingers were not as well endowed as men with bigger index fingers. The study was carried out on patients who had been hospitalized for urological surgery. While they were sedated, scientists measured their manhoods, later reporting their findings to the world."

The Detroit debate did not consist exclusively of penile measurements. Megyn Kelly, perhaps setting herself up for a renewed menstruation attack from Donald, brought up a killer question, almost deliberately trying to provoke him once again. "I understand that your Trump University got a 'D' from the Better Business Bureau and not the 'A' you had claimed. In fact, the Attorney General of New York likened Trump U's plaintiffs in a civil case against you as 'Bernie Madoff victims.'"

Enraged, but controlling his temper, Donald denied her accusation but Rubio, sensing fresh blood, moved in.

"The students [at Trump University] signed up because they believed that Trump was this fantastic businessman who was going to teach them the tricks of the trade," Rubio said. "When they finally realized it was a scam, they asked for their money back."

Moderator Baier tried to embarrass Donald by claiming that top military brass would refuse to administer the harsh measures he demanded (i.e., water boarding and/or killing the families of terrorists) because their enforcement, despite direct orders from the President, would violate the law.

"If I say to do it, they're going to do it," Donald responded, defiantly.

He frequently interrupted his rivals, which brought a "schoolteacher rap" from Cruz. "Donald, learn not to interrupt. It's not complicated. Count to 10, Donald. Count to 10."

Under heavy fire, Donald seemed to back down from previously stated political positions. He claimed that the United States needed highly skilled people, and that he would allow such immigrants, even if Muslim, into the country on an as-needed, case-by-case basis.

He also changed his position on assault weapons, stating that he no longer supported a ban. He refused to authorize The New York Times to release a recording of an off-the-record interview he gave that newspaper. During that session, it was alleged that he said he would be "flexible about an immigration policy."

"You could resolve this issue very quickly just by releasing the tapes," Cruz chided him.

"I've given my answer, Lyin' Ted," Donald snapped.

Columnist Rick Lowry noted how often GOP candidates "paid obeisance to Ronald Reagan. But Trump has set out to kick down the door of the House of Reagan; a structure teetering on the brink of collapse. Much more decrepit than anyone noticed. Someone just old enough to cast his first vote for Reagan in 1980 would be 54 years old today. Trump will, on occasion, reference Reagan, although all he seems to know about him is that he used to be a Democrat—just like you know who."

Bernard Lawrence "Bernie" Madoff (born 1938) is an American investment advisor and fraudster, the admitted organizer of the biggest financial fraud in American history. It defrauded an estimated $65 billion from thousands of investors.

In 2009, Madoff was sentenced to 150 years in prison, the maximum allowed.

Both of Madoff's sons were implicated. One was sentenced to ten years in prison, the other committed suicide by hanging.

After Madoff's arrest, the SEC (Securities and Exchange Commission) was lacerated for its lax and/or inept oversight of improprieties on Wall Street.

"HEY, MITT! KISS MY BLUEGRASS!"
Shrugging off Romney's Thunder, Donald Grabs Kentucky and Louisiana

Mitt Romney, the failed 2012 GOP candidate for President, was all smiles, but not when he vigorously attacked Donald.

In a bit of head-scratching double entendre, Donald zapped back with: "In 2012, he was begging for my endorsement."

"I could have said, 'Mitt, drop to your knees—and he would have.'"

Poa pratensis is commonly known as **Kentucky bluegrass.** The name derives from its flower heads, which are blue when the plant is allowed to grow to its natural height of two to three feet.

When Donald swept to victory in the Kentucky primary, the fact that "bluegrass" rhymes with "ass" gave headline writers a field day.

As the election results came in, it became increasingly obvious that Mitt Romney's venomous attacks on Donald had hardly "dented his fender" with voters. He had eked out victories in both the "Bluegrass State" of Kentucky and in Louisiana, edging out Cruz.

"If loser Mitt had devoted that same energy to winning the presidency four years ago, as he is now trying to destroy our party, he would have won the election," Donald charged. "Republicans such as him are eating their own."

Margins were close, however: Donald won Kentucky with 35.98% with Cruz trailing at 31.65%. In Louisiana, Donald got 41.4% of the vote, with Cruz behind at 37.8%

In the Midwest, Cruz scored an upset in Kansas at 48.2% of the vote, with Donald a distant second at 23.8%. "God Bless Kansas," said a jubilant Cruz, invoking God's intervention once again: "The scream you hear coming from Washington is one of utter terror at what we, the people, are doing together."

Cruz also carried Maine, with 45.9% of the vote, with Donald at 32.6% In Palm Beach, Donald cattily said, "I expected Cruz to do well in Maine. After all, it borders Canada, his birthplace." Donald also used the occasion to attack the politicians in Washington, assailing them for their "incompetent leadership. Those eggheads—half of them can't even tie their shoes."

Hammering home his victories, Cruz urged Rubio and Kasich to drop out of the race.

More and more, "Little Marco" was living up to Donald's characterization of him as a loser. He finished a distant third in Kentucky, Kansas, and Louisiana, coming in fourth in Maine.

As shown by his wins in Louisiana and Kentucky, Trump showed that he could still mix populism and pugnacity, his appeal to the working class seemingly growing month by month.

"Our machine keeps rolling on and on to victory," he proclaimed.

From the Democratic war zones, Bernie Sanders notched a surprising win over Hillary in Kansas, a 36-point lead in the caucus there. He did better in caucuses than in primaries.

"The grumpy old man," as his enemies referred to him, also scored a 12-point victory in the caucus in Nebraska.

But it was a different story in Louisiana as voters turned out to give Hillary a stunning 47-point lead over Sanders.

"Everyone's trying to figure out how to stop Trump," Donald said at a rally in Florida.

In the wake of the latest election, many columnists wrote articles claiming "ONLY CRUZ CAN STOP TRUMP."

But the establishment faced serious reservations about their second-tier candidate, "and not because he's hideously ugly," said Janet Hope, a Republican voter in Lawrence, Kansas, trying to make up her mind which GOP candidate to back. "Trump is too narcissistic; Rubio is cute but dumb; and Kasich's candidacy is a joke."

Columnist Jonah Goldberg wrote: "Cruz's fellow senators don't like him because they don't like him. They say he's arrogant and condescending, a terrible listener and completely uninterested in actually getting anything done that doesn't further his own interests."

Goldberg concluded, "Cruz missed one thing: The black swan known as Donald Trump. Cruz brilliantly made his bed, and Trump leapt into it when Cruz wasn't looking."

Donald's Enemies Rip With a Litany of NAME-CALLING

A well-known journalist, Joe Klein, appeared on Morning Joe, hosted by Joe Scarborough and Mika Brzezinski. Klein claimed that Donald was "operating out of his lizard brain."

Scarborough accused him of suffering from "Trump derangement syndrome," without explaining what he meant.

Mika and Joe had been working hard, overtime. The previous evening, they had hosted an hour-long town hall meeting with Trump.

"It was a classic Trump performance filled with nastiness and ignorance," Klein claimed. "He said he opposed the Trans-Pacific trade deal because of Asian currency manipulation, apparently not knowing that China was not part of the deal. He also said that Germany and South Korea should be forced to pay for American troops protecting them, when they already do pay a share."

***

Reporters across the country set out to investigate why Donald, in spite of his well-publicized flaws, continued to gain support from a wide range of voters across America, and the answers they got were as diverse and eccentric as the American demographic itself.

Donald's political enemies came up with a litany of unattractive names to call the candidate—"Hitler, a buffoon, a phoney, a potty-mouth, pompous, narcissistic, nasty, and ignorant."

But the most vicious was to label him **"a junkyard dog with rabies."**

The popular journalist, Joe Klein, drew the comparison of Donald with a **lizard brain**. What did he mean?

"Lizard brain" is a common phrase for the ancient knob of reflective low-brain cells (the brain stem, cerebellum, and basal ganglia) perched atop the spinal cord. These parts handle basic body functions like breathing, balance, and coordination, and simple survival urges like feeding, mating, and defense.

These contrast with the frontal lobe of a human's brain, the seat of thought and reason.

Billy Fletcher, a GOP voter in New Orleans, said, "Trump is a junkyard dog, and I have no illusions about his character. But I'm 100% behind him. He goes with his gut, and I like that. Rubio is too prissy, Cruz is a lunatic, a religious nutbag. What choice is there? Hillary Clinton? You've got to be kidding!"

Longtime Republican stalwart, Peggy Noonan, wrote in her column: "We are more or less witnessing the end of the GOP as we knew it."

Among American newspapers, the New York Daily News remained Donald's chief editorial adversary. On March 6, it ran a column headlined, "TRUMP IS HITLER." That coincided with the assessment of Louis C.K., a standup Manhattan comedian:

"Trump is an insane bigot," the entertainer said. "He is dangerous. The guy is Hitler. Do you think the Germans in the '30s saw that shit coming? Hitler was just some hilarious and refreshing dude with a weird comb-over who would say anything at all. Hitler was hilarious until he became terrifying."

Louis C.K. wasn't the only critic equating Donald with the Führer. Similar opinions had been expressed by comedian Bill Mahler, as well as by Chris Christie, former New Jersey governor Christie Whitman, and Philadelphia mayor Michael Nutter.

Donald was also criticized by such luminaries as Michael Chertoff, the former secretary of homeland security. Robert Zoellick, the former deputy secretary of state, said, "There's something heartbreaking about the prospect that America's next commander-in-chief may be a global joke, a man regarded in most world capitals as a dangerous buffoon."

Columnist Nicholas Kristof wrote that Donald was "pugnacious, pugilistic, preening, and puerile," and asked for other words to describe him. He claimed that the results poured in like a deluge: "Petulant, pandering, pathetic, peevish, prickly, pernicious, patronizing, Pantagruelian, prevaricating, phoney, presumptuous, potty-mouthed, provocative, pompous, predatory, and so many more, including the troubling 'probably president.'"

"WE SHOULD EXECUTE THAT TRAITOR, BOWE BERGDAHL,
AND FIND THE WHORE WHO INJECTED POISON INTO JUSTICE SCALIA'S BUTT"
—Donald Trump

Throughout his campaign, Donald took some unscripted and alarming" detours way off the political trail. Sometimes in defiance of his handlers, he issued opinions that made headlines.

Such was the case when he called for the "execution death" of Army Sergeant Bowe Bergdahl, who had deserted his military post in Afghanistan in 2009 and was subsequently captured by the Taliban.

"Bergdahl was a traitor," Donald said. "He should be put to death. He endangered the lives of his fellow soldiers."

Attorneys for the disgraced sergeant sent a letter to Donald, requesting an interview in advance of Bergdahl's arraignment for desertion. They expressed their concern that his scathing remarks might deprive their client of a fair trial, to which he was entitled. In an attempt to contain the damage he might have caused, these lawyers were considering either deposing

Donald or calling him as a witness.

The electorate's attention soon shifted to another issue. As one reporter noted, "Bergdahl was small fry when Donald found even bigger fish to fry." By then, Donald had interjected himself into the mystery surrounding the February 13 death of Antonin Scalia, the 79-year-old right-wing justice of the Supreme Court.

Rumors surfaced that the CIA had carried out his murder by hiring a $2,000-a-night hooker, who injected the judge's buttocks with the poisonous contents of a syringe.

Donald claimed that he was shocked by allegations of a cover-up. "As President, I will get to the bottom of this," he promised. "I suspect that something fishy is going on about the judge's death. Let's face it: Scalia's passing is big stuff. It really affects the balance of the court."

William J. Bennett, host of Morning in America, a radio show, said, "Trump is the perfect man to expose any conspiracy because he's not part of the good old boys' club. These run-of-the-mill establishment politicians are all puppets owned by big money. But there's one man who isn't beholden to anyone—and that's Donald Trump."

Bennett's suggestion, widely broadcast over the media, was that Donald, as President, could get to the bottom of a possible conspiracy and expose exactly who murdered Scalia.

Donald Trump wants this man dead! **Bowe Bergdahl** deserted his post in 2009 in Afghanistan and was held captive, caged and tortured, by the Taliban. He was released in 2014 as part of a prisoner exchange for five Taliban members.

On November 3, 2017, military judge Colonel Jeffrey Nance accepted Bergdahl's guilty plea and sentenced him to be dishonorably dischargd, reduced in rank, and fined $1,000 per month for ten months, with no prison time.

The discharge was stayed pending automatic appeal. In June of 2018, General Robert Abrams approved the sentence.

Trump tweeted that "The decision is a complete and total disgrace to our country and our military."

RABBLE-ROUSING HIS TROOPS
With Free Publicity

Instead of paying for expensive political ads, Donald—thanks to the ratings he generated—received huge amounts of free publicity, agreeing to one controversial (and unpaid) TV or radio appearance after another. On March 6, he appeared as a guest on CBS's Face the Nation, calling for new laws on torture.

"I think we are weak. We cannot beat ISIS. We should be at them very quickly. General George Patton would have had ISIS down in about three days. We have to beat the savages!"

He had previously called for a return to waterboarding and other tortures.

"We have to play the game by their rules if we're going to win. You're not going to win if you're soft. I think we have to change the present laws because they are not working. They're killing our soldiers when they capture them. They're laughing at us right now. I would like to strengthen the laws so that we can compete."

In the first week of March, Donald blitzed the "Rust Belt States," campaigning at stops that included Warren, Michigan, where he lamented the loss of American manufacturing jobs that caused many blue collar workers to lose their homes.

He noted that former businesses that used to produce useful products, such as brooms, had been shipped overseas, leaving the American worker stranded with no income.

He delivered speeches in factories which had been shut down in the Middle West.

His appeal was to "Reagan Democrats," who felt their former alliance with Democrats no longer protected their economic interests. "They seem more interested in promoting affirmative action and welfare aimed at minorities," said one discharged factory worker. "We are white, the forgotten class in America."

Columnist Ted Wrobleski wrote of an America infected with "Trumpocalypse," and then evoked for his readers the horror of a Trump presidency:

"What will happen if he gets elected? Rips in the space-time continuum? Seismic disturbances in the Force? Isn't this how The Walking Dead starts? Few presidential elections in recent memory have been this divisive this early. It's husbands against wives in some places. Brother versus sister. Kids against moms and dads. Our new Civil War approaches."

Linda Stasi, the "hot, hot" columnist, wrote, "This GOP election has devolved on the world stage into a literal, yuuuge, balls-out, pissing match. It has friend and foe, all alike, laughing at America and making us all look, yes, not great."

By now, "Zombie Apocalypse" is a familiar phrase and concept. But Donald's political enemies created a new word to describe the consequences of a possible Trump presidency. This illustration depicts what a "**Trumpocalypse**" would actually mean.

QUESTION: As of 2023, what's the newest definition of an STD?
ANSWER: It's STUPID TRUMP DISEASE!

Even during the peak of Rupert Murdoch's vigilant support of Donald Trump, his Media Empire ran occasionally critical stories associated with his gaffes and *faux pas*, as in (*left photo*), the cover of their Sunday edition of July 19, 2015. At the time, however, one liberal commentator warned anti-Trumpers: to be careful: "Before everyone gets all "OMG. the Murdochs are totally breaking up with Trump forever," please remember that occasional breaks with Murdoch, inc., had (occasionally) happened before.

But by 2023, Trump critiques from the frontpage of the **New York Post** (*right photo, above, dated November 10, 2022*) had became more dire. By then, even the (Murdoch-owned) **Wall Street Journal,** in an editorial by Carl Quintanilla, cited Trump for his "perfect record of electoral defeats. He has led Republicans into one political fiasco after another. Trump is the Republican Party's biggest loser. He has flopped in 2018, 2020, 2021, and 2022."

Chapter Eleven

British Pundits Insist that a Trump Presidency Would Lead to
Massive Global Disasters

Donald Rebuts GOP Attempts
to Designate One of their Own as a Third-Party Independent,
Threatening Violent Protests in Cleveland
if Republicans Sabotage His Nomination

Sexual Politics
Cruz Denies Any Association with $1,000-a-Night Hookers

Despite Opposition, Surveys Reveal that Millions of Americans,
Especially Members of the Military, Adore Donald Trump

Protesters Mock Trump and His Campaign Slogans
"Make America Hate Again"

The presidential campaign, such as it was, of Michael R. Bloomberg, three times mayor of New York, began with a whimper and ended, on March 7, with a sigh. He decided not to enter, claiming that a three-way race might lead to the election of Donald J. Trump.

He attacked Donald's "divisive and demagogic campaign," and claimed that if he were elected, it would "compromise the moral leadership of America around the world."

"As it stands now," Bloomberg said, "my candidacy could lead to the election of Trump or Ted Cruz. That is not a risk I can take in good conscience. Trump and Cruz are zealots who would weaken our unity and divide our country."

With his fellow New York billionaire out of the race, Donald could continue his onward march toward the nomination.

On March 8, a densely scheduled evening for primary elections, Donald hit two more home runs, winning both Michigan and Mississippi, where he scored his most decisive victory, wining 47% of the vote, as compared to the deeply evangelical Cruz, who won only 36%.

Cruz, however, carried Idaho with 44% to Donald's 28%.

As the East Coast went to bed, polls were still open in Hawaii.

Trump would later carry Hawaii, Obama's native state, where he had once promised an investigation into "the birther issue."

Rubio was a big loser that night.

As for the Democrats, although Sanders won with a narrow margin in Michigan, Hillary "clobbered" him in Mississippi, taking 83% of the vote. During her campaign there, she accused Sanders of orchestrating an "artful smear" by insinuating that she'd been bought by Wall Street.

After the most recent primaries, Donald set his sights on "destroying" Rubio in the eyes of his home state of Florida. "Little Marco is sweating," Donald told a rally. "It's pouring down."

At a rally in Warren, Michigan, Donald said, "Rubio is going down, and because I wanted to show off what a good athlete I am, I wanted to show with the size of my hands how I could grab him. I didn't want him to get hurt hitting his head going down."

Polls showed Donald leading by twenty points in Florida,

"You know, in Florida, they hate Little Marco so much because of the fact he never shows up to vote in the Senate. He conned the people of Florida into voting for him."

On the campaign trail after Minnesota, Rubio scored a second victory by winning the GOP primary in Puerto Rico. Popular with Hispanics there, he captured all of that troubled island's twenty-three delegates.

By now, Donald had instructed his staff to compile printouts of the barrage of attacks that appeared online and in the press about him every day. These he avidly consumed, often with his morning coffee.

Some of the editorials irritated him more than others. One particularly incendiary piece had been written by Heather MacDonald, a Thomas W. Smith fellow at the Manhattan Institute.

"Instead of engaging with his opponents' ideas, Trump invariably sneers at his rivals' appearance and launches ad hominem insults. Mocking the size of Marco Rubio's ears and bragging about one's sexual organ may be uproariously funny to a seven-year-old boy, but such sandbox tactics should be inconceivable for someone who aspires to the office once occupied by George Washington, Abraham Lincoln, and James Madison."

"Trump is the consummate bully, delighting in kicking people when they are down," MacDonald continued. "Long after Rick Perry and George Pataki were lifeless corpses and of no possible threat to his presidency, Trump continued to entertain audiences by gratuitously mocking Perry's eyeglasses and intelligence, belittling Pataki's political stance, and gloating about how he routed both from the race."

The GOP elite continued on their hopeless quest to stop Trump, spending some $10 million on hostile ads in the crucial state of Florida. These TV spots depicted Donald as a "liberal," a "huckster," and a "draft dodger." On military matters, he was denounced as a "poseur."

Tom Hanton, a former POW in Vietnam, claimed, "Trump would not have survived as a prisoner of war. He would probably have been the first to fold."

To fight back, on March 6, Donald unleashed a savage assault of his own, a 60-second ad denouncing Marco Rubio as "corrupt," accusing him of misusing a Republican credit card as a means of lining his own pockets.

In the ad, a narrator claimed, "As a legislator, the corrupt Marco Rubio flipped on a key vote after making a quick $200,000 deal selling his house to the mother of one of the bill's lobbyists."

The ad also accused Rubio of using the GOP's credit card "to live it up in Las Vegas," and to pave the driveway to his home.

There was more: "Rubio has spent years defrauding the people of Florida," the narrator charged. "The lightweight is a dishonest person. He's a no-show for having missed key Senate votes."

"With these ads, I am doing the people of Florida a great favor by exposing this crook," Donald claimed.

To retaliate, Rubio's forces prepared an ad attacking Donald for using profanities in his speeches to various rallies. Although the actual profanities could not be broadcast on TV, it was clear to viewers that they included "pussy," "shit," "fuck," and "mother-fucker."

The ads were timed to run before the March 15 primary in Florida, which was also the date that voters in North Carolina, Illinois, Missouri, and Ohio would go to the polls.

PUBLICLY RUBIO EXPRESSES REMORSE FOR TAUNTING DONALD
WHO SAYS, "I'M NOT POLITICALLY CORRECT," AND
"UNLEASH THE GENERALS ON ISIS"

On March 10, at Coral Gables, Florida, the twelfth GOP debate, the fourth and final one for CNN, had been scheduled just before the all-important primaries in Florida, Illinois, North Carolina, Missouri, and Ohio.

Moderated by Jake Tapper, and co-sponsored by The Washington Times, the debate was staged at the University of Miami's BankUnited arena. Other moderators included Dana Bash, Hugh Hewitt, and Stephen Dana.

Going into the debate, both Donald and Rubio, Florida's native son, predicted victory in that state's primary. For Rubio, losing his home state could be the death knell of his presidential campaign.

As it turned out, it would be his final debate, as he would suspend his campaign in its aftermath. Or as one commentator said, "For Marco, it was too much, too soon. You don't just arrive in town and start running for President."

Instead of making the debate too personal, as in previous cases, Donald tried to stake out some policy positions: "We have to knock out ISIS. Get rid of it, and then come back and rebuild our country, which is falling apart. I would listen to the generals. Right now, they're not allowed to fight. We're not knocking out the oil because we don't want to create environmental pollution in the air. We used to fight to win."

He also defended his stand against Muslims. "I don't want to be politically correct. We have a serious, serious problem of hate. All across the Middle East, you have people chanting, 'Death to the US of A.' That does not sound like a friendly act to me."

The worst personal jab of the evening came from Cruz. "If you nominate Donald Trump, Hillary Clinton wins."

Most newspapers characterized this debate as low energy. Others referred to it as "surprisingly calm."

"We're all in this together," Donald said in an appeal for party unity. In spite of the moderators pressing him for more details about his policies, he demurred.

Bash pointed out that Social Security was heading toward insolvency in 22 years. Donald claimed he would keep it afloat by cutting fraud and abuse.

Then, Bash raised the point that such measures would save, at the most, only $3 billion out of an expected deficit of $147 billion. Donald then said, "I'd cut foreign aid."

Cruz chimed in, "Your solutions don't work, Donald."

After the debate, Rubio told reporters that he regretted "my schoolyard taunting of Trump." [As witnessed by millions, he had ridiculed the brash, suntanned real estate mogul as "small-handed" (i.e., small-dicked) and made fun of his "orange face."]

It's not something I'm proud of," Rubio told MSNBC. "If I had it to do over again, I wouldn't. If

As President of the United States, Donald claimed he would destroy ISIS.

He denounced Obama for his failure to use the words "Islamic terrorists," and in his speeches, he noted the tide of young people heading to the "caliphate" in Iraq and Syria to become racicalized before returning to the United States and other Western countries.

"These recruits are some of the most dangerous and fanatical adherents to radical Islam," he claimed. "They plan to kill us!"

taunting is what it takes to become President of the United States, I don't want to be President."

Donald ended his appeal to Florida voters by saying, "The Republican Party has a great chance to embrace millions of people that it's never known before. We should seize the chance!"

From a "Pathological" Surgeon and from the Country's Most Famous Transgendered Celebrity Come

PRO-DONALD ENDORSEMENTS

Celebrity approval arrived unexpectedly from a woman who was new on the media scene.

Caitlyn Jenner (previously known as Bruce Jenner) emerged to claim, "Donald would be good on women's issues. As for Hillary, she's a fucking liar."

"Because of Donald Trump's macho attitude," Jenner continued, "some say he would not be a good candidate for women to support. Actually, I think he would be very good for women's issues. I would never vote for Hillary. If she becomes President, the country is over. She's a political hack."

On March 11, the retired neurosurgeon, Ben Carson, who had already dropped out of the race, appeared before reporters in the ballroom of Mar-a-Lago to endorse Donald.

Carson's endorsement came as a surprise. At one point in the campaign, Donald had said that the soft-spoken doctor had "the pathological temperament of a child molester."

At Mar-a-Lago that day, Carson told the press, "Donald and I have buried the hatchet."

Then he announced that he would be joining Donald on the campaign trail. "if the Republicans lose in November, we're surrendering the country to the socialists."

Later, on Fox News, Carson said, "There are two Donald Trumps. There's the Donald Trump that you see on television and who gets up in front of a big audience, and there's the Donald Trump behind the scenes. They're not the same person. One's very much the entertainer, and one is actually a thinking individual."

Cruz must have looked on all this with disdain, as later that day, he defined Donald's supporters "low information voters." One reporter said, "In other words, Cruz thinks Donald's fans are dummies."

Cruz, too, had an endorsement to tout, claiming that he had won the support of Utah Senator Mike Lee, the only member of that body to endorse him, since all the others, including Lindsey Graham, had no kind words to say about the Texas senator.

Around the same time, Cruz picked up yet another endorsement, this time from Carly Fiorina, who had lost her bid to become the presidential nominee. She once said, "That guy (Cruz) would say whatever he needs to get elected."

Now, she sang a different song, one in favor of the man she had previously competed against: "Cruz has fought for re-

Donald appealed to older voters, such as retirees in states ranging from Florida to Arizona.

He promised to save **Social Security**, in spite of warnings that the system was heading for insolvency.

Donald entered a new frontier in the culture wars based on the use of public toilets for the transgendered.

He promised that if **Caitlyn Jenner** visited Trump Tower, she could use any bathroom she preferred.

ligious liberty and is a leader and a reformer," she said.

[Reportedly, she had detested Donald ever since he'd publicly mocked "her ugly face."]

As Donald staged and appeared at rallies across the country, some of his supporters engaged in violent confrontations with protesters.

At a rally in North Carolina, a 78-year-old man, John McGraw, sucker-punched a black protester (Rakeen Jones) at a Trump rally. Whereas security then roughly removed Jones (the victim) from the arena, McGraw then calmly sat down, receiving applause and congratulations from Trump supporters.

"Next time we see him, we might have to kill him," McGraw later told Inside Edition in reference to Jones. "We don't know who he is. He might be a terrorist."

At another rally, Donald seemed to brazenly encourage, even solicit, a violent response from his protesters. A man rose from his seat in the auditorium and, in reference to a nearby protester, started shouting toward Donald, "I'd like to punch that one in the face myself."

In response, Donald said. "If someone punches him [i.e., the protester], I'll pay his legal bills if he gets into trouble."

From the podium, he spoke fondly of the "good old days when the police could rough up protesters without fear of a backlash."

At Mar-a-Lago, the retired neurosurgeon, **Dr. Ben Carson**, appeared before the press to bury the hatchet.

Donald had once made odious charges against the surgeon, but now, with Carson's backing, he hoped to strengthen his position among the more right-wing conservatives and evangelists.

These conflicts took place in Fayetteville, North Carolina, a rally that was disrupted seventeen times, mostly with shouts coming from African Americans, some of whom were handcuffed and forcibly removed from the arena.

On March 10, at a rally in Jupiter, Florida, Donald's campaign manager, Corey Lewandowski, was seen grabbing the arm of Michelle Fields, a reporter from Breitbart News. She had left the confines of the "corral" designated for the Press Corps, and started to advance toward Donald as he was exiting from the Trump National Club. The campaign manager grabbed her arm, bruising it, and nearly yanked her to the floor.

On March 11, Fields lodged a criminal complaint against Lewandowski. A Trump campaign aide said Fields' allegation was "entirely false. I did not witness any such encounter, and I was right there."

However, the event had been caught on video, indicating some sort of physical confrontation between the two antagonists.

Although it was widely publicized in the media, the case was later thrown out of court.

En route to an event in Chicago, Donald and his aides flew to St. Louis, where a rally turned bloody. The clashes occurred in front of the city's Peabody Opera House, leaving one man bloodied and another charged with assault. Pictures of Anthony Cage, a black activist, with his face bloodied, appeared on frontpages around the country.

Before entering the opera house, Trump supporters screamed profanities and racial slurs at the group of largely black protesters gathered outside. Inside, protesters frequently interrupted Donald's campaign speech.

He lamented that police officers were "too kind" in evicting the protesters. "These bad dudes realize there is no consequence for protesting and interrupting our free speech rally."

That night, the St. Louis Police arrested 28 people for disturbing the peace.

"These troublemakers should go home to mommy," Donald said. "They should get a job. They

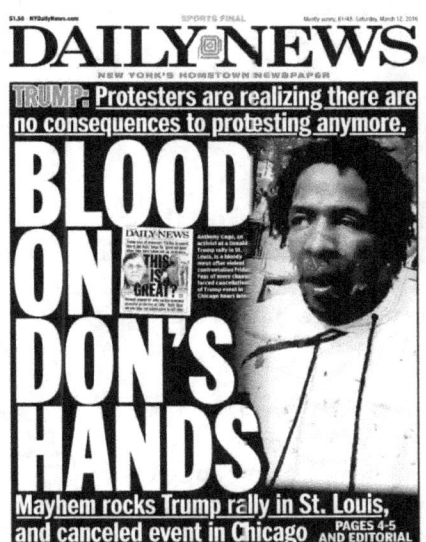

Anthony Cage, bloodied in front of the Peabody Opera House in St. Louis.

An activist, Cage learned the price one paid for attacking Donald's candidacy at one of his rallies.

Reporter **Michelle Fields** broke out of the "barrier" where the press had been assigned and headed toward Donald as he was exiting from a rally.

His campaign manager, **Corey Lewandowski,** perhaps fearing that she might be planning to cause the candidate harm, grabbed her arm to restrain her.

The incident, part of which was recorded on a security camera, became notorious and led to a court case in Jupiter, Florida.

contribute nothing."

The following day, R&B singer Chris Brown issued a call to African Americans to travel in large numbers to Trump rallies to fend off violent attacks from Trump supporters. "Man," Brown said in a video he posted online. "This shit is getting crazy. Black people getting assaulted at fucking rallies where you're supposed to talk at. What you need to start doing? Go together—40, 50 deep. See what they do then!"

Protesters in Chicago shut down Donald's scheduled rally there when violent confrontations broke out on the sidewalks between pro-Trump and anti-Trump brigades, the latter of which was composed predominantly of Latinos and African Americans.

It soon became apparent that Chicago's battle-toughened men in blue were no match for the volatile crowds gathering at the University of Illinois.

Donald and his aides met with the police, and determined that for the safety of tens of thousands, it was better to cancel the rally.

One Donald supporter, Kevin Anand, said, "This is so wrong. Everyone has a right in America to speak. If you don't like Donald Trump, you don't have to vote for him. But some of us want to hear what he has to say. Why should some ugly mob shut us down in a country where free speech is supposed to be guaranteed?"

Reporters noted that the city of Chicago has been run for decades by Democrats and populated by nearly equal thirds African Americans, Latino, and whites, seemingly a volatile mixture as it pertains to any form of politics.

***

Another disturbing incident occurred on March 12, when Donald was addressing a rally in Dayton, Ohio. A protester, Thomas Dimassimo, 22, charged over a fence at the back of the outdoor stage and rushed toward Donald. Four Secret Service agents blocked his access, wrestling him to the ground.

Startled at first, Donald soon regained his composure, telling his audience, "I was ready for him," he said, flashing a double thumbs-up. "But it's much easier for the cops to do it."

Dimassimo was later revealed to be a Bernie Sanders supporter and part of the Black Lives Matter movement. He was charged with inducing panic and disorderly conduct.

Before his attempted attack on Donald, an overview of his Twitter account revealed him sticking out his tongue and tweeting "FUCK YOU, BITCH DONALD TRUMP."

Outside the rally, in Dayton, protesters held up signs that read, "IF YOU SUPPORT TRUMP YOUR DICK MUST BE SMALL." Others proclaimed: "TRUMP IS HITLER'S CHILD."

The Sunshine State Didn't Shine on MARCO RUBIO As, Near Tears, He DROPS OUT

In Ohio, Buckeye Democrats Turn the Tide for GOP's JOHN KASICH

On March 12, Cruz won the most delegates from the state of Wyoming. In Washington, D.C., Rubio narrowly beat Governor John Kasich before the upcoming make-or-break primaries in five large states that included their respective home states of Florida and Ohio.

Republicans are relatively rare in the nation's capital. Their ranks consist mainly of lobbyists, attorneys, and/or Capitol Hill staffers.

In reference to Rubio's strong showing in D.C., reporter Jason Horowitz wrote, "Rubio's victory amounted to what might be the Establishment's last roar at the angry anti-Washington masses, who have dominated the electorate so far. "Rubio carried 37% of the vote with Kasich breathing down his neck at 36%." Cruz and Donald were buried in the Potomac," wrote one reporter.

Wyoming was not a priority on Donald's campaign agenda, as they had written it off from the beginning. "I'll turn over that state to Cruz and his ostrich-skinned cowboy boots," Donald said. "He'll probably look more like a city

Though it had been about a month since **Marco Rubio**'s defeat, he still looked depressed & mournful during this ABC interview.

Friends of the youthful candidate speculated that this son of refugees from Castro's Cuba would seek the presidency once again in 2020.

slicker than a real cowboy."

On March 13, with only two days remaining before the big GOP primaries, polls showed Donald enjoying a safe lead in Florida, but in a dead heat with Kasich in Ohio, where he remained a popular governor.

Before voting began, Kasich claimed, "I will not take the low road to the highest office in the land," an inference that Donald, Cruz, and Rubio would.

In Palm Beach, Ivana, Donald's first wife, voted for her former husband, denouncing Rubio as "a silly boy."

"He is too young, too inexperienced. Hillary just lies a lot. Donald will run the country like a business."

Contradicting previous statements attributed to her, Ivana said, "I have no trouble with Melania as a possible First Lady. Right now, I'm juggling three boyfriends."

In Florida's "winner-take-all" GOP presidential primary, Donald swept to victory, leaving "Little Marco to cry in his Gatorade."

Donald went on to capture the delegate lead in North Carolina and Illinois. On election night, Missouri was too close to call.

With results from Florida pouring in, Donald was declared the winner, with 46% of the vote. (Rubio received only 27%. Cruz trailed at 17%.)

In North Carolina, Donald won 40% of the vote, with Cruz in second place with 37%. In Illinois, Donald led with 39% of the vote, with Cruz at 31%.

At Mar-a-Lago, Donald told supporters, "This is a great evening. We have to bring our party together. We have something happening that actually makes the Republican Party the biggest political story in the world. Millions of people are coming out to vote."

In Florida, the country's most sought-after swing state, Donald walked off with 99 delegates.

In Ohio, thousands of Democrats crossed over to vote in the Republican primary so they could cast a vote for their popular governor. About 7% of the voters identified themselves as Democrats. A majority of those Democrats, some 53%, voted for Kasich, with 40% supporting Donald.

Corey Lewandowski, Donald's campaign manager, boasted that the Democratic defectors represented a national trend. "A lot of voters are changing their party affiliation to vote for Donald. This is a pattern we've seen in state after state. It's a good sign for Donald's campaign and a good sign for the Republican Party."

From the Democratic side of the war zone, Hillary swept to victory in primaries in Florida, North Carolina, and Ohio, bounding back from her upset loss to Bernie Sanders in Michigan.

At this point, she had netted so many more delegates than the Vermont senator that she was ahead by three times what Barack Obama had achieved at this point in the presidential race back in 2008.

We're going to win and go on winning," Donald said. "Win, win, win! Don't worry, Marco. You've got a great future. But it wasn't your time, kiddo."

Then, to the disappointment of his supporters in Miami, Rubio announced that he was bowing out of the race. "America is in the middle of a real political storm—a real tsunami—and we should have seen it coming. This may not have been the year for a hopeful and optimistic message."

After dropping out, Rubio blamed attack ads that had deluged voters in Florida. "I was blitzed," he claimed.

As it turned out, Donald carried Missouri, but only by the slimmest of margins, winning 40.9% of the vote, as opposed to Cruz, who garnered 40.7%.

The day after the results came in from Missouri, Donald issued a warning to the GOP elite. "There will be riots in Cleveland if I am denied the GOP nomination. I think the establishment will have problems like they've never seen before if they deny my supporters. I think bad things will happen."

House Speaker Paul Ryan criticized Donald for suggesting there might be riots in Cleveland in July, but he rejected a proposal that he, personally, should enter the race for the GOP nomination as the party's "anti-Trump alternative."

Donald's swelling roster of victories came with ominous warnings. British analysts predicted that a Trump presidency would be one of the world's ten biggest global risks. The Economist Intelligence unit claimed that a Trump-led government might endanger the world economy, creating chaos in America and abroad and increasing the risk of terrorism across the planet.

***

Donald's ardent supporters recommended various "Law and Order" candidates as his vice presidential running mate.

Choices included the widely discredited Sarah Palin, who had run unsuccessfully with John McCain in 2008, and Rudy Giuliani, the former mayor of New York City.

A surprise choice was **Joe Arpaio,** the anti-immigrant Arizona sheriff sometimes cited as the toughest law enforcer in America. He backed Donald's call for a wall along the southern border.

As more and more politicos perceived that Donald was successfully "locking up" the GOP's nomination in July, there was talk of who he'd pick as his vice presidential running mate.

Polls came up with suggestions: Sarah Palin, the former governor of Alaska; Joe Arpaio, at the age of 83, "America's toughest sheriff;" New Jersey's Governor Chris Christie; his campaign rival Ted Cruz; and former New York City Mayor Rudy Giuliani. Rubio was conspicuously absent from the list.

As campaign tensions mounted, and Donald's enemies grew into the millions, there were death threats delivered to Trump Tower, some of them serious enough to merit investigation by the Secret Service.

As could be predicted, Donald's children also received threats. Such was the case when handwritten letters filled with white powder were delivered to the Manhattan condo of Eric Trump and his wife, Lara, on Central Park South.

Lara opened the envelope and white powder spilled onto her kitchen floor. She summoned help, and the powder was analyzed. It turned out to be lemonade mix.

The letter, signed "X," had been mailed from Massachusetts. "If your father does not drop out of the race, the next envelope will not be fake," its writer threatened.

Then the battleground shifted to a widely publicized confrontation between failed presidential candidate (and former governor of Massachusetts) Mitt Romney and Donald.

Romney announced, in a highly visible snub to Donald, that he would vote for Ted Cruz in the Utah caucus. Romney went on to urge Republicans not to vote for John Kasich, asserting that such votes would only help Donald.

Donald was quick to respond: "Failed presidential candidate, Mitt Romney, the man who 'choked' and let us all down, is now endorsing Lyin' Ted Cruz."

On that same day, Fox News blasted Donald for his "crude and sexist" trashing of their network's news anchor, Megyn Kelly. Donald had called for his supporters to boycott her nightly TV newscast. Donald had tweeted that Kelly was "overrated" and "sick...Her show is not worth watching," he charged.

Fox defended its anchor. In a statement, it charged that "Trump's vitriolic attacks against Megyn Kelly and his extreme sick obsession with her is beneath the dignity of a presidential candidate who wants to occupy the highest office in the land."

In Arizona, a state with 58 delegates to offer its GOP nominee, former governor Jan Brewer endorsed Donald. So did that state's infamous anti-immigrant sheriff Joe Arpaio.

Meanwhile, dozens of columnists nationwide continued to hit Donald in editorials. Linda Chavez wrote: "Donald Trump seems to believe that the way you deal with dissent is to crush it—not with compelling ideas or more reasoned speech, not with dignity in the face of foul threats, but with punches that will see the protesters 'carried out on a stretcher' as they were in the 'old days.' If he keeps predicting violence, he'll likely get it—and the results for our country will be very ugly."

Anti-Trump GOP leaders, minus the war paint, worked behind the scenes to deny him the nomination. A coven of leaders met in Washington to map out a 100-day campaign of attack ads and other means to mow him down, beginning with the April 5 primary in Wisconsin.

They also planned a delegate-by-delegate lobbying to rally anti-Trump forces in the hinterlands. Their tactics were referred to in the press as "guerilla fighting" or "desperate measures."

It was also put forward that another means of defeating Donald would involve the very risky backing of another presidential candidate to run on an Independent ticket. The former governor of Texas, Rick Perry, was evaluated as a possible candidate, as was Tom Coburn, the former senator from Oklahoma.

In an exclusive, an investigative team from the New York Daily News discovered that many members of the military, along with their families, living on or near military bases in the United States, overwhelmingly favored Donald's presidency.

"I love Trump," said a sailor at Camp Pendleton in California. "He's brutally honest, and I like brutal honesty." The sailor also agreed with Donald's policy to bring back torture.

In North Carolina, an Army specialist at Fort Bragg, the nation's largest military base, said, "In my profession—infantry—we're hard-ass, alpha males, get to it, get it done. That's what Donald Trump is."

Even though Donald had growing support in Arizona, and prominent endorsements, he still faced trouble at a Trump rally at Fountain Hills, a suburb of Phoenix. In a scene evocative of a showdown in the Wild West, anti-Trump protesters parked their vehicles in the middle of the rally's access route—in this case, a three-lane highway. Some of the event's more ardent participants chained themselves to their cars in an effort to thwart police officers charged with clearing the blockade. Violence erupted in the searing heat, including an episode involving a Trump supporter who knocked a protester to the ground and then stomped on his body, kicking him.

Back in Manhattan, Trump haters clashed with the police at Trump Tower after marching through Midtown with anti-Trump slogans. The most popular signs were clustered around Columbus Circle and urged protesters to FUCK TRUMP. A shoving match between screaming protesters and men in blue broke out along Central Park South. Cops responded to the refusal of protesters to back down by pepper-spraying them. After in-your-face entanglements with police officers, several of the protesters were handcuffed and arrested.

Who Should Be Cited as a Role Model for
MELANIA TRUMP'S BREASTS?
Jayne Mansfield or Grace Kelly?

As Donald's candidacy began to be taken more seriously, attention focused on his wife, Melania, as a potential First Lay. Many newspapers in their Sunday Styles sections, wandered down memory lane and came up with provocative pictures of her snapped during the early years of the 21st Century. She had been photographed multiple times in outfits with plunging décolletage that exposed virtually all of her breasts except the nipples.

She was not afraid to show off her legs, either, in gowns whose slits practically climbed to "Mount Everest." In 2000, she had provided photographers with a "leg bomb" in a gown years before Angelina Jolie wore an equivalent garment at the Oscars.

In a separate incident, based on an outfit she wore to a gala at the Waldorf Astoria in Manhattan, fashionistas labeled her dress a "baby doll" as her breasts seemed ready to pop out of her shocking pink frock.

In distinct contrast, in February of 2016, voters at a GOP victory party in South Carolina were introduced to a "New Melania." She wore an Antonio Berardi bubblegum pink shift dress that didn't conceal her figure, but kept her breasts safely tucked away.

During a colder month, in Colorado, she was attired in a white and pink dress that covered her upper torso. To emphasize her revised modesty quotient, she'd draped a Christian Dior coat across her shoulders.

In years past, she'd been called "Donald's sex kitten," especially when she posed nude and alluringly positioned on a bearskin rug for the British GQ.

She had also posed in a *va-va-voom* Hervé Leger dress while hawking her jewelry collection on QVC.

Patsy Cisneros, a corporate image consultant, said, "All that cleavage is well and good when you're the third spouse of Donald—but not so acceptable for a presidential hopeful's wife. Melania has become more demure as his campaign's chances have gotten better."

"If Donald wins, designers will be more than eager to dress his wife," Cisneros continued. "If he's elected, there's going to be enormous visibility for designers who dress her. Everyone is going to be throwing clothes at her for her appearances."

***

On March 21, at the Verizon Center in Washington, D.C., at the annual rally of the American Israel Public Affairs Committee, one of the largest pro-Israel lobbying groups in the world, Donald promised he'd bring peace to the Middle East if he were elected President. Then, as part of his speech, he unleashed a verbal broadside against Iran.

"My number one priority is to dismantle the disastrous deal with Iran," he told the audience of 18,000 Jews. "The deal is catastrophic—for America, for Israel, and for the whole Middle East." He also denounced Iran's recent missile tests and spoke of that country's threats against Israel.

The mogul received some of his biggest cheers when he disparaged Obama. He praised Prime Minister Benjamin Netanyahu and endorsed the idea of moving the U.S. Embassy from Tel Aviv to Jerusalem.

He also told the assembly that "my daughter Ivanka is about to have a beautiful Jewish baby."

Earlier that day, he had spoken with the editorial board of The Washington Post, saying that the United States should cut back its funding of NATO. We certainly can't afford to do this anymore. We're spending a lot of our money protecting our so-called Allies."

The next morning, many Jewish leaders attacked Donald's speech before thousands of Jews. Rabbi Shmuel Herzfeld, leader of the oldest synagogue in Washington D.C., the Ohev Sholom congregation (aka The National Synagogue) said, "This man is wicked. He inspires racists and bigots. He encourages violence. Do not listen to him."

***

On March 27, a newspaper headlined a blessed event in the Trump clan as "HEIR TO THE HAIR IS BORN." That was its way of announcing that Ivanka, Donald's 34-year-old daughter, had given birth, with her husband Jared Kushner, to her third child.

The latest grandkid tally is now number eight for "Grandpa Donald."

Ted Cruz did not send congratulations. Instead, he launched a savage attack on the once-again grandfather on Fox News. "Donald is completely ignorant on foreign policy. He's out of his depth, not smart enough to handle America's role in foreign affairs. His presidency would be a disaster for the nation. He just doesn't understand the issues—and I do."

Or so he said.

REPUBLICAN VOTERS EVALUATE THEIR OPTIONS FOR FIRST LADY: A Beautiful Nude? or "A Screeching Harridan from Hell?"

A Super PAC, Make America Awesome, produced a series of Facebook ads targeting conservative Mormon voters in Utah, a state that is about 60% Mormon. The ads assumed that Mormons would be repulsed by direct access to Melania's immodest photos from GQ.

The text associated with this photo trumpeted "Meet Melania Trump, your next First Lady. Or you could support Ted Cruz on Tuesday."

Columnist Seth Mandel weighed in. "People keep saying that this election is a battle for survival for the GOP. Maybe. But if this is how the party of faith and family values fights for its life, it's dead already."

Enraged, Donald blasted back: "Lyin' Ted Cruz just used a picture of Melania from a GQ shot and used it in a campaign ad," Donald tweeted. "Be careful or I will spill the beans on your wife."

In anger, Cruz responded, "Donald, if you try to attack Heidi, you're more of a coward than I thought. Classless."

Cruz denied that he personally was responsible for the controversial ad that went out to voters across Utah.

Then, Donald's aides launched a counterattack. They ran a grotesque picture of Heidi Cruz, making her look, as described by a reporter, "like a screeching harridan from hell." The photograph was run alongside one of an elegant and serene depiction of Melania.

Heidi responded to the attack ad: "I have one job on this campaign, and it's to be helping Ted win the race," she said.

In a voice filled with rage, and an expression contorted with hatred, Cruz lashed back at Donald. "I don't get angry often, but you mess with my wife, you mess with my kids—that'll do it every time."

"Good ol' Texas boy, Ted, practically shit his pants," said a Wisconsin farmer who attended a Cruz rally.

Although Donald had not directly attacked Cruz's two daughters, a cartoon had recently depicted them as monkeys.

Donald's campaign manager, Corey Lewandowski, told the press, "This is Cruz's effort to gain attention to try and stay relevant in the race that he has lost."

A rival candidate, Ohio governor John Kasich, weighed in, calling for families of presidential candidates to be "off limits. We cannot allow these attacks on families," he said on NBC's Meet the Press. "There's got to be some rules, and there's got to be something that gets set there. Some decency."

Lindsey Graham appeared on NBC's Today show. "Hey, guys, knock it off. The world is falling apart. Man up!"

Cruz tried to toss in the final word: "Donald, real men don't attack women. Your wife is lovely, and Heidi is the love of my life."

Then an avalanche of attacks from Democrats poured in: "What in hell does Cruz mean?" asked one voter in Los Angeles.

In one of the more lurid exposés during the campaign for the GOP presidential nod, the *National Enquirer* ran an article charging that **Ted Cruz** patronized $1,000-a-night hookers.

The Cruz campaign vehemently denied the charge.

"His whole campaign was launched with attacks on Hillary. The last time I checked, she was a woman. So you attack her. That means, in your own words, you're not a real man. But I knew that all along, you bastard!"

Another tweeted, "Heidi should be attacked. What poor judgment. She married a loser like Ted Cruz. Pathetic!"

In the wake of the Melania nude photo scandal, the GOP "rat race" devolved into a true mudfight when The National Enquirer came out with an exposé linking Cruz to a string of hookers (aka, "a carnal quintet").

The supermarket tabloid headlined its feature story "FIVE ROMPS THAT WILL DESTROY TED CRUZ." In a two-page spread, Cruz was accused of having sustained five extramarital affairs, including one with a $1,000-a-night hooker, a teacher, and three co-workers.

"The story is bullshit," Cruz said, fighting back and blaming Donald for enlisting his so-called friends at the Enquirer for these startling revelations. They were especially damaging since Cruz had more or less depicted himself on the campaign trail as a "Messenger of God."

"Trump demonstrated that when he's scared, when he's losing, his first and natural resort is to go to sleaze and to go to the slime," Cruz said at another rally in Wisconsin. "And truth has nothing to do with it."

Donald denied that he was behind this "bimbo eruption" suddenly swirling around Cruz's head. The context echoed the sexual revelations associated with Bill Clinton when he was President.

One of Donald's employees at Trump Tower defended his boss, but in a very roundabout way. "If I were married to a dog like Heidi, I'd pay a hooker, too."

Cruz continued to defend himself, "I have never veered to the wrong side of the Ten Commandments. These attacks are garbage. There is no low where Donald won't go."

Instead of being confined to a supermarket tabloid, the exposé made its way not only into the campaign, but into the mainstream press. The Enquirer story detailed one "torrid tryst" inside a closet at a state Republican convention, and another inside the private Republican Capitol Hill Club.

Cruz continued to lament the attacks, calling them "an utter lie, a tabloid smear." He then delivered a strange statement. "Donald may be a rat, but I have no desire to copulate with him."

In a Facebook posting, Cruz wrote: "The Enquirer report is completely bogus and totally unnecessary. They're offensive to Heidi and me, and offensive to our daughters. Trump's consistently disgraceful behavior is beneath the office we are seeking, and we are not going to follow."

The exposé launched at least two million reactions, mostly from Cruz's many enemies. Whether it was true or not, a Washington hooker tweeted, "Ever since he reached Washington to shut down the government, Ted became known as a reliable, $1,000-a-night trick."

A former female aide who had campaigned for him in Houston tweeted, "In the Lone Star State, Cruz has long been known as the Texas horndog."

Donald's camp indulged in some "revenge porn" of their own. An aide discovered that their boss's nemesis, Megyn Kelly, had also posed for GQ, not nude, but wearing a short blackslip dress and red high heels. "A real hooker-like pose," an aide said.

Jennifer Weiner, author of the novel Who Do You Love? wrote: "The would-be first ladies (Melania and Heidi) will survive nudity and mockery, but both of them will be diminished, stripped of their personhood, and reduced to objects. They have been flattened into human baseball cards, to be rated and traded, compared and assessed, and their worth depends not on who they are or what they do, but on how good they look, and how much their husbands love them."

An informal poll in New Orleans, a late night talk show, asked listeners to call in with answers to a question: "Would you like to bed either Melania Trump or Heidi Cruz?"

The one-hundred callers, all of them male, cast every vote for Melania.

***

Ted Cruz had loudly predicted he'd win Arizona—at least until the results were announced. Donald had "scorched" Cruz under the Arizona sun, picking up 46.2% of the vote, as opposed to Cruz's paltry 22.4%.

As one Phoenix merchant said, "In Arizona, we're much smarter than Texans. They were dumb enough to vote for Cruz."

Donald garnered all fifty-eight delegates in that state's winner-take-all primary. He appealed to the voters' anger over immigrants crossing the Mexican border illegally into their state.

As for the Democrats, Hillary (with 60% of the vote) easily won over Sanders, who received only 37.1% of the vote,

***

Based partly on Mitt Romney's endorsement, Cruz was hoping for a win in Utah.

In the wake of the terrorist attack in Brussels, Cruz said, "We need to empower law enforcement to patrol and secure Muslim neighborhoods before they become radicalized."

His remark drew fire from New York City Police Commissioner Bill Bratton: "Stick to running your long-shot campaign—and shut your big mouth. You don't know what in hell you're talking about."

Meanwhile, snoopers from all ends of the political spectrum were working around the clock researching embarrassments to discredit Donald. At the time, he was on the warpath against China's "unfair" advantage in trading with the United States, and was prominently promoting his promise to bring manufacturing jobs back to America.

Then, a reporter made a discovery in Bloomingdale's in Manhattan that would make Donald turn orange in the face: Gawker.com published a photo showing stacks of boxes piled up at the store with Ivanka's footwear brand. Printed on the boxes were the words "Made in China."

Rick Wilson, a die-hard Republican, was a strategist for Rudy Giuliani's short-lived Senate campaign against Hillary. He was in a quandary when faced with a choice of Hillary or Donald.

"Hillary's foreign policy record as Secretary of State may be a disaster, stretching from China to the 'Russian reset' to Benghazi. But on these things she's merely wrong, not unhinged. She'll make a lot of wrong decisions, but they'll be wrong because of caution, calculation, and philosophy, not because of ignorance and instability. It makes a difference."

Made in China

OH DONALD, that's Impossible! A Financial Scandal Associated with IVANKA?

Say that it isn't so?

"Equally important," Wilson wrote, "Clinton will teach Trump's troll party, currently riding a high that they can tell everyone to go to hell and get away with it, a hard lesson. Furious voters' national hissy has finally given them what they want—a pure, blindly stupid avatar of their rage and dissatisfaction."

On March 23, in Palo Alto, California, at Stanford University, Hillary attacked Donald and Cruz, denouncing their reckless rhetoric. "If Trump gets his way, it will be like Christmas in the Kremlin. It will make America less safe and the world more dangerous." Then she vigorously assaulted both of them, claiming their stated goals "will alienate America's closest allies, demonize Muslims, and empower Russia."

The popular columnist Gail Collins summed up the state of affairs for the GOP. "How can things get worse for them? Jeb Bush turned out to be a terrible candidate. Marco Rubio turned out to be an annoying twit. Donald Trump is a nightmare. Something had to be done, and so the solid, steady moderate elite decided that best strategy was to rally around...Ted Cruz. Welcome to worse."

Another missile aimed at the GOP was revealed in a poll released by USA Today/Rock the Vote Poll. It revealed that the Republican Party faced lasting damage by having lost the youth vote—52% would go to Hillary, and only 19% to Donald.

On March 23, Jeb Bush (showing no enthusiasm) endorsed Cruz, calling him a "consistent, principled conservative. For the sake of our party and country, we must overcome the divisiveness and vulgarity of Donald Trump, or we will certainly lose."

One voter, mostly in jest, asked him, "But what do you really think, Jeb?"

A disturbing poll released that same day by Monmouth University revealed that 27% of Trump's supporters would not vote for a different Republican nominee. Many claimed, "If Trump isn't the GOP nominee, we won't even bother to vote in November."

The poll positioned Donald's favorability ratio at 43%, with Cruz at 29%.

Columnist John Podhoretz weighed in on the unlikely possibility that an alternative to Donald would magically appear at the Cleveland convention:

"Cruz has yet to demonstrate that he has a national constituency. Alas for him, the movement he wanted to lead—conservative white people—had its candidate. His name is Trump. Kasich has a following of people who still cry when they listen to 'Eleanor Rigby' and its invocation of 'all the lonely people' and who want a hug because their Aunt Minnie has the shingles."

As Donald increased his wins, millions of American Muslims were said to be "watching the growing horror, fearing for their status in America."

Accordingly, many became alert to the benefits of increasing the numbers of American Muslims who voted. Muslim organizations increased their efforts to add voter registration facilities to their mosques and community centers. "The fear and apprehension in the American Muslim community has never been at this level before," said Ibrahim

In a move designed to anger his campaign manager, **Corey Lewandowski,** Donald hired the controversial **Paul Manafort** to oversee the "delegate-corralling" and media strategy aspects of his race.

This New Englander was battle toughened, having worked on the campaigns of six different Presidents, including Ronald Reagan.

He was also notorious for having lobbied for shady and controversial foreign dictators, including Ferdinand Marcos of the Philippines and Jonas Savimbi, the leader of the Angolan rebel group UNITA.

Hooper, a spokesman for the Council on American-Islamic Relations.

Before September 11, 2001, the majority of Muslims had voted Republican. But during the presidency of George W. Bush, they shifted more or less to the Democrats, with 70% self-defining as Democrats, 11% as Republican.

On March 26, Donald delivered his harshest attack on U.S. allies, who, he insisted "must start paying for their protection." He claimed he would boycott oil from Saudi Arabia and from other oil-producing allies unless they provided troops or funds to fight ISIS. "If Saudi Arabia was without the cloak of American protection, I don't think it would be around."

He also threatened that, if elected President, he would remove American forces from both South Korea and from Japan if they didn't pay more. "It's getting expensive defending the Free World," he said.

"We have been disrespected, mocked, and ripped off for many, many years by people who were smarter, shrewder, and tougher," he claimed.

He also said, to the shock of many, that he would allow Japan and South Korea to develop their own nuclear programs and not depend on America to protect them from China and North Korea. "I would use nukes as a last resort."

Columnist Frank Bruni took a close look at the "Anyone But Trump" movement, especially those "holding their noses and turning to a grotesque choice: Ted Cruz."

"Attila the Hun? True, he was truculent, but what can a spirit do? Torquemada? A tad rigid, yes, but that's what righteousness sometimes looks like. Cruz has gone from the insufferable nemesis of Republican traditionalists to their last best hope. The likes of Mitt Romney, Lindsey Graham, and Jeb Bush have now given him endorsements—or approximations thereof—that will go down in political history as some of the most constipated hosannas ever rendered."

Ann Curry, the former Today anchor, spoke of the media-making Trump: "He is not just an instant ratings, circulation/clock clicks goldmine, he's the mother lode. He stepped up onto the presidential campaign stage precisely at the moment when the media is struggling with deep insecurities about its financial future. The truth is, the media has needed Trump like a crack addict needs a hit."

In a shrewd move, Donald hired Paul J. Manafort to lead his delegate-corralling efforts. The 66-year-old strategist was one of the most experienced in managing nomination fights. He was known for having managed the 1976 Gerald Ford convention in a showdown with Ronald Reagan.

In an about-face, Manafort had performed in a similar capacity for Reagan in 1980. He had also played a leading role in the nominations of George H.W. Bush in both 1988 and 1992.

In a Statement That Enrages Millions of Feminists, Donald Calls for Some Form of
PUNISHMENT FOR WOMEN WHO ABORT

In one of the worst missteps of his presidential race, Donald offended millions with an abrasive comment about criminalizing women who submit to a legal abortion.

"If abortion were illegal," he said, "and a woman went ahead and had one, there would have to be some form of punishment." That was his answer to MSNBC's Chris Matthews after he was presented with a hypothetical question.

"I haven't determined what the punishment should be," he said. "The woman is a victim, as is the life in her womb."

The fallout was instantaneous, beginning with Cecile Richards, president of Planned Parenthood. "His stance, vile and stupid, is about controlling women."

Trump recanted his remarks hours later, after facing immediate, hostile attacks from both the GOP

Appearing on MSNBC with TV anchor **Chris Matthews**, no friend of Donald's, the candidate fell into a trap.

Provocatively, Matthews asked him if abortion were made illegal, would there be some form of punishment for the mother who aborted her child?

Donald shocked millions—and not just women—when he said that there should be "some form of punishment." His casual remark caused outrage across the country.

and Democrats.

Then he fine-tuned his original statement with another statement, "The doctor or any other person performing this illegal act upon a woman would be held legally responsible, not the woman."

"Trump's remarks would drag the country back to the days when women were forced to seek illegal procedures from unlicensed providers out of sheer desperation," said Debbie Wasserman Schultz, chairwoman of the Democratic National Committee.

Jeanne Mancini, President of the March for Life Education and Defense Fund, said, "No pro-lifer would ever want to punish a woman who has chosen abortion. We invite a woman who has gone down this route to consider paths to healing, not punishment."

Columnist Nickolas Kristof wrote: "Maybe Trump in his flip-flopping wavering about women's issues can at least remind us of a larger truth. Whatever one thinks of abortion, criminalizing it would be worse."

MEANWHILE, THE DEMOCRATS WERE RAGING, TOO

The remarkable **Debbie Wasserman Schultz** was a congresswoman from Florida and the chairperson of the Democratic National Committee. She was pro-choice, and a supporter of gun control legislation and the LGBTQ community.

She was the first Jewish congresswoman elected from Florida, and was the co-chair for Hillary Clinton's unsuccessful run for President in 2008.

Although she had done a remarkable job in all offices she'd held, Bernie Sanders demanded that she be removed as chairperson of the Democratic National Committee because "she unfairly favored Secretary Clinton over me."

CHAPTER TWELVE

Hothead Cruz Gets Denounced by the Former Speaker of the House as
"LUCIFER IN THE FLESH...A MISERABLE SON OF A BITCH"
The *NY Daily News* Nicknames Cruz "KING TURD" and "BEELZEBUB"

Donald Threatens to Cut Off the Flow of Billions of Dollars to
MEXICO
and calls for a Massive Buildup of the U.S. Military on the Southern Border

"NEVER TRUMP" GETS BURIED As Donald Scores Big in the Northeast

NYC's Most Anti-Trump Tabloid (The Daily News) Devotes
EQUAL TIME TO HATING CRUZ

After Riots in California, Radical Billionaire, **CHARLES KOCH,**
One of the Staunchest and Most Implacable Conservatives in the World,
Denounces Donald Trump and Ted Cruz and
THREATENS TO SUPPORT HILLARY

"Donald Trump's candidacy is not only fracturing the Republican Party. it's putting more stress on more friendships than any other political development in my experience."
—Peter Wehner

April Fool's Day arrived with a dismal forecast for Donald's campaign aides. If the GOP candidate won the presidential nomination, he would be the most disliked candidate in the thirty-two years since such a poll existed. According to the Washington Post/ABC News poll, Donald registered a whopping 67% unfavorable rating.

Before Donald, in 1992, President George H.W. Bush had been the most disliked candidate, receiving a 57% unfavorable rating in his race against Bill Clinton.

Surveys revealed that Donald's misogyny and fear-mongering had offended or turned off millions of voters.

His unfavorability rating among women was even higher, registering 75%. Among Hispanics, some 85% claimed that they disliked him intensely, mainly because of his stance against Mexicans.

In contrast, although it was nothing to brag about, Hillary received a dismaying 52% unfavorable rating among voters-at-large.

Although she had tended to ignore Donald's attacks on her, she slammed him at a closed-to-the-press Lower East Side fund-raiser in Manhattan. Its guests included one of his worst enemies, Rosie O'Donnell, who said, "Really, I feel like we are watching an id—an id with hair," she said at the event for LGBT supporters.

"I'm hoping," Rosie continued, "that his campaign keeps going until they have insulted every American in every group in every part of the country. We could have a landslide."

Donald had previously publicly insulted her. O'Donnell took the opportunity to strike back at Donald as a loser, comparing him to the Harry Potter villain, Lord Voldemort.

Around the same time, she told the press, "I'm done with marriage." The former host of *The View* made the comment after finalizing a divorce from her second wife, Michelle Rounds.

It wasn't just the Democratic Party who wanted to stop Donald. Among the GOP, the *NEVER TRUMP* movement was growing daily, almost with every controversial utterance he delivered. As one editorial writer described it, "The *NEVER TRUMP* group is trying to sell Republicans on a dangerously reactionary senator (Cruz) as an improvement over a dangerously reactionary businessman."

The *NEVER TRUMP* movement organized and paid for tens of millions of dollars' worth of last-ditch negative ads. Their tenets were embraced by GOP senators and governors, as well as big money donors, political strategists, and grassroots activists.

Senator Lindsey Graham of South Carolina best expressed their dilemma: "Having to chose between Trump and Cruz is like deciding between getting shot and getting poisoned."

Columnist Michael Goodwin suggested that Donald was his own worst enemy on the campaign trail. "His suicide-by-media efforts are of a different sort. He foolishly agrees to long interviews with news organizations that already declared him unfit to be President, and gives them what they want. In his hubris, he provides the rope to lynch mobs."

At long last, Bob Woodward, writing in the Washington Post, revealed how Donald would force Mexico to pay for a border wall. He declared that if elected President, he would cut of the flow of billions of dollars in payments that immigrants sent back, through banking channels and wire transfers, to their home country.

"That would decimate the Mexican economy," he said. "My proposal would jeopardize a stream of cash that would be vital to Mexico's struggling economy."

Woodward went on to speculate that the daring (and legally horrifying) proposal would test the bounds of a President's executive power.

According to Donald, his threat would be withdrawn if Mexico made a one-time payment of $5 to $10 billion for construction of the 1,000-mile border fence.

"Nearly $25 billion was sent home by Mexicans living in the United States in 2015, mostly in the form of money transfers." Donald said, "The majority of that comes from illegal aliens."

***

Several columnists set out to unravel the confounding candidacy of Donald Trump. Eduardo Porter wrote: "The most solid appeal among Repulican primary voters may be what it says about the waning role of religion in American politics. His popularity is a sign that Americans are finally losing their religious spirit, following the long trend in other advanced nations. Trump is not just the least religious Republican in the field, he is perceived as less religious than Hillary Clinton."

Of the many rappers whose lyrics have been inspired by Donald Trump, none burst onto the media scene as decisively as **Mac Miller,** whose hit song, "Donald Trump" sold millions beginning in 2011. Donald threatened to sue him.

When Miller learned that Donald was running for President, he said, "Oh fuck! This is horrible. I have a fucking song with this dude's name and now he's being such a douchebag."

Donald's response? "Little Mac Miller is an ungrateful dog."

A poll by Pew Research Center revealed that less than half of the Republican voters viewed him as religious, given his three marriages and his multiple positions on abortion.

IVANA SAYS: "Donald is The Best Ex I Ever Had"

In a satirical, media-savvy adaptation of Marla Maples' famous remark ["Donald is the best sex I ever had"], Ivana, his first wife, told the media that he was the "best ex I ever had."

Years after her nasty divorce, she had softened her position on Donald, claiming that her "woman-loving ex would be good for America."

She gave an interview from within her opulent seven-story townhouse on Manhattan's Upper East Side, which she had purchased for about $3 million in 1998.

She also asserted her role as a political adviser to her former husband. "We speak before and after his appearances, and he asks me what I think."

"Donald is a fantastic businessman, unlike Obama, who cannot make a decision if his life depended on it."

Although once an immigrant herself, she opposed immigration. She cited an example of a pregnant Mexican girl crossing illegally into the United States. "She gives birth in an American hospital, which is free. The child automatically becomes a U.S. citizen. She then brings the whole family. She doesn't pay taxes. She doesn't have a job. She gets the free housing, she gets the food stamps. Who's paying? You and me."

In her delicate way, Ivana weighed in on the controversy about Donald's small hands.

"Speaking of hands—and other body parts—Donald does just fine in that department," she said. "If there was a problem there, Donald would not have five kids."

TRUMP GETS "CREAMED" IN DAIRYLAND
As Evangelical Cruz Milks the Wisconsin Cow

No good news came out of Wisconsin in the days before the primary there as the state's governor, Scott Walker, endorsed Ted Cruz and right-wing radio hosts flayed Donald.

Cruz was ahead by ten percentage points in the polls, and the STOP TRUMP movement was scoring points.

One highly placed Wisconsin state senator said, "Don't get the wrong idea. We hate that Texan windbag Cruz. But we hate Trump even more. Call our voting for the Texan a marriage of convenience, about as sexually unfulfilling as a lesbian married to a gay male."

However, polls showed that Donald still had a lot of support among white working class voters.

The Wisconsin primaries had been scheduled for April 5. As anticipated, Cruz trounced Donald, getting some 48% of the vote, in contrast to Donald's 34%. Pundits defined it as a major setback for the Trump campaign.

At a victory rally in Milwaukee, Cruz told cheering supporters, "Tonight is a turning point. It's a rallying cry. We have a choice, a real choice."

Hope Hicks, Trump's spokesperson, assailed the winner as "'Lyin Ted.' He's worse than a puppet—he is a Trojan horse, being used by (Republican) party bosses attempting to steal the nomination from Mr. Trump."

On the Democratic front, Bernie Sanders scored his sixth straight victory in the nominating race.

***

On his home turf, New York City, Donald was hoping to sweep to a decisive victory, but his rivals had other plans. At a rally on Long Island, he was greeted with cheers and jeers, a mixed reaction from a crowd filled with nervous unrest in a cavernous film studio peopled with many white, blue collar voters. "It's great to be home!" he said to the raucous crowd.

At this point, Cruz had more or less abandoned hopes for any significant wins in the five boroughs of metropolitan New York, hoping instead for gains upstate where he would meet greater numbers of conservative Republicans.

Ted Cruz carried the primary, beating Donald throughout the dairylands of Wisconsin.

One local reporter wrote, "I'm not surprised. Cruz is a cowpie himself."

Even Cruz had enough sense to know he couldn't win New York City, since he'd made his distaste for the place known.

His campaign recognized that Cruz didn't necessarily have to beat Donald on the mogul's turf, and probably wouldn't succeed even if they tried. Instead, in game of "wait and see," Cruz and his cohorts opted to continue amassing the delegates needed to keep him from accumulating a majority of committed delegates before the Republican convention in July.

"THE MYSOGYNISTIC, HOMOPHOBIC, RACIST VULGARIAN"
(No, We're Not Talking About Donald) IS DEFEATED IN NEW YORK

After attacking Donald in a debate, berating him for his "New York values," the brazen Texas senator, Ted Cruz, got the Bronx cheer as his unappetizing presence arrived in a city he loathed.

He was derided for "crawling back into town seeking votes but also begging for cash."

"Ted Cruz is a hypocrite," said Ruben Diaz, Jr., the Bronx Borough President. "He not only offended New Yorkers, he offended Bronxites, and now he's here looking for money and votes."

When it was announced that Cruz would address the Bronx Lighthouse College Preparatory Academy, students threatened a boycott. In a letter, he was denounced as "misogynistic, homophobic, and racist, a man who uses vulgar language, gestures, and profanity."

In the "Battle for New York," that city's *Daily News,* the most anti-Trump newspaper in the nation, gave equal time to hating Ted. After a string of critical headlines from that publication, Cruz spoke to reporters on his way out of a Brooklyn synagogue. "It's tabloid reporting," he said. "I'm much more interested in the people of New York than what journalists think."

For Donald, April 7 was both a good day and a bad day. The good news involved former mayor, Rudy Giulinai, who announced that he'd vote for him.

The almost simultaneous bad news involved headlines trumpeting: "DON DROOLED FOR BABY DAUGHTER—WHAT A BOOB." It was revealed that he once commented on his one-year-old daughter, Tiffany, whom he had conceived with his second wife, Marla Maples.

In a recycled segment from a 1994 episode of Lifestyles of the Rich and Famous, its host, Robin Leach, asked, "Donald, what does Tiffany have of yours, and what does she have of Marla's?"

"I think that she got a lot of Marla's," Donald replied. "She is a really beautiful baby, and she's got Marla's legs. We don't know whether she's got another part yet, but time will tell." Then he had gestured toward her unformed breasts.

On April 9, hoping for a big win in the New York primaries, Donald traveled the four miles from the glitzy Trump Tower to visit Ground Zero, the memorial to 9/11 in Lower Manhattan. It was his first-ever visit to the memorial.

He was accompanied by his wife, Melania, who was attired in a tight-fitting black pants suit and high heels whose height seemed to equal that of the Trump Tower from which she had descended.

Donald racked up another first, giving $100,000 to the memorial.

After spending a half hour at the site, he left without speaking to reporters.

Although he had prepared for a sweeping victory in the New York primary, he nonetheless blasted the "corrupting" nominating system of the state's Republican Party.

On radio, Donald said, "I guarantee New Yorkers could forget about the Federal government if Cruz is nominated. I won in Louisiana, but lost the delegate race to Cruz because of the nonsense going on, real shenanigans. The system is corrupt."

His delegate wrangler, Paul Manafort, on NBC's Meet the Press, played the Nazi card against Cruz: "He's using Gestapo tactics to wrest the nomination from Trump."

As the New York primary neared, it was revealed that more than half of the record spending on negative advertising was aimed at candidate Donald. More than $132 million had already been spent. Of that amount, some $70 million of it had been configured with the intent of preventing Donald from getting the nomination. Three GOP Super PACS had

OIH VEY! Shamelessly pandering to Jewish voters in Orthodox Brooklyn, **Ted Cruz** tries to make a matzo ball.

After shaking countless hands, he didn't even wash his own hands before handling the dough.

already defined "taking Trump down," as one of their primary goals.

[In contrast to the mega-spenders, Donald would spend just over $16 million on TV ads.]

The anti-Trump PACS were helped by Hillary, who joined in the onslaught on Donald with negative ads of her own. Most of them highlighted his stances on immigration and abortion.

Despite the negative screams, Donald's campaign rolled inexorably onward, earning him the name "Teflon Don."

On April 12, House Speaker Paul Ryan ruled himself out for a presidential bid, squashing speculation that he would emerge at a brokered convention to topple Donald. Pundits speculated that Ryan actually hoped that Donald would be the nominee—and lose—so that he could step in and grab the nomination in 2020, without having a sitting Republican President to run against.

"I will not accept the nomination of our party," Ryan said, echoing the words of Lyndon Johnson in 1968 when he bowed out of that year's presidential race.

The spectacularly non-charismatic Senate leader, Mitch McConnell, whose appearance had been likened to that of a stern Presbyterian deacon, seemed to be reconciling himself to the fact that the Texas senator might be the only one to stop Donald.

"These guys [i.e. the Republican Establishment] are only using Cruz to shut down Donald before they stab Cruz in the back this summer," said Erick Erickson, a right-wing talk show host.

***

To their chagrin, just as the GOP elite was thinking the unthinkable—that is, the nomination of Cruz as the Republican Party's nominee for President—the senator from Texas became the centerpiece for an avalanche of mocking headlines about "BAD VIBRATIONS."

On April 13, it was revealed that Cruz had once defended a Texas law banning the use of sex toys. As part of his struggle for state-wide fame and approval from conservative voters, he had argued that there was no constitutional right to stimulate one's genitals.

In reaction to that revelation, one provocative late-night talk show host told his listeners, "I'm sending Cruz a 12-inch dildo and telling him where to stick it."

Even Cruz's former long-ago roommate from Princeton, Craig Mazin, insisted that Cruz did not always feel that way about sex toys. Without directly saying so, the suggestion was that Cruz had used sex toys himself.

Days before citizens of New York were scheduled to vote in that state's primary, yet another poll revealed that Donald was the most unpopular candidate to run for President in some three decades, and that he was viewed unfavorably by 67% of Americans. Only David Duke, the KKK leader, beat him with an unfavorability rating of 69%.

Ted Cruz didn't win any popularity contests either, reflecting a 53% unfavorable rating, despite his allegations that Jesus Christ, even God, had endorsed him.

Republicans who publicly asserted that they would vote for Donald were often inundated with hate mail. Such was the case with Craig Dunn, the Republican chairman of Howard County, Indiana.

On the air, after being asked if he would support Donald, he replied, "Only if Satan was one vote away from the nomination."

He soon found out how ardent Donald's supporters could be. Almost immediately, he was showered with hate mail, one Donald fan refering to Dunn as "the biggest traitor since Benedict Arnold."

A typical message to Dunn read, "You sorry motherfucker,

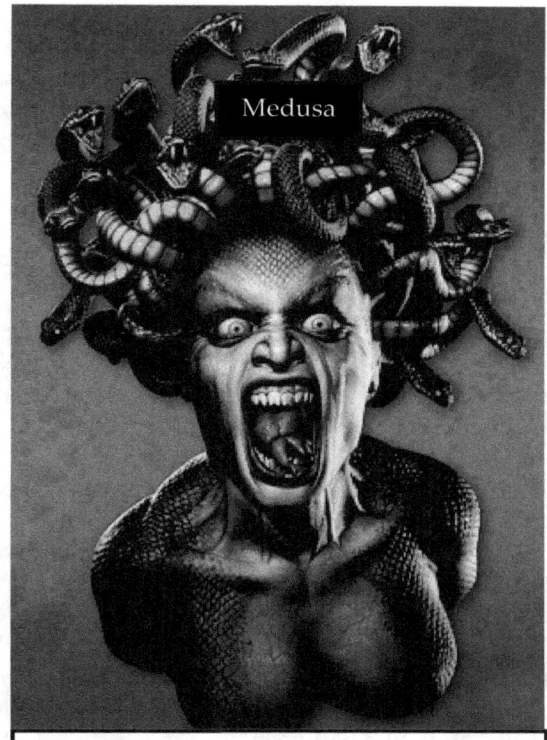

Days before the New York primary, newspapers wrote about Ted Cruz's "friendemies."

Columnist Johan Goldberg said: "Like Perseus pulling Medusa's head out of a sack to petrify his enemies, **Cruz** has been able to dangle the prospect of a President Trump to strike fear in the hearts of even his biggest detractors."

Ted Cruz always claimed that he was a strict believer in following the exact wording of the Constitution.

"At no place does this wonderful document grant citizens the right to use sex toys to stimulate one's genitals. I'm calling for a statewide ban in Texas!"

I hope the worst for you."

Dunn later evaluated that period of his life like this: "My life became a living hell. I received hate email to my business and political accounts. People left hateful messages on my home and my office phones."

The irony is that, as a pledged delegate from Indiana, based on the fine print of Indiana's election laws, Dunn was obligated to vote for Donald, at least on the first ballot.

***

Garry Kasparov, chairman of the New York City-based Human Rights Foundation, released an article suggesting that Donald represents the worst of a great city.

"It's tempting to rally behind him, but we should resist. Because the New York values Trump represents are the very worst kind. He exemplifies the seamy side of New York—the Ponzi schemers and the Brooklyn Bridge sellers, the gangster traders like Bernie Madoff, and the celebrity gangsters like John Gotti—not the hard work and sacrifice that built New York and America. He stands for fake values, debt instead of cash, appearance over substance, gold paint instead of the real thing."

On April 19 as New Yorkers went to the polls to place their votes in the primaries, Donald made history. The results came in a few seconds after voting ended at 9PM.

Donald had swept to victory in his home state, receiving the approval of 89 of the 95 delegates. In a surprise move, with the exception of Manhattan where he lived, he had won every county in the state. [Ironically, it was Kasich who picked up the three delegates from Manhattan.]

In vivid contrast, Cruz—either because of his attacks on the great people of a great city or because most sophisticated urbanites simply couldn't stand him—didn't win any delegates. Not even one.

In the Democratic race, Hillary knocked out Bernie Sanders. He had been born in Brooklyn, but deserted it for the wilds of Vermont. She had been born in Chicago, but ultimately selected New York State as her home address.

During his victory speech at Trump Tower, Donald sounded almost presidential. "Our jobs are being sucked out of our states," he told the faithful who had gathered to cheer.

Then the Queens-born mogul declared his love for his home state to the sound of Frank Sinatra singing "New York, New York."

[Donald had trounced "that right-wing fanatic" as Cruz was known, winning 83% of the vote. His closest competitor was John Kasich with 25%. New York-hating Cruz scored a paltry 15% Cruz supporters were denouncd as "fools" in some quarters, usually because of the candidate's widely publicized distaste for the Empire State.]

For New York, it was a historical moment. The last time the state had been home to each of the two leading presidential candidates was a face-off in 1944 between an ailing Franklin D. Roosevelt and Republican Thomas E. Dewey, who was ridiculed for looking like the tuxedo-clad groom on top of a wedding cake.

***

In the Colorado caucuses, Cruz swept to victory, capturing that state's thirteen right-wing delegates. Donald's people had had no organized national campaign in operation there, virtually giving the state to Cruz.

The losses for Donald were reported as "troubling," although some of his aides diagnosed their loss with: "Cruz appeals to the redneck West more than a city slicker like Donald."

Donald was labeled a sore loser when he complained about it to social media: "The people of Colorado had their vote taken away from them by phony politicians. This will not be allowed."

On AM970's Cats Roundtable Radio Show, as moderated by John Catsimatidis, a former mayoral candidate for New York City, Donald said, "This guy hates New York. He voted against appropriations for New York, for Hurricane Sandy, for other things. Now he's trying to pretend like all this stuff never happened."

CRITICS EQUATE DONALD'S "BELLOW & BLUSTER" SCHTICK WITH "BIGOTRY & BUFFOONERY"
But He's Cited for Allowing Jews and Blacks into Waspy Palm Beach

After his colossal sweep of the GOP primary in New York, the Trump campaign seemed at a crossroads. Whereas he had abundantly proven that he could get votes in popular elections, there now rose a crucially important issue of whether those votes would translate into approval from the Republican Party's convention delegates.

[EDITORIAL NOTE: *Election by-laws vary widely state-to-state, but generally, the Republican Party, unlike the Democratic Party, allows each state to decide whether to use the winner-take-all method or the proportional method of voting in a winner in a primary election. In the winner-take-all method the candidate whom the majority of caucus participants or voters support receives all the delegates for the state.*

Based on the arcane and extremely complex nature of state party election bylaws—a system that Donald repeatedly and perhaps accurately condemned as being "rigged"—the approval of delegates and their pledges of (voting) support for an individual candidate is as important (perhaps more so) than the approval of popular voters.]

Beginning in mid-to-late April, Donald began to focus not just on GOP primary voters—many of them rabidly right wing—but on convention delegates. Cruz was winning the allegiance of some of them by "clod-hopping" across such states as Wyoming.

"This is a multi-level audience play," said conservative talk show host Laura Ingraham. "Trump's message to the voter is that the system is corrupt and has to be changed, and he's the real outsider. To the delegates, he's playing a 'you-better-watch-it' game—because the people are on to you."

It had become clear that Donald was facing a pivotal moment in his quest to reside at 1600 Pennsylvania Avenue. Reporter Jonathan Martin wrote: "Installing political veterans atop his campaign, committing to an eight-figure budget, and at least trying to impose a measure of discipline on himself, Trump appears mindful that if he does not improve his performance, he risks having the nomination snapped from his grasp."

To his rage, Donald tended to be outmaneuvered at grassroots Republican events where insiders, based on arcane election statutes, seemed to delight in thwarting his advances.

"Lyin' Ted Cruz showed he was adept in these little side shows," Donald said. "Stealing delegates doesn't necessarily make him qualified to take over the government. Up to now, he had only succeeded in shutting down the government."

As the campaign went on, more and more political analysts continued to watch Donald's rise and to document his many failures. It was obvious that he was defying Washington consensus to help attract voters, thousands of whom had never supported a Republican ticket before. Yet there were ominous signs, and headlines warned that "TRUMP'S TRIAL BALLOONS CATCHING UP WITH HIM." Pundits concluded that "a style long on gut instincts is finally taking its toll."

Late in March, he had suggested that it might not be a bad idea if Japan and South Korea had nuclear arms.

President Obama ridiculed that remark, and the South Koreans and Japanese feared an arms race. Since then, Donald had changed his tune, saying that he did not want the two American allies to actually get "the bomb."

He also backed down on other headline-generating positions, including his suggestion that women should face some sort of punishment for aborting a child. He also softened his previous statements on torture, agreeing—after a horrified reaction from the media—to respect the law as regards the interrogation of suspected terrorists.

Despite his implied retraction of a few of his earlier positions, Donald's blunt rhetoric continued to attract record-breaking crowds, as many as 25,000 at a rally in Alabama.

He was also drawing unprecedented swarms of protesters. Polls showed that 31% of Republican women claimed they'd be upset if he became the nominee. Nationwide, 73% of women viewed him unfavorably. Threats poured into Trump Tower, as a half dozen Secret Service men stood ready to protect him.

In spite of all his derogatory "fat pig" comments about women, his grip on the nomination seemed to get stronger. On March 26 he tweeted, "Nobody has more respect for women than Donald Trump."

By mid-April, in spite of dire predictions to the contrary, he had won twenty of 32 nominating races. "I'm the biggest story in politics—forget what's his name, that crazy socialist, and fat Hillary."

"Donald is a showbiz guy and reality TV star, and his talk is his schtick," said Christopher Ruddy, a friend. Critics called his "bellow and bluster schtick bigotry and buffoonery."

"People label him as racist," said one Palm Beach socialite who did not want to be named. "But he's opened up Waspy Palm Beach to the Jews. He's even friendly with the blacks."

***

Back on the campaign trail, Donald's chief rival, Ted Cruz, kept "sliming" New York again, hoping to appeal to the rural voters of Pensylvania. "Let me tell you what Trump and his media want to convince everybody: That Pennsylvania is a suburb of Manhattan. Manhattan has spoken, and Pennsylvania will follow obediantly. At least that's what Trump wants you to do."

Donald tweeted his response: "Ted Cruz is mathematically out of winning the race. Now all he can do is be a spoiler, never a nice thing to do. I will beat Hillary."

The "old" Donald Trump resurfaced at a rally at the Indiana State Fairgrounds in Indianapolis. He was back in "red meat form," attacking "Crooked Hillary" and "Lyin' Ted Cruz," whom he likened to a lion's head.

When protesters interrupted his speech, he bellowed to the guards, "Get 'em out! I love waterboarding!"

Was he suggesting that the guards subject the protesters to torture?"

***

The May issue of Fortune revealed that Donald's net worth is $3.72 billion, far less than the $10 billion he claims. The figure was also below the $4.5 billion cited by Forbes the previous October. The lower water estimate of $2.9 billion was set by Bloomberg Politics in May, which caused a lot of speculation about just how rich Donald really was.

In the same edition, Fortune ran a photo of Donald from 2008. In it, as he's talking on the phone, he's clearly "flipping the bird," a universal "fuck you" sign, to a photographer.

While on the subject of money, economists in late April released a report of what "Trumponomics" would look like, revealing that if Donald became President, his tax cuts would benefit the very rich with an average reduction of 12% or perhaps $275,000 each. The bottom 20% of wage earners would see that tax bill reduced by "a hair under 1%." The richest of the rich, they estimated, including Donald himself, would save a staggering $1.3 million annually in taxes.

TOILETS FOR THE TRANSGENDERED
"Where," Republicans Raged, "Should Caitlyn Jenner Squat?"

All of Cruz's hopes were riding on Indiana, where he made crude jokes about new bathroom by-laws that determined where the transgendered, based on new laws in such states as North Carolina, could use only a toilet associated with the gender they were documented with at the moment of their birth.

"What's next?" Cruz lamented. "Donald dressing up like Hillary to get into the little girl's room? Not with my daughters!"

Known for changing his positions, Donald weighed in on the transgender bathroom issue, breaking from mainstream Republican rhetoric endorsed by, among others, Cruz, who was terrified that men dressed as women would invade women's toilets and assault the little girls they found inside.

In marked contrast to his Republican rivals Donald said that transgender people should be allowed to use whatever bathroom they felt comfortable in, including those at Trump Tower.

"Leave it the way it is now," he said. "There have been very few complaints, if any."

He also admitted that the Trump Organization "probably employs some transgendered."

Cruz quickly pounced on him: "Trump is no different from politically correct leftist elites. Today, he joined them in calling for grown men to be allowed to use litle girls' public restrooms."

***

It could safely be said that Donald, of all the candidates seeking the GOP nomination, was the most tolerant to members of the LGBT community, as influenced, no doubt, by his being a native of a very tolerant New York City. But as the campaign deepened, he leaned more to the right on the issue, no doubt to appease and placate his homophobic supporters.

Back on December 21, 2005, Donald had sent congratulations to Elton John and his lover, David Furnish, when they entered into a civil partnership in London.

"I knew both of them, and they got along wonderfully," he said. "It's a marriage thats going to work. I'm very happy for them, If two people dig each other, they dig each other."

As The New York Times pointed out, "Trump is far more acepting of sexual minorities than his party leaders have been."

His rivals, including Ted Cruz and especially Rick Santorum and Mike Huckabee, had made their horrified opposition to same-sex marriage widely known. Marco Rubio, too, had frequently emphasized that he opposed same-sex marriages.

As the nation's (Democratic) Vice President Joe Biden quipped: "There are still a lot of homophobes around, and most of them are running for the Republican nomination."

In 2000, Donald and Rudy Giuliani had been captured on video in a playful "gay mood" when the then-New York City mayor had dressed in drag for a skit at a political roast. Donald pretended to be turned on by "Sexy Rudy," and nuzzled his neck, getting excited at the smell of his perfume.

As late as 2011, Donald, a sophisticated urbanite, had said, "I know many, many gay people. Tremendous people."

As evidence of his tolerance, he was believed to be the first owner of a private resort in Palm Beach (in this case, Mar-a-Lago) to openly welcome a gay couple.

However, as the 2016 campaign deepened, he moved to the right on same-sex marriage, claiming that he believed that the bonds of matrimony should be confined exclusively to a man and a woman. However, he thought it should be left to the States to decide.

[Legal authorities have pointed out that if that were the case, the associated legal and personal complications would be chaotic, unclear, and overwhelming.]

***

Simultaneous with defending the "squatting rights" of Ms. Jenner, Donald took a politically incorrect position. He didn't want to see the engraving of Andrew Jackson removed from the face of the U.S. twenty-dollar bill. He went on to denounce "pure political correctness" the proposal of putting an image of the black civil rights pioneer, Harriet Tubman, in its place.

"I don't like seeing it," he said. "She might be better off on the little-seen $2 bill."

[*A former slave, abolitionist and Union spy, Tubman (died 1913) led hundreds of African Americans to freedom on the Underground Railroad. It was announced by Treasury Secretary Jacob J. Lew that Tubman's image will replace Andrew Jackson's on the bill, and that a series of other bills would likewise be revised to include images of seminal feminists and human rights activists who will eventually include Eleanor Roosevelt, Elizabeth Cady Stanton, and Susan B. Anthony.*]

The New York Times described this development as "the most sweeping and historically symbolic makeover of American currency in a century."

"DONALD KICKS TED CRUZ'S ASS OUT OF NEW ENGLAND"

On April 26, victory parties were hosted for Donald in Pennsylvaia, Maryland, Connecticut, Delaware, and Rhode Island.

Both Donald and Hillary had dominated that round of primary contests. He had swept through five eastern states. On the Democratic front, Hillary had won four. Only tiny Rhode Island, usually a bastion of liberalism with a high percentage of college-age and twenty-something voters, had allied itself with Sanders.

Donald scored the best of all the candidates, with more than thirty percentage points over his rivals, Cruz and Kasich. After the vote, Donald seemed close to his goal. To the horror of his critics, a sudden aura of invincibility shone like a halo around his orange comb-over.

Appearing before adoring hordes at Trump Tower, he said, "When a boxer knocks out the other boxer, you don't have to wait around for the decision."

Peter Wehner, a senior fellow at the Ethics and Public Policy Center, claimed, "The candidacy of Donald Trump is not only fracturing the Republican Party, it is breaking up friendships as well. His candidacy is putting more stress on more friendsips than any other political development in my experience. The dynamic is playing out in public, too. Glenn Beck and Sarah Palin, while not lifelong friends, were once close. No more."

Trying to look presidential Donald gave his first foreign policy speech, with calls for "America First. We will no longer surrender this country, or its people, to the false song of globalism."

He attacked Hillary and Obama as "reckless, rudderless, and aimless." He also called for easing tensions with China and Russia, the defeat of ISIS, and a massive buildup of the military.

***

The battle for the primary voters of Indiana and California intensified. Stopping first in Indiana, Donald renewed his attacks on Hillary, claiming, "She couldn't even get elected to a seat on a city council if she didn't play 'the woman card.'"

The next day, when challenged, he stood by his statement. "In a national election without the woman card, she would get only five percent of the vote."

It was on to California, where he hoped to solidify his quota of committed delegates so he could win on the first ballot at the upcoming GOP convention in Cleveland in July.

An angry mob broke through the steel barricades outside the Hyatt Regency Hotel in Burlingame, near the San Francisco International Airport, in an attempt to disrupt one of his rallies. Donald had to be smuggled in through the rear entrance, under heavy guard.

Outside the Hyatt, protesters threw eggs at the police and shouted obscenities, such as "FUCK TRUMP!" Some illegal aliens, fearing deportation if he became President, waved Mexican flags.

The riot at Burlingame took place the day after another rally, and an almost equivalent protest, in Orange County, near L.A. There, some twenty protesters had been arrested after clashing with the police. Cops appeared in full riot gear to control the angry mob.

In a surprise announcement, the staunchly conservative billionaire, Charles Koch, who had spent millions backing Republican candidates, faced the press. He said that he was "disgusted at the current GOP presidential races. I will not spend a cent on any of the contenders—and that includes Ted Cruz and Donald Trump."

Kansas-born **Charles de Ganahl Koch**, owner of "Dixie Cup" and other products, is the sixth richest person in the world and a major contributor to the Republican Party.

He has expressed his disappointment in the chief rivals seeking the GOP nomination, both Ted Cruz and Donald Trump.

Then he threw out the shocking suggestion that in a desperate move, he might even support Hillary Clinton.

***

In Indiana, during the twilight of his failing campaign, Cruz seemed desperate. As evidence of that, he took the strange position of naming his vice presidential running mate. It was Carly Fiorina herself, a former rival and failed candidate who had previously denounced Cruz when she was running against him.

In October, she had told CNN, "There is no honor in charging up a hill that you know you can't take, only encountering casualties. Cruz is a total phony. He says one thing in Manhattan, another in Iowa. He says whatever he needs to get elected."

In Indiana, in revised circumstances, she was singing a different tune: "The Republican Party is in a struggle for the soul and future of the nation."

Donald's aides ridiculed her selection as a running mate for Ted Cruz. One of them quipped, "The former Hewlett-Packard executive began her failed administration by telling 30,000 employees, 'You're fired!' She even had to steal that line from Donald's hit TV show, The Apprentice."

The most hellish attack on Cruz came not from Donald, but from John Boehner, the former (deeply frustrated and oft-humiliated) Republican Speaker of the House. Now retired and free for the first time to reveal what he really thought, he said, "Ted Cruz is Lucifer in the Flesh...I've never worked with a more miserable son of a bitch!"

This statement, widely dispersed across the nation, was delivered at Stanford University.

In contrast, the speaker said that he had a great affection for Donald. "We regularly hit the links together and are texting buddies."

Cruz shot back. Demurring with false innocence, he said: "The truth of the matter is, I don't know Boehner. I've met him only two or three times in my life."

That statement was so blatantly false that Donald said, "Now I know why I call him 'Lying Cruz.'"

Boehner's attack drew its sharpest fire from an unlikely source, the Satanic Temple. A blog site with which it's associated (the "Friendly Atheist,") posted this comment: "Cruz's failures of reason, compassion, decency, and humanity are products of the Christian faith."

Based in NYC, with a branches in Detroit and California, The Satanic Temple is an atheistic, humanistic, and intensely political group that uses Satanic imagery to promote social justice, egalitarianism, and the separation of church and state.

The group's public statements have attacked fundamentalist Christian organizations that it believes interfere with personal freedom.

Some critics have questioned whether the Satanic Temple is a prank, a satire, or a genuine Satanic cult. Officially, at least, it does not believe in a supernatural Satan, as its associates believe that this encourages superstition that will prevent their ability to remain "malleable to the best current scientific understandings of the material world."

***

As morally and ethically complicated as these issues were, one thing about Trump seemed certain—at least before the 2016 election—as articulated by one particularly outraged reviewer: "After the voters go to the polls in Indiana and California, the race for the nomination will be all over for 'Lucifer in the Flesh.' The press will be on his devil's tail as he, with pitchfork in hand, races back to the Gates of Hell."

Now that **John Boehner** is no longer the Republican Speaker of the House, he is free to speak his mind.

And so he did, ripping into Ted Cruz, "that miserable son of a bitch who was a pain in the ass and shut down our government."

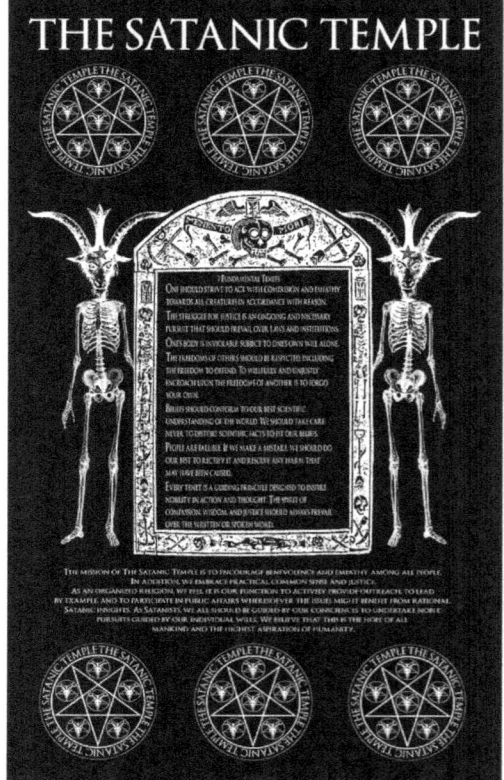

As reviewed by The New York Times, "**The Satanic Temple**, with only a website, some legal savvy, and a clever way with satire, this new, mostly virtual religion has become a sharp thorn in the brow of conservative Christianity."

Supporters cite its founders' most visible success as their creation of a faith-based organization that met all of George W. Bush's "White House Office of Faith-Based and Community Initiatives" criteria for receiving government funds.

Understandably, the group's criteria were repugnant to most of the conservative Christians who had to evaluate them. In the aftermath, many legal arguments arose that rebutted the Bush Administration's sanction of public funding for conservative Christian lobbying groups.

Chapter Thirteen
(May, 2016)

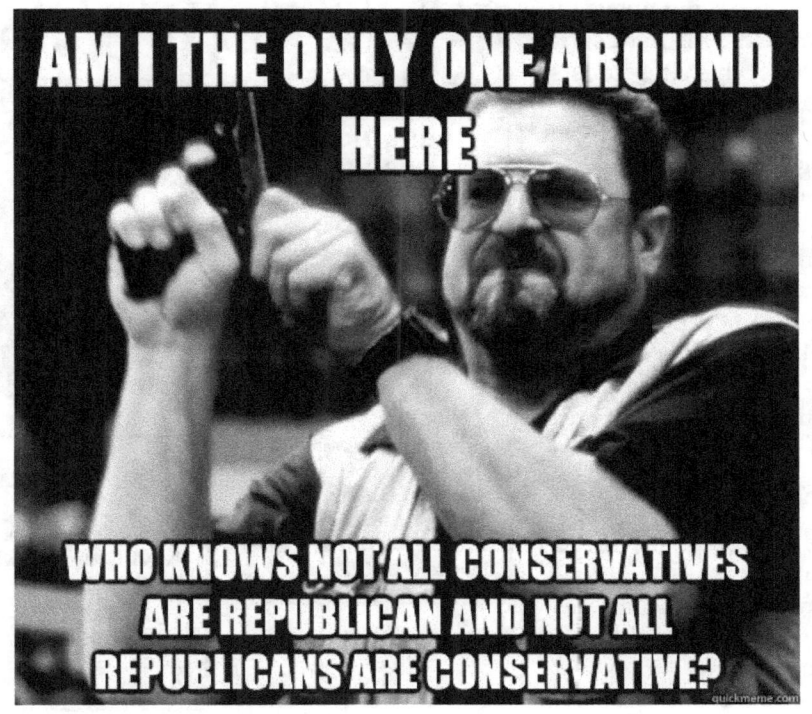

DONALD TRUMP BECOMES THE PRESUMPTIVE REPUBLICAN NOMINEE
In the GOP's Battle Against Hillary, Donald Mocks Her for "Feeling the Bern" From Sanders, Who Won't Give Up His Campaign

"UNHINGED, RANTING, & RAVING"
Ted Cruz is Banished to the GOP's "Elephant Graveyard" As Trump Triumphs in Indiana

DONALD WANTS TO KNOW:
What Was Ted Cruz's Father Doing With Lee Harvey Oswald?

"Running as Trump's Veep Would Be Like Buying a Ticket on the Titanic"
—Senator Lindsey Graham

On May 1, columnist Maureen Dowd released her summary of candidate Donald: "He exudes macho, wearing his trucker hat, retweeting bimbo cracks, swearing with abandon, and bragging about the size of his manhood, his crowds, his hands, his poll margins, his bank account, his skyscrapers, his steaks, and his beautiful wall. He and his pallies, Paul Manafort and Roger Stone, seem like a latter day Rat Pack, having a gas with tomatoes, twirls, and ring-a-ding ding."

As the month began, possible GOP vice presidential running mates were falling all over themselves, fleeing from invitations to be included with Donald on the Republican ticket.

"No chance," said John Kasich. Wisconsin Governor Scott Walker was said to have expressed a viscerally negative reaction to Donald. South Carolina Governor Nikki Haley bowed out without ever having been asked, as did Senator Jeff Flake of Arizona.

"*Hahahahahahahaha,*" wrote Sally Bradshaw, senior advisor to Jeb Bush.

Also indicating a complete lack of interest was Marco Rubio, Senator from Florida, although he's been known to change his mind.

Nonetheless, some potential candidates for the VP slot emerged. They included Chris Christie, Governor of New Jersey, and Senator Jeff Sessions of Alabama. Ben Carson said he might consider it.

From the beginning, most columnists had not taken Donald's candidacy seriously, claiming he'd be "buried" in early primaries by the likes of Scott Walker, Jeb Bush, and Rick Perry.

Of course, that didn't happen. Columnist Michael Walsh gave his forecast, claiming that Donald would be the GOP nominee "absent an alien invasion, the zombie apocalypse, or the sudden re-annexation of California by Mexico."

"Can he beat Hillary Clinton?" Walsh asked. "You're darn right he can."

RUNNING FOR COVER

Fearing disastrous consequences for their political futures, many politicians who otherwise might have been considered as candidates for Donald's vice presidential running mate reportedly went into hiding.

Ducking out were such prominent politicians as **Nikki Haley, Jeff Flake, Scott Walker, Marco Rubio,** and most definitely, **Jeb!.**

COULD IT BE NEWT?

The notoriously controversial former House Speaker **Newt Gingrich** would have been willing to run as Donald's Veep.

"If he needs me, it would be very hard for a patriotic citizen to say no."

TED CRUZ & THE INDIANA PRIMARY
Was it Custer's Last Stand? Or the Battle of the Alamo?

The fight to win the "red" [i.e., mostly Republican] state of Indiana suddenly became scalding hot and bitterly contentious. Cruz and Donald forgot about national issues and dug up every personal scandal that had ever been unearthed, using them as weapons in their attacks on each other.

At a rally, Cruz lambasted Donald as "an amoral narcissist and a pathological liar."

"Donald Trump is a serial philanderer and he boasts about it. I want everyone to think about your teenaged kids. The President of the United States talks about how great it is to commit adultery, how proud he is. He describes his battle with

venereal disease as his own 'personal Vietnam.' That's a quote, by the way, from The Howard Stern Show. Do you want to spend the next five years with your kids bragging about infidelity?"

Donald immediately zapped back with slurs about "Lyin' Cruz."

MEMORIES OF CAMELOT IN CUBA
AND ASSOCIATIONS WITH THE MURDER OF JFK

On May 2, the National Enquirer ran a frontpage exposé—"TED CRUZ FATHER LINKED TO JFK ASSASSINATION."

Rafael Cruz, now a pastor, was reported to have once been a supporter of the Cuban dictator Fidel Castro. But he fled Cuba in 1957 and later disavowed communism.

The tabloid hired photo experts to examine a photo reportedly of Rafael Cruz, which was snapped alongside JFK's assassin, Lee Harvey Oswald, in August of 1963, just months before the President was shot in Dallas. At the time, Oswald was working on behalf of a pro-Castro group, The Fair Play for Cuba Committee.

More than a half-century later, on the campaign trail in Indiana, Donald brought up the question: "What was Rafael Cruz doing with Lee Harvey Oswald?"

As voters went to the polls in Indiana, Cruz became almost unhinged, repeating, loudly, his familiar accusations: "Trump is a pathological liar. He doesn't know the difference between truth and lies. It's a pattern straight out of a psychology textbook. He accuses everyone of lying. He is utterly amoral, a narcissist at a level I don't think this country's ever seen. He's also a serial philanderer. His campaign can't run a lemonade stand."

Donald rejoined with: "Today's ridiculous outburst only proves what I've been saying for a long time. That Cruz does not have the temperament to be President of the United States. Wow, Lyin' Ted really went wacko today. Made all sorts of crazy charges. Not very presidential. Sad."

Seizing advantage, Donald Trump, Jr. said, "That was an impressive meltdown by Cruz. Desperate but impressive. Reminded me of my three-year-old coming off a sugar high."

Late on election night, after 93% of the states' precincts had submitted their tallies, it was announced that Donald had won the Indiana race. He had 54% of the vote, as compared to 37% for Cruz, with Kasich trailing at a paltry 8%.

Donald addressed his supporters with a victory speech at Trump Tower in Manhattan. Unlike Cruz, he showed a certain grace in his triumph: "I don't know if Cruz likes me or if he doesn't like me, but he was one hell of a competitor…a tough, smart guy. We're going to love each other."

Veteran GOP strategist Ed Rollins had predicted, "Indiana was Cruz's last stand. There are no more back doors at the Alamo. If Trump wins, you'll see the air go out of Cruz's balloon. You'll see people jump on the Trump bandwagon."

A national poll showed Donald having a two-point lead over Hillary, 41% to her 39%.

"I will defeat Crooked Hillary," he boasted.

In Indiana, after his defeat, Cruz announced, "I'm leaving the field. We gave it everything we got. But the voters chose another path. With a heavy heart, but with

This picture was dug up of **Lee Harvey Oswald,** the 1963 assassin of John F. Kennedy, and **Rafael Cruz,** the father of candidate Ted Cruz.

Cruz's campaign denounced the photo and article as "another garbage story."

"Trump is detached from reality," Cruz charged, "and his false, cheap, and meaningless comments every day indicate his desperation to get attention and a willingness to say anything to do so."

boundless optimism for the long-term future of our nation, we are suspending our campaign."

Then, in an clumsy attempt to reach for and embrace his wife, he accidentally jostled her with his elbow, another graceless moment in a graceless campaign.

Meanwhile, despite his horrible turnout, Kasich's campaign claimed that their leader was "still in the running"

On the Democratic front, upstart Bernie Sanders had beaten Hillary, sweeping to victory in Indiana and promising "more victories in the weeks to come."

Our favorite columnist, Linda Stasi, released her assessment of the Indiana primary under the headline "Even God could not help Cruz." Then she labeled him "a narcissist who had the balls to call Donald the ultimate narcissist."

As for Cruz's family circle, in a style evoking that of God himself Rafael Cruz had announced to his son's followers that "Jesus personally has anointed my son."

Stasi challenged John Boehner's label for Cruz as Lucifer. "Damien the Omen, son of Satan and a jackal, yes. Lucifer, no."

The columnist then noted that Carly Fiorina, named as Cruz's Vice Presidential running mate, was a bad omen herself. Moving away from the podium after announcing Cruz as "the next President of the United States," she fell off the stage, dropping faster than Cruz's chance at the nomination.

Cruz ignored the fallen, floundering diva, conspicuously failing to come to her rescue.

Some reporters speculated that Cruz lost the basketball-loving Hoosiers when he referred to a basketball hoop as a "ring."

During his abortive campaign attempts for his son, Rafael Cruz had claimed that "gay marriage is a socialist conspiracy" and that "Obama should be forcibly returned to Kenya."

As the results of the Indiana primary came in on May 3, Donald won that state's fifty-one delegates. The Indiana win gave him a delegate count of 1,047. He needed 1,237 to win, so the Indiana victory put him within striking distance of the nomination.

As the New York Daily News trumpeted on its frontpage: "Dearly beloved, we are gathered here today to mourn the GOP, a once-great political party, killed by the epidemic of Trump." It pictured an elephant in a coffin under the head: "REPUBLICAN PARTY: 1854-2016."

The only moderate in the GOP race, John Kasich, Governor of Ohio, also ended his long shot quest for the presidency on May 4, after the Indiana primary. He had portrayed himself "as the only adult in the GOP primary."

He ended his bid for the Republican nomination in Columbus, Ohio. "I have faith that the Lord will show me the way forward and fulfill the purpose of my life." He had presented himself as an optimistic candidate in a gloomy race where his rivals spoke of despair, and Cruz had warned that the nation was going over an "abyss"

Kasich had carried only one state, his own, Ohio.

On May 4, the day after the Indiana primary, Kate Bradshaw wrote: "Ted Cruz, the 'adorably' unlikable teabagger the Republican establishment pushed as a viable alternative to Trump, as it held its nose, dropped out after losing the Indiana primary Tuesday night. Trump was just the sideshow in a GOP clown car stuffed to the gills with nearly 20 others, but now he's the main character."

After Trump carried Indiana, *Time* magazine's Philip Elliot asked the big question: "Does he emerge as this century's Ronald Reagan, who remakes the party's image for a generation, or as someone more akin to Barry Goldwater, who lost 44 states in 1964?"

Donald himself released a pithy opinion: "If I was presidential, only about 20% of you would be here, because it would be boring as hell."

[*Apparently, he saw being unpredictable as an asset, shrewdly appreciating the rowdy nature of his rallies, where music from the Rolling Stones sometimes cranked away on the soundtrack.*

In May of 2016, in a statement to Time *magazine, a spokesperson for the band said, "The Rolling Stones have never given permission to the Trump campaign to use their songs and have requested that they cease all use immediately." The spokesperson went on to say that neither Trump nor anyone from his campaign had asked for permission to use the songs.*

Rolling Stones' songs played at Trump rallies had included "You Can't Always Get What You Want," "Sympathy for the Devil" and "Brown Sugar."

In February, one of Trump's campaign volunteers told a reporter from The New Yorker *that Trump had personally curated the playlist.*]

On May 26, it was revealed that a survey showed that Donald had already bagged the 1,237 delegates he needed to win the GOP nod.

In a delegate count, the Associated Press reported that Donald "was over the top" with 303 delegates at stake in the June 7 primaries. He'd become the presumptive nominee of the Republican Party.

He reacted to his good fortune by chiding Hillary "who can't close the deal," a reference

Mick Jagger—not the typical Republican.

to her ongoing, still inconclusive race with Bernie Sanders.

***

With Donald firmly ensconced as the presumptive GOP nominee, elements from his complicated past resurfaced to haunt him. He had played a supporting role in a 1989 Bo Derek movie, *Ghosts Can't Do It,* an enigmatically suggestive title.

A box office failure, the film was widely panned by movie critics. It did, however, sweep the Razzle Awards, winning trophies for "Worst Picture," "Worst Actress," and "Worst Director" of the Year. For his role in that film, Donald won a Razzle Award as "Worst Supporting Actor."

According to *The New York Times*, the plot "involves a main character dying and becoming a ghost, and his wife drowning a young man so that the spirit of her dead husband can inhabit his earthly body and engage in carnal pleasure—again—and also complete a business deal with Trump."

"Oih vey!" audiences said before staying away in droves.

Before Cruz bowed out of the race, he alerted his supporters that Donald had also inspired a character in Back to the Future II. Its screenwriter said that he based the character of "Biff Tannen" on Donald Trump—"a caricature of a braggadocious, arrogant buffoon who builds casinos with giant pictures of him wherever he looks."

HATE CRIMES INCREASE As Donald Steps Up the Pace of His Anti-Muslim Assaults

In early May, Georgetown University's Center for Muslim-Christian Understanding documented an upsurge in violence against Muslims in the United States. The crimes dated back to the end of 2015, the year in which Donald had demanded a ban on Muslims entering the United States.

This came as no surprise to President Obama, who spoke of the "threats and harassment Muslim Americans faced."

Cited were the murders of three university students in Chapel Hill, North Carolina. "Islamophobia now has lethal effects," the report claimed. Yet GOP polling showed that a large majority of his party's primary voters endorsed the Muslim ban.

Donald came under fire from London's newly elected Muslim mayor, Sadiq Khan. Son of a Pakistani bus driver, he had promised to be "a mayor for all Londoners."

Khan told reporters that he'd vote for Hillary if he were a U.S. citizen. He also stated that "Islam is perfectly compatible with Western values," although millions would disagree with that assessment.

Then he accused Donald of "playing into the hands of extremists. He is ignorant about Islam."

Donald stuck by his ban on Muslims entering the United States, although he said that he might make an exception for Khan, based on his election as

Donald Trump had a small supporting role in one of the worst films ever made, *Ghosts Can't Do It*, a so-called comedy starring **Bo Derek**, depicted above on the 1994 cover of *Playboy*.

As one reviewer wrote, "Trump purses his lips like a condescending sex offender. All two of his scenes are with Bo Derek, and he looks her right in the eye and vows to destroy her. In short, it's not his fault this movie sucks, but he doesn't make it any better."

Sadiq Khan, *(right)*, the newly elected Mayor of London, attacked Donald for threatening to bar Muslims from entering the United States.

Donald suggested he might make an exception for the Lord Mayor. But Khan responded, "I have no desire to be an exception."

London's mayor.

Khan responded, "I have no desire to be an exception."

Unintimidated by his critics, Donald renewed his attack: "I think Islam hates us," he told CNN's Anderson Cooper. "There is an unbelievable hatred of us. We can't allow people coming into this country who possess this hatred of us."

Donald then told Fox & Friends that he might ask New York's former mayor, Rudy Giuliani, to lead a terrorism commission that would block non-citizen Muslims from entering the United States.

"MEXICAN EX-PRES LOSES HIS COJONES"
—New York Daily News

Vicente Fox, former President of Mexico, once emphatically stated that his country would not "pay for that fucking wall."

But on May 5, he apologized. "If I offended you, I'm sorry," he said to the presumptive GOP nominee. He even invited Donald to Mexico to see "what our country is all about. Forgiveness is one of the greatest qualities that human beings have. It is the quality of a compassionate leader. You have to love thy neighbor."

No word emerged from the Trump camp regarding a possible visit South of the Border.

In Washington, Donald celebrated Cinco de Mayo and showed his "love for Hispanics by tweeting a photo of himself grinning over a faux-Mexicano dish while bragging about his business. At the Trump Tower Grill, he claimed that the chef made the best taco bowls around.

Vicente Fox, proud *Mexicano*. The former president of Mexico issued a public statement that his country would not "pay for that fucking wall." But he later apologized for the expletive he had included in his remark.

That led to press attacks that Fox "has no balls" or *cojones*, as they're called South of the Border.

The following day, it was revealed that even though Donald may "love Hispanics," he'd hired an Irish chef to make the taco bowls.

In the wake of the Trump posting, hordes poured into Trump Tower to sample the taco bowl. Before that onslaught, the dish had been featured only on Thursday.

The chef, reporters discovered, was a big white guy named Chris Divine, who claimed, "I'm as Irish as they come."

At the same time that Donald was tweeting expressions of his love for Hispanics, he sent a different message to bankrupt Puerto Rico: "DROP DEAD."

The presumptive GOP nominee didn't think America should bail out the little island nation staggering toward bankruptcy. [Technically, according to some experts, although the island territory is barred from declaring bankruptcy because of a quirk in U.S. law, the financial situation of its crushing debt was dire, indeed.]

"They have far too much debt. Don't forget. I'm the king of debt. I love debt," he told CNN.

Despite his bluster, he offered no solutions to the island's financial predicament, which had catalyzed massive unemployment, driving hordes of islanders to the U.S. mainland, especially to central Florida.

***

By now, more and more Republicans were denouncing their presumptive nominee. On May 5, Senator Ben Sasse of Nebraska called for someone to run against both Hillary and Donald, labeling them "dishonest liberals less popular than dumpster fires." Although insisting, "I'm not the guy," he pushed for a third party option to take on Donald.

"Why shouldn't America draft an honest leader who will focus on 70% solutions for the next four years? You know… an adult."

Sasse said he didn't want to be away from his young children. Most strategists claimed that at this point in the race, a third party run was "a mere pipe dream."

Looking like a "good ol redneck country boy from the wilds of Nebraska," as an Omaha reporter described him, Senator **Ben Sasse** didn't think either Donald or Hillary were suitable to be President of the United States.

Ever since Donald attacked **John McCain**, claiming he was not a war hero since he'd been captured, the Arizona senator made his disdain for "The Donald" known.

The 2008 GOP nominee announced that he was going to boycott the Republican convention.

John McCain, the senior U.S. Senator from Arizona who had been the GOP nominee in 2008, said he would not attend his party's convention. As justification for that radical decision, he cited his fears for his own chances at re-election: "If Donald Trump is at the top of the ticket, here in Arizona, with 30% of the vote being Hispanic, no doubt, this may be the race of my life."

On May 5, House Speaker Paul Ryan issued an extraordinary statement. The nation's highest-ranking Republican, third in line to step in as President, announced that he was "not ready" to endorse Donald. Ironically, he had already been designated as Chairman of the upcoming GOP convention in July in Cleveland, where Donald seemed likely to receive the nomination of the Republican Party.

Those who presumed to know what Ryan was thinking claimed that he viewed many of Donald's remarks as a "toxic brew."

Donald, within an hour, issued a biting rejoinder: "I am not ready to support Ryan's agenda. Perhaps in the future we can work together and come to an agreement about what is best for the American people."

On CNN, Ryan called for "a standard bearer who shares our principles."

[In modern times, a party nominee has never failed to gain the support of both the House Speaker and the Majority Leader of the Senate.]

Then, Donald issued a threat to the Speaker, warning Ryan, "You'll pay a big price if you don't support me."

"It'll be a hot time in the old town today," predicted a newscaster, in reference to the escalating tensions between Donald and key figures within the party that seemed barely able to contain him.

On May 12, Donald was flying to Washington to "woo the reluctant bride," a reference to Ryan.

Many editorial writers described Ryan's dilemma. He faced a splintering GOP with his arch-conservative politics in peril.

Complicating matters, it was speculated that Ryan had a long-term plan to run for President himself in 2020. Forecasters had suggested that during that upcoming election cycle, he might face off against either Ted Cruz and/or Marco Rubio.

Ryan might also have to face Ben Sasse, a "NEVER TRUMP" kingpin. A female staffer who works for Congress gave her opinion. "Ryan looks like that jerk in high school who begged you for a date, whereas Sasse is your real boyfriend."

After meeting with House members in reference to the screams emanating from Republicans about what was described as the impending civil war within the Party, , Ryan said, "To pretend we're unified as a party would lead us to go into the fall at half sprint."

In response, Donald defiantly told the press, "I have no intention of reinventing myself for Mr. Ryan," and announcing that he had "a mandate" to lead the Republican Party.

Then he compared his campaign razzmatazz to the showmanship of Broadway openings and championship baseball games.

"Success begot success and it would be foolish of me to change my behavior now. A lot of voters, millions of them, want Donald Trump to be Donald Trump."

Guy Cecil, chief strategist of Priorities USA, the Super PAC supporting Hillary said, "Trump's rally rants and Twitter brawls are meant to dominate media coverage and public conversation, so that Democratic challengers have less space to break through all the noise. He doesn't want people to talk about his record or positions."

"I have been victorious in twenty-nine states, most recently in Nebraska and West Virginia," Donald said. "People are tired of trade deals that are ripping our jobs apart and taking their wages."

Did the Washington frost eventually melt between Trump and Paul Ryan?

In a chilly meeting, they confronted each other. Donald, however, did not emerge from their meeting with an endorsement. Ryan referred to Donald as "warm and gentle." (Perhaps he'd met an imposter.)

In the wake of their meeting, he told the press, "A process of reconciliation is underway." It was reported that behind closed doors, Donald had backed down on his threat to remove Ryan as Chairman of the Republican National Convention in July.

In a wishy-washy statement, Ryan said, "It is important that we discuss the principles that tie us together."

Ryan and Donald met for 45 minutes, with Reince Priebus "as their chaperone."

One aide reported, "Paul and Donald did not come to blows."

Anti-Trump protesters in Washington confronted the line of cars hauling Donald and his aides to his meeting with Ryan. Donald faced a cabal of undocumented aliens, a coven of women from the protest group Codepink, and a lone man holding a "RABBIS AGAINST TRUMP" sign. Many brandished signs asserting "ISLAMOPHOBIA IS UNAMERICAN."

Throughout America, this sign appeared on various lawns of Republicans, Democrats, and Independents alike.

It was a voter's way of expressing disgust at all Washington politicians, most notably Hillary Clinton and Donald Trump.

***

He might have been holding his nose, but Reince Priebus, the embattled, world-weary Chairman of the Republican National Committee, then launched a defense of the GOP's most likely candidate.

Appearing on CBS's Face the Nation, he said: "Donald Trump has rewritten the traditional playbook of politics. And I don't know if anyone else could have pulled off what he's pulled off over the past year." He suggested that voters didn't really care about his boorish behavior toward women, or his refusal to release his tax returns.

"Voters only care that Trump will create an earthquake in the nation's capital," Priebus continued. Then he admitted that it was "a bit odd" that Trump had pretended to be a public relations rep named "John Miller" and, having adopted that as a persona, had talked about his own exploits, sexual or otherwise. "This is not a big issue with the electorate. All these stories that come out—and they come out every couple weeks…People just don't care."

Columnist Mike Lupica summed it up. "The whole world can scream about prevarication—or even past fornication—and it only makes his supporters scream louder."

Another columnist, Richard Cohen, wrote: "I have concluded that Priebus has no pride, no shame, and, almost certainly, no future. After Donald Trump loses the presidency, the name Priebus will, like Quisling, take on a separate meaning. Poor Priebus bobbed and weaved his way from TV studio to TV studio, on May 15, on a trudge of abasement, a rite of shame."

Donald later commented on his meeting with Ryan. "We talked about the success I've had. Paul said to me that he has never seen anything like it because I'm a non-politician and I beat very successful politicians. He was really fascinated by how I'd won. I said, 'It's just like I have good ideas and I've bonded with people and my people are very loyal.' They will stay through thick and thin, whereas the people that support Little Marco and Lyin' Cruz wouldn't. And if Jeb sneezed, they'd leave."

"CROOKED HILLARY" VS. "DANGEROUS DON"
It Evolved into the Ugliest Political Race of Modern Times

In a May 7 editorial, *The New York Times* wrote: "There's ample reason to expect Clinton vs. Trump to be the ugliest, most cringeworthy contest of the modern era. It promises to be a half year long slog through the marital troubles, personal peccadilloes, financial ambitions, social media habits, and physical appearances of 'Dangerous Don' and 'Crooked Hillary,' two labels that the campaign and their allies are already deploying."

JFK never admitted to marital infidelity, and Bill Clinton had denied everything. But long before he ran for President, Donald, on The Howard Stern Show and in other interviews had admitted to "erotic escapades."

Columnist Frank Bruni wrote: "Trump isn't just any libertine. He's a retro rascal, a throwback to an era and ethic of big suits, paneled boardrooms, thick billfolds, and buxom arm candy. In the context of the pansexual, gender-fluid, Molly-popping millennials who make conservatives shudder, he's a musky whiff of nostalgia, a stubborn ember of patriarchy, a vintage stripe of a sybarite. He's promiscuity steeped in chauvinism and misogyny: More old-fashioned, and more comforting."

***

From a stage, in a swing through the Pacific Northwest during the second week of May, Donald asked a rally in Washington State if they'd noticed how much "nicer" he'd become. Then he ridiculed Senator Lindsey Graham as "a total dope who is constantly on television."

He then proceeded to trash Hillary: "She's married to a man who hurt many women. Bill Clinton was impeached for lying about what happened with a woman. Hillary treated these abused women horribly."

Danielle Allen, a political theorist at Harvard, said, "Trump wants to rumble with Hillary in a battle of the sexes because he believes that it will be losing terrain for her. This is the terrain on which the NEVER TRUMP campaigners largely fought him, and they failed."

"I look forward to debating this crooked woman politician," Donald said.

The snarling candidate also attacked "liberal darling Elizabeth Warren: She's goofy, a fraud, and weak and ineffective. I hope corrupt Hillary chooses her as a running mate. I will defeat both of them."

Warren shot back. "There's more enthusiasm for Trump among leaders of the KKK than from leaders of his own political party. You can beat a bully—not by tucking tail and running, but by holding your ground."

Columnist Maureen Dowd asked Donald about his Twitter feud with Senator Warren.

"You mean, Pocahontas?" Donald asked.

[Warren had claimed that she has Native American blood.]

DONALD AND THE PINOCCHIO QUOTIENT
Politico Revealed a Misstatement of Facts At Least Once Every Five Minutes, Yet Polls Revealed That Trump Fans Seem to Universally Hate Hillary

On the campaign trail, Donald consistently accused Ted Cruz and Hillary of being liars. But Politico examined one week of his speeches and found that on the average, he misstated the facts at least once every five minutes.

Since his designation as the GOP nominee, polls showed him running even with his likely challenger, Hillary, who couldn't shake Bernie Sanders from her tail. A Reuters/Ipsos poll placed her at 41% among likely voters, Donald at 40%.

By now, an alarming trend had surfaced: The majority of voters didn't trust either candidate. Some polls revealed that both of them were among the most hated candidates ever to seek the presidency.

As a means of breaking this standoff, as part of a strategy cooked up from somewhere within Donald's campaign, he decided to not only attack Hillary, but to zero in on Bill Clinton's widely known charges of rape and sexual assault.

In an attack ad, what Juanita Broaddrick had alleged against Bill Clinton in 1998 (about a rape that allegedly occurred in 1978) were resuscitated.

In addition, the charges of sexual harassment from Kathleen Willey, a former White House volunteer, were also fanned back into flames. Accompanied the "news" were photos of the former President sucking on a cigar. (One of the more revolting charges aired by Monica Lewinsky was, as a result of those references to cigars, also revived.)

The pro-Trump ad asked, "Is Hillary really protecting women?"

"Nobody in this country was worse than Bill Clinton with women," Donald charged. "He was a disaster. Hillary was a total enabler."

Of all the candidates running for President, Donald was often awarded with as many as "**Four Pinocchios**" for his statements (and mis-statements) at various rallies.

Max Boot, senior fellow at the Council on Foreign Relations, wrote: "All politicians spin and twist facts to some extent, but Trump's lies are so epic and recurring as to put him in a whole other universe of dissembling—a place where facts are meaningless and the truth can be anything he wants it to be at that particular moment."

DONALD ENDORSES THE NRA
"Gun Nuts Back Nut"
—New York Daily News

On May 20 in Louisville, Kentucky, Donald warned that Hillary would be a great risk if she were elected President. "She would let violent criminals out of prison and disarm law-abiding citizens."

Then he gleefully accepted the endorsement of the notorious National Rifle Association.

Although he had not been a staunch supporter of guns in the past, he stated his new position, claiming that the November election would be a referendum on the Second Amendment.

"Crooked Hillary is the most anti-gun, anti-Second Amendment candidate ever to run for office."

In January, he had called for "ending gun-free zones in school," a position widely denounced as "extremely dangerous." Some reporters called it "time for a playground shootout."

Donald told an NRA rally that he had a permit to carry a gun. "Nobody knows that," he said, "Boy, would I surprise someone if they hit Trump," speaking of himself in the third person. "Heartless Hillary wants to disarm America's grandmothers, leaving them de-

fenseless against murderers and rapists."

Donald left the NRA convention after promising its members that he would repeal Obama gun controls "in the first hour that I am the President."

He also spoke of his big game-hunting sons, Donald Jr. and Eric, "who are both avid hunters and gun owners."

His sons had recently been photographed with their (dead) big game trophies in Africa within a context that evoked the bravado of super-macho Ernest Hemingway in the days prior to his suicide.

"My boys have so many rifles, so many guns, that even I get a little concerned, "Donald said.

He attacked limitations on gun control. "It will never stop an armed killer, a rapist, a genocide tyrant, or terrorist mass murderer with a rolled-up newspaper."

Right-wing NRA boss Wayne LaPierre took the occasion to "belch fire about transgender bathrooms," which in some way he viewed as a terrible threat to all those gun-toting he-men.

JERSEY BOY, CHRIS CHRISTIE
Trump's "Mister Big"

During the GOP debates, no other candidate had been as effective in attacking Hillary as Chris Christie, the governor of New Jersey. It came as no surprise on May 9 when Donald named him as director of his transition team. Headlines announced Christie as "TRUMP'S MISTER BIG," referring, of course, to the rotund governor's massive waistline.

There was speculation that this was the first step to maneuver Christie into position for a top job in Trump's post-election administration, in the event that he would win the November election.

Rumors raged that Christie might be designated as either his vice presidential running mate, or else be named as U.S. Attorney General during the formation of Trump's post-victory cabinet.

Then another potential vice-presidential candidate signaled his interest in running as Donald's VEEP.

On May 22, billionaire Mark Cuban, owner of the Dallas Mavericks, a self-described Independent, revealed that he'd be amenable to being named a vice presidential running mate to either Hillary or Donald.

"Absolutely," he told NBC's *Meet the Press*.

"I think Donald has a real chance to win, and that scares a lot of people. But what's scary about it to me is that you can see him now trying to do what he thinks is right to unify the party."

Cuban also said that he was considering a run for the White House himself one day.

***

Christie's hastily defined duties involved assessing and assembling a team of experts on domestic and foreign policy, and the setup of the nucleus of a new administration to replace the one presently administering the White House.

Naming Christie to the transition team involved the Trump clan in some very awkward moments. On the same team was Jared Kushner, Ivanka's Orthodox Jewish husband, Donald's son-in-law.

A decade before, in his capacity as the U.S. Attorney in New Jersey, Christie had put Jared's father in jail. Charles Kushner had pleaded guilty to eighteen felonies after hiring a prostitute to seduce his brother-in-law as a means of blackmailing him in 2005.

At the time, Christie had attacked Kushner for his "outrageous criminal conduct" and had sought the maximum penalty behind bars.

"Oh, to be a fly on the wall when Jared and Fatso came together in the same room," said a Trump aide who didn't want to be named.

Donald, speaking of his son-in-law, said, "He's a whiz in real estate, but lately, I think he's showing more interest in politics. Perhaps one day he—and not Bernie Sanders—will be the first Jewish President of the United States. Ivanka would be the greatest of all First Ladies."

Hoping to win supporters, Donald became a political chameleon, reversing his positions on the minimum wage and higher taxes for the rich.

Like father, not like son: **Charles Kushner** (left) ended up in jail. Not so his son **Jared** (right).

In an Orthodox Jewish ceremony, Jared married Ivanka and became the father of her three children and the son-in-law of Donald Trump.

When Jared learned that Donald was considering Chris Christie as a possible Veep running mate, he was horrified. It was Christie, then attorney general of New Jersey, who had sent Jared's father, Charles, to jail.

On November 10, 2015, on the Fox Business debate, he'd said: "Taxes are too high, wages too high. We're not going to be able to compete against the world. I hate to say it, but we have to leave it the way it is."

But on May 8, 2016, on Meet the Press, he said: "I don't know how people make it on $7.25 an hour. I would like to see an increase of some magnitude. But I'd rather leave it to the states."

In September of 2015, he outlined his tax plan. "Highest tax bracket would be reduced from 39.5% to 25%. Americans will get a simpler tax code with four brackets: 0%, 10%, 20%, or 25% instead of the current seven."

But also on May 8, speaking to This Week, he said, "I am willing to pay more, and you know what? The wealthy are willing to pay more."

As a means of addressing Donald's wavering policies on amending the tax code and coping with the deficit, on May 22, Maya MacGuineas, president of the Committee for a Responsible Federal Budget, released an editorial with some alarming statistics:

"Donald Trump has promised to pay off the debt in eight years. That would require $28 trillion in savings over ten years. He has also promised to balance the budget, which would require a still hefty $8 trillion in savings. There's a big problem with these promises: His plans to date would cost—not save—$12 trillion. His plans so far are utterly unworkable. There is no painless way to get rid of our debt."

[The United States' debt stands currently at 75% of the GDP. That is the highest it's been at any other time other than World War II. The debt, experts agree, is expected to grow to just under 86% of the GDP by 2026, exceeding the size of the entire American economy within the next 20 years.]

ENRAGING GREENPEACE
Donald Denies Climate Change and Trivializes the Environment

In a May 24 frontpage exposé, the New York Daily News ran a story headlined "EARTH, WIND, & LIAR"

"Trump plays GOP for suckers—calls climate change bullshit, then submits plans for a wall to protect his golf course in Ireland from global warming," the paper claimed.

Previously, Donald had defined climate change as "a con job, or else a fiendish plot by the Chinese."

But in Ireland, it was announced that he wanted to build a two-mile-long seawall at his golf resort to keep out rising tides. Rising sea levels caused by climate change had unleashed storms that had battered the Irish Coast where sat Trump International Golf Links and Hotel in County Clare. Resort officials had said that the beach had been disappearing at the rate of about three feet a year because of rising waters.

**

Hoping to arouse passions in chilly North Dakota, Donald flew into Bismarck, the heart of that region of the country's oil and gas boom. At a rally, he called for "more fossil fuel drilling and few environmental regulations."

He also vowed to cancel the Paris Climate Change Agreement, which committed nearly every nation to curb climate change.

He also vowed to rescind Obama's signature climate change rules and revive construction of the Keystone XL pipeline, which would bring petroleum from Canada's oil sands to the refineries of Texas and Louisiana's Gulf Coast.

In another switch, Donald turned to the very reluctant Republican Party to raise money for the upcoming fall election. Up to now, or so he claimed, he had spent $40 million of his own money on the primaries, although that was much disputed.

He claimed that he would need $1.5 billion as a war chest for the electoral battles to come. For that bundle, he would need fat-cat GOP donors—"no more self-financing."

Many of the major-league donors who had financed Mitt Romney's 2012 run privately told associates, "We're sitting this one out."

MAKING UP IS HARD TO DO
In a Tepid Resolution of Their Feud, Megyn Goes Soft On Donald

During a broadcast on May 17, Fox's TV anchor, Megyn Kelly, and Donald tried to make up…sort of. Some reporters called it "a lovefest," but it really wasn't. Body image experts claimed that both of them artfully concealed it, but they obviously held each other in contempt.

The interview was her first sitdown with Donald since the now notorious August GOP debate, when she had grilled him about "vile remarks he'd made about women." The May 17 interview itself was too tepid to generate many headlines.

Donald still insisted that her original question was unfair. "I was caught off guard because I'd never actually debated before. I don't really blame you because you're doing your thing, but from my standpoint, I don't have to like it."

She pressed him about any regrets he might have had.

"I could have done certain things differently…I could have maybe used different language in a couple of instances. If I hadn't fought back in the way I fought back, I don't think I would have been successful," he said.

In a statement not confirmed, it was reported that after leaving the interview, Donald said, "I think Kelly is just using me to gain more exposure. With my friend Barbara Walters retiring, Kelly's trying to become the next Barbara Walters."

For the most part, Kelly got bad reviews, including an attack from Jennifer Rubin, writing for the *Washington Post.* "She wasn't newsy. It was the sort of gauzy, non-confrontational and unrevealing celebrity interview. In essence, she conceded that Trump had won in her feud with him. Kelly now risks becoming yet another chess piece in Trump's game of intimidation."

REPUBLICANS COALESCE AROUND DONALD
But Popularity Polls Rank Lice and Dumpster Fires Ahead of Both Candidates

Hillary wasn't the only one firing at Donald. During a commencement address at Rutgers University, Obama labeled many of his plans "just plain stupid," decrying the anti-intellectual tone coming from his Republican enemies. "Ignorance is not a virtue. It's not cool not to know what you're talking about."

From the 50,000 people in the audience, Obama drew raucous applause when he said, "Building walls won't change the world, which is more interconnected than before. When you hear someone longing for the good old days, take it with a grain of salt."

He was referring to the time when homosexuals were subject to arrest for being gay, and when civil rights were denied to African Americans, and when women, for the most part, were confined to the kitchen.

In another development, the always outspoken congressman, Long Island's Peter King, wanted to break up the "bromance" between Donald and Vladimir Putin.

On CBS's Face the Nation, King publicly begged Donald to end his infatuation with the Russian dictator. "I'm supporting Trump, but I still have real questions with him as far as national security is concerned."

Facing the inevitability of a Trump nomination in July, many very conservative Republicans, both individuals and groups, were slowly coming around to lend their support. When faced with a choice of Donald or Hillary, many adamantly supported Donald all the way.

As Penny Nance, President of Concerned Women for America put it, "Trump is not my first choice. He's not my second choice. But any concerns I have about him pale in contrast to Hillary Clinton."

Privately, many Republicans, not going on record, said, "I would prefer the Bitch of Buchenwald to Hillary Clinton," naming the Nazi matron of horror who made lampshades out of human skin.

More and more, GOP members were starting to coalesce around their presumptive nominee. However, many qualified their support, saying they did not agree with all of his positions, such as gay rights and abortion rights.

Perhaps the most bizarre poll ever taken, a real eye-popper—revealed that Americans would choose lice over having Trump as President. In popularity rankings, he ranked along with such stomach churners as root canals, traffic jams, and jury duty. In a Public Policy polling survey, voters had a higher opinion of used car salesmen.

Donald's unfavorable rating stood at a whopping 61%. However, the news wasn't all bad for him. He won out over hemorrhoids.

Those who still had a favorable view of Donald went 65% for the theory that Obama was a Muslim. Only 7% agreed that Bible-thumping Rafael Cruz (Ted's father) had been involved in the assassination of JFK. One of the four voters with favorable views of Donald held the view that Supreme Court Justice Antonin Scalia had been murdered.

Occasionally, amid the whirlpool of publicity generated by Donald, Ivana occasionally spoke her mind.

As the mother of three of his children [Donald Jr., Ivanka, and Eric], she said, "The campaign is very hard for them because they all have families," she told the Fashion Institute of Technology. "Don Jr. has five kids and a wife; and he has to be on the campaign trail. Ivanka has three kids. She just gave birth to another baby. And Eric has a wife. It's very, very stressful for them, because they have to follow Donald and support him."

Ivana said she didn't know about Donald's grandchildren, whose ages ranged from eight months to eight years. "They are very young, they understand their grandfather is very important and wants to make a difference, but I am not sure what they think otherwise."

***

Donald's campaign and his missteps made him vulnerable to satire, as columnists devoted oceans of ink to mocking him.

Thomas L. Friedman wrote: "OK, it's easy to pick on his foreign policy. But just because he recently referred to the attack on the World Trade Center as happening on 7/11—which is a convenience store—instead of 9/11, and just because he held 'a major event' in Russia two or three years ago—The Miss Universe contest, which was a 'big, big, incredible event'—doesn't make him unqualified. I'm sure you can learn a lot schmoozing with Miss Argentina. You can also learn a lot eating at the International House of Pancakes. Perhaps he never understood Arab politics until he ate hummus—or was it Hamas?"

***

In May, despite increased pressure, and despite having boasted that he paid "the lowest possible tax rate," Donald steadfastly continued to refuse to release his tax returns.

On Good Morning America, he promised to release his tax returns after they were audited. "You'll learn very little from my returns," he claimed. He told ABC host George Stephanopoulos "My taxes are none of your business. You'll see it when I release them."

If he doesn't release his returns, he will be the first presidential nominee in a half-century who refused to do so. Ted Cruz claimed, "He won't release his returns because they will reveal his business dealings with the Mob."

As May moved on, the attacks on Donald continued. The Wall Street Journal, in an exposé, claimed that despite Donald's claim of being worth $10 billion, he didn't have enough liquid assets to self-finance the fall election. The paper wrote, "His pretax income in 2016 is likely to be about $160 million."

A spokesperson for Trump denied the WSJ's assessment. "It did not take into account cash held by Trump properties."

***

Near the end of May, Donald was on the campaign trail in California. He told a raucous and wildly cheering crowd in Fresno that "I can't stand to hear Hillary screaming into the microphone."

Once again, the police had to escort hecklers from the auditorium. Outside, protesters clashed with Trump loyalists.

"Hillary is a disaster," he told the partisan audience. "She has bad judgment. That was said by Bernie Sanders. He's given me some of my best lines. Crazy Bernie charged that she wasn't qualified to be President. Do you think Hillary looks presidential?"

The crowd responded by roaring its disapproval of her.

***

During the course of May, speculation briefly focused on "the debate that never happened," despite many headlines that trumpeted: "**TRUMP'S 'BERNING' DESIRE TO DEBATE.**"

Trump demanded that the networks shell out as much as $15 million for charity before he'd agree to a showdown with Bernie Sanders.

"Bernie and I would get high ratings in a big arena somewhere," Donald said. "And we could have a lot of fun."

"We are ready to debate Trump, and I hope he doesn't chicken out," said Sanders spokesman Jeff Weaver.

Hillary was skeptical, publicly doubting whether "The Donald" and "Giveaway Bernie" would ever confront one another in a one-on-one debate.

As it happened, the lady was right.

But even though the energy behind the "non debate" fizzled out, Donald relentlessly egged Sanders on, daring him to run as an independent.

"Of course he'd say that," Hillary responded. "I think Ted Cruz should run as a third-party candidate, Marco Rubio as a fourth-party candidate, and John Kasich as a fifth-party candidate."

The Trump camp was in a jubilant mood as a fourth national survey, conducted by the Washington Post and NBC/Wall Street Journal, positioned Trump at 43% and Hillary at 46%, respectively The numbers revealed on 11% surge toward Donald since the results of the previous survey had been announced in March.

In contrast, polls continued to show that many Americans (57%) seemed to dislike both candidates with equally intense fervor.

The same polls showed Bernie Sanders trouncing Donald 54% to 39%.

Perhaps Sanders summed up the dilemma with the greatest precision. As he stated during an interview with ABC News Sunday, "We need a campaign, an election coming up, which does not have two candidates who are really very, very strongly disliked."

THE GRANDEST OLD PARTY ON EARTH
FANTASTIC FEATS!
MAGNIFICENT SPECIMENS
THE WORLD FAMOUS GOP
1860

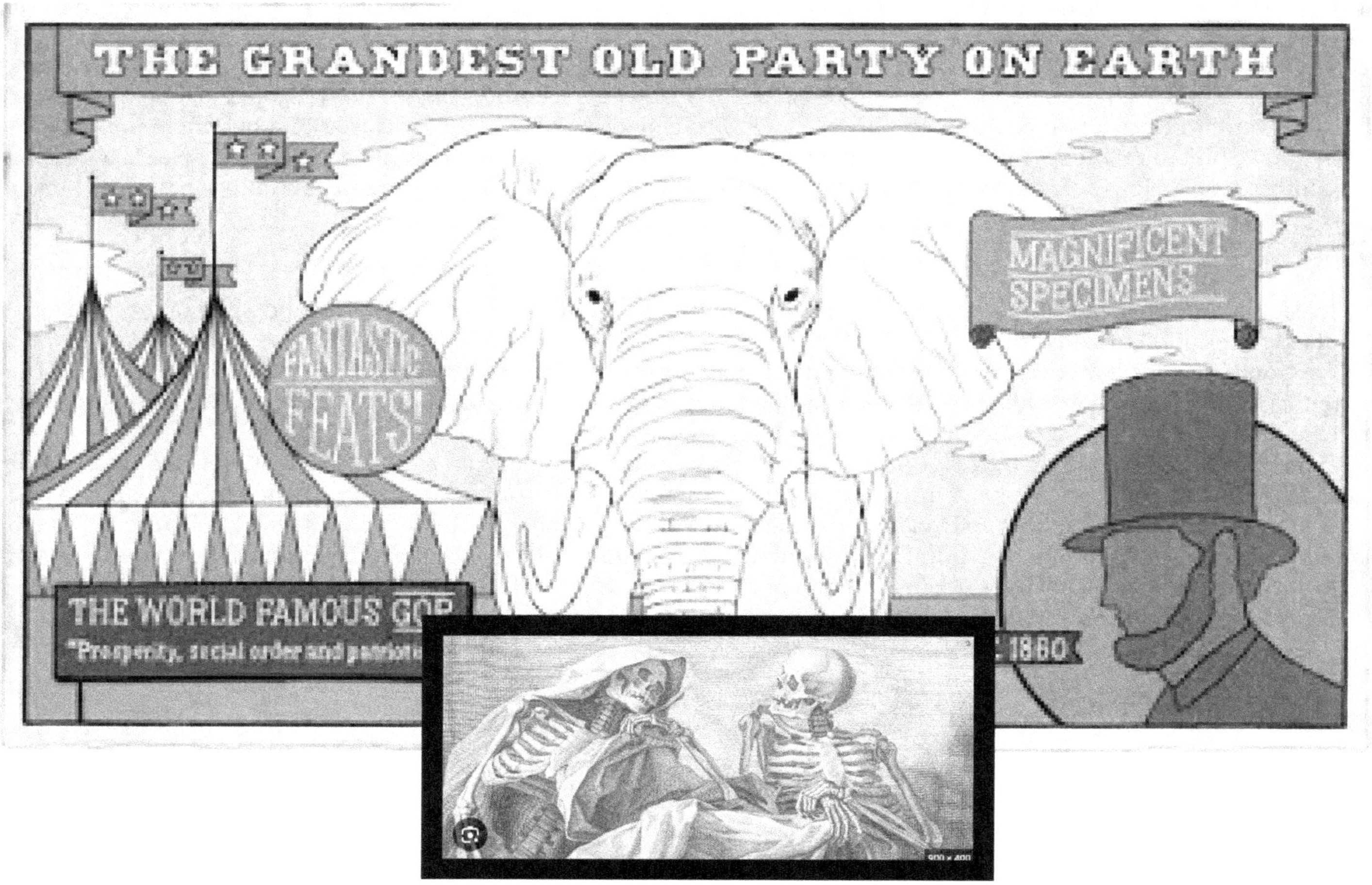

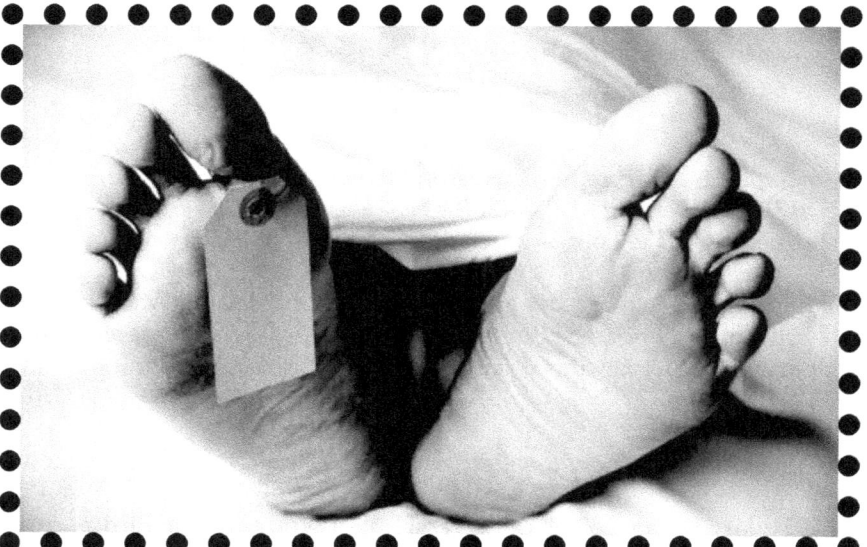

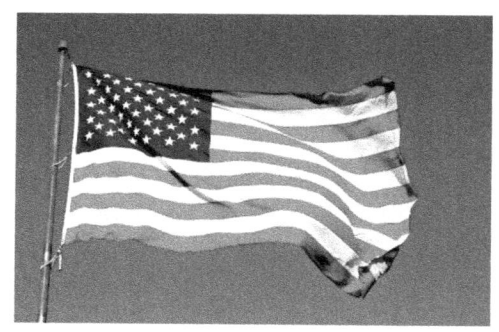

Chapter Fourteen
June and early July, 2016

"HILLARY CLINTON MAY BE THE MOST CORRUPT PERSON EVER TO RUN FOR PRESIDENT"

—Donald Trump

DONALD FIRES HIS CAMPAIGN MANAGER
Ivanka Tells Dad "It's Him (Corey Lewandowski) or Me!"

AN ASSASSINATION ATTEMPT
On Donald Is Blocked By Policeman

June got off to a bad start for Donald Trump, as the lawsuit against his Trump University entered another phase. Judge Gonzalo P. Curiel of the United District Court ordered that documents related to the case be unsealed. That led to unwelcome headlines, some calling the school "SCREW U." Others announced "HOW 'SCHOOL' SOLD TRUMP SNAKE OIL."

The presidential candidate was fighting a California lawsuit in which his school venture was charged with misleading thousands of students who paid up to $35,000 for seminars to learn about his real estate investment strategies.

Documents unsealed revealed that one enticement "script coercion" read: "Do you enjoy seeing everyone else but yourself in their dream house and driving their cars with huge checking accounts? Those people saw an opportunity and didn't make excuses, like what you're doing now."

At a rally on May 27 in San Diego, Donald had attacked the case's presiding judge. "I have a judge who is a hater of Donald Trump. He was appointed by Barack Obama, and I believe he is a Mexican."

The son of Mexican parents, Curiel had been born in Indiana, making him an American citizen.

Legal scholars claimed that by impugning the honesty of the judge in a pending case, Donald could be held for contempt of court.

The promoters of Trump U. told customers that they should "max out" their credit cards to pay the high tuition fees.

The California lawsuit added to Donald's legal woes. At the time, he was also being sued for issues associated with Trump University in New York. That state's Attorney General, Eric Schneiderman, had filed a $40 million suit against Donald in 2013, alleging that the billionaire swindled more that 5,000 students through his school.

In one of the documents, instructors were told how to deal with students who complain about the cost of "tuition." Remind them that Trump is the BEST!" the document instructs.

The controversial for-profit university had been shuttered since 2010. In the ensuing months and at other rallies, Donald continued to attack Curiel, bringing up his "Mexican heritage."

In court testimony, former Trump U managers testified that the business school relied on high pressure sales tactics, hired unqualified instructors, made deceptive "get-rich quick claims, and exploited vulnerable students of varying ages." One struggling couple was urged to charge $35,000 on credit cards, even though it would endanger their economic future.

The "University" had been established in 2005, with Donald owning 93 percent of it.

His lawyers fought back, claiming that complaints were emanating from only a small number of former students. "The vast majority of pupils gave us positive reviews," Donald claimed.

At the time of the Trump U documents release, Donald, during the final days of May, unleased a vitriolic attack on the media, who had been "pestering me with questions about veterans. He called an ABC reporter "a sleaze."

In January, in a feud with Fox, he opted to boycott the GOP debate, which had led to lower ratings for the network. In lieu of attending the debate, he participated in a competing event, a televised fund-raiser nearby, where he announced that he had raised more than $6 million (a sum that included, he said, a personal donation of $1 million) for veterans.

After an investigation, the *Washington Post* reported that he had not made the charitable donation. To show that he had, he produced a photocopy of a check he'd written. It was suggested by many reporters that Donald had been "forced to make the belated donation" after his failure to do so had been exposed in the press.

For a brief time, **Gonzalo P. Curiel** became the most controversial judge in America.

Donald Trump accused him of a "conflict of interest" presiding over a Trump University Class Action Lawsuit because of his Mexican heritage.

He was born in Indiana to Mexican immigrants.

***

In early June, it was revealed that two minor third and fourth-party candidates might tip the outcome of the incredibly close election. They included Jill Stein, who was running as the Green Party candidate; and former New Mexico governor, Gary Johnson, the Libertarian hopeful.

The question undecided was if the involvement of either or both candidates would benefit Donald or Hillary. Johnson was running with another governor, William Weld of Massachusetts. Donald attacked Johnson's running mate, suggesting that "he hits the bottle."

***

Speaking at a Democratic rally in San Diego, Hillary approached the podium with guns blazing, all of them aimed at Donald. She claimed that electing him President would be a "historic mistake." She charged that he was "hopelessly unprepared and temperamentally unfit to be commander-in-chief."

"He is a reckless, childish, and uninformed amateur, who has played at the game of global stagecraft. This is not someone who should ever have the nuclear codes. It's not hard to imagine Donald Trump leading us into a war just because somebody got under his thin skin."

He was sending nasty tweets about her even as she spoke. "Bad performance by Crooked Hillary Clinton," he tweeted. "She doesn't even look presidential. A terrible performance…pathetic."

Columnist Paul Krugman ridiculed Donald on the same day that Hillary attacked him: "No doubt Trump hates environmental protection in part for the usual reasons. But there's an extra layer of venom to his pro-pollution stances that is both personal and mind-bogglingly petty. He has repeatedly denounced restrictions intended to protect the ozone layer because he claims they're the reason his hair spray doesn't work as well as it used to. The Republicans are rallying around this rich guy who worries about his hairdo."

Around this time, Donald was in California, addressing a rally in San Jose that turned violent. As Trump supporters filed into the auditorium, some were pelted with eggs and attacked with heavy objects. Victims showed off their gashes before photographers. Water balloons were thrown, as steel barriers were toppled. Cops in riot gear prevented a full scale attack.

On CBS's *Face the Nation*, Donald admitted that he not only would consider a Mexican judge prejudiced against him, but he also feared bias if the judge were Muslim. He claimed that Judge Curiel should recuse himself from the Trump University case.

Even fellow Republicans, such as the usually friendly Newt Gingrich, claimed that Donald's comments about judges "is one of his worst mistakes yet."

Speaker Paul Ryan said, "I completely disagree with Trump's comments about Curiel."

Mitch McConnell said, "Trump should be working on unifying the party, not on settling scores and grudges."

One lawyer, who did not want to be named, said, "Donald is right. What is all this protest? Of course, judges are some of the most biased people in America—take Clarence Thomas, for instance. Some judges in the South have made their intolerance for homosexuals or African Americans all too obvious."

Even though he'd just attacked Donald for his comments about the Mexican judge, news leaked out on June 3 that Ryan had finally came around and endorsed Donald, although seemingly with great reluctance. "I feel confident that he would help us turn the ideas in our agenda into laws. He would help other people's lives. That's why I'm voting for him this fall."

Ryan said that "Trump's Mexican judge rant is the definition of racist, but I still support him."

HILLARY MAKES HISTORY
JUST AS HER GOP RIVAL FACES HEADLINES LABELING HIM AS "DEADBEAT DON"

Monday, June 6, was a date that will live in American history. Hillary Clinton became the first woman to capture the presidential nomination of a major political party.

After a bruising fight with Bernie Sanders, who was still refusing to abandon the race, she appeared on the brink of an unprecedented moment.

She clenched the Democratic nomination with the support of hundreds of superdelegates. The Associated Press was the first to declare that she had reached the golden number of 2,383 needed to secure the nomination. Advisers to Sanders took a dim view of the AP tally.

A native of North Dakota, **Gary Johnson** was the Libertarian Party nominee for President in the 2016 election.

Starting as a door-to-door handyman, he developed a multi-million-dollar construction firm.

He became the fiscally conservative Governor of New Mexico in 1994 where he was known as "Governor Veto."

THE STEINWAY:

BY SPLITTING THE VOTE, DID SHE SABOTAGE HILLARY'S BID FOR THE PRESIDENCY?

Born in Chicago to Russian Jewish parents, **Jill Stein** was the 2016 nominee of the Green Party for President of the United States, having sought that same office in 2012.

A medical doctor, she was an activist for clean energy, health care, and local green economies. In her articles she calls for "Healthy People, Healthy Planet."

Stein also developed multiple musical albums with co-star Ken Selcer in the folk-rock band "Somebody's Sister."

At a rally in Brooklyn, Hillary appeared before her most ardent supporters. "Tonight caps an amazing journey—a long, long journey. We all owe so much to those who came before and tonight belongs to all of us." Her victory came nearly a century after women won the right to vote nationwide.

Until then, Obama had remained on the sidelines in the Democratic race between Sanders and Hillary. Now, in a move to unite the two warring factions of the Democratic Party, he came out and emphatically endorsed her. In contrast to Sanders' venomous campaign assaults upon her, Obama said, "I don't think there's ever been someone as qualified to hold the office. She's got the courage, the compassion, and the heart to get the job done."

During some closed-door meetings in the Oval Office, Obama presumably tried to channel Sanders' forceful energy into uniting—not dividing—the Democratic Party.

Perhaps he urged him to "cool it with his attacks on Hillary," in the heat of which he'd claimed she was not qualified to be President.

While Hillary, during her moment of triumph, was in her glory, Donald became the focus of negative headlines, including one which read "DEADBEAT DON STIFFED US."

A report listed hundreds of instances in which people working for the Trump organization did not get paid or else were "shortchanged or stiffed" from previously agreed-on wages or fees. It was reported that Donald's organization had violated the Fair Labor Act two dozen times at the Trump Plaza Casino in Atlantic City, based on its failure to pay minimum wage or overtime.

Included among the shortchanged were hundreds of workers, real estate brokers, bartenders, waiters, and other employees, many of them deeply resentful.

Within a climate permeated with bad publicity for Donald and good publicity for Hillary, newscasters opted to release additional polling results. A Fox News poll of independent voters found 32% in favor of Donald, 22% in favor of Hillary, and 23% in favor of Gary Johnson, the Libertarian candidate.

However, in a general election poll of all voters, Hillary maintained a three-point lead. The poll showed an overall drop of support for Donald. Of all the voters polled, 72% reported, "We're angry as hell at Washington, and we're not going to take it anymore."

A Deranged Muslim Psychotic
Massacres 49 at Gay Club in Orlando
Worst Mass Shooting to that Point in U.S. History

A psychotic American-born Muslim and ISIS supporter, 29-year-old madman Omar Mateen, cackled as he opened fire on patrons at a gay nightclub early Sunday morning, June 12 in Orlando, killing 49 of them and wounding many others. It was the deadliest mass shooting in U.S. history. "This guy wanted to kill all of us," said survivor Jeanette McCoy.

The mostly Latino, mostly celebratory night of dancing to salsa and merengue at the Pulse nightclub ended in blood and mayhem.

"The gunman behind the massacre was a bloodthirsty homophobic bigot who was unhinged and unstable," as reported by Daniel Gilroy, and ex-Fort Pierce policeman who worked with him as a private guard. "I never heard him refer to anybody who was black or gay as anything else but niggers and queers," Gilroy said.

The New York Daily News, in a frontpage headline, trumpeted, "THANKS, NRA. Because of your continued opposition to an assault rifle ban, terrorists like this lunatic can legally buy a killing machine and perpetrate the worst mass shooting in U.S. history."

Donald seized the moment, claiming, "I said this was going to happen, and it is only going to get worse." He criticized Hillary for what he claimed was her desire "to dramatically increase admissions from the Middle East."

"Referring to militant Muslims, he said, "We will have no way to screen them, pay for them, or prevent the second generation from radicalizing. The rampage in Orlando is just the beginning."

Donald used the blood-soaked occasion to renew his attacks on Obama, accusing him of not cracking down on Islamic terrorists "because he doesn't

Perpetrator of the Orlando massacre, **Omar Mateen.**

But did this headline, as it appeared on the front page of the *New York Post*, ruin his chances of entering Jihadists' Paradise?

get it, or else because he sympathized with them. Look, we're led by a man that either is not tough, not smart, or he's got something else in mind. There's something going on. Why can't he utter the words, 'radical Islamic terrorists?'"

Then, in an unusual show of temper and anger, President Obama denounced Donald's remarks after the Orlando massacre, calling them "a dangerous mind-set that recalls the darkest and most shameful periods in American history. We hear language that singles out immigrants and suggests entire religious communities are complicit in violence. Where does this stop? Are you going to start treating Muslim Americans differently? That would make us less safe."

Donald used the Orlando massacre as a herald call for more guns in society. "If some of the great people who were in that club that night had guns strapped to their waist or ankle, casualties would have been lower."

Then, rather unconvincingly, Donald also claimed that he would be the best friend that the LGBT community ever had in the White House.

As he made those remarks, Sacramento pastor Roger Jimenez, in reference to LGBT people, preached from his pulpit, "The tragedy is that more of them didn't die. I'm kind of upset that he didn't finish the job, because these people are predators."

Responding to that, a journalist wrote, "Sir, you are a predator of Satan disguised as a follower of Jesus."

Then the blowhard Lieutenant Governor of Texas, Dan Patrick, posted "Man reaps what he sows," referring to the gays of Orlando.

***

In discussing the Orlando massacre, Donald veered from the GOP party line, calling for people on the terror watch list to be barred from buying firearms. His tweet could be interpreted to support some of the measures being pushed by Democrats opposing Republicans in Congress at the time.

In the wake of the massacre, a new poll reflected how disenchanted the electorate continued to be. Only 29% had a favorable view of Donald, as opposed to 43% for Hillary.

According to Bill Cunningham, a New York-based political consultant, "Trump is new to the scene, and he said things that time and time again offended different groups of people. This will be the most negative, vitriolic, mud-throwing campaign ever. It will be negative, negative, negative."

When this poll was released, Donald was at a rally in Dallas staged at Gilley's honky-tonk ballroom, where John Travolta rode a mechanical bull in the 1980 film Urban Cowboy.

"Where's the horse?" Donald called out. "I want to get on that horse."

The occasion marked the first anniversary of his presidential campaign launched from Trump Tower.

He attacked Obama for failing to defeat ISIS, and then promised his adoring fans that, when he became President, that was one of the first things he'd do.

"We'll plaster MAKE AMERICA GREAT AGAIN on a cowboy hat."

His speech was interrupted several times by protesters who were drowned out by his supporters.

Outside the rally, many of his fans came fully armed with assault weapons, which was their legal right. Anti-Trump protesters mocked and/or trivialized them. One young man walked up to an armed Trump supporter and, in a gesture reminiscent of the Flower-Power Hippy protests of the 1960s, placed a daisy in the barrel of his rifle.

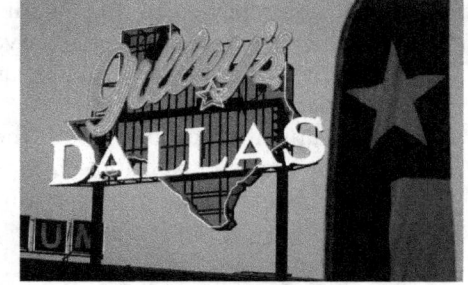

Donald Trump had turned 70 on June 14, and astrologers predicted that "surprises by the bucket load" awaited him in the upcoming year. "They will be good surprises," claimed astrologer Sally Brompton. She advised him to "surround yourself with people whose lust for life is as strong as yours."

Donald had celebrated his birthday quietly with Melania and their son Barron at Ralph Lauren's Polo Bar near Trump Tower.

If elected in November, Donald would be the oldest President ever sworn into office. Before that, it had been Ronald Reagan, who was still a "baby" (aged 69) at the debut of this presidential administration.

In another "birthday development," it was revealed that Russians had penetrated the "Trump file" at the Democratic National Committee's headquarters. The file contained "sensitive private and personal information" which presumably was delivered to the Russian President Vladimir Putin.

During the previous few months, polls had revealed that Donald was doing well with white male voters, many of whom felt disenfranchised and were often out of work. The majority of them were not college educated.

In mid-June, publicity associated with the release of a new book, The End of

WHEN DONALD WENT TO TEXAS

At Gilley's, Dallas' most famous honky-tonk, Donald wanted to ride the mechanical bull made famous by John Travolta in Urban Cowboy.

He also claimed he'd trade in his trucker's cap for a cowboy hat if it had his campaign's rallying cry.

White Christian America, revealed how the white demographic had changed during the last few years.

Author Robert F. Jones released it after going through mountains of surveys to write this "obituary" to the nation's shrinking population of white Protestants, who had dominated the United States since its inception.

Based on eye-popping data, it revealed that in 1993, when Bill Clinton became President, 51% of the U.S. population had identified themselves as white Protestants. By 2014, that figure had declined to just 32% of the population.

Donald's success with such voters, especially those who self-identified as evangelicals, came as a surprise to many. "Although he stumbled through Biblical passages such as 'Two Corinthians,' he seemed to have mastered the more important scripture of the evangelicals." Jones claimed. "He did so by calling towns like Ferguson, Missouri, one of the most dangerous places on earth."

Anti-Trump attacks reached new lows on June 18 when a political action committee, Americans Against Insecure Billionaires with Tiny Hands, released a mocking new video ad:

In a voiceover, a woman asks, "If the White House phone rings at 3AM, could his little hand even pick up the receiver?"

The ad, analyzed and discussed as a news item on MSNBC, also called for Donald "to release his official hand measurements,"

Another woman in the ad then asks, "How can he create jobs if his hands are too small to shake on the deal?"

Then a man questions, "When he decides to launch his nuclear war, will his stubby fingers even be able to push the button all the way down?"

***

In mid-June, news leaked out that delegates who were scheduled to attend the GOP convention in Cleveland were planning a mutiny to stop Donald from ever receiving the nomination. As reported by the Washington Post, their campaign, code-named "Anybody But Trump," would involve a change in the party rules a week in advance of the convention.

One of the components of their plan involve passing a "conscience clause," allowing a delegate to vote for whomever they wanted during a floor tally.

"I think any attempt to overturn the will of the delegates would result in a rebellion," predicted Senator Susan Collins of Maine, who has yet to endorse Donald.

When he got whiff of it, Trump himself defined this cabal of delegates and their plot as "an illegal act."

Nicknamed "Jeff," **Jefferson Beauregard Sessions III** sounds like a name left over from the Civil War.

The Junior U.S. Senator from Alabama was the first senator to endorse Donald Trump, and was considered a possible VEEP nominee.

As a senator, he is loathed by the LGBTQ community, based partly on his demands for a constitutional ban on same-sex marriage.

The "obituary" of **White Christian America** has been written by author Robert F. Jones.

He claimed that the population of those who identified themselves as white Protestants has shrunk to just 32% of the population.

"Any attempt to dump Trump would be a disaster," said one of his strongest supporters, Senator Jeff Sessions of Alabama.

Speaker Paul Ryan, however, granted his fellow Republicans a free pass to dump Trump "if voting for him violates their conscience."

In his rise to power, Donald sometimes benefitted from the gaffes and shortcomings of his Republican opponents. Maureen Dowd, in a June 19 column in The New York Times asserted that for decades, she had seen Donald as a New York celebrity, "not the apotheosis of evil uttered in the same breath of Hitler or Mussolini."

She then referred to Cruz as "a crazy nihilist, a creepy, calculating ideologue;" to Rubio as "a hungry lightweight;" to Chris Christie as "a vindictive bully;" and to Jeb Bush as "a past his sell-by-date scion."

Then she noted: "Trump's obnoxious use of ethnicity only exposed the fact that the Republicans have been using bigotry against minorities and gays to whip up voters for decades."

"YOU'RE FIRED!"
—Donald to Corey Lewandowsky

"YOU'RE HIRED!"
—Donald to Paul Manafort

A major shakeup in Donald Trump's campaign for President occurred on June 22, when his reporter-grabbing campaign manager, Corey Lewandowski, was abruptly fired. Caught unaware, he was brusquely escorted out of Trump Tower by two security guards.

Michael Caputo, a Trump adviser, almost immediately tweeted, "DING DONG THE WITCH IS DEAD!"

Behind the scenes, it was alleged that Ivanka was threatening to distance herself from the campaign if her father didn't ax Corey.

His departure left campaign chairman Paul Manafort in charge. But by now, was he the undisputed leader?

Ivanka was said to have been distressed ever since Corey grabbed reporter Michelle Fields by the arm at a Florida event. An item appeared in New York newspapers that Corey had also gotten into a shouting match on a Midtown Manhattan street with Hope Hicks, the campaign's spokeswoman.

That wasn't all. Ivanka was said to have encountered the final straw when Corey was "caught red-handed trying to plant a negative story about her husband, Jared Kushner."

Donald's oldest son, Don Jr., admitted that his siblings played a major role in Corey's firing. He told Bloomberg Politics: "We're involved in talking with our dad about this, sure. But in the end, my father's always going to make up his own mind."

Donald issued a statement, praising Corey for his past services. "He's a good man, but it's time for a change. I think it's time now for a different campaign. We ran a small, beautiful, well-unified campaign. It worked very well for us in the primaries. But we're going to be a little bit different from this point forward. A little different style."

After his abrupt dismissal, Corey sat for an interview on CNN, in which he had nothing but praise for Donald. He also claimed that he had a "great relationship with Kushner," and

A failed candidate for political office himself, **Corey Lewandowski** was Donald Trump's first campaign manager.

A pond hockey player from Lowell, Massachusetts, he is veteran of a number of nasty political campaigns.

Lewandowski first met Donald in April of 2004 at a poltical event in New Hampshire. Donald was impressed with his aggressive style of campaining, and hired him as his campaign manager in 2015.

Until he was fired, he operated Donald's campaign based on a policy he widely enforced as "LET TRUMP BE TRUMP."

In 2016, the controversial **Paul Manafort** became Donald Trump's campaign manager, replacing Corey Lewandowski.

A veteran of numerous presidential election campaigns, Manafort, a native of Connecticut, was a notorious lobbyist whose clients around the world often included brutal dictators dominating governments and political factions in Nigeria, Somalia, Zaire, Kenya, and Pakistan.

had never tried to plant a negative story about him.

Paul Manafort had been in operational control of the campaign since April 7.

An aide claimed that in the past three weeks, Corey with a baseball bat had been walking around campaign headquarters. "He tapped people on the shoulder with that bat. The guy is fucking nuts. Corey was down to just the interns and the airplane."

Ryan Williams, a Trump critic, said, "The dismissal of Lewandowski shows donors, activists, and party officials that Trump is willing to make significant changes, even if it means parting ways with a trusted political aide."

The grandson of a union printer, Corey had had a long political background, having been a worker on various campaigns. He had twice run unsuccessfully for office himself, once in Massachusetts and again in New Hampshire.

He met Donald in April of 2014 at a political event in New Hampshire. Summoned to Trump Tower in January of 2015, Donald hired him at a salary of $20,000 a month. From the beginning, Corey's motto was "Let Trump Be Trump."

Donald said, "He leaves me alone, but he knows when to make his presence felt."

After he won in Corey's home state of New Hampshire on February 9, 2016, Donald acknowledged the important role Corey had played.

Donald praised Corey as a family man. He'd met his future wife, Alison, when he was in the ninth grade and she in the eighth. She married his best friend in 1998, but he died on a United Airlines flight on 9/11. Corey married her four years later and became the father of their four children.

In April of 2016, another veteran GOP operative, Paul Manafort, was hired. The following month, he was named campaign chairman. It seemed inevitable that Corey and Manafort would clash.

Before linking up with Donald, Manafort had been as adviser to the presidential campaigns of Gerald Ford, Ronald Reagan, George H.W. Bush, Bob Dole, George W. Bush, and John McCain. He was also a lobbyist, having previously worked for such foreign dictators as Ferdinand Marcos, the deposed despot of the Philippines.

Many of Manafort's associations with dictators have been sharply criticized. His company was listed among the top five lobbying firms receiving money from human rights-abusing regimes. Collectively, they were called "the Torturer's Lobby."

One of Manafort's more controversial links involved his previous role as an adviser to Ukrainian president Viktor Yanukovych, even as the U.S. opposed him because of his ties to Russia's Vladimir Putin. In February of 2014, Yanukovych was overthrown by violent protesters, and he fled to Russia.

JARED KUSHNER
Donald's Son-in-Law, a Man With a Past, Many Secrets, and Suspicious Links to the Saudis, Also Rises

No one really understood what **Jared Kushner** did or was doing in the White House. *Vox* magazine defined him as "the most powerful person there not named Trump." Here, he enigmatically appears on the cover of the January 27, 2020 edition of *Time*.

The real power behind the throne in the Trump campaign is said to be Jared Kushner, a business man and real estate investor heading Kushner Properties, which also owns The New York Observer. He is the son of the real estate developer Charles Kushner. Married to Ivanka, Jared spent at least $7 billion on New York real estate from 2007 to 2016.

Reared in an Orthodox Jewish family, he attended Harvard.

His father, Charles, was once arrested on charges of tax evasion, illegal campaign donations, and witness tampering in 2004 He was eventually convicted on all of those charges.

The flagship acquisition for the Kushners is the office building at 666 Fifth Avenue, which father and son purchased.

Kushner joined Donald's campaign initially as a speechwriter and was charged with working on a plan for a White House transition team, should his father-in-law be elected in November. Donald later assigned the transition team roundup to Chris Christie.

As *The New York Times* phrased it, "Kushner has become involved in virtually every facet of the Trump presidential campaign, so much so that many insiders seek him as a de facto campaign manager." There is a certain irony there. For decades, the Kushners bankrolled Democrats seeking office.

The New York Times also pointed out that Jared is now "at the center of a campaign that has been embraced by white nationalists and anti-Semites."

"Jared and I are extremely close," Donald said. "He is an amazing son-in-law, a big and bold thinker."

***

As for Lewandowsky, out of a job, he landed on his feet when it was announced that he'd been hired as a political commentator for CNN. That network's boss, Jeff Zucker, said he was "drooling" to sign up Donald's former campaign manager. For his new gig, CNN was reported to have signed Corey for a fee of half a million annually. A CNN spokesperson denied that figure.

Then it surfaced that Corey had signed a non-disclosure agreement with Donald, making revelation of information about both him and his campaign a violation of his contract.

In the wake of hiring Corey, many CNN staffers were upset to have him join their ranks. Once source asked the question, "Will CNN tell its viewers that before Corey speaks, he is legally prohibited from criticizing Trump?"

It was also reported that CNN anchor, Anderson Cooper, didn't want Corey on his show.

HarperCollins offered Corey a $1.2 million book deal for a revealing insider's look at the Trump campaign. After failing to provide the publisher with his non-disclosure agreement, HarperCollins was said to have withdrawn its offer.

AND IN LAS VEGAS, A BRITISH GUN-GRABBER ATTEMPTS TO ASSASSINATE DONALD TRUMP

At a June 18 Donald Trump rally at the Treasure Island Casino in Las Vegas, Michael Steven Sandford tried to grab a police officer's gun so that he could kill Donald.

Reportedly, the unarmed 20-year-old Brit, in the United States on an expired visa, approached a police officer and politely asked him if he could get an autograph from Donald.

Trying to distract the officer, he then reached with both hands and tried to pull a gun from the cop's holster so he could use it to shoot at Donald, who was speaking.

Sandford appeared in leg irons that Monday in the U.S. District Court in Nevada to face a charge of potential violence on restricted grounds.

According to a Secret Service reporter, the deranged would-be assassin had driven from Hoboken, New Jersey, all the way to Las Vegas, where he parked his car on June 16. His first priority after checking into a hotel was to visit a shooting range for his first-ever lesson in how to fire a gun.

An employee at the range told police that Sandford had fired twenty rounds from a 9mm Glock pistol.

From the Secret Service report, it was revealed that the unhinged Brit said that if he were released from custody, he would make yet another attempt to assassinate Donald. In his possession, a ticket was discovered to Phoenix, where Donald was scheduled to appear the next day.

In England, Sandford's father was interviewed in Portsmouth, where he lived. He told the local paper, the Portsmouth News, that for the past three months, he had become alarmed about his son and his whereabouts. He also revealed that his son was autistic and suffered from Asperger syndrome.

In court, it was exposed that he had suffered from obsessive-compulsive disorder and anorexia. When he was fourteen, he had been hospitalized, but escaped.

It was noted that he had fallen in love with a young woman, a native of New Jersey, and had become

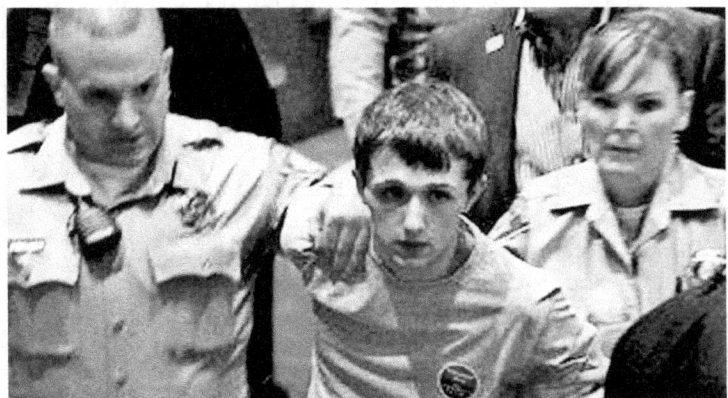

Michael Steven Sandford, British would-be assassin of Donald Trump, perhaps had dreams of entering the history books as a clone of Lee Harvey Oswald.

On June 18, 2016, at a pro-Trump rally, near the podium where Trump was speaking, he tried to grab the pistol of a Las Vegas Metropolitan Police officer, in his words, "to try to kill Trump before he became president." After waiving his Miranda rights, he was charged with disorderly conduct and for being "an illegal alien in possession of a firearm," based on having previously rented a pistol at a Nevada shooting range. (Instructors there reported that he was not a good shot.) Pleading guilty to both charges, he was sentenced to a year in prision, sometimes in solitary confinement and on suicide watch, but released and deported to the U.K after eleven months in custody.

Based on a long history of mental disorders, he later became the subject of a documentary on mental health sponsored by the BBC.

"lovesick." He was so depressed that his father gave him money to fly to the United States to live close to the object of his obsession.

His father had not been able to reach him. "My son doesn't talk much and never about his private life. His attempt on Trump's life came as a total surprise, because he never showed the slightest interest in politics." He also revealed that his son had dropped out of high school at the age of fifteen.

"He has always been a polite and very peaceful boy. I can't believe that he's become radicalized. Maybe he's been blackmailed or something. It's against my boy's nature to do anything like this. Maybe somebody got hold of him and put him up to this. I'm mortified. He's a good boy, but with problems."

DONALD IS CHARGED IN RAPE OF A 13-YEAR-OLD GIRL
WHO ALLEGES, "I WAS HIS SEX SLAVE"

As if Donald's campaign didn't have enough trouble, a bizarre lawsuit emerged in a California court in May.

A "Katie Johnson" filed a bombshell $100 million lawsuit in which she claimed she was repeatedly raped by Donald in 1994 at one of "billionaire pedophile's" Jeffrey Epstein's "sex parties" at a mansion in Palm Beach.

The suit claimed the GOP nominee "took my virginity and that he and Epstein treated me as a sex slave during a horrific four-month period."

Johnson was said to have offered her story to the tabloids, along with photographs of herself, for $25,000. As reported by Radar Online, Epstein's infamous "little black book" did not contain the name of Katie Johnson.

Johnson charged that she and her family were threatened with harm if she didn't give in to sexual demands. The suit further alleged that Johnson and another sex slave, also 13, gave naked Donald and Epstein sexually charged massages in the same room at Epstein's Manhattan residence. The plaintiff said she was enticed with promises of money and a modeling career.

The complaint that was filed stated that a woman, identified in court papers only as "Tiffany Doe," reportedly an employee of Epstein, could confirm Johnson's allegations.

In one alleged encounter, Johnson claims she was tied to a bed by Donald and "forcibly raped." The suit also claimed that he refused to wear a condom, despite her pleas.

"Defendant Trump slapped the Plaintiff Johnson in the face with his open hand and angrily stated that he would do whatever he wanted and that he was in charge," the suit maintained.

It also stated that, "After achieving sexual orgasm, Defendant Trump put his clothes back on, and when the plaintiff Johnson sobbed about being afraid that Defendant Trump had impregnated her, he angrily threw some $100 bills at her and screamed at her 'to get a fucking abortion' with the money."

The complaint also claimed that she had been sexually assaulted by Epstein on three different occasions during that same four-month period, including "one savage attack during which I was beaten, raped, and sodomized by Epstein."

In 2006, Epstein was arrested and accused of sexual abuse by some forty different women, some of whom claimed they were teenagers at the time. None of these women implicated Donald in any wrongdoing.

In February of 2016, Donald publicly referenced Epstein and then went on to drag Bill Clinton into this seedy mess. "Clinton has a lot of problems coming up in my opinion with that famous Caribbean island with Epstein. A lot of problems." He made these remarks at the Conservative Political Action Conference, where he distanced himself from the financier.

Donald allegedly banned Epstein from the Mar-a-Lago Club after he was accused of propositioning an underage teenage girl.

Aquazzura Wild Thing Shoe

Trump Hettie Shoe

AQUAZZURRA'S WILD THING (LEFT) VS. IVANKA'S HETTIE (RIGHT).

You be the judge: Did Ivanka steal the design of the Italian shoe manufacturer? What difference did it make? It generated a boatload of ill will for Ivanka from the Italian fashion industry and from an electorate already convinced of the Trump empire's greed.

Eventually, after a widely publicized court procedure, Epstein drew a sentence of eighteen months for a misdemeanor—soliciting an underage girl. He was released after thirteen months for good behavior.

In California, Donald's lawyer, Alan Garter, claimed that an investigation produced no evidence that "Katie Johnson" actually existed. He cited her address and phone number as false. He also denounced charges associated with Donald's alleged involvement at Epstein's sex parties as completely false.

"The allegations are disgusting at the highest level and clearly framed to solicit media attention, or more likely are politically motivated." Garten said. "To be clear, there is absolutely no merit to these claims, and based on our investigation, no evidence that the person who has made these allegations actually exists."

The case was dismissed by a Los Angeles Federal Judge in May, but resurfaced in Manhattan Federal Court in June.

Katie Johnson's lawyer claims that his client "remains traumatized by the abuse."

The case, as of this writing, remains uncertain.

FOOT FETISHES & LITIGATION NEWS
Aquazzura's Wild Thing Vs. Ivanka's "Trump Hettie"

Her father might be facing charges of rape, but daughter Ivanka, on June 22, was sued by an Italian designer for ripping off his design for a high-end, fringe-toed, and tassel-strapped pair of stiletto high heels. Filed in Manhattan Federal Court, the case alleged that the Trump fashion maven appropriated a popular Aquazzura shoe.

Ivanka's lawyers shot back, "The case is about generating publicity."

"One of the most disturbing things in the fashion industry is when someone blatantly steals our copyright design and doesn't care," claimed a lawyer for Aquazzura, referring to their popular shoe which they had marketed as, "Wild Thing."

Whereas the exclusive Italian original retailed for $785, Ivanka's knock-off design, blatantly marketed as "the Trump Hettie," sold for prices ranging from $600 to $145, depending on the retailer and its backlog of inventories at the time.

Hillary Says:
"AS BANKRUPTER-IN-CHIEF, DONALD WILL NUKE THE U.S. ECONOMY"

All political strategists from both parties were aware of how crucial the African American vote would be in the upcoming presidential election. A Quinnipiac University poll found that Donald's support among "the blacks" (his words) was almost nil, with less than 1% of the vote in a national election. This was in contrast to the 6% that Mitt Romney had garnered in 2012.

In distinct contrast, Hillary polled 91% of the black vote.

With white males, Donald trounced Hillary, winning 56% of their support as opposed to her meager 25%.

At the start of June, Hillary has amassed a fortune of $41 million in her campaign's war chest. On June 23, it was revealed that Donald had only $1.3 in his campaign fund. That was the worst financial report of any major party nominee in recent history.

In another assessment, it was also revealed that Donald had only seventy members on his campaign staff, as opposed to Hillary, who had assembled an army of 700.

At this point in June, the Clintonistas had spent $26 million in attack ads, whereas Trump staffers had not spent anything.

In response to his campaign's low bank accounts, Donald said he might have to tap into his personal fortune to keep his forces parading along. He claimed that he had spent $50 million of his own money during the primaries.

Campaign filings, as required by law, revealed that he had shifted a lot of campaign money back into to his own staff or properties. It was shown that he had reimbursed at least $1.1 million to his businesses and family members for campaign travel costs they had incurred.

Some financial experts raised eyebrows at the numbers and the transactions he claimed. They included $423,000 which had gone to Mar-a-Lago, and more than $170,000 paid out to Trump Tower, in their respective roles as campaign headquarters.

***

Meanwhile, among the Democrats, although Bernie Sanders was still biting into Hillary's flesh, she avoided—for the sake of party unity—attacking him, since she knew she would need the "young Turks" who supported him.

Instead, she aimed her fire directly at Donald, predicting a "recession and global panic" if he ever became President. She outlined a list of his business failures and bankruptcies, with a special emphasis on his dealings in Atlantic City.

She also attacked his suggestion that the United States, as a way out of its debt crisis, might opt to default on its debts, a path of action that could set off a world depression.

"Alexander Hamilton, our first Treasury Secretary, might be rolling over in his grave," she charged. "Maybe we shouldn't expect better from someone whose most famous words are, 'You're fired!' she said. "He's written a lot of books about business. They all seem to end at Chapter Eleven."

In a surprise reaction, Donald threw stones at Hillary's commitment to her religious faith. Speaking at a meeting of evangelical leaders, he said, "There's nothing we know about her faith, or lack thereof, even though she's been in the public eye for years. It's going to be an extension of Obama, but worse. At least with Obama, we had our guard up. With Hillary, you don't know."

In a speech at the Marriott Marquis at New York City's Times Square, he warned evangelicals that the Democrats under Hillary might "sell Christianity down the tubes. Evangelicals especially are under siege."

In all their speeches, Hillary and Donald continued to exchange gunfire. In a speech at the once-robust former steel town of Monessen, Pennsylvania, Donald charged, "The wave of globalization had wiped out totally, totally, our middle class. You can blame Hillary and her trade deals for that."

She shot back at him: "He's one to talk about globalization of American manufacturing jobs." At a rally, she held up a Trump shirt. "It's made in Bangladesh!"

AFL-CIO President Richard Trumka also attacked Donald for "crying crocodile tears about lost jobs and shuttered factories. He embodies everything that is wrong with our current trade policies. He has consistently sent American jobs overseas to line his own pockets with cheap labor."

At another rally, Donald promised that as President, he would withdraw the United States from NAFTA, impose high tariffs on foreign goods, and start a currency war with China. He also promised to scrap the Trans-Pacific Partnership, a twelve-nation trade deal among the United States and its Pacific Rim allies.

He always left his rallies with a promise—"It's time for the American people to take back their future."

***

Since House Speaker Paul Ryan had been critical of Donald, the mogul reportedly took delight when the media compared the conservative Republican to his lookalike, the fictional TV character, "Eddie Munster," from the classic hit TV show, The Munsters, from the 1960s.

In a scathing article in the New York Daily News, Andy Parker blasted Ryan and the other "gutless wonders" of the GOP for failing to take action on gun control. Parker's daughter, Alison, had been a reporter for Virginia TV when she was shot to death on live TV the previous August.

"It was probably snarky of me to compare Paul Ryan to Eddie Munster, but forgive me for being one pissed-off dad doing what I can to save another from the soul-crushing agony I live with every day. Given Ryan's action of the course of the last 24 hours, I'm not sorry I said it. Like the rest of his colleagues in the GOP leadership, Ryan is a coward and an obstructionist and a tool for the National Rifle Association."

"HERE LIES HILLARY (AND LIES & LIES)"

—New York Post

As time marched on, Donald seemed to lose his footing at times. He even delivered several self-inflicted wounds. He attacked a Federal judge, issued a self-congratulatory boast after the terror attack in Orlando, and stepped up his oral assaults on Hillary.

In Manhattan, he appeared at the Trump SoHo Hotel, where he called her "a world class liar," and charged that "she is the most corrupt person ever to seek the presidency. She would destroy the last scrap of our independence. We'd be under her total and complete control."

He also blamed her for all the turmoil in the Middle East. His critics pounced on his remarks, calling them "a patchwork of cable-news-ready sound bites as opposed to the presentation of new ideas."

At another rally, he accused Hillary for the invasion of Libya and "handing the country over to ISIS, the barbarians." He also assailed her for "getting rich by cutting deals with brutal foreign regimes that donated millions to her family's foundation or paid for Bill Clinton's speeches. "She has perfected a politics of personal profit and even theft."

Many pundits claimed that that speech marked the unofficial debut of the general election campaign.

In one of his more outrageous accusations, he claimed that Hillary was probably the victim of blackmail from the Chinese who had gained access to her e-mail account while she was Secretary of State.

Hillary was not the only woman Donald attacked. Elizabeth Warren, the Senator from Massachusetts, assailed Donald in speech after speech. He went after her, stating that to get into Harvard, she had falsely stated that she had Cherokee blood, thus benefitting from Affirmative Action awarded to Native Americans. She said that she was five percent Indian, but was not able to prove that.

In retaliation, Donald mocked her as "Pocahontas." In response, Native Americans attacked him for "using that racist assault."

To retaliate, Warren, campaigning with Hillary in Cincinnati, called Donald "a bigot with a goofy baseball hat."

"Pocahontas is one of the least productive of U.S. senators," he rejoined.

BREXIT
WHEN THE BRITISH SAID "CHEERIO" TO THE EUROPEAN UNION, DONALD SAID: *"WITH A WEAKENED POUND, MORE PEOPLE CAN AFFORD TO STAY AT MY GOLF HOTEL."*

Donald was in Britain, at his newly opened golf resort in Scotland, at the time of the Brexit vote. In a referendum with worldwide implications, Britain had decided to end its association with the European Union.

When he learned that such a move had led to the immediate and historic decline in the value of the British pound, he told reporters, "A weakened pound will make rates at my golf resort more reasonable, and we should benefit financially from the more affordable rates."

The British media responded with fury.

On June 24, news about Britain's decision to exit from the European Union shocked much of the world. A historic decision known as "Brexit," it carried world-shaping consequences, including the possibility of a global economic crisis.

It rattled financial markets and rocked political regimes worldwide. As David Cameron announced his upcoming resignation, the value of the British pound plummeted on financial markets. Britain had brought on itself the dubious honor of being the first country to break from the painstakingly assembled 28-member bloc.

Reporters caught up with Donald in Ayrshire, Scotland, where he had deserted his U.S. campaign trail for promotion of his new golf course and resort on that country's southwestern coast.

Purchased in 2014, Trump Turnberry is a luxury golf course and resort dating back to the 1900s.

"Our friends over here have voted to take back control of their economy," Donald claimed. "Take back their politics and their borders. I was on the right side of that issue, while Hillary, as always, stood with the elite. So did Obama."

Donald pledged that when he became President, he would reverse "the worst legacies of the Clinton era."

He tried to turn the anti-EU vote in Britain into a good sign that might help elect him President. "I think there are great similarities between what happened here in Britain and my campaign in America." He told reporters. "People on both sides of the ocean want to take their country back." He attacked both Hillary and Obama for urging Britain to stay in the EU.

"The American people are tired of seeing stupid decisions and having Swiss-cheese borders," he said.

In Scotland, he faced the inevitable protesters, some of his opponents flying Mexican flags. During the opening ceremonies for Donald's golf course, British comic Lee Nelson held up golf balls emblazoned with swastikas as news cameras spinned.

***

July arrived for Donald Trump like the blast of a firecracker. A Fox News poll had him favored to beat Hillary Clinton by a margin of 43% to 39%. He'd been trailing her by five points.

He held a 14-point lead among men, but trailed her among women voters by 6%. And whereas the candidates were tied among voters under 40, the mogul beat her among older voters.

Meanwhile, Bill Clinton and Attorney General Loretta Lynch came under fire on June 30 for holding a private meeting on a plane at the Phoenix Airport. The parlay came in the wake of an FBI investigation of Hillary's e-mail server, with the implication that Bill Clinton had somehow unduly influenced (or coerced) the Attorney General in the case pending against Hillary.

The impromptu and probably accidental meeting was widely denounced by Donald, even though Lynch emphatically and repeatedly insisted that all that they talked about were golf and their grandchildren.

"Their meeting was terrible," Donald said, "and it was really sneaky. It was something they didn't want publicized as I understand it. Wow. I just think it was terrible. The meeting was so out of bounds even the liberal media's making it a big story."

***

On July 3, agents of the FBI intensely grilled Hillary over the use of her private e-mail server, which she'd used during her tenure as Secretary of State. Meeting voluntarily with her probers in Washington, she reportedly answered all the questions put to her.

In an unconfirmed report, CNN announced that no charges would be brought against her. That immediately provoked an attack from Donald. In the past, he'd called for her to go to jail. He tweeted, "Like I said, the system is rigged!"

"It is impossible for the FBI not to recommend criminal charges against her," he tweeted. "What she did was wrong. What Bill did was stupid!" By that, he referred to Bill meeting Loretta Lynch on the tarmac of the Phoenix airport.

An ad from Donald's campaign machine. But is the **Star of David**, in association with allegations of corruption and cash something that might offend Jews?

The media immediately questioned the judgment of whomever approved the ad.

And although the Trump children's "hipness quotient," as worldly Manhattanites, is said to be off the charts, didn't they know that this might offend?

***

In an informal survey, *The New York Times* revealed their "readers' pick" for Donald's vice-presidential running mate.

The most favored choice for the no. 2 spot was Sarah Palin. [As noted by The Times, "She hates the Establishment and, like Trump, considers herself a maverick."]

Other readers wanted Tennessee Senator Bob Corker because of his much-needed foreign policy experience. Michele Bachman was also a leading contender. ["She's a Trump woman and attractive, with strong Tea Party and evangelical support."]

Chris Christie was an obvious choice for second banana. Ben Carson, Donald's former rival, was described as "capable, steady, classy, and intelligent."

Even though she'd said she didn't want the job, South Carolina's Governor Nikki Haley was also cited. [Haley is "living proof that Donald is not a racist, a misogynist, and a xenophobe," wrote a reader.] The name of Condoleezza Rice bubbled up from obscurity to appear on the list. [An odd choice, she was described by participants in the survey as "honest and charming."]

Newt Gingrich was a heavy favorite ["...a true Washington insider"]. Also cited was Jeff Sessions, the senator from Alabama. Near the bottom of the list was Mary Fallin, the charismatic governor of Oklahoma. The oddest choice was Ivanka Trump ["...smart as a whip and someone Donald will listen to."]

It seemed inevitable that Donald couldn't advance further into July without generating unwanted headlines. On July 2, he ignited a firestorm when he called Hillary "the most corrupt candidate ever" and tweeted an illustration that positioned her face next to a Star of David over a pile of money. He cited a Fox News poll that showed that 58% of respondents thought she was corrupt.

His tweet drew angry responses from around the country, some of them accusing Donald of being an anti-Semitic white supremacist. Moving swiftly, within a few hours, he, or someone on his campaign staff, had replaced the Star of David with a red circle.

He later tried to escape criticism, claiming that viewers had misinterpreted the tweet. "It wasn't the Star of David but a sheriff's star."

No one seemed to be buying that.

***

On the campaign trail, Donald had attacked the presidency of George W. Bush, especially when he was debating Jeb!. He accused the former President of misleading America into its involvement in the disastrous war in Iraq, costing taxpayers trillions of dollars—not to mention the horrible loss of American lives.

In early July, the publication of Jean Edward Smith's new biography, Bush, backed up Donald's complaints against the

43rd President. The first sentence of the book reads: "Rarely in the history of the United States has the nation been so ill-served as during the presidency of George W. Bush."

The biography concludes: "Whether George W. Bush was the worst President in American history will be long debated, but his decision to invade Iraq is easily the worst foreign policy decision made by an American President."

***

On July 5, the FBI director, James B. Comey, recommended that no criminal charges be filed against Hillary Clinton for her handling of classified information when she was Secretary of State.

The announcement came some two hours before she boarded a familiar carrier, Air Force One, with Barack Obama to take her to the crucial voting state of North Carolina, then absorbed over a controversial law about transgenders' use of bathroom facilities.

The FBI found no evidence that she had intentionally transmitted or willfully mishandled classified information, elements necessary to warrant a criminal charge. But although he recommended that no charges be filed, Comey nonetheless rebuked Hillary for her use of a private e-mail address and server.

In his testimony before a Congressional committee—the majority of whose members were hostile Republicans—Comey may have damaged Hillary more than all of Donald's previous attacks on her. The FBI director called into question her ability to function as Commander-in-Chief.

Comey charged that Hillary "was extremely careless in her handling of very sensitive, highly classified information."

Instantly, Donald's campaign went to work preparing attack ads, claiming that Hillary was incompetent to hold down the highest office in the land.

He responded to the FBI director's charges. "Our adversaries almost certainly have a blackmail file on Hillary Clinton. Her lawyers and Bill Clinton have been up to no good. Mr. Comey's findings disqualify her from running for the presidency. Her judgment is horrible. Look at her e-mails."

On August 29, 2015, in Minneapolis, Hillary responded: "I have said repeatedly that I did not send nor receive classified material, and I'm very confident that when the entire process plays out, that will be understood by everyone."

To contradict her, the FBI discovered that of some 30,000 e-mails returned to the State Department, 110 e-mails in fifty-two e-mail chains were determined to contain classified information.

In the wake of the FBI director's testimony, Donald claimed, "The FBI did me a favor. I would rather face Crooked Hillary than Crazy Bernie. Why? Because Hillary is corrupt. The decision to give her a pass is a total miscarriage of justice."

In another development, it was announced that the GOP's fund raisers had raised $51 million to add to Donald's war chest. He chipped in another $3.8 million He claimed that voter disgust over Hillary's escaping prosecution had generated millions to his campaign fund.

"People are sick of the constant scamming of all of us by the Clintons," he charged. He also took the occasion to blast New York Mayor Bill de Blasio, calling him a "maniac, the worst mayor in the history of New York."

James Comey was the seventh director of the F.B.I. He had been appointed to the post in 2013 by then-President Obama.

He received widespread condemnation from Republicans when he announced the results of Hillary Clinton's e-mail controversy.

He said he was recommending to the U.S. Department of Justice that no criminal charges be filed against the former Secretary of State.

Nonetheless, by famously broadcasting these allegations against Hillary so precariously late in the campaign, he earned a notorious footnote in history, with millions of enraged Hillary fans charging that his intervention cost her the presidential election.

Then, in another reckless charge, Donald, on July 6, charged that Hillary offered Loretta Lynch a bribe by promising to reappoint her as attorney general. [There is no evidence whatsoever of this.]

As he attacked Hillary for allegedly trying to bribe her with a cabinet post, reporters continued to press him on his choice of a vice presidential running mate.

"I have a lot of choices," he said, "but at the moment, I don't know, although the time is soon coming where I will have to make a decision."

He named Wisconsin governor, Scott Walker, as a possibility. Scott himself had been an early frontrunner for the GOP nomination, but soon dropped out of the race, using the occasion to attack Donald's suitability as a candidate for the presidency.

IN PRAISE OF DESPOTS:
Some of Donald's Ideas on Foreign Policy

To the horror of the State Department, and perhaps to the consternation of his handlers, Donald was quick to enunciate controversial opinions about some of the planet's most notorious autocrats. Some of his comments enraged many listeners who marveled that he had actually gotten away with uttering them.

SADDAM HUSSEIN, the "Butcher of Baghdad"

Donald: "He was a bad guy, right? Really bad guy. But you know what he did well? He killed terrorists. That was good. He didn't read them their rights. They don't talk. They were terrorists. It was over."

[In contrast, Paul Ryan called Hussein "one of the most evil figures of the 20th Century. He committed mass genocide."

Also in contrast, many national security experts have sharply contested whether the citizens of Iraq murdered by Hussein were terrorists, or merely citizens who protested his authority.]

VLADIMIR PUTIN, Corrupt Thug and Dictator, the "Curse of Russia"

Donald: "We can work together. We'll get along fine."

MOHAMMAR KHADAFY, "The Terror of Libya"

Donald: "Libya would be so much better off if he were still in charge."

KIM JONG UN, the Brutal and Probably Psychotic Dictator of North Korea, Who Threatened the West with a Nuclear Attack

Donald: "Ya gotta give him credit. It's incredible. He wiped out his uncle. He wiped out this one, that one…"

***

"BUT HE'S EASY TO GET ALONG WITH"
Donald Butts Heads With Republican Senators

On July 7, Donald flew into Washington, holding a testy meeting on Capitol Hill, where he "picked fights," according to the press, with some of the leaders of the GOP.

One encounter was with Senator Jeff Flake, Republican of Arizona.

"You've been very critical of me," Donald said to him.

"Flake responded, "Yes, I'm the other senator from Arizona—the one who didn't get captured." [Flake was referring to Donald's charge that John McCain, a prisoner of war in Vietnam, was not a hero.]

He also met with Mark Sandford, Republican senator from South Carolina. Sandford told the press, "I wasn't particularly impressed."

Ben Stasse, Senator from Nebraska, and Mark Kirk of Illinois, each announced that they were not endorsing the GOP nominee.

Donald lashed back, calling Kirk "dishonest and a loser."

Kirk shot back, "He's an Easterner, a privileged bully. Our bullies are made of better stuff in Illinois."

"It was a great meeting that will help Trump unify the GOP," said Rep. Lee Zeldin of Long Island in his evaluation of the contentious exchanges that took place.

It was???

***

On July 8, Micah Johnson, 25, a heavily armed gunman who had served in the U.S. military in Afghanistan, mowed down five police officers in Dallas, allegedly as a "payback" for the shooting of two black men in Louisiana and Minnesota.

A black racist with a hatred of white people, he set out to kill as many policemen as he could. His Facebook profile revealed that he supported the new Black Panther Party, a coven of African Americans who advocated violence against whites and Jews.

At his home in Dallas, police found bomb-making materials, ammunition, ballistic vests, and a personal journal of combat tactics.

The worst mass killing of police officers since 9/11, the massacre seguéd instantly into the political campaign. Donald called the brutal killings "an attack on our country. We must stand in solidarity with law enforcement, which we must remember is the force between civilization and total chaos. Every American has the right to live in safety and peace. We will make America safe again."

The cop killer's Facebook profile shows him dressed in an African dashiki and holding a clenched fist in the familiar stance of a Black Power salute.

AMERICA'S ELITE GETS VOCAL
As Ruth Bader Ginsburg Denounces Trump, Rudy Giuliani Ferociously Supports Him

In the days leading up to the Republican convention in Cleveland, famous American figures, including the oft-revered Supreme Court Justice Ruth Bader Ginsburg and former NYC mayor Rudolf Giuliani, spoke out on controversial, hot-button issues.

Rare for a Supreme Court Justice, Ginsburg said, "I can't imagine what this place would be—I can't imagine what this country would be—with Donald Trump as our President. For the country, it could be four years. For the court, it could be—I don't even want to contemplate that."

She even suggested that with a Trump presidency, it might be time "to move to New Zealand."

She went on to speak about the stalled nomination of Judge Merrick B. Garland. Republican senators had continued to refuse to bring his nomination to the floor.

"I think Mr. Garland is about as well-qualified as any nominee on this court. Super bright and very nice, very easy to deal with. And super prepared. He would be a great colleague."

Revered for her scholarship and contemporary savvy: **Ruth Bader Ginsburg.**

The U.S. Supreme Court Justice set off a firestorm when she made her distaste for Donald Trump known.

***

On another issue, Rudy Giuliani, who had once sought the presidency himself on the Republican ticket, denounced the Black Lives Matter movement, accusing it of ignoring black-on-black crime, for inciting violence against the police, and for promoting racism.

"When you say Black Lives Matter, that's inherently racist," he said on CBS's Face the Nation. "White lives matter. Asian lives matter. Hispanic lives matter."

"They sing rap songs about killing police officers, and they talk about killing police officers, and they yell it out at their rallies and the police officers

Former New York City Mayor **Rudy Giuliani,** a politician legendary for his oratory and political showmanship.

His rhetoric angered African Americans. "The police are the ones saving black lives," he said. "Black Lives Matter is not saving black lives. It's the police officers doing it."

hear it."

"When there are sixty shootings in Chicago over the Fourth of July and fourteen murders, Black Lives Matter is nonexistent. Do black lives matter or only the very few black lives that are killed by white policemen?"

Giuliani went on to accuse the Black Lives Matter movement of "painting a target on the back of police officers." On MSNBC, Giuliani said that the swell of protests and demonstrations in response to black men being shot and killed by cops has led to "divisiveness and anti-police rhetoric. I think the reasons there's a target on police officer's backs is because of groups like Black Lives Matter that make it seem like all police are against the blacks. They're not."

"The police are the ones saving black lives," he said. "Black Lives Matter is not saving black lives. It's the police officers doing it."

BUT DONALD, ON GAY RIGHTS, WHERE ARE YOU, EXACTLY?
"Does an "Urban Sophisticate" Like Donald Trump Really Care Who Someone Marries or Where They Go to Take a Piss?"
—a GOP Delegate from New York

Although gay rights was a hot-button issue for the GOP, Donald seemed to want to avoid getting involved. Social conservatives opposing same-sex marriage and abortion rights had dominated GOP platforms of the past, as in 2012.

Donald himself has claimed, "tremendous friendship with the gay community." Gays, in fact, have not been singled out for attack in his speeches, and thousands in the GLBT community supported him. At times, Donald has also criticized all those laws trying to prevent transgendered people from using the public restrooms of their choice. In fact, he received a supportive call from Caitlyn Jenner, the former Olympic athlete previously known as Bruce Jenner.

Many GOP delegates argue that their party can no longer afford to alienate people by taking intolerant positions on gay rights.

But these moderate voices face almost hysterical opposition. Cynthia Dunbar, delegate from Virginia, has compared the gay rights movement to Nazism.

A rival delegate said, "Ms. Dunbar should sit down and read a book about the history of the Nazi party."

A delegate from Missouri, Hardy Billington, went so far to take out an ad in his hometown newspaper, claiming that homosexuality kills people at two to three times the rate of smoking. [Of course, this was ridiculous.]

Mary Frances Forrester of North Carolina suggested that "the homosexual agenda is trying to change the course of western civilization." Perhaps she confused gays with ISIS.

Lanhee J. Chen, who led Mitt Romney's platform efforts in 2012, said: "The bigger problem for the Trump people and the Republican National Committee is the fact there are these major disagreements between where Trump is on some of these issues and where the activist base of the Republican Party is."

Of course, Donald could take the position of Bob Dole, the Republican nominee in 1996. When he was asked about the official platforms and ideologies endorsed by party members during that election cycle, he said, "I never read it."

THE RACE WARS: Donald Self-Defines as "THE LAW AND ORDER" CANDIDATE

On July 11, at a campaign rally in Virginia Beach, Donald responded to the killing of two black men by the police in Minnesota and Louisiana, and of five police officers gunned down in Dallas.

Lacking his usual fire-and-brimstone approach, Donald said, "We must stand in solidarity with law enforcement, which we must remember is the force between civilization and total chaos. I am the law-and-order candidate," he declared, echoing a campaign slogan that put Richard Nixon into the Oval Office in the tumultuous election of 1968, in the wake of the assassination of Martin Luther King Jr. and Robert Kennedy.

Hoping to sound presidential, Donald said, "The attack on our Dallas police is an attack on our country. Our whole nation is in mourning. Yet we have also seen increasing threats against our police and a substantial rise in the number of officers killed in the line of duty."

"We must remember the police are needed the most where crime is the highest." He cited Chicago as a case of a violence-plagued city with a high crime rate where blacks often murder fellow blacks.

"Every kid in America should be able to securely walk the streets of their own neighborhood without harm. Everyone will be protected equally."

His ardent supporter, Chris Christie, backed him up. "We need a President who once again will put law and order at the top of the priority of the presidency of the country."

Christie also used the occasion to get in some digs at Hillary. "She is weak, ineffective, pandering and—as proven by her recent e-mail scandals, which was an embarrassment not only to her, but to the entire nation as a whole—she's either a liar or grossly incompetent. It's probably both."

***

On July 12, Donald, on TV, watched with great skepticism as Vermont Senator Bernie Sanders endorsed Hillary as the Democratic nominee for President. In spite of that, she faced angry Sanders supporters who held up signs, "NEVER HILLARY." Both candidates, even though they might not really like each other, seemed to unite against a common foe: Donald Trump.

"I intend to do everything I can to make certain she will be the next president," Sanders said.

"There goes Crooked Hillary and Crazy Bernie trying to trick voters," Donald said.

"We are joining forces to defeat Donald Trump," Hillary proclaimed.

Donald also took the occasion to denounce Justice Ruth Bader Ginsburg as a "disgrace" after she voiced her criticism of him. "I think she should apologize to the court. I couldn't believe it when I saw it."

He predicted that her comments against him would backfire, giving him the election. "It's so beneath the court for her to be making statements like that. It only energizes my base even more. I would hope that she would get off the court as soon as possible."

ANGRY CAUCASIANS DEFEND TRUMP
THE DONALD: LAST STAND OF THE WHITE MAN

In a rare frontpage lead story in the July 14 edition of The New York Times, Nicholas Confessore wrote an article headlined "TRUMP MINES GRIEVANCES OF WHITES WHO FEEL LOST."

Sounding more like an editorial than a straight news story, he claimed: "In countless collisions of color and creed, Donald J. Trump's name evokes an easily understood message of racial hostility. Defying modern conventions of political civility and language, Mr. Trump has breached the boundaries that have long constrained America's public discussion of race."

The article revealed work done by Michael J. Norton, a professor at the Harvard Business School. He suggested that "whites have come to see an anti-white bias as more prevalent than anti-black bias, and that these people think further black progress is coming at their expense."

In another study by Michael Tesler, a political scientist at the University of California, it was revealed that many whites believed that "blacks play the race card or else are racist themselves."

"GOP CAVES IN TO TRUMP'S WALL OF SHAME
PORN'S A HEALTH CRISIS, BUT COAL IS CLEAN"
—New York Daily News

On July 14, it was announced that the platform committee of the GOP had drafted a list of controversial, far-right proposals, which were a nonbinding document that had to be approved at the Republican Convention in Cleveland.

Many editorial writers found the proposals more appropriate for a convention in 1948.

According to the draft of their official platform, the GOP approved a wall "covering the entirety of the southern border."

Donald gloated over their endorsement of his wall, claiming "It will make America safe again."

The proposed platform did not say how the wall would be financed.

Other proposals called for "special scrutiny" of people entering the United States from "regions associated with Islamic terrorism."

Appealing to the most conservative of Republicans, the document also warned that pornography is a "public health crisis."

At the same time that porn was defined as dangerous to one's health, the use of coal was deemed "a clean energy source."

The committee also adopted measures that supported the teaching of the Bible in public schools, and a measure rejecting Charles Darwin's Evolution of Species as a scientific theory.

In spite of the Supreme Court's legalization of same-sex marriage, the platform stripped virtually all support and rights from America's gay community. It supported adoption agencies which refused to work with gay couples, and also endorse the rights of parents to seek the widely discredited tenets of "conversion therapy" for their gay children.

In Springfield, Illinois, Hillary said that "the party of Lincoln has now become the party of Trump. His campaign adds up to an ugly, dangerous message to America."

Day Four of the RNC Convention in Cleveland, **Trump** kisses **Ivanka** amid a forest of Stars and Stripes in a staged rite of political passage that spectators found either inspiring, creepy, or terrifying, depending on their loyalties.

On May 30, 2017, the edgy, sometimes badass *comedienne* and social critic **Kathy Griffin** posted to her Instagram and Twitter accounts a video of herself holding a blonde wig attached to a Halloween mask drenched in ketchup and styled to look like the severed head of Donald Trump. Melania Trump later cited her son Barron's "panic" when he saw the image on TV.

Trump World and Griffin's employers at CNN immediately "went crazy," firing her from her New Year's Eve gig in Times Square with Anderson Cooper and placing her on security watch for her perceived threat on the life of a U.S. President.

The video and its photos derived from an off-handed session with photographer Tyler Shields, known for "artfully shocking" commercial imagery. Under extreme duress and roars of disapproval, Griffin hastily removed the images from her social media accounts, apologizing but later "recanting" her apology.

Her attorney, Lisa Bloom, stated, "Like many edgy works of artistic expression, the photo could be interpreted different ways. But Griffin never imagined that it could be misinterpreted as a threat of violence against Trump. That was never what she intended. She has never threatened or committed an act of violence against anyone."

Accusing the Trump family of "trying to ruin my life forever," Griffin wrote: "I captioned this with 'there was blood coming out of his eyes, blood coming out of his ... wherever,'" referencing comments Trump had made about Megyn Kelly.

In the aftermath of the hurricanes, most of America's Republican "talking heads" as well as liberals who included Anderson Cooper and Chelsea Clinton denounced her, and most of her comedy tours and TV gigs were cancelled.

In the years that followed, Griffin survived to give many interviews (including one widely broadcast on PBS) about the "nuclear reaction" generated by her photos. "Stop acting like my little picture is more important than talking about the actual atrocities that the president of the United States is committing."

In November 2017, on *Skavlan*, she said "I take that apology back by the way. I take it back big time". She went on to say that she had received "a lot of bad advice at the time." On November 4, 2020 (her 60th birthday and the day after the 2020 US presidential election), Griffin once again posted a photo of her posing with a model of Donald Trump's bloody, decapitated head.

A Trump-era spin on **Medusa with Perseus**

EPILOGUE

PRELUDE TO CLEVELAND
Donald Trump Claims That as President, He'll Urge Congress to Declare
WORLD WAR III

Donald Veers to the Extreme Right & Names
EVANGELICAL HOOSIER, INDIANA GOVERNOR MIKE PENCE
As His Veep Running Mate

THE ODD COUPLE
A Homophobic, Bible-Thumping Misogynist is Donald's Choice as The Man Who's a Heartbeat Away from Being President

At last, on July 15, the world learned that Donald J. Trump had named Tea Party favorite, Michael Richard Pence (called "Mike") to be his vice presidential running mate in the 2016 presidential election.

Newspapers noted that in 1988, George H.W. Bush had named another Hoosier, Danforth Quayle, as his Veep. A former radio talk show host, Mike called himself "Rush Limbaugh on decaff."

In his selection of this Born Again Christian, Donald had more or less abruptly rejected two highly visible and highly competitive finalists, New Jersey governor Chris Christie and former House Speaker Newt Gingrich.

To accept the invitation from Donald, Pence had to end his re-election campaign as governor of Indiana. Polls showed that he would have lost the race anyway because earlier and very expensive errors in judgment he had made during his administration of his state.

The liberal press had a field day writing satirical headlines about "Magic Mike." They included:

THE DONALD'S RUNNING WITH STUPID!

~

TRUMP-PENCE MATCH MADE IN HATER HELL

~

DONALD, PICK THE TEA PARTY FANATIC AND LOSE MORE SUPPORT

~

REMEMBER: A PENCE IS WORTH ONLY A PENNY

~

MIKE PENCE WANTED TED CRUZ TO BE PRESIDENT

~

POLL SHOWS NINE OUT OF TEN AMERICANS WANT TO KNOW: "WHO IN HELL IS MIKE PENCE?"

~

THE GREAT WHITE DOPE AND THE HOOSIER HOMOPHOBE

~

A RIGHT-WING TRIFECTA— RACIAL HATRED, RELIGIOUS HATRED, AND SAME-SEX HATRED

~

PARTY OF GOP SWITCHES INITIALS TO *BIFF*: BIGOTS, IDIOTS, FASCISTS, AND FOOLS

***

It was July 14, Bastille Day, in the French Riviera city of Nice. Revelers were parading along the seafront promenade enjoying the fireworks when suddenly, a crazed 31-year-old Muslim fanatic from Tunisia started driving a large ice truck down the crowded boulevard. He massacred eighty-four men, women, and children, and injured another 100 or so along the length of his deadly mile-long path. He killed them with an automatic rifle and also by crushing them under the wheels of his truck. His slaughter of innocents came to an end when French police assassinated him.

The resort's waterfront esplanade was transformed into a field of bloody, twisted bodies, pulverized beneath the wheels of this death machine.

In New York, Donald had been set to announce his vice presidential running mate at 11AM at Trump Tower, but postponed his appearance to honor the victims in Nice.

Speaking to the press, Donald claimed that as President of the United States, he would go before Congress and ask for a declaration of World War III to battle the Islamic terrorists. "I would, I would," he vowed. "We're dealing with people without uniforms. I'll also focus on restricting immigration and getting NATO more involved."

Angry that his choice for Veep had been prematurely leaked, he finally got around to formally designating Mike Pence, the controversial governor of Indiana, as his vice presidential running mate. He denied reports that almost up until the last minute, he "kept wavering in his choice."

A poll revealed that nine out of ten Americans had never heard of Pence. These same people would soon be filled in on stands he had taken both as a congressman and as an unpopular governor.

One of the first polls taken after the announcement discovered that only 12% of voters claimed that Pence's name on the ticket would make them more likely to vote for Trump. Most of this support came from evangelicals who didn't find Donald Trump "all that religious" in spite of his protestations.

None of these evangelicals had ever doubted the faith of Pence. As a congressman, he used to read passages from the Bible to either an empty chamber, or perhaps to an audience of only two or three fellow congressmen.

The Hillary Clinton campaign certainly knew who Pence was, and its administrators were shocked that Donald had made a selection of such a "right-wing nutbag, the most extreme pick in a generation." As a comparison, Barry Goldwater in the 1964 campaign against Lyndon B. Johnson was cited. Clintonistas attacked Pence's extremist views on abortion, gun rights, immigration, the LGBT community, and the minimum wage.

John D. Podesta, Hillary's campaign manager, said, "Trump has reinforced some of this most disturbing beliefs by choosing an incredibly divisive and unpopular running mate known for supporting discriminatory policies against millions of Americans and his failed economic policies as governor of Indiana."

"As a politician, Pence has a rich history of marginalizing women," said Mary Stech, spokesperson for "Emily's List," a pro-choice group. "As regards women, he shares something in common with Donald Trump. Together, they are a perfect storm of classic out-of-touch GOP extremism. For the very few women still not convinced that Trump isn't a threat to women, Governor Pence should do it—these two men are not to be trusted."

To the LGBT community, Pence was among the most loathed politicians in America. Not since the Third Reich went down in flames in the spring of 1945 had such anti-gay rhetoric been heard in America

In 2002, Pence stated, "Congress should oppose any effort to recognize homosexuals as a discreet and insular minority entitled to the protection of anti-discrimination laws similar to those extended to women and ethnic minorities." As it was assessed at the time, he wanted to strip away the rights of millions of tax-paying American citizens.

Gay activist Paul Bristol said, "This corn-fed Hoosier boy really hates our guts and holds us in utter contempt. History may one day record that Donald J. Trump took leave of his senses in nominating this Midwestern psycho. The Trump children should have known better even if daddy was an idiot. They were said to have vetted Pence. Could they be as stupid as dear ol' dad?"

Shortly after Trump's announcent of **Mike Pence** as his Veep nominee, *The Advocate* described their campaign banner—superimposed next to Pence delivering a speech during his less-than-spectacular stint as governor of Indiana— as "curiously sexual," based on how the shaft of the "T" seems to penetrate the hole in the "P."

"In choosing Pence," wrote one reporter, "Donald Trump selected a politician who has scars from the kinds of ideological fights that electrify social conservatives. He has support from evangelicals who aren't sure they can stomach Trump."

Lynn Evans, who had campaigned against Pence in Indiana every time he'd run for office, said, "If Trump becomes President and is assassinated, and Pence becomes President, and is informed of an imminent nuclear attack, instead of retaliating, he'd probably get down on his knees and ask Jesus to save America."

"Pence dodged the bullet in our state," wrote one reporter. "Had he run for re-election as governor of Indiana, he would have gone down in flames. He and Danforth Quayle could go out and get drunk together—no, not that. Pence avoids places where alcohol is served, viewing it as some kind of devil's brew."

Although Pence's selection as a potential Veep was viewed with mounting horror by millions, the Tea Party defined him as a hero. Senate Leader Mitch McConnell said Pence was "a great choice. We look forward to enthusiastically supporting the ticket."

Ironically, in December of 2015, Pence had opposed Donald's call to bar Muslims from entering the United States. The governor referred to it as "offensive and unconstitutional."

House Speaker Paul Ryan said that he rejoiced after hearing that Donald had picked a "good movement conservative. Clearly Mike is that. No one will challenge his conservative principles."

Ryan's backing of Pence was to be expected. As a former congressman, Pence had favored Ryan's plan for America—low taxes on the rich, free trade, and a trimming of the Social Security net.

In newspapers across the country, "Letters to the Editor" boxes were flooded with e-mails. Michael G. Sivler of New York wrote: "Pence is the obvious choice, given the Republican platform. He's anti-women, anti-gay, anti-poor, and anti-immigrant. He is not merely right wing. He's cruel, racist, and uncaring."

S.C. Palepu, also of New York, claimed that "the choice made sense since Donald didn't want a running mate to steal the limelight from him like Newt Gingrich or Chris Christie might have done. Mike Pence has the personality, the charisma, and the star wattage of a rutabaga."

Many pundits claimed that Donald's selection of such a staunch anti-gay, anti-abortion social conservative at least would be a complicated gamble, attracting the most extreme of evangelicals but alienating millions upon millions of moderate and independent voters.

Columnist David Brooks mocked Donald's endorsement of Pence: "With his selection, Trump launched his verbal rocket ship straight through the stratosphere, and it landed somewhere on the dark side of Planet Debbie. It was truly the strangest vice presidential unveiling in recent political history. Ricocheting around the verbal wilds for more than twice as long as the man he was introducing, Trump even refused to remain on stage and gaze on admiringly as Pence flattered him. It was like watching a guy lose interest in a wedding when the bride appeared."

The press had been mocking Christie as "Trump's lap dog." Apparently, according to some reporters, he'd made a last-ditch plea to Donald to name him, but was rejected. He'd been one of Donald's earlier backers, having dropped out of the race for President himself.

"He tried so hard to get the Veep nod, but ended up not just losing badly in the presidential stakes, but looking so much weaker than before," said Ed Rollins, longtime GOP strategist.

"Christie's rejection was death by humiliation," said Andy Borowitz, the New Yorker humor columnist. "Slow, twisting, and played out in public, like a reality show elimination."

At the time of his loss of the Veep nod, Christie's approval rating as governor of New Jersey had sunk to a dismal low of 26 percent.

As for Newt Gingrich, he reportedly said "I knew all along that I was too smart for Donald. He feared that as his Veep, I would outshine him on the campaign trail."

Donald told the press he might find a position for both Gingrich and Christie in his new government.

As a side note, Haskel Lookstein, was the prominent New York rabbi who had supervised the conversion of Ivanka Trump to Judaism before her marriage to Jared Kushner. It had been announced that he would deliver one of the opening prayers at the Republican Convention in Cleveland. But when criticism of his involvement with Donald's campaign increased, he withdrew his offer of a public appearance, asserting that the preannounced invocation "had become too political. Politics divides people. It does not bring them together."

Throughout the campaign, reporters had called Donald, among other labels, "borderline pathological" or even "the Michelangelo of Deception."

For decades, he had been known for exaggerating money claims. For example, appearing on a TV interview with Larry King, he claimed he was paid $1 million for a speech. Actually, he got $400,000 for that speech, an impressive enough figure.

As one reporter noted, "With all the lies he's told, he has the cojones to call Hillary a liar. Compared to him, she's the Goddess of Truth."

The Washington Post fact-checked forty-six of Donald's statements. They determined that there was something misleading with 70% of them, an error rating worth four Pinocchios, an abysmal record.

One liberal newsman, a cynical one at that, wrote: "On July 15, as Trump announced what a great guy and governor Mike Pence of Indiana was, he told the greatest lie yet. Pence is great all right, if you go in for a homophobic, Bible-thumping misogynist to the right of Joseph Goebbels."

So Ya Wanna Unify the GOP?

PUNDITS SLAM THE VOTING RECORD OF MIKE PENCE
Sometimes, His Stands Were So Far Right That They Were Incompatible with Positions Endorsed by Donald

"Just who is this Mike Pence?" voters wanted to know.

Born in Columbus, Indiana, one of six children, Mike Pence was the son of a gas jockey. His grandfather had emigrated from Ireland through Ellis Island to become a bus driver in Chicago.

Pence earned a law degree from Indiana University in 1986 and later became a right-wing radio talk show host, adopting Rush Lindbaugh as his role model, but without Rush's bite. "He talked about the weather and how the chickens were laying," wrote one critic.

He spearheaded two unsuccessful campaigns for Congress—in 1988 and again in 1990, but was trounced by longtime Democratic incumbent Phil Sharp. Eventually, he won a congressional seat in November of 2000 and was re-elected four more times by safe margins. He campaigned on "a return to the GOP values of the 1994 Republican Revolution." In 2009, he was elected to become the Republican Conference Chairman, the third highest ranking GOP leadership post.

Deserting Congress, Pence ran and won the Republican governorship of Indiana in 2012.

He continues to maintain that he is "a Christian, a conservative, and a Republican in that order." The former altar boy had once considered entering the priesthood.

A champion of traditional family values, he married his wife, Karen with the jet black hair, in 1985 and they have three children—Michael, Charlotte, and Audrey. When Pence was a congressman, the family lived in Arlington, Virginia.

A Democratic strategist in Indiana (who did not want to be named) said, "As First Lady, or Second Lady, as the case may be, Karen Pence would adhere to the political beliefs of Grace Coolidge and Lou Henry Hoover. But instead of being a fashion maven like Jacqueline Kennedy or Nancy Reagan, she would follow the dress code—not the politics—of Bess Truman, actually more like Mamie Eisenhower."

Politically, Donald and Pence are miles apart. That's why the press consistently referred to them as "The Odd Couple" [a reference to a 1968 film starring Jack Lemmon and Walter Matthau about two incompatible divorced men living together].

Most often, Pence's political stances are based on ignorance. Long after the government confirmed that cigarette smoking could cause cancer, he mocked their alarm. In 1998, he announced the statement as "hysteria—smoking doesn't kill. Time for a quick reality check." Perhaps he was the one needing the reality check.

As one reporter from Indianapolis wrote, "Pence wants us to get lung cancer."

After announcing Pence as his Veep, Donald praised his accomplishments in Congress, earning even more Pinocchios.

During a twelve-year career in Washington, Pence did introduce 90 controversial bills and resolutions. Not one of the Pence bills ever became law. Even his fellow GOP congressmen rejected them.

In 2003, he launched a ferocious attack on the LGBT community, calling for "an audit to ensure that Federal money not be given to organizations or any group that celebrated and encouraged the types of behaviors that facilitated the spreading of the HIV/AIDS virus." Shockingly, he advocated that Federal money be directed instead toward the discredited "conversion therapy" programs aimed at turning homosexuals into heterosexuals.

He also called for the removal of gays and lesbians from the military. "Homosexuality is incompatible with military service because the presence of homosexuals in the ranks weakens unit cohesion." In 2010, he urged that the policy of "Don't Ask, Don't Tell" not be repealed, again citing unit cohesion as his motivation. He also opposed the 2009 Matthew Shepard Hate Crimes Act, claiming that by endorsing it, President Obama wanted to advance a radical homosexual agenda. He wanted pastors to be free to express Biblical views on the issue of "homosexual behavior," which, in essence, called for their deaths.

Of course, he opposed same-sex marriage and advocated a nationwide constitutional ban on it, or else an overturn of the 5-4 Supreme Court Ruling. He also opposed civil unions and any government recognition of homosexuals at all.

He continued with his rants that no Federal funding should be used to aid people with HIV/AIDS unless programs were established to "change the sexual behavior of these people."

One columnist asked, "Exactly what does Pence advocate? Praying away the gay at some Nazi concentration camp? The Nazis found the gas chamber quicker."

Pence detested gay people, but loves guns. The NRA gave him an "A+" for his votes against any form of gun control. In Congress, he voted to ban lawsuits against gun manufacturers and to loosen regulations on Interstate gun purchases, including on assault weapons.

He also endorsed a Trans Pacific Partnership and other trade pacts such as NAFTA that Donald has consistently campaigned against.

As for NAFTA, Pence said, "I believe it's the only thing Bill Clinton has ever done that I agree with. Trade means jobs."

In striking contrast, Donald had defined NAFTA as "the worst economic deal in the history of America."

In Congress, Pence had defied his fellow GOP members when he attacked such signature programs as "No Child Left Behind" and a Medicare prescription drug benefit.

As one critic said, "He attacks women's rights to control their own bodies, tells gays who they can love, and now he wants poor people who can't afford much needed drugs to die. What a guy!"

As a congressman in 2006, Pence had proposed an immigration compromise by creating a guest worker program. He faced intense opposition from his fellow Republicans, and the bill died like a plucked wildflower. Instead of a wall, he advocated building a fence along the Mexican border.

Pence has been one of the leading attack dogs opposing Planned Parenthood, advocating that the government refuse Federal funding in spite of the good work they do providing reproductive health care and saving women's lives in their health clinics. His stance was based entirely on the subsection of their organization that focuses on abortions, even though no Federal funding was used for that purpose.

At one point, and with a sense of outrage, he cited video footage which purported to show a Planned Parenthood clinic "harvesting body parts of a fetus."

It turned out that such footage was a fake: The videographers who tampered with the footage and faked it were later indicted on a charge of tampering with a government record. Pence did not apologize to Planned Parenthood.

Pence stirred up an even bigger uproar in March of 2016 when, as governor, he advocated a stringent abortion measure. The law that he advocated would have barred abortions motivated solely for reasons associated with the fetus's race or gender. It would also have barred the availability of an abortion based on the diagnosis that the fetus suffered from a disability such as Downs syndrome.

It also would have made the receipt, sale, or transfer of fetal tissue a felony.

For these and for other positions he adopted, Pence came under fire from women's groups. Subsequently, a Federal judge issued a preliminary injunction to block the proposed law as endorsed by Pence.

On March 26, 2015, Pence was introduced to millions of Americans for the first time when he signed into Indiana law the notorious so-called Religious Freedom Restoration Act. Critics called it "freedom to discriminate against gay people." News about its negative implications almost instantly went viral.

The statewide law was condemned nationwide by everyone except evangelicals.

Companies doing business in Indiana not only denounced the bill, but threatened to withdraw business from the state. The mayors of Seattle and San Francisco each announced their respective bans of state business travel to Indiana.

Powerful CEOs notified Pence that they were pulling their conventions out of Indiana, citing the new laws as insulting and injurious to the well-being of their employees and/or customers. Ultimately this wave of cancellations and bad publicity cost the state economy some $60 million in lost revenues. Angie's List announced it would cancel a $40 million expansion at its headquarters in the state.

The fallout and negativity generated by Pence was so severe that pundits who had traced his political career predicted its imminent demise.

Bowing to the pressure, he agreed to "fix" the bill, revising the law so as not to discriminate against the GLBT community. Evangelicals attacked him for backing down. In the meantime, Indiana still has laws that discriminate against LGBT people in unemployment benefits and housing.

"Pence's Law," as it came to be known, generated so much attention that Obama mocked it at the annual 2015 White House correspondents' dinner. He joked that he and Joe Biden had become so close that if they came to Indiana, chances were that they would not be served a pizza.

***

As the Republican nominee for Veep, Pence will offer no comfort to millions of people who fear the oncoming devastation of global warming.

As governor of Indiana, he threatened to disobey the Federal government's orders to lower carbon emissions. "The government rules will raise electricity costs for Hoosiers," he claimed. "That will result in less reliable electricity and impede economic growth and prosperity in Indiana and the rest of the country."

He also claimed that the Clean Power Plan was "ill conceived and poorly executed." He further accused the Environmental Protection Agency of going beyond its legal authority in enacting the rules of the plan. He announced that as Governor, he'd join several other Red states in trying to block the Clear Power Plan in Federal courts.

Pence and Donald appeared uncomfortable in each other's presence as they faced a joint appearance on CBS's 60 Minutes where they were interviewed by journalist Lesley Stahl. She immediately zeroed in on foreign policy and how Donald had condemned Hillary for voting for the war against Iraq and how she had urged U.S. intervention in Libya.

Ironically, Pence—of whom Donald seemed to abundantly approve—had advocated almost exactly the same positions. When challenged with this, Donald seemed to duck the question, as Pence squirmed.

Stahl then said, "In other words, Hillary is to be condemned and Pence is given a pass?"

Pence not only endorsed the U.S. military intervention in Iraq, but, as a member of the Foreign Affairs Committee, had made annual visits to both that country and to Afghanistan. In 2007, he was ridiculed for a remark he made while visiting a market in Baghdad. "It reminds me of a normal outdoor market in Indiana in the summertime."

Only months before, men, women, and children had been blown apart in a bomb attack at that very market he visited.

However, Donald and Pence were on the same page when the governor tried unsuccessfully to prevent Syrian refugees from settling in Indiana.

On 60 Minutes, Donald said, "We're going to declare war on ISIS. We have to wipe it out." He also stated that he would use "brains and brawn" to defeat Islamic terrorists. "We'll need very few troops on the ground. We're going to have unbelievable intelligence, which we need right now and don't have."

He blamed Hillary for the rise of ISIS. "She invented these terrorists with her stupid choices. She is responsible for ISIS. She led Obama because I don't think he knew anything. I think he relied on her."

"As Bernie Sanders claimed, she's got bad judgment," Donald charged. "So bad. She's got bad instincts."

He also said he would call on Turkey to play a larger role battling ISIS. "Ankara alone could eliminate ISIS."

In announcing his choice of Pence as a "job creator," Donald failed to call attention to the announcement by Carrier, Inc., a manufacture of air conditioning and refrigeration units, that it was pulling its manufacturing facilities out of Indianapolis and moving them to Monterrey, Mexico. That meant a loss of 1,400 American jobs.

Chuck Jones, the head of the union representing the steelworkers who will lose their jobs when Carrier moves beginning in 2017, was asked for an opinion about the Trump-Pence ticket.

"Those 'job creators,'" he said. "All that duo needs is a circus tent."

During a Pence interview on 60 Minutes, he blamed Hillary and Obama for the attempted military coup in Turkey, with its subsequent loss of life. "The larger issue here is declining American power in the world."

William Kristol, the editor of the conservative *Weekly Standard*, said, "Pence and Trump will probably conceal their differences on the cam-

Visitors were urged to boycott the state of Indiana after Governor Mike Spence signed a law **(the Religious Freedom Restoration Act)** that made it legal for businesses to turn away LGBTQ customers.

As a result of that boycott and the tsunamis of negative publicity for Indiana that followed, the state lost $60 million in revenues, and set an example for how NOT to run a state government.

paign trail and stick to about the only thing they agree on—that Obama was a horrible President and Hillary was a horrible Secretary of State."

***

In all the hysteria surrounding the Pence selection on the eve of the convention, Donald still had time to comment on other personalities making news.

He defended the Fox media mogul, Roger Ailes, against charges of sexual harassment brought by former anchor Gretchen Carlson. She claimed in a court document that she had to refuse his sexual advances.

In an interview with the *Washington Examiner*, Donald said, "Trust me, Ailes is no perv. I think the accusations against him are unfounded, based on what I've read. Totally unfounded."

He took delight when Ruth Bader Ginsburg, Justice of the Supreme Court, apologized for her criticism of his candidacy. She told the press her comments against him were, "Ill-advised—and I regret making them."

On July 17, as Republican delegates were packing their bags and heading for Cleveland, news erupted about an ambush against police officers in Baton Rouge, Louisiana. That city had been the scene of daily protests following the shooting of a black man, Alton Sterling, reportedly at point blank range while he was being restrained by local police.

On that sleepy Sunday morning, a deranged African American, a former Marine, shot and killed three policemen and wounded three others.

The killer, Gavin Eugene Long, wore a Ninja-like black mask as he went on his murderous rampage. It was later revealed it was his 29th birthday, and he was a self-described member of the Nation of Islam.

Campaigning as the law-and-order candidate, Donald declared that "America has become a divided crime scene."

President Obama issued a call for calm in the wake of the shootings by police officers of two African American men and the subsequent massacres of police officers in both Dallas and Baton Rouge.

After listening to the President, Donald tweeted, "He doesn't have a clue. How many law enforcement people have to die because of lack of leadership in our country? We demand law and order!"

***

Hours before the convention opened in Cleveland, Donald reportedly threw a "temper fit" over his "showbiz plans" for the gathering. He had wanted the flamboyant boxing promoter, Don King, to address the convention, but his proposal was vetoed. The chairman of the Republican National Committee, Reince Priebus, reminded Donald that King has once stomped a man to death and had been convicted of manslaughter. Donald finally gave in.

He also wanted Tom Brady, the New England Patriots' quarterback, to address the convention, but Brady, it appeared, was not available. Nor interested, perhaps. Donald was also said to have requested Bob Knight, Indiana University's men's basketball coach, but he didn't make the GOP speakers' lineup either.

Donald also wanted Kathleen Willey to appear and to recite her claim that in the 1990s, while in the Oval Office, Bill Clinton allegedly groped her.

Nikki Haley, governor of South Carolina, was said to have turned down an invitation to speak as well.

One highly visible competitor who agreed to speak at Donald's party was "Lyin' Ted Cruz," perhaps hoping that he could be the Republicans' nominee in 2020.

***

On the day the convention opened, Donald proclaimed, "It's going to be the classiest, the greatest, and most amazing convention in the history of conventions—like a real spectacle with a showbiz edge."

"Hillary might have Barbra Streisand or possibly Meryl Streep, but we've got Antonio Sabato Jr., Scott Baio, even Willie Robertson of *Duck Dynasty*."

Whatever Donald did, he didn't plan to re-invite Clint Eastwood, who appeared in 2012 and delivered a rambling speech to an empty chair that he pretended held Obama. It was a sad spectacle and was ridiculed across the nation. The GOP was seen as a party of "cranky old white men yelling at ghosts," in the words of reporter James Poniewozik.

DAY ONE
OF THE REPUBLICAN NATIONAL CONVENTION
Monday, July 18, 2016

GOP DELEGATES CONVENE IN CLEVELAND
"An Alamo of Aggrieved Counterattacks as Custer Seeks Revenge"

FASHION & THE CULTURE WARS

What Trump Fans Were Wearing in Cleveland

RANCOR AND HARD-EDGE RHETORIC
Launch Fiery Gathering as Protesters Rant Outside: "LOCK HER UP!"

MELANIA TRUMP, FIRST LADY IN WAITING
Is Charged with Plagiarism, Stealing Words and Phrases from Michelle Obama

THE GOP ADOPTS ITS MOST HOMOPHOBIC PLATFORM IN HISTORY: "Gays Should Be Stripped of All Rights Except Taxation"

"It Was Like Putting Lipstick on a Pig"

—the Ghostwriter of Donald's *The Art of the Deal*

The timing could not have been worse for The Donald. On the eve of the Republican Convention in Cleveland, Ohio, the author who "ghosted" The Art of the Deal for Donald attacked the presumptive GOP nominee for President of the United States.

Donald had long maintained that his famous book, which had roosted on The New York Times bestseller list for 51 weeks, was his second favorite book after the Bible.

His ghost writer, Tony Schwartz, admitted that he felt deep remorse for "putting lipstick on a pig." He claimed that he regretted portraying the real estate mogul in a positive light, stating a firm belief that the election of Donald as President of the United States "might lead to the decline of Western Civilization."

Donald had split the $500,000 advance in royalties from Random House with Schwartz. During its preparation, a period that lasted about eighteen months, Schwartz had met frequently with Donald.

"The money came as a huge windfall for me," Schwartz said. "But I knew I was selling out. Literally, the term was invented to describe what I did."

Today, Schwartz, who runs a consulting firm, recalled his frequent meetings with Donald—in his office, in his Manhattan apartment, in Palm Beach, and in his private helicopter. He claimed that Donald suffered from an attention deficit disorder. "He could not focus for long on any subject other than his own self-aggrandizement for more than a few minutes. If, as President, he had to be briefed on a world crisis in the Situation Room, it's hard to imagine him paying attention for very long."

The author admitted that he wrote a memoir which was "a fable of fame and fortune woven mainly from falsehoods or euphemisms that Trump created."

"Donald Trump is a hateful, one-dimensional blowhard, who is pathologically impulsive, obsessed with publicity, self-centered, and so cold he pisses ice water."

"Lying is second nature to him. More than anyone I have ever met, he has the ability to convince himself that whatever he is saying at any given moment is true, or sort of true, or at least it ought to be true."

Schwartz admitted that he'd made a "Faustian bargain" in ghosting the book for the mogul. "I was caught between the Devil and the higher side."

While researching the book, Schwartz spend days listening to Donald on the phone, often fighting with attorneys, bankers, or reporters. "The experience was draining for me. Even more draining was trying to make Trump appear as a sympathetic character. Rather than the just hateful or, worse yet, one-dimensional blowhard that he was." He deliberately left out unflattering details

After the great success of the book, Donald offered the author a chance to write a sequel for a third of the profits. Schwartz turned down the "second ghost job."

In the *New Yorker*, Donald attacked Schwartz. "Wow! That's great disloyalty, because I made Tony rich. He owes me a lot. I helped him when he didn't have two cents in his pocket. It's great disloyalty. I guess he thinks it's good for him—but he'll find out it's not good for him."

Schwartz, appearing on *Good Morning America*, said, "I feel it is my civic duty to speak out against Trump" He also claimed that he was pledging all of his 2016 royalties due him to charities supporting immigrants and victims of torture. "I like the idea that the more copies that The Art of the Deal sells, the more money I can donate to the people whose rights Trump seeks to abridge."

It was later announced that Donald planned to sue Schwartz in a suit that demanded the return of all the royalties paid out so far.

***

The city of Cleveland was tense on the night of Sunday, July 17. The Cleveland Republican National Convention was set to open the following afternoon.

The theme of Monday's confab of delegates on the first night was to "Make America Safe Again."

Outside the Quicken Loans Arena, the atmosphere felt anything but safe. At least part of the fear was based on Ohio's controversial open-carry law, allowing people to walk around fully armed.

Police chief Calvin Williams had appealed to Ohio's governor, John Kasich, to issue a temporary ban on that state law. But the former presidential candidate claimed that he lacked the authority to suspend the law.

Newspaper headlines proclaimed "LET THE CIRCUS BEGIN—ANYTHING CAN HAPPEN."

"Bring 'em on," said Cleveland Mayor Frank Jackson. "Have no fear. The people of Cleveland are not strangers to unrest and demonstrations and protests."

The forecasts were dire: "BLOOD WILL FLOW IN THE STREETS OF CLEVELAND."

Agitation from at least 10,000 protesters, both pro- and anti-Trump, had been anticipated. Groups ranged from those calling for a communist overthrow of the government to Bible-thumping Born Again right-wing religious zealots, some of them predicting the fast-approaching End of the World.

The controversial Black Lives Matter movement was expected to show up in full force, denouncing cops as "fat pigs who should be fried like bacon."

"All these gun-toting protesters piling into our city is total insanity," said Steve Loomis, head of the Cleveland Police Patrolmen's Association.

In June, Cleveland's mayor, Jackson, took out a $50 million insurance policy, a precaution to protect his city in case of massive destruction of property.

Members of the KKK supporting Donald were expected to arrive, as were the rather threatening new Black Panther Party, a radical nationalist coven. The Oath Keepers, another radical anti-government group, were due to arrive as well. This cabal was composed mostly of heavily armed former members of the military.

In August of 2015, Donald Trump insulted and embarrassed John Kerry and Barack Obama by saying that they should read and learn from his book, **The Art of the Deal,** as an antidote to screwing up their negotiations with Iran and the rest of the world.

Lower photo. Just before the convention in Cleveland, ghostwriter **Tony Schwartz,** who wrote the book in Donald's name, forcefully rejected the book's premises and announced publicly, "I would have titled the book *The Sociopath.*"

Motivated by images of the terrorist attack which had recently devastated Nice, in France, the city had taken precautions to prevent a massacre. Police officers placed barriers or barricades along key streets and intersections leading into the downtown neighborhoods near and around the Arena.

More than 3,000 Ohio policemen would be on the scene, outfitted with state-of-the-art gear and body cameras. This force was beefed up by 4,000 security officers from various government agencies, including hundreds from the FBI. Officers arrived from locations ranging from Florida to California.

The pugnacious former Senator from New York, Alfonse D'Amato, predicted that the officers were needed to prevent a calamity. "Some of the hooligans will be armed," he said. "So I think we are going to have riotous conditions caused by these absolute degenerates who don't give a damn about the values of this country and are trying to rip us apart."

In an appearance on Fox News on July 17, RNC chairman Reince Priebus was more optimistic: "Every convention has its share of problems and protests," he said. "Obviously, this has been a pretty politically charged environment over the past year. So we are taking extra precautions to prevent violence in Cleveland."

Before the convention opened, Paul Manafort, Donald's chief adviser, attacked Kasich for refusing to support Donald after he won the nomination. "Kasich is embarrassing our party in Ohio. It's a disgrace he's not showing up for the Republican convention in his own state."

As anticipated, the evening was marked by fiery speeches, beginning with venomous attacks on Hillary Clinton. One delegate from Delaware said, "Don't print my name, but Hillary is getting blamed for the massacres of police, the Nice slaughter, all the earthquakes or volcanic eruptions, any loss of jobs, for all poverty, for any terrorist attacks against U.S. citizens, for her husband's infidelities, and for secret deals with some of the most horrible dictators on the face of the planet. I never realized she had such power."

The *#NeverTrump* movement, still mostly aligned with the failed candidacy of Ted Cruz, staged chaos on the convention floor. The insurgent delegates tried to push forward a roll call vote to overturn previously agreed-upon rules supported by pro-Trump forces. It would deny Donald's enemies a chance to stir up a fight during prime time TV at the first night's session. Most of the fight was over whether delegates would be "bound" to vote for Donald based on previous elections and caucuses. These rebels wanted to be cut free of any obligations forged during the primaries. "We want to be allowed to vote our conscience," became their oft-repeated, anti-Donald rallying cry.

The pro-Trump forces booed the anti-Trump insurgents, and the Republican National Chairman hastily denied insurgents' demand for a roll call with a voice vote.

Dissidents had submitted petitions from nine states, which, according to party rules, would have, in most "normal" circumstances, forced a roll call vote. That tactic didn't work. When their requests were denied, the Colorado delegation stormed out in protest, followed by angry delegates from both Virginia and Utah.

BENGHAZI…AGAIN
"I Blame Hillary Clinton Personally For the Death of My Son"
—Patricia Smith

The tumultuous night led off with speeches by emotional parents who had lost their offspring at the "murdering hands" of illegal immigrants. That was followed by Marine Corps veterans who had fought in the attack on Benghazi in Libya and lived to tell about it.

The most emotional speech of the evening came near the beginning. It was delivered by the nearly hysterical Patricia Smith, the mother of Sean Smith, one of the four U.S. soldiers who had died during the attack on the U.S mission in Benghazi in 2012.

"I blame Hillary Clinton personally for the death of my son," she claimed, even though the charge was outrageous. Nonetheless, she brought tears to many delegates, as one representative from Georgia later said, "Ms. Smith was preaching to the choir, and most of us knew that Hillary was not personally responsible. Only a fool would believe that, but we cheered her on anyway because all of us hated Hillary."

"The entire campaign comes down to a single question," Smith said. "If Hillary Clinton can't give us the truth, why should we give her the presidency?" She paused to notice a hand-painted sign in the audience urging its reader to "LOCK HER UP!"

"That's right," Smith said. "Hillary for prison. She deserves the stripes!"

Midway through Smith's vengeful rant for her dead son, Donald interrupted the Fox News broadcast and spoke personally to Bill O'Reilly, the leading Fox News anchor. He was later criticized for interrupting Smith's speech, since most Republicans around the country were watching the Fox News broadcast of the convention instead of MSNBC's or CNN's.

STUMPING AND TRUMPING
PRIME TIME BLAHS AT THE RNC

THE REPUBLICANS ANNOUNCE THEIR KEYNOTE CONVENTION SPEAKERS: D-LIST ENTERTAINERS FROM SHOW BIZ'S DEAD ZONE BREATHLESSLY WITNESSING TO MILLIONS ABOUT DONALD: A CALVIN KLEIN UNDERWEAR MODEL AND A HAS-BEEN FROM *HAPPY DAYS*

Donald had promised convention-goers that exhibitions of "show biz star power" would be sizzling onstage and rooting for him at the Convention, but all the big names in Hollywood, including Barbra Streisand, seemed to have run away in droves and in many cases, migrated toward Hillary. So instead of super stars, Donald rounded up what the *New York Daily News* headlined as "HAS-BEEN D-LISTERS TO KICK OFF SIDESHOW CONFAB."

Sabato

Antonio Sabato Jr., whom aging female delegates and the few log cabin gays remembered for his provocative "underwear revelations" for long-ago Calvin Klein ads, came onto the stage, still looking good after all these years.

He was remembered for his role in the soap opera, *General Hospital,* and he has also appeared in reality shows, including *My Antonio,* in 2009. In the latter, various young women competed to be his girlfriend.

From the podium, he spoke of his immigrant status, asserting that he'd arrived in the U.S. from Rome in 1985, the son of an Italian father and a mother from what was then known as Czechoslovakia. He'd been granted citizenship in 1996. "I took no shortcuts—it was legal," he proclaimed, as he invoked the teachings of Jesus Christ, with a call to protect the future of the nation's children.

He went on to attack the previous eight years of the Obama administration, making the claim that the rights of Americans had been trampled upon.

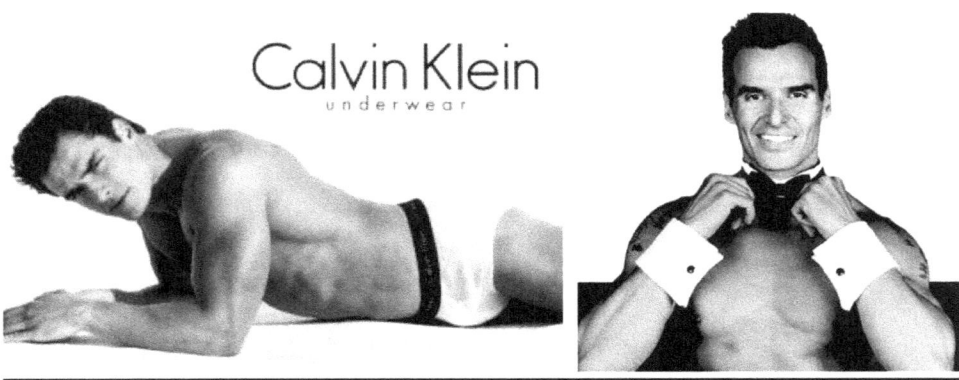

Hillary Clinton could persuade and enlist A-list legends such as Barbra Streisand or Meryl Streep to promote her candidacy.

In contrast, for "star power" of his own, Donald had to turn to former Calvin Klein underwear model **Antonio Sabato Jr.** On the right, he appears as a Chippendale dancer.

Baio

Remembered by older delegates from the time he was 16, actor and TV director Scott Baio also made an appearance. He'd been cast as The Fonz's cousin, Chachi Arcola, in the hit TV series, *Happy Days,* which went off the air in 1984. He had also played a role in the TV sitcom, *Charles in Charge,* which premiered on CBS in 1985 and ran for 126 episodes.

Born in Brooklyn in 1960, Baio was a political conservative. He had campaigned for Ronald Reagan at a young age, and had also attended his state funeral.

In 2012, he'd endorsed Mitt Romney, claiming, "I can't tell whether Obama is dumb, a Muslim, or a Muslim sympathizer."

Baio said, "America is an easy place to get to, but it's important to know what it means to be an American. It doesn't mean getting free stuff."

That charge was met with wild applause from delegates who loathed the welfare system and food stamps. "Being American means sacrificing, winning, losing, failing, succeeding, and sometimes doing things you don't want to do, including hard work, in order to get where you want to get."

Baio had attracted Donald's attention when he sent out, via Twitter, a now-notorious photograph of Hillary. She was shown in front of a banner which read "COUNTRY."

Front cover, April, 1979, of *Tiger Beat* magazine, documenting the peak years of teen idol and boy band hottie **Scott Baio**. one of whose big hits was "How Do You Talk to Girls?" Biao made two records, the second and final of which was released in 1983.

At the Cleveland Republican Convention, this refugee from the long defunct TV series, *Happy Days*, vigorously endorsed the candidacy of Donald Trump.

So a decades-old TV gig on *Happy Days* and an unchivalrous use of the C-word makes you a celebrity?

Depicted above is **Scott Baio's Twitter**—the one that attracted the attention and approval of Donald Trump. It propelled him from show biz obscurity to prime time as a keynote speaker at the RNC.

Her body covered up the "O" in the banner, and the two final letters of "COUNTRY" were cut off. That left her in front of wide letters that collectively spelled "CUNT."

[Below the photo, a caption read: "So There's a Letter Blocked. What Difference Does It Make?"]

ROBERTSON

Also as a speaker at his convention, Donald invited a quasi-celebrity, Willie Robertson, of the hit TV show, *Duck Dynasty*. As one reporter said, "Bearded Willie was hauled out to appeal to the hicks and the rednecks, or are those two terms redundant?"

Giving an embarrassing speech attacking political correctness, Robertson said, "Heck, I don't even know if they know how to talk to people in real America." No doubt, he was referring to Hillary and Obama. "They don't hunt and fish and pray. They just don't get it. Today, in a lot of ways, America is in a bad spot, and we will need a President who will have our back."

CLARKE

It was to be a night promoting Donald as the candidate of Law and Order, with appeals to the mostly all-white audience. For the sake of appearance, Donald had tapped two African Americans to rebuke black protesters—specifically the Black Lives Matter movement.

David A. Clarke Jr., the sheriff of Milwaukee County in Wisconsin, and a sometimes commentator on the Fox network, attacked the Black Lives Matter movement, proclaiming, "Blue Lives Matter."

He praised police officers around the country. "So many of the actions of the Occupy Movement and the Black Lives Matter transcend peaceful protest and violate the code of conduct we rely on." That remark brought cheers from the floor.

Clarke also received a robust round of applause when he praised the acquittal in Baltimore of Lt. Brian Rice in the alleged manslaughter death of Freddie Gray, which had led to nights of rioting, burning, and looting in that city.

GLENN

Belonging to that rare breed, an African American Republican, Colorado delegate Darryl Glenn, in a race for the Senate, said, "Someone with a nice tan needs to say too, 'All Lives Matter.'"

MCCAUL

Texas Rep. Michael McCaul, a member of the House Homeland Security panel, asked the delegates, "Are you safer today than you were eight months ago?"

MANIGAULT

In a bizarre appointment, Donald named Omarosa Manigault, his director of African American outreach for his campaign. She had been the most controversial and outspoken guest on the first season of *The Apprentice*, making two appearances. She lost both times.

A reporter confronted her with the awful "near zero" support Donald had among African Americas. She admitted that the Trump campaign for the black vote "will be an uphill climb."

COTTON

Senator Tom Cotton of Arkansas came on stage to deliver his own military credentials and those of his family. He claimed that America "needs a commander-in-chief who calls the enemy by its name and enforces 'red lines' ruthlessly."

GIULIANI: "BLUE LIVES MATTER"

The most impressive law-and-order speaker of the night was Rudy Giuliani, who delivered the fiery speech of this career, the evening's biggest hit.

He, too, endorsed Blue Lives: "What I did for New York in lowering crime, Donald will do for America. The police don't ask if you're black or white, they just come to save you. We reach out with love and compassion to those who have lost loved ones in police shootings, some justified and some unjustified. People fear for themselves. They fear for their police officers who are being marked instead with a target on their backs. We pray for our police officers in Dallas and Baton Rouge and their families, and we say thank you to the Cleveland Police Department for protecting us."

He attacked Obama for his failure to identify Islamic terrorists. "Our enemies see us as weak and vulnerable because of him."

Delivering a full throated endorsement of Donald, Giuliani said, "In the last seven months, there have been five major Islamic terrorist attacks on us and our allies. We must not be afraid to define our enemy. It is Islamic Extremist Terrorism. The vast majority of Americans do not feel safe. They fear for their children."

A consummate showman, the former mayor built to a crescendo, as he shouted and waved his arms, getting the delegates to rise to their feet.

Although lauded by most of the delegates, Giuliani did not receive universal praise from newspaper columnists. Mike Lupica wrote: "The former New York mayor looked as if he were some cartoon, exploding head-ring announcer on Monday Night Raw. It was as if he thought he could arm-wave and stammer and shout himself back into political relevance with this bogeyman speech, at one point screaming, 'They're coming here to kill us!' It is always reassuring to hear this guy act like some expert at protecting anybody from terrorism. The next time he does that for anybody will be the first time."

MELANIA LOOKED GOOD…
Until Two Hours Later

At the end of Giuliani's speech, Donald himself appeared in a blue-tinged theatrical fog, like Batman in a movie. He was back-lit in silhouette as he showed up to the sound of Queen's "We Are the Champions." It was a precedent-breaking move, as most nominees in the past didn't appear until their acceptance speech in the final night of their respective conventions.

He told the clapping delegates, "Oh, we're going to win. We're going to win big."

He had come onstage to introduce the guest speaker of the evening, his stunning ex-model wife, Melania Trump. Beautifully made up and coiffed, she appeared in a white haute couture gown.

Her appearance would be the highlight of the evening. A headline the next day read: "DONALD TRUMP'S WIFE MORE ELEGANT THAN MERYL STREEP."

She had come to praise her husband. "I know he will make a lasting difference," she told the delegates who seemed awed by her beauty and regal poise. "Donald has a great and deep and unbending determination and a never-give-up attitude. If you want someone to fight for you and for your country, I can assure you he's the guy."

"My husband offers a new direction, a welcoming change, prosperity, and greater cooperation among peoples and nations Donald intends to represent all of the people. That includes Christians and Jews and Muslims. It includes Hispanics and African Americans, and Asians and the poor and middle class."

"As First Lady, I will help women and children who need it."

Then she returned to praising Donald again. "He has a kinder, gentler side. That kindness is not always noted, but it is there for all to see. That is one reason I fell in love with him to begin with."

Her carefully rehearsed speech was met with a standing ovation except from the still bitter Ted Cruz faction. As one Colorado delegate complained, "Donald has a pretty wife, and Ted does not. But Donald is not extreme enough for most of us. He wants to deport illegal aliens. I'd prefer to round them up and shoot them. It's cheaper that way. Don't quote me."

It was approaching 11PM when the "Pig Castrator from Iowa," Senator Joni Ernest, appeared. In her attack on Hillary, she spoke to a half-empty arena.

"Hillary Clinton cannot be trusted," Ernst charged. "Her judgment and character are not suited to be sitting in the most powerful office in the world."

As she made those remarks, Hillary had just concluded addressing the NAACP's annual convention. Donald had rejected an invitation to address the assembly of African Americans.

"There is no justification for directing violence at law enforcement," Hillary said. "As President, I will bring the full weight of the law to bear in making sure those who kill police officers are brought to justice."

In the meantime, a reporter was doing some fact-checking. Parts of Melania's speech had a familiar ring. She thought she'd heard it before.

A national scandal was about to erupt.

THE GOP's OFFICIAL 2016 PLATFORM
"Terrifying, Out of Date, and to the Right of Atilla The Hun"

The official platform adopted by the Republican delegates seemed to pass quietly under the radar screen, but it was one of the harshest and most socially conservative ever written, with homosexuals coming under the same heavy fire as the terrorists who threatened the safety of the United States.

The platform stated, "Five unelected lawyers robbed 320 million Americans of their legitimate constitutional authority to define marriage as the union of one man and one woman."

The bigoted report also stated: "The Court twisted the meaning of the 14th Amendment beyond recognition. To echo Scalia, we dissent. We, therefore, support the appointment of justices and judges who will respect constitutional limits on their power and respect the authority of the states to decide such fundamental social questions."

The platform endorsed traditional families over "modern families. Every child deserves a married mom or dad." The report also endorsed the application of widely discredited "conversion therapy" procedures as "therapy" for gay minors. It granting any parent the legal power to subject a young son or daughter suspected of becoming a gay man or lesbian to medical and psychological treatment in an attempt to alter their sexual orientation. [*Widely discredited by, among others, the State of California, this form of coerced behavior alteration has often ended in suicide.*]

In another assault, the Republican platform endorsed the right of any business to discriminate against gays and refuse to grant them services if that conflicted with a business person's religious views.

As anticipated, the platform drafters came down hard on the right of a woman's right to choose, granting almost no ground for a woman to abort a fetus, even if giving birth might lead to a woman's death.

The platform also called for the Bible to be taught in public schools, and asked for state or national legislators to use the Christian religion as a guide in lawmaking.

It also advocated that female soldiers be removed from combat, and rejected any need for gun control.

The platform adopted its most extreme position on the use by transgendered person of public toilets.

The "social and cultural revolution" being imposed on America by the Obama administration was attacked. Obama was accused of "wrongly defining sexual discrimination to include sexual orientation and other categories." It called for states' rights in determining the use of restrooms, locker rooms, and other facilities. The government was accused of drafting a mandate that was "at once illegal and dangerous, ignoring privacy issues."

The platform attacked Obamacare and criticized the "radical anti-coal agenda advocated by Democrats."

It also endorsed Donald's controversial call for building a wall along the southern border with Mexico.

The extreme right-wing advocacy of the platform drew fire from the liberal press, and even from the more enlightened conservative press, too.

The editorial board of The New York Times came down hard on the GOP platform, labeling it "one of disruption and damage. It rivals Donald Trump for shock value. It goes with the most extreme version of every position and is tailored to Trump's impulsive bluster. Ideologues pushed through a raft of plans to banish any notion of moderation. The planks of 2016 have been fashioned as underpinnings for Trump jingoism. The GOP used to insist it was a "big tent' open to one and all. Now, it's a Big Wall party braced by a destructive platform out of touch with American lives and devoid of the common sense the nation needs for any form of political progress."

DAY TWO
Of the Republican National Convention
Tuesday, July 19, 2016

GOPers "CLINCH THE DONALD DEAL"
As Don Jr's. Symbolically Defining Vote "Throws Dad Over the Top"

SHOWTRIALS: "LOCK HER UP!"
Chris Christie, Puts "Lying Hillary" on Trial, without Representation, at a Televised Kangaroo Court, as Thousands of Agitated Republicans Scream for Blood

Within an hour of delivering her speech before the convention, Melania came under fire. Ugly charges of plagiarism arose, with allegations that she had borrowed complete passages of the speech that First Lady Michelle Obama had delivered at the Democratic National Convention in 2008.

It's not definite, but Jarett Hill, an out-of-work journalist watching the convention on his laptop from a Starbucks in L.A. may have been the first "detective" to note the similarities in the two speeches.

Most of the plagiarized passages concerned the importance of hard work and honesty. Sometimes, a complete paragraph was used with only minor changes or else a repetition of three words repeated verbatim as in "integrity, compassion, and intelligence."

Reporters at the *Huffington Post* discovered the similarities and tried to reach the Trump campaign for a comment. Their queries went unanswered.

It was not clear how much of the speech Melania had written herself. She was known to speak five languages, of which English was her fifth. Sometimes, in TV interviews, she had made such errors in grammar as "he don't."

Hours before delivering her speech, she was interviewed by Matt Lauer aboard the Trump jet. Standing beside her husband, she made the claim that, "I wrote most of the speech myself with as little help as possible."

By Tuesday morning, the day after her worldwide mega-exposure, Melania's plagiarism had become the story of the day, even "Trumping" the news of Donald's nomination. But instead of headlining that triumph for which he'd struggled for months, The New York Times devoted its lead story to the plagiarism charge.

It seemed that Ivanka's husband, Jared Kushner, Donald's son-in-law, had originally commissioned veteran speechwriters John McConnell and Matthew Scully to write the remarks for Melania. They had written George W. Bush's speech to the nation that he delivered on September 11, 2001.

Their draft was delivered to Melania, and the two men heard nothing. When they watched her on TV, they admitted that almost none of their original draft had been used.

Reportedly, Melania had been disappointed in the speech they had crafted and wanted it reworked.

It appeared that she had turned to a different writer for help.

When confronted with charges of plagiarism, the Trump campaign aides buckled down and went into denial, at first admitting nothing.

Stuart Stevens, who had written speeches for Mitt Romney in 2012, commented on the charges. "It's like some guy trying to paddle across a river in a rowboat who shoots a hole in the boat."

Experienced speechwriters sometime avail themselves of several programs which are available online and, in some cases, free—including DupliChecker—which are capable of catching a plagiarism. Yet such computer applications were not used by Melania or her associates.

Chris Christie, the former attorney general of New Jersey, stated that had such a case come before him, he would not bring charges of plagiarism against Melania. "Ninety-three percent of the speech was original," he claimed.

Jeffrey Lord, a Trump supporter, appeared on CNN shifting the blame away from Melania. Overall, however, he downplayed the controversy. "Let's face it: This is not Benghazi."

Jason Miller, a spokesman from the Trump campaign, defended the integrity of Melania's speech. "Her team of writers took notes on her life's inspiration, and in most instances included fragments that reflected her own thinking. That included her immigrant experience and her love of America which shone through in her speech, which made it such a success with the convention."

His statement was followed by a supportive tweet from Donald himself. "It was truly an honor to introduce my wife, Melania. Her speech and demeanor were absolutely incredible. Very proud!"

Sean Spicer, RNC's chief strategist, shrugged off the charges. "The phrases in question are so pedestrian, they're used in the throwback cartoon My Little Pony. They're also used by singers Kid Rock and John Legend, so were talking about seventy words."

Campaign manager Paul Manafort weighed in, too. "There's no cribbing from Michelle Obama's speech," he said on CNN. "To think that she'd be cribbing from Michelle Obama is crazy."

Donald's former campaign manager, Corey Landowsky, who had been fired, stated that if Manafort had vetted Melania's speech, and approved it, he, too, should be fired.

Don Trump Jr., took a different slant from Manafort. "Melania's speech writers should not have done it," he said, virtually admitting there was plagiarism after all.

Many newspapers published side-by-side extracts from Melania's speech on Tuesday night at the Cleveland convention, and Michelle's speech from 2008.

MELANIA: "You work hard for what you want in life. Your word is your bond and you do what you say and keep your promise. You treat people with respect."
MICHELLE: "You work hard for what you want in life. Your word is your bond and you do what you say and keep your promise. You treat people with dignity and respect."

MELANIA: "We want our children in this nation to know that the only limit to your achievements is the strength of your dreams and your willingness to work for them."
MICHELLE: "We want our children—and all children in this nation—to know that the only limit of your achievement is the reach of your dreams and your willingness to work for them."

Reports that Melania had stolen from Michelle set off a series of angry tweets from African Americans.

"All the Trumps do is attack Obama, and now they're caught swiping from Michelle," wrote Elija Yett of Ohio. "The next thing we'll hear is Melania giving the 'I Have a Dream' speech."

Yasmin Yonis wrote, "I'm not surprised that Melanie (sic) plagiarized from Michelle. White women have spent centuries stealing black women's genius, labor, babies, and bodies."

One musician tweeted, "It's totally predictable. White people always steal from blacks. Elvis Presley got his entire sound from Little Richard."

Many reports noted that even Donald's campaign slogans of "America First" and "Make America Great Again" were stolen from Pat Buchanan and Ronald Reagan.

Press criticism of Melania's speech was often negative, as reflected by this comment in the *Washington Post*. "Melania's speech was so platitudinous—a gauze collection of assurances that her husband, Donald Trump, is 'kind and fair and caring' and will 'never, ever let you down'—it could have been delivered by any spouse about any candidate."

LOCK HER UP!
Vindictive and On Stage, The Spurned Governor of New Jersey Depicts Hillary in Kangaroo Court as a Murderous Ma Barker...or Lizzie Borden

Chris Christie waddled onto the stage, barely recovered from his rejection as Donald's vice presidential running mate. Since he couldn't attack "the main man" he decided instead to light a fire under Hillary Clinton and to "convict" her in a mock trial.

The former Attorney General from New Jersey, himself involved in a raft of upcoming litigation for Bridgegate, Christie once again became a prosecutor, indicting the former Secretary of State for all her alleged crimes. Delegates, like members of a bloodthirsty mob, were asked to call out GUILTY OR NOT GUILTY from the floor at the end of each of his indictments.

Of course, in every case, the delegates shouted "GUILTY" followed by roars from the Republican faithful to "LOCK HER UP," a phrase which became the oft-repeated rallying cry of the evening.

In reference to Hillary, Christie charged, "She cared more about protecting her own secrets than she did about protecting America's secrets. And then she lied about it over and over again."

"We're going to present the facts to you tonight sitting as a jury of her peers, both in this hall and in your living rooms across the nation. He then followed with a distorted list of her professional and personal failures.

He mocked her for "cozying up" to Vladimir Putin and for supporting the brutal murderer and dictator, Syria's Bashar al-Assad. "She set the stage for the rise of ISIS during her tenure as Secretary of State," he claimed.

He brought up her e-mail scandal, drawing on the testimony of the FBI director, James Comey, who had recently appeared on "the hot seat" before a congressional committee. After presenting the evidence, Comey said the FBI would not recommend that she be indicted.

"Let's look around the world at the violence and danger of every region that has been infected by Hillary's flawed judgment," Christie said.

Listening to Christie's rants on TV, Hillary was not amused at the mock trial *in absentia*, where she could put up no defense. She hit back with a snarky tweet about the governor's Bridgegate-derived legal troubles. "If you think Chris Christie can lecture anyone on ethics, we have a bridge to sell you."

The governor of New Jersey, **Chris Christie,** conducted a kangaroo court trial that judged and convicted Hillary Clinton in absentia from onstage at the GOP convention in Cleveland.

The verdict screamed repeatedly from the floor from the rowdy delegates?: A lifetime in prison for her.

***

After a tumultuous campaign, with charges and countercharges and threats by the "Dump Trump" delegates, the time had come for the actual nomination. It had for some time been made clear that Donald had the 1,237 delegate votes needed to make him the nominee. Nonetheless, there were many attempts to sabotage the count.

That brought an element of suspense to the tense evening, as the media watched to see what disgruntled delegates from Colorado or Alaska would do.

The controversies were shot down as Donald was formally crowned as the GOP's presidential nominee.

In honor of the nominee's home state, the delegates from New York were allowed to cast its votes out of order. That way, New York would be credited as the entity that provided its bombastic native son the 1,237 votes needed. As head of the New York delegation, Donald Trump Jr., cast the deciding vote that "threw Dad over the top."

From the floor, Don Jr. smiled at his siblings, Ivanka Kushner and Eric Trump, before making his announcement. "Congratulations, Dad, we love you."

As he said that, the house band broke out in a jazzy rendition of Frank Sinatra's "New York, New York." Overhead, the Jumbotron displayed fireworks.

"It's not a campaign anymore," Don Jr. said, "It's a movement." Then, *#1 Son* pledged to put New York, which had not voted Republican during a presidential election year in 32 years, in play. But the road to the presidency, of course, would be an uphill battle.

Not everyone was rejoicing. Donald's chief rival, Ted Cruz, perhaps with an eye to a presidential bid in 2020, met with donors and activists at a reception across the street from the arena.

The roll call reflected discontent. In normal times, the Ohio governor, John Kasich, would have visibly and triumphantly positioned at the head of his state's delegation. But he was conspicuously absent, having refused to endorse Donald for President.

Senate Majority Leader Mitch McConnell of Kentucky appeared on stage a number of times, but his presence was met with scattered boos. After all, he represented the Washington Establishment which Donald was running against.

House Speaker Paul Ryan, third in line to assume the presidency, was viewed as the GOP's bright hope for 2020. He, too, appeared, reminding the delegates of his past arguments with Donald. Nonetheless, he was on hand, appearing ready to endorse him, claiming, "Democracy is a series of choices."

After the roll call, it was learned that 721 delegates had cast their votes for other candidates, mostly for Ted Cruz, but also for Marco Rubio and John Kasich. The convention showed the most discontent since 1976 when Ronald Reagan's forces battled the sitting President Gerald Ford, who assumed the position after Richard Nixon had resigned over the Watergate scandal and Vice President Spiro Agnew had stepped down after being exposed for having accepted bribes.

At the conclusion of the vote, Donald appeared on the screen. "Today has been a very, very special day watching my children put me over the top earlier," he said. "I'm so proud to be your nominee for President of the United States, and I look forward to sharing my thoughts with you on Thursday night about how to build a brighter future of all Americans."

After the vote, many Cruz supporters walked out of the building. Kendal Unruh, one of the anti-Trump leaders, said, "It's just not me who's going to take this defeat personally. There is so much discontent here tonight."

Before the evening ended, Ryan returned to the stage to deliver a passionate plea for unity within his fractured party. "Let's see this thing through," he shouted at the delegates. "Let's win this thing. Let's show America our best." His appeal had many delegates rising to their feet, at least those who had remained in the arena.

***

The most electrifying moment in the hall came when Don Jr. was presented as the featured speaker of the evening. He delivered a rousing speech that savaged Hillary and heaped praise onto dear old dad.

"When people tell my Dad it can't be done, it gets done. When people tell him something is impossible, that triggers him into action. For my father, impossible is just the starting point."

"You want to know what kind of President he'll be?" Junior asked. "Let me tell you how he ran his businesses, and I know because I was there with him by his side at the job sites, in conference rooms from the time I could walk. Dad didn't hide behind some desk in an executive suite. He spent his career with regular Americans."

The 38-year-old went on to say, "He hung out with the guys on construction sites, pouring concrete and hanging sheetrock. Dad listened to them and he valued their opinions as much and often more than the guys from Harvard and Wharton locked away in offices away from the real work."

"We didn't learn from the MBAs. We learned from people who had doctorates in common sense. It's why we're the only children of billionaires as comfortable in a D10 Caterpillar as we are in our own cars."

Speaking in a rapid-fire dialogue, as was his custom, Don Jr. got the loudest applause of the evening.

He took the usual GOP positions, attacking Obamacare and gun control, as he called for American energy independence.

He falsely claimed that as President, Hillary would "Take away the guns of Americans." He also mocked present gun control laws. "Just look at how effective these laws have been in such inner cities as Chicago. Seventy people were murdered last month alone and over 3,400 American lives were lost there since the Obama administration took office in 2009."

Donald's second daughter, Tiffany *[the daughter derived from the union of Donald with his second wife, Marla Maples]* spoke next.

At the podium, addressing Republican delegates and the nation at large, she was "all blonde, sweetness and sugar," in the words of one delegate. Her job involved revealing he personal side of her formidable father.

"He wrote sweet notes on my report cards and words of advice," she claimed. "I always look forward to introducing him to my friends," She claimed that "he was always there for me when I needed him."

After the roll call, Donald ended up with 1,725 delegates. Just weeks before the convention, pundits had predicted he would not get the 1,237 needed, and that it would be an "open convention." They were wrong.

Donald announced, "Together we have achieved historic results with the largest vote total in the history of the Republican Party. This is a movement, but we have to go all the way."

"GOD WILL ABANDON AMERICA IF HILLARY IS ELECTED PRESIDENT."

—Ben Carson

The evening was peppered with dull speeches, with sober discussions of conservative principles interspersed with attacks on Hillary.

Ben Carson, the African-American neurosurgeon who had dropped out of the race to back Donald, charged that Hillary was "attempting to deceive poor blacks. She would continue with a system that denigrates the education of our young people, puts them in a place where they're never going to be able to get a job, where they're always going to be dependent, and where therefore they can be cultivated for their votes. This is not what America is about"

As anticipated, Carson provided no real evidence against the former Secretary of State to back up his claims.

Fred Brown, who chairs the National Black Republican Council (yes there is such a group), spoke to the press. He said he'd been a regular at GOP conventions since the 1970s. "I think the 2016 convention in Cleveland is the whitest in my memory."

Meanwhile, at his ranch in Texas, George W. Bush watched the convention with dismay. He told friends, "I am worried that I will be the last Republican President. History may record that."

He feared that Donald's inflated ego and bizarre stands would cause irreparable harm to our party. "We might just disappear like the Whigs."

DAY THREE
OF THE REPUBLICAN NATIONAL CONVENTION
Wednesday, July 20, 2016

AS TRUMPKINS BOO AND WIFE HEIDI FLEES CONVENTION HALL
TED CRUZ REFUSES TO ENDORSE DONALD

"LYIN' TED" STICKS IT TO DONALD
DASHING UNITY HOPES FOR THE GOP

"CUT & PASTE" AIDE, FALLING ON HER PEN, ACCEPTS BLAME FOR
MELANIA'S PLAGIARISM

NATO
TRUMP ANNOUNCES THAT HE MAY NOT DEFEND AMERICA'S "DEADBEAT ALLIES" UNLESS THEY PAY THEIR FAIR SHARE

LACKLUSTER INDIANA GOVERNOR
MIKE PENCE & OTHER SECOND BANANAS PROMISE TO MAKE AMERICA FIRST AGAIN

In one of the more reckless decisions of the Donald campaign, the embittered senator from Texas, Ted Cruz, was allowed—apparently without restrictions—to address the assembled delegates at the Republican National Convention on Wednesday night, July 20.

At first, he was cheered by the Trumpkins, who erroneously believed that he'd come to Cleveland to throw his support behind Donald, that he would "bury the hatchet" after the carloads of venom each had unleashed upon the other during the course of the tumultuous campaign.

But as his speech unfolded, the early days of the campaign when Cruz had locked Donald in a bear hug quickly became a distant memory.

Treachery from Inside the Convention: Ted's Final, Prime-Time Effort to
CRUZ-I-FY DONALD

He opened with rambling rants about the U.S. Constitution and the need for evangelicals to discriminate if they didn't want to serve a homosexual.

He didn't phrase it that bluntly, relying instead on code words such as "religious liberty," but his followers knew what he meant.

In vain, however, the Trumpkins kept waiting for "red meat" as his speech neared its end. Many of them were expecting a triumphant conclusion in the form of a resounding endorsement for Donald.

None ever came. Instead, in an astonishing anti-climax, the defiant Cruz urged delegates to "vote your conscience," and the anti-Trump cabal knew what that meant.

Immediately, Trumpkins turned on him, almost booing him from the stage with their cadenced chants of "TRUMP! TRUMP! TRUMP!"

The loudest and most intense rage came from the New York delegation, which had been strategically positioned close to the podium. With a wry smile, Cruz sarcastically said as the live television cameras whirled, "I appreciate the enthusiasm of the New York delegation," [*What he probably really meant to say, but opted not to, was, "I hope you'll all be delivered instantly to the Gates of Hell."*]

"Freedom matters, and I was part of something beautiful," he said.

[*No he wasn't. He ran a vicious smear campaign against Donald, calling him names which had included "pathological liar."*]

Fearing for Heidi's safety amid the hostile crowd, security guards rushed her from the arena. One delegate screamed in denunciation "GOLDMAN SACHS" at her, a reference to the Wall Street firm she'd been associated with. Other less tactful delegates called her a "Texas bitch" or "a Texas cunt."

As Cruz ranted, the Trump siblings sat in stone-faced silence as they watched "the man they loved to hate" grandiosely fall short of endorsing their father.

As Cruz neared the end of his speech, the boos increased in volume and intensity.

At this point, as a means to sabotage his rival's domination of the moment, Donald made an dramatic appearance in the arena. As he advanced toward his seat in the VIP section, he delivered a "thumbs up" to the chanting crowd, many of whom cheered his authoritarian entrance, contributing to a confusing medley of boos and cheers simultaneously permeating the arena.

Peter King, a Congressman from Long Island, was the first to launch a post-speech attack on Cruz. "He's a disgrace. He's a self-centered liar and fraud. Lyin' Ted! I never trusted him. I never liked him, and I think he's disqualified himself from ever being considered as the Republican nominee for President."

Backstage, two security guards had to restrain a man who wanted to physically assault Cruz.

Expressing his contempt for Cruz, one delegate said, "What we needed was a pitchfork and some torches. Perhaps we should have tarred and feathered him"

Laurie Powell, a delegate from North Carolina, had been a Cruz supporter, but after his speech she turned against him, yelling, "Cruz is an asshole! He's not our nominee! What he needed to do tonight is get behind our nominee. He put himself above our party. As far as I'm concerned, the jerk's political career is over and done."

A Cruz alternate delegate from the senator's home state of Texas, Toby Walker, defended the failed candidate with some soothing platitudes: "What they did to him was really cruel. I think he did a great job trying to unite the party."

[*He did such a great job that the next day, one newspaper headlined the night as "CIVIL WAR."*]

Walker continued his defense of Cruz: "My heart breaks for him, and his campaign and his wife and two little girls. The boos aren't fair. His speech was exactly what we needed from him to unite the party."

[*Many reporters analyzed Cruz's speech as the opening gambit of his campaign for the presidency in 2020.*]

Gingrich

In a limp explanation, in an attempt to camouflage the depths of the insult to Donald, former House Speaker Newt Gingrich, who was the speaker scheduled after Cruz, told the delegates, "You misunderstood the senator. Ted Cruz said you can vote your conscience for anyone who will uphold the Constitution. In this election there is only one candidate that will uphold the Constitution." And in that phrase, there was no doubt that he was referring to Donald Trump.

No one was buying Gingrich's attempts to soften the blow. Unity of party was the last thing they heard in Cruz's bitter rant.

What Cruz did succeed in doing was to take the spotlight off the evangelical Indiana Governor Mike Pence. Tomorrow's headlines would focus mostly on Cruz, with only minor copy about the uncharismatic Pence.

Walker

Another failed presidential candidate, Scott Walker, governor of Wisconsin, came onstage to address the delegates. He spoke in a very loud voice, perhaps hoping to sound decisive and forceful. He didn't want to be accused of being a low-energy candidate like Jeb!. Walker, too was rumored to be looking for another run for the White House in 2020.

"Trump knows there is a better way forward," he said with absolutely no sincerity. He veered into the delegates' favorite subject, an attack on what a "criminal" Hillary Clinton was. He claimed that if she were more of a Washington insider, she'd be in prison. The delegates rose to their feet to cheer that remark, even though it made no sense.

"America, you have the choice," Walker said. "You decide. You deserve better."

Perhaps that was a chastisement for the voters having rejected him.

Rubio

Another failed candidate, Marco Rubio of Florida, didn't bother (or wasn't asked) to fly to Cleveland for the convention. Instead, he sent a videotaped, pre-vetted address to the delegates, throwing his weight behind Donald, and telling his fans that it was "time to unite."

What he meant, wrote a Miami reporter, was that the time to unite would be in 2020 when he ran once again for the presidency.

From the Podium, In Anticipation of the 2020 Elections, A NEW CROP OF AMBITIOUS CONSERVATIVES SPIN FOR RECOGNITION

In addition to the likes of Scott Walker and Ted Cruz, many Republican politicians appeared on stage not so much to sing the praise of Donald, but as a preview of their own run for the White House in 2020.

Such was the case with Senator Tom Cotton of Arkansas. "I'm the only politician here this week that married a girl born in Iowa."

He later admitted he was pandering, knowing that Iowa was the first state to select a candidate for President in the 2020 race.

One reporter said, "There were so many hopefuls waiting in the wings for the 2020 race. The convention was filled with not so subtle wooing and chit collecting. Many delegates privately told me that they suspected that Hillary would win the White House for the next four years. Would daughter Chelsea get her old room back? That was the question."

Laura Ingraham

Conservative talk show host Laura Ingraham fared better, receiving at one point a standing ovation. "All you boys with wounded feelings and bruised egos, we love you, but you must honor your pledge to support Donald Trump." She was chastising not only Cruz, but Jeb Bush and Ohio governor John Kasich for their refusal to support the GOP nominee.

Talk show radio host **Laura Ingraham** gave the Nazi salute at the Republican Convention. Or was it a wave goodbye?

The convention probably wasn't the best venue for such a gesture, since many of Trump's fanatics had been yelling "Sieg Heil" that night.

Rick Scott

Florida governor Rick Scott, with his Yul Brynner coiffure, also addressed the delegates. "Perhaps I know that some of you have reservations about my friend Donald Trump," he said. "Sometimes, he's not polite. He can be a bit rough, and to some people, he can be a little direct. But this election isn't about Donald Trump or Hillary Clinton. It's about the very survival of the American dream. Any candidate is better than a Democrat. It's time for Americans to put down their partisan banners and do the right thing for this country."

"Instead of the 16 or 17 candidates who ran for the GOP nomination in 2016, I suspect there will be at least thirty candidates in the 2020 Race for President.

All the 2020 hopefuls seemed to be racing to court Sheldon Adelson, the Las Vegas magnate who invests millions in GOP political campaigns.

Even Mark Cuban was discussed as a possible candidate for 2020. He is the wealthy owner of the Dallas Mavericks. David Carney, a GOP strategist, said, "Donald Trump has given the Mark Cubans of the world a road map."

Paul Ryan

Of all the possible candidates for the Republican Party's presidential nomination in 2020, House Speaker Paul Ryan appeared to be a favorite. He told the delegates, "The Republican Party is a ship floating on populism right now. I stand opposed to those of us who profit off anger, outrage, and dark emotions for short-term goals."

That appeared to be a dig at Donald's candidacy.

Ryan's reluctant and wavering support for Donald turned off a number of voters. Eric R. Carey of Arlington, Virginia, said: "A once promising politician, Paul Ryan has lost his way. Given that his entire public career has been one of shameless advancement of his incoherent budget policy, migration of wealth to the already rich, and, above all, himself, an accurate assessment of him would be of a transparent, valueless self-promoter who found his place in an equally empty political home."

Eric Trump

Eric Trump also addressed the convention. Although his speech was not memorable, many delegates found him more personable than his older brother, Don Jr. Eric seemed the most charitable of the Trump children, since he runs the Eric Trump Foundation, which helps finance St. Jude's Hospital.

Eric provided specifics about how his father had rescued failing government projects, citing his rescue of Central Park's derelict Wollman Rink, site of a famous ice-skating scene in the hit romantic drama *Love Story* (1970).

Eric told the delegates: "Throughout my father's career, he has been called upon by government to step in and save delayed, shuttered, and grossly over-budgeted public projects, everything from the exterior of Grand Central Terminal in Manhattan to the iconic old post office in Washington, D.C."

"It's time for a President who has always been the one to sign the front of the check—not the back," Eric said.

One delegate from New Hampshire said, "I thought Eric gave a great speech, although I don't really remember what he said. One thing I do recall. He said Donald was his best friend."

All that a delegate from Minnesota recalled was that Eric said that he and his relatively new wife were considering raising a family. "He's very good looking," she said, "and very rich."

In contrast, Don Junior's speech had made him a star. Some members of the New York delegation told him he should follow in the footsteps of Rudy Giuliani and run for mayor of New York City, taking on the sitting mayor, Democrat Bill de Blasio.

Manhattan GOP leader Adele Malpass said, "I like the sound of 'Mayor Trump.' Perhaps the sound of 'Governor Trump.'"

"For Don Jr., the sky is the limit," said John Antoniello, who heads the Republican Party on Staten Island.

More About Melania

Although Cruz's non-endorsement dominated the nation's headlines the following morning, commentary about Melania's plagiarism of Michelle Obama's 2008 speech to the Democratic convention continued to generate headlines. As had been predicted, a member of the Trump Organization stepped forward "to fall on the sword."

Taking the blame was Meredith McIver, 65, a former ballet dancer who had joined the Trump Organization in 2001. Since then, she had become Donald's favorite author, ghostwriting—in his name—such Trump-centric hits as Trump: How to Think Like a Billionaire, and Trump: How to Get Rich.

McIver issued her mea culpa and told the press that although she had offered to resign, Donald had instructed her to stay on. "I feel terrible for the chaos I have caused," she admitted. "I apologize to Mrs. Obama. No harm was meant."

"Melania and I discussed many people who inspired her and messages she wanted to share with the American people," McIver said.

The writer claimed that during phone conversations with Melania, Mrs. Trump had read passages to her from other writings that had inspired her. "I wrote them down and later included some of the phrasing in my draft that ultimately ended up in the final speech. I did not check Mrs. Obama's speeches. That was my mistake."

Donald himself has never been sued for plagiarism in any of the books he wrote. However, he once threatened to sue Barack Obama for "stealing my words."

He was talking about 2011, when Obama "used my tough talk about trade relations with China."

On Fox News, Donald had threatened to sue the President. "It was almost my language he used in a speech, grounds for a lawsuit. A lot of people have said that Obama's talk was almost taken word for word from my playbook."

"Incidentally, Joe Biden is an admitted plagiarist," Donald charged.

He was referring to the Vice President's admission that he lifted lines from a speech by Neil Kinnock, the British politician. Biden had confessed to the plagiarism after a speech he delivered during his unsuccessful run for the presidency in 1988.

Magic Mike

During its advance planning, Day Three of the RNC had been choreographed as a showcase for Mike Pence, a world-class opportunity for the prospective Veep to introduce himself to millions of Americans who had never heard of him before.

But ironically (and anti-climactically), it would not be Pence, but Cruz who dominated the headlines the next day.

Pence was aware that he was not a charismatic figure. Seeming to admit how dull he was, he announced from the podium, "Trump is a man known for his large personality, colorful style, and lots of charisma. So I guess he was looking for some balance on the ticket."

Columnist Kyle Smith would later write, "Pence is the Superego of Donald's Id."

"Donald Trump is someone who doesn't quit," Pence lauded from the podium. "Trump is tough. He perseveres. How about his amazing children? Aren't they something?"

Although Pence was said to have spent twelve hours locked away in his hotel suite working on his speech, it contained no surprises. He got the biggest applause when he attacked Hillary, using the refrain that she would, if elected President, "be giving Obama a third term in office."

Rhetorically, he announced that the GOP ticket for 2016 represented a "rendezvous with destiny." Then he added a word of caution: "None of us should think for one second that this should be easy. You know this won't be America's first glimpse of the Clinton machine in action, as Bernie Sanders can tell you. Democrats are about to anoint someone who represents everything this country is tired of," Pence said.

***

In an evaluation of the convention, one editorial writer said, "All week, speaker after speaker has painted a vision of a country imperiled by black nationalists, cop killers, immigrant murderers, Muslim terrorists, and criminal Democrats. Other than that, a good time was had by all until Lying Ted Cruz took the microphones."

Several thousand Trumpkins at the convention had vengefully screamed "LOCK HER UP!," lacerating Hillary for her alleged criminal activity.

An adviser to the Trump campaign, Al Baldasaro, a New Hampshire state representative and a Marine Corps veteran, had an even harsher punishment in mind. He called for Hillary to be executed for treason.

"She should be put in the firing line. She is a disgrace for the lies that she told those mothers about how their children got killed over there in Benghazi. She also dropped the ball on over four hundred e-mails requesting backup security. Hillary Clinton is nothing but a piece of garbage."

As always, columnist Linda Stasi summed up the dynamic of the convention with the most acid evaluation ever:

"Air kissing and ass kissing, airheads and heirheads, cheeseheads and cheeseballs, the Joker & the Dark Knight, countless white supremacists and eighteen black delegates. Nazi salutes and thumbs up, hip grabbing and back slapping. Make America Great Again and lock her up. Christie's kangaroo court and elephants acting like asses, Lucifer in flames and Trump in fog, Muslim banning and Muslims for Trump. Damn! I'm going to miss the Republican National Convention—this is the best show since Hamilton."

DAY FOUR
Of the Republican National Convention
Thursday, July 21, 2016

Gloom and Chaos as the Convention Nears Its Final Moments
DONALD ATTACKS IMMIGRATION & CRIME
"I AM THE VOICE OF LAW & ORDER!"

"LUCIFER—HE'S BACK!"
—John Boehner, in reference to Ted Cruz's Atomic Fallout

Gay Republican Delegates from Washington, D.C. Swim in
A SEA OF HOMOPHOBES

THE TRUMP QUINTET: A NEW GENERATION OF REALITY TV

Donald's Children Emerge as Convention Celebrities With Comparisons to the Kennedy Clan of the 1960s

As the month of July sweated its way to the dog days of August, and as the four-day GOP Convention in Cleveland unfolded, "The Impossible" happened. Against all odds, Donald J. Trump was going to become the Republican nominee for President of the United States.

Although there would be hopeless last minute attempts to block his candidacy, it seemed inevitable that Donald battle Hillary Clinton for the presidency.

Of course, a war chest was needed, but that was beginning to happen. During the previous month, the Trump coffers of gold had grown from a low of $1.3 million to $26 million in campaign contributions, as reluctant Republican donors were beginning to dig deep.

Nearly every major newspaper in America articulated an ominous concept associated with this most problematic of elections: Both Donald and Hillary carried too much baggage, too many negatives. Negative ratings, in fact, for both candidates had reached an alltime high.

Most voters were presented with the repellent choice of voting for whichever candidate they hated the least. It would be a case of picking the lesser of two evils to move into 1600 Pennsylvania Avenue on the 240th anniversary of the Republic.

Finally, as the fourth day of the convention opened, Thursday, July 21, delegates heard speaker after speaker, including Rudy Giuliani, who mostly expressed variations of the same theme: All of them despised Hillary, viewing her as "corrupt" and a "criminal deserving a lock-up."

Ranting demands to confine her in leg irons were heard throughout the Quicken Loans Arena in Cleveland.

America was no longer Ronald Reagan's shining city on a hill. If you believed the convention's speakers, the Republic was mired in a swampland of gloom, doom, and chaos run by inept leaders who were born in other countries, perhaps darkest Africa.

To warm up the crowd, Rudy Giuliani, the former mayor of New York, appeared before the crowd to deliver an impassioned and fiery speech. Surpassed only by Chris Christie, he became the second most powerful voice demanding the imprisonment of Hillary. Naturally, he brought up her e-mail scandal.

"If the Republicans take over the White House, we'll reopen the case. I'm really sick at what the Clintons have gotten away with."

"If Donald Trump becomes President, we'll bring her to trial. It is not double jeopardy. The statute of limitations is not up yet."

Giuliani, a ferocious former prosecutor, told delegates, "I'd like to be the attorney selected to prosecute her for high treason in giving away America's secrets to its deadliest enemies."

***

The surprise guest speaker of the convention's fourth and final evening was Peter Thiel. The billionaire co-founder of PayPal stunned the convention with: "Every American has a unique identity. I am proud to be a gay man. I am proud to be a Republican. But, most of all, I am proud to be an American."

His comments, to the shock of many watching from far away, were greeted with loud applause from the floor.

"I don't pretend to agree with every plank in our party's platform," Thiel said. "But fake culture wars only distract from our economic decline, and nobody in this race is being honest about it, except Donald Trump."

Then the 48-year-old billionaire likened himself to Donald, claiming, "We are not politicians, but both of us are builders. And it's time to rebuild America."

In addition to his self-defined status as a gay male, Thiel also belonged to another minority group: He was a Trump supporter from Silicon Valley. That made him what was called "a species of humans so endangered it might be called extinct."

"If a vote were taken tomorrow in the Silicon Valley, I bet Hillary Clinton would win about 95% of the vote," said one executive who did not want to be named.

Thiel had recently made national news when it was revealed that he had provided the financial support for Hulk Hogan's legal fight against Gawker Media, which bankrupted

Out, loud, and proud computer techie **Peter Thiel,** one of the only people from Silicon Valley to stump for Trump.

that exposé media firm.

"Techies" tended to view most of Donald's positions as abhorrent. Although he runs a notorious (and very sophisticated) Twitter campaign, most men and women who work in Silicon Valley viewed the GOP nominee as "an ignoramus." It was reported that most techies also evaluated Donald as a "kind of kryptonite."

Donald claimed that as President, he would enlist Microsoft founder Bill Gates to help him close down and deny casual access to essential parts of the Internet. He also promised to force Apple to manufacture iPhones in America, and he also threatened Amazon with an anti-trust investigation.

It seems that most techies are Democrats. In fact, one Mozilla CEO was forced out of his position when it was revealed that he had contributed to a campaign opposing same-sex marriage.

Thiel's remarks were mostly warmly received by the nineteen delegates representing Washington, D.C. A third of the delegation from the nation's capital were either gay or lesbian. They were still voting with the Republican Party even though it had just written a platform attacking gay rights, gay parenthood, and transgender issues.

These delegates had wanted some language inserted into the platform condemning discrimination against gays and acknowledging that they were often targets for murder from the Islamic Caliphate. All of their requests for revisions to the Republican platform had been rejected.

In high-profile contrast, the Democratic Party Platform, since 1980—the year that Ronald Reagan, no friend of gay people, had risen to power—had consistently called for general civil rights for the LGBT community.

The Washington, D.C. delegates applauded Thiel as one of their won, but most of the arena broke into shouts of "USA! USA! USA!" that were intended as a sign of their approval for the gay tycoon.

Christian Berle, an environmental policy analyst from Washington, D.C., said, "The GOP is becoming more and more narrow and more and more spiteful. I had to struggle to remain a Republican, as most of my gay friends have left the party. I have to ask myself every day: "Why am I a Republican?"

Jose Cunningham, the chairman of the Washington, D.C. delegation at the convention, said: "I'm gay, Latino, American, pro-life, and evangelical. Why didn't Trump put me on the stage?"

***

Much of the news on Thursday (the convention's last day) and Friday continued to focus on Ted Cruz's notorious campaign speech and his failure to endorse the GOP candidate for President. A reporter caught up with the disgraced and booed candidate as he headed back to Texas on a plane. "I won't vote for Hillary Clinton," Cruz said, "and I'm not going to endorse Donald Trump like some servile puppy dog. He targeted both my wife and father during the primary race, and those insults I can't forgive."

At a breakfast meeting on Thursday, July 21, the final day of the convention, with delegates from Texas, Cruz was booed by many in the audience, some of whom frequently interrupted his remarks chanting "TRUMP! TRUMP! TRUMP!"

Charles Krauthammer, the popular columnist and Fox TV talking head, defined Cruz's convention speech as "the longest suicide in American history."

Carl Paladino, former New York gubernatorial candidate, tweeted a picture of Donald talking into the ear of the Texas senator. It was captioned: "After I move to the White House, I'll hire you to mow the lawn."

Paladino said, "Cruz could have blown the roof off the building, attained statesman status, and be appointed to the Supreme Court under a Donald Trump administration. But he chose to implode with self-love."

Jeff Roe, Cruz's campaign manager, appeared on the Chris Stigall Show on Philadelphia radio. He claimed that Chris Christie had "lost his political testicles" when he endorsed Donald. That was a counterpunch for the New Jersey governor's denunciation of candidate Cruz on a previous night.

Most voters appeared disgusted with Cruz's campaign speech, as reflected in "Letters to the Editor" columns in newspapers across the country.

John Guonagura wrote: "Cruz is a modern-day Benedict Arnold—a traitor to his party. Politics is a dirty game, and Cruz is as low as it gets. The Texas battle cry was, 'REMEMBER THE ALAMO!' Now it should be 'FORGET TED CRUZ!'"

Marie Giovanniello wrote, "How sad that Ted Cruz has lived up to his pathetic shortcomings."

Nicholas A. Langworthy, chairman of the Erie County (NY) Republican Party, said "Cruz slit his own throat. He is finished in national Republican politics."

THE DAUGHTER ALSO RISES

With her straight blonde hair, her winning smile, stunning looks, and lovely pink frock, Ivanka Trump addressed the convention before Donald came out. Positioned as "the crown jewel of the Trump campaign," Donald had saved her appearance for last, thinking she would be the most impressive of his speech-making children.

The 34-year-old, the recent mother of her third child, she had converted to Judaism when she married real estate mogul Jared Kushner.

From the podium, as broadcast to millions, Ivanka claimed Donald would be "a boon to women. As President, my father will change the labor laws that were put in place during a time in which women were not a significant part of the work force. He will focus on making quality child care affordable and accessible for all."

"At our family's company, there are more female executives than male. Women are paid equally for work that we do and, when a woman becomes a mother, she is supported—not shut out."

For fifteen minutes, Ivanka spoke lovingly of Donald to loud applause. "Politicians talk about wage quality, but my father has made a practice at his company and throughout his career fighting for equal pay for equal work, and I will fight with him."

She had been positioned as a vital component in the evening's lineup, a speaker who would trumpet the best aspects of Donald to women voters. His favorability rating among women at the time was near a low of 24%.

Throughout her speech, Ivanka referred, frequently and repetitively, to "my father."

"I grew up constructing Lego skyscrapers at the feet of a man who was building the real thing," she said.

"Like so many of my fellow millennials, I do not consider myself categorically Republican or Democrat. More than party affiliation, I vote based on what I believe is right for my family and my country. Sometimes, it's a tough choice. That is not the case this time. Come January, 2017, all things will be possible again."

After listening to both Eric and Ivanka speak on different nights, it was obvious to delegates that brother and sister were on the same page about recognizing what a magnificent builder their father was.

When not at the convention hall, Ivanka and her husband, Jered Kushner, were often seen at the fourth floor hotel suite of billionaire casino magnate Sheldon Adelson. He always had a banquet of kosher food spread out—no pigs in a blanket, no lobster rolls.

After four of Donald's children had addressed the delegates, many reporters emphasized their similarities to images of the Kennedy clan in the 1960s.

DONALD'S CONVENTION ADDRESS
Thursday, July 21, 2016

Addressing a rocky and divisive convention in Cleveland on its final night, Donald Trump proclaimed, "I'll be a strongman!" Crime and violence that today afflicts our nation will soon come to an end," he promised. "Beginning on January 20, 2017, safety will be restored."

"The problems we face now—poverty and violence at home, war and destruction abroad—will last only as long as we continue relying on the same politicians who created them. A change in leadership is required to change these outcomes. There can be no prosperity without law and order. Hillary Clinton is proposing mass amnesty, mass immigration, and mass lawlessness."

He painted an America dipped in blood, a misdirected country that had suffered from a 50% increase of policemen killed in the line of duty during 2016 alone. He blamed it on "the rollback of criminal enforcement by Obama."

He also used the occasion to attack Hillary for her "legacy of death, destruction, and weakness."

"America is a nation of believers, dreamers, and strivers that is being led by a group of censors, critics, and cynics."

He accused Obama of "using the pulpit of the presidency to divide us by race and color. He has made America a more dangerous environment for everyone."

He also vowed to champion the cause of "The Forgotten American" and to destroy Radical Islamic Terrorism.

When he spoke of illegal immigration, there were chants of "BUILD THE WALL! BUILD THE WALL! BUILD THE WALL!"

He received massive approval when he spoke about recent killings of police officers. "I have a message to every last person threatening the peace on our streets and the safety of our police. When I take the oath of office next year, I will restore law and order to our country."

In many ways, Donald reminded voters of a President delivering a speech during wartime.

"It is time to show the whole world that America is back—bigger and better and stronger than ever."

In the Quicken Loans Arena, with a thicket of U.S. flags stanchioned behind him, he seemed to portray himself as a Messianic figure who would rescue America from three principal evils—illegal immigration, Global Radical Islamic Terrorists, and urban crime "which makes it unsafe to walk the streets of America."

"I can fix it," he boasted, a comment that would later be mocked by Hillary for suggesting that he could do it alone.

David Gergen, an adviser to four U.S. Presidents, said: "Trump puts forward the same iron fist of Richard Nixon. But Nixon clothed his in a velvet glove. Trump, however, threw away that glove."

The 70-year-old mogul used dark imagery in his portrait of a rotting America. At times, his voice was filled with anger when he spoke of an America humiliated around the world. "Any politician who does not grasp the danger is not fit to lead the country."

Yet he shocked many delegates from Red States when he transgressed the Republican's homophobic platform and vowed to use his power to protect LGBT citizens from "violence and oppression of a hateful foreign ideology," referring to the execution of gay people in the Muslim world. "Many times, they were beheaded, stoned to death, or thrown from tall buildings."

Amazingly, the audience applauded, in contrast to when a gay American soldier, addressing delegates via a videotaped recording, was booed at the convention that nominated Mitt Romney in 2012.

"I have to say, that as a Republican, it is so nice to hear you cheering for what I just said," Donald said, in reference to his remarks about protecting gays.

In his self-portrayal as a savior for his people, he said, "Every day I wake up determined to deliver a better life for the people all across the nation that have been ignored, neglected, and abandoned."

***

Many editorial writers were disappointed that he didn't use the occasion to present a detailed plan for change. "As always, it was an empty sales pitch," claimed one reporter.

The ever critical *New York Times* lashed out against him: "He has sought advantage by playing to disaffected people's worst instincts, inventing scapegoats and conspiracy theories, waging and inciting vicious attacks on those who disagree with him. He is a poisonous messenger for a legitimate demand: That an ossified party dedicate itself to improving working people's lives, instead of serving the elite."

Even after such a forceful speech, many delegates left the arena still hesitant about a vote for Donald. As Governor Gary Herbert of Utah put it, "I'm going to vote for Mike Pence, and Donald Trump comes along with the package."

Before the delegates filed out of the convention all that fateful evening, Donald delivered a ringing call to protect the American children of the future: "To every parent who dreams for their child, and every child who dreams for the future, I say these words to you tonight. I'm with you, I will fight for you, and I will win for you."

In his closing remarks, Donald said, "To all Americans tonight, in all our cities and town, I make this promise:

WE WILL MAKE AMERICA STRONG AGAIN.
WE WILL MAKE AMERICA PROUD AGAIN.
WE WILL MAKE AMERICA SAFE AGAIN.
AND WE WILL MAKE AMERICA GREAT AGAIN."

On July 23, just two days after Donald's grim message to American voters on the final night of the RNC in Cleveland, his arch-opponent, **Hillary Clinton,** announced her running mate for Veep, former Virginia governor, now Senator **Tim Kaine.**

A NEW PHASE IN THE DONALD WARS HAD BEGUN.

POST-CONVENTION POSTSCRIPT

For The Donald, for His Entourage, for the Republicans, & for the Nation:
Chaos, Confusion, Turmoil, Rage, & Despair

"I'm told every day to be nicer. But is that what America really wants?"

—Donald Trump

On the front cover of its edition of August 22, 2016, *Time* magazine, with a banner headline saying "MELTDOWN," depicted a dripping wax effigy of Donald Trump.

The article claimed, "Since the convention in Cleveland, Trump has done almost nothing right by traditional standards. He has picked fights with senior Republicans and Gold Star parents, invited Russian spies to meddle in U.S. democracy, and appeared to joke about gun enthusiasts' prematurely removing a U.S. president from office. He's shuffled campaign messages like playing cards and left GOP elders fretting that he lacks the judgment to be Commander-in-Chief. During a dismal two-week stretch, he surrendered a narrow lead over Democratic nominee Hillary Clinton and now trails by an average of eight points in recent nationwide polls."

One senior Hillary adviser said, "Trump can set himself on fire at breakfast, kill a nun at lunch, and waterboard a puppy in the afternoon. And that doesn't even get us to prime time."

In the wake of the GOP convention, Donald was at the center of one spectacular misstep after another.

In a bizarre rant on July 27, from a podium during a televised speech, he extended an invitation for Russia to commit espionage against Hillary and her Democrats, and to hack her e-mails. "Russia, if you are listening, I hope you are able to find the 30,000 Hillary e-mails that are missing. You'll find some beauties."

His phraseologies were immediately denounced as "treasonous" by security experts, and as a "new low" by news industry pundits.

House Speaker Paul Ryan immediately condemned the rant, denouncing Russia as a "global menace led by a devious thug. Putin should stay out of American elections."

On editorial writer suggested that the invitation he had extended to the Russians for the continuation of their espionage would be defined as grounds for impeachment if Donald Trump were elected President: "This is something a lot more serious than Bill Clinton getting a blow-job in the Oval Office."

With avid interest, Donald had watched the Democratic convention in Philadelphia. Although he was infuriated by nearly everything he saw, he had been enraged by one testimonial more than by any other: that of Khizr Khan, the Muslim father of a 27-year-old soldier killed in Iraq. Khan had ripped into Donald with, among others, the accusation that whereas military families had made ultimate sacrifices and endured oceans of suffering, "You, Mr. Trump, have sacrificed nothing."

The Khan family's son, Captain Humayun Khan, had been killed in 2004 by suicide bombers in Iraq after he'd waved his soldiers back and away from harm. For his bravery, he'd (posthumously) earned the Bronze Star and Purple Heart.

At the Democratic National Convention, at the podium, Khizr's wife, Ghazala, clad like a conservative Muslim woman, in a blue headscarf, had positioned herself silently and supportively beside her husband.

Khan's emotional denunciation of Trump was one of the highlights of the final night of the Democratic Convention. The event was climaxed by Hillary's address to the nation wherein she accepted her historic nomination for President.

Khan had articulated the feelings of Muslim Americas who had been repeatedly outraged by Donald's anti-Muslim pronouncements and rhetoric.

Shortly after the Khans' address to the nation, Donald reacted with white-heated venom, belittling and publicly trivializing them: "The father did all the talking because the mother was forbidden to speak because of her religion," he charged.

Khan shot back that his wife had not spoken because she was too overcome with grief at the death of her son.

As national coverage of the incident intensified, Governor John Kasich of Ohio—long an outspoken opponent of the Republican nominee, lashed out once again with, "There's only one way to talk about Gold Star parents: With honor and respect."

As July neared its end, Donald continued to horrify and amaze. When he appeared on ABC-TV's This Week for an interview with George Stephanopoulos, he made a spectacularly embarrassing foreign policy gaffes:

"Putin is not going into Ukraine, OK, just so you understand. He's not going into Ukraine, all right? You can mark it down. You can put it down."

[Donald's lack of understanding of the situation horrified insiders throughout the diplomatic community. Way back in 2014, in a move condemned by the Free World, and based on directives emanating directly from Putin, Russia had already invaded the Crimea, and had, since then, effectively annexed it from Ukraine.]

As the very hot month of August roared in like a fiery lion, so did campaign rhetoric. In an unusual move for a sitting President, Obama urged GOP leaders to withdraw their endorsements of Donald, describing him as "unfit to serve as President."

The month wasn't looking good for Donald. Stories appeared that described how Republican leaders were looking for ways "to replace loudmouth on the ticket," although it was not immediately made clear just how that would be accomplished. Loyal staffers were reported to be "almost suicidal," based on the potty-trail of gaffes perpetrated by their autocratic boss.

[A defender for Donald emerged at around this time in the form of 86-year-old Clint Eastwood. In Esquire magazine, he said he supported Donald—"The good, the bad, and the ugly." Eastwood then went on, in print, to bash America's "pussy generation."]

***

As if matters weren't complicated enough, simultaneous with the harshest of the backlashes against Donald, Melania's past suddenly came roaring back to haunt her.

It was revealed that way back in 1995, the would-be First Lady had been an undocumented and illegal worker. She had posed for nude fetish-industry photos on the fringes of the sex industry. This discovery was in marked contrast to her previous claims that she had arrived in the U.S. for the first time in 1996.

This new information, and the unearthing of these erotic, now widely distributed photos, revealed that her previous statements had been untrue. Had Donald's immigration policies been in effect at the time the photos had been snapped, she would have been deported.

In a daring exposé, the usually pro-Trump tabloid, the *New York Post*, in its edition of July 31, 2016, ran, on its front cover, a nude photo of Melania snapped in Manhattan in 1995. The nipples of her ample breasts are covered with blue paste-on stars, and she uses both hands to cover her (otherwise naked) vagina, with some pubic hairs showing.

On page 3 of that same edition, *The Post* had positioned a view of Melania's derrière. She's wearing only high heels.

The racy photos were taken by French fashion photographer Jarl Alé Alexandre de Basseville.

[Describing himself as "The Prince of Normandy, and a descendant of the 1st king Harald of Norway," he was born in Bordeaux, France, on July 8th, 1970. In a statement he made to the press, he said, "I am completely against this world, and I don't understand why girls fuck with old guys to afford a Chanel, Louis Vuitton, or Hermès bag. The fashion industry has become the biggest pimp ever."

Was he referring to Melania? Actually, he praised her, calling her "a super great and fantastic personality."]

The Post, in its edition of the following day, ran additional, even more shocking erotic photos, depicting Melania as a player in a lesbian romp with an also-naked Emma Eriksson, a gorgeous Scandinavian nudie. From the rear, she embraces Melania with arms that encircle her torso at a point just below her breasts. In another photo, the Viking goddess is depicted wearing a low-cut long robe designed by the notorious John Galliano. She raises a whip as if preparing to beat Melania, who's dressed in a skin-tight gown and high heels.

***

Around August 7, as the dog days of midsummer caused landscapes across the country to shimmer with perspiration and heat, Donald's poll numbers plummeted. Predictably, Donald went on the offensive.

As if he could see clairvoyantly into the future, he claimed that if he lost the presidency in the upcoming November election, it would be based on it having been "rigged" in favor of Hillary.

Trump advisor Roger Stone predicted *[or threatened, depending on your point of view]*, "The government will shut down if they *[the Democrats]* attempt to steal this and swear Hillary in."

John Pitney, a former GOP operative, also weighed in: "Given the history of Trump rallies, there is some potential for violence if Hillary is elected."

On the campaign trail, Donald had taken to calling the Democratic nominee, "Hillary Rotten Clinton."

"The voter ID situation has turned out to be a very unfair development. We may have people voting ten times. It's inconceivable that you don't have to show identification in order to vote."

***

Another blow hit the Trump campaign on August 8, as fifty of the country's top GOP national security officials signed a pact claiming that Donald "lacks the character, values, and experience to be President of the United States. He would put at risk the country's national security and well-being," the document stated. "He would be the most reckless President in American history."

As this document was released, Donald flew into depressed Detroit to deliver a speech outlining his economic agenda and tax changes. He claimed that his plans for the economy would spur economic growth and bring new jobs. He called Hillary "The Steward of Stagnation." His plan included deep tax cuts for the rich, himself included. He then went on to promise the disruption of long-standing trade agreements with other countries…"We can't fix a rigged system by relying on the people who rigged it in the first place."

***

As August deepened, Hillary's attacks on Donald grew ever harsher. Frequently and publicly, she questioned his mental and emotional stability, asserting that it would be dangerous to turn over America's nuclear codes to such a deranged personality. "Imagine him in the Oval Office facing a real crisis," she said. "A man you can bait with a tweet is not a man you can trust with nuclear weapons!"

***

In defiance of the Republican National Committee virtually screaming for Donald to become more presidential, he delivered a suggestion [or was it a threat?] that echoed, instantly around the world.

The *New York Daily News*, on its front page, summed it up like this: "When Trump hinted gun-rights supporters shoot Hillary, he went from offensive to reckless. He must end his campaign. If he doesn't, the GOP needs to abandon him."

During a speech in the crucial "swing state" of North Carolina, Donald had delivered a jaw-droppingly enigmatic remark that horrified virtually everyone:

"Hillary wants to essentially abolish the Second Amendment. By the way, and if she gets to pick

Supreme Court Judges, [there's] nothing you can do, folks. Although the Second Amendment people…maybe there is. I don't know."

Reporters interpreted his remark as a suggestion that gun advocates should aim (and shoot) their weapons at Hillary. True loyalists in the crowd applauded, but others among his supporters appeared shocked. Of course, the National Rifle Association quickly tweeted its continuing endorsement of their combustible candidate.

Literally millions of Americans, led by Senator Elizabeth Warren, condemned Donald's call to arms: Warren tweeted, "Donald Trump makes death threats because he's a pathetic coward who can't handle the fact that he's losing to a girl."

Anti-Trump groups, including the Democratic Coalition Against Trump, demanded an investigation by the FBI, arguing that Donald should be arrested for attempting to incite violence, perhaps even encouraging an assassination of his opponent.

POST-ELECTION POSTSCRIPT

On November 8, 2016, Donald Trump Seized Control of "THE DIVIDED STATES OF AMERICA"

On the morning of the presidential election, Tuesday, November 8, 2016, the *New York Post*, Donald Trump's hometown newspaper, depicted a young woman on its frontpage, holding her nose. The headline read: VOTE FOR THE ONE YOU DISLIKE THE LEAST.

Poll after poll showed that the Republican candidate, Donald Trump, and his Democratic challenger, Hillary Clinton, were the two most disliked people ever to seek the office of President of the United States.

Across this vast nation, millions flocked to the polls in the wake of an extraordinarily nasty presidential race, battling until the 11th hour.

Hillary Clinton, the first woman ever to be nominated by a major party, and Donald Trump duked it out in battleground states that included North Carolina, Florida, Pennsylvania, Ohio, Michigan, and Georgia.

As the sun rose that morning, most national polls had Clinton leading by 3 to 6 percentage points. Democrats were confidant, the Trump camp not so jubilant, fearing defeat. Their contender denounced in advance, "IT'S A RIGGED ELECTION BY CROOKED HILLARY!"

As the early election results began to pour into television stations on that fateful Tuesday night, millions of people across the world tuned in to watch the news.

Then the unthinkable happened. Trump was going to win, even though he trailed behind, with Clinton garnering an estimated 1.5 million more of the popular vote. But what mattered was the Electoral College, in which Trump swept to victory.

He became the 45th President of the United States, in part, by capturing the vote of the nation's alienated white blue-collar workers, many of whom had lost their livelihoods after their jobs were shipped overseas.

Trump's victory was a stinging rebuke to the Democratic Party and its leadership. Millions of American women had their hopes dashed about Clinton breaking the glass ceiling and becoming the first woman president.

At the age of 70, the real estate mogul became the oldest man ever elected president, slightly older than Ronald Reagan when he had taken office.

Many black activists called the massive outpouring from Trump a "white backlash."

Millions of horrified TV viewers in Europe woke up to hear the news. Their reaction appeared in "Second Coming" headlines across the Continent. One German newspaper proclaimed "**THE COMING OF THE APOCALYPSE.**" A London tabloid asked: "**OH GOD, AMERICA, WHAT HAVE YOU DONE TO US?**"

Pundits claimed that the election foreshadowed that the United States in the future would focus on its own affairs, leaving the rest of the world to fend for itself.

Throughout his campaign, Trump had billed himself as as an outsider, determined to "drain the swamps" in Washington. He had run a scandal-soaked campaign, filled with embarrassing revelations about his past, only a few of which would probably have destroyed a normal candidate.

In rally after rally during his slapdash campaign, he had attacked minority groups on the basis of their race and religion. He had mocked Clinton as "the most corrupt and crooked individual ever to seek the presidency."

The New York Times admitted, "It's true that racism and misogyny played a large role in Trump's campaign of erratic tweets and rambling speeches, deemed politically incorrect as he attacked Muslims, John McCain ("not a war hero") and even the disabled."

Trump's election led to protests, sometimes violent, on the streets of large American cities. Assassination threats poured in, but the President-elect roared ahead, (reluctantly) preparing to switch residences from the glitzy Trump Tower in Manhattan's center to the more modest (and perhaps more restrictive) digs at 1600 Pennsylvania Avenue.

Ever since he was a pugnacious out-of-control boy with big teeth growing up in Queens, New York, Donald always proclaimed, "I get what I'm after."

And so it came to be.

Many editorial writers issued a warning by digging up an old saying, "Beware of what you want, for you shall surely get it."

Trump at last had it, but what would he to do with it?

As he faced the beginning of the first year of his presidency, his campaign promises and threats had piled up into a foreboding mountain, and dozens of compelling questions remained unanswered.

Would he follow through on this promises and threats, as expressed on the campaign trail?

With Republicans in control of both the Senate and the House, he, as a Republican president, had become a force who could even change—through the appointment of ultra-conservatives—the balance of power on the Supreme Court.

UNCLEAR AND UNANSWERED:

Would he punish women who seek an abortion?

Would he eradicate crime, drugs, and murder in such cities as Chicago and Baltimore?

Would he build a wall along the southern border, and persuade or coerce Mexico to pay for it?

Would he deport millions of illegal aliens? Would he deport Muslims?

Would he, in his own words, "bomb the shit out of ISIS?"

Would he prosecute Hillary Clinton and send her to jail?

Would he bring jobs back to the towns and cities of Rustbelt America?

Would he lower taxes on the very rich?

Could he be trusted to preside over America's arsenal of nuclear weapons?

Would he continue his "bro-mance" with Putin? Would he activate a trade war with China?

Would he abandon our NATO allies for not paying their fair share?

Would he invalidate the North American free Trade Agreement?

Would he repudiate the international agreement made in Paris on climate change? And

Would he tear up the agreement with Iran that prevented it from developing a nuclear weapon?

"STICK AROUND AND WE WILL SEE," SOOTHSAYERS SAID AT THE TIME.

AND SO WE DID

CONCLUSION: Regardless of how voters interpreted the outcome of the November 2016 Presidential election, there is one thing on which most people agreed: Despite methods and style that millions, worldwide, found odious, Donald J. Trump secured a permanent, deeply entrenched position for himself within the history of the Republic. Today, more than ever, he's a unique and historically important figure who's vital to an understanding of the American Experience.

"GOD'S REVENGE ON US"

—Jimmy Carter, on the election of Donald Trump

DARWIN PORTER

Darwin's interest in politics and the celebrities who dominate it began at an early age, during World War II, when sometimes horrifying updates about U.S. wins and losses on the battlefields of Europe and the Pacific sent hearts racing and cultural divides fluttering in hotly contested elections.

Later, as an aspirant journalist who edited the student newspaper (*The Miami Hurricane*) at the University of Miami, then-teenaged Darwin became the recipient of a scholarship that was haphazardly administered by then-Florida Senator **George Smathers**, an intimate "wenching companion" of JFK.

Within a few years, in a climate where meeting politicos was relatively free of barriers and the security issues associated with it today, young Darwin interviewed and mingled with A-list politicos who included **Eleanor Roosevelt; former U.S. President Harry Truman, JFK** and **Jacqueline Kennedy**; the many-faceted **Gore Vidal**; and figures important to the (sometimes spectacularly corrupt) local politics of South Florida.

His interest in politicians was contiguous with a fascination for movie stars, each of whom seemed to court approval from the same voters. Thus was launched his lifelong fascination with celebrity, the high-octane variety that America produced with a frenzy unmatched anywhere else in the world.

Even as a precocious nine-year-old, Darwin met entertainers and politicians through his mother, **Hazel**, a charismatic Southern girl whose husband had died in World War II. Migrating from the Depression-ravaged valleys of western North Carolina to Miami Beach during its most ebullient heyday, Hazel became a personal assistant to the vaudeville comedienne **Sophie Tucker**, the kind-hearted "Last of the Red Hot Mamas." One of her greatest fans was a young **Ronald Reagan**, who showed up at her night club gigs paying his respects to "Miss Sophie." Later, one of Darwin's female friends—we'll call her Margaret—sustained a long-time affair with **Bebe Rebozo**, the best friend of **Richard Nixon**. Information about the flaws and indiscretions of both of them flowed freely.

Politicians were not the only big game wandering through glittering landscapes of young Darwin's South Florida—there were plenty of show-biz flora and fauna, too. Loosely supervised by his mother, Darwin was regularly dazzled by the likes of **Judy Garland, Dinah Shore,** and **Frank Sinatra.**

At the University of Miami, Darwin edited the school newspaper, raising its revenues, through advertising and public events, to unheard-of new levels. He met and interviewed **Eleanor Roosevelt** and later invited her, as part of a sponsored event he crafted, to spend a day ("Eleanor Roosevelt Day") at the university, and to his delight, she accepted. Years later, in Manhattan, during her work as a human rights activist, he escorted her, at her request, to many public functions.

YESTERDAY, WHEN HE WAS YOUNG

DARWIN PORTER
A social historian fascinated by biographies and the ironies of the American Experience.

On another occasion, he invited **Lucille Ball** and **Desi Arnaz**, then at the pinnacle of their fame and popularity, to the University. On campus, after the photographers and fans departed, Lucille launched a bitter attack on her husband, accusing him of having had sex the previous night with two showgirls. Because of that and other upsets that unfolded that day, Darwin learned early in his life that Lucille Ball and Desi Arnaz were definitely not Ricky and Lucy Ricardo.

After his graduation, Darwin, in a graceful transition from his work as editor of the University's newspaper and his sponsorship by **Wilson Hicks** (Photo Editor and then Executive Editor of *Life* magazine) became a Bureau Chief of *The Miami Herald* (the youngest in that publication's history) assigned to its branch in Key West. At the time, the island outpost was an avant-garde literary mecca and—thanks to the Cuban missile crisis—a flash point of the Cold War.

Key West had been the site of **Harry S Truman**'s "Winter White House," and Truman returned a few months before his death for a final visit. He invited young Darwin for "early morning walks" where he used the young emissary of *The Miami Herald* to "set the record straight" about the politics of postwar America.

Through Truman, Darwin was introduced and later joined the staff of **Senator George Smathers** of Florida. Smathers' best friend was a young senator, **John F. Kennedy**. Through "Gorgeous George," as Smathers was known in the Senate, Darwin got to meet **Jack and Jacqueline** in Palm Beach. He later wrote two books about them—*The Kennedys, All the Gossip Unfit to Print*, and one of his all-time bestsellers, *Jacqueline Kennedy Onassis—A Life Beyond Her Wildest Dreams. [A commemorative new edition of that sold-out biography was released in 2022 as* JKO: Her Tumultuous Life & Her Love Affairs.*]*

Buttressed by his status as *The Miami Herald*'s Key West Bureau Chief, Darwin met, interviewed, and often befriended celebrities who included **Tennessee Williams. Ernest Hemingway, Tallulah Bankhead** *[a lifelong Democrat who worked tirelessly for the ongoing re-election of the Roosevelts]*, **Gore Vidal** *[who ran for public office in a failed bid for election as a member of the New York State House of Representatives]*, **Truman Capote, Carson McCullers**, and a gaggle of other internationally famous writers and entertainers: **Cary Grant, Rock Hudson, Marlon Brando, Montgomery Clift, Susan Hayward, Warren Beatty, Christopher Isherwood, Anne Bancroft, Angela Lansbury**, and **William Inge.**

Eventually transferred to Manhattan, Darwin worked for a decade in television advertising with the producer and arts-industry socialite **Stanley Mills Haggart**. In addition to some speculative ventures associated with **Marilyn Monroe**, they also jointly produced TV commercials that included testimonials from **Joan Crawford** *[then feverishly promoting Pepsi-Cola]*; **Ronald Reagan** *[General Electric]*; and **Debbie Reynolds** *[Singer sewing machines]*. Other personalities they promoted, each delivering televised sales pitches, included **Louis Armstrong, Lena Horne, Rosalind Russell, William Holden,** and **Arlene Dahl,** each of them hawking commercial and in some cases, political, products and causes.

Beginning in the early 1960s, Darwin joined forces with the then-fledgling **Arthur Frommer** organization, playing a key role in researching and writing more than 50 titles and defining the style and values that later emerged as the world's leading travel guidebooks, *The Frommer Guides*. Darwin's particular journalistic expertise on Europe, New England, California, and the Caribbean eventually propelled him into authorship of (depending on the era and whatever crises were brewing at the time), between 70 and 80% of their titles. Even during the research of his travel guides, he continued to interview political and show-biz celebrities, discussing their triumphs, feuds, frustrations, and political visions. At this point in their lives, many were retired and reclusive. Darwin either pursued them (sometimes through local tourist offices) or encountered them randomly as part of his extensive travels. **Ava Gardner, Lana Turner, Hedy Lamarr, Ingrid Bergman, Ethel Merman, Andy Warhol, Elizabeth Taylor, Marlene Dietrich, Bette Davis, Judy Garland,** and **Paul Newman** were particularly insightful.

Porter's biographies—at this writing, they number sixty-three— have won thirty first prize or "runner-up to first prize" awards at literary festivals in cities or regions which include New England, New York, Los Angeles, Hollywood, San Francisco, Florida, California, and Paris.

A resident of New York City, where he spent years within the social orbit of the Queen of Off-Broadway (the eccentric and very temperamental philanthropist, **Lucille Lortel**), Darwin is currently at work on a series of books with eyebrow-raising revelations about the dazzling personalities who kept the lights sparkling both On and Off Broadway in the 60s and 70s.

DANFORTH PRINCE

A graduate of Hamilton College and a native of Easton and Bethlehem, Pennsylvania, he's president and founder *[in 1983]* of the Porter and Prince Corporation, the entity that produced the original texts and updates for dozens of key titles of **THE FROMMER GUIDES**—travel "bibles" for millions of readers during the travel industry's go-go years in the 80s, 90s, and early millennium.

He also founded, in 1996, the **Georgia Literary Association**, precursor to what morphed, in 2004, into **Blood Moon Productions**, the corporate force behind dozens of political and Hollywood biographies. Its vaguely apocalyptic name was inspired by one of Darwin Porter's popular early novels, *Blood Moon*, a thriller about the false gods of power, wealth, and physical beauty. In 2011, Prince was named "Publisher of the Year" by a consortium of literary critics and marketers spearheaded by the J.M. Northern Media Group.

Prince has electronically documented his stewardship of Blood Moon in at least 50 videotaped documentaries, book trailers, public speeches, and TV or radio interviews. Most of these are available on YouTube.com and Facebook (keyword: "Danforth Prince"); on Twitter (#BloodyandLunar); or by clicking on **BloodMoonProductions.com**.

DANFORTH PRINCE

BLOOD MOON WANTS READERS TO KNOW THAT THE DONALD IS NOT THE ONLY BENEFICIARY OF CELEBRITY POLITICAL "ANALYSES" FROM PORTER & PRINCE.

THEY'VE FOCUSSED ON DEMOCRATS, TOO! FOR MORE INFORMATION ABOUT EACH OF THE TITLES WHOSE COVERS APPEAR IMMEDIATELY BELOW, PLEASE CONTINUE FLIPPING THROUGH THE FINAL PAGES OF THIS BOOK.

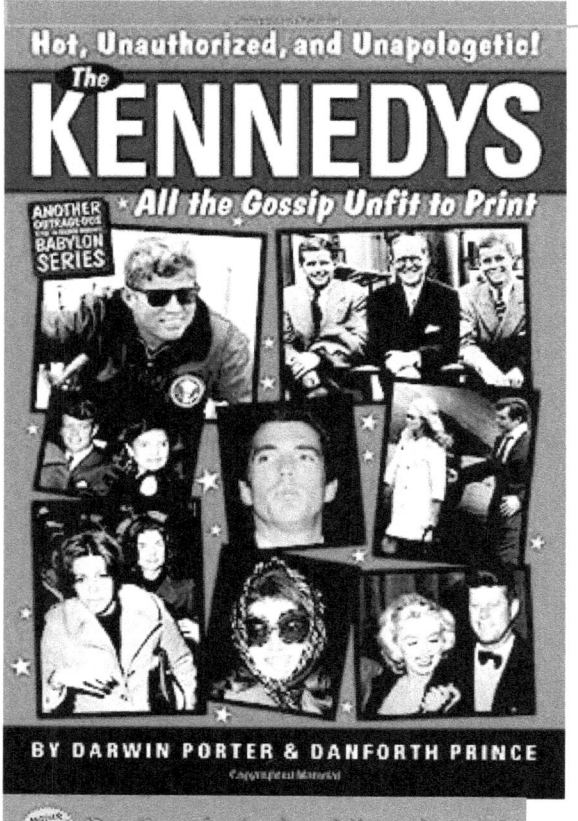

AMERICA!

THERE'S NO PLACE LIKE HOME

LUCILLE BALL & DESI ARNAZ

BECAME THE MOST CELEBRATED DUO IN THE HISTORY OF TELEVISION

Half of America gathered every Monday night around the little black box in their living rooms to watch the antics of Lucy and Ricky Ricardo, a Cuban bandleader with his wacky, high-spirited wife.

The early struggles of Lucy and Desi were epic. As a girl, she at times was literally chained in her backyard in Jamestown, New York. As a teenager, she broke away and earned a reputation as "The Jamestown hussy," riding around with Johnny DeVita, a local hoodlum.

Born to wealth and privilege in Cuba, Desi, at the age of twelve, was escorted to the local bordello by his father to lose his virginity.

His family lost everything in the Cuban Revolution and fled to America. In Miami, Desi got a job cleaning out canary cages. He was eventually hired by bandleader Xavier Cugat because, "I beat hell out of those Afro-Cuban drums."

Meanwhile, in Manhattan, Lucy was struggling to break into show business, hustling "sugar daddies" and stage-door Johnnies who gave her money and gifts. Once, when desperate, she became a nude model. "A gal's gotta eat."

In the 1930s, she made it to Hollywood and worked making films for RKO. The executives used her as a gussied-up hooker to "entertain" out-of-town film exhibitors.

[Ultimately, she got her revenge. In one of the most ironic "fiscal revolutions" in show-biz history, she bought the studio.]

Drifting to Hollywood, Desi spotted Lucy on a sound stage "dressed like a two-dollar whore who had been badly beaten by her pimp." Their tempestuous marriage, characterized by long separations, staggered along for two decades.

By the early 1950s, the careers of both Desi and Lucy had headed south. There was a lot of resistance among TV executives who objected to his Cuban accent. But *I Love Lucy* was launched nevertheless and shot up in the ratings like a rocket, morphing into the most successful sitcom in TV history.

"With gold arriving in wheelbarrows" (Desi's words), they bought the four-block RKO Studios. Desilu Productions was launched, becoming the largest motion picture and television studio in the world.

In 1960, after their divorce, Lucy appraised her husband: "He is a Jekyll and Hyde type. He drinks, gambles, and chases the broads from thirteen to thirty, even Carrie Fisher. He's awash in broads, lots of booze, and that gay actor, Cesar Romero, is his devoted slave. Desi is destructive, but always building something. If it's big, he has to break it down."

"Love?" she asked. "I was always falling in love with the wrong man. Even Desi."

Desi, too, summed up his many years of marriage: "We were anything but Lucy and Ricky Ricardo on the tube. Those guys had nothing to do with us. Lucy and I dreamed of success, fame, and fortune. Guess what? ***It all led to hell.***"

LUCILLE BALL & DESI ARNAZ

THEY WEREN'T LUCY AND RICKY RICARDO

VOLUME ONE (1911-1960)
OF A TWO-PART BIOGRAPHY

Darwin Porter and Danforth Prince
ISBN 978-1-936003-71-6
Softcover, 530 pages, with photos,
available everywhere now

THE SAD & TRAGIC ENDING OF LUCILLE BALL

VOLUME TWO (1961-1989)
OF A TWO-PART BIOGRAPHY

Darwin Porter and Danforth Prince
ISBN 978-1-936003-80-8
Softcover, 550 pages, with photos, available
everywhere now

Judy Garland & Liza Minnelli

Too Many Damn Rainbows

Judy and Liza were the greatest, most colorful, and most tragic mother-daughter saga in show biz history. They live, laugh, and weep again in the tear-soaked pages of this remarkable biography. Darwin Porter and Danforth Prince have compiled a compelling "post-modern" spin.

According to Liza, "My mother—hailed as the world's greatest entertainer—lived eighty lives during her short time with us."

Their memorable stories unfold through eyewitness accounts of the typhoons that engulfed them. They swing across glittery landscapes of euphoria and glory, detailing the betrayals and treachery which the duo encountered almost daily. There were depressions "as deep as the Mariana Trench," suicide attempts, and obsessive identifications on deep psychological levels with roles that include Judy's Vicky Lester in *A Star is Born* (1954) and Liza's Sally Bowles in *Cabaret* (1972).

Lesser known are the jealous actress-to-actress rivalries. Fueled by klieg lights and rivers of negative publicity, they sprouted like malevolent mushrooms on steroids.

As Judy faded into the 1960s, Liza roaringly emerged as a star in her own right. "I did it my way," Liza said. She survived the whirlwinds of her mother's drug addiction with a yen for choosing all the wrong men in patterns that weirdly evoked those of Judy herself.

For millions of fans, Judy will forever remain the cheerful adolescent (Dorothy) skipping along a yellow brick road toward the other side of the rainbow. Liza followed her down that hallucinogenic path, searching for the childhood, the security, and the love that eluded her.

Judy Garland, an icon whose memory is permanently etched into the American psyche, continues to thrive as a cult goddess. Revered by thousands of die-hard fans, she's the most poignant example of both the manic and depressive (some say "schizophrenic") sides of the Hollywood myth.

Deep in her 70s, Liza is still with us, too, nursing memories of her former acclaim and her first visit as a little girl to her parents at MGM, the "Dream Factory," during the Golden Age of Hollywood.

Judy Garland & Liza Minnelli: Too Many Damn Rainbows
Darwin Porter & Danforth Prince
Softcover, 6" x 9", with hundreds of photos. ISBN 9781936003693
Available Everywhere Now

The Seductive Sapphic Exploits of
Mercedes de Acosta
Hollywood's Greatest Lover

IF YOU ASSUMED THAT THE GREATEST LOVERS ARE MEN, some of the most famous "cult goddesses" of the early- and mid-20th-Century might emphatically disagree.

At Magnolia House, in the final years of her life, the celebrated, notorious, and once-fabled Spanish beauty, **MERCEDES DE ACOSTA** (1892-1968) was a frequent visitor. To Darwin Porter, she confessed and recited fabulously indiscreet stories about her romantic same-sex exploits among the theatrical and cinematic elite of New York, London, Paris, and Hollywood.

*It reveals "Sapphic Standards" from the heyday of Silent Film and the early Talkies that no other book—even her own (*Here Lies the Heart, *published in 1960)— ever dared to make public.*

Mercedes de Acosta's love affairs were with women, each a figurehead in art, the theater, and the filmmaking and literary scenes. They included Greta Garbo, Marlene Dietrich, Nazimova, Gertrude Stein, Alice B. Toklas, Eva Le Gallienne, Tallulah Bankhead, Jeanne Eagels, Katharine Cornell, Eleanora Duse, Isadora Duncan, and both of Valentino's wives. This is probably the best portrait of *avant-garde* Broadway and early 20th-century filmmaking ever published.

Read all about it in the most recent installment of Blood Moon's MAGNOLIA HOUSE SERIES

The Seductive Sapphic Exploits of
MERCEDES DE ACOSTA
Hollywood's Greatest Lover

Darwin Porter and Danforth Prince   ISBN 978-1-936003-75-4.
A pithy, photo-packed softcover with 474 pages and many dozens of photos
available now from Ingram's Lightning Source and Amazon.com

LOVE TRIANGLE
Ronald Reagan, Jane Wyman, & Nancy Davis

HOW MUCH DO YOU REALLY KNOW ABOUT THE REAGANS?

THIS BOOK TELLS EVERYTHING ABOUT THE SHOW-BIZ SCANDALS THEY DESPERATELY WANTED TO FORGET.

UNIQUE IN THE HISTORY OF PUBLISHING, THIS SCANDALOUS TRIPLE BIOGRAPHY focuses on the Hollywood indiscretions of former U.S. president Ronald Reagan and his two wives. A proud and Presidential addition to Blood Moon's Babylon series, it digs deep into what these three young and attractive movie stars were doing decades before two of them took over the Free World.

As reviewed by Diane Donovan, Senior Reviewer at the California Bookwatch section of the Midwest Book Review: "Love Triangle: Ronald Reagan, Jane Wyman & Nancy Davis may find its way onto many a Republican Reagan fan's reading shelf; but those who expect another Reagan celebration will be surprised: this is lurid Hollywood exposé writing at its best, and outlines the truths surrounding one of the most provocative industry scandals in the world.

"There are already so many biographies of the Reagans on the market that one might expect similar mile-markers from this: be prepared for shock and awe; because Love Triangle doesn't take your ordinary approach to biography and describes a love triangle that eventually bumped a major Hollywood movie star from the possibility of being First Lady and replaced her with a lesser-known Grade B actress (Nancy Davis).

"From politics and betrayal to romance, infidelity, and sordid affairs, Love Triangle is a steamy, eye-opening story that blows the lid off of the Reagan illusion to raise eyebrows on both sides of the big screen.

"Black and white photos liberally pepper an account of the careers of all three and the lasting shock of their stormy relationships in a delightful pursuit especially recommended for any who relish Hollywood gossip."

In 2015, LOVE TRIANGLE, Blood Moon Productions' overview of the early dramas associated with Ronald Reagan's scandal-soaked career in Hollywood, was designated by the Awards Committee of the HOLLYWOOD BOOK FESTIVAL as Runner-Up to Best Biography of the Year.

LOVE TRIANGLE: Ronald Reagan, Jane Wyman, & Nancy Davis
Darwin Porter & Danforth Prince
Softcover, 6" x 9", with hundreds of photos.   ISBN 978-1-936003-41-9

> **THIS BOOK ILLUSTRATES WHY *GENTLEMEN PREFER BLONDES*, AND WHY MARILYN MONROE WAS TOO DANGEROUS TO BE ALLOWED TO GO ON LIVING.**

Less than an hour after the discovery of Marilyn Monroe's corpse in Brentwood, a flood of theories, tainted evidence, and conflicting testimonies began pouring out into the public landscape.

Filled with rage, hysteria, and depression, "and fed up with Jack's lies, Bobby's lies," Marilyn sought revenge and mass vindication. Her revelations at an imminent press conference could have toppled political dynasties and destroyed criminal empires. Marilyn had to be stopped…

Into this steamy cauldron of deceit, Marilyn herself emerges as a most unreliable witness during the weeks leading up to her murder. Her own deceptions, vanities, and self-delusion poured toxic accelerants on an already raging fire.

> *"This is the best book about Marilyn Monroe ever published."*
> —**David Hartnell**, Recipient, in 2011, of New Zealand's Order of Merit (MNZM) for services to the entertainment industry, as defined by Her Majesty, Queen Elizabeth II.

Winner of literary awards from the New York, Hollywood, and San Francisco Book Festivals

"Darwin Porter is fearless, honest and a great read. He minces no words. If the truth makes you wince and honesty offends your sensibility, stay away. It's been said that he deals in muck because he can't libel the dead. Well, it's about time someone started telling the truth about the dead and being honest about just what happened to get us in the mess in which we're in. If libel is lying, then Porter is so completely innocent as to deserve an award. In all of his works he speaks only to the truth, and although he is a hard teacher and task master, he's one we ignore at our peril. To quote Gore Vidal, power is not a toy we give to someone for being good. If we all don't begin to investigate where power and money really are in the here and now, we deserve what we get. Yes, Porter names names. The reader will come away from the book knowing just who killed Monroe. Porter rather brilliantly points to a number of motives, but leaves it to the reader to surmise exactly what happened at the rainbow's end, just why Marilyn was killed. And, of course, why we should be careful of getting exactly what we want. It's a very long tumble from the top."

—ALAN PETRUCELLI, Examiner.com, May 13, 2012

> # MARILYN: DON'T EVEN DREAM ABOUT TOMORROW
> SEX, LIES, MURDER, AND THE GREAT COVER-UP, BY DARWIN PORTER
> ISBN 978-1-936003-79-2   A Revised Edition of Darwin Porter's Investigative Classic from 2012
> *MARILYN AT RAINBOW'S END*

CARRIE FISHER & DEBBIE REYNOLDS
PRINCESS LEIA & UNSINKABLE TAMMY IN HELL

It's history's first comprehensive, unauthorized overview of one of the greatest mother-daughter acts in showbiz history, Debbie Reynolds ("hard as nails and with more balls than any five guys I've ever known") and her talented, often traumatized daughter, Carrie Fisher ("one of the smartest, hippest chicks in Hollywood"). Evolving for decades under the unrelenting glare of public scrutiny, each became a world-class symbol of the social and cinematic tastes that prevailed during their heydays as celebrity icons in Hollywood.

It's a scandalous saga of the ferociously loyal relationship of the "boop-boop-a-doop" girl with her intergalactic STAR WARS daughter, and their iron-willed, "true grit" battles to out-race changing tastes in Hollywood.

Loaded with revelations about "who was doing what to whom" during the final gasps of Golden Age Hollywood, it's an All-American story about the price of glamour, career-related pain, family anguish, romantic betrayals, lingering guilt, and the volcanic shifts that affected a scrappy, mother-daughter team—and everyone else who ever loved the movies.

"Feeling misunderstood by the younger (female) members of your gene pool? This is the Hollywood exposé every grandmother should give to her granddaughter, a roadmap like Debbie Reynolds might have offered to Billie Lourd."
—Marnie O'Toole

"Hold onto your hats, the "bad boys" of Blood Moon Productions are back. This time, they have an exhaustively researched and highly readable account of the greatest mother-daughter act in the history of show business: Debbie Reynolds and Carrie (Princess Leia) Fisher. If celebrity gossip and inside dirt is your secret desire, check it out. This is a fabulous book that we heartily recommend. It will not disappoint. We rate it worthy of four stars."
—MAJ Glenn MacDonald, U.S. Army Reserve (Retired), © MilitaryCorruption.com

"How is a 1950s-era movie star, (TAMMY) supposed to cope with her postmodern, substance-abusing daughter (PRINCESS LEIA), the rebellious, high-octane byproduct of Rock 'n Roll, Free Love, and postwar Hollywood's most scandal-soaked marriage? Read about it here, in Blood Moon's unauthorized double exposé about how Hollywood's toughest (and savviest) mother-daughter team maneuvered their way through shifting definitions of fame, reconciliation, and fortune."
—Donna McSorley

Winner of the coveted "Best Biography" Award from the 2018
New York Book Festival

CARRIE FISHER & DEBBIE REYNOLDS,
UNSINKABLE TAMMY & PRINCESS LEIA IN HELL
Darwin Porter & Danforth Prince

630 pages Softcover with photos. Now online and in bookstores everywhere
ISBN 978-1-936003-57-0

This is What Happens When A Demented Billionaire Hits Hollywood

HOWARD HUGHES
HELL'S ANGEL
DARWIN PORTER

From his reckless pursuit of love as a rich teenager to his final days as a demented fossil, Howard Hughes tasted the best and worst of the century he occupied. Along the way, he changed the worlds of aviation and entertainment forever.

This biography reveals inside details about his destructive and usually scandalous associations with other Hollywood players.

"The Aviator flew both ways. Porter's biography presents new allegations about Hughes' shady dealings with some of the biggest names of the 20th century"
—*New York Daily News*

"Darwin Porter's access to film industry insiders and other Hughes confidants supplied him with the resources he needed to create a portrait of Hughes that both corroborates what other Hughes biographies have divulged, and go them one better."
—*Foreword Magazine*

"Thanks to this bio of Howard Hughes, we'll never be able to look at the old pinups in quite the same way again."
—*The Times* (London)

Winner of a respected literary award from the Los Angeles Book Festival, this book gives an insider's perspective about what money can buy —and what it can't.

814 pages, with photos. **Available everywhere now.**
ISBN 978-1-936003-13-6

LANA TURNER

The Sweater Girl, Celluloid Venus, Sex Nymph to the G.I.s who won World War II, and Hollywood's OTHER Most Notorious Blonde

Beautiful and Bad, Her Full Story Has Never Been Told. UNTIL NOW!

Lana Turner was the most scandalous, most copied, and most gossiped-about actress in Hollywood. When her abusive Mafia lover was murdered in her house, every newspaper in the Free World described the murky dramas with something approaching hysteria.

Blood Moon's salacious but empathetic new biography exposes the public and private dramas of the girl who changed the American definition of what it REALLY means to be a blonde.

Here's how CALIFORNIA BOOKWATCH and THE MIDWEST BOOK REVIEW described the mega-celebrity as revealed in this book:

"Lana Turner: Hearts and Diamonds Take All belongs on the shelves of any collection strong in movie star biographies in general and Hollywood evolution in particular, and represents no lightweight production, appearing on the 20th anniversary of Lana Turner's death to provide a weighty survey packed with new information about her life.

"One would think that just about everything to be known about The Sweater Girl would have already appeared in print, but it should be noted that Lana Turner: Hearts and Diamonds Take All offers many new revelations not just about Turner, but about the movie industry in the aftermath of World War II.

"From Lana's introduction of a new brand of covert sexuality in women's movies to her scandalous romances among the stars, her extreme promiscuity, her search for love, and her notorious flings - even her involvement in murder - are all probed in a revealing account of glamour and movie industry relationships that bring Turner and her times to life.

"Some of the greatest scandals in Hollywood history are intricately detailed on these pages, making this much more than another survey of her life and times, and a 'must have' pick for any collection strong in Hollywood history in general, gossip and scandals and the real stories behind them, and Lana Turner's tumultuous career, in particular."

Lana Turner, Hearts & Diamonds Take All
Winner of the coveted "Best Biography" Award from the San Francisco Book Festival

By Darwin Porter and Danforth Prince
Softcover, 622 pages, with photos. ISBN 978-1-936003-53-2
Available everywhere, online and in bookstores.

SCARLETT O'HARA,

DESPERATELY IN LOVE WITH HEATHCLIFF,

TOGETHER ON THE ROAD TO HELL

Here, for the first time, is a biography that raises the curtain on the secret lives of **Lord Laurence Olivier**, often cited as the finest actor in the history of England, and **Vivien Leigh**, who immortalized herself with her Oscar-winning portrayals of Scarlett O'Hara in *Gone With the Wind*, and as Blanche DuBois in Tennessee Williams' *A Streetcar Named Desire*.

Dashing and "impossibly handsome," Laurence Olivier was pursued by the most dazzling luminaries, male and female, of the movie and theater worlds.

Lord Olivier's beautiful and brilliant but emotionally disturbed wife (Viv to her lovers) led a tumultuous off-the-record life whose paramours ranged from the A-list celebrities to men she selected randomly off the street. But none of the brilliant roles depicted by Lord and Lady Olivier, on stage or on screen, ever matched the power and drama of personal dramas which wavered between Wagnerian opera and Greek tragedy. Damn You, Scarlett O'Hara is the definitive and most revelatory portrait ever published of the most talented and tormented actor and actress of the 20th century.

Darwin Porter is the principal author of this seminal work.

"The folks over at TMZ would have had a field day tracking Laurence Olivier and Vivien Leigh with flip cameras in hand. Damn You, Scarlett O'Hara can be a dazzling read, the prose unmannered and instantly digestible. The authors' ability to pile scandal atop scandal, seduction after seduction, can be impossible to resist."

—THE WASHINGTON TIMES

DAMN YOU, SCARLETT O'HARA
THE PRIVATE LIFES OF LAURENCE OLIVIER AND VIVIEN LEIGH

Darwin Porter and Roy Moseley

Winner of four distinguished literary awards, this is the best biography of Vivien Leigh and Laurence Olivier ever published, with hundreds of insights into the London Theatre, the role of the Oliviers in the politics of World War II, and the passion, fury, and frustration of their lives together as actors in the West End, on Broadway, and in Hollywood.

ISBN 978-1-936003-15-0   Hardcover, 708 pages, with about a hundred photos.

DONALD TRUMP
WAS THE MAN WHO WOULD BE KING

This is the most famous book about our incendiary ex-President you've probably never heard of.

Winner of three respected literary awards, and released three months before the Presidential elections of 2016, it's an entertainingly packaged, artfully salacious bombshell, a scathingly historic overview of America during its 2016 election cycle, a portrait unlike anything ever published on CANDIDATE DONALD and the climate in which he thrived and massacred his political rivals.

Its volcanic, much-suppressed release during the heat and venom of the 2016 Presidential campaign has already been heralded by the Midwestern Book Review, California Book Watch, the Seattle Gay News, the staunchly right-wing WILS-AM radio, and also by the editors at the most popular Seniors' magazine in Florida, BOOMER TIMES, which designated it as one of their BOOKS OF THE MONTH.

TRUMPOCALYPSE: *"Donald Trump: The Man Who Would Be King* is recommended reading for all sides, no matter what political stance is being adopted: Republican, Democrat, or other.

"One of its driving forces is its ability to synthesize an unbelievable amount of information into a format and presentation which blends lively irony with outrageous observations, entertaining even as it presents eye-opening information in a format accessible to all.

"Politics dovetail with American obsessions and fascinations with trends, figureheads, drama, and sizzling news stories, but blend well with the observations of sociologists, psychologists, politicians, and others in a wide range of fields who lend their expertise and insights to create a much broader review of the Trump phenomena than a more casual book could provide.

"The result is a 'must read' for any American interested in issues of race, freedom, equality, and justice—and for any non-American who wonders just what is going on behind the scenes in this country's latest election debacle."

Diane Donovan, Senior Editor, California Bookwatch

Donald Trump, The Man Who Would Be King
Winner of "Best Biography" Awards from book festivals in
New York, California, and Florida
by Darwin Porter and Danforth Prince
Softcover, with 822 pages and hundreds of photos. ISBN 978-1-936003-51-8.

Available now from Ingram, Amazon.com and other purveyors, worldwide.

LINDA LOVELACE

INSIDE LINDA LOVELACE'S DEEP THROAT
Degradation, Porno Chic, and the Rise of Feminism

The most comprehensive biography ever written of an adult entertainment star, her tormented relationship with Hollywood's underbelly, and how she changed forever the world's perceptions about censorship, sexual behavior patterns, and pornography.

Darwin Porter, author of more than thirty critically acclaimed celebrity exposés of behind-the-scenes intrigue in the entertainment industry, was deeply involved in the Linda Lovelace saga as it unfolded in the 70s, interviewing many of the players, and raising money for the legal defense of the film's co-star, Harry Reems.

In this book, emphasizing her role as an unlikely celebrity interacting with other celebrities, he brings inside information and a never-before-published revelation to almost every page.

"This book drew me in..How could it not?"
Coco Papy, Bookslut.

The Beach Book Festival's Grand Prize Winner for Best Summer Reading of 2013"

Runner-Up to "Best Biography of 2013" The Los Angeles Book Festival

Another hot and insightful commentary about major and sometimes violently controversial conflicts of the American Century, from Blood Moon Productions.

Inside Linda Lovelace's Deep Throat, by Darwin Porter
Softcover, 640 pages, 6"x9" with photos.
ISBN 978-1-936003-33-4

PINK TRIANGLE

The Feuds and Private Lives of
TENNESSEE WILLIAMS, GORE VIDAL, TRUMAN CAPOTE,
& Famous Members of their Entourages

Darwin Porter & Danforth Prince

This book, the only one of its kind, reveals the backlot intrigues associated with the literary and script-writing *enfants terribles* of America's entertainment community during the mid-20th century.

It exposes their bitchfests, their slugfests, and their relationships with the glitterati—Marilyn Monroe, Brando, the Oliviers, the Paleys, U.S. Presidents, a gaggle of other movie stars, millionaires, and international débauchés.

This is for anyone who's interested in the formerly concealed scandals of Hollywood and Broadway, and the values and pretentions of both the literary community and the entertainment industry.

"A banquet... If PINK TRIANGLE had not been written for us, we would have had to research and type it all up for ourselves...Pink Triangle is nearly seven hundred pages of the most entertaining histrionics ever sliced, spiced, heated, and serviced up to the reading public. Everything that Blood Moon has done before pales in comparison.
Given the fact that the subjects of the book themselves were nearly delusional on the subject of themselves (to say nothing of each other) it is hard to find fault. Add to this the intertwined jungle that was the relationship among Williams, Capote, and Vidal, of the times they vied for things they loved most—especially attention—and the times they enthralled each other and the world, [Pink Triangle is] the perfect antidote to the Polar Vortex."

—**Vinton McCabe in the NY JOURNAL OF BOOKS**

"Full disclosure: I have been a friend and follower of Blood Moon Productions' tomes for years, and always marveled at the amount of information in their books—it's staggering. The index alone to Pink Triangle runs to 21 pages—and the scale of names in it runs like a Who's Who of American social, cultural and political life through much of the 20th century."

—**Perry Brass in THE HUFFINGTON POST**

"We Brits are not spared the Porter/Prince silken lash either. PINK TRIANGLE's research is, quite frankly, breathtaking. PINK TRIANGLE will fascinate you for many weeks to come. Once you have made the initial titillating dip, the day will seem dull without it."

—**Jeffery Tayor in THE SUNDAY EXPRESS (UK)**

PINK TRIANGLE—The Feuds and Private Lives of Tennessee Williams, Gore Vidal, Truman Capote, and Famous Members of their Entourages

Darwin Porter & Danforth Prince
Softcover, 700 pages, with photos   ISBN 978-1-936003-37-2   Also Available for E-Readers

THOSE GLAMOROUS GABORS
BOMBSHELLS FROM BUDAPEST

Zsa Zsa, Eva, and Magda Gabor transferred their glittery dreams and gold-digging ambitions from the twilight of the Austro-Hungarian Empire to Hollywood. There, more effectively than any army, these Bombshells from Budapest broke hearts, amassed fortunes, lovers, and A-list husbands, and amused millions of voyeurs through the medium of television, movies, and the social registers. In this astonishing "triple-play" biography, designated "Best Biography of the Year" by the Hollywood Book Festival, Blood Moon lifts the "mink-and-diamond" curtain on this amazing trio of blood-related sisters, whose complicated intrigues have never been fully explored before.

***

"You will never be Ga-bored…this book gives new meaning to the term compelling. Be warned, Those Glamorous Gabors is both an epic and a pip. Not since Gone With the Wind have so many characters on the printed page been forced to run for their lives for one reason or another. And Scarlett making a dress out of the curtains is nothing compared to what a Gabor will do when she needs to scrap together an outfit for a movie premiere or late-night outing.

"For those not up to speed, Jolie Tilleman came from a family of jewelers and therefore came by her love for the shiny stones honestly, perhaps genetically. She married Vilmos Gabor somewhere around World War 1 (exact dates, especially birth dates, are always somewhat vague in order to establish plausible deniability later on) and they were soon blessed with three daughters: Magda, the oldest, whose hair, sadly, was naturally brown, although it would turn quite red in America; Zsa Zsa (born 'Sari') a natural blond who at a very young age exhibited the desire for fame with none of the talents usually associated with achievement, excepting beauty and a natural wit; and Eva, the youngest and blondest of the girls, who after seeing Grace Moore perform at the National Theater, decided that she wanted to be an actress and that she would one day move to Hollywood to become a star.

"Given that the Gabor family at that time lived in Budapest, Hungary, at the period of time between the World Wars, that Hollywood dream seemed a distant one indeed. The story—the riches to rags to riches to rags to riches again myth of survival against all odds as the four women, because of their Jewish heritage, flee Europe with only the minks on their backs and what jewels they could smuggle along with them in their decolletage, only to have to battle afresh for their places in the vicious Hollywood pecking order— gives new meaning to the term 'compelling.' The reader, as if he were witnessing a particularly gore-drenched traffic accident, is incapable of looking away."

—*New York Review of Books*

THOSE GLAMOROUS GABORS
Bombshells from Budapest,
by Darwin Porter & Danforth Prince
Softcover, 730 pages, with hundreds of photos
ISBN 978-1-936003-35-8

ROCK HUDSON

IN THE DYING DAYS OF HOLLYWOOD'S GOLDEN AGE, ROCK HUDSON WAS THE MOST CELEBRATED PHALLIC SYMBOL AND LUST OBJECT IN AMERICA.

THIS BOOK DESCRIBES HIS RISE AND FALL, AND THE INDUSTRY THAT CREATED HIM.

Rock Hudson charmed every casting director in Hollywood (and movie-goers throughout America) as the megastar they most wanted to share PILLOW TALK with. This book describes his rise and fall, and how he handled himself as a closeted but promiscuous bisexual during an age when EVERYBODY tried to throw him onto a casting couch.

Based on dozens of face-to-face interviews with the actor's friends, co-conspirators, and enemies, and researched over a period of a half century, this biography reveals the shame, agonies, and irony of Rock Hudson's complete, never-before-told story.

In 2017, the year of its release, it was designated as winner ("BEST BIOGRAPHY") at two of the Golden State's most prestigious literary competitions, the Northern California and the Southern California Book Festivals.

It was also favorably reviewed by the *Midwestern Book Review*, *California Book Watch*, *KNEWS RADIO*, the *New York Journal of Books*, and the editors at the most popular Seniors' magazine in Florida, *BOOMER TIMES*.

ROCK HUDSON EROTIC FIRE
By Darwin Porter & Danforth Prince
Softcover, 624 pages, with dozens of photos, 6" x 9"
ISBN 978-1-936003-55-6

Available everywhere now

BILL & HILLARY
So This Is That Thing Called Love

CONFUSED ABOUT HOW TO INTERPRET THEIR RAUCOUS PASTS?
THIS UNCENSORED TALE ABOUT A LOVE AFFAIR THAT CHANGED THE COURSE OF POLITICS AND THE PLANET IS OF COMPELLING INTEREST TO ANYONE INVOLVED IN THE SLUGFESTS AND INCENDIARY WARS OF THE CLINTONS.

"This is both a biographical coverage of the Clintons and a political exposé; a detailed, weighty exploration that traces the couple's social and political evolution, from how each entered the political arena to their White House years under Bill Clinton's presidency.

"Containing gossip, scandal, and biographical sketches, it delves deeply into the news and politics of its times, presenting enough historical background to fully explore the underlying controversies affecting the Clinton family and their choices.

"Sidebars of information and black and white photos liberally peppered throughout the account offer visual reinforcement to the exploration, lending it the feel and tone of both a gossip column and political piece - something that probes not just Clinton interactions but the D.C. political milieu as a whole.

"The result may appear weighty, sporting over five hundred pages, but is an absorbing, top recommendation for readers of both biographical and political pieces who will thoroughly enjoy this spirited, lively, and thought-provoking analysis."

—THE MIDWEST BOOK REVIEW

***

Shortly after its release in December of 2015, this book received a literary award (Runner-up to Best Biography of the Year) from the New England Book Festival. As stated by a spokesperson for the Awards, "The New England Book Festival is an annual competition honoring excellence in books, with particular focus on projects that deserve closer attention from the academic community. Congratulations to Blood Moon and its authors, especially Darwin Porter, for his highly entertaining analysis of Clinton's double-barreled presidential regime, and the sometimes hysterical over-reaction of their enemies."

BILL & HILLARY—SO THIS IS THAT THING CALLED LOVE
Softcover, with photos. ISBN 978-1-936003-47-1

BURT REYNOLDS
PUT THE PEDAL TO THE METAL
How a Nude Centerfold Sex Symbol Seduced Hollywood

In the 1970s and '80s, Burt Reynolds represented a new breed of movie star.

Charming and relentlessly macho, he was a good old Southern boy who made hearts throb and audiences laugh. He was Burt Reynolds, a football hero and a guy you might have shared some jokes with in a redneck bar. After an impressive but tormented career, rivers of negative publicity, a self-admitted history of bad choices, and a spectacular fall from Hollywood grace, he died in Jupiter, Florida, at the age of 82 in September of 2018.

For five years, both in terms of earnings and popularity, he was the number one box office star in the world. *Smokey and the Bandit* (1977) became the biggest-grossing car-chase film of all time. As he put it, perhaps as a means of bolstering his image, "I like nothing better than making love to some of the most beautiful women in the world." Perhaps he was referring to his romantic and sexual involvements with dozens of celebrities from New Hollywood. More unusual dalliances occurred with Marilyn Monroe, whom he once picked up on his way to the Actors Studio in New York City. Love with another VIP came in the form of that "Sweetheart of the G.I.s," Dinah Shore, sparking chatter. "I appreciate older women," he once said in a moment of self-revelation. According to Sally Field, "Burt still lives in my heart." But then she expressed relief that, because of his recent death, he never read what she'd said about him in her memoir.

Men liked him too: He played poker with Frank Sinatra; shared boozy nights with John Wayne; intercepted a "pass" from closeted Spencer Tracy; talked "penis size" with Mark Wahlberg; went "wench-hunting" with Johnny Carson; and threatened to kill Marlon Brando, to whom his appearance was often compared. He also hung out with Bette Davis. ("I always had a thing for her.")

His least happy (some said "most poisonous") marriage—to Loni Anderson—was rife with dramas played out more in the tabloids than in the boudoir. According to Reynolds, "She's vain, she's a rotten mother, she sleeps around, and she spent all my money."

This biography—the first comprehensive overview of the "redneck icon" ever published—reveals the joys and sorrows of a movie star who thrived in, but who was then almost buried by the pressures and insecurities of the New Hollywood. A tribute to "truck stop" America, it's about the accelerated life of a courageous spirit who "Put His Pedal to the Metal" with humor, high jinx, and pizzazz. He predicted his own death: "Soon, I'll be racing a hotrod in Valhalla in my cowboy hat and a pair of aviators." On his tombstone, he wanted it writ: "He was not the best actor in the world, but he was the best Burt Reynolds in the world."

BURT REYNOLDS
PUT THE PEDAL TO THE METAL

Darwin Porter & Danforth Prince; ISBN 978-1-936003-63-1; 450 pages with photos.
Available Everywhere Now

PETER O'TOOLE

HELLRAISER, SEXUAL OUTLAW, IRISH REBEL

When it was published, early in 2015, this book was widely publicized in the *Daily Mail,* the *New York Daily News,* the *New York Post,* the *Midwest Book Review, The Express (London), The Globe,* the *National Enquirer,* and in equivalent publications worldwide

One of the world's most admired (and brilliant) actors, Peter O'Toole wined and wenched his way through a labyrinth of sexual and interpersonal betrayals, sometimes with disastrous results. Away from the stage and screen, where such films as *Becket* and *Lawrence of Arabia,* made film history, his life was filled with drunken, debauched nights and edgy sexual experimentations, most of which were never openly examined in the press. A hellraiser, he shared wild times with his "best blokes" Richard Burton and Richard Harris. Peter Finch, also his close friend, once invited him to join him in sharing the pleasures of his mistress, Vivien Leigh.

"My father, a bookie, moved us to the Mick community of Leeds," O'Toole once told a reporter. "We were very poor, but I was born an Irishman, which accounts for my gift of gab, my unruly behavior, my passionate devotion to women and the bottle, and my loathing of any authority figure."

Author Robert Sellers described O'Toole's boyhood neighborhood. "Three of his playmates went on to be hanged for murder; one strangled a girl in a lovers' quarrel; one killed a man during a robbery; another cut up a warden in South Africa with a pair of shears. It was a heavy bunch."

Peter O'Toole's hell-raising life story has never been told, until now. Hot and uncensored, from a writing team which, even prior to O'Toole's death in 2013, had been collecting under-the-radar info about him for years, this book has everything you ever wanted to know about how THE LION navigated his way through the boudoirs of the Entertainment Industry IN WINTER, Spring, Summer, and a dissipated Autumn as well.

Blood Moon has ripped away the imperial robe, scepter, and crown usually associated with this quixotic problem child of the British Midlands. Provocatively uncensored, this illusion-shattering overview of Peter O'Toole's hell-raising (or at least very naughty) and demented life is unique in the history of publishing.

PETER O'TOOLE
HELLRAISER, SEXUAL OUTLAW, IRISH REBEL
DARWIN PORTER & DANFORTH PRINCE
Softcover, with photos. ISBN 978-1-936003-45-7
Available Now

PAUL NEWMAN

THE MAN BEHIND THE BABY BLUES
HIS SECRET LIFE EXPOSED

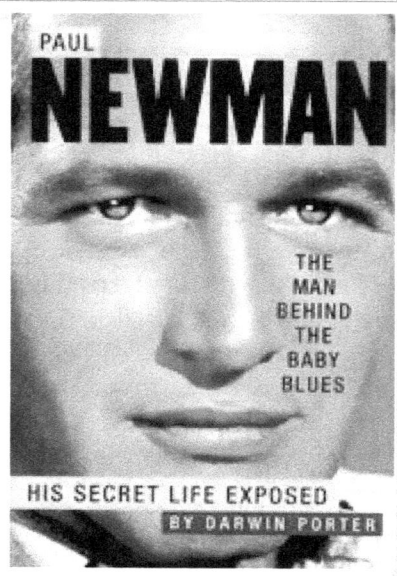

Drawn from firsthand interviews with insiders who knew Paul Newman intimately, and compiled over a period of nearly a half-century, this is the world's most honest and most revelatory biography about Hollywood's pre-eminent male sex symbol.

This is a respectful but candid cornucopia of once-concealed information about the sexual and emotional adventures of an affable, impossibly good-looking workaday actor, a former sailor from Shaker Heights, Ohio, who parlayed his ambisexual charm and extraordinary good looks into one of the most successful careers in Hollywood.

Whereas the situations it exposes were widely known within Hollywood's inner circles, they've never before been revealed to the general public.

But now, the full story has been published—the giddy heights and agonizing crashes of a great American star, with revelations and insights never before published in any other biography.

***

"Paul Newman had just as many on-location affairs as the rest of us, and he was just as bisexual as I was. But whereas I was always getting caught with my pants down, he managed to do it in the dark with not a paparazzo in sight. He might have bedded Marilyn Monroe or Elizabeth Taylor the night before, but he always managed to show up for breakfast with Joanne Woodward, with those baby blues, looking as innocent as a Botticelli angel. He never fooled me. It takes an alleycat to know another one. Did I ever tell you what really happened between Newman and me? If that doesn't grab you, what about what went on between James Dean and Newman? Let me tell you about this co-called model husband if you want to look behind those famous peepers."

—Marlon Brando

PAUL NEWMAN, THE MAN BEHIND THE BABY BLUES,
His Secret Life Exposed, by Darwin Porter
Recipient of an Honorable Mention from the New England Book Festival
Hardcover, 520 pages, with dozens of photos.
ISBN 978-0-9786465-1-6   Available everywhere now.

JAMES DEAN
TOMORROW NEVER COMES
HONORING THE 60TH ANNIVERSARY OF HIS VIOLENT AND EARLY DEATH

America's most enduring and legendary symbol of young, enraged rebellion, James Dean continues into the 21st Century to capture the imagination of the world.

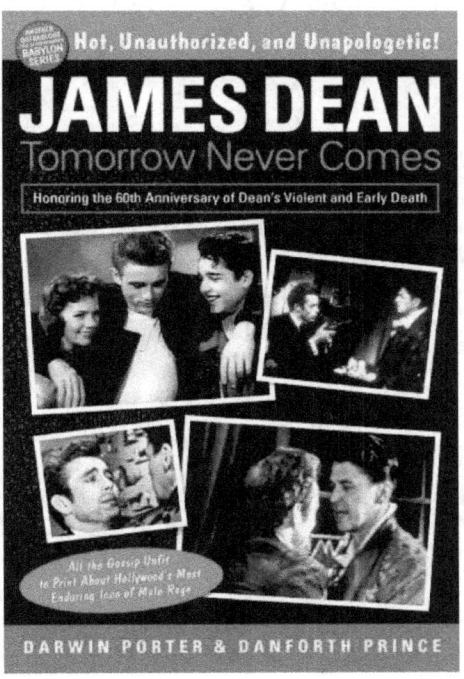

After one of his many flirtations with Death, which caught up with him when he was a celebrity-soaked 24-year-old, he said, "If a man can live after he dies, then maybe he's a great man." Today, bars from Nigeria to Patagonia are named in honor of this international, spectacularly self-destructive movie star icon.

Migrating from the dusty backroads of Indiana to center stage in the most formidable boudoirs of Hollywood, his saga is electrifying.

A strikingly handsome heart-throb, Dean is a study in contrasts: Tough but tender, brutal but remarkably sensitive; he was a reckless hellraiser badass who could revert to a little boy in bed.

A rampant bisexual, he claimed that he didn't want to go through life "with one hand tied behind my back." He demonstrated that during bedroom trysts with Marilyn Monroe, Rock Hudson, Elizabeth Taylor, Paul Newman, Natalie Wood, Shelley Winters, Marlon Brando, Steve McQueen, Ursula Andress, Montgomery Clift, Pier Angeli, Tennessee Williams, Susan Strasberg, Tallulah Bankhead, and FBI director J. Edgar Hoover.

Woolworth heiress Barbara Hutton, one of the richest and most dissipated women of her era, wanted to make him her toy boy.

Tomorrow Never Comes is the most penetrating look at James Dean to have emerged from the wreckage of his Porsche Spyder in 1955.

Before setting out on his last ride, he said, "I feel life too intensely to bear living it." *Tomorrow Never Comes* presents a damaged but beautiful soul.

JAMES DEAN—TOMORROW NEVER COMES
DARWIN PORTER & DANFORTH PRINCE
Softcover, with photos. ISBN 978-1-936003-49-5

BLOOD MOON'S RESPECTFUL FAREWELL TO A GREAT AMERICAN MOVIE STAR

KIRK DOUGLAS
MORE IS NEVER ENOUGH

OOZING MASCULINITY, A YOUNG HORNDOG SETS OUT TO CONQUER HOLLYWOOD

Of the many male stars of Golden Age Hollywood, Kirk Douglas became the final survivor, the last icon of a fabled, optimistic era that the world will never see again. When he celebrated his birthday in 2016, a headline read: LEGENDARY HOLLYWOOD HORNDOG TURNS 100.

He was both a charismatic actor and a man of uncommon force and vigor. His restless and volcanic spirit is reflected both in his films and through his many sexual conquests.

Douglas was the son of Russian-Jewish immigrants, his father a collector and seller of rags. After service in the Navy during World War II, he hit Hollywood, oozing masculinity and charm. Conquering Tinseltown and bedding its leading ladies, he became the personification of the American dream, moving from obscurity and (literally) rags to riches and major-league fame.

The *Who's Who* cast of characters roaring through his life included not only a daunting list of Hollywood goddesses, but the town's most colossal male talents and egos, too. They included his kindred hellraiser and best buddy Burt Lancaster, John Wayne, Henry Fonda, Billy Wilder, Laurence Olivier, Rock Hudson, and a future U.S. President, Ronald Reagan, when winning the highest office in the land was virtually unthinkable.

Over the decades, he immortalized himself in film after film, delivering, like a Trojan, one memorable performance after another. He was at home in *film noir*, as a western gunslinger, as an adventurer (in both ancient and modern sagas), as a juggler, as Tennessee Williams' "gentleman caller," as a Greek super-hero from Homer's *Odyssey*, and as roguish sailor in the Jules Verne yarn, exploring the mysteries of the ocean's depths.

En route to his status as a myth and legend, his performances reflected both his personal pain and the brutalization of the characters he played, too. In *Champion* (1949), he was beaten to a fatal bloody pulp. As the sleazy, heartless reporter in *Ace in the Hole* (1951), he was stabbed with a knife in his gut. As Van Gogh in *Lust for Life* (1956), he writhed in emotional agony and unrequited love before slicing off his ear with a razor. His World War I movie, *Paths of Glory* (1957) grows more profound over the years. He lost an eye in *The Vikings* (1958), and, as the Thracian slave leading a revolt against Roman legions in *Spartacus* (1960), he was crucified.

All of this is brought out, with photos, in this remarkable testimonial to the last hero of Hollywood's cinematic and swashbuckling Golden Age, an inspiring testimonial to the values and core beliefs of an America that's Gone With the Wind, yet lovingly remembered as a time when it, in many ways, was truly great.

KIRK DOUGLAS: MORE IS NEVER ENOUGH

Darwin Porter & Danforth Prince; ISBN 978-1-936003-61-7; 550 pages with photos. Available everywhere now

Available Now From Blood Moon: The Comprehensive, Unauthorized Exposé that Every Survivor of the Sexual Revolution Will Want to Read

Hugh Hefner, the most iconic Playboy in human history, was a visionary, an empire-builder, and a pajama-clad pipe-smoker with a pre-coital grin.

In 1953, he published his first edition of *Playboy* with money borrowed from his puritanical, Nebraska-born mother. Marilyn Monroe appeared on the cover, with her nude calendar inside.

Rebelling against his strict upbringing, he lost his virginity at the age of 22.

His magazine, punctuated with nudes and studded with articles by major literary figures, reached its zenith at eight million readers. As a "tasteful pornographer," Hef became a cultural warrior, fighting government censorship all the way to the U.S. Supreme Court. As the years and his notoriety progressed, he became an advocate of abortion, LGBT equality, and the legalization of pot. Eventually, he engaged in "pubic wars" with Bob Guccione, the flamboyant founder of Penthouse, which cut into Hef's sales.

Lauded by millions of avid readers, he was denounced as "the father of sex addiction," "a huckster," "a lecherous low-brow feeder of our vices," "a misogynist," and, near the end of his life, "a symbol of priapic senility."

During his heyday, some of the biggest male stars in Hollywood, including Warren Beatty, Sammy Davis, Jr., Mick Jagger, and Jack Nicholson, came to frolic behind Hef's guarded walls, stripping nude in the hot tub grotto before sampling the rotating beds upstairs. Even a future U.S. president came to call. "Donald Trump had an appreciation of Bunny tail," Hef said.

Hefner's last Viagra-fueled marriage was to a beautiful blonde, Crystal Harris, 60 years his junior. "There's nothing wrong in a man marrying a girl who could be his great-granddaughter," he was famously quoted as saying.

This ground-breaking biography, the latest in Blood Moon's string of outrageously unvarnished myth-busters, was the first published since Hefner's death at the age of 91 in 2017. It's a provocative saga, rich in tantalizing, often shocking detail. Not recommended for the sanctimonious or the faint of heart, and loaded with ironic, little-known details about the trendsetter's epic challenges and the solutions he devised.

PLAYBOY'S HUGH HEFNER
EMPIRE OF SKIN

by Darwin Porter and Danforth Prince
978-1-936003-59-4

Blood Moon Productions proudly announces its compilation of lurid, vintage scandals from the Golden Age of Camelot.

It's in the form of a new edition of Darwin Porter's classic 2014 biography of the most watched, most enigmatic, and most controversial woman of the 20th Century,

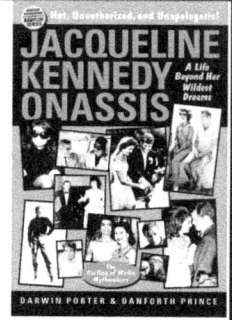

JACQUELINE KENNEDY ONASSIS
Her Tumultous Life & Her Love Affairs

JACKIE INVADES WASHINGTON BABYLON, EUROPE, and BEYOND

This is a new edition of the most compelling compilation of cash-soaked ambition, sexual indiscretion, and social embarrassment about a former first lady ever published,

Available now from **Ingram** and from **Amazon.com** worldwide, in honor of one of America's favorite Valentines

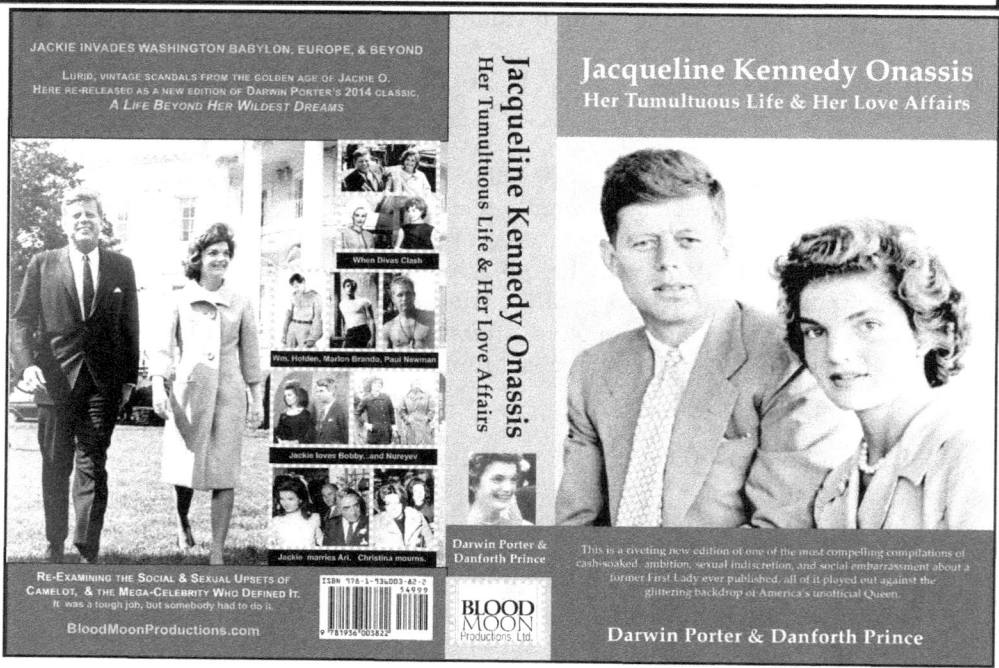

JAQUELINE KENNEDY ONASSIS
Her Tumultuous Life & Her Love Affairs
ISBN 978-1-936003-82-2   Originally published in 2014 as
A LIFE BEYOND HER WILDEST DREAMS by Darwin Porter & Danforth Prince
700 fascinating pages with hundreds of photos

Conceived in direct and sometimes defiant contrast to the avalanche of more breathlessly respectful testimonials to the life and legacy of "America's Queen," this book is the latest installment in Blood Moon's endlessly irreverent MAGNOLIA HOUSE series.

RE-EXAMINING THE SOCIAL AND SEXUAL UPSETS OF CAMELOT AND THE MEGA-CELEBRITY WHO DEFINED IT.

It was a tough job, but somebody had to do it.

www.ingramcontent.com/pod-product-compliance
Lightning Source LLC
Chambersburg PA
CBHW081740100526
44592CB00015B/2240